D1207936

Battle for the Ruhr

Battle for the Ruhr

The German Army's Final Defeat in the West

Derek S. Zumbro

UNIVERSITY PRESS OF KANSAS

940, 5421
Zum

© 2006 by the University Press of Kansas

Published by the University Press of Kansas (Lawrence, Kansas 66045), which was organized by the Kansas Board of Regents and is operated and funded by Emporia State University, Fort Hays State University, Kansas State University, Pittsburg State University, the University of Kansas, and Wichita State University

Library of Congress Cataloging-in-Publication Data

Zumbro, Derek S.
  Battle for the Ruhr : the German Army's final defeat in the West / Derek S. Zumbro.
    p.   cm. — (Modern war studies)
  Includes bibliographical references and index.
  ISBN 0-7006-1490-7 (cloth : alk. paper)
  1. Ruhr Pocket, Battle of the, Germany, 1945.   I. Title.   II. Series.
  D756.5.R8Z97 2006
  940.54'21355—dc22   2006015008

British Library Cataloguing-in-Publication Data is available.

Printed in the United States of America
10 9 8 7 6 5 4 3 2 1

To Karen,
Kristopher, and
Kristin

CONTENTS

Photograph sections follow pages 108 and 260.

ACKNOWLEDGMENTS

I would like to extend my sincere appreciation to Suzanne Marchand, David Lindenfeld, and Stan Hilton of Louisiana State University for their support throughout this project. Suzanne Marchand contributed numerous hours reviewing the manuscript, and her recommendations proved to be invaluable for the development and completion of the project. I would like to express my gratitude to both Andrew Wiest and Bradley Bond of the University of Southern Mississippi, as well as to Kathi Jones of Shaw Air Force Base, for encouraging me to pursue this project at its inception. I would also like to give my heartfelt thanks to Max Wind in Munich, my long-time friend Gottlob Bidermann, and the Hebestreit family in Dornstetten/Aach for their support and assistance during many months of work and research in Germany. Additionally, Hans-Georg Model provided me with invaluable details regarding his father's military career. Most notable among the many contributors to this project were Field Marshal Model's former staff officers, Winrich Behr and Günther Reichhelm. Both men contributed many hours and exhibited infinite patience during an exhaustive series of interviews that extended over a period of many months; their support throughout this project cannot be overstated. My special thanks also extends to Willi Mues of Erwitte, who generously provided research material from the extensive archive accumulated by him over a number of years for his own outstanding work on this subject. Willi Mues also donated many hours of his time in personally escorting me throughout the area of Lippstadt while explaining events that occurred in the Ruhr-Sauerland in 1945. His contribution of archival materials and his knowledge of the campaign proved to be essential for the timely completion of this project.

INTRODUCTION

In late April 1945, the German economic and military infrastructure was in the final throes of total collapse. The Anglo-American armies stood at the Elbe River, awaiting the imminent encirclement of Berlin by Soviet forces. Far to the south, SS General Karl Wolf was negotiating the surrender of all German forces in Italy. Isolated pockets of German troops continued to exhibit signs of resistance, mostly in combating Soviet forces that were marching ever deeper into western Europe. Far to the west of the apocalyptic events taking place east of the Elbe, a tiny contingent of German soldiers on the Rhine, representing the last vestiges of the Wehrmacht's once-formidable Army Group B, were bringing their own participation in the war to an end.

On the afternoon of 21 April 1945, Field Marshal Walter Model, commander of Army Group B, spoke briefly to a trusted staff officer before handing him an envelope containing a final letter to family members, his wedding ring, and several other personal possessions. He then walked a short distance into a densely wooded area south of the Ruhr city of Duisburg, drew his service pistol, and ended his life. This action also served to officially and irrevocably end the existence of Army Group B. Some two years previously, in early February 1943, Germany had received the inconceivable announcement that Field Marshal Friedrich Paulus had surrendered the Wehrmacht's Sixth Army at Stalingrad. At that time, Model had remarked to his son, Hans-Georg, "A German field marshal doesn't surrender ... such a thing is not possible." Model could not have known that he, like Paulus, would one day witness the total annihilation of his forces.

Although he is not the primary focus of this work, by virtue of his position Walter Model is a pivotal figure in this story. The enigmatic officer's meteoric rise to field marshal was not without merit. On no less than five separate occasions, he had been dispatched to save a collapsing front in Russia. Finally, in late summer 1944, Model found himself again sent into a chaotic situation to save Wehrmacht forces from irrecoverable defeat. No one could have predicted that his last assignment would span a period of eight months, during which his battered divisions conducted an arduous and costly retreat across France and Belgium to the borders of the Reich. This narrative follows the fate of Model's forces as they were pursued, methodically encircled, and finally destroyed by Lieutenant General

Omar Bradley's Twelfth Army Group and Field Marshal Bernard Montgomery's Twenty-first Army Group. This relatively short span of time saw the retreat across France to the borders of the Reich, Montgomery's debacle at Arnhem, the vicious series of engagements in the Hürtgen Forest, the fall of Aachen, the Ardennes Offensive, the breaching of the Rhine, and finally the encirclement and destruction of the army group in the Ruhr Valley.

The war ended in April 1945 for the field marshal and some 300,000 Wehrmacht soldiers serving with Army Group B. Yet Model represents more than simply a senior military officer in command of an army group that was destined for destruction. In many regards, he may well represent the general community, civilian and military, within Germany under the Third Reich. According to contemporary sources and those who knew him well, Model chose to distance himself from the political intrigue and malfeasance that characterized Adolf Hitler's government. Many Germans, like Walter Model, certainly benefited from the series of events that led up to the war and marked its early phases. Yet choosing to distance oneself from the iniquitous traits of a regime, especially while benefiting from its actions, does not mitigate the lack of moral responsibility that accompanies any reward. The same system that provided a nation with a temporary, albeit illusory, sense of destiny and greatness resulted in the deaths of some 50 million people. The accountability for the cataclysm must be shared by those who served to sustain Hitler's policies, regardless of the perceived insignificance or indirectness of their contribution.

By some accounts, this is a story that should not have been written. The military events and chronology of the Ruhr Pocket campaign have been examined and documented in a number of earlier sources, and questioning the value of research that examines a well-documented military campaign has merit. However, the campaign involving the destruction of Army Group B in the Ruhr Pocket is not the sole focus of this work; rather, it can be considered a necessary component. Unlike many contemporary history projects, this book does not focus on a single, precise argument but instead encompasses and illustrates a dramatic series of events that create a unique story of human experience. The emphasis is not on the names, numbers, and dates that identify military units and specific events but on the nature of the campaign at the ground level. Most important to American readers, the volume exhibits how the U.S. Army, in the role of an invading foreign power, was encountered by the enemy soldiers and civilians in northwest Germany in the spring of 1945. The lack of an American perspective in this account cannot be attributed to oversight or neglect; it reflects the concentration on experiences and views of the defeated German populace.

The GIs of World War II are widely accepted in American culture as citizen-soldiers who, when called on, made selfless sacrifices in a successful, though costly, endeavor to preserve their nation's freedom. The purpose of the narrative offered here is to provide the reader with another perspective without detracting from that fundamental conviction. This is the story of the defeated. The narrative follows the events as experienced by "ordinary citizens" and "ordinary soldiers" as their neighborhoods and homes were enveloped in destruction and their villages became battlefields. It is the story of children pressed into service as Hitler's final levy during the closing hours of a monumental defeat and of desperate fathers and mothers attempting to save their sons from being sacrificed at the eleventh hour for an iniquitous cause. Communities and farmyards, often left scarred by the engagements that engulfed them, became littered with the refuse of war; villages and towns were rendered smoldering ruins as columns of American vehicles rolled relentlessly toward Berlin, leaving the inhabitants at the mercy of the anarchy that followed in their wake. The story also reveals the mass graves and the unspeakable conditions suffered by foreign laborers, prisoners of war (POWs), and political opponents of Hitler's policies, thus providing the Allied soldiers with an unprecedented perspective on the enemy they were confronting. The irrefutable defeat looming over Hitler's followers in the closing hours of the war did little to deter genocidal and sadistic policies. To the contrary, the imminent collapse served, in some instances, to spur abominable practices to unparalleled extremes.

In addition to revealing the impressions left by the soldiers of the U.S. Army on inhabitants, fugitives, and POWs in the Ruhr Pocket, this story reveals the identities of specific characters who have been discussed in previous works yet never identified. The last hours experienced by the officers summarily executed for the loss of the Remagen bridge are revealed in detail. The fate of those officers, at the hands of Lieutenant-General Dr. Rudolf Hübner's *fliegenden Standgericht* ("flying courts-martial"), is described by surviving witnesses. This account also reveals something about Field Marshal Model's acquiescence to Hitler's dominance of military affairs. Hübner's tribunal spread terror throughout the units associated with the loss of the Remagen bridge, and Model himself was not spared the indignity of interrogation. Yet the field marshal seems to have borne the intrusion and disruption without discernible protest—a phenomenon that may illustrate the ruthless nature of Hitler's regime, sustained by legions of those who blindly served him. A single incident may serve to redeem the field marshal's actions, if only to a limited extent. When the inquisitors turned their sights on Günther Reichhelm, one of Model's most trusted staff officers, the field marshal declared that Reichhelm was not guilty of any offense and demanded that he be left alone. According to Reichhelm, Model was outraged at the behavior and interference of the tribunal, and yet, the field marshal tacitly relented to the presence of Hübner's inquisitors as they continued to careen about Army Group B tyrannizing subordinate units.

Model's conspicuous acquiescence to the presence of Hübner's tribunal remains inescapable, yet this demeanor may also have been indicative of the overwhelming resignation felt by Model following the ill-fated Ardennes Offensive. Although this reaction may have been characteristic of the attitudes held by the senior German officer corps under the rule of Adolf Hitler in 1945, it did not specifically address the general military values in the west; of course, the question of how American or British officers might have reacted in similar circumstances remains unaddressed and thus unanswered.

The core of this story can be regarded as history "from below." Captain Wolf Koltermann, the commander of the Tiger tank company that engaged General Maurice Rose's advance units in the hills south of Paderborn, is identified not through American accounts as recorded in previous memoirs, unit histories, and after-action reports but through German testimony of what occurred during the engagements. The death of General Rose in that encounter has been examined in detail in previous sources, including an official congressional war crimes investigation. Yet to a large extent, personal information regarding the German troops involved in the tragic and highly publicized death of the popular American commander remained obscure. Koltermann and other soldiers of his unit, Panzer Battalion 507, confronted the Americans in a series of vicious engagements during the final hours of the U.S. First Army's march to Lippstadt, and their story provides the reader with a new perspective on the events that occurred in the days before the meeting of the U.S. First and Ninth Armies. The German soldiers are no longer represented as undefinable, anonymous opponents but are finally provided identities with which they can be associated.

Lengthy interviews with Günther Reichhelm and Winrich Behr revealed the inner reflections and previously unreported conflicts of Walter Model's intimate circle of staff officers as they confronted the imminent destruction of their army. Behr, the sole surviving witness of Model's last hours, initially stated that he had little to contribute regarding the official events leading to the demise of the army group. However, more important for the focus of this work, the former cavalry officer was able to recall in great detail his own experiences during the encirclement and eventual dissolution of Army Group B. Behr succinctly recalled the closing days of the field marshal's life as Model and a small number of staff personnel wandered within the confines of an ever-shrinking pocket while evading Allied soldiers intent on bringing the shattered remnants of a once-invincible German army into captivity. Günther Reichhelm, Model's Army Group B operations officer, was flown out of the Ruhr Pocket on personal orders from Hitler to assume duties as chief of staff with General Walther Wenck's Twelfth Army. Reichhelm, who in 1945 ranked among the youngest colonels in the Wehrmacht, succinctly portrayed the foreboding atmosphere he encountered deep within the

Führerbunker in Berlin as he attempted to describe the catastrophic situation in the Ruhr to Adolf Hitler. Such pivotal events remain vivid in the memories of an ever-decreasing number of participants and witnesses to the collapse of the Third Reich, and as such, they have been recalled with precision and consistency.

A variety of primary and secondary sources were used in researching this project. Numerous local histories were consulted, which required extensive travel throughout the Ruhr Valley and the Sauerland where, some sixty years previously, the events described in the story evolved. Archives were searched, witnesses to specific events were located, and numerous official documents were examined for information pertinent to this study. Not surprisingly, personal accounts occasionally conflicted with official U.S. Army after-action reports: official army reports, like the fading memories of aging veterans and witnesses, are not infallible. However, the purpose of this work is not to reveal discrepancies and dispute the army's official record but rather to illustrate how events were observed and remembered by others.

Interviews with members of Model's staff revealed more about the attitudes held by the beleaguered officers and the harrowing environment they experienced than official records could ever portray. In the closing months of the war, Reichhelm recalled, those on the army group's operational staff were compelled to combat Allied armies and their own supreme command simultaneously, while existing on sparse rations, little sleep, and copious amounts of ersatz coffee. Reichhelm reported how Hitler's insistence on committing Germany's last reserves to the ill-fated Ardennes Offensive left Model "white with rage" and how the failure of the operation, predicted by the field marshal, produced a despondency in the commander from which he never recovered. The capture of the Ludendorff Bridge at Remagen by the U.S. First Army has often been regarded as a milestone in the course of the war in Europe. However, in providing his perspective of the event, Winrich Behr simply stated, "Of course it offered sensational headlines for the Allied press, but as far as we were concerned it was insignificant and even inevitable. We failed to prevent the Americans from crossing the Atlantic, and we had even failed to prevent the crossing of the English Channel ... with their growing strength and the continued deterioration of our own forces, we knew that there was little that could be done to prevent the Allies from crossing the Rhine wherever they wished."

The retreat of Army Group B across France and Belgium and, ultimately, to its end in the Ruhr Pocket clearly exhibits the rapid deterioration of the Wehrmacht, especially during the final months of the war. The army group's final months fully supports Omer Bartov's portrayal of the "demodernization" of the Wehrmacht. Additionally, the actions of Hübner's tribunal following the loss of the Ludendorff Bridge at Remagen directly exhibit Bartov's "perversion of discipline," as does the willingness of Model to acquiesce to Hübner's inquisitors as they interrogated officers under his command. The capture of the bridge by U.S. forces resulted in the sentencing to death by firing squad of six German officers, two of whom were sentenced in absentia. The sentencing represents an insignificant number relative to the thousands of German soldiers executed by the Wehrmacht during World War II, but it is indicative of the terror the Nazi system continued to inflict on civilians and indeed many of its own soldiers, particularly in the closing months of the conflict.

Interviews with surviving soldiers of Army Group B revealed the extent to which the Allied strategic bombing campaign immobilized German forces and contributed to the rapid deterioration of their combat effectiveness. As the Allies systematically reduced Model's encircled divisions, Wehrmacht supply depots containing immense fuel and ammunition reserves were demolished by retreating German forces due to lack of transport. This occurred in instances when, only a few miles distant, armored units and artillery batteries were immobilized and rendered ineffective due to lack of fuel and ammunition. Thousands of gallons of gasoline and tons of artillery projectiles cannot be transported, even for short distances, without proper vehicles or functional railways; even horse-drawn batteries require an extensive logistics train to remain operational. The paralysis of transportation assets in the closing weeks of the war often proved to irretrievably degrade the capabilities of the Wehrmacht, even at local levels. Moreover, the tendency of some forces to fiercely defend against further encroachments into the homeland was sometimes offset by the inclination of other less determined troops to don civilian clothing and disappear among the civilian populace. After six years of war, many of Hitler's most steadfast soldiers viewed the dismal situation as hopeless once the Americans and British penetrated the borders of Germany, and they reacted accordingly.

Another aspect of this story extends beyond the accounts of civilians living beneath the bombs or the postwar memoirs in which aging soldiers reflect on their experiences in the war in Europe. As an interview with former tank commander Ludwig Bauer illustrated, combat reaches an unforeseen level of intensity when troops are fighting on home soil. Bauer described the dilemma faced by German tank crews when, forced to engage seemingly endless numbers of enemy armored units, they were compelled to ignite farmhouses and villages with phosphorus projectiles in order to silhouette the oncoming tanks. To spare homes or farmsteads would have risked the imminent destruction of their own units by a numerically superior opponent. To illuminate the attacking force by reducing German homes to cinders—and likely killing the inhabitants—provided the soldiers an advantage that could have meant the difference between survival and death. Such conduct on foreign soil would have been accepted without hesitation; however, the situation was complicated when the measures taken would likely result in the deaths of civilians in the soldiers' own country.

Juxtaposed to this recollection are the documented accounts of civilians being executed by German officials for displaying white flags at the approach of Allied forces. However, even the callousness of such actions cannot always be taken at face value. A soldier given the responsibility of depriving a strategic area to the enemy cannot, in all cases, relinquish this responsibility when to do so means endangering his own troops. Accounts of American and British forces shooting German prisoners for having continued to resist after white flags were exhibited are numerous, as are instances in which Allied soldiers died because of the deception of a cornered and desperate enemy. Enraged, war-weary Allied soldiers were seldom inclined to investigate the reasons resistance was encountered following the exhibition of surrender, particularly if they suffered what they perceived to be needless casualties as a result of deception. Nor did they care that it may have been frightened civilians who had displayed white flags, albeit without the authority to do so.

A subtle comparison of German troops and equipment with the material wealth of the Americans remains at the forefront of the narrative. Whether explicit or implied, a comparison is unavoidable given the great disparity in numbers and material. The Wehrmacht, contrary to wartime propaganda and conventional belief, was never more than 20 percent motorized. The bulk of the forces, including logistics and artillery units, relied solely on rail and horse-drawn transport. As historian Dennis Showalter wrote, a full-strength, first-wave infantry division in 1939 possessed over 5,000 horses but fewer than 600 trucks. But the lack of mechanization, particularly in the early stages of the war, was not indicative of an unprepared or ill-equipped Wehrmacht. The German army was superior or equal to most military forces that existed in 1939, when few ground forces had evolved substantially from their nineteenth-century or World War I forebears. The common perception of a contest between enormous, motorized armies during World War II reflects the massive industrial capability that the United States brought to bear against opponents in all theaters of the war. The immense production capacity, particularly in aircraft and motorized vehicles, enabled the U.S. Army to quickly revolutionize the conduct of war. The inherent material disparity between German and Allied forces increased notably after mid-1943. By the spring of 1945, what little cohesion remained in the German force structure was rapidly disintegrating, whereas the Allied forces—supported by the immense production capability of the United States, which was protected by geographic isolation—continued to accelerate.

When writing about World War II, particularly from the perspective encompassed by this project, one inevitably faces criticism from numerous quarters.

Historians and researchers risk becoming immersed in their subject matter and thus losing the perspective of a general audience of readers. This is especially true when discussing Germany and Nazism in the Third Reich. It is not the purpose of this narrative to provoke contradiction on a subject that is controversial by its very nature. Much of this story is intended to provide insight into a little-discussed aspect of the war: the way in which the defeated enemy experienced and viewed the U.S. soldier as a conqueror. To undertake such a project for the benefit of any audience may prove to be a controversial and difficult endeavor. Yet this remains a compelling chronicle of human experience that must be presented, if for nothing less than to acknowledge and fulfill the demands of historical record.

Chapter 1

Retreat to the Reich

By August 1944 the situation for the German army in France was grim, if not catastrophic. In northern France, the German Wehrmacht was fighting for survival. The Anglo-American forces had carried out the greatest amphibious operation in history in Normandy on 6 June 1944. The Americans had conducted subsequent landings on the southern coast of France on 15 August. In Normandy, the Americans and British had broken out of the beachhead on the Cotentin Peninsula, and at Caen, the British forces had finally penetrated the German front. The Allied armies were prepared to sweep across France toward the German border.

At the onset of the Allied invasion, the German armies were commanded by highly respected and renowned commanders. The commander-in-chief of the German armies in France and the Low Countries (Oberbefehlshaber West [OB West], or Supreme Commander, West) was Field Marshal Gerd von Rundstedt. His forces totaled approximately sixty divisions of various strength and reliability. The divisions were assigned to two army groups, the largest of which was Army Group B, under the command of Field Marshal Erwin Rommel. Rommel's forces consisted of the Seventh Army occupying Normandy and Brittany, the Fifteenth Army in Pas de Calais and Flanders, and the LXXXVIII Corps in Holland. Army Group H, under command of General Johannes von Blaskowitz, consisted of the First and Nineteenth Armies, located in south and southwest France.

The Fifteenth Army had waited for the main Allied invasion to occur at Pas de Calais for seven weeks following the invasion in Normandy. The German high command had been convinced that the landings on 6 June were a feint, that the main Allied effort was destined for Calais, and that Lieutenant General George S. Patton was in England preparing to launch this massive assault. Thus, while nineteen German divisions remained in Calais anticipating an invasion that never materialized, less than 100 miles away the remnants of Army Group B were fighting viciously to contain the Allied beachhead. General Omar Bradley referred to this successful deception plan as "the biggest single hoax of the war."[1]

Disagreement between the two senior German commanders had only made a defense more difficult. Rundstedt believed that the best strategy for defeating the invasion force was to allow the Allies to gain a foothold and then destroy the beachhead. He insisted that German defenses should consist of a thinly held line along the beaches with a strong, mobile armored reserve that could be mobilized to eliminate the landing force. Rommel strongly believed that the only chance to deny the Allies success was to destroy their forces on the beaches before they could create and reinforce a beachhead. His experiences in Africa had revealed to him the hopelessness of fighting against an overwhelming enemy whose virtually unlimited airpower rendered every movement impossible. The disagreement in strategy led to the positioning of strong infantry defenses along the beaches, with the armored units held far to the rear in reserve. The compromise resulted in a defensive posture that pleased neither of the two commanders and weakened the overall strategy. The full strength of the panzer divisions was not committed to the landing until long after the beachhead had been consolidated.

As the Allied beachhead grew stronger, Rommel and Rundstedt appealed in vain for Hitler to release the divisions in Calais for a massive counterattack to eliminate the Allied forces. Hitler, fearing that the main attack was still imminent, refused. Finally, at the end of June, Rundstedt stated that he could no longer accept the responsibility of his position without authority to act accordingly. Hitler responded with a letter expressing his concern for the field marshal's health. Rundstedt submitted his resignation the following day.

On 7 July, Hitler dispatched Field Marshal Günther von Kluge, former head of Army Group Center in Russia, to be Rundstedt's successor. The change in command brought no relief. By 11 July, less than five weeks after the landings, Army Group B had lost almost 100,000 men in Normandy, including more than 2,000 irreplaceable officers. Oberkommando der Wehrmacht (OKW, or Supreme Command, German Armed Forces) had scraped together a mere 6,000 reinforcements to replace the lost regiments. More than 200 tanks were lost; only 17 replacements were received. Despite the reputation that preceded Kluge from the Eastern Front, the optimism that he initially brought to the battlefield in Normandy soon evaporated. Even he could not deny that the German defenses could not hold indefinitely. The perilous situation could collapse at any time, and the imminent breakout would leave the Allies streaming across the open country of northern France toward Germany.

In his second week after assuming command in the west, Kluge met with another disaster. On 17 July, Rommel was inspecting the precarious front in an attempt to read the next intentions of the Allies. Late that afternoon, he visited the headquarters (HQ) of the I SS Panzer Corps, under command of SS General Josef "Sepp" Dietrich. The two officers—one a former Nazi street brawler, the other an archetypical professional military officer—discussed the abysmal situation confidentially. The conditions under which the German forces were now attempting to stem the Allied advance were affecting even the blind faith of Dietrich, one of the founding members of Hitler's SS bodyguard regiments. Following the terse meeting, Rommel climbed into his imposing Horch staff car and ordered the driver to return to headquarters.

In an attempt to avoid the marauding fighter-bombers, the driver proceeded along secondary roads, where massive trees concealed the lanes between hedgerows. At length, they cleared the bocage and sped onto the open main road toward Vimoutiers. Within seconds, the speeding vehicle was spotted by a patrol of Spitfires. Rommel's shouts to the driver to take cover came too late. The fighters screamed toward the staff car at low level and opened fire with machine guns and cannons, spraying the vehicle with shrapnel and .50-caliber bullets as the Horch careened along the road at high speed. The severely wounded driver fought to maneuver the swerving car before losing control and slamming into a tree. Rommel was thrown from the open vehicle and struck the pavement. The hero of Africa barely survived the accident, suffering a shattered skull. Thereafter, Kluge assumed a dual role as both commander-in-chief of German forces in the west and as commander of Army Group B.

Many of the senior German officers now found themselves facing two battles. With their limited resources being consumed by the Allied advance, politics began to take a toll. The professional staff officers were aware that with the success of the Allied landing in Normandy, the defeat of Germany was imminent. The Wehrmacht might have been able to halt the onslaught of the Soviet army in the east, but it lacked the resources to stall the massive Red Army while fighting in Italy and France simultaneously. The only way to save Germany from total destruction was to negotiate a separate peace with the Anglo-American Allies. Thus, Hitler had to go.

Some weeks earlier, on 20 July 1944, Colonel Klaus Graf von Stauffenberg had placed a briefcase packed with explosives in Hitler's briefing room in East Prussia. Within minutes of Stauffenberg's departure from the conference room, the bomb exploded and demolished the wood-framed building. However, Hitler survived the blast. In the aftermath of that July assassination attempt, investigations and accusations of complicity took on epidemic proportions as the Gestapo implicated an increasing number of senior officers in the failed coup.

The Allies continued to try to free themselves of the beachhead and push into the open country, where their fully mechanized armored divisions could prevail. To break the impasse, they planned a massive air assault to bomb a path through the German lines. Operation Cobra called for a fleet of aircraft to strike the German units that were still tenaciously dug into the hedgerows, where they stubbornly refused to yield ground. The extraordinary operation entailed the use of heavy bombers for tactical air support; 1,500 heavy bombers, 396 medium bombers, and 350 fighter-bombers were committed to the plan.[2]

On 25 July, the air armada struck. More than 2,000 aircraft pounded 5 square miles of hedgerows, turning the Normandy farms into a moonscape. The carpet of bombs opened a swath through the German lines through which twenty-one fully motorized U.S. divisions poured, breaking out of the static warfare in the hedgerows onto open terrain. Kluge had been ordered by Hitler to hold all ground, and as the Americans flowed past his decimated army under the cover of aircraft, the surviving panzergrenadiers on both flanks of the corridor remained mired in their foxholes.

With a withdrawal of his forces expressly forbidden, Kluge sought another solution, reasoning that perhaps an attack could prevent the looming catastrophe. If the German forces could drive a wedge through the Allies to the sea from Mortain to Avranches, the U.S. Third Army would be severed from Omar Bradley's Twelfth Army Group and Bernard Montgomery's Twenty-first Army Group. The move would separate both Allied army groups from their breakout positions. The plan was an all-or-nothing gamble. By driving west through the U.S. Third Army, the German Seventh Army was exposing its entire southern and northern flanks to strong enemy forces. If the Allies succeeded in turning the German flanks, they would halt the attack with the German forces in the open, and little would stand between the Anglo-American troops and the borders of the Reich. On 7 August, Kluge launched his attack to split the Allied forces that were advancing south and southeast. The attempt to drive to the sea failed, and Omar Bradley saw "an opportunity that comes to a commander not more than once in a century."[3] Kluge's fears were realized as the Allies began closing the noose around the German Seventh Army between Falaise and Argentan.

By 11 August, Kluge knew that the gamble had failed, and on the next day, the Seventh Army was in flight. Montgomery had made slow progress against fanatical resistance, and an 18-mile gap remained open north of Falaise, through which thousands of German troops poured to escape the noose. Bradley, concerned that the U.S. and British armies might strike one another head-on in the chaos, refused permission for Third Army commander George Patton to drive northeast to close the gap. Patton was anxious to do so, but Bradley was also concerned that Patton's forces would become extended too far to be able to contain the Germans. With nineteen German divisions escaping from the pocket, he conceded that it was better to continue with the initial Allied plan than to expose Patton's line to penetration in any number of places.[4]

In mid-August, Kluge requested that Major Winrich "Teddy" Behr, an experienced reconnaissance officer, accompany him on an unexpected trip to Paris.

During the journey from La Roche–Guyon to Paris, Behr kept a close watch on the skies for any sign of Allied aircraft, and little was spoken between the two officers. Kluge was quietly distracted and distant as the vehicle sped south. The sky remained devoid of enemy aircraft, and they reached their destination without incident. Kluge directed the driver to a Wehrmacht medical facility, where he disappeared for some thirty minutes. On returning to the waiting vehicle, the field marshal explained to Behr that he had had a short visit with his son-in-law, a medical officer assigned to the facility. The officers then returned to La Roche–Guyon, again without encountering the normally ubiquitous fighter-bombers.[5]

Several days after Kluge's mysterious trip to Paris, the telephone rang at Chateau La Roche–Guyon, in which Army Group B's staff headquarters was located. The officer who answered responded to the caller's questions, explaining that Field Marshal von Kluge was on a tour of the front. The rough voice on the telephone identified himself as Field Marshal Walter Model and brusquely demanded directions to La Roche–Guyon. This request was followed by a string of sharply worded questions demanding to know why it was necessary to follow only the north bank of the Seine, why the Seine bridges were unusable, where the enemy forces were located, and how was it possible that the enemy had made such progress.[6]

The exasperated aide transferred the call to Army Group B's operations officer, Colonel Hans Georg von Tempelhoff, and to the chief of staff, Model's old acquaintance Lieutenant-General Hans Speidel. The aide suspected that Model, known as the *Terrorflieger* ("terror-pilot") among staff officers, was taking command in the west.

Model's reputation had preceded him from the Eastern Front. On five separate occasions, he had pulled Wehrmacht divisions from the abyss of total defeat. He had proven his abilities to conduct a withdrawal, stabilize a front, and reestablish a cohesive defensive line—first in 1942 in the Rshev Salient, then in the Orel Salient in 1943, and again while commanding Army Group North in the Baltic, in East Galicia, and in White Russia in 1944. His ability to save his forces from certain destruction had brought him a promotion to field marshal, the highest traditional rank in the German army, in March 1944. Now, in August 1944, Hitler had again called on Model's skills to save the catastrophic situation in Normandy.

Model's past successes did not come without cost. On the front, his reputation gave the soldiers facing the enemy renewed confidence, and he was known for maintaining close contact with the troops, who led a precarious existence under the guns. Within the staff officer corps, however, Model had developed a reputation as an enigmatic commander who drove his officers as hard as he drove himself. Because of his refusal to condemn or even discuss Germany's disastrous political situation, he was also considered by some as a fervent Nazi. Yet these detractors were not present when heated confrontations occurred between Model and Hitler regarding military strategy in the face of imminent defeat. Despite the events of the past months, Model remained steadfast in his refusal to introduce politics into his method of leading an army.

Hitler bestowed on Model the diamond clasp to the Knight's Cross on 16 August 1944 and praised his performance in Russia, remarking that the German people were grateful for his service to the country. Model, accompanied by his aide, Lieutenant Graf zu Stolber-Rossla, immediately flew to Paris. In the French capital, the field marshal spoke briefly with Lieutenant-General Dietrich von Choltitz, the newly appointed military commander of the German forces in the city. The general had acquired a reputation on the Eastern Front for unquestionable loyalty, and Choltitz had been personally chosen by Hitler to either defend or destroy Paris. The Führer had ordered that the capital be held at all costs, and Model desired to hear about the situation from the local commanders. From Paris, the field marshal traveled to his new headquarters in St. Germain, where he was briefed by Chief of Staff General Günther von Blumentritt.

At St. Germain, Model was provided with news of a shocking situation. Of the three armies assigned to his Army Group B, the Seventh Army and a large part of the Fifth Panzer Army, representing some 100,000 troops, were threatened with entrapment in the massive pocket between Mortain and Falaise. General von Salmuth's Fifteenth Army, situated on the channel coast, was also in danger of being cut off and annihilated. The sky above the pocket was thick with smoke billowing from columns of burning German tanks, artillery batteries, and support vehicles. Allied fighter-bombers hurled themselves through openings in the black clouds to pounce on anything that exhibited movement. The roads were lined with dead and dying men and horses, the corpses and carcasses rapidly putrefying in the summer heat. Allied pilots flying high above the battlefield reported that they were overwhelmed by the stench of death even at altitudes of several thousand feet.

Model was shocked by these reports. This was northern France, not the Eastern Front, and beyond Normandy, there existed little to stop the Allies from reaching the German border. An entire German army group was in the process of being annihilated only a few hours' distance from the German frontier. Additionally, the political briefing by Hitler had been ominous at best. Kluge, whom Model had been sent to replace, was now suspected of contacting the Allies in an attempt to discuss a separate peace proposal. On 15 August, the day before Model was assigned to assume command in the west, Kluge had remained out of touch for approximately twelve hours during a tour of the front in the area of Mortain-Falaise. Hitler's mistrust of his generals had intensified following the

20 July assassination attempt, and he was suspicious of Kluge's prolonged absence from his headquarters. The thought that Kluge might have been delayed because of the Allied fighter patrols that were impeding every German movement was dismissed. Additionally, Hitler had lost confidence in the commander's ability to stop the Allies. He was also convinced that Kluge was attempting to defect, and he emphatically made this belief known to Model.

Several hours after his abrupt telephone call to the Army Group B headquarters, Model's vehicle pulled into the courtyard of the Chateau La Roche–Guyon. The field marshal's car was accompanied by two large, open trucks, each carrying a number of heavily armed security personnel. As the escort personnel sprang from the trucks and established a perimeter around the courtyard, one of Kluge's aides, watching from an upper-floor window, looked at Tempelhoff and asked, "Well … are we going to be arrested? Now we're in for an experience."[7]

Model immediately marched into the headquarters, where he fumed in silence most of the afternoon while waiting for Kluge's return. In the meantime, General Blumentritt, chief of staff at Supreme Headquarters West, arrived from St. Germain. In the early evening, Kluge at last appeared, and the two field marshals withdrew from the nervous staff officers into a separate room and spoke with one another in private. The two chiefs of staff, Speidel and Blumentritt, waited in the outer foyer, expecting to be called at any moment.

Model reappeared and looked disgustedly at the two officers before sarcastically asking them if they had been sleeping. Additional rude comments followed. Model received less than tactful answers in response before he stormed from the room. With typical Swabian humor, Blumentritt turned to Speidel and stated that he probably should order a bottle of champagne for the two of them, as it would be of no further use to try to speak with the field marshal for the remainder of the day.

Meanwhile, another victim crossed Model's path. Lieutenant-General Fritz Bayerlein, commander of the decimated Panzer Lehr Division, had arrived to discuss the disposition of his severely mauled unit. The Panzer Lehr had borne the brunt of the carpet bombing that had initiated Operation Cobra. The remnants of the division, those men who had somehow survived the horror that had descended on them from squadrons of B-17 bombers, were without the heavy weapons needed to face the mechanized Allied divisions. Additionally, many of them were psychologically devastated by their experience under the carpet bombing. On seeing Bayerlein, Model came to a halt and rudely asked why he was not with his division. Bayerlein retorted that his division had to be withdrawn from the front to be restructured and reequipped. Model responded with sarcasm: "My dear Bayerlein! In the east the divisions remain on the front to be reequipped, and so shall it be done here from now on! Your units will remain where they are."[8]

At length, the staff officers of the army group were introduced. Colonel von Tempelhoff briefed Model on the situation at the front and found him to be rude and sarcastic. Colonel Leodegard Freyberg, the Army Group B adjutant, received special attention: Model looked at him closely and asked if they had been previously introduced. "Yes, Herr Feldmarschall," he responded dryly. "I served with the Field Marshal at the IV Army Corps; I have been well informed about the Field Marshal." Model responded only with his customary aloofness and a slight, insincere smile.[9]

During the night after Model's arrival, the majority of the staff personnel transferred to their new location at Margival, giving way to the waves of American tanks that were pushing relentlessly forward. Model, as was typical, remained behind to be among the last to depart. Field Marshal von Kluge stayed overnight, accompanied by his aide and driver. His small party of escorts prepared to depart for Germany the following day. German field marshals traditionally remained on active service for life, but Kluge had already received notice that he had been transferred from the active army to the reserves. The speed at which his relief from command had taken place caused him to consider the probable fate that lay before him: discharge from the army followed by the ordeal of arrest, interrogation, and an eventual death sentence issued by the People's Court.

The morning of 18 August found Model following his standard practice of departing promptly at 6:00 for a tour of the front. He directed his driver to take him to the headquarters of the Fifth Panzer Army for a conference with General Heinrich Eberbach and the two SS generals, Sepp Dietrich and Paul Hauser. Their discussion centered on resolving the crises in the Mortain-Falaise Pocket, which had been reduced to an area 36 miles wide by 18 miles deep. The narrow corridor toward the east through which troops could escape was being bitterly defended against the Americans pushing hard from the south and the Canadians and British from the north.

Sepp Dietrich, commander of the I SS Panzer Corps, elected to avoid facing the temperamental field marshal and sent his chief of staff, Major-General Rudolph Christoph Freiherr von Gersdorff, in his stead. Gersdorff, the former Intelligence officer (Ic) of Army Group Center on the Eastern Front, attended the meeting with reluctance. He had previously served with Model, whom he contemptuously regarded as a "full-blooded Nazi."[10]

In La Roche–Guyon on 19 August, Colonel von Tempelhoff conducted his inspection of the chateau at sunrise, as was his routine, and Field Marshal von Kluge prepared to return to Germany. The soft echo of American artillery fire sounded on the horizon, a constant reminder that the Germans' presence in the ancient chateau was reaching an end. The American forces had already crossed the Seine and were closing on Vernon and Mantes. Kluge would have to drive north to avoid encountering the enemy columns. In Kluge's room, Tempelhoff observed the field marshal's uneaten breakfast still on a table.

Kluge departed La Roche–Guyon with his small party as the sun was rising. Tangermann drove the field marshal's car, which was accompanied by a small security detachment. As the vehicles bounced along the roads rutted from the passage of heavy armored columns, Kluge was observed murmuring to himself, and the accompanying officers heard him say, "I cannot survive this, I simply cannot bear leaving my soldiers to their fate now, in this situation."[11]

They reached the forest of Compiègne by early afternoon and halted under the foliage for a rest. Kluge paced back and forth and continued to speak of how he could not bear to return to Germany under the circumstances. Tangermann attempted to calm him and advised the field marshal that he would feel better if he got some sleep. After an hour, they drove on toward the east, over the battlefields of World War I, and by midday, the party was west of Verdun. Kluge again requested that the party halt for a rest, and between Clermont-en-Argonnes and Dombasle, the convoy pulled to the side of the road in a favorable location. A blanket was spread several yards from the vehicles, and Kluge rested in the shade and busied himself writing a letter. After several minutes, he called to Tangermann; as the officer approached, he handed him the letter in an envelope and requested that it be mailed to his brother, Lieutenant-General von Kluge, adding that the party should prepare to depart in about fifteen minutes. As Tangermann walked back to the vehicles to prepare for their departure, Kluge slipped a tiny, glass cyanide capsule into his mouth. Within seconds, the field marshal lay dying.[12]

In La Roche–Guyon, Model reacted with cold stoicism on hearing of Kluge's death. He dispatched Colonel Freyberg to Seventh Army headquarters to inform Kluge's son, Lieutenant-Colonel Günther von Kluge, of his father's death.[13]

The following day, General Speidel approached the field marshal and broached the subject regarding the attitude Model had exhibited toward the staff officers immediately after his arrival on 17 August. They had known one another for many years, and between the two officers, such things could be discussed with candor. Model admitted that he may have been too harsh in his initial treatment of the staff. Speidel then began to discuss the overall situation on the front and suggested that it might be best to negotiate with the western Allies in order to win a free hand against the Soviets. Model hesitantly concurred and then was silent for a moment before he abruptly ended the discussion by responding, characteristically, "Well, let's stay out of politics."[14]

On 19 August, the day Günther von Kluge committed suicide, Montgomery succeeded in linking with American forces to close the Falaise Pocket, trapping a large part of the German Seventh Army. The trap was not sprung between

Falaise and Argentan, however, but 15 miles to the east of Falaise at Chambois. The battle area of Falaise was strewn with the corpses of thousands of German soldiers, and thousands more Wehrmacht troops were being processed by the Allies as prisoners of war. However, although the men were demoralized and suffering due to immense losses of equipment, the delay in closing the pincer and sealing the pocket had enabled much of the Seventh Army to succeed in escaping the noose.

Like his predecessors, Field Marshal Model was faced with the impossible task of halting the overwhelming might of the Allied armies. Within twenty-five days after the landings on 6 June, the Allies had put more than 1 million troops ashore, supported by 560,000 tons of materiél.[15] Most senior German officers were aware that unless the situation changed dramatically, they were going to lose the war. German industry could not match the overwhelming numbers of tanks, artillery pieces, aircraft, and other materials being produced by the Allies. Moreover, the German sources of manpower were exhausted; the badly decimated units were being augmented by half-trained foreign volunteers and teenagers. The insurmountable Allied strength, coupled with the high command's refusal to give the western commanders freedom of action, had decimated the army group. Approximately 130,000 men had been lost, either killed or captured, in the Falaise Pocket. At Amiens, one of the army group's most talented leaders, General Eberbach, was taken prisoner by the Americans, along with his entire staff. The remains of the eleven divisions that comprised the Seventh Army were supposed to regroup in the area of Somme–St. Quentin to be reequipped; the area was overrun by the Americans before the plan could even be set into motion.

In the meantime, Paris had fallen. On 20 August, Hitler had issued his orders to either hold the city or ensure its destruction. Model had forwarded the message to the Paris commander, Dietrich von Choltitz, without comment. On receiving reports that the resistance organizations within the city were rising up against the German occupiers, Hitler again sent a message, on 23 August, restating his demand that Paris be either held or destroyed.

In stark contrast to his reputation, Choltitz, lacking sufficient troop strength to defend the city, ignored Hitler's demands to destroy the capital. On 25 August, he surrendered to elements of General Philippe Leclerc's French 2nd Armored Division following a preemptive uprising by the Maquis (the French Resistance), which resulted in a highly unusual, albeit temporary, cease-fire between the Maquis and Choltitz's German forces. In the face of the catastrophe confronting his army group, Field Marshal Model seemed to take little notice, and he no longer busied himself with the issue of Paris. He had left the matter of Hitler's *Führerbefehl* (Führer Order, a directive personally from Hitler) to either hold or destroy the city to his chief of staff, Hans Speidel. The collapsed front, with superbly equipped Allied armies pouring toward the east, was of more concern to him than political objectives, and Model, like his American counterpart Omar Bradley, considered Paris of little strategic military value.

The following day, Model was confronted by another of his generals. Colonel-General von Salmuth, commander of the Fifteenth Army, strongly recommended that the entire army group be withdrawn behind the Seine before it was too late to avoid total destruction. He feared that within a few days, it would no longer be possible to cross the river with heavy weapons and tanks, which would leave the already badly mauled army group completely stripped of combat capability. Model voiced his opposition to Salmuth's proposal. The heated discussion continued until the field marshal pointedly refused to consider a withdrawal. Shortly thereafter, Salmuth was relieved of his command, and the Fifteenth Army was passed to General Gustav von Zangen.

The German army continued to give ground under pressure from the Allies. The end of August found the Army Group B staff located in the "White Castle" at Havrincourt. Meanwhile, the specter of 20 July continued to haunt the senior officers of the Wehrmacht. At one point, Colonel Freyberg, Model's senior adjutant, informed the field marshal that he had an incoming call from the chief of army personnel, Major-General Wilhelm Burgdorf, regarding Model's chief of staff, General Speidel. Burgdorf advised Model that Hans Speidel was to be relieved of his duties: his name had surfaced during the investigation of the assassination attempt. A verbal altercation between Model and Burgdorf ensued, during which the field marshal advised Burgdorf that he and his men were in the middle of a battle in which the army group was fighting for its existence. Burgdorf remained adamant and asked who Model would like to have as a replacement. Responding heatedly, Model asked for evidence that Speidel was involved in the conspiracy. The sharp exchange continued, with the field marshal losing his composure and telling Burgdorf that he was not interested in hearing about why, at this critical point of the war, his chief of staff was being relieved of his duties: "This is nonsense! I can't replace my Chief of Staff right now, and I demand that this order be withdrawn! Tell that to the Führer! Suspicions … Do you have proof? This is nonsense." The conversation ended with Model slamming down the phone receiver. He then turned to Freyberg. "They've all gone crazy. Speidel is supposed to go," he said, fuming but resigned. "It has something to do with 20 July, some kind of political nonsense."[16]

Knowing that Speidel's transfer was inevitable, Model chose the chief of staff of the LXXXIX Corps, Colonel Ullrich, as Speidel's relief. To his chagrin, Ullrich could not be located; he was assumed to have been killed or captured in the ongoing chaos of the destruction in Normandy. Several days later, without prior notification from Berlin, General Hans Krebs appeared unannounced at the Army Group HQ to serve as Speidel's relief. Krebs was an experienced staff officer with a sound reputation, and his arrival provoked no comment from the field marshal.

On 3 September, Model hosted a farewell dinner for Speidel in the new staff headquarters at Chaudefontaine. Model's speech was short but characteristically heartfelt. He later advised Freyberg to maintain a respectable distance from Speidel until the issue surrounding his departure was resolved. On the day the altercation with Burgdorf over Speidel's relief from duties had occurred, the People's Court had condemned three officers to death for complicity in the 20 July plot: the former military governor of France, General Karl Heinrich von Stülpnagel; his chief of staff, Colonel Hans-Otfried von Linstow; and the senior quartermaster west, Colonel Eberhard Finckh. Model later received a letter from the widow of Colonel Georg Schultze-Büttger, who had also disappeared in the wave of terror following the assassination attempt. Frau Schultze-Büttger requested assistance in locating the whereabouts of her husband; Model forwarded the letter to the Office of Army Personnel. "I'm going to stay clear of this," he said to his adjutants. "I don't want to have anything to do with it."[17]

Model's arrival had been marked by the fleeing German forces coming to a halt, and the demoralized troops were now reorganizing to present a strong defensive front. As the Allies closed with the border of Germany, Model demanded a reinforcement of twenty-five new divisions, five or six of which were to be armored. With the full knowledge that the forces he demanded were not available, he nevertheless attempted to stress the critical situation on the Western Front to the high command. In response to his incessant calls for reinforcements, he received two panzergrenadier divisions and two armored brigades. The troops he required to stem the Allied advance had long since disappeared in the vastness of Russia. The remnants of the units that had escaped death or capture in the east were now being relentlessly destroyed in France.

The Allies captured Antwerp on 4 September. The Anglo-American forces had begun experiencing severe supply problems of their own as they quickly distanced themselves from Normandy during their eastward pursuit. Despite the attempt by General Dwight D. Eisenhower to keep the German armies reeling in defeat, the Wehrmacht was starting to recover and stabilize its situation after the Normandy debacle. Even with the immense losses suffered by Germany since the D-Day landings, the British and Americans had noted an increase in German resistance that slowed their race across France to a crawl. Omar Bradley, frustrated at the resistance his forces were suddenly encountering just when the German army had appeared to be teetering toward total collapse, attributed the newfound stubbornness of the German defense to a little-known "Prussian" whom Hitler had decorated the previous year for halting the Russians at the Vistula. It was reported that this new commander had taken control of Army Group B following Kluge's death.[18]

On 5 September, Field Marshal Gerd von Rundstedt, the patriarch of the German officer corps, was recalled to assume senior command in the west, leaving Model free to fully commit himself to Army Group B. Model, relieved that his impossible dual responsibility had come to an end, now concentrated on extricating his army group from the tenacious Allies and regrouping for a defense of the Reich. His first briefing with Rundstedt took place in a pharmacy in the ancient town of Stadtkyll. He advised Rundstedt that the estimated strength of the Allies now stood at 61 superbly equipped, fully motorized divisions. The Allies were supported by a massive fleet of 16,000 aircraft. Opposing this gigantic force were 3 to 4 exhausted panzer divisions and 10 decimated infantry divisions whose every move was met by destruction from the incessant fighter-bombers that controlled the skies.[19] The Twenty-first Army Group, under Field Marshal Montgomery, appeared ready to push through Holland and threaten the Ruhr, while the Twelfth Army Group, under General Omar Bradley, was advancing across Belgium toward the German border.

On 7 September, General Hans Speidel was arrested by order of Reichsführer SS Heinrich Himmler for suspicion of treasonous activities. Despite the immense burdens he faced on the front, Model was aware of the arrest of his former chief of staff; news of such reprisals spread quickly through the nervous officer corps. The field marshal ordered his aide, SS Sturmbannführer (Major) Heinz Springer, to arrange a meeting with Sepp Dietrich, with whom Springer had served in Russia. The meeting was to be confidential: they were to meet alone, in a place where they could speak without being observed.

Springer selected an isolated residence overlooking a vineyard near Namur. The field marshal requested that Springer remain present during the meeting. During this period of inquisition and distrust, it was important for all parties to conversations to have reliable witnesses. Model characteristically broached the purpose of the meeting directly. "My dear Sepp Dietrich, you are aware that on 7 September they arrested Speidel. This is impossible, especially now, with the problems we are facing. We can't do without him. Rundstedt needs a chief of staff who understands our situation here. You, Sepp Dietrich, still have influence with the Führer." He paused before continuing, "I would like to ask you to use this influence on behalf of Lieutenant-General Speidel." Dietrich promised that he would attempt to intervene on Speidel's behalf, and the officers then spoke briefly of unrelated matters before ending the meeting.[20]

On 11 September, less than twenty days after the liberation of Paris, American forward elements reached the German border near Aachen. On the same day, the U.S. Third Army was joined by the U.S. Seventh Army, which had driven from southern France after pushing Blaskowitz's Army Group G eastward toward Germany. The Allies now held a solid, impenetrable line from Switzerland to Holland. However, even the great material superiority of the Anglo-American armies had limits. At the point of breaching the frontiers of Germany, the Allied troops were forced to a halt because of severely extended supply lines.

In September, Field Marshal Montgomery, commander of the Allied Twenty-first Army Group, drafted a plan for the British Twenty-first Army to break through the German defenses of the Maas, Waal, and Lower Rhine. Without consulting his American counterpart, Omar Bradley, Montgomery flew to Eisenhower's headquarters to brief the supreme Allied commander of his remarkably daring plan. Bradley was shocked when he learned of the plan through his Twenty-first Army Group liaison officer several days after its approval by Eisenhower, and he remained steadfastly opposed to the concept.[21]

Code-named Market-Garden, the operation called for a massive Anglo-American airborne drop to secure bridges in Holland and to open a 60-mile-wide corridor through which Allied forces could push into Germany and secure the Ruhr area, simultaneously moving east across the open plains of northwest Germany. This assignment fell to the 82nd and 101st Airborne Divisions under Generals J. Gavin and Maxwell Taylor, respectively, and the British 1st Airborne Division under General R. E. Urquhart and the Polish Parachute Brigade under General Sosabowski.

There were five major waterways to be crossed on this route: two canals north of Eindhoven; the Meuse River, 24 miles beyond the canals; the Waal River at Nijmegen, some 8 miles beyond the Meuse; and finally, the wide Lower Rhine at Arnhem, some 20 miles from the open German border. The Americans were to secure the bridges in the areas of Eindhoven-Greve-Nijmegen, the British and Poles were to seize the bridges in Arnhem and the Lower Rhine. It was a daring gamble that, if successful, would enable the Allies to outflank the Siegfried Line defenses and cross the Rhine onto the plains of north Germany.

On Sunday, 17 September, the Army Group B staff was in the Park-Hotel in Oosterbeek, Holland. Field Marshal Model was conducting a briefing when the sky suddenly filled with aircraft. The German forces in the area were accustomed to Allied aircraft. Holland lay directly in the flight path of the heavy bomber squadrons that routinely pounded the Ruhr industrial area farther to the southeast. However, at 2:00 p.m., the air at Oosterbeek was rent with explosions. Windows shattered, and plaster from the ceiling rained on the staff personnel as they took cover on the floor. A second wave of bombers struck as staff officers ran from the building into the garden to observe the vast armada passing overhead. Colonel Tempelhoff, Army Group B operations officer, appeared and breathlessly reported to Model that at least two divisions of paratroopers were landing in the area. The field marshal immediately called for an emergency evacuation. Officers and aides feverishly gathered maps and documents as Model ordered the staff to meet in Terborg.

Terborg was situated along the route from Arnhem to Emmerich, and the army group staff set to work repelling the Allied force. Model's first objective was to contact SS General Wilhelm Bittrich's II SS Panzer Corps in Dötinchem, which had been heavily hit by the air attack. He ordered Bittrich to secure the Rhine bridges and to organize all available units to counter the assault. Bittrich quickly committed a battle group from the 9th SS Panzer Division "Hohenstaufen" and an SS training battalion to destroy the British concentrations.

In the other areas under assault from the paratroopers, the situation was more acute. Colonel-General Kurt Student, commander of the First Parachute Army, had experienced a similar attack. Student requested permission to demolish the massive Waal bridge to deny it to the Allied assault force; Model adamantly re-fused to allow the destruction. Student's fears were realized when, several days later, the bridge fell into the hands of the American paratroopers working with the forward elements of the British Guards Armored Division. The bridges at Greve and Eindhoven soon fell to the Allies. Then came the German counterat-tack amid problems within the Allied forces. General Brian Horrocks was unable to establish contact between his armored units and the airborne units before the stronger German forces began to decimate the pockets of isolated paratroopers.

On Monday, 18 September, Model personally directed the counterattack against the British parachute units located between Oosterbeek and Wolfheeze. General Urquhart's paratroopers, lacking contact with the armored units, were quickly reduced. The assault by the Polish brigade arrived on 21 September—too late to reinforce the isolated British forces. The following day, Horrocks ordered the British and Polish forces to attempt to break out of the ever-tightening net in the area of Arnhem. Of the 9,000 British paratroopers dropped into the Arnhem bridgehead, less than 2,500 escaped to reach Allied lines.[22]

Operation Market-Garden would be the last major defensive victory for Model. The OKW report of 27 September indicated that 6,500 Allied troops were taken prisoner, 30 antitank guns were captured, and 1,000 gliders were destroyed. German antiaircraft units reported 100 aircraft were shot down.[23] The thousands of Allied and German dead littering the area bore testimony to the vicious fighting that had occurred. Omar Bradley had opposed the operation in favor of a campaign against German forces guarding Antwerp and the Scheldt es-tuaries. The Allied supply lines were badly strained, and the lack of fuel reserves had forced the Americans and British to slow their advance toward the Westwall, known to the Allies as the Siegfried Line. With the failure of Market-Garden, the proposed campaign against the Scheldt was abandoned. The Antwerp harbor, so urgently needed to alleviate the supply problem, remained closed to the Allies until 26 November.

While the battle in Holland was raging, the battle for Aachen had begun. During the first week of September 1945, units of Major General Clarence R. Huebner's 1st Infantry Division, the Big Red One, reached the outskirts of the city. The German commander of Aachen, Colonel von Osterroth, assumed the role of combat commander, a dubious title at best. His available forces had no heavy weapons, and moreover, the bunkers and fortresses of the vaunted Westwall had long been neglected. Many installations were secured and locked, and the locations of the keys to reinforced structures were often a mystery. Some of the bunkers had been broken into and plundered; others were almost submerged in water. A message sent at the end of August by Field Marshal Model directing Military Districts VI and XIII to prepare defenses on the Westwall had apparently had little effect.

Although the area of Aachen was assigned to General Erich Brandenberger's Seventh Army sector, the city itself was the responsibility of Lieutenant-General Ferdinand Schack's LXXXI Corps. Theoretically, the corps was fully armed, but in fact, it consisted only of a collection of remnants of troops of various divisions that had been hurriedly assembled after the debacle in Normandy. The skeletal remains of the 183rd Infantry Division were ordered to defend the city. Model was aware that the Allies could launch another daring attack through the Cologne basin on the Rhine between Cologne and Düsseldorf. To counter this threat, he ordered the 116th Panzer Division, under Lieutenant-General Graf Gerd von Schwerin, to reinforce Aachen.

The arrival of combat troops contributed to the panic spreading among the city's inhabitants. The local authorities prematurely ordered the destruction of munitions factories, even one of which could have produced enough small-arms ammunition to supply half of Army Group B for weeks.[24] The civilian population was ordered to evacuate the city, and among the first to flee were the *Kreisleiter* ("district political leader") and the chief of police.

General Schwerin's oncoming tanks were met by columns of refugees fleeing the city. Schwerin immediately ordered the civilians to return to their homes. The possibility of an Allied attack on the city was still remote, and he needed the streets clear for an unimpeded approach by his forces. He then dispatched a carefully worded letter to the commander of the forces opposing him, General J. Lawton Collins, commander of the U.S. VII Corps. Appealing to Collins to avoid unnecessary civilian casualties, Schwerin advised him that the people of Aachen had not been evacuated and that fighting in the city should be avoided.

The *Gauleiter* of the Cologne-Aachen district, Josef Grohe, was chagrined by the flight of his subordinates and other party functionaries. In attempts to salvage his blemished reputation, he seized on the letter Schwerin had dispatched to the American forces, embellished on the incident, and forwarded a scathing report to his political superiors. In the wake of the 20 July assassination attempt, any suggestion of traitorous activity drew immediate attention. On 16 September, General Franz Mattenklott, assistant commander of Wehrkreis VI (Military District VI) in Münster, appeared unannounced in the city. He had been dispatched by order of Reichsführer SS Himmler to investigate the report from Grohe, who had falsely reported to his Nazi Party officials that Schwerin's 116th Panzer Division had fled the city, leaving it defenseless.

Mattenklott's orders were to stabilize the critical situation by arming the Aachen police with light antitank weapons to stop the American advance. General Schwerin met with Mattenklott and briefed him on the critical situation in the city. The exasperated Schwerin explained that the loss of civilian lives had to be avoided, thus justifying the letter to his opponent. However, this explanation proved to be unsatisfactory. On 17 September, Schwerin was ordered to report to General Schack, whereon he was further interrogated under suspicion of traitorous activity. Meanwhile, Field Marshal Model, engaged in battling the Market-Garden airborne assault from his headquarters in Oosterbeek, sent word to Schwerin that the general should be prepared to face arrest and conviction through the People's Court. Schwerin heeded the warning. Model continued to busy himself with fighting the Allied airborne forces in Holland.

After several hours of questioning by General Schack's inquisitors, Schwerin returned to his division, where he promptly relocated his headquarters deep within the maze of an ever-changing front and remained out of contact with higher authorities.[25] After three days, he was finally contacted by General Brandenberger, who advised him that he was under arrest and now under the jurisdiction of OB West in Koblenz. With this action, Schwerin was also immediately placed under the jurisdiction of Model and Rundstedt. Despite the immense power at his disposal, Himmler theoretically could not officially cross the administrative lines. Schwerin's arrest by army authorities serving under Model placed the general out of reach of the Nazi headhunters, at least until his military case could be resolved.[26]

The case of Schwerin in Aachen was indicative of an increasing conflict between party functionaries and military officers that became more acute as the Allied armies neared the borders of the Reich. Power hungry and often militarily incompetent, the Nazi officials were placed in command of the paramilitary units being used to augment the Wehrmacht in defending the homeland. Responsible for mobilizing the Volkssturm, the party had prepared for the eventuality by hoarding weapons, fuel, and supplies that could have been better used by the army, which was constantly plagued by shortfalls in every category.

Following the 20 July assassination attempt, Himmler had been placed in command of the replacement army, under which new units were formed. The new People's Army, or Volksheer, consisted of units scraped together from the skeletal remnants of once-proud divisions, the bulk of whose troops now lay in countless unmarked graves throughout Europe or languished in prisoner-of-war cages across two continents.

Many civilians barely concealed the disdain they felt for the Golden Pheasants, as the senior Nazi Party officials were known. With many suspecting that the end of Nazi rule was approaching, this attitude was sometimes hardly concealed by army officers. Model characteristically remained aloof and distanced himself from the whirlwind of political issues. The military, he emphasized, had to remain apart from politics; it was not the responsibility of the soldiers to change political conditions, nor was it in their power to do so. His responsibility was to hold the front. So he tolerated the presence of the Gauleiters and kept his opinion of the distasteful politicians largely to himself.[27]

The field marshal worked tirelessly to draw additional forces together for his defense of the Reich. Model took the opportunity to request more forces directly from Dr. Joseph Goebbels when the propaganda minister visited the Rhine and Ruhr districts. Goebbels met with the field marshal at his army group headquarters in Fischelen near Krefeld. Over dinner, Model explained that the catastrophic situation his troops had been facing several weeks ago had been temporarily stabilized but that he was in desperate need of at least two complete divisions and 100 tanks. The land bridge in Holland between Eindhoven and Nijmegen was now in British hands, and the threat had to be countered. Model suggested that the propaganda minister could advise the Führer of the shortfalls; perhaps this connection could produce the needed forces.

The discussion proved fruitless. Goebbels, in an astonishing exhibition of candor, revealed to the field marshal that he no longer believed the rising production figures routinely provided by Armaments Minister Albert Speer; no additional supplies would be forthcoming. Furthermore, supplies of fuel and deliveries of important war materials had been seriously disrupted beneath an incessant carpet of bombs dropped from fleets of Allied aircraft. Even if Model were to be given the 100 tanks he requested, it remained doubtful that he could receive the fuel needed for them. The Germans had reached a point where supply became unpredictable; they were fighting with whatever came available from week to week and even from day to day.[28]

The fighting in the area of Aachen increased in intensity. For Hitler, the city held an importance of mythic proportions. Aachen was the burial site of Charlemagne, and the Führer was determined to deny the Allies the grave of the legendary emperor, whom he considered one of his spiritual forebears. The supreme commander, west, and the commander of Army Group B, Rundstedt and Model, respectively, were bound by instructions emanating directly from Hitler's headquarters. The command of the 116th Panzer Division was assumed by Colonel Siegfried Freiherr von Waldenburg following the fiasco leading to Schwerin's arrest. The former Aachen battle commander, Osterroth, was relieved on 30 September by Colonel Max Leyherr, commander of Grenadier Regiment 689. The 116th Panzer Division was taken out of the line to receive other assignments and was replaced by the 245th Volksgrenadier Division, which had recently arrived from Prague.

At the end of September, the American XIX and VII Corps attacked Aachen, with the intent of encircling the city. Between 8 and 15 October, Model attempted to prevent the encirclement by counterattacking with the 116th and 3rd Panzergrenadier Divisions, reinforced with heavy tank and tank destroyer battalions. On 10 October, Lieutenant General Courtney Hodges dispatched three intermediaries to attempt to convince Leyherr to surrender. This appeal was accompanied by a psychological campaign directed at the Wehrmacht soldiers and the citizens of Aachen through loudspeakers and leaflets urging them to abandon the hopeless contest. A delegation of prominent citizens appeared at the colonel's headquarters and appealed to Leyherr to heed the surrender request. In the midst of the once-splendid city that was quickly being reduced to a hideous pile of blackened rubble, the colonel again refused. Model had previously denied a request from Leyherr on 3 October to permit him to surrender and thus spare the city further destruction.

On 12 October, Leyherr received his reward for his unwavering obedience to Hitler's directive for self-immolation. The maze of investigations in the wake of the 20 July assassination attempt now suggested that he, too, was involved in the conspiracy. It was noted that Leyherr was the son-in-law of the former German chief of the General Staff, Franz Halder, who had been linked to the conspiracy. This close relationship automatically placed him under suspicion. During the course of the investigation, he was relieved of his command; his replacement was Colonel Gerhard Wilk, commander of the 245th Volksgrenadier Division.[29]

At the time of the investigation, Leyherr had established his headquarters in the cellar of the renowned Quellenhof Hotel, which had been reduced to a smoldering shell during the fighting. Colonel Wilk transferred the new command post to a massive bunker complex on Förster-Rütscher Strasse. Half of the city was now a field of ruins, and the citizens of Aachen, in an attempt to bring the incessant torment to an end, were emerging from their cellars to advise the advancing American units of German military positions. Women and elderly men tried to persuade Wehrmacht defenders to exchange their uniforms for civilian clothing and wait for the Americans. The American infantrymen reached the cathedral quarter in the heart of Aachen and discovered that the clerics had remained in the city, unlike the Nazi functionaries, who had fled. An SS battle group that had been fighting fiercely within the ruins eventually vanished without a trace beneath the artillery barrages and encroaching waves of U.S. soldiers.

Colonel Wilk radioed Army Group B for permission to break out of the encirclement. Model responded that Wilk was expected to "hold to the last man." On 24 October at 11:38 a.m., Colonel Wilk sent his last radio message to the Seventh Army. Accompanied by 300 surviving defenders, he then emerged from the ruins to surrender to the U.S. 26th Infantry Regiment.[30]

In the late phases of the struggle for the city of Aachen, news reached Army Group B that Field Marshal Erwin Rommel had died unexpectedly en route to a hospital in Ulm. Model's reaction to the death of his predecessor was stoic; the two officers had had very little personal contact during their careers. Hitler ordered a state funeral; Colonel von Tempelhoff was dispatched to Ulm to represent Model's Army Group B. Field Marshal von Rundstedt conducted the funeral oratory, and Germany mourned the loss of the legendary hero of the Afrikakorps. The public remained unaware of the cause of Rommel's death, and at the time, the true reason behind the unexpected passing was known to neither Rundstedt nor Model. Rommel had been involved, albeit inactively, in the 20 July conspiracy, and his knowledge of the conspirators' activities had been discovered during the subsequent series of inquisitions and arrests.

Rommel was a national hero and one of the few generals who did not belong to the distrusted *Junker* class. Hitler had agreed that he should be permitted to commit suicide rather than face the People's Court. This was not necessarily a magnanimous gesture on the Führer's part, for Hitler wished to avoid the embarrassment and political fallout that Rommel's involvement in the 20 July *attentat* would bring if made public. In return, the field marshal would be provided a state funeral, and his family would be spared the notorious *Sippenhaft*—the punishment of family members for an individual's crimes. Additionally, the family would continue to receive Rommel's pension. His death was conveniently attributed to the wounds he received in Normandy. Although Rundstedt later learned what had happened, it is unknown whether Model ever knew the true cause of Rommel's death.

In October, Model was successful in transferring his operations officer, Colonel von Tempelhoff, and his intelligence officer, Colonel Freyberg, from his staff. Neither regretted parting ways with the field marshal. Freyberg experienced one last insulting exchange during a dinner with the senior *Bürgermeister* of Krefeld. Model asked Freyberg a question regarding an artillery officer who was serving with a certain regiment. The colonel responded that he had little contact with the division and regimental commanders and that he had even less contact with specific battery commanders. Model turned to the Bürgermeister and remarked frostily, "You see what kind of people I have to work with. The man has no idea about personnel matters." Freyberg retorted that throughout his long career as a staff officer, he had received many officers' evaluations to the contrary. Model stared at him coldly for several seconds before raising his glass and remarking, "So ... *Prost*, Freyberg."[31]

Colonel von Tempelhoff was relieved by a General Staff officer intimately familiar with Model's peculiarities. Lieutenant-Colonel Günther Reichhelm had served with him during the massive defensive battles on the Eastern Front and was thus accustomed to the field marshal's egocentrism. Freyberg's replacement, Colonel Theodor Pilling, assumed duties as Model's intelligence officer after recovering from a severe wound received while serving as commander of Grenadier Regiment 513 on the Bessarabia Front. Both officers were considered by some staff members to be favorites of the field marshal. However, their favored status was not without merit. Model's most reliable officers had long since learned to disregard his volatile temper and abrasive manner and had developed an intuition as to how and when to approach their controversial commander.

Reichhelm was greeted coldly by some members of Model's army group staff. Tempelhoff, Reichhelm's predecessor, had been very popular with the other officers and had often served as a buffer between the abrasive field marshal and his staff. Reichhelm had served with Tempelhoff in the prewar years with Artillery Regiment 3 in Frankfurt an der Oder, and some of the officers attributed his rapid promotion through the officer ranks to favoritism from Model. The army group staff officers were unaware that Reichhelm's first encounter with Model had been less than pleasant. His initial contact with the future field marshal occurred in Russia while he was serving on the staff of the XXIII Corps. In the wake of the failed attempt to capture Moscow, Model was ordered to replace Colonel-General Adolf Strauss as commander of the Ninth Army. During the course of Reichhelm's early briefings, Model unexpectedly surfaced at the XXIII Corps headquarters. Shortly after Reichhelm began his situation report, Model launched into a demeaning diatribe concerning the correct manner in which briefings should be conducted. He demanded that Reichhelm, as with all of his staff officers, not only brief him on a situation but also provide at least three alternative plans for resolving the specific problem at issue. Reichhelm explained that there could be no solution when equipment was lacking, all ammunition and fuel had been expended, and there were no replacements for the mounting casualties. This response provoked a torrent of abuse from Model. Reichhelm abruptly ended the encounter by throwing the files and maps onto the floor in exasperation and storming from the room, slamming the door behind him.[32]

He expected a formal reprimand—or worse—for his uncharacteristic outburst. Such a shocking display of insubordination could carry severe penalties in any army, and the Wehrmacht, with a well-earned reputation for draconian discipline for any infraction, was no exception. He waited with dread for what the future under the temperamental field marshal would bring. The outburst appeared to have had the opposite effect. In the months that followed, Reichhelm developed as close a working relationship as was possible with the enigmatic field marshal. Thereafter, each time Model was transferred to a new command, Reichhelm was inevitably called to serve on the field marshal's staff.

Despite the frosty reception initially received by Reichhelm from some of the Army Group B officers, he was not without friends and acquaintances who were serving with Model's staff. The staff Ic, Lieutenant-Colonel Michael, had served with Reichhelm in the same artillery regiment, and the two of them were the same year group (sharing the same year of birth). Reichhelm had also been a guest of Michael's parents in 1932 during a trip through Germany that took him to Heidelberg. Their relationship became strained, however, while serving with Model's staff in the Münstereifel. Michael was known to be an unabashed womanizer, and true to his character, he had developed a relationship with a young woman from a prominent family in the area. In the evenings, following Model's return from his daily tour of the front, Reichhelm was additionally burdened with justifying Michael's frequent absences. Eventually, Reichhelm ordered that a telephone cable be established from the staff headquarters to the young woman's residence so that the officers could forewarn Michael of the field marshal's arrival and he could thus reappear in time for the evening briefings.

Reichhelm also quickly developed a close friendship with Major Winrich Behr. Major Behr had accompanied Field Marshal von Kluge on his impromptu trip to Paris, perhaps to obtain the cyanide capsule that Kluge used to commit suicide after being relieved as OB West in August 1944. As with many of the officers who served together during times of adversity, Reichhelm and Behr could discuss without inhibition the politics of the Nazi government as well as the ever-deteriorating military situation. Unlike some of the other officers on Model's staff, Behr was also considered by the field marshal to be among his most trusted staff members. The positive relationship could not be attributed to Behr's diplomatic demeanor or an intuition for Model's attitude. The major was, however, similar to the field marshal in his directness. Model seemed to have a penchant for young officers who did not hesitate in the face of confrontation and those he could trust to provide him with an honest, even if somber, appraisal of any situation.

Like many other officers who, by fall 1944, had served in various capacities during more than five years of war, Winrich Behr seemed to have led a charmed life. The cavalry major had proven himself more than once on the battlefield in times of adversity. He had won the Knight's Cross, Germany's highest award for bravery or merit, while serving with Erwin Rommel in Africa. Transferred from

Africa to the Eastern Front, Behr was assigned to the Sixth Army staff as an aide to Field Marshal Friedrich Paulus. At the height of the Stalingrad debacle, he had been selected by Paulus to be flown out of the pocket to personally brief Hitler on conditions facing the beleaguered army. Fully aware of Hitler's distrust of the high command, Paulus chose to send him because he felt the young officer would appeal to the dictator. Behr was also an experienced cavalry reconnaissance officer who was intimately familiar with the privations and hardships endured by the dying army at Stalingrad. The trip to Berlin had spared him the fate of the quarter million troops trapped at Stalingrad with Paulus's army, but it had proven fruitless. The vaunted Sixth Army perished.[33]

The destruction experienced by the Wehrmacht during the final months of 1944 was having its effect on the army's discipline. On 29 October, Model issued a message to his commanders expressing his concern about the deterioration of discipline within the borders of the Reich, particularly the thefts committed by soldiers; he noted that reports about German troops misappropriating civilian property continued to surface. He added that the previous orders regarding such activities were apparently being ignored or simply not forwarded to the frontline units, and he reemphasized that regulations on the requisition of property for the conduct of the war were to be strictly observed. Any unauthorized requisition or misappropriation of property would constitute theft, he warned, and would be severely punished. Extreme cases would be punished by execution.[34]

On 28 October, Hitler summoned the chiefs of staffs of both OB West (Lieutenant-General Siegfried Westphal) and Army Group B (General Hans Krebs) to Berlin for a conference. There, he unveiled his plans for the Ardennes Offensive, the astonishing scheme for a new offensive that would decide the war in the west. On 2 November, Model and Rundstedt met with Westphal, Krebs, and the commanders of Army Group B to discuss the possibilities of the offensive. Krebs recommended what was termed the small solution: attack the Americans' salient in the area of Aachen to cut their lines and isolate the forces east of the Maas River. However, Hitler's plan involved a large solution, calling for the capture of Antwerp with a massive strike through the Eifel in the thickly wooded Ardennes and over the Maas. This plan would deny the Allies their vital supply link and simultaneously sever the Allied forces in northern Belgium and southern Holland. Model and Rundstedt remained silent during the briefing of Hitler's plan; both commanders knew that they lacked the offensive capability to even consider such a far-reaching scheme.

The bulk of the responsibility for carrying out Hitler's Ardennes Offensive was placed on Army Group B. The main thrust was assigned to the Sixth SS Panzer Army under SS General Sepp Dietrich, reinforced with two SS panzer corps. The other forces involved in the attack were the Fifth, Seventh, and Fifteenth

Armies. In Holland, Army Group H was situated to secure the Maas Front. The plans required bringing together fourteen Volksgrenadier divisions; four parachute divisions; twelve Volksartillerie corps consisting of two regiments each; four self-propelled flak regiments; three or four assault gun brigades; and a number of miscellaneous forces, including heavy artillery, heavy armor and antitank battalions, and combat engineer units. Despite a large fuel allotment strategically hidden in the Rhine area, Model expressed grave concerns about the fuel situation, knowing that the tortuous roads through the Eifel presented myriad problems even in favorable weather. When attempting to traverse the ice-covered forest routes in winter, the fuel situation would be precarious.

The entire operation was shrouded in strictest secrecy. All preparations were conducted under the code name *Abwehrschlacht* ("Defensive Battle"). Model was convinced that the plan to reach Antwerp could succeed only if certain conditions existed. Total surprise had to be achieved. Allied aircraft had to remain grounded by bad weather. And the forces allotted for the offensive had to actually materialize.

Until 10 November, the operation was known only to the army commanders and their chiefs of staff and operations officers. On a selective basis, other staff personnel were gradually introduced to the plan. The offensive was spearheaded by two special operations. Operation *Greif* involved SS Colonel Otto Skorzeny, the commando who had rescued Benito Mussolini from his captors in Italy in a daring glider action on 12 September 1943. His forces, working under the code name *Panzerbrigade 150*, were to infiltrate the U.S. Army's rear areas disguised in American uniforms to disrupt communications, redirect traffic, and create general havoc in the rear echelon. The second operation was an airborne drop involving up to 1,000 paratroopers under the command of Lieutenant-Colonel von der Heydte. The airborne forces were to seize the primary road junctions in advance of Dietrich's Sixth Panzer Army. A deception plan was devised that involved sending agents disguised as German army deserters and members of a Communist resistance cell into the American lines. They were to reveal to Allied intelligence officers a major troop concentration developing northeast of Aachen. This information would, it was hoped, divert American and British reserves from the main thrust through the Eifel.

Model and Rundstedt continued to press Hitler to settle for the small solution. But the Führer insisted on carrying through the large solution, believing that the field marshals were fixed on an offensive that carried no strategic value. Always the gambler, Hitler disregarded the advice of the officers, who were well aware of the enemy's overwhelming strength and of the Wehrmacht's weaknesses. The arguments between Model's headquarters and Berlin began to take on a more heated tone. General Hasso von Manteuffel overheard one discussion during which Model said to Colonel-General Alfred Jodl, chief of the Wehrmacht General Staff, "You can tell your Führer that Model will not carry out these types of orders!" Nevertheless, the planning continued, and the days were marked by frenzied activity in preparing for the offensive that would decide the outcome in the west.[35]

On 2 November 1944, the U.S. First Army launched another offensive to attempt to turn the northern wing of the German Seventh Army southeast of Aachen and break through onto the Cologne plateau. The "third battle of Aachen" was fought bitterly in the hills and impassable terrain of the Hürtgen Forest and near Vossenack. The fighting increased on 16 November with a push by the Americans toward the Rur sector between Düren and Jülich in an attempt to capture the Urft and Rur dams.

The day the November offensive was launched, Model was holding a defensive briefing in the Schlenderhan Manor, west of Cologne, with the commanders and staffs of the Fifth Panzer and Seventh Armies. The field marshal received a telephone call at the start of the briefing from the deputy commander of the LXXIV Corps, who excitedly reported that the Americans had pushed toward Germater-Vossenack. The situation was critical, and he was in immediate need of the Seventh Army reserves to stabilize his crumbling front. Model remained calm, quietly dispatched the commanding general of the LXXIV Corps to the scene, and continued with his briefing.

The vicious fighting in the hills and valleys of the Hürtgen Forest persisted into the third week of November. The German front continued to hold as the Americans waded deeper into the line of destroyed villages and shattered, barren trees in an area in which the bitter engagements now resembled the static warfare of World War I. Although the grueling German resistance was inflicting enormous casualties on the American forces, the constant fighting was costing Model irreplaceable reserves. Hitler was already planning that these troops, decimated in terms of both men and material, would be used for the Ardennes Offensive.

On 2 December, Model and Reichhelm flew to Berlin again for a conference with Hitler. Also present were Manteuffel and Dietrich, both of whom had been selected to command the armored formations that would lead the Ardennes Offensive. In the Reich Chancellery, they were met by the Wehrmacht deputy chief of staff, General August Winter, and Colonel-General Heinz Guderian. The conference was marked by Guderian's disapproval of any offensive action in the west. He was adamant that to deploy the last major reserves the Wehrmacht could bring together against the Americans and British would only result in their fruitless destruction. Convinced that pitting the German reserves against the overwhelming power of the Allies in the air and on the ground was wasted effort, he argued that these forces should be used against the Russians in the east.

Jodl remained silent throughout most of the discussion. Soon, the conference degenerated into a heated confrontation between Field Marshal Model and the Führer. With his cold, emotionless demeanor, Model stubbornly insisted on the small solution; Hitler consistently countered with a flat refusal. At length, in the face of Model's obstinacy, Hitler characteristically employed a compromise. He accepted the field marshal's argument in part. The large solution would remain the primary plan, but in the event it failed, they would fall back on the small solution. It was clear that the goal of seizing Antwerp would remain the gamble on which everything was staked. Hitler additionally promised air support of up to 4,000 aircraft—an astonishing promise that no one believed could ever be fulfilled even if he was serious in his pledge.[36]

Model's assessment that the army was in no condition to launch the offensive was countered by Hitler, who insisted that fuel would not be a problem because a fuel line was to be established across the Rhine. Thus, Model's army group remained shackled to Hitler's planned offensive. Ultimately, however, the promised support failed to materialize: of the fourteen panzer divisions promised, ten were eventually made available; of the fourteen promised infantry divisions, approximately eleven severely understrength divisions were present; of the four paratroop divisions required, only two were provided. Of the various additional elements critical to the effort—including self-propelled guns, engineers, and heavy artillery—only 60 percent were available. And the shortage of fuel for the mechanized units remained a serious concern. The total strength available to Model for the offensive stood at approximately 1,800 tanks and assault guns, the same number as had been lost during the summer debacle in Normandy.[37]

On 15 December, a priority message arrived from Hitler's headquarters specifically forbidding the movement of any armored forces from east of the Maas toward the north.[38] Hitler clearly remembered Model's insistence on a limited offensive, and he personally dispatched the written order to ensure that the field marshal did not spoil his offensive by preparing to carry out the small solution. Model curtly responded that all forces were committed to Antwerp.

At first light on 16 December, the offensive began. A thick cover of fog denied the Allies their air support, and the offensive struck the U.S. VII Corps with full surprise. The American lines were torn open in numerous positions as the VII Corps sector was overrun by German forces emerging from the dark forests of the Ardennes. General Omar Bradley's headquarters erupted in a frenzy of activity as commanders attempted to throw together a defense. Field Marshal Montgomery, whose forces were on the northern flank of the offensive, had been preparing to depart for Christmas leave in England.

The Allies reacted with surprising speed as the German airborne attacks missed their targets by wide margins. Otto Skorzeny's commandos, dressed in U.S.

uniforms, were quickly neutralized. However, the fear of the oncoming Germans had its effect. Panic-stricken American troops, many without previous combat experience, fled toward the rear as far as Sedan. Through the tumult, however, some of the vastly outnumbered American units stood firm. Most important, the strategic crossroads and strong points at Bastogne and St. Vith continued to hold, causing the German columns to detour along secondary roads and placing them further behind their vital timetable.

The developments over the next several days revealed that the two corps and four panzer divisions of the Sixth SS Panzer Army were mired in the area of Elsenborn-Krinkelt. Manteuffel's Fifth Panzer Army moved quickly and covered more distance toward its objective, yet the troops failed to dislodge the American defenders at the important Bastogne crossroads. Officers from General Anthony McAuliffe's 101st Airborne Division met emissaries dispatched from General Heinrich Freiherr von Lüttwitz's XXXVII Panzer Corps. Lieutenant Henke, one of the German officers who plowed through the snow carrying a large, white flag toward the American lines, delivered a written message requesting that the Americans avoid further losses and bloodshed by surrendering to the overwhelming German forces encircling them. McAuliffe simply responded, "Nuts," and then ordered that the bewildered emissaries be sent back to their own lines.[39] The bulk of the Fifth Panzer Army remained mired around Bastogne as long as the Americans continued to hold their ground. The forward elements of the 2nd Panzer Division pushed westward, reaching to within 3 miles of Dinant. On 21 December, the bitterly contested town of St. Vith finally fell to the German forces.

As the Americans realized that this was no spoiling attack but a major offensive with far-reaching goals, they began to react decisively. To better coordinate a defense that would be followed with a counteroffensive, the U.S. First and Ninth Armies on the north shoulder of the German penetration were transferred from Bradley's Twelfth Army Group to Field Marshal Montgomery's Twenty-first Army Group. Although the transfer was operationally expedient, it resulted in further friction between the British field marshal and his American counterparts. Canceling his plans to visit Britain, Montgomery is reported to have strode into First Army headquarters "like Christ coming to cleanse the temple." After the German offensive was halted and Allied forces had regrouped, Montgomery further alienated his allies on 7 January by his remarks at a press conference, in which he asserted that he had saved the Americans from a perilous situation and described that effort as "one of the most interesting and tricky I have ever handled."[40]

Initially, Manteuffel's Fifth Panzer Army made good progress, followed by the successes of the Seventh Army. The Fifteenth Army in the Rur bridgehead remained mired on poor roads, rendered almost impassable by heavy traffic and abysmal weather. The Sixth SS Panzer Army, which spearheaded the main offensive, encountered numerous difficulties in the narrow, icy roads that twisted through the forests of the Eifel. Numerous vehicles were stopped on open roads, unable to traverse the steep, ice-covered gradients. In the area of Elsenborn, American forces resisted bitterly, causing the forward elements of the 1st SS Panzer Division to fall behind schedule. The 1st SS Panzer Division "Leibstandarte Adolf Hitler" pushed through past Malmédy before being encircled by an enormous American counterattack. Short of fuel and ammunition, the panzergrenadiers were forced to destroy their remaining armor and slog through the snow toward the east, leaving their dead in the frozen forests and abandoning their wounded to an enraged enemy. The advancing Americans discovered the bodies of seventy-one American soldiers at a road crossing near Malmédy; they had apparently been shot after being taken prisoner. Many American units reacted in kind.[41]

On 22 and 23 December, the weather cleared, and the skies were soon filled with squadrons of Allied fighter-bombers. The Americans quickly recovered from the initial shock of the assault and began a systematic reduction of the pocket in the Ardennes. The supply situation became hopeless for the Germans, and the roads and fields were littered with abandoned or burning Wehrmacht vehicles. On 23 December, Model met with Reichsminister Speer, and they held a lengthy conversation regarding Germany's armaments situation. Eventually, Model peered at the armaments minister from behind his monocle and coldly stated that it "was over." Speer did not respond. The context of this remark remains speculative.[42]

Christmas Eve found Model and Günther Reichhelm driving on ice-covered roads in an unflagging effort to salvage what forces remained after the failed offensive. To be moving during daylight hours was fraught with danger; the Allied *Jabos*, or fighter-bombers, blanketed the skies and pounced on any activity observed on the roads and snow-covered fields below. Model's selected route took them through an open area, approximately 12 miles in length, between the towns of Blankenheim and Stadtkyll. Shortly after setting out, the accompanying communications van was struck by a team of fighter-bombers and destroyed. The Germans abandoned the burning vehicle on the roadside. They made slow progress along the frozen roads, swerving from the route periodically as they were compelled to seek cover from the incessant attacks by the fighter-bombers. At length, a pair of roaming aircraft caught the tiny convoy on an open road with no nearby concealment. The field marshal, along with Reichhelm and other members of the party, were forced to abandon the vehicles on the road and throw themselves on the ground in an open field. The aircraft raked the stranded vehicles with machine-gun fire and banked against the clear winter sky to return for another attack. Model and Reichhelm lay prone in the snow and watched as the field marshal's staff vehicle went up in flames. As the pair of aircraft made a final pass, they flew low over the officers lying in the field and wagged their wings in a salute to the prone soldiers before disappearing over the treetops.[43]

The staff officers arrived at Model's advanced command post in Blankenheim as darkness fell across the Ardennes. The harrowing experience had lasted eight hours, during which they had driven a distance of 12 miles. That they had narrowly escaped with their lives was not lost to them: the officers had been spared by anonymous fighter pilots who were unaware that one of the German soldiers they had forced to seek cover on an open field was the commander of an entire Wehrmacht army group. The rest of the night was spent pouring over situation maps by candlelight in the Blankenheim schoolhouse.[44]

Model's worst fears were realized when the offensive stalled. On 27 December, Hitler belatedly ordered the small solution to be put into motion. It was, however, too late for any hope of success; many of the forces needed for the plan were reduced to frozen corpses under a blanket of snow in Belgium. The material and transport assets required to conduct the offensive had been burned, captured, or abandoned for lack of fuel. The German divisions, bled white in the constant fighting since June, continued to fall back toward the Rhine.

In early January 1945, Model's aide, SS Major Heinrich Springer, accompanied the field marshal on his routine tour of the shattered front. In the late evening, they passed a ragged column of *Landsers* trudging slowly through the mud toward a distant crossroads, and Model ordered his driver to halt. Springer exited his vehicle and joined the field marshal as he approached the haggard soldiers. Surprised by the appearance of the field marshal, the men drew to attention and saluted. Model asked them a number of questions. How long had they been without sleep? How long ago did they last have warm rations or a change of clothing? He learned that the small group of ragged soldiers represented the remaining strength of an infantry company. What had happened to the rest of the company? Model asked. A sergeant shook his head. "Gone. Dead. Wounded. Captured. Gone, Herr Feldmarschall." The men exchanged salutes, and the field marshal and his aide returned to the waiting vehicles. Model requested that Springer join him in his vehicle, and the staff car proceeded up the road. After several moments, Model broke the silence. "Springer," he said with resignation, gazing at the snow-covered hills through which the road was taking them, "a commander must regard his soldiers as he regards his children. And you know, things are very bad for them now."[45]

Chapter 2

Destroying the Ruhr

Germany possessed two major industrial areas that were essential to the war. In February 1945, the strategically important mines and factories of Silesia had fallen to the Soviet army. In the spring of 1945, the industrial cities of the Ruhr Valley, representing the last sources of essential war material and coal, were threatened with capture by American and British forces.

The Ruhr Valley lies east of the Rhine in northwest Germany. The Ruhr River flows from its source in the Sauerland, the hills of which lie south and southeast of the valley, and west-northwest to its confluence with the Rhine at the industrial city of Duisburg. It is at this confluence that the traditional heartland of German industry is located. Fueled by enormous coal deposits, the area known as the *Ruhrgebiet* ("Ruhr region") is situated between Bonn and Remagen in the south and the fortress town of Wesel in the north. The region is flanked on the south by the Sieg River, which flows west from the town of Siegen through the hills and forests of the Sauerland to meet the Rhine at Bonn. It is bordered on the north by the Lippe River, which flows west from the Teutoburg Forest through the plains of the Münsterland to join the Rhine at Wesel. East and northeast of the Ruhr Valley lies the Teutoburg Forest, a dense expanse of rolling hills and forests in which, in the year A.D. 9, the Roman general Varus met defeat at the hands of a Germanic chieftain named Arminius.

The Ruhr Valley between the Sieg and Lippe Rivers boasts a concentration of strategically important, heavily populated municipalities such as Düsseldorf, Duisburg, Essen, Wuppertal, Lüdenscheid, Solingen, and numerous smaller towns that rose to prominence during the Industrial Revolution. A number of canals were created in the nineteenth century to expedite the transfer of large volumes of coal from Ruhr towns and cities to the Rhine, the most prominent being the Rhine-Herne and the Dortmund-Ems Canals. These extensive waterways run roughly from east to west through the Ruhr district, augmenting the Sieg, Ruhr, and Lippe Rivers as important transportation routes.

The Ruhr Valley, Germany's primary source of coal and steel, produced 80 percent of Germany's coal, and the war industry required a supply of no less than

22,000 freight cars of coal per day. By the end of November 1944, the coal shipments had been reduced to 5,000 cars per day.[1] Although Armaments Minister Speer had succeeded in increasing material production from 1943 until the latter months of 1944, the bombing campaign against the vital transportation network was strangling the German war effort.

Initial attempts to cripple German manufacturing centers proved unsuccessful. On 12 October 1942, the British Royal Air Force issued a memorandum outlining the Allied policy regarding mass bombing of German cities. Emphasis shifted from the unsuccessful efforts to destroy the German war-making capabilities; the new goal was to undermine the morale of the civil population and simultaneously disrupt rail transportation through precision bombing. It had been decided that the will of the German people to continue the war had to be broken. British Air Marshal Sir Arthur Harris firmly asserted that, given enough aircraft and ordnance, the war could be brought to a victorious end by April 1944.[2]

The general strategy was a primary item of discussion during the Casablanca Conference held by the Allies in January 1943. The combined planning staffs belatedly concluded that airpower alone would prove insufficient to force a German surrender. Furthermore, a massive bombing campaign would have to be launched to weaken the enemy in preparation for a land invasion of the European continent in 1944. For the first time, the bombing campaign of German industry was stated to be "an essential prerequisite" to the impending invasion.[3]

After Casablanca, a directive was published by the Combined Chiefs of Staff to direct the operations of the British and U.S. bombing campaigns. The opening statement of general intent, common to all military directives, clearly emphasized that the destruction and disruption of enemy military and industrial systems and the undermining of the morale of the German people would be primary objectives. On reissuance of this directive to the Allied Bomber Command, Harris changed the wording to state that the principal mission would be to destroy the morale of the German people, not the industry.[4] The alteration of a succinct military directive for further promulgation is not done without careful consideration. With a simple change of wording, the emphasis was shifted from a combined goal of destroying the German military and industrial capacity while degrading the German will to continue resistance to a primary goal of destroying civilian morale in the Bomber Command campaign.

The British never questioned that Germany would be bombed following the outbreak of war. As early as 10 May 1940, while the German forces were pushing into France, the British cabinet was debating whether the Ruhr industrial area should be attacked. The following day, the decision was made to launch air attacks against military targets. During the night of 12 May, an air raid was conducted by British bombers on the city of Mönchengladbach, and four days later, the air attacks began against the industrial heart of the Ruhr Valley.[5]

Attacking congested population centers were not a new concept. Following World War I, some military strategists asserted that future wars would be conducted by aircraft alone. A *New York Times* editorial outlined how, in future conflicts, entire industrial areas would be destroyed, with heavy losses among the civilian inhabitants. Major General Sir George Aston accurately predicted that the heaviest losses in these campaigns would not be among military combatants but would be borne by the civilian inhabitants of the urban areas. With detached, military aloofness, he wrote, "Is it not more merciful in the end to wipe out whole families, rather than to kill the best of their manhood only, leaving the terrible gaps in each family life?"[6]

As early as May 1940, former Chief of Air Staff Lord Trenchard advised Prime Minister Winston Churchill that in waging a successful war against Germany, morale counted most; he added that the British should take advantage of the German predisposition for "hysteria and panic." Pursuant to this theory, the service chiefs directed the air squadrons to attack "German transportation and morale" one week prior to Harris's assignment as chief of Bomber Command.[7]

Fulfilling the predictions of prewar theorists and airpower proponents, the main focus of the raids was the heavy population centers of the Ruhr: few cities would suffer destruction as severe as that inflicted on cities in Germany's industrial heartland. The targeting staffs carefully studied the German transportation network, collected and assessed data on Germany's industry and communications systems, and identified the weak links for destruction.

By spring 1945, aerial reconnaissance photographs revealed the Ruhr and its environs to be devastated. Essen and Gelsenkirchen were 51 percent destroyed, Dortmund and Duisburg 65 percent, Cologne 70 percent, Bocholt 89 percent, and Wesel 97 percent.[8] In one raid alone, the U.S. Eighth Air Force attacked the area of Düren with 1,000 B-17s and 243 B-24s, dropping more than 4,000 tons of ordnance. The Americans were quickly followed by the British Royal Air Force, which deposited an additional 3,000 tons on the hapless city.[9]

With the overwhelming material wealth employed by U.S. forces, much of the destruction that occurred far from viable targets could be attributed to indifference and poor training. After the cessation of hostilities, the armed forces openly admitted the shortcomings in all branches. Regarding the targeting of German cities and industry, officials of the U.S. Air Force wrote: "Many officers who were impressed into intelligence duties in commands and higher echelons had little knowledge of military staff procedures or of the functions and responsibilities of intelligence at those levels."[10]

In 1942, the *Heimatflak*—the national homeland antiaircraft defense units—were established when it became apparent that the Wehrmacht and traditional civil defense organizations lacked enough personnel to protect the German cities. Able-bodied citizens were conscripted for duty to fill quotas with the local flak units, and their assignments required that they serve on their batteries a minimum of one week out of every three. This commitment was required in addition to their routine employment. If not serving with the flak units, they were often compelled to serve as security personnel in the factories, where legions of foreign laborers toiled under adverse conditions for the German war effort.

Citizens were required to retain gas masks within reach at their offices and workplaces, and work was often interrupted by air raid drills during which all workers were required to don the masks. Early in the war, demonstrations and short courses instructing the civilians in how to extinguish fires with shovels and simple piles of sand were held periodically. It was soon realized, however, that such demonstrations were little more than a cruel farce, for the cities were reduced to cinders under the weight of massive assaults conducted by the hundreds of heavy B-17 Flying Fortresses, B-24 Liberators, and British Lancasters that dropped thousands of tons of incendiary bombs.

The civilian inhabitants of these areas often found themselves more affected by the war and living more dangerously than their fathers, sons, and brothers who were serving in the Wehrmacht on numerous fronts. By May 1943, the city of Duisburg had suffered almost 200 bombing raids and had experienced more than 600 air alarms as fleets of Allied bombers routinely darkened the skies above the Ruhr. A single raid during the night of 13 May 1943 either damaged or completely destroyed more than half of the homes in the city.[11]

The destruction of entire cities and towns also affected the morale of the conquerors as they penetrated the Reich. When the British forces approached Dülmen, one diarist recorded the devastation and suggested the inherent danger lurking in the ruins: "I have reckoned with death every day for weeks, yet I always escape from death with the feeling that I have turned away at heaven's door." At this same time, a British war reporter wrote, "We have come to recognize the ruins in this war. We have learned to tell the difference between those ruins [of buildings] destroyed by bombs and those destroyed by shells, fire or explosions. In England we have never experienced a city that is totally extinguished, entirely empty and abandoned—as empty as Pompeii, a city that, from one end to the other, bears the stench of a rubbish heap and from within the only sound heard is water dripping somewhere among the rubble."[12]

With the escalation of the bombing, the casualties suffered by the Allied airmen increased accordingly. To reduce losses among the aircrews, it was decided to target numerous locations simultaneously, thus scattering and weakening the antiaircraft defenses. So-called second-priority targets were selected to draw the flak batteries from the industrial cities. Some 3,500 people were killed in an air raid on Wuppertal-Barmen during the night of 30 May 1943 after eighteen heavy flak batteries had been withdrawn to defend other cities. During this raid, 644 heavy bombers dropped more than 1,800 tons of bombs. The raid essentially wiped Barmen off the map.[13]

In 1943, in an attempt to alleviate the destruction, the Germans initiated a program for dispersing the industrial targets, thus rendering them more difficult to locate and destroy. Ironically, this effort provided the Allies with some measure of success in disrupting production: the Allied bomber commands estimated that the dispersal program cost the Germans more in terms of actual production than would have been lost to the bombs. Had the factories remained concentrated, they would have been easier to supply and the transport of finished products could have been better coordinated.[14]

Phosphorus was the favored tool of destruction used by the Allied bombers. In thirty-four months of air raids, 1,000 high-explosive bombs and 150,000 incendiary bombs were dropped on the city of Essen, home to the renowned Krupp steel-manufacturing complex. Some 1,500 homes were damaged or destroyed, and 600 inhabitants died. Over the next five months, the Allied planners increased the pressure on the German cities. In the accelerated campaign, 4,500 high-explosive bombs and a half a million incendiaries were dropped on Essen, killing 1,600 inhabitants and destroying almost 9,000 homes.[15]

A typical attack employed about 500 heavy bombers. The squadrons began turning up on the runways in England at sunset. With hundreds of throbbing engines, the fleets of aircraft, loaded with more than 1,000 tons of high-explosive and incendiary bombs, taxied down runways and took off in an unprecedented display of technological and industrial might. The nightly targets were typically rail networks, factories, airfields, flak positions, and the residential areas of the inner cities. Most often, the heavily populated city centers bore the brunt of the attacks.

The fleets routinely passed over the coast of Holland, turned toward the city of Dorsten, and altered course toward the heart of the Ruhr industrial area astride the Rhine. Forward air observation positions noted the approach of the streams of bombers and calculated the altitude, direction, and numbers of attackers. The information was relayed over military and civilian switchboards to the antiaircraft commands located to the rear. The air raid sirens began to wail as the pertinent information was further relayed to flak batteries. Civilians not already dwelling underground wearily made their way to the cellars and air raid shelters. The stairwells in hospitals were choked with patients and staffers as they crowded into the cellars and other shelters. Nonambulatory patients were carried along dimly lit passages on litters and stretchers to the relative safety of the shelters as the first planes made their final approach to their targets.

As the droning of the motors increased and the target city was overflown, the first *Christbäume* ("Christmas trees") were dropped to mark the targets for the oncoming waves of bombers. The brightly burning flares hung over the city for long minutes, indicating to the people below that they were once again on the Allied target list.

The crews of the flak batteries sprang into action, manning their high-velocity guns. Teenaged boys feverishly adjusted the fuses on heavy 88-mm antiaircraft projectiles designed to detonate and scatter clouds of shrapnel at the reported altitude of the invaders. As the aircraft approached the Ruhr, they were intercepted by German night-fighters that dived and punched their way into and through the ranks of bombers, attempting to shoot down individual aircraft and to break up the flight patterns. Searchlights traversed the black sky, powerful pillars of yellow light seeking the bomber formations. Young girls manning the battery switchboards in nearby bunkers reported the positions of the aircraft as the information was relayed to them. Over Dorsten, the bombers were met by brilliant bursts of flak, fired from 88-mm batteries and rapid-firing 20-mm positions manned by elderly men, fifteen- and sixteen-year-old boys, and foreign volunteer laborers. The explosions of the 500-pound bombs were heard through the pounding of the heavy flak. The earth shook, concrete shelters quivered, and gas lines burst as the shrieking bombs descended and exploded.

Clusters of elderly men, women, and children cowered within the dim confines of the shelters. Screams filled the darkness with each explosion. The inferno could be observed for miles from the target's center. Villagers in outlying areas heard the soft rumble of faraway detonations over the faint wail of sirens. They felt the vibrations of exploding ordnance, and the distant skyline was illuminated by the eerie glow of flames from which pillars of searchlight beams extended skyward into blackness.

The fear and deprivation felt by the inhabitants within the targeted cities was often tempered by the youthful exuberance of teenagers assigned responsibilities far beyond their age. In early 1943, Willi Boemer, a member of the class of schoolboys who had been assigned to a flak battery as a *Luftwaffenhelfer* ("Luftwaffe assistant or auxiliary") in the Essen suburb of Vogelheim since 15 February 1943, excitedly wrote, "I have been issued a helmet and I am now authorized to stand outside [the bunker]." He was one of three students who were killed by a direct hit on their position the night of 5 March 1943.[16]

In the aftermath of the 15 February raid on Essen, fireman Emil Leiermann requested directions from his superiors on where to begin combating the flames.

The chief simply waved his hand with resignation and exhaustion. "Go to Steeler Strasse," he replied wearily. "Which building number?" the fireman asked. "Just pick one of the fires" was the response.[17]

The inhabitants were also responsible for assisting in extinguishing isolated fires, but many of them remained in their cellars. During the night of 15 February, a housewife in Röttenscheid scribbled a quick note to her brother: "The City Hall, Cramer and Meermann, Woolworths and the Germar Theater are burning, and there is no telling what else. But it will be much, much worse. The poor, poor people! Right now, at half past midnight, we can still hear the detonations."[18]

Irma Ditges later wrote of a raid on Cologne: "It was hardly five minutes before the first bombs began to fall on the right bank harbor area near the south bridge. The bombs that fell into the Rhine caused subsurface pressure waves, so that one had the feeling of being tossed back and forth like a ship at sea. We lay on the floor and believed that our end had come, the carpets of bombs fell again and again. We felt our bunker receiving hits." The people in Ditges's shelter attempted to leave the heavily damaged structure when silence signaled the end of the raid, but enormous I beams and heavy iron fittings had been blown in front of the bunker entrance by the pressure waves of the exploding bombs, making it impossible to exit without assistance from outside. A small flak detachment was located near the bunker, and the soldiers, assigned to protect the south bridge, knew that people were in the bunker. They cut through the iron beams with blowtorches, freeing the trapped inhabitants several hours later. On emerging, the people saw for the first time the total destruction: the area was nothing but a field of craters. The bunker had held only by the last few inches of reinforced concrete.[19]

Following a raid during the night of 6 May 1943, 20,000 Cologne inhabitants were ordered to evacuate their homes—or what was left of them—for the ruins remained saturated with unexploded ordnance. Many of the bombs left behind after the waves of attackers had passed were armed with time-fuse detonators. These bombs did not explode on impact but buried themselves deep into the rubble, their fuses methodically ticking away until the bombs detonated with murderous effect. The unexpected detonations often occurred in the midst of firefighters and rescue workers attempting to free civilians entombed in bunkers, long after the sounds of the aircraft and flak had subsided.

The city of Essen suffered its heaviest raid on Sunday, 11 March 1945, less than two months before Germany's unconditional surrender. Fritz Schlessmann, the district Nazi Party leader and Reich defense minister, was celebrating his forty-fifth birthday deep in his command bunker near Essen's Walter-Sachsse-Weg. Under the protection of reinforced concrete, he had little to fear from the heaviest Allied bombs. Eleven-year-old Inge Peters played with her sisters Gerda and Hannelore near the entrance to the "Freedom" air raid bunker, a two-story tunnel system buried 25 feet beneath the railway station. The massive facility was equipped with a kitchen, break rooms, bunk rooms, a medical clinic, and a morgue. The shelter had been meticulously planned with numerous entrances and exits, and air was supplied through an integrated ventilation system. Some 1,500 inhabitants routinely fled the remains of their homes to take refuge in the facility. Many had taken up permanent residence in the underground chambers, living a semicivilized existence deep beneath the rail tracks.

As Defense Minister Schlessmann celebrated his birthday, a massive wave of Allied bombers was reported over the coast of Holland. It was clear that they were en route to another rendezvous with the Ruhr. German soldiers, foreign laborers, and women and children gazed upward from the countryside between the Ruhr and Holland as streams of bombers, escorted by swarms of fighters, droned toward the southeast in the direction of Essen. The initial alarm was passed to the central communications network, complete with details on distance, altitude, and approximate number of aircraft.

Fifteen-year-old Heribert Stuhlreyer, leader of a Hitler Youth gun crew on flak position 462, received the warning at 2:00 p.m. as the aircraft approached the 10-kilometer mark. The teenaged gun commander issued orders through his microphone as the crews of six 105-mm antiaircraft artillery pieces located on the garden cemetery in Essen-Huttrop feverishly prepared for action.

Within seconds, the aircraft were overhead. Sunlight gleamed off the delicate, silver strand of bombs dropping though open bays beneath the fuselages of the B-17s and descending on the city. The fleet struck the rail station, the Krupp facilities, the Folkwang Museum, the Deutschlandhaus, and the city's opera house. The central fire command facility and the numerous exhibition halls were lost in clouds of smoke and debris. An ominous lull settled briefly in smoke-blackened skies as a squadron departed the targets and was soon followed by another formation of bombers.

Deep in the Freedom shelter, the walls trembled and the air filled with dust as the emergency lighting failed amid screams of terror and desperate prayers. Maria Kolberg crouched next to Inge Peters and her sisters; the terrified women heard a Volkssturm soldier, who had been en route to his assembly point when the raid began and had thus sought quick refuge in the shelter, mutter softly, "Today they're going to finish us."

As the droning aircraft disappeared over the horizon, Essen remained blanketed by a massive cloud of dust and debris that blocked the sun and left the vast field of ruins shrouded in a ghostly darkness. The bombing mission had lasted fifty-five minutes. This raid, heavier than any previously experienced by the benumbed inhabitants, had been concentrated on areas that had escaped previous attacks. Rellinghauserstrasse, Moltkestrasse, Ruettenscheiderstrasse, Alfredstrasse, Kruppstrasse, and Bismarckstrasse—the prominent pedestrian and traffic arteries through the city—were now unidentifiable fields of smoking ruins. Over the next several days, recovery crews wrapped 900 bodies in paper shrouds for burial in a mass grave.

Explosive-ordnance disposal teams, the *Sprengkommandos*, were activated to comb through the rubble. In Essen, twenty-four-year-old Lieutenant Bruno Werdelmann volunteered to serve on a bomb disposal team during his recuperation from a severe wound received at the front. The young officer was not new to war—he had been wounded on four separate occasions—and facing a different form of imminent danger posed no new threat to the trained chemist. On 11 March, Werdelmann drove toward Essen with a fireman and two concentration camp inmates who had volunteered for the dangerous work. Hazardous duty was considered a means of improving the dim chances of survival for the political prisoners by receiving better food in payment for their deadly work. As the team approached Essen, they observed an ominous black cloud blanketing the horizon, and soon, their ragged Opel Kapitän and aging BMW were stopped by piles of fresh rubble blocking their path. They immediately set to work.

The prisoners did not deactivate the bombs; the technical work was the responsibility of the officer. Their job was to assist in locating the 500-pound containers and free them from the rubble with hand shovels. Werdelmann would then descend into the crater to unscrew the fuse and detonator while the other workers retreated a safe distance. The priority was to locate and disarm bombs at or in the immediate vicinity of strategically important facilities such as railway junctions, waterworks, industrial facilities, and major roadways.

The first bomb to be disarmed was a dud, or *Blindgänger*, located on the Meisenburgstrasse. Werdelmann instantly recognized it as an American general purpose (GP) 500-pounder. Descending into the crater left by the impact of the heavy container, he slowly unscrewed the M-101 fuse located in the nose of the large and still-warm cylinder before carefully entering data in the specified columns of his logbook. The bomb was methodically recorded as number 64. In the "points" column, Werdelmann wrote the number 3. If he accumulated 450 points, he would be rewarded with the Iron Cross First Class. With 2,000 points, he would receive the German Cross in Gold. On this afternoon, the officer disarmed two additional unexploded bombs, one on the same street and another in front of the police barracks.[20]

Heinrich Weinand, imprisoned as an active opponent of the Nazi Party, had avoided transfer to a concentration camp by volunteering to serve with the ordnance disposal unit in the nearby town of Kalkum. His team was en route to Essen by 6:30 a.m. the following day, and the silhouette of the city soon came into view.

The first bomb damage they observed was negligible, and they drove through the streets until they reached the blackened rubble that had once been the blocks of the inner city. The disposal team, long accustomed to the sights of destroyed cities, ignored the stench of death and the corpses scattered through the ruins as they searched for the bombs. The first one they located was a Blindgänger, and it was soon disarmed and prepared for later removal. The team was searching for the next bomb when they were shaken by an immense detonation. One of the first time-delay bombs had exploded deep within a nearby building. With a shrug, they returned to their vehicle and proceeded to the next location of a reported dud. They found it buried within an air raid shelter a short distance from the badly torn bodies of a man and woman. After a cursory examination, they quickly decided that the bomb would have to remain in place—it was armed with a deadly time-delay fuse and could explode at any moment.[21]

Of the 11 March raids, one woman noted in a letter, "In thirty minutes [the city of] Essen has become a small town"; she closed with the words, "There's no point in coming back here." Another woman later wrote, "It was the heaviest bombing in Germany. During the night placards appeared throughout the area advising the populace that no one was authorized to depart Essen and Kettwig. The authorities soon reconsidered the decision, changed their minds, and everyone was relieved when the women and children were permitted to leave."[22]

Many of the inhabitants became accustomed to a subterranean existence in the cellars and bunkers as all semblance of a normal routine disappeared in flames, explosions, and ruin. Entire city blocks collapsed under storms of glowing phosphorus, and the shelters became stifling, asphyxiating tombs as the city blocks burned. Without lights and trapped in the stifling confines where unbearable heat robbed them of oxygen, panic-stricken masses often stumbled through the darkness in an attempt to escape suffocation in the shelters. Blinded by heat, smoke, and phosphorus fumes, they staggered from cellars onto streets that had become rivers of burning, molten asphalt. In their panic, some sank ankle-deep in the morass before collapsing and rolling in agony, their bodies becoming sticky masses of seared flesh and singed hair. Their screams rapidly subsided within cocoons of glowing asphalt. In the larger public air raid shelters, mass hysteria often overwhelmed the crowds, and in the darkness, many people were crushed under the feet of mobs attempting to escape the torment.[23]

An eerie silence fell on the cities as the waves of bombers subsided, leaving only the whispers of flames, the sporadic detonations of time-delay fuses on high-explosive bombs, and the earth-shaking rumble of collapsing buildings as the flames devoured entire city blocks. Survivors stumbled from cellars and air raid shelters to stagger aimlessly through the ruins, speechless, shocked, and confused. Occasionally, all the occupants of a shelter were found asphyxiated, lying in heaps in the concrete caverns where, in their panic, they had attempted to flee when robbed of oxygen by the sea of flames. The bodies of the dead remained in collapsed cellars and bunkers, mutely awaiting removal.[24]

Many citizens were entombed when the escape routes from the shelters were filled with rubble or collapsed. Long after the war, during construction work in Rosenheim, surprised workers uncovered a narrow stairwell descending into an industrial pump facility where they found the mummified corpse of a German soldier sitting on the steps as if waiting for the day the rubble would be removed. His Mauser rifle rested across his knees, and he was still fully outfitted in his duty uniform, complete with regulation steel helmet, bayonet, and cartridge belt. Identity papers in his tunic pocket identified him as a musician from Heidelberg. Entombed in the stairwell during a raid, he had taken a seat on the stairs to await rescue—or death—and slowly lost consciousness in the dark confines of his grave.

Following a major raid on Essen, Inge Schroeder wrote of scenes she observed during her daily route to the women's *Reichsarbeitsdienst* ("Reich Labor Service") office:

> Human limbs extended from the piles of rubble, days-old corpses lay strewn about, a nun collected body parts.

Robert Jahn noted the conditions of one of the Krupp factories as Allied ground forces closed on the area:

> You stumbled over ruins and filth, the rubble of buildings, bent, twisted, melted steel girders. The massive steel girders, industrial machinery, rails, roofs, everything lay tossed together in a macabre display of a dying industry. And in the middle of all of this, incoming artillery rounds fired from invisible Allied batteries beyond the field of ruins continued to impact. No one thought of clearing operations, the bombs had completely destroyed the road surfaces and disrupted and ruptured the underground facilities.[25]

Only under the most optimal conditions could an effective rescue effort be organized after a bombing. Representatives from local emergency organizations were centrally located in bunkers or relatively secure facilities, with telephone communications to their subordinate units. Couriers, often Hitler Youth members, were standing by to relay messages in the event telephone lines were disrupted. The organizations responsible for taking part in the rescue and evacuation of casualties were composed of members of police units and fire brigades, hospital representatives, utility personnel, and German Red Cross representatives. The official organizations were augmented by soldiers on leave, Nazi Party paramilitary volunteers, foreign laborers, and prisoners of war. Their first priority was to provide emergency medical aid to those injured during the attack or in subsequent events and to transport them to safety. Emergency first aid stations, complete with surgery capabilities, were organized and set up in the areas deemed to have suffered the most casualties. Inhabitants who had lost their homes were assigned to shelters or encouraged to seek refuge with friends and relatives. Items of value that could be retrieved were pulled from the rubble at the first opportunity to prevent further economic loss to those who had lost their homes. Communications with higher authorities, essential for requesting assistance from neighboring districts, were often disrupted during the bombing. The communications facilities were rapidly repaired, and contact was reestablished outside the affected area. At length came the gruesome task of locating, identifying, and burying the dead.

Removing the dead as quickly as possible from the populated areas was essential in preventing outbreaks of disease, and relatives were anxious to learn the fate of missing family members. In 1944, sixteen-year-old Kurt Stasyk of Drolshagen found himself en route to the heavily bombed Ruhr area to assist in clearing and organization operations. Seated on open, flatbed railcars, he and 200 other members of his Hitler Youth company were transported from the relatively untouched periphery of the Ruhr into the nightmare moonscape of the central industrial regions. The teenagers were overwhelmed at the sight that greeted them as they passed through devastated rail junctions and block after block of ruins. The train crawled through fields of blackened rubble where cities once stood. On arrival at a railhead in Essen, the boys were immediately organized into squads for locating and removing the dead from cellars and collapsed buildings. Entire city blocks were cordoned off to inhibit looting and access by unauthorized persons.[26]

The squads of Hitler Youth teenagers, fire brigades, and foreign laborers worked side by side in digging through the rubble. The work continued for a week, during which the boys piled decomposing bodies, severed limbs, and unidentifiable clumps of flesh onto carts for possible identification and removal and burial. Breathing was difficult in air choked with thick smoke from burning facilities and the fumes of phosphorus gas that had settled in low areas. Groups of corpses packed tightly together could sometimes be located by the stench of decaying flesh emitting from under tons of rubble. Working with shovels and picks, the teenagers removed layers of roofing tiles, bricks, mortar, and concrete to uncover the bodies of the dead lying in every conceivable configuration. Some small groups had simply died from asphyxiation, and their bodies remained intact but clumped together like macabre statues; others were little more than flattened layers of decaying bodies that had been crushed to a pulp under tons of collapsing concrete, now recognizable as human only by the blood-caked clothing that clung to the decaying flesh. Many of the corpses that were roasted by incendiary bombs had shrunken to barely discernible nude figures little more than 3 or 4 feet in length, shriveled to hairless masses of burned flesh and protruding, blackened bones.[27]

The bodies were dragged to the waiting carts, where any identifying features were noted and samples of clothing were taken for later efforts by survivors to determine the fate of missing relatives. The location was noted to assist in identification, which was no easy task when all recognizable features of streets and buildings had been obliterated. In areas where movement was difficult, the bodies were lashed to planks or dismantled doors so they could be dragged, pushed, and carried through the ruins. Where available, bulldozers cleared paths through the mounds of ruins, pushing collapsed buildings, incinerated belongings, and corpses into massive piles along the roadways when rapid clearing of the streets was necessary for the movement of essential troops and equipment.[28]

Some of the boys broke under the strain of smelling, viewing, and handling the dead. They collapsed as strength left their limbs, shaking uncontrollably and gasping for breath in the foul stench of rotting flesh. They sank within the ruins and curled into the fetal position, unable to speak but screaming unintelligibly and tearing at their filthy uniforms in an attempt to remove all traces of the corpses they had borne through the piles of ruins. Many refused to eat the sparse rations that were provided from food sources found in the rubble or immediately vomited anything they consumed in the foul air. The swollen cadavers of horses, cattle, and house pets were piled onto a makeshift grating assembled from railroad ties and then were doused with coal oil and set alight. Starving and confused dogs roaming through the rubble were shot by soldiers and policemen. As the days passed, the number of workers dwindled as the nightmare took its psychological and physical toll. In the end, only those with great tolerance or those who had become numbed by their grisly work remained to continue piling the bodies on carts for removal.[29]

By the spring of 1945, the Allied ground forces were pushing over the Rhine. Many inhabitants in the Ruhr anxiously awaited the arrival of the American and British forces, believing that would bring an end to the torment and relief from the ceaseless air raids. In the closing weeks of the war, the skies over German cities were darkened by the armadas of Allied aircraft that kept the entire Ruhr paralyzed.

When the Allies marched into the unearthly landscape that had been the city of Essen, in April 1945, they found an immense field of ruins unfit for human habitation. Even in the residences that remained occupied, more than 3,000 cellars were filled with sewage. The drainage lines ruptured by the bombings caused uncontrollable flooding of toxic waste. Some 58 percent of the water lines were no longer functional, more than half of the homes were either completely destroyed or rendered uninhabitable, and only 3.4 percent of the dwellings remained undamaged. The gas utility system was destroyed, three-fourths of the public transportation system was immobilized, and the buses and streetcars were reduced to scorched shells strewn randomly throughout the city. Electric power was nonexistent, and with sunset, the city became a darkened, silent field of destruction. More than 6,500 bombs had destroyed 571 industrial facilities, as well as 18 Catholic and 15 Protestant churches. The incessant attacks created a macabre cycle of rebuilding, relocating, and renewed destruction in a deadly contest of wills between the Allied Bomber Command and German industry workers. A German worker summed up the attitude of the inhabitants: "Today we have finished rebuilding the plants, and tomorrow the bombers will come again."[30] Flak assistant Roland Streck, serving with Flak Battery 462 on the Essen-Frintrop water tower, wrote to a friend about the conditions following an air raid: "Hardly a cellar is still intact, it is as if the city has again been tossed upside down. The inner city has become hell … even the fighter-bombers are active, one can easily recognize them as Thunderbolts."[31]

The German citizens were among the more fortunate living among the devastation—they were permitted the luxury of retreating to shelters and cellars during the days and nights of terror. Most cities and towns lacked sufficient shelter for the inhabitants, who often relied on their own cellars for safety. The personal cellars offered minimal protection at best and were usually modified with a fire door and additional beams reinforcing the ceiling. The cellars were officially required to have two exits, which was usually accomplished by hammering an opening though the wall that separated one's cellar from the neighbor's. A simple curtain was usually installed over the openings between the chambers for privacy. Members of ten-year-old Elenore Kötter's family in Düsseldorf modified their cellar in the customary fashion. They blocked the street-level windows against bomb fragments and chiseled a simple door through the wall into the neighboring cellar. They attempted to reinforce the crumbling walls and ceiling with heavy wooden timbers after a 500-pound GP bomb exploded several hundred feet from their makeshift shelter. Elenore's uncle, a Wehrmacht sergeant who had been wounded at Stalingrad and was home on convalescent leave, was shocked when he inspected the facility to which the family was entrusting their lives. "That place is a death-trap!" he exclaimed. "Stay out of there and go to the public shelter!"[32]

The Allied air armadas delivered more than high explosives, time-delay fuses, and incendiaries. Since the earliest days of the war, British propaganda units had dropped tons of leaflets on German cities for the purpose of demoralizing the population and swaying public support away from Hitler's policies.

The leaflets were first delivered to Germany's soldiers and civilian population by unmanned balloons set adrift on air currents that carried them into German territory. One of the problems associated with unmanned craft coasting on thermal currents was that the heavily populated industrial areas—containing the very people at whom the leaflets were targeted—produced updrafts that blocked the prevailing currents. This situation was especially acute when heavy bombing raids reduced entire city blocks to a sea of flames.

The British resorted to simply packing bundles of leaflets alongside the bombs in the aircraft. When the bomb bays opened, the leaflets would fall free to be blown over a wide area. This method fell far short of the goal of distributing leaflets where the population was most dense. The bombs fell faster than the leaflets, and the ascending air currents resulting from the flames produced by the incendiaries would push the leaflets up and out of the intended area.

From early 1941, a small bomb container (SBC) was utilized. The SBC system featured a canister that was installed in the aircraft bombing system; each container could hold approximately 72,000 leaflets. The containers were not dropped but were electrically opened to release the payload into the plane's airstream. The Americans refined this method to deliver even more leaflets. In 1944, Captain James L. Monroe of the U.S. Eighth Air Force experimented with enclosing bundles of leaflets within cardboard illumination-bomb canisters. For the American purposes, this proved to be the most effective method. The containers fit into a standard bomb rack and were designed to open at an altitude of approximately 1,200 feet. The 8-inch by 10-inch leaflets remained confined to a relatively small (2.5-square-kilometer) area, and a single B-17 Flying Fortress or B-24 Liberator could deliver as many as 960,000 leaflets in twelve Monroe bombs.[33]

Early in the war, the leaflets were largely ignored by the Nazi authorities. In view of the astonishing Wehrmacht successes in that period, any attempt by the Allies to persuade the German populace that the war was lost was considered by the Nazi government as insignificant at best. During the first months of 1940, a simple brochure titled *Was tue ich im Ernstfall?* (What Must I Do in an Emergency?) was distributed with the monthly allotment of ration cards. The brochure was printed under the direction of Reichsführer SS Himmler and included instructions regarding the proper handling of enemy propaganda leaflets. The finder of any such leaflet was instructed to mark it as "enemy propaganda" and deliver it to the nearest police station. There was no mention of a penalty for possessing or reading the material.[34]

On 12 January 1940, Himmler again issued an order regarding Allied leaflets, under the heading "Found Enemy Leaflets and Dissemination of Same." The Gestapo was responsible for enforcing the directive, as well as for collecting and disposing of the propaganda material. When the leaflets appeared in any specific area, the local party leaders, working with various Nazi paramilitary organizations, were instructed to collect the material. Usually, members of the Nazi youth organizations—the Jungvolk and Hitler Youth—were set to work combing the area and collecting any leaflets found. The materials were then destroyed by the local authorities.

For most of the war, there was no official penalty for possessing the leaflets, but any person who did posses the material was liable for immediate arrest under various charges. The arrests could take place under charges of committing a variety of crimes, depending on the circumstances under which one was arrested. Grounds for arrest varied from high treason to rendering assistance to the enemy, and penalties ranged from simple arrest and release to lengthy prison sentences. Extreme cases carried the penalty of confinement in a concentration camp or even death if rendering aid to the enemy was substantiated. On 4 February 1944, four years after his initial instructions for the disposal of Allied leaflets, Himmler issued an order clearly making the collection, possession, or dissemination of Allied propaganda material a state crime.[35]

The general population observed the messages delivered in the leaflets with humor but later, as the war turned against them, with sobering stoicism. Despite the torrents of rhetoric from Propaganda Minister Joseph Goebbels, most Germans became aware that the war was lost as the German army suffered defeats on every front and the enemy forces drew relentlessly nearer. The restriction imposed by the authorities on possessing enemy propaganda leaflets was only one of myriad restraints on individual civil liberties.

The bombing of Germany's heavily populated areas took its toll on historical and cultural treasures. In towns and cities dating from the early Middle Ages, innumerable historical artifacts and artworks were destroyed in the flames. Others were transported from the industrial cities to outlying areas for storage and safekeeping. When the bombing campaign intensified, even the small towns became targets for endless waves of four-engine bombers, and as the Allied ground forces approached, the swarms of fighter-bombers targeted strategic and tactical sites. The safest places for storing priceless artifacts were the coal and iron-ore mines throughout the area.

The town of Siegen became a focal point for the storage and safeguarding of an unusual number of cultural artifacts and art treasures. Oberbürgermeister (Senior Mayor) Alfred Fissmer of Siegen took the treasures from the Aachen Cathedral into his custody, including the shrine containing the bones of Charlemagne. Also hidden deep within the Siegen tunnels were the treasure of Münster with the golden madonna; the holy shrine from the Siegburg church; the contents of the Rheinische Landesmuseum in Bonn; the Aachen Suermondt Museum collection; the art from the Cologne churches; numerous works from the Wallraf-Richartz Museum in Cologne; the Trier Cathedral treasures; and numerous altars, tapestries, paintings, sculptures, and associated items from throughout the Rhineland.[36]

The Siegen mines contained treasures estimated to have a combined value of more than 4 billion reichsmarks. The items were transferred to a collection point on order of Graf Metternich, Hitler's Rhineland provincial conservator. Graf Metternich's attention was directed toward the extensive Siegen mines during his search for a secure storage facility where the treasures would remain safe from the Allied bombs. He was particularly attracted to the Hainer Hüttenstollen, a tunnel system that ran some 30 to 40 feet beneath the old district of the city. Under the direction of Oberbürgermeister Fissmer, the tunnels were equipped with a climate-control system and renovated with retaining walls to separate the storage facility from the air raid bunkers that were also constructed within the system.[37]

The demand for raw materials to support the war grew as the Allies targeted and destroyed the Germans' capability to obtain the metals needed to produce armaments and equipment. As the demand increased, officials were compelled to seek secondary sources. Eventually, the churches and cathedrals fell victim to the shortages. Church bells were requisitioned for their metal content, which was desperately needed for military use. The bells, many of which represented centuries of cultural heritage and historical craftsmanship, were collected at designated points to be transported to smelting firms. Regulations regarding the requisition of such artifacts authorized that up to 50 or 75 percent of the bells should be removed from a bell tower with multiple bells. A church record in Morsbach recorded that during the dismantling of the belfry, a large crowd gathered with excitement as the bells were lowered to the ground. The children squealed and ran among the workers; some of them chalked their names on ancient bells destined for the smelter, oblivious to the fact that another part of their culture was being sacrificed to Hitler's war.[38]

In some instances, specialists were assigned to render plaster casts of the engravings and inscriptions on bells considered culturally and historically significant. The war would not last forever, and the casts would someday be needed for reproducing the treasures. Although numerous churches sacrificed their bells to the war effort, a number of bells mysteriously escaped the smelting ovens and were located in the postwar era. After an extensive search, the bells of Morsbach were discovered in a Düsseldorf harbor facility and were returned to the town in October 1947.[39]

As it became apparent that the Luftwaffe was not able to halt the waves of Allied bombers, measures were taken to evacuate women and children from the areas most likely to suffer the heaviest bombing. These evacuees soon flooded the outlying farms and villages, placing an additional strain on crowded living facilities and limited food resources. The children were often enrolled in the *Kinderlandverschickung* program, in which school-age children were organized into groups and sent to nonthreatened areas; there, they lived in dormitory-style quarters and continued to participate in school courses. The evacuation efforts were only partially effective, as many women did not desire to leave their husbands for extended periods and soon returned to their homes or took up temporary residence with friends or relatives. Homesickness, ill treatment of urban evacuees by local inhabitants, overcrowded quarters, and insufficient food resources all contributed to the desire to return home despite the inherent dangers. Many families did not want to entrust their children indefinitely to the care and supervision of the Nazi Party organizations and soon sent for them or personally retrieved them from the state-sponsored children's program.

The exodus of nonessential populations from the cities left the vast fields of ruins almost devoid of life. The orders for the evacuation of Cologne came from Nazi Party officials following a massive, thousand-bomber raid on 14 October 1944. Women, children, and elderly inhabitants were transported from the Rhineland city to designated collection areas in the nearby Westerwald or as far away as Thuringia and Saxony. Between September and November 1944, the population in Cologne shrank from 445,000 to 254,000. By the year's end, the city was reduced to 178,000 inhabitants. In early March of 1945, the American troops entered an almost deserted area that had been transformed from a city with a population of half a million to a sea of rubble containing 40,000 inhabitants.[40]

Hitler's goal of establishing a purely Aryan society in the heart of Europe had turned Germany into one of the most ethnically diverse nations on earth. More than 7 million foreign workers were employed in wartime Germany to labor in mines and factories that had been stripped of the German workers who had been called to the Wehrmacht. By August 1944, 20 percent of the working populace in Germany was officially designated as foreign labor, and there was a distinct emphasis on placing these workers in industries requiring heavy labor. Half of the people employed in agriculture were foreigners, mostly French POWs and, to a lesser extent, Polish and Soviet civilians. In the construction, mining, and steel industries, every third worker was from an occupied country or territory. This workforce consisted of men and women from almost twenty countries; 2 million of them were POWs and more than 5 million were civilians recruited or conscripted for the war industry. Of the 7 million foreigners in Germany, 2.8 million were from the Soviet Union, 1.7 million from Poland, 1.3 million from France, and approximately 600,000 from Italy. Fifty percent of the laborers from Poland and the Soviet Union were women, whose average age was twenty.[41]

At the time of the invasion in Normandy in June 1944, 250,000 foreign civilian laborers and 75,000 prisoners of war were engaged in the heavy Ruhr industry, mostly in coal mines and the steel industry. The use of foreign workers, particularly those from eastern Europe, was regarded by the Nazis as a temporary measure to meet wartime requirements, and the hapless laborers were often treated accordingly. The Nazi government established strict guidelines and regulations for the employment and treatment of the foreigners, particularly those from the east. The Poles, engaged in heavy mining and steel industries, were harshly affected by these measures. Polish laborers were confined to work camps, where they remained segregated from the general population. Fraternization between Poles and Germans was strictly forbidden. Polish laborers were required to wear a distinctive P on their clothing, and their life in Germany was marked by crowded and unsanitary living quarters, poor rations, and low pay. Relationships between Polish men and German women were punishable by death. Polish workers were forbidden to use public transportation, to enter German restaurants, or to stay overnight in any dwelling other than their designated barracks.

Similar restrictions were placed on workers from the Soviet Union. They were required to wear a badge identifying them as *Ostarbeiter* ("eastern laborers"), and they were deported by the hundreds of thousands from captured territories to fill quotas in the war industry. The Soviet workers were primarily engaged in the coal-mining industry, where they labored underground without relief for weeks. They endured appalling conditions deep within the labyrinths of the mines, where they were valued by their overseers on a par with the horses used by the Wehrmacht. They were sources of labor whose care was required only to maintain their ability to work. By August 1944, 40 percent of all miners in the Ruhr were foreign laborers, of whom three-fourths were from eastern Europe. One German miner in the industrial town of Recklinghausen reported: "If you arrived early at the mine, you could see how the Russians arrived. To the right and left marched an overseer with a rubber truncheon in hand, and they were quick to use them on those that were too slow. There were even other foreign miners who beat them. For once they had someone under them, upon whom they could take out their frustrations."[42]

The hordes of foreign workers in Germany were also officially separated into ethnic and racial groups or classes. Those at the top of the hierarchy were the workers from western Europe, the *Westarbeiter*. These workers from France, Belgium, and Holland enjoyed a status not afforded to the chattel from the east. The Westarbeiter were usually provided pay and rations that, although meager, generally equaled those of their German counterparts. Others who received special treatment, similar to the Westarbeiter, were the workers from countries friendly or allied with Germany, such as the Balkan and Mediterranean nations. At the bottom of the hierarchy were the laborers from Poland and the Soviet Union, including prisoners of war. The soldiers who had been fortunate enough to survive initial capture and subsequent imprisonment in massive POW pens in the east now found themselves laboring for the German war effort.

The laborers assigned to farms were more fortunate than those condemned to spend countless weeks in dark mines or to endure the saturation bombing in the industrial centers. The farmers could provide relatively ample quantities of food, even in a country that was quickly becoming "demodernized" by the war. Gasoline for farm machinery became almost nonexistent, and most labor had to be performed by hand. In contrast to the farm laborers, other workers were often compelled to survive on a daily ration of thin soup augmented with a small slice of black bread. The monotonous rations seldom varied, despite the intense physical labor endured by the workers. As the bombing of transportation systems and logistics networks took effect, many of the workers were reduced to starvation diets. An additional advantage to working outside the cities was relative safety from the air raids that had become a horrifying, constant fact of life since the bombing of the industrial centers escalated in 1943.

The foreign laborers in the cities were unprotected in densely populated areas, where space in shelters and reinforced cellars was at a premium. Small slit trenches that offered only a semblance of protection were occasionally constructed near the labor camps, but for the most part, the foreigners had no option but to remain in their wooden barracks. In March 1943, a French worker in Essen wrote home: "That was the thirty-fifth alarm since 20 December, they are here almost every evening. You can believe me when I tell you that it's not amusing when the barracks shakes like a house of cards. We can only remain in our rooms, as we don't have a shelter nearby."[43]

With the intensification of the bombing, the conditions for the foreign laborers, never acceptable even in the best of cases, continued to deteriorate. As the factories that employed them were bombed out of existence, the workers were transferred to other locations. Due to the disruption of transportation systems, these workers often had to embark on forced marches, which further exhausted the malnourished prisoners and seriously strained lodging, food, and transportation resources. The advance of the Allies from the west in late 1944 and early 1945 forced the evacuation of thousands of laborers from their workplaces in the Ruhr factories. The unfortunate workers were transported or marched for weeks deeper into Germany, causing severe overcrowding and hunger in work camps that lacked food and shelter for their overwhelming numbers.

In an attempt to escape the terrible conditions of the camps and the near-starvation conditions under which they toiled, many of the workers chose to risk death by fleeing their workplaces. The Nazi officials sought to discourage such attempts by imposing severe penalties, and they put all resources to work in an effort to control the mass of foreigners. By the summer of 1944, 90 percent of all arrests made by the Gestapo involved foreigners, and the influx of the "criminal" elements placed great strain on local law officials and magistrates. During the final months of the war, gangs of foreign workers and German petty criminals banded together to pursue illegal activities, including black marketing, theft, robbery, and homicide. As the Allied front drew ever closer, crimes increased among concentrated gangs of foreign laborers who were able to escape their overseers in the chaos of the bombed cities. The disruption of communications and transportation networks and general administrative chaos enabled them to disappear in the waves of refugees that swept over the cities and countryside. In response to the breakdown of civil order, the Gestapo summarily executed foreigners apprehended while conducting illegal activities, without benefit of trial. In the bombed cities, looting was often punished by immediate execution, and reports of the executions of Germans and foreigners apprehended while searching the rubble for valuables became commonplace.

Many laborers deserted their workplaces to avoid being transported deeper into Germany as the Allies approached and were forced to rely on theft or join criminal gangs as a means of survival. The gangs armed themselves with weapons stolen from soldiers or looted from destroyed military and police installations. The plunderers, often operating in gangs but sometimes working alone or in pairs, would slink through the ruins during the night, taking with them anything of value that could be easily carried. Any police actions were hampered by the conditions of the cities and strict blackout regulations. Police units, many of which had been stripped of military-aged men for service in the Wehrmacht, were under great strain to provide manpower for even routine duties. Germans apprehended in the act of plundering often identified themselves as family members searching for clues as to the whereabouts of relatives. With a lack of communications and a breakdown of administrative networks, it was difficult to immediately confirm or disprove such claims.

As the situation deteriorated throughout the war and it became evident that the outcome would not favor Germany, many foreign workers chose to desert or to be intentionally less productive. Execution was routine for foreign workers if they were apprehended by the authorities while absent from their camps or workplaces without authorization. Laborers who were condemned to the mines and heavy industrial facilities faced imminent starvation or death from diseases that swept through their crowded camps. The knowledge of this fate served to make them particularly desperate to avoid capture. Their punishment, when captured, was also intended to serve as an example to others.

In December 1944 the Fortasraki Gang, led by eastern laborers in Cologne, united with the German-led Bauer Gang to conduct a campaign of organized crime. In time, they were cornered and compelled to engage in a desperate skirmish with the Gestapo. The leader of the Fortasraki and a small number of followers were able to elude the authorities during the subsequent roundup, and they made their way from Cologne through Wuppertal to Essen. There, they stole packages from railcars loaded with military mail until they were finally captured following a shoot-out with the Essen police.[44]

German teenagers organized into gangs of Edelweiss Pirates, which served as a loosely knit opposition to the hated Hitler Youth organization that all boys were required to join. Members of these gangs were often armed and could present a danger to the authorities, as they did not fear the use of violence. One of their victims was Ortsgruppenleiter Söntgen who, according to a report of the Cologne Gestapo bureau, was fatally shot as he was riding a bicycle. The murder launched an intensive cordon and search of the area, leading to the arrest of an "Edelweiss terror group" as well as the apprehension of numerous foreign laborers who had fled their workplaces. Eleven Soviet and Polish workers were executed on 25 October 1944 as a result of the action, followed by the executions of thirteen German teenagers from the industrial suburb of Ehrenfeld. The condemned were publicly hanged without trial. Among the executed was sixteen-year-old Bartholomaeus Schink, a local boy who had sought refuge in the ruins to avoid mandatory labor duties on the vaunted Westwall.[45]

The crimes of looting, common theft, listening to Allied radio broadcasts, and possession of enemy leaflets for the purpose of dissemination often resulted in execution. In an astonishing exhibit of self-absorption, a former judge recalled, "We often had to put in overtime to prosecute crimes, write the sentencing reports. Crimes as insignificant as stealing an alarm clock or demeaning statements about the Hitler regime would often cost the accused his life. We sometimes signed these sentences, that had nothing to do with justice, with heavy hearts, sometimes in tears. The executions would then take place in the well-known Klingelpütz prison."[46]

Following the capture of the heavily damaged industrial cities by the Allies, the gangs continued to plague the British and American authorities. Of particular temerity was Willi Herold, a nineteen-year-old Wehrmacht corporal from Lutzena. In the fall of 1944, Herold deserted from his unit, obtained the uniform of a Wehrmacht captain, and organized a gang of German army stragglers to form the notorious Einheit Herold near the Dutch border. While impersonating a Wehrmacht officer in April 1945, he succeeded in taking control of the Aschendorf concentration camp, where he instigated the summary execution of numerous inmates. In 1946, Herold was finally captured by the Allied occupation authorities and indicted on ninety-eight counts of murder. His criminal career ended with a death sentence from a British court.[47]

The deterioration of control and civil authority during the closing weeks of the war were recorded by a diarist in the Westphalian town of Cösfeld. As the Allied troops closed on the town, he wrote:

Many have abandoned the city, but they return in the evening to their homes to sleep, even in the middle of the rubble. Daylight-fearing ghosts slink everywhere, plundering under the cover of darkness, and not only the liberated Russians are involved in the thievery. The Cösfeld rail facility is nothing more than a pile of rubble, and the extensive clearing work conducted by thousands of workers that takes place every night is useless. Sources of food have become a burning question. Where are the brown [uniformed] gentlemen who are responsible for all of this? They don't let themselves be seen any more, and perhaps it is better for them. They, with their idiotic orders! Most of them have no talent for leadership whatsoever, and always end with the words "Either this order will be carried out, or you can count on being shot on the spot!" They themselves, however, the gentlemen from the *Kreisleitung*, have already prepared everything to flee in the direction of Annaberg to the *Gauleitung*. The warm weather is over— now a cold, damp wind is blowing. The foreign workers—the Flemish, the French, Italians and also Ukrainians—were taken to Schöppingen by five guards. It is a caravan of misery. Of the soldiers who are lingering about the farmyards, only one officer candidate exhibits any morale to continue. Most of the others have even thrown away their weapons.[48]

Many of the Westarbeiter from Holland, Belgium, and France were lured to Germany early in the war by promises of favorable working conditions, sufficient rations, and pay comparable to their German counterparts. This government initiative offered skilled laborers the opportunity to feed their families and to escape the deprivations the Nazi occupation had brought to their own countries. The majority of laborers, however, particularly those from eastern countries, did not go to Germany voluntarily. Forced by Nazi occupiers to fill labor quotas, the provisional governments in Poland and the occupied areas of the Soviet Union compelled thousands of workers to report for deportation to Germany. For others, it was a matter of survival—either volunteer for work in Germany or starve. Packed into freight cars in Poland or the Soviet Union, the workers were transported to the industrial areas of Silesia in eastern Germany or to the Ruhr in the west, where, regardless of health or other physical needs, they were immediately assigned to the work camps that had been established to serve the mines and factories. There existed more than 300 labor camps in Essen, and the city swarmed with foreigners imported to work for the Nazi war effort.

Like much of Europe during World War II, the Ruhr cities were conspicuously devoid of Jews. The deportation of Jews to ghettos outside Germany was initiated in 1941. Most of the country's Jewish inhabitants found themselves en route to Poland, where they vanished from sight in the labyrinth of the Nazi concentration camp system. To facilitate administrative tasks in locating, identifying, and accounting for all Jews to be deported, the Gestapo required that they be registered and that all their belongings—including household goods, real estate holdings, bank accounts, clothing, works of art, jewelry, and liquid assets—be provided to the authorities. All Jews destined for deportation were compelled to surrender all property to the German authorities, most of which became the property of the Reich's finance office. The confiscated property was often used for later distribution to Germans who had lost their belongings during the bombings.

The deportations could not be concealed from the inhabitants of the cities. The Jews were marched from assembly areas to the train stations during the day, within view of all inhabitants. Their residences were confiscated by the government and made available to Germans whose homes had been destroyed. The official procedures for the deportations required that the information pass through myriad official channels, and the logistics for the shipments of human cargo required the involvement of numerous officials and government workers. Among those aware of the deportations in large cities were staff personnel in the Gestapo's main office, the police departments, the court officials, the rail system employees, some local SS units, the finance departments, various branches of the government banks, the German Red Cross, numerous assistants, and not least of all the neighbors of those who simply vanished.

The Jews received implicit instructions regarding the deportation procedures. Each person was permitted a small suitcase or rucksack for belongings, including a fourteen-day supply of food. A three-day supply of food was to be wrapped in a wool blanket, together with a spoon and plate or bowl. All other belongings were confiscated. On reporting for deportation, all food and medicine had to be surrendered, ostensibly for later distribution by the German Red Cross.

The first deportation of Jews from Essen began on 27 October 1941, when 262 individuals were transported to the Lodz Ghetto in Poland. A total of nine transports occurred in 1941, 1942, and 1943. The early transports took Jews from the Ruhr to various camps in Lodz, Minsk, Riga, Izbica, and Theresienstadt. In 1943, the trains, heavily loaded with human cargo destined for death, took the Jews directly to Auschwitz. Keeping track of the Jews was not difficult—they were easily identified through ration card registration files, on which a large J was stamped in red ink. In Essen, 1,225 Jews were issued ration cards in September 1940. By October 1941, the number had fallen to 1,039, and within thirty days, the number was reduced to 795. The numbers declined even further as more deportation trains departed to the east, and between March and November 1942, the total number of cards issued fell from 721 to 111. In September 1943, the last deportation train left Essen en route to Theresienstadt, leaving only 39 Jews remaining to be issued ration cards in the city.[49]

Although the daily life in the cities was marked by the absence of the Jews, there was within the Ruhr a sizable Jewish population that was still fleetingly seen by inhabitants. During the summer of 1944, some 500 female concentration camp inmates were transported by railcar to Essen to meet the ever-growing demand for workers in the Krupp factories. At first, the women were housed under canvas shelters near the Gelsenkirchen-Horst refinery, where they were required to clear mounds of rubble following air raids. They were later transferred to a barracks located on Essen's Humboltstrasse. The women were divided into work groups and housed in four barracks that were furnished with rough-planked bunks and straw-filled sacks for mattresses. They were awakened every day at 4:00 a.m. for the journey to the factory. A sparse breakfast of bread and marmalade was initially issued, but this soon fell victim to the food shortages that ravaged the Ruhr, and the women existed on meager rations of cabbage soup and bread. When the public transportation system became a permanent casualty to the bombing, the women were compelled to walk the distance down the Humboltstrasse and over the Krupp and Helenenstrasse to the Bottroper Strasse, where most of them worked in the Krupp Walzwerk.[50]

Seventeen-year-old Engelbert Ayon was among the Jews transported from Essen to Izbica in Poland. His parents, in a German-Jewish mixed marriage, received the first correspondence from their son sometime after 25 April 1942. The small card bore a simple, terse message:

Dear Parents, We arrived in good order. I am living with Ewald and Walter, for whom I am also writing, as they do not have any post cards. Please give the address to their parents. We are allowed to receive money in amounts up to one hundred Reichsmarks, and packages up to two kilograms are permitted. We can obtain anything here with money. Otherwise everything is all right, and I assume all is well with you. I send many greetings and kisses. Your son, Engelbert Ayon. Also the best greetings from Walter. We will all soon write to everyone. Heartfelt greetings, Ewald.

A second post card was dated 3 July 1942. Written with pencil, it bore only a short message: "I am healthy, I am doing well. Sincere thanks for the mail. Engelbert." The final card received by Engelbert Ayon's parents, dated 9 August 1942, also bore simple words: "I am healthy, I am doing well. Sincere thanks for the mail. Engelbert." In the lower left margin of the last two cards was the mark of a censor. His parents heard nothing more from him. With the surrender of Germany on 8 May 1945, Engelbert Ayon was officially declared deceased.[51]

Chapter 3

Into the Rhineland

The failure of the Ardennes Offensive had a profound impact on the disposition of Field Marshal Model. His tone lost much of its sharpness; he was less quick to react to impending change; he appeared at times to be resigned to the fate that was befalling Germany. While German forces were experiencing mass attrition in the west, events were occurring on the Eastern Front that would directly affect the remaining conduct of the war. On 17 January, Warsaw was evacuated by the Wehrmacht forces. The evacuation was conducted without Hitler's knowledge, and on hearing of the fall of the city, the Führer flew into an uncontrollable rage. He remained obsessed with the loss of Warsaw for the next several days and intent on punishing the General Staff officers and any others who might have been responsible. Colonel von Bonin, the chief of the Army Operations Section, was arrested, as were two of the staff officers working with him. The three officers, along with Army Chief of Staff Heinz Guderian, were subjected to days of interrogation by the Sicherheitsdienst (SD), the Reich Security Service. Bonin found himself incarcerated in a concentration camp, where he remained until the end of the war.

The incident produced a new order from Hitler on 21 January, which was disseminated to the commanders-in-chief, corps commanders, and divisional commanders for implementation. Henceforth, Hitler was to be personally involved with decisions to carry out any operational movements. Every plan for evacuating or withdrawing from any position, regardless of level or intensity, had to first receive his approval. Every plan for surrendering any position, any local strong points, or so-called fortresses required his authorization. Furthermore, all such plans had to be submitted to Hitler with sufficient time to enable him to intervene personally and issue counterorders if deemed necessary.[1] With this order, the final crippling of the Wehrmacht became official doctrine. No German officer was at liberty to move any forces at his command without Hitler's direct approval. To do so was to risk relief from command, arrest, and possible execution.

The catastrophe facing the German armies on both the Eastern and Western Fronts brought uneasiness among German military leaders at all levels. Not only

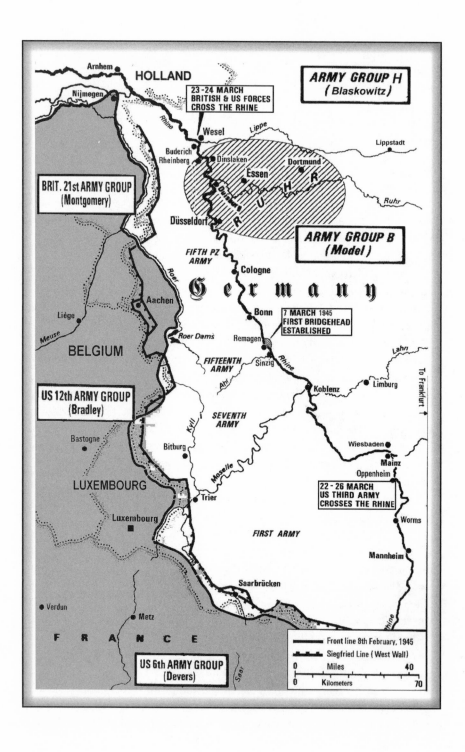

Arnhem
Nijmegen
HOLLAND

ARMY GROUP H
(Blaskowitz)

23-24 MARCH
BRITISH & US FORCES
CROSS THE RHINE

Wesel
Lippe
Lippstadt

Buderich
Rheinberg
Dinslaken
Dortmund
Essen
R U H R

BRIT. 21st ARMY GROUP
(Montgomery)

Düsseldorf

Ruhr

ARMY GROUP B
(Model)

FIFTH PZ
ARMY

G e r m a n y

Cologne

Aachen

Liège

Bonn

7 MARCH 1945
FIRST BRIDGEHEAD
ESTABLISHED

Roer Dams

Remagen

Lahn

BELGIUM

FIFTEENTH
ARMY

Sinzig
Ahr
Rhine
Koblenz
Limburg

To Frankfurt

US 12th ARMY GROUP
(Bradley)

SEVENTH
ARMY

Bastogne

Bitburg

Wiesbaden
Mainz
Oppenheim

LUXEMBOURG

Luxembourg

Trier

22 - 26 MARCH
US THIRD ARMY
CROSSES THE RHINE

Worms

FIRST ARMY

Mannheim

Saarbrücken

Verdun

Metz

F R A N C E

US 6th ARMY GROUP
(Devers)

Saar

—— Front line 8th February, 1945
▬▬ Siegfried Line (West Wall)

0   Miles   40
0   Kilometers   70

Meuse
Roer
Kyll
Moselle

did they become increasingly critical of the decisions made in Berlin, they also found themselves threatened by a system that consistently brought retribution for any expression of displeasure with the regime. Field Marshal Model, known for his insistence on distancing himself from political issues, acted accordingly. At one time, General Heinrich Freiherr von Lüttwitz, commander of the XXXXVII Panzer Corps, attempted to engage the field marshal in a discussion concerning the political situation they were facing. The attempt was rebuffed by Model without reservation. Lüttwitz, an outspoken officer whom the soldiers had nicknamed "the Horse Trader," was burdened with a reputation for criticizing Hitler and the Nazis. To make matters worse, Lüttwitz was a member of a Prussian-Silesian Junker family with a long, esteemed military heritage—the very type of officer held in great disdain by the German Führer in Berlin and the Nazis with whom Hitler surrounded himself. Model immediately admonished Lüttwitz for his attitude and even dispatched Colonel Reichhelm to the XXXXVII headquarters with a letter clearly explaining that Lüttwitz was henceforth forbidden to engage in politically motivated discussions with the field marshal. Included in the admonishment from Model was an invitation to dinner.[2]

On 24 January 1945, the staff celebrated the field marshal's fifty-fourth birthday in his headquarters, situated in a hunting lodge deep in the Eifel. General von Manteuffel and Model's chief of staff, Colonel Pilling, arranged for a surprise visit by his seventeen-year-old son, Hans-Georg, who was serving on the Eastern Front as an officer candidate with the elite armored brigade Grossdeutschland. The two staff officers were unsure of how the unexpected visit would be taken by Model; he usually disdained any privileges beyond those officially accorded an officer of his rank: for the conservative and traditional field marshal, to abuse his position for a special privilege would be unthinkable. The visit, however, proved successful. The son of the field marshal remained only a short time before returning to the east. It would be their last meeting.[3]

The friction between the American and British military leaders did not dissipate with their success in defeating the Ardennes Offensive. The situation created by the Battle of the Bulge (the U.S. Army designation for the Ardennes Offensive) had shifted the focus of the Allied thrust from Bradley's Twelfth Army Group to Montgomery's Twenty-first Army Group in the north. After eliminating the Bulge, Eisenhower left the U.S. Ninth Army under Montgomery's command, and Bradley's Twelfth Army Group was required to relinquish additional divisions to support the Ninth Army. Bradley was convinced that he should maintain control of the bulk of the Allied forces, with which he could strike through the remnants of the Wehrmacht forces, reeling from the defeat in the Ardennes, to turn toward the north and trap those Germans currently facing Montgomery. For his part, Montgomery was convinced that the Allies lacked the strength to conduct a broad sweep toward the Rhine, and he was insistent that emphasis should be placed on his Twenty-first Army Group in the North. With the Americans supporting his southern flank, the British could push across the Rhine onto the wide, open expanse of the northern German plain and strike for Berlin. Eisenhower, however, continued to stay on track with his broad-front strategy, in which both Bradley and Montgomery would push toward the east slowly but steadily, destroying German forces positioned between the Allies and the Rhine. He intended to establish a line of defense on the west bank of the Rhine, to be followed up with a massive crossing of the river. In addition to a push by Montgomery across the northern plain, he planned to have the First and Third Armies under Bradley cross the Rhine south of the Ruhr Valley and then link up with Montgomery's forces east of the Rhine.

The stubborn German defense thwarted any illusions that Bradley or Montgomery might have held regarding a quick, decisive thrust toward the Rhine. As the Anglo-American forces brought more strength to bear against the Wehrmacht, Army Group B succeeded in extracting itself from pending destruction, albeit with immense losses. It was clear to Field Marshal Model that mounting a defense west of the Rhine with the few forces available would be fruitless. On 7 February, he met with a number of his senior commanders to discuss the dismal situation. Present were General Blaskowitz, commander of Army Group H, and General Alfred Schlemm of the First Parachute Army, as well as the commanders of the Fifteenth and Fifth Panzer Armies. The briefing revealed grim statistics. There were overall shortfalls in fuel. It was impossible to organize any reliable transfer of reserves on short notice when necessary. The conditions facing the individual soldiers were abysmal, and the men were exhausted and overtaxed. Aside from the bleak situation on the front, every soldier was aware of the destruction that was occurring in his home city on a daily basis as squadrons of bombers passed overhead en route to Germany.

On 9 February 1945, Commander-in-Chief West Gerd von Rundstedt reported to Hitler that he no longer possessed the forces necessary to recover those areas of Germany that had been overrun by the Allied forces. His entire strength, including the combined forces of Army Group B, totaled the equivalent of some six and one-half divisions. At best, he could attempt to halt the advance by preventing a breakthrough. To maximize the effectiveness of his forces, Rundstedt requested permission to take independent action in conducting limited, local withdrawals to solidify defenses and concentrate his forces in favorable terrain. The Führer, he added, could rest assured that such action would be taken only when deemed absolutely essential for holding the front. Whenever possible, he would attempt to gain permission prior to any withdrawals.

Rundstedt received a measured response the following day. Only limited, local withdrawals were authorized for stabilizing sectors of the front—and only if absolutely necessary. The surrender of any line of fortifications or city was absolutely forbidden. "Perhaps the enemy can assault a line of fortifications or a city, but they will never be evacuated," the message read. "This is an order directly from the Führer."[4]

The seriousness with which the perceived lack of resolve to defend German territory was taken was expressed by Robert Ley, leader of the German Labor Front. Ley accused the Wehrmacht of failing to properly defend the Ordensburg Vogelsang, an elaborate education facility used by the Labor Front as a training and conference center. The loss of the facility was, in addition to an embarrassment for Ley, an immense, personal financial loss for the leader. His accusation required an investigation into the circumstances involving the loss of the facility to Allied troops. The commander of the LXXIV Corps, General Erich Straube, faced a court-martial for losing the facility, as did one of his division commanders and the commander of an artillery regiment. General Gustav von Zangen, commander of the Fifteenth Army, was assigned by Model to serve as judge. Zangen found the officers not guilty. When reviewing the case, Model refused to accept the judgment and proceeded to conduct his own investigation, which even involved personally touring the area in which the events had occurred. At length, Model agreed that the officers were not guilty of any offense.[5]

In addition to the lack of adequate forces to defend the area west of the Rhine, the army group was stripped of a large number of essential units, which were to be transferred to the Eastern Front. A complete panzer army command staff, two panzer corps staffs, four panzer divisions, two mechanized brigades, three artillery corps, and three mortar brigades withdrew from their positions and began the fateful journey across Germany to face the Soviet army. With this move, the army group lost a third of its remaining strength. The group's staff was aware that a successful defense west of the Rhine was impossible with the forces at hand, and the doctrine of holding every yard of ground only contributed to the difficulty.[6]

On 16 February 1945, Model was ordered to report to Hitler in Berlin. The discussion that took place between the field marshal and the Führer was not shared with any of the staff officers. As he was departing, Model requested permission to return to the front by way of Dresden, the capital of Saxony. Suspicious, Hitler asked why he needed to go to Dresden—the city was to the south of Berlin, in the opposite direction of the Rhine front. The field marshal informed him that his family resided in the Weisses Hirsch quarter of the still-burning city. During the night of 13 February, thousands of Allied bombers had incinerated Dresden, and Model had heard nothing from his family since that fateful night. It was not known if his wife and daughters had perished during the destruction, in which tens of thousands of inhabitants and refugees had died. Hitler responded that he had been unaware that the field marshal's family was in Dresden, and he expressed concern for their well-being as he gave approval for the detour to the south. Model hurried from the headquarters, anxious for information regarding his family. Soon enough, he would be immersed in the business of attempting to stabilize a front that could not be saved.

In Dresden, he met his wife and daughters in the family's undamaged villa; the Weisses Hirsch area had miraculously escaped the devastation wrought on the city by the air armada. His only son, seventeen-year-old Hans-Georg, was not present for the gathering; he remained at the front in service with the Grossdeutschland brigade. The field marshal quietly advised the family to visit relatives in the west. His brother was an attorney in Mühlhausen in Thuringia; they would be welcome there. Greatly relieved that they were safe, he then made the long journey through the darkness back to the Lower Rhine.[7]

The German high command was determined to defeat the enemy west of the Rhine with support of the Westwall, the crumbling series of bunkers and tank obstacles dating from the prewar years. An organized defense of the Rhine and even the drafting of a plan to evacuate forces over the river was strictly forbidden. Hitler asserted that if any plans were made and defenses were constructed east of the Rhine, the troops would become obsessed with the idea of falling back behind these defenses and thus fail to mount a tenacious defense of the Reich's western borders. Not until the first week in March, with the Allies some 12 miles from the Rhine, was a subordinate staff authorized to initiate defenses east of the river with replacement units and Volkssturm battalions.

Of particular importance was the defense of the Rhine bridges. The bridges and ferries were designated for use by specific armies, corps, and divisions within their defined areas. The long retreat of the Wehrmacht back to German soil brought the military organizations into conflict with one another. The administration of the river crossings remained under the control of the local military district commanders, which placed them beyond the command of the active military units. In early February 1945, the control of the crossings was transferred to the army groups, from where they were subordinated to specific military units. Nonetheless, not a single soldier, artillery piece, or armored vehicle was permitted to withdraw to the safety of the east bank of the Rhine.

At the end of February 1945, Major Friedel of the Wehrmacht high command recorded:

The defensive battle west of Cologne remains of foremost importance.
Some of the important observations: It appears certain that the enemy,

primarily the British, as observed since the beginning of the invasion, will adhere to his methodical method of fighting: Determine a limited goal of attack, prepare for a break-through in the area with heavy artillery fire with use of enormous amounts of artillery ammunition. In the attack that follows the armor is used less for a break-through than for local neutralizing of resistance, then securing the captured territory with more artillery barrages ahead of slowly advancing armor and infantry units. The front-line troops are of the opinion that only in isolated instances can the Allies be prevented from reaching their daily objectives.[8]

During the night of 23 February, the American forces along the Ruhr front between Düren and Roermond unleashed a massive barrage on the makeshift Wehrmacht defenses remaining west of the Rhine. Under the umbrella of artillery fire, the Allies pushed thirty divisions along a 40-mile front toward the east. The advance threatened to encircle and destroy all remaining defenders between the Rur and Rhine Rivers. The advance was marked by the dismal scene of columns of disarmed soldiers in field-gray marching toward the west, hands held high over their heads, or assisting sick and wounded as they made their way into the POW cages.

The roads leading to the great Rhine city of Cologne were also under incessant attack from Allied airpower. One inhabitant, observing the approaches to the city, wrote: "In bright sunlight the American *Jabos*, mostly the fast, twin-fuselaged Lightnings, fell upon their ground targets like falcons. I could clearly see how they released the five hundred pound bombs, which fell to the earth like strands of silver pearls. Then one could hear the detonations and see the cloud from the explosions rising like mushrooms in the distance."[9]

Despite the extensive damage inflicted on Cologne by fleets of aircraft during the months of bombing campaigns, a large civilian population remained within the city, many of whom were working urgently to prepare for the Allied onslaught.

With the advance toward Cologne, the American forces encountered for the first time the last-ditch levy scraped together by Nazi functionaries for defending the Reich—the Volkssturm. Along the Militärring, the major road encircling the city, the Volkssturm units were at work digging tank trenches and foxholes in preparation for the coming battle. Poorly armed elderly men and teenaged boys prepared to meet the Americans with obsolete small arms and Panzerfausts. Most had received only rudimentary training. The units, armed with a variety of rifles predating World War I, were sparsely supplied with a handful of ammunition. The shortage of supplies rendered it impossible to fire the weapons with live ammunition. Training had been conducted in a simulated manner; the live ammunition was saved for the serious business of killing Allied soldiers. Most of the Volkssturm troops wore little in the way of uniforms; the majority were clad in civilian clothing and sported reluctantly donned armbands printed with the national emblem and the words *Deutsche Wehrmacht*. The lack of steel helmets required the erstwhile defenders to wear their civilian caps, among which a smattering of alpine-style Hitler Youth headgear could be seen.

At the end of February during a meeting of district party authorities, the leading local functionary in the Nazi Party, Kreisleiter Schaller, announced that Cologne would be defended. On 1 March 1945, his superior, Gauleiter Josef Grohé, had ordered the evacuation of women and children and all other non-combatants. It was his last official act as Gauleiter in the city. On 5 March, after the Hohenzollern Bridge was demolished by retreating Wehrmacht troops, the Gauleiter climbed into a boat and fled to the east bank of the Rhine. He later took refuge with other party officials in Bensberg Castle.

The order for evacuation was ignored by many of the inhabitants, who were eager only to see the war—and their misery—come to an end. Despite the approaching front, the citizens of Cologne exhibited a remarkable level of morale, punctuated by moments of resignation and humor. An often, though surreptitiously, repeated rhyme in the city during the closing days went: *Es geht alles vorüber, es geht alles vorbei, auch Adolf Hitler, mit seiner Partei* (It will all be over, it will all be past, also Adolf Hitler, with his party).[10]

The defense of Cologne was less strategic than symbolic, for little remained that was worth defending. The last major air raid occurred on 2 March 1945. At 10:00 a.m., a fleet of British Halifax and Lancaster bombers approached. A swarm of fighter-bombers led the way, attacking tactical targets that included the air raid warning system. The staff of Cologne's flak defense system had been transferred from headquarters in the Post stadium to the east bank of the Rhine; few had suspected that the Allies would expend more material on the field of ruins that had once been the Rhineland's proudest city. The fleet of bombers passed at low altitude over a company of reluctant Volkssturm soldiers.

Volkssturm soldier Willy Weirauch, shocked by the spectacle of the oncoming aircraft, waited expectantly for orders from his elderly commander. Without a word, the group of teenagers and elderly reservists began tossing aside their antiquated firearms and running desperately for cover. No sooner had they gained the dubious safety of an air raid bunker than a massive explosion rent the air. The breathless Volkssturm members were thrown to the concrete floor by the blast; the steel doors of the bunker were ripped from their frames and hung warped and useless. The roar of the explosions deafened their ears, and the pain from the air pressure was excruciating. The bombs fell without interruption. The air would momentarily clear as one squadron passed overhead en route to the city center, but within seconds, a follow-on attack would pass overhead. The soldiers discerned the sounds of screaming bombs over the roar of the explosions as the attackers progressed farther east into the heart of Cologne.

The raid lasted sixty minutes. Most of the inhabitants who had not previously fled the city were surprised by the attack, and the lack of warning produced catastrophic results. Caught in the open, people sought any form of shelter as the bombers flew overhead. Those who reached the safety of the crypts within the badly damaged St. Gereons Church crowded together in the darkness and attempted to wait out the attack, with screams, cries, and prayers penetrating the air over the sounds of droning motors and exploding bombs. The earth shook and the church tower swayed with the pressure waves, but the walls of St. Gereons continued to hold.

Other Cologne inhabitants were not so fortunate. The cleric of St. Georgs Church in the Waidmarkt was buried beneath the rubble of his building. Hundreds of others lay submerged beneath shifting rubble or were entombed in collapsed cellars. That afternoon, the city suffered another, albeit smaller, air raid conducted by some 150 aircraft.[11]

The soldiers of Willy Weirauch's Volkssturm unit remained huddled in the cellar after the droning of bombers faded in the distance, and then slowly, the group began exiting the shelter. Finding himself alone in the bunker, Weirauch stared at the floor in the dim light and pondered the situation. Not knowing whether his parents had survived the raid, he wanted only an end to the torment of life amid the ruins. With his right hand, he reached to his left shoulder, grasped the Volkssturm armband, and tore it from his jacket. Tossing the insignia to the floor, he sprang from the bunker and headed toward his home. His brief service as one of Hitler's soldiers had come to an end.[12]

The air raid of Friday, 2 March, was the last endured by the citizens of Cologne. But that raid served to increase the confusion that prevailed in the city as the advancing Allies drew nearer. The victims of the attack were hastily buried wherever possible. Any remaining air defense units began transferring their equipment and personnel to the east bank of the Rhine. Most transport was conducted over the still-standing Hohenzollern Bridge. The other major bridge spanning the Rhine in the city, the Hindenburg Bridge, was no longer available. Heavily damaged by previous raids and weakened by masses of refugees and heavy traffic, it had collapsed into the Rhine on 28 February, carrying an undetermined number of soldiers and refugees into the river.

The railway authorities received instructions to transfer all undamaged rolling stock to the east bank. Isolated soldiers, traveling alone or in small groups, threaded their way through the ruins in the direction of the Hohenzollern Bridge, intent on not being abandoned on the west bank in the face of the oncoming

Allies. Many of the soldiers who were from the area elected to discard their Wehrmacht uniforms and slip into the surrounding countryside to await the end of the war among friends or family members.

German soldiers were not the only people seeking refuge from the oncoming Allies. After weeks of haranguing the populace to fight to the last man, the Nazi Party officials were fleeing toward the east in increasing numbers. As late as 4 March 1945, the Nazi officials in Cologne had advised the local German military commander that the city had to be fiercely defended. "The Volkssturm can stop the American tanks with Panzerfausts," they had announced.[13]

The actions of many officials, however, belied their propaganda. Nazi offices became scenes of frenetic activity as files and documents were burned to keep incriminating evidence from falling into the hands of the Americans. Distinctive brown and gold uniforms, trimmed with swastika armbands that evoked an earlier age for the Nazi leadership, were hastily tossed out of windows to lie in the streets and alleys. Nazi banners, parade regalia, and the obligatory oversized photographs of the Führer that were found in all official buildings were hastily buried or burned by nervous inhabitants. The bible of the Nazi Party, Hitler's *Mein Kampf*, was purged from residences and shop windows. There were no Nazis in Cologne: the Allies would find only innocent victims of Nazi oppression.

As Volkssturm members and foreign laborers on the outskirts of the city constructed long, winding trenches and tank traps with shovels and picks, files of refugees passed en route to the Rhine and the safety of the east bank. One resident wrote of the exodus:

> The people make their way over the roads from the front area. Horses,
> wagons, a cow tethered with a halter, piles of linens bundled in sheets
> and tied with string to hand-carts. Farm wagons have been converted to
> temporary shelters, swaying wooden contraptions with peep holes. And
> there are the women limping on wounded feet as they proceed onward with
> painful faces, benumbed by artillery barrages, tormented by the bombs.
> There are the children, penal battalions, flocks of prisoners, a caravan of
> misery, of hunger, of thirst and of hopelessness.[14]

During the night of 3 March, Allied aircraft dropped thousands of leaflets over the tortured city. At sunrise, the inhabitants emerged from their cellars and bunkers to find rubble-clogged streets littered with the small notes imploring the citizens to disobey the directives of the Nazi leaders. The Allies were asking them not to evacuate the city and advised them that they had nothing to fear from the Allied troops. It made little difference to most of the residents; they were weary and hungry, and there no longer existed a means of fleeing the city even if they wanted to do so. Besides, it was clear that fleeing over the Hohenzollern Bridge to the east half of the city would only delay the inevitable.

At 7:00 a.m. on Monday, 5 March, the American 3rd Armored Division launched a final advance on Cologne. The GIs, under the command of General Maurice Rose, cautiously felt their way toward the heart of the city. The experienced soldiers did not fully expect to find the city empty: there would be defenders. They were not mistaken. Waiting for the advancing GIs were remnants of General Friedrich Köchling's LXXXI Corps, consisting of units from the 363rd Volksgrenadier Division, the 9th Panzer Division, and the 3rd Panzergrenadier Division. The total strength of his forces represented approximately two regiments. Kochling's defenses comprised two main lines of defense. The Militärring, the roadway encircling the city's perimeter, was defended by the regular military forces at his disposal. The next line of defense was the "green belt," which was defended by policemen, fire department personnel, and any paramilitary units that had not already evaporated in the face of the oncoming American tanks. The units were augmented by the final Volkssturm levies of old men, boys, crippled individuals, and disabled veterans who were still capable of carrying a weapon. The Allied intelligence reports that the German army was now reduced to stragglers and last-ditch conscripts was of little comfort to the U.S. infantrymen moving cautiously through the ruins. They had long ago learned that even an aged reservist could be deadly if he was determined to make the ultimate sacrifice for Hitler in an obviously lost war.

Despite the dangers awaiting in the blocks of rubble ahead of the advancing Americans, they could not delay in moving ever eastward toward the Rhine. The Hohenzollern Bridge still lay ahead, beyond the twin spires of the Cologne Cathedral. The goal was to advance with enough speed to capture the bridge intact. However, the Wehrmacht had become skilled in leaving a path of destruction in its wake, and thus, the infantrymen and tank crews held few illusions that an intact bridge would be standing for them.

Encountering resistance after penetrating the Militärring, the lead armored elements destroyed an 88-mm antitank position and plowed forward, raking buildings and possible resistance locations with machine-gun and tank fire. Resistance increased as the lead elements penetrated deeper, toward the heart of Cologne. Antiaircraft guns fired from fixed embrasures until overrun by tanks or destroyed by infantrymen probing their way through the ruins. The dead and wounded of both sides were left in the wake of the advancing units. The commander of the 9th Panzer Division, Major-General Harald Freiherr von Elverfeldt, fell before American guns as his rear guard was decimated.

The Cologne citizens cowering in cellars detected the noises of an approaching battle with a mixture of fear and relief. They were relieved that the fighting would soon end and that for them, peace (albeit under occupation by enemy forces) would begin. Their feelings of relief were dampened by memories of Nazi propaganda that reported Allied plans to deport Germans for slave labor, as well as the rumors of rapes and murders. After all, they concluded, an enemy who would relentlessly incinerate entire cities filled with civilians was capable of anything. However, if nothing else, the arrival of the Americans would bring change, and most survivors were convinced that life could not get any worse than all they had endured over the last weeks. They had arrived at a point where they believed "an end with terror is preferable to terror without end."[15]

After a series of skirmishes with scattered German units on the outskirts of the city, the American columns halted at the green belt, the inner road network that encircled the oldest section of Cologne. There, they consolidated their forces, evacuated the wounded, replenished fuel and ammunition, and prepared to assault the inner city the following day. The inhabitants in the outer ring huddled in their cellars, shocked at the display of military might they had witnessed. The night of 5–6 March resounded with the unintelligible shouts of commands in English, the rattling of half-tracks, and the rumble of heavy armored vehicles taking position in the ruins.

As the sun rose on Tuesday, 6 March, the columns moved out of their positions toward the heart of the city. Curious onlookers began to emerge from their shelters to observe their conquerors, and they gathered in small groups to discuss their fate. American reconnaissance aircraft, circling lazily in a clear sky over the blocks of rubble, reported any suspected enemy positions to the armored units below. The streets remained ominously silent; no German defenders moved to repel the cautious but relentless advance of the enemy forces. The evidence of a German military presence was sparse, but the streets still bore mute witness to the last deadly air raid on the city. The American soldiers discerned the stench of death that emanated from the ruins and mixed with the familiar smell of exhaust fumes, cordite, and cosmoline. Hardened by months of combat, they paid little notice to the mangled corpses of bomb victims that still lay in their path.

Toward the inner city, resistance slackened, and the tanks increased their speed. Onlookers began gathering at intersections to view the column of American vehicles, flanked by ranks of infantrymen, snaking through the city. White flags mushroomed from windows and rooftops. Most of the inhabitants were unaware of the progress made by the Allies over the past days. There had been no electricity since the last major air raid, and they hungered for information regarding the latest developments determining Germany's fate. As the American point elements penetrated deeper into the heart of Cologne, the last German military units cleared the Rhine and sought the temporary safety of the east bank, leaving a ragged rear guard behind. American infantrymen were approaching the banks of the river when the city was rocked by a massive explosion. The Hohenzollern Bridge, the pride of Cologne and the vital link between the east and west sectors of the city, plunged into the Rhine.

The column slowly approached the twin spires of the 700-year-old Cologne Cathedral, left a blackened shell by the numerous bombing raids over the course of the war. The magnificent structure, the enduring symbol of the city, had suffered extensive damage during a raid in 1943 but had remained standing. The cathedral had sustained hits from twelve high-explosive bombs, countless incendiary bombs, and nineteen artillery rounds.[16] It now served as a beacon for the oncoming Americans. The bark of a heavy weapon broke forth from the concealment of a nearby building, and the lead Sherman rocked to a halt and burst into flames. A second Sherman quickly rotated its turret and opened fire on the German Panther, putting it out of action with a direct hit. The German crew bailed from the smoking vehicle and disappeared into the surrounding ruins. The Americans proceeded cautiously. Suddenly, the tankers and infantrymen were met by the sight of a vast expanse of water flowing through the ruins. Far away to the east, they could discern other fields of ruins beyond their reach, separated by the water. The U.S. First Army had reached the Rhine.

The Allies quickly consolidated their hold on the west bank sector of Cologne and in the surrounding countryside. Large numbers of inhabitants had been evacuated to Saxony and Brandenburg during October and December 1944 to escape the incessant artillery barrages. Trenches were dug to the south and west of the district; railway bridges had been destroyed. Medical personnel evacuated many of the wounded to a large hospital complex in Rheindahlen. The wounded were loaded onto horse-carts and the few remaining motorized vehicles and in some cases were moved in hand-carts. Motorized vehicles pulled by horses became a common sight; meager fuel supplies were carefully rationed, and many units had long since exhausted their resources. Numerous injured soldiers, their wounds exacerbated by the movement, bled to death during the long march and were pulled from the wagons. Stripped of identification tags and documents so that their family members could be notified of their fate, the dead were often abandoned by the roadside to be disposed of by the advancing Americans.

There was no escape from the relentless enemy. On 24 February, the first artillery rounds began falling on Rheindahlen, followed by a bombing raid. A schoolteacher recorded on that date:

> The first artillery rounds on Rheindahlen. At midday bombs were dropped on the city without causing too much damage. I did not risk conducting the 14:00 lecture. The entire situation remains tenuous and nerve-wracking. At dusk I went to the Beecker Strasse where the lecture was to take place

in a private residence. Only one student appeared very late for the class. In order for the children to have to go only a short distance to classes we are conducting the lessons in small groups in nearby restaurants, homes and bunkers.[17]

At the end of February, the entire Army Group B front collapsed. Unable to hold the Rhine approaches with his three weakened armies, Model ordered a senior engineering staff to be organized for the evacuation of irreplaceable equipment over the Rhine between Koblenz and Düsseldorf. Forced to acknowledge that the west bank could no longer be held indefinitely, Hitler relaxed the order that forbade the withdrawal of military units behind the Rhine, and the evacuation of nonessential staff personnel began. However, he directed that the combat units were to continue resisting the Allied forces on the west bank.

The small towns and villages in the path of the oncoming American First and Ninth Armies to the west and northwest of the Ruhr were experiencing the initial phases of total collapse. During the day, it was impossible to move freely on open roads. The squadrons of fighters patrolled the skies in advance of the armored columns, destroying any target that presented a potential threat to the tanks or infantry. Food became scarce with the disruption of transportation facilities, and the population remaining in the threatened areas began to consume their carefully hoarded reserves. The public utilities began to experience disruptions that took ever longer to restore. As the Allied armies drew nearer, the power and gas lines often failed altogether, as the facilities were destroyed under the weight of bombing raids or artillery barrages. Many of the inhabitants attempted a last-minute flight to rearward areas east of the Rhine, away from the oncoming enemy and the unknown fate that awaited them at the hands of the invaders.

For many, the decision to flee ahead of the Americans came too late. Gasoline for the private vehicles not already requisitioned by the Wehrmacht was impossible to obtain. Evacuation by rail carried its own risks; everyone was aware that the public transportation system offered an easy and favored target for marauding fighter-bombers. Additionally, special permits were required for use of the public transportation systems; the surviving railcars were largely reserved for the transport of troops and equipment.

The Rhineland town of Lobberich was under evacuation orders in the face of the American advance. The town was to be defended, and all nonessential residents were ordered to leave. On 25 February 1945, Arnold Frank recorded in his diary:

Corporal Fischer is with us, together with two comrades. They brought two bottles of rum with them. At 01:00 Fischer has to depart for Sonsbeck, a courier is never free from duty. The Volkssturm has been on alert for days. Every night troops pass through our streets, retreating from the enemy. The German front is broken. Volkssturm level IV was called up this week to their assembly point near Berg Ingenhoven—they are the last reserves. At exactly 12:00 I reported as ordered and met about two dozen members of my unit. Some personnel were busy digging tank trenches. As the clock struck twelve they measured the depth of the trench—it met the required specifications— and everyone took off. A couple of the Volkssturm men followed at a distance, then one after another they disappeared in the direction of home, until I was one of the last ones still standing there. As the senior person remaining on the site I issued the order "toward home—march!" My service with the Volkssturm thus came to an end.[18]

A light rain began to fall as the Volkssturm units disintegrated. The rain con-tinued through the night and into the following morning. A bedraggled soldier detached himself from his retreating company long enough to ask Frank to repair the soles of his sodden boots. While the soldier patiently waited, Frank nailed the soles and asked if a major at the market square had picked him up. The soldier shook his head with a puzzled look. Frank advised him that the major was round-ing up all retreating soldiers who could not produce marching orders; a defense of Lobberich was being organized. Frank soon completed his task, handed the boots to the waiting soldier, and glanced through the door, from where he ob-served a number of German paratroopers hastily piling equipment onto a vehicle drawn up in front of a nearby shop. It was apparent that the Allies had once again broken through.[19]

In the town of Kempen, Bürgermeister Mertens ordered the civilians to evac-uate the town for the outlying areas. Thirty-two of the civilians were assigned as lookouts from the water tower in three-hour shifts, with orders to report any enemy activity to the police station. The first and second levels of Volkssturm were mustered. The third, consisting of the youngest members, was ordered to Krefeld. The fourth was not called, for there were no weapons with which they could be armed.[20]

On 2 March, the distant droning of observation aircraft wafted faintly over Kempen throughout the day as the Americans drew nearer. That afternoon, ar-tillery rounds began falling. The old Propstei Church was destroyed by a direct hit. The Kellersohn Hotel, Haus Platen, the Rathaus, and numerous buildings in the vicinity of the train station were destroyed. At 2:00 p.m., a large column of olive green vehicles was observed approaching from Voest. The column sud-denly braked to a halt, and numerous soldiers were seen rapidly abandoning the vehicles. The Americans took cover in roadside trenches and waited expectantly.

The road remained quiet; no German soldiers were anywhere to be seen. Near the village of Vorst, the local Volkssturm had assembled to secure the Gulder road. That evening, an officer appeared with a group of approximately fifty soldiers and occupied the freshly dug defenses. He inquired about the strength of the Volkssturm unit. "Nine men" was the reply.

"How are you armed?"

"With a carbine and four Panzerfausts."

"How have you been trained?"

"We each fired the carbine once, and we watched a demonstration of how to use a Panzerfaust."

Shaking his head, the officer ordered the men to leave the weapons in the trenches and assemble for a briefing. As the motley collection of elderly men gathered, the officer announced that they were being held "in reserve" and promptly sent them home.[21]

An American infantry patrol encountered heavy resistance as they advanced in the direction of Krefeld and approached the village of Kehn. A small group of Wehrmacht soldiers had fortified themselves in the Steiger and Kaiser farm buildings, from where they fired until their ammunition was exhausted. The officer, in charge of five surviving soldiers, called into a cellar where the farm families and the laborers had sought shelter. He advised the civilians that it was over, their ammunition was expended. One of the farmers volunteered to approach the Americans to inform them that the German soldiers wished to surrender. As the Germans filed into the farmyard with upraised hands, the American soldiers smashed the rifles of the newly captured prisoners and relieved them of their watches. An angry American soldier ripped the officer's shoulder boards from his tunic and threw them into the mud before herding the prisoners up the road with upraised hands amid kicks and blows from rifle butts.[22]

Hitler continued to issue orders regarding the conduct of the war in Army Group B's beleaguered sector as the situation deteriorated by the hour. Immediately after the capture of Krefeld, he reiterated his order that under no circumstances was any Rhine bridge to fall into the hands of the Allies. It was also made clear that should such an event occur, the sector commander was to be held personally responsible; there were to be no excuses, and no justification for such an occurrence would be accepted. Additionally, bridges were to be retained intact and passable as long as feasible. They were to be destroyed only to prevent their seizure by enemy forces. The bridges remained necessary for the transport of supplies and the evacuation of wounded from the bridgeheads on the west bank, and their early destruction would doom any forces that remained in the area.

The order served to hasten the annihilation of those German units holding the shrinking bridgeheads on the west bank. Thousands of war-weary troops found themselves compressed into small bridgeheads that offered a target-rich environment for the fighter-bombers. American artillery batteries concentrated their fire on crossroads and strategic terrain features, bringing death and destruction with every attempt by the Germans to move out of their defenses. Disabled tanks were abandoned for lack of spare parts; other fully intact vehicles were left by the roads or hidden from view under the protection of trees, where they remained due to the lack of fuel. Artillery pieces were abandoned along the roadsides when the prime movers became immobilized. Ammunition dumps that had been carefully concealed from fighter-bombers for weeks fell victim to the acute lack of transport and were abandoned or demolished as the Americans pressed forward. The roads were lined with scorched shells of destroyed vehicles, dead horses, and the shattered remnants of Wehrmacht wagons that had fallen victim to artillery bursts or fighter attacks.

One after another, the German cities and town fell to the Allied armies. On 2 March, Mönchengladbach, Roermond, and Venlo fell. The gateway to the Ruhr industrial cities situated along the west bank of the Rhine was opened. On 3 March, Neuss and Krefeld fell. General Alfred Schlemm, commander of the First Parachute Army, attempted to salvage the remnants of his forces as they were pressed ever closer to the Rhine. He received instructions to establish defenses for a bridgehead along the west bank of the river, extending from Krefeld in the south to Wesel in the north, and to hold his positions at all costs. Losing control of the Rhine along the Ruhr Valley would mean losing the last possibility for continuing the war for even a limited time. The coal for the harbors of Hamburg, Bremen, and Wilhelmshaven had to be transported along the Rhine and through the Lippe Canal south of Wesel, then farther through the Dortmund-Ems Canal to the northeastern cities. If American forces gained control of the west bank of the Rhine in the Ruhr sector, this lifeline would be severed; what little remained of German industrial and military activity in the harbors would grind to a halt after the on-site supplies of coal were exhausted.

The receipt of Hitler's order was especially troubling to General Schlemm, for he was responsible for no less than nine bridges in his sector. He transferred his headquarters to the Rhine town of Rheinberg for better command and control of the bridges and established radio communications with each bridge in his sector for close monitoring. Any delay that enabled the Americans to seize a bridge would result in a military catastrophe for which he would be personally responsible.

The seriousness of Hitler's order was almost tested on 3 March. A forward unit of the U.S. 84th Infantry Division pushed toward the Rhine in the area of Hüls, meeting increasing resistance as it neared the river. The German forces in the area, under command of General Rodt, were attempting to hold the

Ürdingen bridgehead with remnants of artillery and flak reserve units and had been compressed into an area running from Bockum to Kapellen. It was clear that the bridgehead could not be held and that the Americans would reach the Rhine within several hours. Combat engineers feverishly prepared the bridge for demolition. As engineers made final preparations, they discovered that the electric cable essential for detonating the charges within the framework of the bridge was badly damaged. The engineers worked feverishly to replace several yards of cable as the bridge came under artillery fire and fighter-bomber attacks. Thirty-nine German soldiers died in the desperate attempt to repair the damaged cable. At length, Americans appeared on the west approaches and, under a hail of fire, assaulted the bridge, killing or driving the survivors onto the east bank. The American troops stormed forward and almost gained the east approaches before being driven back by strong counterfire. A seesaw battle ensued until a Wehrmacht truck, laden with explosives, drove under the pilings and demolished a 100-yard section of the bridge. At 6:00 a.m. the following day, the air was rent by an enormous explosion as the retreating Germans completed the destruction of the bridge and denied the Americans their prize.[23]

Another close call occurred at the Homberg road bridge in the Ürdingen bridgehead. General Schlemm grew increasingly nervous as he followed the situation reports and tracked the locations of the American units as they closed on the area. When it became apparent that the American tanks were nearing the bridge, he radioed the on-scene commander and ordered him to destroy the structure. Ten minutes later, he picked up the radio again and demanded to know if the bridge had been demolished. To his astonishment, the officer replied that he had not carried out the order: he advised the general that a colonel at the scene refused to permit the order to be followed. Enraged, Schlemm screamed into the radio transmitter. "Who in the hell is this colonel who is countermanding my order?" he shouted. "I am the army commander, and I am ordering you to destroy the bridge immediately!"

The radio remained silent for a moment as Schlemm waited anxiously for a reply. Finally, the voice of the officer broke the silence: "The colonel says that he is not under your command, Herr General. He says that he is assigned to Field Marshal Model, and that the bridge is not to be destroyed."

Schlemm digested the unbelievable discourse in stunned silence for several seconds. The Americans were approaching the bridge embankment, what few defenders remained west of the bridge could be considered as good as lost, and now an unknown colonel had appeared from nowhere and was countermanding his order. The general lost all composure. Jumping to his feet, he screamed into the handset that if the bridge was not demolished immediately, he was going to show up down there and "personally shoot not only that colonel, but everyone else at the bridge!" Within seconds, a massive explosion reverberated along the length of the river in the Ruhr Valley as the Homberg Bridge rose from its girders and then collapsed into the swirling currents of the Rhine.[24]

As the Americans closed on the river in the area of Wesel, they met stiff resistance from remnants of the renowned Panzer Lehr Division that had remained behind as a rear guard. Near the town of Veen, American and German tanks clashed in one of the final battles between armored units west of the Rhine. Sergeant Eduard Job of the Panzerjäger Lehr Battalion 130 was lying in wait for the approaching Americans when he observed a U.S. armored unit approaching to within close range of his hidden tank. As Job attempted to rotate the gun to follow the movement of an approaching Sherman, the mechanism refused to give way. Suddenly, the tank commander ordered him to fire; the gun remained silent. At that moment, the Sherman fired on Job's tank, but the round cracked overhead, missing the turret by inches. The frantic commander continued to scream for Job to fire, but the gunner could not bring the gun to bear on target. Desperately attempting to locate the cause of the malfunction, Job discovered that one of the gun projectiles stored in the turret had fallen against the rotating gears and was jamming the gun's mechanism. Job frantically freed the gears of the projectile, sprang upright in the gunner's position, rotated the gun, and fired. The Sherman burst into flames as Job sought a second target. One of the American armored vehicles approached rapidly from behind the burning Sherman, firing as it moved with small-caliber weapons. Job fired again, and the tank rocked to a halt as it, too, became enveloped in smoke.

The German tank turned and departed toward the town of Rheinberg, leaving the two disabled American tanks in its trail. Realizing that the goal of the Americans was to reach the ferry near Rheinberg, the crew assumed that other armored units would be penetrating German positions behind them. Intent on protecting the ferry landing as long as possible to permit the Panzer Lehr infantrymen to escape the shrinking bridgehead, the Panzerjäger sped toward the Rhine.

The tankers rolled through the town of Rheinberg toward the ferry landing and suddenly spotted three Shermans that had broken through the outer line of defenses. Eduard Job observed one of the tanks bearing down on them, and he opened fire from a range of 50 yards. The projectile struck the Sherman squarely below the turret, and the American tank careened blindly forward at rapid speed. Before the Panzerjäger could turn to avoid the impact, the two tanks collided almost head-on with a deafening crash. As both heavy vehicles slammed to a halt, Sergeant Job and the other crew members of the Panzerjäger were catapulted forward, falling against ammunition and equipment within the confines of the turret. The Sherman appeared to have been jolted from its path by the collision, and the heavy vehicle now proceeded to rake the Panzerjäger along the length of its right flank before breaking free and blindly colliding with a nearby building. The walls of the structure collapsed on the tank, partially burying the steel colossus under masonry as the American crewmen frantically opened the hatches and scrambled free.[25]

In the first week in March, the Army Group B headquarters staff was en route to cross the final barrier in the west. Model's staff navigated the congested roads toward the Rhine, where the personnel planned to cross on one of the few remaining ferries at Andernach. As they drew closer to the river, the road became increasingly congested with straggling units, extending along the roadsides in long, marching columns or riding in vehicles of every description. Horse-drawn wagons crammed with wounded soldiers and evacuees sought the safety of the far bank. The congestion on the narrow roads was exacerbated by throngs of civilians pushing hand-carts and leading children toward the east. Columns of infantrymen filed through the mud, shoulders bent under the weight of field equipment as they plodded toward the illusion of safety.

The crowds of refugees and retreating troops slowly parted in the path of the vehicles bearing the insignia and pennants of the army group staff. Toward the front of the convoy rode Field Marshal Model. In his company was Major Winrich Behr, the staff officer who had accompanied Model's predecessor, Günther von Kluge, on the impromptu trip to Paris in August. The staff officers were relieved that the sky remained black with thick, low-lying clouds that denied the tempting target of congested, snarled roads to the Allied fighter-bombers.

Despite the pennant bearing crossed batons conspicuously displayed on the fender of the field marshal's vehicle, the convoy made only sporadic progress through the throngs of refugees converging on the ferry landing. Losing patience at the delays, the field marshal leaned forward. "Listen, Behr," he said sharply with characteristically clipped words, "I have to get to the other side. I want you to stay here and bring order to this mess. Keep a vehicle, organize a defense, and get this cleared up. You know what to do. I'll send someone to relieve you when I get to the other side." As Behr sprang from the vehicle, Model added, "I'm designating you as the combat commander of Andernach. Do whatever you have to do to take care of this."

Thus, Winrich Behr suddenly and unexpectedly found himself the official combat commander of the small town on the Rhine. The major motioned for his vehicle to break from the field marshal's column and to pull to the side of the road. Glancing through the columns of soldiers filing past, he seized two young officers and ordered them to bring organization to the throng of civilians and soldiers at the ferry landing. It was not an easy task. Myriad vehicles attempted to jostle their way through the crowd for a place on the ferry. Behr was determined that the combat equipment would have priority; the air was filled with ensuing arguments and confrontations. The small group of officers labored at the ferry crossing the remainder of the day and late into the night.

At some time during the night, the area was rent with a massive explosion. Assuming that the ferry had struck a mine, Behr hurried to the scene and found that the ferry had simply disappeared in the darkness, leaving a column of vehicles and dozens of soldiers waiting on the west bank. Certain that the ferryboat would not be returning, Behr set about attempting to organize a defense; the American units could not be far away, and it was possible that the skies would clear. Cloudless skies would bring all traffic to a halt under an all-too-familiar swarm of fighter-bombers. As dawn approached, he walked the length of the road leading from the river to the first road junction. He began stopping all men in uniform and directing them to a nearby collection point. Quickly establishing an impromptu chain of command, he assigned an officer to be in charge of the group. Ordering the officer to halt all combat personnel and engage them in manning defenses, he departed to check on conditions at the Rhine.

Two hours later, he returned to the road crossing only to find that his makeshift defense unit had evaporated into the surrounding countryside. The soldiers at the crossing were not inclined to obey orders issued by this unknown, medal-bedecked major who had unexpectedly commandeered them. The retreating landsers did not relish the prospect of sacrificing themselves at the behest of the anonymous Knight's Cross holder; in their eyes, he was obviously a fanatic who would probably get them killed in what were clearly the last days of a hopelessly lost war.

Behr stopped to ponder the grim situation. His driver and vehicle had already been dispatched to the opposite bank. The American fighter-bombers or advanced armored elements could appear at any moment, and he was now stranded on the west bank. While considering various options, he was approached by a middle-aged reservist wearing the rank of a Wehrmacht major. The officer introduced himself as Behr's relief; he had been dispatched on orders of Field Marshal Model to relieve Behr and assume duties as battle commander of Andernach. The two officers spoke of the situation in which they found themselves. Defeat was looming for Germany; divisions could not be "stomped out of the ground" by the generals to secure victory.

The conversation became an honest assessment of how the two officers viewed their prospects. The reserve major lived nearby, and the Americans would soon be arriving. He was deeply concerned about his wife and children. Behr pondered the situation. The major would be left here with no weapons and no forces with which to establish a defense. Even if he managed to scrape together a weak group of defenders, Behr knew that it would only result in the American armored units and aircraft shooting the entire town of Andernach to pieces. At length, Behr looked at the major. "Go home," he advised the officer. "It could cost you your head, but to stay here is not an option. Take off and go home to your family. Besides," he motioned about them at the abandoned crossroads, "you have nothing here with which you can perform your duties." He then returned the officer's salute and walked toward the Rhine.[26]

Behr slowly made his way downstream in search of a crossing to the east bank. As he approached the small resort town of Weissen Thurm, he noted that the Rhine bridge at that location had been destroyed. However, a tangle of girders still protruded above the swirling brown water, providing a precarious foot bridge high above the river. He cautiously began making his way high above the Rhine along the steel girders. Several yards ahead of him, a small group of young soldiers from a retreating flak unit felt their way cautiously toward the opposite bank. Suddenly, two of the teenagers slipped from the rusted iron girders, plunged into the water far below, and disappeared in the swiftly moving, icy current. "This is no way to end the war," Behr thought to himself. He turned and slowly inched his way back toward the west bank. Along the way, he was forced to halt and yield to several Wehrmacht soldiers who were edging their way across the girder. The landsers inched past the major as they navigated the dizzying height and continued in the opposite direction. Behr was chagrined that he, an experienced combat veteran and holder of Germany's highest decoration for valor, was compelled to ignominiously retreat to the western shore.

No sooner had he reached the west bank than he heard the cough of a nearby engine. To the major's surprise, a small boat with a sputtering outboard motor, navigated by two boys clad in brown Hitler Youth uniforms, emerged from the riverbank. The teenagers were ferrying isolated stragglers to the safety of the east bank. Behr climbed into the waiting boat, joining a wounded officer whose head was swathed in bloody bandages, and the party slowly traversed the wide expanse of the Rhine.[27]

Chapter 4

Crossing at Remagen

During the closing days of February 1945, the Allies were consolidating their positions on the west bank of the Rhine, opposite the last elements of the German armies that had filtered over the river. The remnants of the Wehrmacht in the west were facing the most powerful combined might of troops and technological strength the world had ever seen. Eisenhower was in command of some 4 million soldiers in three separate army groups. His forces consisted of eight armies made up of twenty-one corps and seventy-three fully mechanized divisions. Three-fourths of the troops were Americans; the remainder were a mixture of British and British Commonwealth forces, French troops, and various colonial units. There were six tactical air commands with more than 17,000 aircraft, of which 5,000 were fighter-bombers and 7,000 were medium and heavy bombers.[1]

By early March 1945, most of the German army in the west had retreated to the east bank of the Rhine. The troops remaining on the west bank, constituting a rear guard, were facing inevitable destruction by the Anglo-American forces if they failed to cross the river. The forces consolidated under OB West, Field Marshal Gerd von Rundstedt, were attempting to reinforce their positions on the east bank. In the north, Army Group H, commanded by Colonel-General Johannes von Blaskowitz, was deployed in Holland and along the Lower Rhine. To the south of Blaskowitz's forces, extending from the northern Ruhr Valley to south of the Westerwald (which lay south of the Ruhr Valley), was Field Marshal Model's Army Group B. Army Group G, under SS Colonel-General Paul Hauser, was deployed to the south of Army Group B in Alsace and in the Saar area. General Erich Brandenberger's Nineteenth Army held the southernmost front in southwestern Germany along the Upper Rhine.

Eisenhower intended to face Model's army group with Montgomery's Twenty-first Army Group in the north and Bradley's Twelfth Army Group immediately to the south. The two Allied army groups formed an impenetrable line along the Rhine from Holland to Koblenz. These units were responsible for neutralizing German forces in the Rhineland and preparing for follow-on crossings over the Rhine. One of the primary objectives was to seize the Ruhr, the large industrial center vital to Germany's war capability. Without the Ruhr to supply the Wehrmacht divisions, the German army's capacity to continue to resist would quickly become exhausted.

The advance into the Rhineland had been hampered by the flooding of large areas when the Germans opened the locks of the Roer River dams. On 3 March, Montgomery's forces linked up with Bradley's Twelfth Army Group at Geldern. Other elements rapidly closed on the banks of the Rhine in an attempt to trap as many German forces as possible by denying them access to river crossings.

Hitler had previously demanded that the borders be defended west of the Rhine River along the Westwall (the Siegfried Line). Believing that the German soldiers would attempt to retreat behind the Rhine and hide in defensive positions, he had refused to permit the construction of defenses east of the river. Field Marshal Model constantly requested that preparations be made for a withdrawal behind the Rhine; his forces were too weak to halt an Allied advance west of the river. However, Hitler remained adamant that the defense of the German border west of the Rhine had to be maintained.

On 2 March 1945, Army Group B established a staff at Schloss Bensberg for conducting the Rhine defenses. The officer responsible was infantry General Joachim von Kortzfleisch; his chief of staff was Major Rudolf Schulz. One of their primary objectives was to secure the bridges over the Rhine and thereby enable the remaining German forces to cross to safety. They were to ensure that the bridges did not fall into Allied hands. One of the bridges for which they were responsible was the Ludendorff Bridge at the small Rhineland town of Remagen.

The bridge was constructed during World War I as a means for expediting traffic and communications in the Remagen area over the river. Designed by Mannheim architect Carl Wiener, the imposing structure was a dual-track railway bridge that connected the Ahr railroad with the rail network east of the Rhine. The bridge, named after the first quartermaster of the Imperial German Army, Erich von Ludendorff, was designed with three demolitions chambers built within each of the two massive piers supporting the bridge spans. The chambers had been filled with concrete during the French occupation of the Rhineland in the 1920s. The bridge spanned the Rhine in a north-south direction for a length of 300 yards. The east bank of the bridge ended at a 350-yard tunnel beneath an imposing cliff known as the Erpeler Ley. Beyond the tunnel, the route followed a steep ravine for some 500 yards before intersecting the Niederlahnstein-Troisdorf railway.[2]

The demolition charges vital to the defense of the bridge had been removed from the structure in 1940 and stored in the Pfungstadt depot near Darmstadt. Following the Allied invasion of France in 1944, efforts were made to prepare the bridge for destruction. In the autumn of 1944, German Staff Sergeant Jacob

Kleebach was dispatched to the Pfungstadt depot to recover the demolitions charges. To his chagrin, he found that during the war, the explosives had mysteriously vanished. Subsequent investigation revealed that the charges had ostensibly been expended for other uses. Replacement charges were hastily manufactured to the original specifications and were positioned on the bridge on 6 March 1945.

The following day, the engineer detachment constructed an antitank trench on the west bank of the Rhine along the railway embankment to impede any unexpected road traffic. One firing circuit was prepared for demolition; a second was still under construction at 2:00 p.m. on 7 March. The demolitions charges consisted of 600 kilograms of TNT. The firing plan called for the main charge to be initiated by a command-detonated, electrical firing device. A secondary firing device was to be prepared for use in the event the primary device failed or if immediate destruction of the bridge prior to completion of the primary preparations should be necessary. An additional 600 kilograms of explosives were requested for use with the secondary device, but by 11:00 a.m. on 7 March, the engineers had received only 300 kilograms of commercial Donarit.[3]

Present at the bridge was a combat engineering company under the command of forty-eight-year-old Captain Carl Christian Friesenhahn. The noncommissioned officer (NCO) formerly responsible for preparations at the bridge, Sergeant Kleebach, was integrated into Friesenhahn's new force of engineers. The engineering company was subordinate to Battalion 3, Pionier Regiment 12, under the command of Major August Kraft, whose command post was at the nearby village of Bendorf-Sayn. The unit had been placed under the operational command of Zangen's Fifteenth Army on 1 March 1945.

The bridge security forces consisted of forty-six convalescent soldiers from Infantry Replacement and Training Battalion 80, headquartered in Koblenz. The company was under the command of forty-year-old Captain Willi Oskar Bratge, who had been assigned as combat commander of Remagen in December 1944. An additional force consisting of a reduced company from Technical Battalion 1 and Railway Engineering Company 103 had been responsible for maintenance on the bridge since the autumn of 1944. On 5 March, all maintenance personnel were placed under the administrative command of the 12th Company, Engineer Regiment 12.[4]

The ground defense force was augmented by antiaircraft defenses, which consisted of 37-mm and 20-mm flak batteries supported by one heavy railway flak battery from 1st Heavy Railway Flak Detachment 535 and a smoke company. In February 1945, the defenses had been strengthened by the arrival of a new antiaircraft rocket unit, irreverently referred to as the beer crate flak by the gunners because of the open framework of the rocket launchers. The rocket launcher crews were assigned to Flak Training and Test Detachment 900 and were trained to operate the new weapons at Rerik on the Baltic coast before being deployed for operations with the rockets. The 1st Battery was deployed for railway transport protection, the 2nd Battery remained in a semimobile status, and the 3rd Battery was deployed to Remagen as a stationary unit. The batteries were organized into crews of five men for each rocket launcher, with a sergeant in command of every crew. The rocket projectiles were stored in a temporary magazine in Remagen and in a sawmill at Kretzhaus. A 3-ton truck was used to transport the rockets to the battery positions. The rocket battery remained operationally independent from the conventional flak commands in the area of Remagen and was placed under the senior commander at Ehrenbreitstein Citadel in Koblenz.[5]

The commander of the 120 men assigned to the 3rd Battery was Lieutenant Karl Heinz Peters. The battery personnel were deployed in positions near the Römerhaus, situated on the hillside between Erpel and Orsberg, and on the Erpeler Ley. Lieutenant Peters had established his command post in the Schulz Hotel at Unkel and later in the Fuhrmann Gasthof in Bruchhausen. The enlisted personnel of the battery were living in private quarters at Orsberg and in the meeting room of the Zur Erpeler Ley Gasthof.

As the Allied forces closed relentlessly on the banks of the Rhine, concern for the bridge preparations increased. General Wolfgang Pickert, commander of the III Flak Corps, inspected the rocket battery in late February and judged the rockets to be of dubious value for antiaircraft purposes. On 6 March, the total ground troop strength for the defense of the bridge stood at thirty-six men and was composed solely of the security company of convalescents. The local Volkssturm had been activated, but Bratge received word that most of the men assigned to the district Volkssturm were not to be found. The local units that were previously mobilized had received orders to defend the roadblocks at the Apollinaris Church on the Remagen-Birresdorf road. The Wehrmacht training facility for the Hitler Youth reported that during the night of 6–7 March, the teenagers from year group 1928 had been withdrawn to another sector on the east bank of the Rhine.[6]

At 9:00 p.m. on 6 March, the bridge commander, Captain Friesenhahn, reported that the bridge was prepared for destruction, and Captain Bratge requested that it be opened to vehicular traffic. Friesenhahn stated that it was not yet possible to open the bridge, as he had received a message from the Reichsbahn (Reich railway system) authorities that some twelve trains were scheduled to cross over the bridge during the night. He added that the bridge could probably be cleared for vehicular traffic at 5:00 a.m. the following day, 7 March.

Bratge continued to be concerned with every update of enemy positions. He placed a telephone call to the Army Group B staff and requested that his situation report be forwarded immediately to the Ia, the army group operations officer. He reported that the Americans had reached the area to the west of Birresdorf with heavy strength and that an Allied push toward Remagen on the morning of 7 March was expected. He also informed the army group staff that his only defenses consisted of a thirty-six-man company and that all other alarm units planned for the defense had been transferred elsewhere.

The staff officer brushed aside Bratge's concerns, stating that the enemy push was directed toward the Bonn-Cologne-Düsseldorf area. The enemy armored units that had been reported to Bratge were considered to be nothing more than forces securing the American right flank. Bratge, however, was unconvinced. He argued that the forces were stronger than mere flank security warranted. Growing weary of the discussion with the unknown captain on the phone, the staff officer became impatient. "I really believe, Herr Hauptmann," the officer responded sarcastically, "that you have your pants full." Furious, Bratge slammed down the receiver.[7]

Unbeknownst to Bratge, the flak units in the area had also been withdrawn. The alert condition for the Remagen area had been downgraded, and the entire flak command, with the exception of the antiaircraft platoons located at Erpel and at the Krupp sand quarry, had been withdrawn during the night of 6–7 March. The three single-barreled guns on the bridge itself remained in position, but the two 20-mm guns on the Erpeler Ley heights were withdrawn, thus degrading the bridge defenses to an even greater extent than Bratge was aware.[8] At 2:00 a.m. on 7 March, Bratge was persuaded by his adjutant to attempt to rest, for there was nothing further that could done to improve the situation at that point. The weary captain still had reason for concern. His reports indicated that strong American armored forces were approaching his position, and the reinforcements promised to him had been transferred elsewhere. Major Kraft, commander of the engineering unit, was continuing to prepare the bridge for demolition. Bratge went into a neighboring room and lay down, intending to be awakened at 4:00 a.m.

Captain Bratge was awakened at 3:00 a.m. by the sounds of approaching vehicles, and he rose to investigate. It was highly unusual for motorized units to be approaching the bridge when it was clearly not opened for vehicular traffic. To his alarm, he discovered that a Wehrmacht motorized column had disregarded his sentries, had plowed through the checkpoint, and was stubbornly driving toward the bridge. The vehicles were filled with rear-echelon supply and administrative troops intent on reaching the safety of the east bank. Their remaining weapons had already been eagerly surrendered to the combat units behind them, and their primary goal was to put distance between themselves and the oncoming Sherman tanks. Bratge hurried to the checkpoint to halt any further passage of vehicles. During an altercation with the retreating troops, the exasperated captain had to draw his pistol and shoot the tires of two vehicles that refused to stop.

The vehicles that had passed through the checkpoint prior to his arrival crowded onto the bridge, halting all traffic for some 100 yards. Considering the numbers of troops and vehicles attempting to gain access to the bridge, it was clear that the sergeant assigned to control the traffic would not be able to manage the situation alone. Bratge set about organizing the traffic and clearing the bridge.

Documents were examined, with drivers required to produce the correct movement orders. Mixed among the trucks were several flak units with orders to proceed to the Bonn-Cologne-Düsseldorf area. The absence of any combat troops, with which Bratge had hoped to augment his sparse defenses, was conspicuous. Waiting to cross the bridge were two badly damaged but still-mobile tanks and one tank that was battle-worthy but had expended its ammunition; a check with the other armored vehicles revealed that they, too, had no ammunition available. At 5:00 a.m., the remaining vehicles slowly began inching over the bridge to safety.[9]

On 7 March, the Wehrmacht's LXVII Corps received an order from Zangen's Fifteenth Army that placed the Remagen bridgehead "immediately" under the corps command. With expectations of a major American push against the Remagen area, the corps was directed to send an officer with General Staff experience to take command of the bridgehead. Major Hans Scheller received the dubious distinction of being assigned to take command of the bridgehead as senior officer in charge. He received personal orders from General Otto Hitzfeld, commander of the LXVII Corps, who appointed him commander of Remagen, with several specific assignments. His tasks included assembling a defensive force from units that were retreating over the bridge, preparing the bridge for demolition, and ensuring destruction of the bridge as soon as the Americans arrived at the western approaches.[10]

On 6 March, the U.S. III Corps, under the command of Major General John Millikin, continued to press forward toward the Rhine. The Ninth Armored Division, under Major General John W. Leonard, was assigned to push toward the Remagen–Sinzig–Bad Neuenahr area. Lieutenant Colonel Leonard Engeman commanded a task force (TF) of the 9th Armored Division's Combat Command B. The task force consisted of the reduced 14th Tank Battalion, the 27th Armored Infantry Battalion, and an engineer platoon from the 9th Armored Engineer Battalion. A Company of the 27th Armored Infantry Battalion was under the command of Second Lieutenant Karl H. Timmermann, a young officer from the Midwest whose German-born mother had emigrated to the United States as a war bride after World War I. Timmermann's company was accompanied by an armored platoon from the 14th Tank Battalion under the command of Second Lieutenant John Gromball.

That morning, the combined tank platoon and infantry company advanced from Meckenheim through Adendorf, Fritzdorf, Överich, Niederich, Leimersdorf, and Birresdorf; from there, they pressed onward toward the Ludendorff Bridge at Remagen. The force reached Överich at 11:00 a.m., where they surprised two German soldiers who had unwisely stopped at the village and entered a building at Landskronerstrasse 29. The unsuspecting landsers were eating lunch when they heard the alarming news that the Americans had already entered the town. The soldiers immediately dropped their lunches and attempted to start the wood-burning engine of their vehicle. The primitive engine failed to ignite, and as the Americans drew near, the two soldiers abandoned the vehicle and attempted to flee across a field to the shelter of the woods below the village. The approaching Americans raked the running figures with a barrage of small-arms fire; the fugitives dropped in the tall grass of the field.

Their flight was observed by a number of civilians hiding behind the Schaefer family barn in Niederich, and the terrified villagers watched as the fleeing soldiers fell under the gunfire. Maria Bolling was following the incident from a window in a nearby house on Hofstrasse. She saw the soldiers as they abandoned their vehicle and disappeared out of view behind the corner of a building. The morning stillness then erupted in gunfire.

Running to the group of villagers standing behind the barn, Maria could hear a voice across the field calling in German for help. Several elderly men refused to go to the soldiers' aid, frightened that they would be mistaken for combatants by the nervous Americans. After a short discussion, Maria Schaefer and Maria Bollig obtained a pole from the barn and draped it with a bedsheet. Holding the makeshift flag aloft, the two women proceeded across the field to the soldiers. They found one of the men badly wounded, and the women dragged him back to the shelter of the house on the Hofstrasse. The second soldier, attempting to avoid detection by the Americans, crawled behind them in the concealment of the grass.

The Americans were arriving in ever-increasing numbers, and soon, numerous vehicles of various descriptions were halting by the roadside. The heavily armed strangers approached the buildings of the village and took the uninjured soldier prisoner. The wounded soldier was carried by the inhabitants to an upper floor of the house on the Hofstrasse, where he died from his wounds during the night.[11]

The villagers determined from the man's documents that he was twenty-three-year-old Johannes Hirsch from Pomerania. The Americans soon confiscated the body and laid it alongside the railway overpass near Ringen, where it rested for several days before the villagers were permitted to bury it in the Ringen cemetery.[12]

On Wednesday, 7 March, shortly after the American patrol surprised the German soldiers in Överich, Major Scheller, accompanied by Captain Vasel, departed from the German corps headquarters for Remagen. General Hitzfeld then transferred his headquarters to Altenahr, approximately 20 miles away.

The dawn broke with a gray sunrise, accompanied by a cold drizzle. The low cloud cover was welcomed by the Germans, who knew that the inclement weather would bring a respite from the air attacks by fighter-bombers. The German columns continued to wind their way along the narrow roads and crowded across the Ludendorff Bridge. Among the vehicles slowly traversing the river crossing were the straggling elements of Field Marshal Model's staff, who were en route from Bad Tönisstein to their new headquarters, located in the Westerwald region near Weyersbusch and Rimbach.

At 10:00 a.m., an enormous explosion echoed along the length of the Rhine Valley as thousands of rounds of antiaircraft rocket ammunition on the Viktoriaberg Heights were demolished by withdrawing Wehrmacht forces. The lack of available transport had required the destruction of the rockets; the batteries had already been transferred to the east bank and out of the Remagen area. The congestion on the bridge increased as more units sought a river crossing. The bridges in Cologne and Bonn, further to the north, already lay as tangled wreckage in the Rhine. All of the ferries were sunk or had been rendered inoperable. Captain Bratge attempted repeatedly to make radio contact with higher headquarters without result and was unaware of the most recent enemy movements.[13]

Major Scheller arrived at the bridge during the late morning hours and was briefed by Bratge on the situation at the bridgehead. Just before noon, the two officers left the railway bridge and proceeded to the St. Anne Convent, where Scheller ordered that the bridge be prepared for demolition. The major knew that the situation would have to be closely monitored and that the bridge had to remain intact as long as possible to allow the remainder of the LXVII Corps to cross the Rhine. The security forces at the bridge continued to stop various troops heading east in an effort to assemble a defense force on the west bank. The Americans had to be delayed in their advance toward the approaches to the bridge.

While observing the activities at the bridge, Bratge recommended that the security company on the Viktoriaberg Heights be transferred for better command and control. Major Scheller approved of the recommendation and ordered the transfer of the security company.[14]

At 11:25 a.m., a courier breathlessly appeared at the command post and reported that the security company had engaged American forces in the woods by the Reich Labor Service camp. Members of the security company, in the process of moving their locations, had engaged an American patrol. After a short exchange of small-arms fire, the Americans had immediately withdrawn.

Major Scheller and Captain Bratge acknowledged the courier's report and continued their orientation briefing. The major then asked to examine the bridge. Scheller was obviously disturbed by the lack of adequate forces for defending the bridge and its approaches. The two officers discussed their predicament, and Bratge recommended that the east bank of the Rhine be reinforced both upstream and downstream. Under the present conditions, he explained, the Americans could cross the Rhine at any point in boats, which were numerous in the area, and easily outflank the German defenses to capture the bridge from the east bank. Scheller disagreed with the recommendation and continued to attempt to glean security forces from the columns that rolled toward the east.

The two officers discovered a machine-gun crew among the retreating troops, and Scheller ordered the five infantrymen to be positioned at the west approaches with their weapon. Just after noon, the major crossed to the west side of the bridge only to find that the five infantrymen, like so many of the retreating forces, had disappeared into the Rhineland countryside.[15]

Just before 1:00 p.m., Scheller issued the order to transfer the command post inside the tunnel. Bratge occupied himself with transferring the post and all classified materials from the St. Anne Convent to safety. While the transfer was in progress, a soldier from the bridge security company appeared on a bicycle and reported that the American tanks had broken through the German positions on the Birresdorf-Remagen road. As Bratge approached the bridge with the remnants of the headquarters staff, Captain Friesenhahn reported the bridge was ready for demolition. To the officer's consternation, the remaining units of the security company, who were supposed to withdraw to the bridge, were nowhere in sight. He ordered the bridge commander to assign two groups of soldiers for close defense; one group was to secure the road leading to the bridge approaches from Sinzig, to the south, and the other group was to secure the northern approach from Birresdorf-Cologne. At 1:10 p.m., Bratge dispatched a runner to report to the bridge security company with the instructions to fall back to the bridge.[16]

Thirty minutes later, the bridge was suddenly raked with small-arms fire. Sergeant Rothe, from the security company, crept over the bridge through the hail of gunfire to report that the Americans had overwhelmed the company and had captured the entire unit. Members of the company had been making their way along the Hohlweg road when they had been surprised by several American tanks that had previously broken through the Birresdorf road. The Americans had opened fire on the company, but Rothe managed to escape capture. While running through a hail of fire on the Koblenzer Strasse and again on the railway embankment, he had been struck three times by American bullets.

Captain Friesenhahn recrossed the bridge as heavy machine-gun and tank fire sent ricochets and white-hot shrapnel through the rail tracks spanning the

Rhine. He reached the east bank and frantically searched for Bratge to request permission to demolish the bridge. Finally locating the captain inside the tunnel entrance, Friesenhahn advised him that the American tanks had reached the Becher factory, not far from the approaches to the bridge. As Friesenhahn was reporting, Bratge observed several olive drab tanks appear on the Alten Strasse in Remagen, from which the vehicles had a clear field of fire to the bridge and the tunnel entrance. He watched helplessly as the tanks rotated their turrets and brought their guns to bear on the east bank. Within seconds, the tunnel entrance was enveloped in 76-mm fire from the distant Shermans.

Bratge had to request permission from Scheller to initiate the main charger. He raced to the major, reported that the Americans were approaching the bridge from the Becher factory, and requested to demolish the structure. Some forty-five minutes elapsed between Friesenhahn's return from the west bank and the moment when permission was obtained to detonate the primary charge on the bridge. Bratge noted that the time was 3:20 p.m. when Scheller gave the order to demolish the bridge. At that, Bratge raced to Friesenhahn, who was nervously waiting with the electrical firing device. As Bratge dashed to within shouting distance, he called for Friesenhahn to detonate the charges.

Friesenhahn shouted for everyone to take cover. Bratge pressed himself against the inside wall of the tunnel entrance and waited expectantly. Several minutes passed in silence: the electric firing device had failed. It was attempted again—and again—but the bridge remained intact. The charges had not detonated. Friesenhahn desperately called for a volunteer to go onto the bridge to initiate the secondary demolition charge. An NCO from Cologne, Sergeant Anton Faust, stepped forward. No novice to war, he had served with Field Marshal Paulus's Sixth Army on the Eastern Front and, after being seriously wounded during the vicious fighting in Stalingrad, had been evacuated from the ruins of the destroyed city. As Faust prepared to cross onto the bridge, he was joined by a young private from the engineering company who refused to watch him go alone. "I'll take the upstream side, you take the downstream side," he said as they prepared to dash into the line of fire. "If something happens to either of us, the other will be there to help."[17]

The two soldiers began racing along the rails spanning the bridge. On reaching the location of the emergency demolitions charge, they pulled the igniter of the manual firing device and waited to ensure that the time fuse was burning. As the acrid smell of the burning fuse wafted into the air, the two soldiers sprinted back to the tunnel through the increasing machine-gun fire. To Friesenhahn's relief, a muffled roar erupted as the emergency, secondary charges detonated some thirty minutes after the main charge had failed. The small group of engineers watched with nervous anticipation as the massive steel girders of the bridge lifted slightly from the piers. Then, to their horror, the heavy structure settled back into place.

As the dust slowly cleared, Friesenhahn was shocked to see the bridge was still intact. The lesser charge of 300 kilograms of Donarit that had been delivered, instead of the requested 600 kilograms of military explosives, had proven inadequate to destroy the bridge.

Friesenhahn raced to the tunnel and reported to Captain Bratge that the demolitions attempt had failed. At that moment, another report arrived advising Bratge that the Americans were on the embankment and were attempting to mount the western span. Bratge dashed to the far end of the tunnel, where he pushed his way through a swarm of civilians until he located Scheller.

The major was incredulous when Bratge advised him of what had happened. The two officers decided to attempt a counterattack against the approaching Americans. Scheller disappeared as Bratge, with the assistance of a sergeant, began pulling soldiers from the crowd of civilians in the tunnel to form an assault force. As Bratge seized the soldiers, the NCO quickly organized them into a cohesive unit. After assembling an impromptu assault force, Bratge instructed the sergeant to return to the tunnel exit and bring Scheller back with him.

Bratge then ordered a soldier to begin burning classified documents. As the soldier ignited the stacks of files, a chorus of protests erupted from the civilians, who feared that the flames would ignite the gasoline fumes emanating from the fuel cars inside the tunnel. The soldier ignored the protests and continued carrying out the order. Within seconds, the Wehrmacht sergeant returned from the tunnel exit and breathlessly reported that Scheller was nowhere to be found.

"Open your eyes!" Bratge yelled back. "Major Scheller is at the tunnel exit!"

"Herr Hauptmann," the exasperated soldier responded over the clamoring civilians and the sound of small-arms fire that were now echoing through the tunnel. "I said, Major Scheller isn't there!"

Bratge brushed past the sergeant and raced toward the tunnel exit. As he searched for the major in the throng of refugees, he was advised by several of the civilians in the tunnel that he had departed toward the nearby village of Unkel. The major's absence left Bratge as senior combat commander. Realizing that a hail of gunfire was raking the mouth of the tunnel near the bridge and the surrounding area, he knew that a direct counterattack with the forces at hand was impossible. The only alternative was to withdraw to the nearby settlement of Orsberg.

Collecting the small force about him, Bratge headed for the tunnel exit, away from the bridge. As the soldiers attempted to leave the shelter of the massive granite structure, they were met by a hail of small-arms fire, followed by the explosions of numerous hand grenades. Bratge knew that he was too late: the Americans had already flanked their position at the base of the Erpeler Ley. Now, the soldiers and the mob of clamoring, terrorized civilians in the cavernous structure were cut off from any exit and trapped in the tunnel.

At 5:00 p.m., another attempt was made to break through to freedom, but by that point, the Americans had brought machine guns into position and had the tunnel entrance near the bridge and the exit completely sealed. Every movement observed by the American infantrymen sent bullets and grenade fragments ricocheting through the confines of the tunnel. As the situation worsened, the civilians increased their protests, punctuated with screams, curses, and cries. They began seizing the soldiers, attempting to disarm them, and imploring the officers to surrender. The crowd started to panic when a man and a child were struck by small-arms fire, heightening the confusion in the tumultuous surroundings.

Bratge consulted with the other officers, and he made it clear that he no longer felt able to carry out his duties as battle commander. The fuel tanks within the tunnel could be ignited at any moment by the tracer bullets bouncing through the structure, and all of the civilians were in imminent danger. As he was speaking, he noticed movement at the far end of the tunnel, near the entrance. A civilian had improvised a white flag and was waving it within sight of the Americans, who were waiting outside, weapons at the ready. As the last civilians crowded from the tunnel with their hands above their heads, Bratge ordered the soldiers to destroy their weapons and to leave the tunnel.

Captains Bratge and Friesenhahn were the last to depart from the tunnel, at 5:30 p.m., as the German defenders surrendered to the American forces outside. The Americans were now in possession of a badly damaged but still passable bridge over the Rhine. The German prisoners were quickly employed by the GIs as litter bearers to carry the wounded across the Ludendorff Bridge to the west bank. The prisoners were directed by U.S. Army Staff Sergeant David M. Keith of the medical platoon assigned to the 27th Armored Infantry Battalion. Within several minutes of surrendering, the wounded were taken to an aid station near the Becher furniture factory. The German prisoners, after carrying the wounded to the west bank for medical care, were taken to the St. Anne Convent, where they were held for further processing and transport.[18]

The commander of the U.S. 27th Armored Infantry Battalion immediately dispatched Lieutenant Jack H. Liedike with B Company and Lieutenant William E. McMasters with C Company over the bridge to reinforce the newly gained bridgehead. The two companies were instructed to seize the Erpeler Ley heights that commanded the area and to establish a defense of the bridge.[19]

The news of the capture of the Ludendorff Bridge was met with astonishment and disbelief by the officers at the Army Group B headquarters. Of immediate concern was the need to determine the strength of the American hold on the east bank and to launch an attack to destroy the expanding bridgehead. Colonel

Günther Reichhelm, the army group operations officer, was concerned that the bulk of the LXVI and LXVII Corps, still attempting to slow the advance of the Americans on the west bank, would be cut off and destroyed if the Americans now succeeded in establishing a firm bridgehead. He immediately seized a telephone and set to work expediting the transport of the two corps to the east bank of the river.

North of Remagen, in Bensberger Manor, the news of the fiasco at the bridge reached the headquarters of General von Kortzfleisch. Leaping into a staff car, he and his operations officer, Major Schulz, sped toward the east bank village of Erpel. As they passed through Siegburg, they happened on a heavily laden train carrying the armored vehicles of the Feldherrnhalle Panzer Brigade 106. The brigade consisted of a fully equipped panzergrenadier battalion, reinforced with ten tanks and a number of armored personnel carriers. It was en route to Bonn, several miles north of Remagen, where the troops were to be employed in reinforcing the bridgehead still held by German units. Kortzfleisch located the brigade commander, Lieutenant-Colonel Ewers, and explained that he needed to redirect the unit to Remagen to break the tenacious hold the Americans had on the east bank. It would not be difficult to do with the strength at hand, for the Americans had not had time to put a quantity of armor over the river, and the bridge was only a few miles away. By the next day, Kortzfleisch explained, it would be too late: once the skies cleared, American aircraft would prevent any Wehrmacht forces from even approaching the Ludendorff Bridge.

General von Kortzfleisch contacted Model, who had been advised of the capture of the bridge. The field marshal remained calm as he discussed the situation with his general. Permission to use the Feldherrnhalle Panzer Brigade was denied; Model had already discussed this with Berlin. The field marshal had requested to utilize the tanks to eliminate the bridgehead, but his request was made in vain; the tanks were to continue toward Bonn to counter a perceived threat from American forces in that area.

Model directed Kortzfleisch to employ elements from the 11th Panzer Division and the Panzer Lehr Division, both of which were still in the area of Düsseldorf, to destroy the bridgehead. However, this presented a very questionable option. The divisions had been vastly weakened during the withdrawal to the Rhine; they lacked ammunition and fuel. The most difficult aspect would be the transport of forces from Düsseldorf to the village of Erpel, directly across the Rhine from Remagen. Kortzfleisch, however, did not argue. Model apparently did not feel that the capture of the bridge was of great significance, and he appeared confident that the bridgehead could easily be eliminated.[20]

For the U.S. First Army, everything had suddenly changed. Eisenhower's original plan for the First Army units to drive south to link up with Patton's Third

Army near Koblenz was altered. Now, with an intact bridge over the Rhine, everything was pushed toward Remagen.

The craters caused by the preliminary demolitions charge and the failed emergency charge in the railbed were quickly filled with debris to clear the path for armored vehicles. As the hours lapsed, the American forces on the east end of the bridge continued to increase in numbers, and near midnight, Brigadier General William M. Hoge personally took command of the bridgehead. The American engineers of the U.S. 9th Armored Engineer Battalion worked through the night in removing the still-intact explosive charges from the bridge and clearing a path for bridge traffic.

In the early morning hours of 8 March, tanks and tank destroyers began rolling over the bridge onto the east bank. One of the tank destroyers slid from the precarious track on the bridge where the secondary, emergency demolitions charge had detonated. The vehicle temporarily blocked further bridge traffic until it could be freed at 5:30 a.m.[21]

The Germans feverishly prepared a counterattack while the American engineers strengthened their tenuous hold on the bridgehead. Just before 1:00 a.m. on 8 March, less than eight hours after the first Americans had crossed the Rhine, a squad of Wehrmacht assault engineers advanced from the village of Unkel to attempt to destroy the bridge. A short but intense firefight ensued when they encountered American security forces, and several Germans were taken prisoner. The remainder of the squad returned to Erpel and reported that the American presence was too strong for an assault to succeed with the limited resources at hand.

Several hours later, the Germans made a second attempt to destroy the bridge. A combat patrol of some sixty men, under the command of Lieutenant Auch, had been preparing to assault the bridgehead since late in the evening of March 7. Three trucks, dubiously powered by wood-burning engines, were taken to Hönningen and loaded with ammunition. The patrol was organized into three groups led by experienced NCOs. Lieutenant Auch received orders from Major Herbert Strobel, commander of the engineer regiment, to proceed to the village of Kasbach, where he was to meet with an officer to receive a briefing on the situation.

The small convoy headed for Kasbach, moving slowly along the darkened road with blacked-out headlights. At length, they arrived at Kasbach, where the demolitions were unloaded. Lieutenant Auch conferred with the officer at the scene, and then they proceeded to a residence at the edge of the village, from where they could observe the terrain near the bridgehead. Auch was informed that the Americans were also occupying the tunnel, and the two officers briefly discussed the options available to them for the assault on the bridge.

A short time later, Auch parted company with the officer and returned to his patrol, which was preparing to proceed to the bridge. They reviewed their plan of action before moving through the darkness along the railway embankment toward the bridge. As they approached to within 150 yards of their target, the patrol suddenly came under intense small-arms fire from the tunnel entrance and the railway underpass. Fire was returned, but with their presence compromised, the mission had clearly failed. Lieutenant Auch and several men succeeded in making their way back to Kasbach, where he reported on the events at the bridgehead before being ordered to return to his unit.[22]

Daybreak found the bridge securely in American hands. During the night, the U.S. 482nd Antiaircraft Battalion had assumed responsibility for the bridge defense. The Americans intensified their efforts to strengthen their bridgehead. The strength of the battalion was increased to three batteries, each with three platoons, and by the afternoon of 8 March, the antiaircraft guns were in position on both sides of the Rhine. They soon received reinforcements from the 413th Antiaircraft Battalion, which deployed several 90-mm guns on the west bank. Combat engineer units quickly began ferry operations, and by 9 March, there were no fewer than five ferries of the 86th Heavy Engineer Pontoon Battalion operating over the Rhine. The engineers began constructing a treadway bridge some 600 yards downstream from the badly damaged Ludendorff Bridge, and the soldiers continued working through heavy German artillery fire. Within thirty-six hours, the treadway bridge was opened for traffic; more men and material began streaming toward the east.

While the Americans were pushing men, vehicles, and support material over the Rhine, the Germans continued their attempts to destroy the bridgehead. A series of fighter missions were launched, and eight of the ten aircraft fell victim to American antiaircraft guns. German combat swimmers were dispatched to the Remagen area to take explosives onto the bridge by traversing the icy, swift current of the Rhine; all attempts failed. German artillery batteries began using their last reserves of ammunition on the bridgehead, and throughout 8 and 9 March, an average of one artillery shell impacted near the bridge every two minutes. The meager allocation of artillery ammunition was soon depleted. By 10 March, three days after the bridge had fallen to the Americans, the German artillery positions were reduced to sending only one shell every four to five minutes.

The U.S. efforts were not without casualties. During the construction of the 1,080-foot treadway bridge, the American forces had forty men killed and wounded. The material losses included cranes, trucks, and thirty-two of the eighty-four pontoon units that were used to construct the temporary bridge.[23]

On 10 March, the U.S. 51st Engineer Battalion, under the command of Lieutenant Colonel Harvey Fraser, set to work constructing a second pontoon bridge over the Rhine near Linz. This bridge was completed in less than thirty hours, and by nightfall on 11 March, more troops and equipment were pouring over the Rhine.

The heavy military convoys ceaselessly traversing the damaged Ludendorff Bridge began to take a toll on the weakened structure. On 12 March, traffic was halted in order to conduct repairs and to strengthen the framework. While the repairs were made, a 40-ton Bailey Bridge was assembled 500 yards to the north, or downstream, of the Ludendorff Bridge. At last, on 17 March, the battered structure suddenly collapsed into the Rhine, carrying a number of American soldiers to their deaths. By that time, however, the three bridges constructed over the river by the U.S. engineers were in full use.

Major Scheller, accompanied by two second lieutenants, left the bridge at approximately 5:00 p.m. on the afternoon of 7 March, as the Americans were seizing control of the east bank. At about midnight, he resurfaced at the headquarters of the LXVII Corps and reported directly to General Kortzfleisch and to the staff operations officer, Major Rudolf Schulz, whose headquarters were located in a school building in Kalenborn. Scheller described the capture of the bridge by the Americans and attributed the failed attempt to demolish the bridge to the severed electric firing cables. He then added that he had gone onto the structure with the engineers to attempt to attach an emergency demolitions charge but that this plan had not succeeded. After failing to demolish the bridge, he then attempted to organize a defense on the east bank, which proved to be unsuccessful in pushing the Americans from the span. Scheller explained that he had been compelled to leave the area to report the incident to higher command.[24]

After being dismissed by General Kortzfleisch, Scheller departed from the staff buildings and went to a storeroom, where, overcome by exhaustion, he immediately fell asleep. He had been at the bridge site without sleep for two and a half days. He was not familiar with the area and had been permitted very little time in which to organize the defense. He had also overlooked the telephone inside the tunnel, from which he could have contacted higher command. This oversight, which proved to be fatal for him, could also be attributed to his lack of familiarity with the assets immediately at hand.

One or two evenings later, Scheller again recounted the events at the bridge to a number of senior officers at an inn, the Gastwirtschaft zur Post, in Weyersbusch. Pacing back and forth in the room, the distraught major attempted to explain in detail what had occurred. Frau Hirschäuser, a young female communications auxiliary, recorded the events as described by Scheller for approximately thirty minutes before the major had completed his account. After the other officers departed, she paused, looked up from the desk, and whispered, "If I were you I would try to get some work clothes and hide in the Westerwald."[25]

Scheller returned to his old unit, the LXVII Corps, sometime during the night of 10–11 March. The staff had relocated to Altwied, and he resumed duties with the other staff officers. At 8:50 a.m. on 11 March, Field Marshal Model appeared at the headquarters, accompanied by the Army Group B intelligence officer, Colonel Pilling. Scheller was again questioned regarding what had occurred at the Ludendorff Bridge. While retelling his account, he was interrupted by the field marshal, who brusquely stated, "Well, now we have one who is guilty." Model then announced to Scheller that he was under arrest. The shaken major was transported to Army Group B headquarters in Rimbach to await his fate.[26]

Luftwaffe Field Marshal Albert Kesselring, whom the Allies had nicknamed "Smiling Albert," had stubbornly defended the boot of Italy against the Allies for months. Kesselring's defense had proven him a master innovator under the most adverse of conditions: the Allied advance in that theater had invariably been frustrated by the Wehrmacht's effective use of mountainous terrain and stubborn defensive tactics. Kesselring now received an unexpected order to report to the *Führerhauptquartier* ("Führer Headquarters") in Berlin on 8 March for a personal audience with Hitler.

Kesselring arrived in Berlin the following day and was informed by Field Marshal Wilhelm Keitel that he was to replace Rundstedt as OB West. He accepted this news begrudgingly. He advised Keitel that his presence was still needed on the Italian Front and that he lacked the background knowledge needed to perform to his fullest extent against the Allies on the Western Front. Keitel expressed an understanding of Kesselring's reservations but advised him that Hitler was adamant; the Führer was convinced that he possessed the qualities now needed to stabilize the situation along the Rhine. Kesselring was then admitted to Hitler's presence, where the two of them were left alone to discuss the situation.[27]

Hitler was determined to dismiss Rundstedt. The dictator believed the elderly field marshal represented a by-gone era and was an obsolete scion of Kaiser Wilhelm's imperial officer corps. Hitler deemed him too "old and weak" to deal with the issues at hand; a younger, more flexible commander was needed, one who was experienced in fighting the western Allies. The American seizure of the Ludendorff Bridge was the last straw for him. Hitler expressed to Kesselring his understanding of the difficulties of such an assignment at that point in the war. However, he was confident that Kesselring would do everything "humanly possible" to stabilize the situation.[28]

Kesselring departed from Berlin during the night of 9–10 March and drove to the OB West headquarters in Ziegenberg. There, he was met by the OB West chief of staff, General of Cavalry Siegfried Westphal, who briefed him on the situation. The news was deeply disturbing but not unexpected. Some fifty-five decimated German units were facing approximately eighty-five superbly equipped, fully motorized American, British, and French divisions. The average strength of the German divisions had sunk from a nominal strength of 12,000 to some 5,000 troops. The few panzer divisions were in a better situation, with an average strength of between 10,000 and 11,000 men. However, they were in large part immobilized because of the lack of fuel and vehicles. On average, the German divisions were having to defend a front using approximately 150 men for every mile. The troops were physically exhausted and tired of war. The soldiers' concern for their families in the devastated cities, particularly in the eastern regions of Germany where the Soviet forces were now inflicting unimaginable horrors on the populace, was having a devastating effect on morale.[29]

Gerd von Rundstedt was replaced by Field Marshal Kesselring on 10 March. Characteristically, Hitler did not send reinforcements to Army Group B, but he did order the establishment of a *fliegender Standgericht*, a special courts-martial commission, to investigate the loss of the Ludendorff Bridge and to punish those responsible. It was made clear that the commission would be directly responsible only to the Führer. The special courts-martial were granted unlimited power for convicting anyone found guilty, but there was no provision for commuting any sentence; executions were to be carried out immediately. It was not deemed necessary to provide anyone accused with legal representation or counsel.[30]

Hitler assigned Lieutenant-General Rudolf Hübner as senior member of the commission. Hübner had volunteered for service in World War I and had finished the war as a lieutenant. Between the wars, he had worked as a dentist, and with the dissolution of the Treaty of Versailles in 1935, he had returned to military service and was accepted into the Wehrmacht as a captain. He had no training as a legal officer and was, for all practical purposes, unqualified to serve in the role assigned him by Hitler.[31]

Hübner's briefing with Hitler lasted approximately one hour, during which the dictator described the basic situation at the front and the importance of Hübner's assignment. Hitler stressed the importance of holding the Western Front, as he expected a rupture in the relations between the Soviet Union and the western powers to occur at any time. Despite the conditions, it was imperative that discipline be maintained at all costs. Hübner then left Berlin and drove to the Wehrmacht personnel office in Hannoversch Münden, where he was joined by several officers assigned to serve as assistants and associate judges.[32]

Hübner and his staff surfaced on 10 March at the headquarters of OB West in Ziegenberg, where they participated in a farewell dinner for Rundstedt. During the meal, a discussion of the Remagen bridgehead was unavoidable, and according to witnesses, Kesselring exacerbated the situation when he openly stated that "Remagen is a crime that could lead to the collapse of the entire front!"[33]

On 11 March, General Hübner appeared at Model's headquarters with his "flying special courts-martial." He was also accompanied by Colonel Obermayer, a former classmate of Model's operations officer, Colonel Reichhelm. Model was the first to be interrogated, an ordeal that lasted throughout the day and resumed the following morning. After being questioned for some eight hours, the field marshal was "white with fury and speechless with indignation" when he stormed from the room. As Model prepared to leave the building, Hübner indicated that Reichhelm would be the next in line. Model halted abruptly, glared icily toward the inquisitors, and in unmistakable terms stated, "Colonel Reichhelm doesn't need to be questioned. He had nothing to do with this, and did exactly as I would have done. You can leave him alone."[34]

Hübner immediately directed his aim at other victims. Model assigned his staff legal officer, Colonel Felix Janert, to accompany the court-martial staff. Janert was not intended to serve as a member of the staff but was to function as an observer for the army group. On 11 March, Hübner interrogated General von Kortzfleisch at the general's headquarters in Hennef. An interrogation of Lieutenant-General Richard Wirtz, the Army Group B commander of engineer forces, followed.

The following day, 12 March, interrogations of individual soldiers who had participated in the defense of the bridge area and had escaped capture were conducted at Rimbach. Captains Bratge and Friesenhahn were tried in absentia. Bratge received a death sentence; Friesenhahn was acquitted. During the morning of 13 March, the interrogations and trials of Major Scheller and Lieutenant Peters took place in Rimbach. Both officers were found guilty and sentenced to be executed. That afternoon, the initial interrogations and trials of Major Kraft, the battalion commander under whom Friesenhahn's 12th Company had been assigned, and Major Strobel, the commander of Engineer Regiment 12, were initiated. The trials continued through the morning of 14 March at Oberirsen in the Gastwirtschaft zum Grund.

Major Strobel was found guilty in that he failed to take proper measures to regain control of the bridge following its capture. General Hübner believed that the regimental commander should have been farther forward and would thus have been able to react in a more decisive, rapid manner. Additionally, Strobel had remained at his command post after the capture of the bridge. Instead of dispatching one of his own staff officers to investigate the incident and to institute the appropriate countermeasures, he had sent Major Kraft.

Strobel had taken command of the regiment five days prior to the capture of the bridge. On 6 March, the evening before the capture, the Remagen bridgehead had been transferred to the command of the newly established Combat

Commander Bonn/Remagen, and this change further complicated the matter of who was in charge of the forces at the bridge. Strobel first learned of the capture of the structure on the evening of 7 March, and he took immediate action in attempting to recover the bridge, although he was no longer part of the operational chain of command. The fact that he did not personally proceed to the bridge to oversee operations should not have been an aggravating factor. For the commander to have done so would have resulted in further neglect of organizing and preparing follow-on action.[35]

Major Kraft, commander of Battalion 3, Pionier Regiment 12, was subordinate to Strobel's regiment. He suffered the same fate as Strobel. Kraft was sentenced to be executed because he had not ensured that the proper communications existed between his command post and his subordinate company at the bridge. Like Strobel, he had not personally gone to the bridge to oversee the counteraction after the capture by the Americans. Neither had he sent an officer from his staff. He had first received word of the capture at 9:00 p.m. on 7 March, some four hours after the bridge was in American hands. Although he was not assigned responsibility for the security of the bridge, he had immediately volunteered to lead a counterattack against the growing American bridgehead. Major Strobel had declined this offer and instead had ordered Kraft to concentrate on the security of the four remaining Rhine bridges in his sector and to ensure that a similar incident did not occur. Kraft immediately departed from his command post and inspected the security preparations at the other bridges; he returned to his command post in the village of Sayn, some 25 miles from Remagen, during the evening of 8 March.[36]

Lieutenant Peters was sentenced to execution because he had failed to prevent his classified weapons, the antiaircraft rockets, from falling into the hands of the Americans. Additionally, he had left the battery, his place of duty, and had remained out of touch with his subordinates and superiors for an extended period of time. For Hübner, this was reason enough for execution.[37]

Scheller was sentenced to execution because he, as the senior officer on the scene, did not ensure the timely destruction of the bridge. He was also found guilty of leaving the area during the fighting there. In doing so, he surrendered authority to a junior officer and then absented himself from his command for several days.

General Hitzfeld, Scheller's immediate superior, attempted to defend the major's actions. Based on Scheller's account of what had happened at the bridge and his participation in attempting to demolish the bridge, the general was even considering awarding him with a medal.

When Scheller had first arrived at the bridge to take command at 11:15 a.m. on 7 March, the security company in Remagen was already reporting contact with the enemy. Scheller had had no time to receive a proper briefing on the situation or on the strengths and weaknesses of the forces assigned to defend the bridge. He had departed from the scene only after all attempts to destroy the bridge had failed. His primary concern following the failure to destroy the bridge was to report what had occurred to the corps as soon as possible so that troops could be diverted to eliminate the weak American bridgehead. Arguably, he had never officially replaced Captain Bratge as combat commander of Remagen and thus should not have been held responsible for what had occurred at the bridge, despite his seniority in rank. Scheller had a difficult time explaining his absence between when he had first reported the incident to his corps, on the evening of 7 March, and when he reappeared at the corps headquarters on 10 March. When he reappeared, Field Marshal Model was on the scene, and he was placed under arrest.[38]

The night of 12 March, Colonel Obermayer of Hübner's staff and Colonel Reichhelm shared Reichhelm's quarters near the staff operations building. The two classmates and longtime friends discussed the issues in detail, and the distraught Obermayer broke down in tears, exclaiming that he could not fathom why he had been selected to participate in the disgusting mission. He asserted that he was certain to take the position opposite Hübner, whom he despised, regarding the disposition of the cases against the officers.[39]

During the second week in March, one of the numerous German units withdrawing into the Westerwald area before the American advance was ordered to provide seven soldiers for a firing squad. The soldiers assigned to the squad were informed that the officers to be executed were convicted of war crimes; further details were not given. On 14 March, the firing squad was joined by a sergeant. The execution was monitored by a judicial magistrate, assigned by OKW.

The officers to be executed were not afforded the presence of clergy. That morning, the men departed from the village for a nearby wooded area. The firing squad, led by the sergeant, proceeded ahead of Major Scheller and Lieutenant Peters, the first of the convicted officers to be executed. Rank insignia had been removed from their uniforms, and their tunics hung loosely without belts. The group entered the small copse and drew up in a file. The officers were positioned approximately 10 yards in front of the firing squad. The order to attention was announced. The magistrate walked up to the officers and read a passage from the verdict, then drew his pistol and stepped aside. The commanding officer called further orders, and the command to fire soon followed. After the bodies of the officers collapsed under the hail of rifle bullets, the magistrate stepped forward and fired a shot into the backs of the heads of the prone figures. The squad then retired to the village. The gruesome scenario was repeated for the executions of Majors Kraft and Strobel.[40]

At about 10:00 a.m. on 14 March, farmer Wilhelm Schumacher was inspecting one of his fields near the village Im breiten Tal when he saw activity near a wooded area. Curious as to what was happening, the forty-six-year-old farmer approached for a better view. He observed an officer being led into the woods by a group of soldiers. Several minutes after the soldiers disappeared from sight, the farmer heard a shot or a volley of fire; never having served in the military and being unfamiliar with firearms, he could not determine if the sound was a single shot or a volley. A short time later, the soldiers reappeared from the woods and returned to the village. Schumacher continued with his work in the field, then noticed that the group of soldiers had returned. The scenario was repeated. The group disappeared into the woods, a shot or shots were heard, and the soldiers reappeared and returned to the village. Unaware that he had witnessed the executions of four Wehrmacht officers, Schumacher turned back to his work.[41]

Many of Model's staff officers met the news of the capture of the bridge at Remagen with resignation. The immense superiority held by the Allies had taken its toll since the landing in Normandy, nine months prior to the capture of the bridge. The Rhine had long been a symbolic barrier for Germany, but given the extensive material advantage of the Allies, the river was by no means a serious military obstacle. With their complete control of the skies, combined with immeasurable material superiority, the Allies could cross the river at practically any point of their choosing.[42]

However, Remagen was not an optimal site for a river crossing. Opposite the town and extending toward the northeast lies the expanse of forested hills and valleys known as the Sauerland. Common lore suggests the name given to this foreboding region derives from the old Germanic term *sur*, meaning "difficult." The Sauerland is a part of the greater Rhenish area known for slate quarries, coal mines, and the blue-gray Westerwald pottery. The Sauerland consists of the rough terrain of the Bergische Land in the west, the mountainous Rothaargeberge in the south, and the Eggegeberge in the east, where the Sauerland meets the Teutoburg Forest. The ravines and woodlands form a geographic border between Westphalia and Hesse and encompass an expanse of rugged terrain marked by numerous rivers and streams. The area did not present a favorable bridgehead from which the U.S. armored divisions would launch an offensive.

The capture of the Ludendorff Bridge was quickly followed by a series of other debacles. On 8 March, the constantly shrinking Bonn bridgehead on the west bank of the Rhine was lost. The Feldherrenhalle Panzer Brigade 106 was unable to stem the Allied onslaught, and the armored strength of the brigade was squandered in Bonn rather than being diverted to the south to eliminate the tiny American bridgehead across the river from Remagen. The combat commander of Bonn, Major-General Richard von Bothmer, took independent action and evacuated his staff and the remainder of his decimated force to Beuel, on the right bank of the Rhine opposite Bonn, to prevent their capture. As a result of this action, he was sent before a special court-martial and found guilty. He was subsequently sentenced to six years' imprisonment and reduction in rank. An officer who came from a family with a long tradition of military service to Germany, Bothmer had lost his wife prematurely, and his only son had been killed on the Eastern Front. He now found himself, in the eyes of Hitler's government, a criminal. Unable to come to terms with what was occurring, the overwrought officer shot himself.[43]

As the American forces consolidated their foothold on the east bank of the Rhine, German forces were organizing to repulse the bridgehead. The troops were still classified as divisions, but months of battle in France, in the Ardennes, and during the slow withdrawal to the east bank had decimated their strength. Still bearing their numerical designations, they were now considered by the German staff officers as mere battle groups or elements, fully lacking in the way of men and material to be judged battle-strength divisions.

Farther to the north, in the Niederrhein (the Lower Rhine area), were Lieutenant-General Wend von Wietersheim's 11th Panzer Division; the 3rd Panzergrenadier Division, under Major-General Walter Denkert; and the once-vaunted Panzer Lehr Division, now under command of Major-General Horst Niemack. The withdrawal across the Rhine had proven to be difficult; the forces had little motorized support due to the lack of adequate fuel supplies. The small amount of remaining fuel was carefully rationed or held as a tactical reserve, and thus, the divisions were, for all practical purposes, immobilized.

The remnants of the 9th Panzer Division were able to cross the Rhine in the area of Cologne. The fierce battles for the city had brought the American forces up to the very banks of the river. The few remaining facilities in Cologne that had survived countless air raids were effectively destroyed in the fighting, and the commander of the 9th Panzer Division, Colonel Zollendorf, had taken command after his predecessor, Lieutenant-General Harald Freiherr von Elverfeldt, was killed in action during the fierce fighting in the city center.

With the American forces now firmly on the east bank of the Rhine in the Remagen bridgehead, paramilitary units began mustering their forces to repel the invaders. On 9 March, the battalions of Freikorps Sauerland received mobilization orders. Some members of Battalion 14 mustered in a school building in the village of Dahlbruch. Each of the erstwhile soldiers was issued a military field cap, a woolen jacket, gray field trousers, a ration bag, a wool blanket, and a zinc identity disk. Antiquated, long-barreled Austrian Steyer rifles and a handful of ammunition completed their inventory of battle equipment. The men filed to a nearby field, where they received cursory instruction in the use of the unfamiliar rifles.

The lessons were repeatedly interrupted by air alarms as Allied fighter-bombers targeted the nearby rail station at Kreuztal. After marching from Dahlbruch to the village of Grund, they were bivouacked in the local schoolhouse, where they received a sparse issue of rations. Local farmers from the surrounding country-side provided the reluctant troops with potatoes and bread. As the elderly soldiers gnawed the cold provisions, they observed columns of refugees pulling hand-carts piled with belongings attempting to escape the oncoming front.[44]

In an indication that the end for the Ruhr was approaching, other inhabi-tants of the heavily bombed city of Essen began preparing for an evacuation. In the south labor barracks, located on Essen's Humboltstrasse, 500 Jewish women began packing their meager belongings. The SS overseers had received orders to begin evacuating the labor camps near the front. The Americans had crossed the Rhine at Remagen, and strong Allied forces were massing in the areas of Rheinberg and Xanten, threatening the immediate areas of the labor facilities in the Ruhr cities east of the Rhine. The work provided by the women was now of little value to the Nazi hierarchy anyway: their workplaces in the massive Krupp facilities had been reduced to rubble. The camp kitchen issued three days' ra-tions to the inmates for their journey toward the east, consisting of 1,600 small loaves of bread and minute portions of minced meat and sausages. The miser-able column marched to the ruins of the train station under a dense cover of fog, and the freight cars, filled with human cargo, were soon steaming away from the devastated city.[45]

The railway authorities had estimated that the journey would take a maxi-mum of three days. However, the odyssey from the threatened area lasted some six days, during which the rations were quickly depleted. The train carried the ill-fated cargo on a winding route over Weimar, through the Hartz Mountains and was eventually directed north, where it bypassed Hannover. The constant air raids were disrupting all schedules and made reliable communications and transport plans impossible. Almost a week after the train had departed from Essen, it pulled into the small town of Bergen-Belsen. As the Jews were marched into the mas-sive concentration camp, the SS guards who accompanied them were stopped at the gates. The sentry advised them that only the Jews could enter — the guards had to be kept at a distance. Within the camp, a massive outbreak of typhus had occurred.[46]

Field Marshal Walter Model: "A German field marshal does not surrender." (Photo courtesy Günther Reichhelm)

Field Marshal Albert Kesselring, who replaced Field Marshal von Rundstedt following the capture of the Ludendorff Bridge at Remagen by the U.S. First Army. (Photo courtesy Willi Mues)

Field Marshal Gerd von Rundstedt was Supreme Commander, West (OB West), until replaced by Field Marshal von Kluge following the failure to repel the invasion at Normandy. Later recalled by Hitler to reassume command in the west, he was again relieved of his post within days after the loss of the Ludendorff Bridge. (Photo courtesy Bundesarchiv)

Model during a briefing with Waffen SS officers. This photograph was probably taken in Russia in 1943 or early 1944. (Photo courtesy Max Wind)

Major Winrich Behr, at the time of his service with Rommel's Afrikakorps. He later served with Field Marshal Paulus at Stalingrad, was reassigned to Rommel's staff in Normandy, served with Field Marshal von Kluge after Rommel's debilitating wounding when attacked by Allied aircraft, and saw his final Wehrmacht service with Model's staff. After the war, Behr rose to the position of assistant secretary general of the European Economic Union in Brussels. (Photo courtesy Winrich Behr)

Model (left) and Major Winrich Behr during the Ardennes Offensive, December 1944. (Photo courtesy Winrich Behr)

Field Marshal Erwin
Rommel (left) and Major
Winrich Behr, Normandy,
April 1944. (Photo courtesy
Winrich Behr)

Günther and Renate
Reichhelm at their
wartime wedding on 4
July 1942. (Photo courtesy
Günther Reichhelm)

(Above and left) Reichhelm
and his favorite mount,
Nation, in 1939. (Photos
courtesy Günther Reichhelm)

(Top) Model and Army Group B staff officers after the failed Ardennes Offensive, January 1945. Third from left is Lieutenant-Colonel Günther Reichhelm; second from right, Field Marshal Model; far right, Major Winrich Behr. (Bottom) Field Marshal Walter Model and Reichsminister Albert Speer. On 20 and 24 March 1945, Speer was at Model's headquarters in Altenkirchen to discuss circumventing Hitler's scorched-earth directive, which entailed destroying the infrastructure of the Ruhr. Model agreed that the order would not be carried out. Left to right: Colonel Günther Reichhelm, General Hans Krebs, Speer, Colonel von Blodnitz, Model, Major Winrich Behr. (Photos courtesy Günther Reichhelm)

(Left) Field Marshal Model and Reichhelm, early in 1945. (Below) Photo taken during an impromptu visit to the Model family residence in Dresden during the summer of 1944. From left to right: daughters Christa (partially hidden) and Hella, Field Marshal Model, and his wife, Herta. Standing behind the Model family are Lieutenant-Colonel Günther Reichhelm and Dr. Leuthold, the family physician. Not shown is the field marshal's son, Hans-Georg. (Photos courtesy Günther Reichhelm)

(Top) Hunger in the Ruhr: German civilians butchering a Wehrmacht horse killed by artillery fire. (Photo courtesy Willi Mues) (Bottom) The push toward the Rhine, 24 February 1945: German prisoners stream over a pontoon bridge as the U.S. First Army advances beyond the Roer River in the Rhineland.

(Top) An American infantryman inspects a neutralized German machine-gun position during the advance toward the Rhine. (Left) A GI falls to a hidden German sniper as U.S. infantrymen cross a tread-bridge in the Rhineland.

(Right) The spires of the famous Cologne Cathedral rise in the distance as U.S. armored units make their way through the destroyed city toward the Rhine. (Below) U.S. infantrymen file past the body of a German lieutenant lying on a street in Cologne.

(Top) A German Panther served as a rear guard for withdrawing Wehrmacht forces before being disabled by an antitank gun as American forces closed on the Hohenzollern Bridge in Cologne. The Cologne Cathedral is seen behind the burning vehicle; the Hohenzollern Bridge was destroyed by German engineers before it could be seized. (Bottom) An American patrol from the 11th Armored Division enters the town of Andernach on the Rhine on 9 March 1945. The original caption of the Signal Corps photograph stated that the troops were under fire from a sniper hidden in the building on the left.

(Above) View from the west of the Ludendorff Bridge spanning the Rhine at Remagen. Beyond the bridge rises the Erpeler Ley, the east bank ridge under which a rail tunnel led to the village of Erpel. The twin pairs of towers flanking both the east and west approaches to the bridge can be clearly discerned in the photograph. (Below) Captured Luftwaffe personnel carry a wounded soldier toward the west over the bridge at Remagen while U.S. infantrymen, laden with combat equipment, trudge toward the east. The railway bridge was planked to accommodate motorized traffic, quantities of which were rapidly pushed over the bridge to secure the bridgehead on the east bank.

View from inside the tunnel running beneath the Erpeler Ley. Surprised by the sudden appearance of American armored units during the afternoon of 7 March 1945, the German defenders sought shelter in the tunnel from intense tank and small-arms fire as they attempted to detonate explosives on the bridge. Trapped within the structure when a unit of the U.S. 9th Armored Division gained the east bank and flanked both ends of the tunnel, most of the German defenders surrendered. Their commander, Captain Willi Bratge, was sentenced to death in absentia for failing to destroy the bridge; he survived the war as a U.S. prisoner of war.

A mobile antiaircraft battery stands watch at the western approach to the bridge at Remagen. During the night of 8 March, five German aircraft were reportedly shot down as they attempted to destroy the bridge after its seizure by U.S. First Army forces.

11 March 1945. German prisoners file along the railbed at Erpel on the east bank of the Rhine. The Ludendorff Bridge leading west to Remagen can be seen spanning the Rhine in the background.

Chapter 5

Crossing at Wesel

As the Allies were building up the bridgehead at Remagen for a breakout toward the east, two massive operations to cross the Lower Rhine north of the Ruhr Valley were in progress. Field Marshal Montgomery was methodically planning his crossing of the Rhine with characteristic thoroughness. At his disposal were some 1.25 million troops. The forces were organized into nine British divisions assigned to the British Second Army, twelve American divisions of the U.S. Ninth Army, and eight divisions of the Canadian First Army. Two divisions from the First Allied Airborne Army augmented the assault force. The ground forces were supported by some 5,500 artillery pieces.[1]

In preparation for the crossing, extensive air raids were conducted on rail bridges, viaducts, power plants, communications facilities, marshaling yards, and antiaircraft positions. Every asset at the disposal of the Allies was utilized to paralyze the German ability to counter any crossing over the Rhine.

Operation Plunder, the plan for ground troops to cross the river, had been in preparation for months and had caused more than a little friction between the British and American high commands. On 5 March, General William H. "Bull" Simpson had proposed an assault utilizing his Ninth Army between Duisburg and Düsseldorf; from there, the Allies could create a massive bridgehead in the heart of the Ruhr district. These plans were preempted on 7 March by the unexpected capture of the Ludendorff Bridge at Remagen. Every commander wanted to be the first to cross the Rhine, and the seizure of the bridge did little to dampen the rivalry between U.S. and British forces farther north.

The German troops in the area of the Lower Rhine had already suffered devastating losses by the time the bridge to the south at Remagen was seized. On 3 March, the advancing British and Canadian troops had linked up with the U.S. Ninth Army at Geldern, west of Wesel. The last passable bridge on the Lower Rhine was the railway bridge at Wesel. An Allied air raid had already destroyed the Rheinbaben road bridge there on 14 February, leaving only the bitterly defended rail bridge to be captured, if possible.

The German forces continued to be compressed into an ever-shrinking bridgehead west of Wesel. On 5 March, the Canadians were 2 miles from Xanten. On 6 March, the American 35th Division captured Rheinberg. The Germans evacuated supply and administration units to the east side of the Rhine; wounded personnel were transported over the river by ferry at Büderich. Hitler ordered all combat units to remain west of the river and to continue to defend the bridgeheads.

General Schlemm, commander of the First Parachute Army, received the unenviable task of defending the bridgehead west of Wesel and was personally responsible for ensuring that no combat-capable soldier was prematurely withdrawn to the east bank. By 6 March, the Germans were still clinging to a bridgehead some 10 miles wide and 8 miles deep west of the Rhine. They were suffering unbearable losses in dead and wounded before Schlemm reported to the army group that the troops remaining in the bridgehead had to be immediately evacuated or there would be no forces left in his command with which to defend the east bank. When reminded of Hitler's order to hold the west bank at all costs, Schlemm requested that the supreme command dispatch an officer to his army to obtain firsthand knowledge of the situation. In the early morning of 7 March, a lieutenant-colonel bearing carmine General Staff insignia appeared at Schlemm's HQ and personally observed the disaster in the making. That evening, Schlemm received authority to evacuate the bridgehead.

The Wesel railway bridge had been modified with heavy wooden planks in 1939 for use by both road and rail traffic. Despite repeated attempts by the Allied aircraft to destroy the structure, it had remained intact and was extensively used for the evacuation of the bridgehead. Numerous ferries and boats had been assembled nearby for additional transport of German forces, and low-hanging clouds prevented the Allied aircraft from flying missions against the withdrawing troops between 7 and 10 March.

The withdrawal of German forces to the east bank of the Rhine took place under relentless pressure from the American and British forces. The German artillery batteries, supply units, heavy weapons, and wounded soldiers continued to pour over the bridge, while infantry units, now hopelessly decimated and disorganized, continued to offer resistance to the oncoming Allies. The British captured Xanten on 8 March, and Alpen fell the same day. General Schlemm remained on the bridge throughout the night of 9–10 March, personally directing the somber withdrawal of Wehrmacht forces interspersed with civilians pushing hand-carts piled with belongings.

On 10 March, as the Allies closed on the remaining German forces crossing the Wesel bridge, a company from the U.S. 134th Infantry Regiment climbed aboard Sherman tanks and rolled along Reichsstrasse 58 to capture the town of Büderich before being stopped short of the Rhine by artillery and mortar fire. This drive, although failing to reach the Rhine, enabled the Americans to link up with British troops near Ginderich. At 7:00 a.m. that morning, General Schlemm, fearing that Allied armored units could burst through the thin line of remaining defenders and capture the bridge, ordered its destruction. To his relief, the Allied forces closed the last distance to the bridge cautiously, enabling many of the German soldiers to cross the Rhine by ferry. Several hours later, the Americans pushed from Büderich to Fort Blücher and captured the last of the defenders. With the seizure of the fort, there no longer existed any active German troops on the west bank of the Rhine.

On 13 March, Allied units took positions on the left bank, where they could observe any movement along the east bank. The British 3rd Infantry Division occupied Hönnepel and Vynen, and the Scottish 52nd Lowlanders were in positions between Vynen and Büderich. The American 75th Division was situated between Büderich and Homberg. The Allies attempted to use all terrain features and available buildings as observation points, but there was little left to observe. The German forces, long accustomed to the overwhelming Allied air strength, had become experts at camouflage and concealment. Movement was rarely detected during daylight hours, for all German transport and defense preparations were conducted after nightfall or when visibility was hampered by thick fog. This strategy did not, however, deter the artillery batteries of both sides in their attempts to neutralize any potential observation points. The tower of the Xanten Cathedral offered a panoramic view of the east side of the Rhine, and within days, the German gunners had riddled the structure with holes to discourage its use by Allied observers. Similarly, the church towers in Wesel and Bislich were destroyed by Allied gunners to prevent their use by Germans for the same purpose.

The Allied artillery batteries in the assault sector were directed to eliminate fortified positions and prevent the movement of troops and supplies to the defenses opposite the Allied-held bank. The banks of the Rhine resounded with the roar of artillery day and night as the gunners fired on carefully planned targets. The Allies also attempted to provoke the German artillery batteries into returning fire and thereby reveal their positions prior to the assault. The Germans refused to be enticed into the trap and remained silent during most of the preparations.

Concerned that civilians or spies in civilian clothing might report the Allied buildup to the German forces on the east bank, the Allied troops evacuated all civilians from the area in preparing for the assault over the Rhine. Telephone communications remained intact between the towns and villages on both sides of the Rhine, and despite strict curfews and restrictions on movement, inhabitants could always find a means of slipping across the river to report Allied activities. Approximately 24,000 civilians were evacuated from the villages and towns near the Rhine to the town of Bedburg, where they found temporary shelter in homes, barns, and tents.

Clandestine missions were conducted to gain intelligence about the enemy forces and preparations, with both sides dispatching reconnaissance patrols over the river on a nightly basis. The U.S. 75th Infantry Division reported their patrols were bringing in an average of four prisoners from the east bank every night, and encounters between German and Allied patrols became commonplace. The Allied forces also gained information from deserters who, convinced that the war was lost, often attempted to reach relatives west of the Rhine. Some soldiers from parts of eastern Germany already overrun by Soviet forces felt they no longer had any reason to continue fighting. Sometimes alone but often in pairs or small groups, they would cross the river and surrender to American and British units patrolling the west bank.

From 15 to 21 March, the Allied troops systematically enveloped the entire Rhine front opposite the Ruhr in artificial fog during daylight hours. After 21 March, in the final preparations for the Rhine crossing, the fog became a permanent presence. Produced by portable generators using a mixture of oil and water heated in massive boilers, the impenetrable, odorous clouds were pumped into the area without interruption. Troops and civilians alike suffered from respiratory problems beneath the thick, greasy vapor. Eye and respiratory infections disabled numerous soldiers, and many more were weakened by incessant nausea and vomiting caused by the toxic smoke. One Twenty-first Army Group report noted, "Our soldiers would prefer that the Germans could see them."[2]

The Allies assembled a massive array of vehicles and weapons for the crossing. Landing craft of every conceivable type, including commandeered ferries and civilian boats, were waiting to carry the assault forces to the east bank. The U.S. Navy provided thirty-six assault craft large enough to transport heavy tanks: the landing craft were brought from the Antwerp harbor by canal and on trucks, accompanied by naval officers and sailors. Large quantities of amphibious armored personnel carriers, or buffaloes, were assembled with armored vehicles for laying bridges and cables.

The material was moved forward during hours of darkness. By 23 March, the British forces had amassed 32,000 vehicles in the assault area, including almost 700 tanks. For the cross-river assault, a combined force of 250,000 combat troops was planned. The British forces were supported by 30,000 tons of bridging material, 60,000 tons of ammunition, and 28,000 tons of various other supplies. The American Ninth Army alone assembled 138,000 tons of supplies for the attack.[3]

Opposite the massive force on the east bank of the Rhine was General Schlemm's First Parachute Army. Most of the 100,000 men under his command were well aware of the overwhelming Allied force they were facing. Many soberly realized they had little or no chance of stopping the Allies should Eisenhower refuse to consider separate negotiations with Germany. Others continued to await the promised wonder weapons that were expected to turn the tide in favor of Germany. Ultimately, however, the Germans had little on which they could pin any real hope.

The harried staff officers continued to request reinforcements, supplies, and ammunition. Their pleas were answered with threats from Berlin and empty promises about wonder weapons. Hitler explicitly directed that any soldier who surrendered without having suffered disabling wounds or without exhibiting irrefutable evidence that he had fought until all means of resistance was exhausted would be considered a deserter. Any family members still located within the shrinking confines of the Reich were to be held responsible for the actions of the soldier on the front. In cases where dishonorable or traitorous conduct was substantiated, payments of wages and issuance of rations to the subject's relatives would be suspended. The high command made it clear that the order to this effect was to be immediately disseminated to all troops. The directive accompanied Hitler's scorched-earth order, according to which all military, industrial, communications, and transportation facilities as well as all food supplies were to be destroyed to prevent their capture by the Allies. Hitler's armaments minister, Albert Speer, who was responsible for carrying out the order, attempted to persuade the Führer that the plan would cause mass starvation and death from disease throughout Germany. Hitler responded, "It is better to destroy these things ourselves ... the people have proven themselves the weaker, and the future belongs to the stronger population in the east. After the war only the weaker will have survived, the best have fallen."[4]

General Schlemm's First Parachute Army, scraped together from myriad sources, varied widely in quality. The army of defenders consisted of the 6th, 7th, and 8th Parachute Divisions of the II Parachute Corps, with a total strength of 16,000 men (approximately a third of the nominal strength). The city of Wesel was occupied by a diverse array of troops, the nucleus of which was created around flak units manned by teenaged boys and foreign volunteers whose main responsibility had been to operate the 81 heavy and 200 light flak guns in and around the city. The flak units were reinforced by Volkssturm, navy, and security units, all of which were assembled under the dubious title Festung Wesel ("Fortress Wesel").

With his refusal to yield ground to the Allies, Hitler had proclaimed Wesel a fortress. The events of recent months had repeatedly exhibited the folly of relying on encircled forces to stop or even deter an Allied advance. The fortress philosophy was based on the theory that large numbers of enemy divisions would remain committed to reducing the fortress, thus causing the enemy to expend valuable divisions in a static role and relieving pressure from the front. In fact, however, the policy had the opposite effect. Creating beleaguered pockets of resistance simply left large numbers of combat troops surrounded and destined for defeat. The encircled divisions were no longer effective for holding any length of a steadily eroding defensive line in the east or west. Hitler had proclaimed numerous surrounded cities as fortresses, almost all of which had eventually surrendered with little noticeable impact on the Allied advance.

The city of Wesel was placed under the command of Major-General Friedrich Deutsch. Other Wehrmacht units in the area were the 180th Infantry Division, the 190th Infantry Division, and, farther to the rear, Division Hamburg, which had been raised early in 1945 in the city of Hamburg from young recruits and soldiers discharged from hospitals. This division had experienced heavy equipment losses even before it was transferred from Hamburg to the Rhine. During one Allied air raid against rail installations and military facilities on the day prior to the transfer, the division's engineer battalion lost 90 percent of its horses and almost half its equipment.[5]

Although most of the German units had suffered immense losses during the withdrawal to the Rhine and their stubborn defense of the bridgehead, the tenacious, last-ditch effort they mounted had enabled large quantities of heavy artillery to be transferred to the east bank. The Rhine front between Duisburg and Emmerich had approximately 800 artillery and heavy antiaircraft pieces. The XXXXVII Panzer Corps, under command of General Freiherr von Lüttwitz, was held in reserve farther to the rear. Lüttwitz's corps, consisting of the well-known 116th "Windhund" Panzer Division and the 15th Panzergrenadier Division, was to be used in the event of a breakthrough by the attackers.

Although both divisions were of excellent reputation and were well known to the Allies, they suffered critical shortfalls in irreplaceable equipment. The 116th Panzer Division, one of the foremost and best-equipped German divisions on the Western Front, reported less than 40 operational tanks in service. The entire Army Group H, along the Lower Rhine front, was in no better condition than Model's Army Group B on its southern flank. Like Army Group B, it consisted of divisions in name only. Not one division resembled another, all varied in numbers of troops and equipment, and there no longer existed any effective form of standardization among the units. Regardless of designation or number of vehicles on hand, most remained immobilized for operational purposes because of critical fuel shortages. When a vehicle became nonserviceable or communications equipment failed, there was no replacement available and no means to obtain vital parts. The Wehrmacht had become a defensive army, with little mobility, intermittent communications, and chronic shortages of ammunition.

The decimated combat units were increased to nominal strength on paper by incorporating all available paramilitary, political, and police units that could be scraped together. They were of little combat value and represented only columns of figures in Wehrmacht reports, lacking in proper training, equipment, and supplies. The most critical personnel shortages were in the ranks of experienced noncommissioned and junior officers.

The Germans were fully aware that a crossing was going to take place along the Lower Rhine plateau. A crossing north of the Ruhr would enable the totally mechanized Allied armies to speed eastward across favorable, flat terrain. On 20 March, General von Blaskowitz heightened the alert status of Army Group H in expectation of an attack. Although the exact site of the landing remained unclear, the Germans were aware that an operation was impending and that they could do little to stop it in any case. The Allies had embarked on extensive deception maneuvers, and the Americans had even assembled an army of decoys on the heights above Krefeld, constantly shifting positions and creating the illusion that a massive buildup was to take place in that area.

Farther to the north, across the Rhine from Emmerich, was the Canadian First Army. The terrain presented an excellent opportunity for a crossing in that area, and the Germans expected an airborne drop as well. They were, however, unable to observe much of what was occurring on the bank opposite Emmerich because everything was blanketed in the impenetrable artificial fog. The lack of radio communications from the usually effusive Allies served as an ominous warning. A noticeable increase in air attacks on German flak positions in the Lower Rhine sectors also indicated that an airborne landing was planned. The problem the Germans were facing was that the entire area was an almost indefensible, flat plain consisting of vast expanses of farmland with few dense population centers. Northern Germany was ideally situated for an airborne operation, and the Germans had few forces with which they could attempt a defense of the expansive area.

At the heart of the Allied plans to cross the Lower Rhine was the ancient fortress town of Wesel. The town had seen an inordinate increase in activity since the Allied attempt to cut off Holland during the ill-fated Operation Market-Garden in September 1944. As the front drew ever nearer, columns of Wehrmacht soldiers streamed through Wesel in growing numbers. Labor brigades had been organized by order of Kreisleiter Kentrat to build defenses farther west on the Dutch border near Goch. Students were mustered from the schools and elderly men taken from the flak units in Wesel for this backbreaking service. The labor camps were ordered to provide foreign laborers for the work as well, hundreds of whom died of disease and exposure in primitive camps near Rees during the winter.

The evacuation of women and children from Wesel began in earnest as the Allied troops drew nearer and the bombing raids increased. The numbers of Wesel inhabitants had risen perceptibly with the influx of thousands of refugees from the west side of the Rhine, many of whom had abandoned their homes in areas occupied by Allied troops. The early weeks of 1945 were marked by intensely congested roadways and rail systems, and the transportation problems were exacerbated by incessant air attacks from roving patrols of British and American fighter-bombers that pounced on anything that moved.

On 16 February 1945, the Allies launched the heaviest air raid to date against Wesel, consisting of three separate missions. The attack left the residential area an uninhabitable pile of rubble as wave after wave of bombers passed overhead. The explosions were so concentrated that the steel doors of air raid shelters blew inward and were torn from their fittings. Women collapsed as their nerves broke under the strain, and children screamed and cried as they clung to anyone within reach. A policeman shot his daughter, his wife, and then himself as they cowered under the hail of bombs.

As the first alarm sirens wailed, twenty-four-year-old Inge Büsching seized the two bags of clothing and valuables that she always had prepared for such occasions. Holding tightly to the hands of her two children, she fled to the nearby Rathaus ("city hall") with her mother. The Rathaus cellar, the closest public air raid shelter in her neighborhood, was filled to capacity. They hurried onward to the National Socialistische Verein (National Socialist League [NSV]) cellar, which they found overflowing with other women and children. After several minutes, the bombs began to fall. The cellar shook, and the lights were immediately extinguished. During the bombardment, someone located a flashlight; others lit candles and lanterns with matches. As the all-clear siren sounded, the people crowded in the cellar made their way onto the street, where they were met by an indescribable scene of horror. The stunned populace wandered onto a wasteland of burning rubble where, only minutes earlier, large buildings had stood. The air was filled with smoke and the muffled thud of delayed explosions in the distance. Two mutilated horses and a dead Wehrmacht soldier lay on the Marktplatz near the entrance to the Rathaus. Inge stared at the dead soldier with horror and shielded her children's eyes from the scene as they picked their way along the street toward their home. They proceeded through the rubble for several minutes before she realized that, in the darkness of the shelter during the raid, someone had stolen one of her bags.[6]

On the morning of the raid, Pauline Breuer toasted slices of white bread and packed them along with several articles of clothing in rucksacks for her children. Government regulations required that each child be provided with food and clothing in the shelters. The family home on the Flemmingstrasse was without a shelter; the houses along the street had no deep basements for such use. The residents had received permission to take refuge in the large, vaulted cellar beneath the villa of the Hardt family, who had fled the city for the duration of the war. As the sirens began to wail and the streams of aircraft approached, Pauline gathered her children and hurried to the Hardt cellar, carrying her infant in a basket. As they descended the steps, they found a mixed crowd of refugees and soldiers had gathered in the narrow confines of the stairwell.

The group waited in the cellar throughout the morning as the sirens continued to wail, and in the early afternoon, the infant began to cry with hunger. Pauline's sister, Maria Erkens, decided to leave the shelter to refill the baby's bottle and obtain more food. Minutes passed, and Maria did not return. Pauline, accompanied by her children, climbed up the stairs and opened the door to see the sky black with aircraft with strings of bombs trailing from the open bays below their fuselages. Terrified, they slammed the door and stumbled back into the depths of the basement as the detonations began. Seconds later, a cacophony of screams, explosions, shrieking sirens, and crashing buildings rent the air. The soft murmur of praying could be heard intermittently through the sounds of destruction and terror. Pauline repeatedly told herself to remain calm for the sake of the children.

At long length, they stumbled up the cellar stairs into air choked with dust and smoke. The mangled corpses of inhabitants and the cadavers of horses lay strewn on the streets, and she attempted to avert her children's eyes from the horror as they gazed about in shock. She made her way toward their home with the children in tow, only to find that it no longer existed. She met the neighboring Clausen family, who had also lost their home, and after a frantic, brief discussion, the distraught neighbors decided to attempt to get to their pastor's home in Marienthal. A short time later, they flagged down a Wehrmacht truck carrying charcoal to Raesfeld and left the ruins of the city.[7]

The nuns of the Josefshaus der Schwestern School at the city's Brüner Tor had taken refuge in the basement of their building shortly before the first bombs fell. The din of explosions grew louder, and suddenly, after a muffled roar, the shelter was plunged into darkness. Dust filled the air, and the explosions were now muted, as if far away: they realized that the entrance to the cellar had been buried. Eventually, a light appeared above them, and the nuns and others in the cellar scrambled toward the beacon. A rescue party of some twenty soldiers had been directed to the location by the clerics of the convent. As they emerged from the ruins, the nuns were shocked by what remained of the city.

Speechless, they seated themselves on the trunks of fallen trees and attempted to quench their thirst from the only water available, the washwater from the kitchen basin that had somehow remained intact through the raid. Seven of the nuns had managed to climb to the surface. Sister Ermenhilde was heard calling from the cavern—her legs were trapped beneath a slab of masonry—but there was no sound from the others who had not made it to the surface. After three hours of feverish labor, Sister Ermenhilde was freed, miraculously uninjured. Another casualty, Fraulein Bückmann, was carried to the surface with multiple fractures in her legs. As the women pleaded with the soldiers to rescue the nuns who remained in the cellar, they were told that the others—Sisters Angela, Marita, Humilita, and Servatia—were all dead. The rescuers had to turn their attentions to saving the living.[8]

After the fleet of bombers had departed, clerics Pröbsting and Schell managed to tear the tabernacle from the ruins of their building and carry it to safety. The tabernacle key and the sacristy had disappeared in the maelstrom. The survivors who had emerged from the shelter were gathered above the entombed nuns when someone began screaming that more aircraft were arriving. The priests and the soldiers quickly dived into the cellar; other survivors scattered like frightened birds as the bombs began to fall.[9]

Police captain Wilhelm Schyns had just appeared at the Brüner-Tor-Platz to assist in recovery efforts when the next waves of aircraft descended. Schyns hoped that the new bombs would contain only time-delay fuses, thus giving the rescue workers at least a limited period in which to continue their efforts before the bombs began detonating. However, his hopes proved to be fruitless. The new loads included heavy, high-explosive, and incendiary bombs equipped with impact fuses, and the already devastated city was again rocked with explosions and consumed with flames. Windowpanes in buildings as far away as Essen and Krefeld—cities that had withstood countless previous raids—shattered with the impact of the pressure waves emanating from Wesel.[10]

As the aircraft departed from the city, the authorities began recovering inhabitants, treating the injured, and disposing of the dead. Many survivors immediately fled the city for the farmlands and outlying villages: anywhere was preferable to the nightmare that Wesel had become. Amid exploding bombs equipped with time-delay fuses, police and fire brigades began attempting to rescue trapped inhabitants and extinguish the fires that threatened to consume them. Civilians physically capable of assisting were conscripted to shovel rubble from the entrances of buried shelters. No means of communications existed to reach the world beyond the parameters of the city, for all facilities had been destroyed. A policeman cautiously picked his way through a moonscape of bomb craters and mounds of debris to reach the badly damaged Lippe Bridge; after gingerly crossing the river, he succeeded in making telephone contact with other towns in the Ruhr to request assistance.

Soon, help was arriving over the still-intact Hünxe-Krudenburger bridge—but not before Wesel was hit by yet another attack. The late-afternoon assault was fully unexpected and arrived without warning. All air raid warning systems had been destroyed in the previous raid or were severed from external communications and power facilities. After several minutes, it was over. A large number of inhabitants had previously fled the city and had thus escaped near-certain death, but the rescue workers, taken by surprise while attempting to clear collapsed cellars and shelters, were caught in the open when the bombs fell. The city was strewn with mangled bodies, and the cries of the injured wafted over the ruins.

The remaining workers who were uninjured were helpless to aid the wounded. There were no means of lifting layers of concrete and tons of rubble, no means of caring for and transporting the victims. Work parties that were organized prior to the raid were now leaderless, with no means of communicating with one another. The entire area now consisted of unrecognizable city blocks of blackened ruins, crushed bodies, hundreds of injured, and small bands of dazed workers stumbling blindly though the heat, dust, and smoke.

Eventually, limited assistance began arriving from other towns. A police major from Oberhausen brought a rescue brigade and immediately began organizing the forces. Rescue parties started digging through the mounds of debris where inhabitants might be buried. The local officials who had survived the last raid were familiar with the locations and layout of many of the shelters, now concealed under tons of rubble, and they advised the teams on where to begin searching for anyone who might be alive under the ruins.

That night, fires began raging through the devastated city. What remained of Wesel's finance building began to burn. The Heuber Garrison, long a symbol of Prussia's military presence in Westphalia, glared brightly as the flames spread. The massive grain silo belonging to the Kempen shipping firm went up in flames, and the city blocks along the Rhine were obliterated. Little firefighting equipment had survived the series of raids intact, so there existed no means of extinguishing the flames. Explosions continued to rock the area throughout the night as bombs equipped with time-delay fuses and those that had failed to explode on impact detonated in the flames. The explosions threw showers of sparks into the sky, spreading the inferno wherever they landed and causing unstable skeletons of buildings, weakened by the bombing and fires, to collapse, making further attempts to fight the fires futile.

By dawn, the only signs of life in the stricken city were isolated teams of workers who still dared to attempt to rescue those buried beneath the rubble. The teams uncovered corpses and laid them aside without cover. With so few means of transport left, whatever was available had to be reserved for the badly injured. The work never stopped as the dead and wounded were carried to the surface. The crews worked without food or water. The need for water was especially acute, for the blinding clouds of dust hanging in the air from pulverized masonry choked their throats and lungs. All water lines in the city were destroyed or blocked, so any available water had to be transported to the work locations in carts or carried over mounds of broken buildings.

Convinced that all Allied targets in Wesel had been destroyed after the series of raids on 16 February, teams of rescue workers from the surrounding areas descended on the city. Nothing could have survived intact, and even the Allies, who possessed a seemingly endless supply of everything, would not risk aircraft and crews to attack a city that was already completely destroyed. The teams worked throughout the next day and night. More rescue equipment and additional firefighters were brought in from surrounding areas to attempt to extinguish the flames that continued to spread. Believing that the terror was finally at an end, inhabitants emerged from the surrounding countryside where they had taken refuge and returned to the stricken city. They trickled back into the field of ruins on foot, singly or in small groups of family members and neighbors, pulling small hand-wagons or leading horse-carts borrowed from farmers in hopes of recovering any items of use or value from the remains of their homes.

On Sunday, 18 February, the waves of bombers reappeared over Wesel, dropping tons of explosives and scattering the knots of returnees and rescue workers. The scarce rescue and transportation equipment disintegrated in the explosions as the city was again tossed and tormented. After the aircraft faded in the distance, the reorganization effort resumed. Some of the workers refused to return. For many, the loss of family members had been confirmed, and most had relatives who were still unaccounted for. The dwindling teams of workers returned to the piles of rubble, where they attempted to locate the entrances to air raid shelters and listened with sound-enhancing equipment for any signs of life beneath the ruins.

The groups that remained at the scene received instructions to bury the dead after sunset, when the risk of attack by bombers or fighter aircraft was considerably lessened. All recent raids had occurred during daylight hours, and darkness was expected to bring a few hours' reprieve. The recovery efforts, however, had to take place during the day, despite the danger posed by the bombers or by fighter aircraft that continued to strafe the city indiscriminately; it proved impossible to conduct the work in darkness. The bodies had to be located, wrested from the rubble, and then hauled through streets choked with debris or dragged and carried over mountains of crushed buildings to a collection point. The transport of the corpses was problematic, for the bodies were heavy and there were no litters or other equipment to assist in the task. The remains were pulled or carried to collection points, where small groups were assigned to try to identify each corpse or note the location and description of the site where the body had been found for possible identification later. The bodies were then loaded onto carts for removal to the cemetery.

Some of the horse-drawn carts experienced problems of another nature. The horses, unaccustomed to the stench and the strange conditions, became unruly and almost uncontrollable. The drivers were compelled to lead the frightened and confused animals through darkened, narrow paths in the rubble at night. During daylight, the horses were taken out of the city: the drivers were acutely aware that the horses were a favorite target for the Allied fighter aircraft. Meanwhile, the workers continued to be harassed from the skies as smaller yet still deadly air raids continued to fall on them. Many of the corpses, lying in the scattered collection points and awaiting transport to the cemetery, were again buried under rubble shifted by exploding bombs. Following the departure of the raiders, the bodies had to be relocated and brought to the surface again.

After experiencing several consecutive air raids, the workers and inhabitants took no further chances. The waves of aircraft returned on 20 February and then again on 24 February. It seemed as though whenever the work parties assembled and began their grisly task of recovering bodies—it was firmly believed no one was still alive under the tons of rubble—aircraft would materialize, sending the groups fleeing in all directions. Fighter-bombers continued to dive without warning on small convoys and groups of people en route to the city. Once the work parties scattered in panic before the aircraft, it was extremely difficult to regroup. Many workers abandoned the task, believing it illogical to continue to risk lives simply to recover the dead. Some locations were abandoned after preliminary work to recover survivors resulted in failure—there simply were no survivors in many locations. In the large shelters in the Hotel Escherhaus, the Esplanade garrison, Hotel Schuhmacher, Torfstrasse, the Stadtwerke, the Stems brewery, and numerous other locations, efforts were abandoned when it became clear that no living persons remained.[11]

It was common practice for inhabitants to have small valuables packed in bags and ready to take to the air raid shelters. Bulkier items were often stored in cellars for safekeeping. Armed with this knowledge, looters descended on the ruins in their search for anything of value that could be easily concealed. Many people, taken by surprise by the massive raid, had forgotten their packed bags in the panic to seek shelter and had escaped only with their lives. The looters became adept at slithering through tiny cellar openings in the rubble, and they developed an instinct for locating concealed corners in the mounds of debris where valuables might be hidden or where an intact stairwell could be found to gain access to the interiors of homes. Workers sometimes discovered the dead after the looters had already announced their presence by leaving the corpses without wallets, wedding rings, watches, and jewelry. The thieves almost always left evidence of their work—the telltale turned-out pockets of the shredded clothing on the dead.

Some of the looters were captured in the act or were found to have valuables on them that clearly belonged to others. The valuables were confiscated, to be logged and stored for eventual return to the owners if they or their family members were still alive. The suspected looters were taken to the nearest intact law enforcement facility—usually in Bocholt or Dorsten.

Elfriede Emmerichs had fled the city following the February raid that had heavily damaged her home but left many possessions intact. She, along with others from the neighborhood, returned every morning in an attempt to retrieve valuables from the sea of ruins. She was able to recover most of her possessions in a series of trips in and out of the city, first carting away porcelain, crystal, silver, clothing, and various necessities. She then concentrated on recovering books, typewriters, and almost ninety jars of preserves. The recovered items were carried to her temporary residence in Drevenack through a precarious journey that required her to repeatedly abandon the cart and dive into roadside ditches to avoid the fighter-bombers that preyed on every moving target.

Foreign laborers, deserters, and the customary criminal elements were not the only ones engaged in looting. On 18 March, when Elfriede again returned to the ruined city to recover any remaining items, she was surprised to find about twenty German paratroopers in her home. The group of stragglers, some of the last demoralized troops who had recently fled over the Rhine from the west bank, had ransacked the home. What they could not cart away, the soldiers had destroyed—smashing furniture, dumping the contents of wardrobes and drawers, ruining carpets, and wrecking anything that had survived the air raids. The soldiers, many of them drunk, offered no apologies or explanation for the devastation. For Elfriede—despite the air raids, the rations, and the many notices she had received about the deaths of friends and relatives serving on many fronts over the past years—it was not until that moment that the realization the war was finally lost swept over her. She knew that all hope was gone when her own country's soldiers wantonly destroyed what they were supposed to protect.[12]

The city of Wesel continued to be subjected to air attacks, though none reached the intensity of the 16 February raid. Between 6 and 23 March, limited air raids were launched against the piles of rubble, but they inflicted little damage, as most facilities had long since been pulverized time and again. As the front drew nearer, the attacks by fighter-bombers increased, and eventually, the city and surrounding area came under artillery fire.

On 23 March, British Prime Minister Winston Churchill flew to the front, much to Field Marshal Montgomery's chagrin. Churchill had long planned to be present when the last great offensive that would carry the Allied troops over the Rhine and into the heart of Germany was to occur. Montgomery was of the opinion that the prime minister should be detained at headquarters as long as possible. Like most military commanders, he did not relish the prospect of having the leader present on the battlefield, especially when, despite overwhelming Allied material superiority, something might go wrong.

Officially, the Germans were once again pinning their hopes on static defenses and a handful of hastily organized units: flak regiments; makeshift artillery positions; the 2nd, 7th, and 8th Parachute Divisions; the 84th and 180th Infantry Divisions; the 15th Panzergrenadier Division; various Volkssturm battalions; and two weakened panzer divisions with ninety-two tanks northwest of Emmerich. They were facing an enemy that was numerically ten times their strength.[13]

The dubious line of defenses with which the Germans intended to halt the Allied drive was optimistically named the *Westfalenwall.* In fall 1944, Dr. Meyer, the Gauleiter of Westphalia, had communicated to Hitler that he was constructing an impassable barrier and requested approval and authority to continue his defense project. Hitler had consented, and the population was set to work with shovels and spades constructing a series of shallow ditches and foxholes running in a line from Ahaus to Stadtlohn, Südlohn to Borken, and Bocholt and beyond to Wesel. The German authorities now expected to stop the world's most powerful mechanized armies with a series of roadside ditches and one-man foxholes. The defenders of the *Rheinfront* consisted of approximately 24 German soldiers of questionable quality per mile. Supporting the personnel were an average of 0.06 barrels of antiaircraft weapons per mile; 0.5 barrels of artillery; and a maximum of 1 tank, usually low on fuel, per mile.[14]

Just before 4:00 p.m. on Friday, 23 March, the artificial-fog generators along the Rhine suddenly fell silent. From his Twenty-first Army Group HQ in Walbeck, Field Marshal Montgomery announced the code words *two if by sea* to launch the largest combined amphibious and airborne operation since D-Day. At 5:00, Generals Eisenhower, Simpson, and Anderson watched from the tower in Lintfort as the Allied artillery batteries opened fire. At 6:00, a second barrage was sent to the east bank of the Rhine; another massive barrage blanketed the bank one hour later. The German positions were enveloped in heavy-caliber shellbursts from more than 1,300 artillery pieces situated on the west bank between the towns of Hönnepel and Büderich. Their targets were some 1,000 German positions that were to be neutralized in preparation for the crossing. The targets included artillery positions, observation points, command-and-control centers, supply depots, assembly areas, crossroads, and any other facility or terrain feature deemed essential to a defense. Additionally, German positions directly on the bank of the Rhine came under a hail of direct fire from more than 1,000 antiaircraft guns. The east bank exploded and boiled under a shower of artillery and antiaircraft shells.[15]

At 9:12 p.m., two corps of the British Second Army and one corp of the U.S. Ninth Army began crossing the Rhine, illuminated by searchlights, between Rees and Wesel. Within minutes, they had established a foothold on the east bank. Bulldozers were set to work leveling the massive Rhine levee and establishing a roadway for the mechanized units crossing in amphibious vehicles. The British 15th and 51st Infantry Divisions formed the spearhead of the crossing at Rees, and they succeeded in putting their entire strength over the Rhine within fifteen minutes. Two miles to the west of Wesel, 1 and 5 Commando Brigades crossed in assault craft with the intent of capturing Wesel from the north.

At 10:20 p.m., 200 British bombers attacked the unfortunate city once again, dropping thousands of bombs on the German defenders and inhabitants ahead of the assault force. The city was then attacked by troops of 5 Commando Brigade, who found little more than ruins in their path. The assault troops met little resistance as they crossed over the Rhine under cover of the artificial fog, and the great barrier was breached. Farther north, the Canadians waited for their orders to cross. At Xanten, the Scots had established a wide bridgehead within thirty minutes of the first crossing.

At 2:00 in the morning of 24 March, three regiments of the U.S. 30th Division crossed between Wesel and Rheinberg. Slightly over an hour later, the assault troops of the U.S. 79th Division crossed the Rhine after a massive barrage of almost 2,000 tons of explosives that fell on the German 180th Infantry Division and the 2nd Parachute Division. Like their British counterparts to the north, they met little resistance from the pulverized defenses.

More crossings were conducted farther north, where 2,000 guns opened fire on German defenses on the east bank. As the barrage subsided, the British XXX Corps and two Canadian divisions crossed and hardly slowed their advance as they passed Emmerich toward the towns of Millingen, Bienen, Isselburg, and Anholt.

Generals Eisenhower, Simpson, and Anderson and Prime Minister Churchill observed the crossing of the Rhine from the headquarters of the XVI Corps, located in Büderich. They were provided a sweeping view of Allied forces from the balcony of a home near Büderich as the final major barrier along the route to Berlin was breached. When Eisenhower excused himself to return an urgent telephone call from General Bradley, Churchill took the opportunity to escape the confines of the headquarters—and Eisenhower's restraining presence—and cross the Rhine himself. Montgomery, Churchill, and several American commanders were transported by assault craft to the east bank near the bridge at Wesel, where they wandered about for some thirty minutes before setting out for the west bank. The party's hopes of proceeding to Wesel by boat were dashed when the launch captain advised them that the passage was blocked by a chain across the river; the chain had been positioned to deter any German attempt to disrupt the crossing by floating mines downriver to the operations area. As a result, the party was compelled to return to shore and proceed by motor vehicle to Wesel.[16]

In Berlin, Hitler received word at 3:15 a.m., 24 March, that the Allies had crossed the Rhine at Wesel and that the Lower Rhine front was collapsing. A quick briefing with staff officers revealed that there were no reserves—all available units were already committed to the fight. The few German defenders who were situated within the assault area were stunned to silence by the massive artillery bombardment. Over the rumble of artillery, the occasional sounds of a desolate machine-gun position, interspersed with erratic rifle fire and isolated grenade blasts, reverberated erratically along the riverbanks and over the open fields of the Lower Rhineland.

Despite the torrent of artillery shells impacting on the east bank, the German defenders beyond the riverbanks began to react. The Americans, south of Wesel, had struck the void between the sectors held by Army Group H and Army Group B. Farther downstream, to the north, the British were unfortunate in encountering the remnants of Schlemm's First Parachute Army. Sporadic but intense firefights began to break out among the wood-lines and the roadsides as the British attempted to consolidate and strengthen their hold on the east bank.

That evening, the ground assault began against Wesel. The city, almost devoid of life since the massive bombing in February, was commanded by General Deutsch. The commando brigade formed for this assault was composed of elements from 46 Commando Brigade of the Royal Marines and 6 Commando Brigade of the Royal Army. With a combined strength of 1,800 combatants, this force was tasked with capturing the city.

Under the protection of an intense artillery barrage, the marines of 46 Commando crossed the Rhine a mile and a half north of Wesel in buffalo amphibious troop carriers, meeting only intermittent small-arms fire. By 10:30 p.m., the entire assault force of both 6 Commando and 46 Commando had completed the crossing and made preparations to assault Wesel.

To eliminate any remaining resistance, the city was again struck by a bombing raid as the commandos prepared to attack. Some 200 bombers dropped more than 1,100 tons of explosives on a city that had long since been reduced to rubble. Any intact buildings that had survived the February raids were now destroyed. Roadways that had been laboriously carved through piles of ruins were again choked with debris. Electric power and communications lines were destroyed, and flak batteries and military facilities were neutralized.

The British troops observed the air attack from their assembly area on Grav Island near the Rhine. The troops of the commando brigade separated into two columns as they departed from the bridgehead. As the sounds of aircraft motors died, followed only by explosions from time-delay bombs and the crackling of flames, 6 Commando began filing through the darkness toward Wesel. The marines of 46 Commando struck east, intending to capture the large Keramag factory on the city's northernmost outskirts. As the last British forces departed from Grav Island, German artillery rounds began to strike the landing area, hitting only deserted beaches but sending a signal to the commandos that the German defenders were aware of their landing and were awaiting their next move.

The British 6 Commando made its way slowly into the outskirts of Wesel, crossed over the Resser Landstrasse from the northwest, and penetrated deeper into the ruins. A detachment from 6 Commando pushed farther toward the south over Mölderstrasse. The troop leaders quickly realized that the meticulously prepared maps, with objectives and roadways carefully identified and marked, were now useless. The Allied bombing raids had left nothing intact: no buildings were identifiable, and streets, if they existed at all, could not be recognized. The ground the soldiers crossed looked more like the battlefields of Verdun than a once-thriving city. Businesses and residences were reduced to blackened silhouettes of rubble, and any open spaces were pockmarked with giant, water-filled bomb craters that reflected the intermittent flames leaping skyward as pockets of ruins smoldered and burned. The troops met little resistance apart from occasional small-arms fire that was quickly neutralized. The city appeared almost devoid of life.

On capturing the core of the city, 6 Commando dispatched patrols throughout the area to eliminate any further resistance. Members of one patrol encountered resistance as they unknowingly approached the headquarters of the Wesel military commander near Wylackstrasse. Realizing that the command bunker was severed from any escape route, Major-General Deutsch took command of one squad of defenders and ordered Lieutenant-Colonel Ross to command another unit, consisting of staff personnel. The fighting continued throughout the night. At approximately 3:00 a.m., Deutsch and several members of his staff fell to machine-gun bursts as the ring around Wesel continued shrinking. At 8:00 a.m. on 24 March, Lieutenant-Colonel Ross finally surrendered the city.[17]

The Royal Marines of 46 Commando were less fortunate, as they encountered heavier resistance from nests of survivors continuing to lurk in the rubble. They gingerly made their way toward their objective, combating the flashes of gunfire that repeatedly broke the darkness, until they reached the Keramag factory. After infiltrating the interior of the large facility, they were not amused to find that they had been given the task of capturing—and now defending—a factory full of ceramic toilet bowls.

During the same night, from 23 to 24 March, another crossing was taking place south of Wesel. At 1:00 a.m., fire erupted from 600 American artillery pieces and shells rained on the east bank to open Operation Flashpoint, the crossing of the Rhine by elements of the U.S. Ninth Army. Within an hour, more than 65,000 rounds had impacted on German positions east of the Rhine, preparing the way for the crossing by the U.S. 30th Infantry Division. Under cover of artillery, the 119th Infantry Regiment crossed from the town of Büderich, the 117th Regiment crossed south of the Lippe intersection, and the 120th Regiment crossed at Rheinberg in plywood assault craft. As the boats approached the east bank, the artillery barrage shifted farther to the east, leaving only a moonscape behind. Every two minutes, another wave of assault craft packed with 30th Infantry soldiers reached the east bank. Within two hours, other battalions followed, as the assault phases progressed with barely any resistance from German forces. Amphibious tanks reached the far bank, sealing the crossing. Now, north of the Ruhr, as in the south at Remagen, American soldiers were east of the Rhine.[18]

At 3:00 a.m., another crossing was taking place farther south, by the U.S. 79th Division. The first waves of infantrymen crossed between Rheinberg and Orsoy in scarcely forty-five minutes. Near the village of Bislich, situated between Xanten and Vynen, the Scottish 15th Division launched Operation Torchlight and crossed the river under cover of British artillery. The Scots were ferried across the river in more than 100 amphibious vehicles that followed assault lanes marked by tracers fired from British antiaircraft guns. The attackers met only sporadic, uncoordinated resistance during the crossing. The few casualties suffered were inflicted by land mines that had escaped the artillery barrages.

At 2:00 a.m., the sounds of machine-gun fire mixed with the explosions of artillery shells in Bislich. The villagers, cowering in their cellars, prayed for an end to the torment as white-hot shrapnel and tracers set buildings alight. Many residents were forced to expose themselves to the deadly barrage when fleeing the burning buildings. A number of civilians ran to the assistance of a neighbor named Leo Stuckmann, helping to pull him from his burning home and to retrieve a few articles of clothing that could still be salvaged from the flames. Stuckmann had received a wound in his back and was being cared for by neighbors as the sounds of tanks approached. Frenzied voices calling in English could be heard through the shooting, coupled with the sounds of heavy boots running through brick-paved streets.

A number of German soldiers had taken refuge in the cellar belonging to Willi Meyboom, and soon, an officer appeared and brusquely ordered them out of the shelter to engage the enemy. As the handful of troops emerged from their cellar, they were struck by a burst of machine-gun fire from a British tank. The Allied attack proceeded similarly in other nearby settlements. One man who had fled the village for the safety of the small settlement of Flüren was attempting to leave his cellar when he was shot by the attackers. In Tannenhaeuschen, a woman was caught in a burst of fire that severed both her legs. Her fourteen-year-old son raced to her side and attempted to render aid while screaming for help; her neighbors failed to hear his pleas over the bursting shells or dared not risk being hit by the rain of bullets and shrapnel that filled the area. Alone, the teenager watched helplessly as his mother died. The clamor of cries and shooting began to fade as the wave of attackers swept through the village. By 2:30 a.m., the Scots were firmly on the east bank and were combing the village for German troops who had fled their positions to seek refuge in basements.[19]

The fighting swept through the villages along the Rhine as the Allied soldiers regrouped. The British and American troops organized assaults against isolated, stubborn defenders and called for additional artillery and air support. Many areas changed hands a number of times. As files of exhausted, disillusioned Wehrmacht soldiers entered farms and hamlets, the inhabitants met their arrival with trepidation. To avoid plundering, the farmers provided the soldiers with provisions, opening their cellars to the retreating forces in hopes that the unwelcome guests would soon vanish. Any indication that the soldiers were establishing defenses provoked vigorous protests. The inhabitants were aware that any resistance encountered by the Allies would result in the destruction of their homes and farmsteads.

Many inhabitants were taken into custody by the Allied soldiers and evacuated to the banks of the Rhine, where they were cursorily searched for weapons. Apparently satisfied that there were no combatants among them, the soldiers soon released the civilians. More than 200 demoralized prisoners were captured in Bislich, most of whom were serving with the German 84th Division. The 84th was one of the Wehrmacht divisions that had suffered high casualties during the withdrawal to the Rhine, and most of the prisoners appeared relieved that, for them, the war was over.

As dusk fell on the village of Haffen on 24 March, 2 miles downstream from Bislich, Colonel von Peller und Ehrenberg waited in his command post. Knowing that the Rhine crossing was to take place at any time, the artillery officer shared a bottle of cognac with his staff to alleviate the tension. As the sun set, a tremendous artillery barrage fell upon the banks of the Rhine. Windows burst and doors were sprung from their mountings as waves of shell-bursts swept toward Bislich, and the artillerymen knew what was coming. The staff hurried into the cellar, where the communications equipment was being manned by radio operators.

A nearby artillery observation post reported the west bank was covered in thick fog, rendering observation of the enemy forces impossible. The foremost positions along the east banks of the Rhine were now free of the Allied artillery fire that had pounded the area moments earlier. The entire house in which the staff was located shook and tossed, and more reports arrived announcing artillery fire creeping toward the hinterland. The immense blanket of explosions made it impossible to man the artillery batteries, and isolated posts no longer reported; the area remained shrouded in silence. No runners could traverse the hail of fire to provide an updated situation report. From the information arriving by radio, the colonel calculated that the main thrust of the attack would take place somewhere within his right sector. Given the sounds of enemy activity being reported, he deduced that his foremost positions were able to offer little resistance. Just that afternoon, he had approved a request from one of his lieutenants to escape the confines of the staff quarters and spend a few hours with one of the observation posts—the eager young officer had desired to be farther forward.

The intense barrage continued unabated throughout the evening. Around midnight, the colonel and his staff received word that construction of a pontoon bridge was in progress near Rees, under protection of heavy artillery. The German batteries tried to fire on the west bank opposite Rees, with the result that the fire falling on their own positions increased. Casualty reports began arriving, and the Allies continued the bridge construction without interruption. The Allied antiaircraft positions on the opposite bank put everything that moved under fire. At 2:00 a.m., the young lieutenant who had been so eager to get closer to the enemy reported that the assault forces were closing on his position with amphibious tanks; preparations were being made to engage the attackers. The position then fell silent. The colonel soon noted that the other observation posts suffered a similar, ominous fate.[20]

The soldiers of General Schlemm's 7th Parachute Division were determined to keep the invaders from gaining a foothold on the east bank. They had the advantage of being familiar with the terrain—a vital advantage when attempting to conduct military operations in darkness. A number of the Allied amphibious vehicles had become mired in the soft mud of the Lower Rhine, and the delay had assisted the defenders in their preparations. Additionally, they had been warned of the impending attack through the artillery preparations.

One of the objectives for the Scots was to capture the Hübsch Manor, an imposing structure encircled by a number of smaller dwellings and farm buildings. The estate occupied a rise surrounded by woods and fruit orchards, and the German paratroopers had prepared to defend the position. The Scottish Argyll and Sutherland Highlanders suffered high losses in taking the small plantation, but from there, they were able to fan out along the hinterland and neutralize further opposition. The town of Haffen was taken, and more casualties were suffered by the Allies in capturing the tiny settlement of Lohrwardt, where the Germans had dug defenses into the cluster of buildings, well protected by shrubbery and trees surrounded by a flat plain. It was not until late afternoon on 24 March that the settlement was in British hands, after the German paratroops had withdrawn in the face of approaching British armor that threatened them with encirclement.

While the Germans were stubbornly defending their positions between Wolfskath and the Hübsch estate, the British forces continued to pour supplies and men over the Rhine. The defenders forced the Allied troops to remain sheltered below the banks of the river; any movement over the berm instantly drew a hail of small-arms fire. Medics feverishly tended the wounded who continued to be carried into the tiny bridgehead. An evacuation was not possible due to accurate German mortar fire raining on the amphibious vehicles crossing the river.

Lance Corporal J. Donovan and Private W. Begbie, two medics serving with the 10th Battalion, Highland Light Infantry, crossed the Rhine with D Company and soon observed a German medic emerge from a battered position. Approaching the company under a white flag, the German explained that his unit had a large number of wounded who required immediate assistance. After a short discussion, the two Allied medics agreed to accompany him back to the German lines, hoping that they would be able to persuade the Germans holding the sector to surrender. At the first location, they attempted but failed to convince the small group of defenders to throw down their arms. They were then led toward the rear, where they met with a senior German officer whose only English words apparently were "English very good!"

The two medics set about assisting the wounded, who were flowing into the command post as the Allied artillery concentration increased; eventually, it became so intense that the Germans believed they had been targeted by an air raid. After several hours, it became clear that the Germans were preparing for a withdrawal. As the last group of officers prepared to depart, the commander made arrangements for the two medics to return to their lines. He then thanked them for their assistance and departed. The staff had assembled three vehicles for transport, two of which were immediately destroyed in a new barrage. The remaining officers squeezed into the one remaining vehicle and disappeared toward the east. As the rear guard prepared to depart, Donovan and Begbie tried to persuade them to surrender, but the offer was sullenly declined.[21]

As dawn approached, Allied forces continued streaming over the Rhine. Fifteen-year-old Alfons Meyboom was waiting out the invasion in his parents' farmhouse near the village of Marwick while a shower of artillery shells covered the area. The wife of the local Dutch milkman, who had taken shelter in a neighboring cellar, was struck in the eye by shrapnel and was being cared for by other members of the family when the first Scottish soldiers arrived. The tiny group of civilians were huddled in the cellar when a pounding on the door brought them to their feet. A voice called in a strange accent, "Nix deutscher Soldat?" Alfons quickly replied that only civilians were present. Soldiers in khaki uniforms entered the cellar to inspect the frightened civilians. A citizen of Wesel who had taken refuge at the farmhouse after losing his home to the bombing raids was relieved of his watch. The group of soldiers then departed, leaving a medic in the cellar to assist in caring for the wounded woman. The medic appeared to be very sympathetic and constantly shook his head, muttering, "All for the führer." More soldiers poured into the neighboring cellar, and throughout the night, the farm family could hear the static of a radio.

The following morning, a soldier reappeared in the cellar, and Alfons was granted permission to care for the family horse. As the boy prepared to go outside, the soldier advised him to remove his cap, for it closely resembled the German army forage caps; wearing it in the open might have been dangerous, given the tenuous situation. Alfons climbed the cellar stairs and was shocked to see his home full of soldiers in the midst of preparing breakfast. The men ignored his presence but seemed to be in a humorous disposition. As the boy left the house to care for the horse, he saw that the garden surrounding the farmstead was pock-marked with foxholes. Several soldiers were laying out large, triangular recognition panels to reveal to Allied aircraft that the farmhouse was occupied with friendly forces. The sudden booming of a nearby weapon startled him, and Alfons saw that a gun crew had erected a heavy machine gun in the family vegetable garden and was firing at an unseen target in the direction of Lekkerfeld.[22]

The Allied forces began to construct bridges across the Rhine while the fighting was in progress. It was essential to establish bridgeheads as quickly as possible, for without bridges, the landing forces had to depend on amphibious vehicles for reinforcements and supplies. To the south, in Rheinberg, where Americans had conducted their early-morning crossing, the Allies encountered less resistance and were able to establish a treadway bridge by evening. The British forces crossing at Rees were delayed by staunch German resistance in the town. They were eventually able to establish a pontoon bridge, and at the close of 24 March, the Allied forces were firmly over the Lower Rhine and had established bridgeheads along the length of the river north of the Ruhr.

Despite the efforts of Nazi officials, who continued to threaten and harangue the populace to resist the advancing Allies, very few citizens refused to accept that the end was near. Some 50 miles to the east of the Rhine crossings, in the extensive medical center of Ahlen, Wehrmacht medical officer Paul Rosenbaum tracked the developments with growing concern. He had already engaged Kreisleiter Wemhöner in a heated confrontation when the party official demanded that the wounded in the hospitals be ordered to man the barricades. Rosenbaum remained steadfast in his refusal. "I won't order any wounded personnel to sacrifice themselves in the senseless defense of this city," the doctor argued. "We should raise a Red Cross flag instead."[23]

On Sunday, 26 March, the inhabitants of Bocholt were officially informed that all males between the ages of sixteen and twenty were to report to the city

Volkssturm battalion for duty. Failure to follow the order would result in execution. Messengers were dispatched from house to house to ensure that all inhabitants were aware of the order. Several hundred erstwhile Volkssturm soldiers were assembled in three companies. The conscripts were placed under the direction of Colonel Primus, commander of the paratrooper regiment assigned to defend Bocholt.

The mood of the Bocholt Volkssturm was less than optimistic. Only one of every three soldiers was issued a rifle, for which there was a shortage of ammunition. One entire company possessed only two U.S.-manufactured machine guns, and few of the conscripts had any idea how to operate the foreign weapons. Scattered within the same company were a total of twenty-one Panzerfausts and twenty-five hand grenades.[24]

In preparation for the Allied onslaught, the Gauleiter and Reichs defense commissar of the district, Dr. Meyer, ordered all important technical and utility facilities to be destroyed and the area to be evacuated. In the village of Borken, Pastor Reinstaatler sorrowfully buried the victims of the latest bombing raid and advised the mourners that, because of the constant air attacks, any additional burials would have to be delayed until the following day. Between the villages of Bienen and Millingen, the 2nd Company of the Bocholt Volkssturm was easily overwhelmed by the paratroopers of the British 6th Airborne Division. The Volkssturm defenders had lost their meager will to resist after discovering that, in addition to having only a limited supply of Panzerfausts with which to stop the Allies, they had also been issued harmless training grenades. Farther to the east, in Münster, some of the 23,000 inhabitants remaining in the city plundered the Cörde supply magazines to obtain as much food as possible before the inevitable arrival of the Allies.[25]

Chapter 6

Operation Varsity

Field Marshal Montgomery's dramatic crossing of the Lower Rhine was supported by a number of airborne operations. The planning for the airborne drops, Operation Varsity, had begun following the catastrophe at Arnhem in September 1944. Some six months later, in the early morning hours of 24 March 1945, thousands of soldiers of the 17th Airborne Division near Paris were placed on alert. At 7:17 a.m., the first transports, packed with troopers of Airborne Regiment 507, rolled down the runways en route to a wooded area northwest of the Rhineland town of Dorsten. Behind them followed Regiment 513 and Glider-Infantry Regiment 194, with the task of capturing and holding the Issel Canal. To the southeast of Brussels, the air armada was joined by British airborne forces en route from England. The joint force consisted of more than 1,500 transport aircraft, 1,300 gliders, and more than 2,000 escorts. Their mission was to deliver 40,000 airborne troops to the battlefield, who were to link up with the ground forces already engaging the Germans east of the Rhine.

The German defenders had little with which to oppose the legions of Allied aircraft. The Luftwaffe had less than 100 fighters available, and most remaining German air assets were committed to defending cities and strategic targets against the 2,500 heavy bombers and 900 medium bombers that were attacking Germany on that day.

The German defenders on the east bank of the Rhine were still clinging to many of their positions on the morning of 24 March. The British and American troops had established a foothold in the three bridgeheads at Wesel, Bislich, and Rees, but the Germans were immobile and thus lacked the ability to push them out of the east bank bridgeheads. The GIs and British forces had entered a tenuous phase of the operation—they had to hold their positions until reinforcements arrived, either by a secondary Rhine crossing or from the air.

A number of German artillery positions had survived the heavy shelling and air raids and were attempting to sever the bridgeheads from their lifeline on the west bank. Theoretically, it should only have been a matter of time before the German communications networks and transportation assets recovered from the initial shock of the invasion and began to bring armor, albeit extremely limited, on the narrow strips of territory tenaciously held by the Allied troops. It does not take a large number of tanks to destroy positions held by lightly armed infantry: in combat, the rumble of approaching tanks, with their heavy-caliber cannons, machine guns, and communications equipment, often induces panic in troops who are well within range of the armored vehicles' weapons yet too distant to defend themselves. It was therefore essential for the Allied troops clinging to the east bank to receive heavy weapons as soon as possible. The overwhelming Allied airpower, especially the fleets of fighter-bombers that were screaming over the treetops, pounced on any perceived target and had rendered the German forces all but immobile during daylight hours. However, once darkness approached, it would not be difficult for the Germans to destroy the bridgeheads if they could bring more troops forward. The fighter-bombers could not destroy what they could not see.

At 9:30 a.m., an enormous artillery barrage was unleashed on the German flak and artillery positions. After approximately twenty minutes, the sounds of bursting artillery rounds faded, and for several long minutes, silence, punctuated by the piercing rattle of distant small-arms fire, descended over the area. Soon, however, a new and ominous sound was discerned by the German forces, as the droning of hundreds of heavy aircraft motors increased.

The troops and inhabitants of the Lower Rhine were accustomed to fleets of aircraft passing overhead en route to their targets in the Ruhr or deeper into the heartland of Germany, and the shrieking sounds of fighter-bombers diving on targets of opportunity had become almost commonplace. The drone of motors reverberating across the pastures and potato fields that morning was almost routine. Before long, waves of aircraft appeared in the clear morning sky, passing low over the defenders. The Germans could do little more than crouch in their trenches, cellars, and foxholes and watch as the sky to the east filled with hundreds of white, blue, and green parachutes.

The air armada crossed the Rhine between 9:50 and 10:00 a.m., where they were met by heavy flak fired from the line of antiaircraft batteries previously established to protect the Ruhr industrial area to the south. A number of the aircraft struck by flak veered from the formations and crashed to the earth. But the majority remained fixed on their course. Within minutes of crossing the Rhine, the green lights appeared in the transports, and the paratroops prepared to drop.

One of the main objectives was the foreboding Diersfordter Forest, approximately 3 miles from the banks of the Rhine. The forest was a long stretch of impenetrable trees and undergrowth in which German troops had established defenses. These sites could be used for counterattacks against the weak bridgeheads, and it was essential that the German positions hidden under the dense, green canopy be neutralized.

Two reinforced airborne divisions were to be dropped onto a series of drop zones, or DZs, on the north, south, and east perimeters of the forest. The airborne drop was intended to surprise the defenders and trap them between the paratroops and the bridgeheads on the Rhine. If the Germans concealed in the Diersfordter Forest could be cut off, they could then be eliminated before they could bring more strength to bear on the bridgeheads. The area of operations represented a rough triangle between the towns of Wesel, Mamminkeln, and Mehrhoog.

General Lewis Brereton, commander of the First Allied Airborne Army, was determined to avoid the catastrophe experienced in September 1944 during Operation Market-Garden in Holland. The airborne landings would take place only after the bridgeheads had been established to avoid encirclement and destruction of the lightly armed paratroopers by the Germans. However, artillery barrages aimed at the hinterland to support the Rhine crossings would not be possible if airborne troops were already on the ground in the area.

The airborne operation was to take place during daylight hours. Even before the Market-Garden fiasco, experience had proven that pilots had more difficulty with orientation in night drops, and consequently, the troops were scattered and could not locate their planned assembly points in the darkness. Brereton was insistent that all soldiers were to be dropped on the same day, that the airdrops and the glider landings would be closely coordinated, and that the targets would be assaulted simultaneously, rather than dropping the paratroops first to secure landing areas for the gliders. Additionally, the airborne troops were to be dropped directly on their targets, thus avoiding the need to cross expanses of enemy-held territory to gain the objectives. Consequently, it was necessary to neutralize as many antiaircraft positions as possible. The objective was not for the airborne forces to establish a bridgehead but rather for them to link up with bridgeheads already held by land forces to strengthen and consolidate the Allied presence on the east bank.

The operations were carried out by the U.S. 17th Airborne Division and the British 6th Airborne Division, both assigned to the XVIII Airborne Corps under the command of Matthew B. Ridgway. The troopers of both divisions were battle-experienced veterans, many of whom had participated in the airborne operations in Normandy almost ten months previously. A large number of the troops had recently gained experience during the fighting in Belgium and Holland.

Despite the inherent dangers in conducting the airborne operation, the Allies were confident they could overwhelm the beleaguered defenders with a combined British-American strength of more than 20,000 airborne combatants. The British

6th Airborne Division consisted of two parachute brigades, each having a strength of more than 1,800 men, including a staff company equipped with four 76-mm mortars and four heavy Vickers machine guns. In addition to the parachute brigades, the division included an airborne brigade of 2,600 men equipped with twelve 76-mm mortars, four heavy machine guns, and a company of eight 57-mm antitank guns. Added to these lightly armed units was the 53rd (Worcestershire Yeomanry) Airlanding Light Regiment, equipped with twenty-four 75-mm howitzers and four 105-mm mortars; an airborne reconnaissance regiment with eight Locust battle tanks, eight motorcycles, and four jeeps; a pathfinder company; antiaircraft batteries; an airborne engineer company; an airborne logistics company; a communications company; the 195th Airlanding field ambulance; two parachute field ambulances; a military police company; and an intelligence and information team.[1]

The U.S. 17th Airborne Division, commanded by General William M. Miley, consisted of two regiments of 2,364 men each, forming a total of six battalions. Each of the battalions was augmented by a support company with an 81-mm mortar platoon and two .30-caliber machine-gun platoons. The 194th Glider Infantry Regiment fielded 3,000 troops, including the regimental staff, an antitank company, and three infantry battalions. The 17th Airborne was the first division in the European theater to be equipped with the new 57-mm recoilless rifles, intended to compliment the standard 75-mm light howitzer. The division was also equipped with twelve 57-mm antitank guns, twelve 75-mm antitank guns, and thirty-six .50-caliber antiaircraft machine guns. In addition, the division was assigned four airborne artillery battalions with twenty-four 75-mm howitzers, an airborne engineer battalion, an airborne communications company, a medical company, a reconnaissance company, a supply company, a replacement and repair company, and a military police platoon.

The bulk of the equipment for the British troops was to be delivered by some 400 Horsa gliders and almost 50 massive Hamilcar gliders packed with weapons, vehicles, and troops, all of which were towed by bomber aircraft. The Americans were using more than 900 smaller Waco gliders, each of which could carry 14 men, a jeep, or a howitzer. The Wacos were towed in pairs by C-47 transport aircraft. The combined British-American force had more than 1,300 gliders towed by almost 900 aircraft.

The paratroopers were provided with 650 transport aircraft, most of which were 18-man C-47 Dakotas. The remainder were new C-46s, which were receiving their baptism on this operation. The C-46s were capable of carrying 36 paratroopers each; the "sticks"—groups of paratroopers assigned to jump together—sprang from doors on each side of the aircraft for a faster, more accurate delivery.

An uneasy calm, broken only by the droning of the aircraft engines, settled over the area as the artillery barrage lifted on the pastures and fields. At 10:20 a.m., the first gliders of the 194th Glider Infantry circled to earth and broke through the underbrush in the wooded area west of the Issel Canal bridges. The aircraft immediately met a torrent of fire from hidden German positions. Some of the gliders landed in open areas or crashed through farm fences. Others descended into heavily wooded areas where they broke into pieces, scattering equipment and the bodies of the paratroopers over wide areas. A number of the fragile aircraft were riddled with holes from numerous small arms, crashing into heaps of crumpled canvas and equipment long before reaching their landing zones.

Accompanying the gliders, in separate formations, were transports carrying thousands of paratroopers. Lieutenant Max Mohr was positioned between the villages of Bergerfurth and Mehrhoog with Battalion 1, Fallschirm-Artillerie Regiment 7, as the transports appeared in the sky. The officer had been engaged throughout the previous days reconnoitering the area and carefully noting all locations in his sector that would be favorable for an airborne drop. He had taken special notice of a rectangular area on his map between central Mehrhoog in the north and the Diersfordter Forest in the south. Noting that the Allies would probably identify it as a drop zone, he transferred three batteries of antiaircraft artillery to the concealment of nearby woods, within easy range of the possible landing area.

On the morning of 24 March, the artillery barrage lifted at approximately 10:00, and Mohr's suspicions were confirmed by the sound of approaching aircraft. The lieutenant immediately sprang from his bunker and was met by the terrifying sight of hundreds of variously colored parachutes hanging in the air. In the distance, he could hear the rattling of small-arms fire accompanied by explosions as heavy flak batteries sought low-level targets. Mohr sped to his number two battery, situated in a small copse west of Reichsstrasse 8, and found his gun crews frantically rotating the barrels of the weapons toward the east, behind their positions. The battery immediately opened fire on the open ground in front of the third battery sector in an attempt to relieve the beleaguered crews, who were under heavy attack in a small area of trees known as Hingendahl's Woods. The ill-fated third battery was directly in the drop zone of the British and Canadian paratroops assigned to neutralize and secure the DZ for follow-on landings.

The paratroopers immediately located the source of the heavy fire, and they attacked the battery from the south edge of Diersfordter Forest. The first attack was unsuccessful, and the commander of the paratroopers' B Company, Major Kippin, fell mortally wounded in the German fire. As the fighting increased in intensity, more British forces converged on the area to neutralize the zone. Within an hour, the copse was secured and the German positions were filled with dead and wounded.[2]

Bitter fighting continued throughout the area as sticks of paratroopers descended. The Canadian 1st Parachute Battalion was widely scattered as the transport pilots overshot the drop zones in their attempt to survive the antiaircraft fire. The air surrounding the falling parachutes cracked with the sound of bullets rising from the woods below. Many of the troops, swinging in their harnesses, were carried directly above the German positions by a gentle breeze that sent them into the sights and effective range of the enemy weapons. The woods reverberated with the explosions and ripping bursts of vicious, close-quarters combat. Lieutenant Colonel Nicklin, the Canadian battalion commander, was found dead in his harness, hanging from the crown of a tree. The battalion chaplain, Captain Kenny, was killed before his body touched ground.

The Germans fired at any target in the sky, desperate to kill as many of the invaders as possible before they landed. For ground troops, paratroops represent an extraordinary foe. Almost always composed of volunteers with high morale who are dedicated to their mission, their units are specially trained to overcome adversity and to fight against numerical odds. To the ground forces who find themselves the target of an airborne operation, a paratrooper is a dangerous and viable enemy as long as he is mobile and unwounded. Trained for combat in small units with little material support, airborne troops represent the best of a quick-reaction force that will kill the enemy wherever the enemy can be found. For the paratroopers swinging below their canopies as they descended toward the German defenses, there was no surrender. The German troops, especially the veterans of Normandy and Market-Garden, realized that if the enemy reached the ground safely and gained the cover of trees or sheltering terrain features below their line of sight, they would rapidly organize into combat groups and proceed to eliminate the pockets of defenders.

The survivors of the deadly drop quickly assembled into platoons and companies. They were guided to their rallying points by colored clouds of smoke billowing from portable smoke pots. Clearing the drop zone as quickly as possible, they proceeded toward their objectives in the village of Bergerfurth and in Diersfordter Forest. During the clearing operations, the paratroops came under fire from German positions in the copses to the north and from the village of Mehrhoog as they attempted to retrieve wounded from their drop zone before the areas were cleared.

The first American paratroopers of the 507th Airborne Regiment descended to earth near Diersfordt. The 507th, the 464th Parachute Artillery Battalion, and the three infantry battalions were to secure drop zone "W" (DZ W), north of Grav Island. Visibility was lost due to heavy smoke billowing along the Rhine, caused by the artillery barrages and the bombing raid on the hapless town of Wesel. Unable to see the DZ, the pilots waited an extra ninety seconds before switching on the green light that signaled the paratroopers to drop. The men were strewn northwest of Diersfordt between Schüttwich and the perimeter of Diersfordter Forest.

On touching ground, the battalion commander, Major Paul F. Smith, was quick to gather a force of men and attack a nearby artillery position. The remainder of the force, led by the regimental commander, Colonel Raff, assaulted an artillery battery adjacent to the forest. During the capture of the battery, his men killed fifty-five Germans and took numerous prisoners. The colonel then mustered more men for an attack against Schloss Diersfordt, an ancient manor surrounded by massive trees, a cemetery, and numerous buildings. After approaching the estate through the heavily wooded terrain, the American paratroopers discovered that the position had been previously attacked by the 3rd Battalion of the 507th Airborne Regiment. The 2nd and 3rd Battalions of the 507th Airborne Regiment, together with the airborne artillery battalion, had landed on DZ W near Flüren. The troops of the 3rd Battalion, originally assigned to take the manor and secure the surrounding buildings, had made their way through the Diersfordter Forest and had attacked their objective, using their new 57-mm recoilless rifles to disable a pair of German assault guns. In the area of Diersfordt, they captured some 300 prisoners, including a staff officer from the 84th Infantry Division.[3]

The last paratroopers descended to earth at 1:04 p.m., and contact was soon established with the British commandos fighting near Wesel. The British 6th Parachute Division linked up with the forward elements of the 15th Division to capture the village of Hamminkeln, south of Wesel. Of the invading forces, the 51st suffered the highest casualties. The men of that division found themselves engaged in heavy fighting against German paratroopers in the fully destroyed town of Rees, and the commander of the British division died in the fight. After suppressing the German defenders in Rees, the 51st pushed farther toward the east. By the afternoon of 24 March, the British troops were on the approaches to the Münster plateau, south of where the Canadians had succeeded in creating a large breakthrough between Millingen and Anholt.

The U.S. 513th Airborne Regiment was the fourth and last unit to be dropped into the Lower Rhine area. The troops were dropped from seventy-two C-46 transports; their target was drop zone "X" (DZ X), the wide expanse of fields and pastureland between the Wesel-Emmerich and Wesel-Bocholt railway lines. The planes were met by heavy antiaircraft fire while flying over the smoke-covered drop zone. Attempting to avoid destruction by the intense flak, the pilots lost orientation and scattered the three battalions over a wide area near Hamminkeln. The wide expanse of open area had previously been designated landing zones "P" and "R" and had been assigned to the British gliders. Fourteen of the transports were shot down before they were able to return to their bases. An additional thirty-eight limped out of the battle area, their fuselages riddled with holes from the heavy flak encountered over the Lower Rhine.[4]

The paratroops of the 513th organized into small battle groups and secured the landing zone for the oncoming gliders. They succeeded in neutralizing a number of flak positions, possibly sparing the British a large number of casualties. The 600 men and twelve 75-mm field guns of the 466th Airborne Artillery Regiment, intended to follow up the airborne drop at DZ X, arrived over the drop zone in the cumbersome C-47s and were strewn across both sides of the Wesel-Emmerich railway. As the paratroopers of the 513th had missed this DZ and thus failed to neutralize the German positions nearby, the artillerymen immediately came under heavy fire from still-intact antiaircraft batteries and isolated German units. The Germans had to be cleared from their defenses along the trees and hedges lining the railway. As the gliders intended for LZ S began to sail to earth during the engagement, many were struck by incendiary rounds and were consumed by flames, with the troops unable to free themselves from the wreckage. As minutes passed, the Americans were able to bring their mortars and .50-caliber machine guns into action, and within a half hour, the landing zone was neutralized. The artillerymen were able to establish positions 300 yards west of the Hamminkeln-Wesel road, where they opened fire on preplanned positions.

Wilhelmine Renken, from the nearby village of Lackhausen, had experienced the war firsthand over the preceding weeks. Lackhausen had suffered an extraordinarily heavy air raid the night of 7 March, during which waves of aircraft had appeared at five-minute intervals to drop tons of bombs on the hapless inhabitants, leveling buildings and setting fires in the ruins. The following morning, she and her family had emerged from their cellar and fled the town for Hamminkeln to stay with relatives. On the evening of 22 March, artillery barrages blanketed the area from Hamminkeln to Bislich while Wilhelmine crouched in a cellar with another woman, two children, and her seventeen-year-old niece. Her thoughts were with her husband, who was serving with a provisional defense unit near Bislich, and her eldest daughter, who was serving somewhere with a flak unit. As the barrage increased in intensity, she nervously scribbled a last note to her family members, rolled it tightly, and stuck it into a beer bottle, which she then concealed some 40 yards from the house in a location the family had previously discussed.

As she was returning to the house, she observed two German soldiers approaching the residence, their helmets and shouldered rifles silhouetted against the burning horizon. In the process of positioning an assault gun near the home, the soldiers advised her that enemy troops had already entered the town. Allied patrols had reached the school on the Brüner Landstrasse, and the soldiers' unit had been dispatched to defend the sector. The situation for the civilians remained very precarious. Other than this advice, the two men could offer no assistance.

The shelling subsided with the arrival of dawn. The familiar drone of approaching aircraft could be heard, and the civilians cowering in the cellar were gripped with fear and uneasy expectation. To their surprise, however, no bombs were released and no explosions could be discerned. As the rumble of engines grew louder, several of the women glanced out of the cellar window, where they were horrified to see hundreds of gliders circling the sky. The gliders seemed to descend without direction or specific purpose, landing at random wherever one happened to glance. The women watched a number of Allied soldiers with upraised arms being led away by the German gun crew several hundred yards from the house. Within minutes, they heard a pounding on the door and were soon gruffly ordered out of the cellar in a mixture of English and broken German. They found themselves marching into the field with hands held high above their heads.

The civilians were led onto an open field behind the Bossigt Manor, where they took cover from several marauding fighter-bombers. Their heavily armed guards joined in firing across the field at an unseen target, and soon, a small group of German soldiers timidly approached, carrying a white cloth suspended from a stick. The air continued to crack with bullets flying overhead, and the tiny group of civilians pressed close together as someone began reading from a Catholic prayer book. The others joined Wilhelmine in prayer. Suddenly, a man nearby was struck by a bullet, and several American soldiers appeared and dressed the wound before carrying him away on a stretcher.

Soon, the first dead were carried across the field. The lifeless bodies in khaki left trails of blood on the short grass. That evening, the detainees were permitted to return to their home, and it became clear why they had been forced to leave. The building was pockmarked with bullet holes, and the entire area was covered with shell craters. Small armored vehicles, many still burning, lay scattered through the neighborhood. The smell of scorched flesh and blood hung in the air. Near the German gun lay the mangled corpses of the two Wehrmacht soldiers who had attempted to warn them of the oncoming engagement.[5]

Within forty minutes, the Allies had dropped almost 10,000 paratroopers over the Diersfordter Forest, and the sky filled with gliders bringing reinforcements in men and material. From a distance, the gliders appeared to be hanging almost motionless overhead, barely moving on air currents as they circled and descended to earth. Skidding on fuselages and towing break chutes, they plowed through thickets and farm fences before sliding to a stop. Many of the planes were riddled with bullet holes before completing their descent; others came under fire as they slid through fences and trees, tearing off wings and ripping long holes in the canvas and wood frames. Others plowed into farmers' fields, skidding hundreds of yards and leaving long furrows in the dark Westphalian soil before coming to a gentle stop.

The German positions that had survived the artillery barrages and assaults by paratroopers now sprang into action. The fields and tree lines came under fire from hidden mortar positions. Fountains of soil exploded skyward as the mortars impacted in the landing area. Some of the gliders, heavily riddled with bullet holes and trailing long strips of fuselage fabric as they descended to earth, struck heavily, slid to a stop, and remained still, all those on board either dead or wounded. Others attracted ground fire as the troops poured from the battered aircraft. Red tracer bullets bounced and streaked across the open ground as German machine gunners sought their targets. Many of the gliders burned fiercely, the screams of trapped inhabitants lost in the sounds of roaring flames and exploding ammunition as thick clouds of greasy black smoke billowed upward.

The target for the almost 600 gliders transporting the 194th Airborne Infantry Regiment and the 680th and 681st Airborne Artillery Battalions was LZ S. This zone extended from the village of Blumenkamp toward the east, over the Issel River, where the 300 troops of the 194th were assigned to secure a series of bridges over the river. Glider pilot Roger Krey noticed that the left motor of the C-47 towing his aircraft was trailing a thick cloud of smoke as they approached the LZ. The transport's motor soon stopped, leaving the propeller twisting slowly in the slipstream as the aircraft labored to continue pulling its cargo of troops and equipment. His copilot, Bill Lane, sought to find an opening in the smoke shrouding the ground beneath them, although it was clear that they had crossed the Rhine and had to be over their target area. Both gliders released their towing cables, and the aircraft sank slowly through the screen of smoke. As they penetrated the oily cloud, they observed a multihued expanse of earth rising to meet them. The gliders came under German automatic-weapons fire on clearing the smoke screen, with red tracers appearing to rise lazily to meet them from the expanses of foliage. As Lane fought to keep the aircraft on course through the smoke and machine-gun fire, he was astonished to hear the eleven soldiers in the fuselage break into a chorus of "Hail, Hail, the Gang's All Here." The pretentious singing continued until a 20-mm antiaircraft round suddenly exploded directly in front of the nose of the glider, saturating the air with splinters of white-hot shrapnel and extinguishing the nervous bravado that, only seconds earlier, had filled the aircraft.[6]

Feeling a burning sensation, Krey realized that he had received shell splinters in his head, neck, and shoulder, and his copilot had been struck in the foot. As he regained composure, he noted that the aircraft was still airborne and flyable, and he continued to steer it toward the earth. Suddenly, the splintered windshield was filled with brilliant sunlight, and the two pilots were shocked to see the tall mast of a power pole looming before them, from which a large number of tightly stretched, high-tension wires were extended. Too low to glide over the lines, they guided the aircraft below the wires in an arch, increasing the speed dangerously until the pilot pulled the red handle to release the brake chute, bringing the speed under control. He then pulled the yellow release lever, and with a lunge, the brake chute was cut away as Lane steadied the aircraft for a landing. The glider struck the earth with a thud and slid across a wide expanse of open field before coming to a stop. The two pilots realized that they were still taking fire as their passengers piled from the two doors in the fuselage of the glider.

The pilots unbuckled their safety belts, grabbed their weapons, and lurched back toward the doors to exit the aircraft. Not knowing from which direction they were taking fire, they waited several seconds before springing out of the aircraft and throwing themselves on the ground. Luckily, they had chosen to exit through the starboard door, which faced away from the hail of fire that surrounded the aircraft. Lying on the ground, Krey knew at once that their situation was tenuous. Both the lieutenant and the platoon sergeant, the senior of the ten infantrymen in the machine, had exited through the left door and been struck instantly by automatic-weapons fire. As they both lay immobilized in the line of fire, the lieutenant screamed over the sound of the shots for the pilots not to do anything that might attract more fire to the beleaguered platoon. The pilots were left with no alternative but to lie helpless by the aircraft and wait.[7]

The German gunners were drawn to new targets as more aircraft descended to earth. One of the nearby infantrymen called to the pilots that it would be best to try to shift positions. After retrieving mortar ammunition from the glider, the infantryman and the pilots dashed to the safety of a nearby tree line.

Landing zone S remained under sporadic fire most of the afternoon. Groups of infantrymen assembled and began to assault their objectives, herding groups of prisoners with upraised arms into assembly areas. The airborne artillery battalions recovered their guns, established firebases and battery positions, and were soon lending support to the infantry.

At noon, some 300 gliders carrying troops and support equipment approached landing zone N under fire. LZ N lay to the north of DZ X and formed a rough triangle between an area known locally as the Schwarzen Wasser, the Diersfordt rail station, and the Am Weissenstein inn. The immediate area had been secured by the artillery battalion that had been misdropped, but beyond the perimeter of the LZ, many German antiaircraft positions remained active. One of the gliders, packed with explosives intended for the 139th Airborne Engineer Battalion, was struck by incendiary bullets on approach, causing the aircraft to explode with a massive roar. Other gliders, attempting to avoid the hail of fire directed at them from unseen batteries, impacted at excessive speeds and broke apart, scattering men and equipment along their path. Yet sufficient numbers of the gliders made it safely to earth to enable crews and staffs to immediately set about performing their tasks. An entire field medical unit was transported to the landing zone in fifty gliders, and the medical facility, complete with surgical capabilities, was operational within an hour of landing. German prisoners, many of them relieved to have fallen safely into captivity, were set to work bearing the wounded. Wehrmacht medical officers and medics, previously quartered at the large Huvermann farmhouse, worked alongside American surgeons tending to wounded German soldiers in some of the tents.

British glider formations came under fire as they approached their designated landing zones. As a formation approached landing zone O, one glider was struck by a burst of antiaircraft fire and simply fell apart, scattering men and equipment across the sky at an altitude of 2,000 feet. At the Hamminkeln rail station, a German antiaircraft battery was overrun by British forces after the Germans attempted to defend their position in vicious close combat. Other British units were assigned to seize the small railway bridge over the Issel, and still others targeted the road bridge on the east bank of the Issel leading to the town of Ringenberg. By 11:40 a.m., the British forces assigned to LZ O had secured all their objectives, at the cost of more than 100 killed and many more wounded. By day's end, the battalion commander, Lieutenant Colonel Carell-Brown, reported that all four companies had lost almost half their operational strength.

Heavy fighting enveloped the area of Hamminkeln as gliders descended on LZ U to the southeast and LZ R to the southwest of the small town. At LZ R, the American 513th Regiment, inadvertently dropped on the wrong LZ, joined forces with British paratroops to clear and secure objectives. The Allied forces secured LZ P near the village of Köpenhof, designated for the British staff and support units, and prepared to receive the Hamilcar and heavy Horsa gliders. The British landing was not without problems. More than half of the gliders, many carrying armored vehicles in the Horsas, landed outside the landing zone. The American forces had previously cleared the zone of enemy forces, and by 11:00 a.m., the staff and supply personnel were conducting their duties near the LZ.

Gliders also descended on drop zones A and B, where British paratroopers had earlier landed under a blanket of smoke. Some twenty large Hamilcar gliders, originally destined for LZ P, landed at drop zones A and B. A number of the aircraft crashed on landing, killing the occupants and destroying the valuable equipment. The pilot of a massive Horsa carrying medical personnel and equipment underestimated the altitude and speed, and his glider burst on landing, killing or injuring all the medical personnel on board. In the nearby village of Bergerfurth, the Canadians captured 700 German prisoners before establishing a command post in the village schoolhouse. The medics situated an aid station in the village church, using the pastor's kitchen and living quarters as operating rooms. The main sanctuary was heavily damaged by shelling and small-arms fire, with the floor covered with broken glass, splintered pews, damaged religious artifacts, and scorched hymnals. Several dozen German prisoners were set to work cleaning the main building to be used as a medical reception area and for treating the lightly wounded. Other prisoners were tasked with digging trenches and earthworks. By 2:30 p.m., the surgical facility was in operation, supplied by materials carried by the paratroops during their jump or flown in by glider. Every man assigned to the medical staff had carried a unit of plasma along with surgical instruments. Ether, chloroform, penicillin, sulpha, Pentothal, and other medical supplies were carried by the medics in their jump packs as they were inserted into the DZ. Within forty-five hours of establishing the field hospital, staff surgeons Major Daintree-Johnson and Major Miller had performed twenty-eight operations, enabling twenty-three badly wounded soldiers to survive.

At 1:00 p.m., the throbbing of heavy motors was again heard approaching from the west as waves of Liberators approached the Diersfordter Forest. On this occasion, hundreds of bombers, dropping to less than 500 feet, released thousands of supply containers that descended to earth on parachutes that were color-coded to indicate their contents. The supplies, destined for specific drop zones and landing zones, were strewn widely throughout the area. Some 600 tons of Allied equipment were strewn over the Diersfordter Forest, of which only about a third could be recovered by the American and British troops. The difficulties encountered in retrieving the supplies were exacerbated by hidden antiaircraft guns that, despite detailed preparations by the Allies, remained stubbornly active. The large, low-flying Liberators made easy targets for the German gunners, who opened fire with automatic weapons loaded with high-explosive and incendiary ammunition. More than 100 aircraft were struck with shrapnel and shell splinters as they flew over the target area before limping back toward the west. A total of 15 aircraft crashed or made emergency landings after crossing to safety west of the Rhine.

By the afternoon, the defenders in the Diersfordter Forest were isolated, cut off from the bulk of the German forces. Most of the Allied objectives had been secured within three hours after the onset of the airborne operations. The town of Hamminkeln, controlling an important road junction north of Wesel, was finally in British hands. Many of the town's citizens cowered in their cellars for most of the day; a sizable group took refuge in the large ice vault of the Kloppert brewery just outside the town perimeter. As the British forces slowly made their way toward Hamminkeln, they forced the inhabitants out of their bunkers and cellars, taking into custody a number of men they suspected of being German soldiers who had hastily donned civilian clothing.

By Saturday evening, the British had collected some 300 women and children in the town's evangelical church, where they remained separated from a smaller number of men who were under watch in another room. The civilians were isolated in the confines of the church until the following day, when artillery shells fired from German batteries near Ringenberg began falling in the area. When the British troops attempted to establish an artillery observation team in the church tower, they provoked a wave of protests from the women, who believed that they would be further endangered by the presence of the observers. A Dutch officer in British uniform who was serving as a translator attempted to calm the crowd. He was explaining that the German forces were aware the church was occupied by civilians when an immense artillery shell detonated adjacent to the churchyard, sending plaster and shattered glass to the floor. The crowded hall rang with cries and screams as more shell splinters crashed through the windows and struck the heavy masonry. The air filled with dust and smoke, and the clamor grew as the crowd desperately sought shelter.

Fearing that the conditions inside the church would only lead to injury and death, the British guards opened the doors and permitted the crowd to leave to seek shelter in a more protected building. The women and children fled through the sounds of artillery shell-bursts to the Kloppert brewery cellar. Others found shelter in the large vaulted cellar of the Neu Gasthof. The inhabitants remained clustered in these shelters until the next day, when the British authorities permitted them to return to their homes. The residents then learned that during the artillery barrage, three women, a boy, and one of the men who had taken shelter in the Neu hotel cellar had been killed; a girl had lost a leg; and others had suffered less extensive injuries.

Klara Brömmling cowered behind her home with her parents, six siblings, and a German soldier in a homemade air raid shelter as the paratroopers began descending from the sky, followed by waves of gliders. Her father tied a white handkerchief to a short stick and waved it frantically as the group emerged from the shelter with their arms over their heads. The British soldiers separated the uniformed soldier from the civilians and led him away; the family was herded into the foyer of the home.

The first squad of soldiers was followed by others, and the residence was soon filled with strange soldiers wearing flat helmets and khaki uniforms. The family was advised that they were to be transported to the Catholic church at 7:00 p.m. That evening, all inhabitants of the Sossmühlenstrasse were taken to the chapel, where they joined some ninety-eight other civilians. They were provided a meal of bread, butter, sausage, and milk. Klara and her neighbor, Christine Zerene, prepared sandwiches while her mother made coffee. Throughout the night and following day, small-arms fire reverberated through the area, shells impacted, and soldiers came and went. A British observer remained perched in the church bell tower; when an elderly man attempted to depart by a side door, he received a wound in the leg. Klara was eventually told to accompany several British soldiers to the van Nahmen and Köster stores in an attempt to locate food. They found only a small quantity of sausage, rice, and sugar.

The constant shelling of Hamminkeln and other Allied-held areas confirmed the inhabitants' fears that the fighting would continue. The Wehrmacht had not conceded the Allied bridgeheads on the east bank of the Rhine as lost. The paratroopers clung to the positions gained in the landings and linked up with the infantrymen probing farther inland from the landing areas, but the tenuous hold on the east bank could be broken at any time. As of dawn on 24 March, there still was no heavy Allied armor on the Lower Rhine bridgeheads, and the danger of a German counterattack was acute.

The scattered German units, separated by airborne units and the expanding bridgeheads, made sporadic attempts to strike back at the Allies. Unable to communicate effectively and paralyzed during daylight hours by swarms of fighter-bombers, small patrols of German soldiers crept through wooded areas, probed villages and towns, and positioned snipers in advantageous positions in an attempt to contain the invasion. However, the sense of hopelessness grew as the Allies strengthened their grip on the east bank. Without an organized counterattack supported by armor, many of the Germans realized that the Allies were there to stay.

During the night of 24–25 March, the American force that had established makeshift defenses along the Issel was augmented by a number of glider pilots with only rudimentary infantry training. The pilots established their defenses near a local inn known as Am Lauerhaas, situated on the Wesel-Brünen road. As darkness fell, a group of German stragglers banded together and left the outskirts of Wesel with the intention of penetrating the perimeter toward the northwest and thereby escape the noose created by the airborne landings.

Lieutenant Bull Ryman had piloted his glider onto the expanse of open field near the road earlier in the day, and together with several other airmen, he decided to spend the night in a foxhole near an abandoned German farmhouse. The foxhole was well concealed by heavy undergrowth. Nearby was a massive bomb crater that offered them a free field of fire if needed. After consuming a sparse meal of K rations, the men curled up under the protection of the thicket and attempted to sleep. It was not an easy endeavor. The night skies were alive with intermittent flares shooting skyward. Isolated rifle shots were heard, and machine guns fired bursts of tracers that ricocheted and bounced against the black horizon. Ryman was startled awake by a hand pressed firmly against his mouth, but before panic overcame him, he realized it was another member of the tiny force who was whispering unintelligibly. He was slowly able to discern the face of one of the crewmen, only inches from his own, and the soldier put his finger to his lips. The pilot lay still and realized that he, too, could hear muffled voices and hurried footsteps moving close by. Reaching to his chest, he cautiously removed his .45 service automatic from his shoulder holster and with pounding heart forced himself to lie still until the unintelligible voices and rapid footsteps faded into the darkness.[8]

In the nearby town of Drevenack, Elfriede Emmerichs bid farewell to the Schless and Bauhaus families, who had elected to pack a few remaining possessions and flee the area. They had already heard rumors of the Rhine crossings at Rees, Bislich, and Wesel, and they had even been told that following a series of bitter firefights, the British troops had been driven from Wesel. Now, on Palm Sunday, they witnessed the unwelcome arrival of Wehrmacht troops. In the early dawn, they were alerted by the presence of dozens of German soldiers, who dug earthworks near the house and established machine-gun positions. The troops collected quantities of ammunition and stacked numerous field-gray Panzerfausts. During a hasty conversation, the women received the impression that the soldiers were thoroughly demoralized; some indicated that they carried white handkerchiefs with them and intended to surrender at the first opportunity. One of the older soldiers attempted to persuade his superior to permit him to depart on a bicycle to visit to his family in Bocholt, whom he had not seen since the previous November. The plea was refused.

Fleets of aircraft passed overhead during the late morning, flying on the customary eastward course. The artillery fire had ceased, and in the distance, numerous gliders were seen circling like flocks of vultures, slowly descending to disappear behind distant trees and terrain features. Several of the slow-moving aircraft were struck by German flak projectiles, and the damaged aircraft trailed long plumes of black smoke as the rhythmic pounding of distant antiaircraft batteries reverberated softly through the area.

As the hours passed, the group of women and children heard new rumors that the British were in Dülmen, only 2.5 miles distant. The evacuees had already packed their bags and had loaded a hand-cart with possessions. However, they resisted the idea of leaving the familiar shelter of the home. That evening, they decided to wait, and the group crowded into the cellar to sleep.

At two o'clock in the morning, Elfriede was startled awake by footsteps and shouting voices. She rushed to the front door and cautiously opened it to find a very young and frightened flak lieutenant accompanied by a sergeant. The nervous soldiers asked directions to the Luels's farm. They explained that, unable to find the roadway in the darkness, the vehicle towing their antiaircraft gun had capsized in a ditch, so they were desperately seeking a team of horses. The lieutenant also added that they were assigned to establish an antiaircraft position nearby; they had been ordered to defend their position to the last man. Elfriede quickly explained the way to the farm, and the two disappeared into the darkness.

She closed the door behind them and returned to the cellar, where she hoped to gain at least a few minutes of sleep.[9]

The occupants of the cellar were again awakened at 4:00 a.m. Loud voices were heard outside the home, and the unwelcome hammering on the door resounded through the crowded rooms. Elfriede's father and uncle made their way through the darkened building and hesitantly opened the front door. For several long minutes, hushed voices were heard from the doorway. Tension continued to build before the two men returned to the waiting civilians. The strangers at the door had brought instructions from the *Ortsbauernführer* ("district farm leader") that all inhabitants were to be evacuated. One of every four farmers was required to organize the livestock into herds, and the animals were to be driven toward the east in the direction of Minden. The two farmers only shook their heads in resignation.[10]

As the bridgeheads continued to slowly expand, the attackers and defenders became interspersed, adding to the confusion that descended on the Lower Rhine. The Canadian Highland Light Infantry began probing the outskirts of the village of Bienen, where the multitude of buildings offered both attackers and defenders concealment. After the first careful probes by foot patrols, the Canadian infantrymen were followed by light armored personnel carriers as the village erupted in firefights between isolated German troops and the methodically advancing Canadians.

Maria Becker and her family had been hiding in the cellar of her home in Bienen on the previous Friday when a German soldier requested that they move to the vaulted cellar of the Aryus inn. There, they found Maria's sister crowded within the confines of the structure, along with what appeared to be the entire civilian population of the village. They spent a largely sleepless night in the stifling confines, and at daylight, they were jolted out of a slumber by the piercing sound of tank tracks clattering on the brick pavement. Several German armored vehicles were taking position in the narrow streets near the churchyard, one of which had driven into a large manure pile, a typical feature of German farmyards. The vehicle nosed into the stinking morass and burrowed forward, burying itself up to the crests of the tracks for added concealment. Shortly thereafter, a swarm of fighter-bombers descended on the village in numerous strafing runs, blasting the houses with machine-gun fire and dropping bombs on suspected targets.

One of the tanks that had parked next to Maria's parents' home exploded into flames as a bomb struck the vulnerable deck armor, sending hot metal and exploding ammunition for dozens of yards in all directions. The screams of the trapped tank crew quickly subsided as the vehicle was consumed by flames. The refugees cowered in the cellar as bullets and shells crashed through walls and windows above them. Suddenly, a German paratrooper who had also taken refuge in the

Aryus inn stormed up the stairwell, leaped onto a sputtering phosphorus shell, and hurled it out the window before it could ignite the building. The soldier had heard the hissing of the phosphorus above the din of ordnance exploding beyond the building. The projectile would have burst at any second, sending white-hot fragments in all directions and immediately engulfing the building in flames.

The civilians who had been hiding in the cellar, knowing that the Allied infantry was drawing nearer, attempted to hang a white sheet from an upstairs window of the inn, but they retreated back to the corner of the cellar under threats from one of the paratroopers. The soldiers did not desire to surrender, but all were aware of what would occur if they chose to stay and offer resistance. The village would be destroyed, and many people would possibly lose their lives; at the very least, there would be numerous injuries.

At long last, the paratroopers, tired of hearing the pleas from the civilians, decided to withdraw. They gathered up their arms and equipment and stomped up the steep stairwell to the large dining area of the inn, where they waited hesitantly while shells continued to fall nearby. Suddenly, a shell slammed through a wall and exploded, leaving dead and wounded strewn about the floor. One of the dead was Heinz Otto, a flak soldier who had been quartered in the neighborhood and was well known to the civilians hiding in the cellar. Another soldier known only to the civilians as Mössthaler tumbled down the staircase, badly wounded from shell splinters. The group of women carried the him into the cellar and laid him on the floor, where they attempted to bind his wounds with strips of cloth torn from a bedsheet. For several minutes, he screamed and convulsed with pain while crying for his mother. The women were unable to staunch the bleeding, and the soldier's cries grew weaker as he slowly bled to death. Chaos engulfed the inn as other wounded were carried in or were helped to make their way into the cellar, where the women spent the next several minutes attempting to render them aid.

Canadian infantrymen appeared shortly after the shell exploded in the building. The first to arrive were weary, nervous, and impatient. A giant figure clad in a rain-soaked khaki uniform kicked the door open and, over the shrieking of the wounded lying on the cellar floor, demanded to know if any German soldiers were present, calling, "Hands up! Soldat hier?!" The women and elderly men raised their arms and, in a chorus of broken English, attempted to explain that there were only civilians and badly wounded in the cellar. A teenaged Russian laborer named Sonya who had been occupying the cellar with her German overseers greeted the Canadians excitedly, knowing that she was finally liberated from her servitude.

The Canadians inspected the crowded cellar and stripped the wounded soldiers of their rings and watches before calling for medics to remove them from the building. The bodies of Heinz Otto and the other dead soldier were dragged outside to an unknown location. The wounded were then carried upstairs and loaded onto a truck parked outside the inn, where they remained until the following day. Long hours passed as the sounds of traffic and multitudes of soldiers meandering their way through the village continued. Hungry and exhausted, the refugees remained locked in the stifling confines of the crowded cellar. As hours passed, the fumes from expended ammunition, smoke from burning buildings, and the smell of dried blood became unbearable, and they covered their mouths and noses with handkerchiefs in an effort to breathe. During the night, more exhausted Canadian soldiers poured into the inn, where they threw themselves on the floor and fell into a deep sleep. The refugees remained pressed together in a corner of the cellar, listening to the low, haunting cries emanating from the wounded lying in the bed of the truck outside.[11]

The German forces, unable to halt the relentless expansion of the bridgehead and the linkup between airborne forces and the reinforced infantry units crossing the Rhine, were now in the process of disintegration. The woods and villages were filled with unorganized bands of stragglers, some of whom continued to offer sporadic resistance when led by experienced officers or NCOs. Other groups, consisting of elderly men, young boys, or foreigners who had been pressed into service with the Wehrmacht, chose to disappear and make their way back to their families or simply waited until the waves of Allied units engulfed them.

Elfriede Emmerichs remained in the shelter of her temporary home in Drevenack as the cellar filled with even more evacuees. That afternoon, she and several other women braved the explosions and dashed across the farmyard to care for the cattle locked in the barn before scurrying back to the safety of the cellar. Shortly before 6:00, they discerned the voices of children outside, and they opened the door to find Frau Neuhaus with a farmworker and Frau Scheiper with three children. The new arrivals explained that their own homes were constantly under fire and that Frau Scheiper's husband had been badly wounded by shell splinters. He had been evacuated by German soldiers that morning. No one knew where he was or even if he was still alive.

The group crowded in the dwelling only caught fragments of sleep whenever possible as distant battles raged. That afternoon, small-caliber mortar rounds, a light weapon as compared to the long-range artillery, had begun impacting nearby, indicating to the refugees that events were changing. Late in the evening, another group of German soldiers appeared and settled into the kitchen. Dirty, unshaven, and exhausted, the men presented a picture of defeat and demoralization. Elfriede was surprised to find a teenager named Willi Bruch from her neighborhood among the group. Willi was well known in the area, and he had been assigned to a mortar squad. Morose and defeated, the teenager wearily stated, "Today I fought for my country," and he bitterly spoke of how groups of grenadiers had surrendered en masse in Wesel. "Three companies from a single battalion ... No one wants to fight anymore ... Who wants to die at the last hour?" Presently, an NCO appeared, and with dragging feet and sagging shoulders, the tiny group of soldiers gathered up their weapons and filed out the door to disappear into the night.

Some new arrivals brought the total number of evacuees crouched in the cellar to eighteen. To escape the stifling conditions, Elfriede decided to sleep in the attached workshop, where she could at least lie down even though actual sleep was impossible. The shell-bursts continued at a distance, with errant explosions echoing nearby. She dozed off during the night and was awakened by a narrow beam of light flickering through the room. Springing upright with fear, she observed the dim silhouette of a German soldier standing near her. The stranger had squeezed through a cellar window and was obviously disappointed to find the building occupied. Shining his flashlight in various directions, he surveyed the contents of the room while he explained that the women should leave as quickly as possible. "It's terrible," he said. He described how the nearby woods were "filled with Poles and Russians ... in Obrighoven all homes were burned, women were beaten with rifle butts ... terrible things happened." He made it clear that they should flee to a safer area and that the Wehrmacht could no longer protect them. After inspecting the contents of the dwelling, the soldier disappeared. Following his departure, Elfriede was only filled with disgust with the knowledge that, in all probability, the last German soldier with whom she would speak was a straggler surprised in the act of looting.[12]

Chapter 7

Breakout toward the East

During Operations Plunder and Varsity across the Lower Rhine, the American casualty rate was 10 percent, the British more than 30 percent. Despite the heavy losses, Montgomery's Twenty-first Army Group now stood firmly on the east bank of the Rhine, where it established a wide front to be used as a bridgehead for sweeping across the north German plateau.

The Allies succinctly summed up the dire situation for the German population in millions of leaflets that were dropped over Germany on 28 March. Outlining the circumstances on both the Western and the Eastern Fronts, the leaflets read:

> The Situation
> on 28 March 1945
> WEST FRONT
> All German soldiers remaining on the left bank of the Rhine between Switzerland and Holland are prisoners of war of the Allies.
>
> Marshal Montgomery's bridgehead near Wesel is 35 kilometers wide and in some areas 20 kilometers deep. New units are streaming without interruption over numerous newly constructed bridges to the east bank.
>
> In the Remagen bridgehead General Hodge's troops have penetrated the German defensive front and have advanced 36 kilometers to Limburg on the Lahn. The city itself is in Allied hands.
>
> General Patton's advance over the Rhine at Oppenheim led to the fall of Darmstadt two days ago. The advanced armored elements of the Third U.S. Army have crossed the Main near Aschaffenburg. Other American units have entered Frankfurt.
>
> Until now more than 10,000 German soldiers have become prisoners of war every day during the month of March.
> EAST FRONT
> In East Prussia the German resistance in the area of Frischen Haffs has collapsed. During the past two days the Russians have captured 21,000 prisoners of war in this area.

South of Oppeln Marshal Schukov's forces have captured Leob-
schuetz and Neisse and after crossing Upper Silesia have penetrated
Czechoslovakia.

North of the Plattensee in Hungary the Russians have captured the
important transportation network Papa and are positioned 65 kilometers
from the Austrian border.[1]

With the crossings at Remagen and Wesel, the Allied armies now stood at
both the right and left flanks of Model's Army Group B. All attempts to destroy the
bridgehead in the south, at Remagen, had failed, and the Americans continued to
push increasing numbers of men and equipment over the Rhine. On 26 March
1945, the Allies orchestrated two simultaneous breakouts toward the east from the
Remagen and Wesel bridgeheads.

The German forces found it impossible to establish a defensive line to the
front of the rapidly moving Allied columns. Along the southern flank, the forward American elements were moving so quickly that the tanks bypassed every
point at which the Germans attempted to establish a defense. Within hours, the
American columns had passed Altenkirchen, Höhr-Grenzhausen, and Dierdorf,
and the post office switchboard operator in Montabaur reported American tanks
on the autobahn north of the city. Resistance had been reduced to isolated engagements by numerous small units, many of whom were simply fading away into
the hillsides of the Sauerland. An intact bridge was seized over the Lahn River at
Limburg, further opening the way on the autobahn toward Frankfurt.

As the American columns approached the town of Brilon, a hastily assembled unit of newly conscripted teenagers found themselves in a Wehrmacht basic
training center, or *Wehrtüchtigungslager*, anxiously attending a briefing by their
commander. "A small American unit has succeeded in escaping the fighting near
Remagen," he explained, "and [is] advancing toward this area from the south.
Within the next hours, you will prove that the Führer can rely upon you."

The teenagers, all between the ages of fifteen and seventeen, donned heavy
leather and canvas field equipment in a school building. During the previous
several weeks, they had received instructions in map and compass reading, small-
arms training, and lessons on communications procedures. After every bombing
raid, during which the classes were interrupted and the cohesion was lost for
several hours, a number of the young warriors disappeared into the surrounding
towns and countryside to attempt to return to their homes. Those who remained
found it increasingly difficult to believe in the promised "final victory" as they
observed the daily decimation in their ranks. Even the most basic necessities
became difficult to obtain. For several weeks, their diet had been reduced to a

watery cabbage soup, and the students found themselves shivering in thin, poor-quality uniforms in unheated buildings.

They noticed, too, that the attitudes of their instructors had grown increasingly somber. The teaching cadre consisted of battle-experienced officers and NCOs, most of whom had suffered debilitating wounds at the front. The instructors had now changed their casual work uniforms for combat equipment, and the students were hastily issued small-caliber training rifles. Several pistols were distributed, and a sprinkling of model 1898 Mauser rifles were obtained to augment their meager supply of weapons. Cases of hand grenades were removed from the storage bunkers; the wooden containers were opened, and the explosive primers were inserted for use. The threadbare company was issued two rapid-firing MG-42 machine guns, and several of the tallest students were given antiquated Czech rifles that almost dragged on the ground when carried by their slings over the shoulder.

The boys marched from the schoolyard through the narrow streets of Brilon. Desperate voices called softly to them from slightly opened doors and windows: "Boys ... take off, the Amis are coming. Get in here and change clothes!" But the files of frightened teenagers marched onward, their faces expressionless as they peered from under large Wehrmacht helmets that failed to conceal the apprehension in their eyes.

Hour after hour, they marched in textbook fashion. Suddenly, they received the unexpected order to reverse their direction, and they marched back to a village they had previously passed. Word quickly circulated through the nervous ranks that the Americans had arrived — three tanks and several jeeps. With pounding hearts, the trembling boys sought refuge in the foliage along a rise flanking the road, and soon, the rumble of approaching vehicles, accompanied by the ominous grinding of steel tracks, was heard. Peering through the brush, they counted the three tanks that had been reported. And then came more. An endless column of monstrous, olive-colored tanks rolled along the road, their ranks broken only by half-tracks and massive trucks filled with more troops.

Suddenly, an explosion split the air, and a cloud of smoke rose into the sky as a tank was struck by a Panzerfaust. With screaming brakes and engines grinding to a halt, the column stopped abruptly, and dozens of soldiers in rounded helmets sprang from the vehicles and took shelter in the roadside ditches below the boys' position. The machine guns and cannons on the tank turrets turned menacingly as they sought targets in the dawn, and seemingly in unison, all guns opened fire on the surrounding area.

The teenagers pressed themselves deeper to the earth as they prayed to survive the next moments. Within seconds, the terrain features and all buildings within sight had been riddled with fire from dozens of automatic weapons. As the firing slowly faded to intermittent bursts, the boys heard a hushed voice ordering them to throw away their weapons. The terrorized youths continued to lie motionless as several of the instructors raced toward the column of vehicles with upraised arms. "Don't shoot! Don't shoot!" they shouted desperately. "There are only children here—they aren't soldiers—only children!"

The bursts of fire faded until silence descended on the roadside, broken only by the occasional clatter of cartridge cases falling from the armored vehicles and the low throbbing of heavy engines. The first boys rose to their feet with their hands held high overhead as a tank wheeled from the column and approached the hedgerow, its exhausts belching smoke and the Detroit engine roaring over the clatter of heavy tracks. Other teenagers staggered to their feet on trembling legs. When all had risen from their positions, they began staggering forward under the load of combat equipment, urged on by GIs in khaki jackets toward the rear of the column. The boys were quickly herded onto the roadside, where a number of black soldiers, accompanied by guards with submachine guns at the ready, stripped them of their leather harnesses and cartridge belts, tossing the gear onto the roadside. Their clothing was quickly rifled, their rings and watches disappeared into the pockets of the captors, and their wallets were cursorily examined before being tossed on the ground.

The boys were led along the road to a nearby village, where they were motioned into a barn. As the group filed into the building, several of the boys slipped out the rear before guards were posted, and they quickly fled to the concealment of a hedgerow bordering an apple orchard. As dawn was breaking, the four escapees crept to a farmyard, where the farmer permitted them to seek shelter in his barn. He later provided them with a sparse meal of bread and milk, and the boys dozed in the straw until dusk. Still in their uniforms, the band of fugitives struck out through the darkness toward Brilon.

Sure that they had at long last cleared the American columns, the boys split into pairs as they made their way to their familiar villages and neighborhoods. One of the boys, confident that he had reached safety, strode boldly along a bend in the road and suddenly found himself confronted by a number of American soldiers manning a checkpoint. The teenager attempted to walk past, smiling innocently, until he was brought to a sharp halt by a command shouted in an unfamiliar language.

"You SS! You Hitler Youth!" one of the strangers exclaimed menacingly in broken German. "You hang!" The soldiers implied that they were searching for a convenient tree limb from which to hang the woeful teen. The boy attempted to explain with a trembling voice that he was on his way home. He stuttered "Mother—home—hunger" and suddenly remembered a phrase from his school-book English. "You are gentleman!" he nervously exclaimed to a huge soldier standing before him. The menacing group of soldiers broke into laughter, and one of the figures stepped forward, winked to those around him, and blurted in broken German, "Take off ... maybe you find your mother before we find a tree!" Stammering his gratitude, the boy disappeared down the cobblestone street in the direction of home.[2]

The Wehrmacht's 9th Panzer Division, situated along the south flank of Model's army group, was quickly overrun by the American onslaught. Lieutenant Heinz Bauer had concealed his tank platoon in a village several miles south of Olpe, where the exhausted soldiers hoped to get some rest before again engaging the enemy armor. The crews immediately sank into a deep sleep, unaware that within hours, the area would be under American occupation. Several hours after sunrise, Bauer awoke in the upper floor of the residence where they rested to the unfamiliar sound of voices in the street below. Rising from the bed, the tank commander was shocked to see a column of American soldiers advancing on each side of the empty street, along which numerous white flags were hanging listlessly in the still morning air. Several of the GIs were inspecting the massive Panther tank parked adjacent to the residence, and the soldiers had obviously already ransacked the belongings carried in the turret by Bauer's tank crew. The inquisitive troops examined the Germans' field packs; letters and photographs lay scattered on the ground. The rations stored in the ammunition racks, carefully hoarded by the crew, were passed from the turret to curious GIs below.

Shocked by the turn of events, Bauer sped from the room to awaken the other crewmen. He was brought to an abrupt halt by the sound of English voices from within the residence. The Americans were only footsteps away, and Bauer, seeking concealment, turned and sped up the stairwell into the attic. With a pounding heart, he glanced cautiously out the window to his tank below. The Americans were arriving in increasing strength, and many thoughts raced through his mind as he attempted to determine what action to take. At length, an American soldier climbed out of the open turret, pulled a grenade from his field gear, and dropped it behind him into the open hatch as other infantrymen with shouldered rifles halted to watch. The grenade detonated with a muffled explosion, and a wisp of smoke floated from the interior of the tank. The crowd of curious GIs moved onward, leaving the street empty again.

The tank commander knew that he was facing only two choices. He could remain where he was, to be discovered and taken prisoner, or he could attempt to return to his own lines. The second option, he realized, could only be accomplished with the tank, for the American columns were obviously passing through the village in strength; he concluded the nonchalant soldiers were not merely a reconnaissance patrol but were already present in at least company strength.

Bauer quietly descended the stairs, halting every few steps to listen for the sounds of enemy soldiers. The residence appeared to be empty, so he continued until he reached the ground floor. Through the window of the front room, he observed the gray bulk of his tank only several yards away; the smoke that had previously ascended from the open turret had cleared. Listening intently, he again discerned distant voices approaching and knew that he had to act quickly.

Cautiously swinging open the door, he crept toward the tank, climbed aboard the chassis on his stomach to avoid being observed by the nearby enemy soldiers, and slid head first into the driver's seat. As the voices grew louder, he struggled to right himself, at length managing to turn in the cramped space until he sat upright in the seat. Careful to avoid creating any noise, he slowly lowered the steel hatch.

The voices grew louder and more distinct as the soldiers approached. With a trembling hand, Bauer placed the ignition key into the aperture before realizing that the Americans were boarding the tank again. Sitting motionless, hardly daring to breathe, the panzer lieutenant heard a curious American soldier clamor into the turret behind him. The soldier examined the interior for several minutes before exiting the tank. Then, others gathered around the vehicle, smoking cigarettes and conversing calmly. Through the driver's aperture, Bauer observed more columns of American infantrymen winding through the street. Several of the GIs standing before the tank leaned against the massive steel chassis as they calmly continued their conversation. With trepidation, Bauer turned the key, pressed the accelerator, and pushed the ignition button.

The roar of the 500-horsepower engine filled the air as the massive motor sputtered and sprang to life. The startled Americans standing before the tank jumped and stared speechless at the massive vehicle. Bauer pushed the transmission into gear, and the tank jolted forward. The American soldiers reacted quickly after their initial surprise. As they scattered before the tank, the air immediately filled with shouts as the engine roared and the tank surged forward. Bauer desperately attempted to shift the transmission into a higher gear but found that the gear shift lever continued to spring from the road gear into neutral. Cursing, Bauer slammed the lever into first gear, and the tank crawled forward, the heavy steel tracks grating against cobblestones.

The experienced tank commander noted the chatter of small-arms fire over the roaring engine, and he was aware of the familiar rattle of bullets striking the armor. Concentrating on clearing the fire, Bauer pressed the accelerator to the floor and, with the engine screaming in protest, swung the vehicle onto a side street. A dull explosion against the chassis told him that he had been hit with a large-caliber weapon, but the tank crawled forward as Bauer discerned the acrid smell of burning oil and paint. The tank suddenly rumbled clear of the village, and, ignoring the screaming transmission, Bauer left the firing behind him as he accelerated down an open road.

As the tank cleared the last houses, he searched the horizon for a sign of the German lines. In the distance, he observed a row of slate-tiled rooftops in a distant village, and he noted that the houses were clear of any white flags. The lack of flags indicated that the Americans were not yet occupying the area before him. He was confident that he was approaching the division's new defense line when a dull explosion filled the air, and the tank trembled to a halt. He knew instantly that he had received a hit from a heavy-caliber gun.

Bauer had experienced the destruction of his tank in combat on eight previous occasions; the sounds and smells were familiar to him. Most discernable was the sharp smell of white-hot steel, present only when the heavy armor was struck by an antitank shell. The explosion was not earsplitting but simply the loud thud of a heavy projectile burning its way through the steel plate. A wave of heat engulfed him as he attempted to open the hatch to freedom before realizing that he was trapped. Mustering all his strength, he managed to swing the hatch upward several inches, far enough to realize that the heavy camouflage netting on the turret had fallen forward and was resting with its full weight on the opening.

The heat within the confines of the turret increased as Bauer struggled to free himself from the inferno. Gasping for oxygen that was being rapidly consumed by the flames, the tank commander felt himself growing weaker and was flooded with the realization that, after so many years of surviving and after eight previous escapes from a disabled tank, he was now dying in the manner he so often had feared. The flames engulfed the tank, and Bauer, gasping for air, felt the agonizing heat grow more intense as he struggled to remain conscious. With a final effort, he again strained against the trapped hatch cover, and suddenly, it lifted free. The heavy netting, ignited by the blast of the antitank shell, had finally burned enough to disintegrate and fall away from the chassis. Feeling himself losing consciousness, Bauer struggled to his feet and twisted his way through the opening to freedom.

Some 200 yards away, an infantry officer from the 9th Panzer Division watched intently as the familiar profile of a tank approached the unit's concealed positions. Through his field glasses, the officer recognized the long, sloping glacis plates that characterized the Panther tank, and he was curious as to why the vehicle was approaching his location directly from the American-occupied area. Fifty yards to his right, the morning calm was suddenly broken by the sharp crack of an antitank gun. Through his field glasses, the officer observed the tank grind to a halt under a rising column of smoke. Horrified, he realized that the antitank position, manned by young and inexperienced gunners, had destroyed one of their own tanks.

With his glasses fixed on the burning tank, the lieutenant observed a figure clad in an unmistakable Wehrmacht panzer uniform emerge from the driver's hatch through the raging flames. The burning figure dropped from the chassis and rolled on the ground as the ammunition and fuel in the tank began to explode, sending fragments of steel skyward. Screaming at the antitank gun crew to hold their fire, he ordered several landsers forward where the figure was writhing on the ground. Two infantrymen immediately sprang from their defenses and raced across the open ground, where they found Bauer alive but suffering from burns on his exposed face and hands. Knowing that they could receive fire at any moment from American soldiers, the two landsers grasped the tank commander under each arm and dragged him to the safety of their lines. As they collapsed on returning, they hardly realized that during the race in the open, which had probably lasted several minutes, not a shot had fallen.[3]

When the American First Army captured the bridge at Remagen, fourteen-year-old Ewald Fischer from Castrop-Rauxel had recently arrived back in his hometown from the Black Forest in southwest Germany, where he had spent many months involved with the Kinderlandverschickung program. On his return home, he was immediately conscripted for military training, but his mother sent a note explaining that he could not comply due to illness. The following Tuesday, he began his work with the Castrop-Rauxel city administration, with his first assignment being to remove posters placed throughout the town by anti-Nazi resistance members urging the city to capitulate without resistance.

As he and another trainee made their way through the town's deserted streets, isolated artillery shells could be discerned falling at random. As they approached the train station, they came on a paratrooper crouching near a roadblock who, cursing at their carelessness, urgently warned them to take cover. The heavily armed soldier pulled them into the concealment of the roadblock and motioned for them to look up the street. They peered, uncomprehending, through a tiny opening in the barrier until the soldier directed their attention to the distant muzzle of an American tank pointed silently but ominously in their direction.

The boys hurried home as the sounds of artillery shells echoed through the streets. En route to his neighborhood, Fischer passed the orphanage near the Catholic church, and he stopped long enough to help a young doctor carry equipment out of the burning structure into the street. After the flames became too intense to risk saving any more furnishings, he started toward home again. A Wehrmacht courier on a motorcycle provided him with transportation for the remaining 2 miles.

Ewald and his mother spent the afternoon burying his Jungvolk uniform, swastika flags, and a small-caliber hunting rifle in the garden. The intensity of the shelling increased as darkness fell, and they spent a restless night in the shelter of their cellar. During the night, they drifted into a fitful sleep and awoke at dawn to an ominous silence. Fischer felt his way through the dim light of the stairwell and climbed to the living quarters, where he peered out onto the street. Some 50 yards away, he observed an American soldier. The heavily armed infantryman moved cautiously along the side of the street and halted before the window of a neighboring house. Raising his weapon, he smashed the window with his rifle butt, then disappeared into the building.

Fischer hurried to the stairs and called to his mother, "The Amis are here!" She hurried up the steps and immediately attempted to force the teenager into a dress, fearing the consequences if the enemy soldiers were to find the fourteen-year-old at home. With shouts of protest, he broke free and quickly put an end to his mother's clumsy attempt to disguise him. The women then cowered behind the cellar door after extracting a promise from Ewald that he would remain in the washroom until they were sure that no danger was present.

Suddenly, a knock was heard on the outer door of the washroom, and Ewald gingerly opened the door to find himself staring into the muzzle of a rifle. He raised his hands as a pair of large American soldiers pushed him back from the door and entered the residence. Other sweat-stained, heavily armed Americans followed. They searched the building, crowding the inhabitants into the kitchen. On eyeing the crucifix hanging in the living room, one of the soldiers dryly remarked, "No Nazis here." One of the GIs discovered a swastika armband during the search, and the incriminating symbol was unceremoniously nailed to an armoire with a kitchen knife.

That afternoon, the Americans established a command post for an artillery battery in the home. The residents remained confined to the cellar. They were surprised by the generosity exhibited by one of the unshaven soldiers, who provided them with genuine coffee, and they were later allowed to venture into the living room. A huge black soldier sat at the piano playing a soft, unidentified melody. Other soldiers gathered about the instrument and sang with eyes glistening in the candlelight. For the first time, the inhabitants realized that the horror was over—they no longer had to fear the bombers overhead or the return of vengeful Nazi Party officials. The following day, the bodies of twelve German soldiers were collected near his home, and Ewald Fischer was among the onlookers as the lifeless corpses were rolled into a shallow hole in the earth and covered with soil.[4]

Reports filtered into Model's headquarters from the area of Marburg that the American columns, after streaming east out of the Remagen bridgehead, had swung toward the north. It was now clear that the closing of the pincers around the army group had begun. The field marshal vainly continued to request permission to withdraw the forces still waiting expectantly on the Rhine between Bonn and Cologne and move them east in an attempt to halt the closing of the pocket.

On 29 March, Hitler issued an order expressly forbidding further withdrawals. Any commander, regardless of the circumstances, would be held responsible for forces that relinquished any territory, and disobedience would be punishable by death. The order was widely disseminated by public radio and affected all military personnel, civil authorities, and party officials.

There was still a chance to delay the inevitable collapse. If the high command acted quickly, there would be time enough to save the imperiled army group. It was no longer possible to break through to the south, for the Americans' drive out of Remagen toward the east ensured that their flanks were being protected against such a move. Farther to the east, near the front of the advancing column, the flanks of the advancing armored units would be weakest. It might still be possible to attack toward the southeast from Winterberg, through the rough terrain of the Sauerland, toward Kassel. A successful breakthrough toward Kassel would sever the point of the American attack and enable the reestablishment of contact with German forces east and southeast of the quickly developing pocket.

On 28 March, General Fritz Bayerlein, the commander of the LIII Corps, was ordered to report to Model's headquarters east of Olpe. Bayerlein was an experienced officer who had fought the British and Americans in Africa and throughout the long retreat across western Europe. As the former commander of the Panzer Lehr Division, Bayerlein fully understood the overwhelming material superiority of the Americans and their tactics. Many officers whose experience was gained primarily on the Eastern Front were unaccustomed to fighting against the combination of overwhelming odds in men and armor supported by an effective air campaign that crippled all movement and made supplies difficult, if not impossible, to obtain.

Bayerlein arrived at Model's headquarters just before midnight. The field marshal greeted him with the dismal news that the entire army group was on the verge of being encircled in the Ruhr area and in the northern Sauerland. He advised Bayerlein that the American thrust had turned north at Marburg and was now in the area of Warburg-Niedermarsburg.

As the two officers examined the bleak situation on a large-scale map, Bayerlein received orders to prepare to assault the American left flank. He was to push out of the area of Schmallenberg to the east or northeast and link up with a newly established SS unit, SS Brigade Westfalen, to cut off the American drive. The troops placed under his command for the breakout attempt were a battle group from the Panzer Lehr Division consisting of an engineering battalion, Panzergrenadier Regiment 902, and various units from an armored battalion. The units were already en route from the area of Düsseldorf. Bayerlein was also to receive the Panzer Lehr battle group engaged near Siegen, the 3rd Panzergrenadier Division from the area of Siegen-Wissen, and units from Heavy Panzer Battalions 654 and 506. Additionally, the 176th Infantry Division was to be transported to his command by truck from the area of Düsseldorf. The attack was to take place as soon as possible, and Model expected to receive details of the concept of the breakout plan no later than noon on 29 March.

Model's staff officers were unable to provide any information regarding the American advance in the area of Winterberg. They only knew that Berleburg remained in German hands and that a weak Luftwaffe battle group was located somewhere south of Winterberg. No one knew whether the strategically important heights and road junctions at Winterberg were in American hands. Winterberg was traditionally a resort town—complete with ski lifts, tourist hotels, and lodges—surrounded by rolling hills and woods. All approaches were narrow, winding roads that favored the defenders and made air reconnaissance difficult. Formerly selected as a site for the 1936 Winter Olympics, the resort town was now witness to the end of an army.

On 29 March, General Gustav von Zangen's Fifteenth Army, holding the southern sector of the Ruhr, could no longer contact its units in the area of Breidenbach-Wolzhausen. The various units, consisting mostly of Volkssturm and replacement battalions, had apparently disappeared in the haze of a collapsing front as the American forces overran sectors before the Germans could establish a defense. The sound of vehicular columns, including numerous tanks, were reported to be streaming east from Breidenstein toward Battenberg. Similar reports were received of columns of tanks and half-tracks to the southeast of Biedenkopf, where the Fifteenth Army staff and Communications Battalion were located. With this report, the staff personnel realized that they and the entire Fifteenth Army Communications Battalion were cut off from the army group.

Hurriedly packing classified files and seizing sensitive equipment, they fled for the concealment of a wooded area southwest of the town. From the woods, they observed endless convoys of trucks, tanks, and half-tracks pouring toward the northeast. Lying beneath the trees, they avoided the prying eyes of the reconnaissance planes that circled overhead as Biedenkopf was occupied by American forces. However, within several hours, they had reestablished radio contact with the army group and with LXVII Corps. Keeping the radio communications to a minimum so as not to betray their location, they were advised that the corps command post was now located in the area of Vogelsberg.

Knowing that it would only be a matter of time before their location was discovered, they began to move as the sun set behind the hills of the Sauerland. The soldiers had determined that the Americans typically drove with a space of a mile or more between the separate convoys. After full darkness, they estimated when one convoy passed, and judging that it would be several minutes before the next arrived, they began feeding onto the roadway in small groups between the American vehicles.

They drove slowly enough not to close on the American column ahead of them and made good headway through the hilly terrain, keeping the dimly lit convoy lights barely visible. They continued streaming between the American convoys until almost 100 German vehicles were on the road. After following the route far enough to clear the territory now occupied by the Americans, the vehicles turned off the main road to make their escape. They crossed fresh tracks of Sherman tanks interspersed with the smaller tracks of the personnel carriers. The ruse succeeded for most of the fugitive vehicles until late in the night, when a courier on a motorcycle, driving ahead of a Wehrmacht truck, called out to what he supposed was a German convoy ahead. It was, in fact, an American unit, and the rear guard of the escaping convoy was taken prisoner.

By the following day, 30 March, most of the Fifteenth Army staff had succeeded in clearing the American lines. They arrived in the town of Altenhundem at dawn, after a nerve-wracking night of driving surreptitiously behind enemy vehicles. That afternoon, Model appeared at the command post in Altenhundem, where he ordered an immediate establishment of a defensive line on the east perimeter of what was rapidly developing into a pocket. He additionally briefed his plans for an attack out of Winterberg toward the east with Bayerlein's LIII Corps to sever the American advance toward Paderborn and to reestablish contact with units of the Eleventh Army near Kassel.[5]

Bayerlein's LIII Corps, under command of Gustav von Zangen's Fifteenth Army, realized that the army staff was missing. It was assumed that Zangen's entire staff had been overrun and captured during the rapid advance of the American armor. Model had assigned General Tocholte, his staff artillery officer, as Zangen's replacement, and Tocholte established a headquarters in Schüllar, north of Berleburg.

Bayerlein left Model's headquarters at 3:00 in the morning of 30 March and drove to the area of Schmallenberg. Over the next hours, he established the corps command post in Milchenbach and continued toward Winterberg. At an intersection in Gleidorf, he intercepted units of the Panzer Lehr Division en route from Düsseldorf, as well as the staff of the Panzerjäger Battalion en route from the Sieg front. He immediately ordered these units to secure the areas of Oberkirchen and Winterberg but to leave the town of Winterberg free of troops. Winterberg was known to be full of refugees, and the resort town had a number of hospitals overflowing with sick and wounded soldiers and civilians. After driving throughout the area to get a firsthand view of how the organization and preparation for the attack should proceed, he continued to the headquarters of the Fifteenth Army to brief his staff. He then drove to Berleburg and met with the battle commander of the unit to brief him of his intentions.

Bayerlein knew that the troops would have to arrive and react with great speed if the plan was to have any chance of success. The American columns were growing stronger by the hour, and unless the weather took a turn for the worse, the Allied air activity would intensify. The general decided that if the forces arrived in time, the breakout would be launched late in the evening of 30 March or in the early morning hours of 31 March. The attack would have to take place east of Winterberg along the narrow secondary roads, with the initial goal of securing the Hallenberg-Medebach road, which would deny the Americans important road networks.

With the scant forces available, he was able to assemble only two weak assault groups, which could risk making the attack only on small secondary roads and in darkness. The Winterberg forestry officials provided a forester who knew every detail of the area. At 1:00 p.m., Bayerlein met with the commanders of Pionier Battalion 130 and the Panzer Lehr's Battalion 2 and ordered them to reconnoiter the assault area, to station their forces east of Winterberg, and to be prepared to launch the attack that evening or during the early morning of the next day. Meanwhile, his staff established the new corps command post in the Hotel Höher Asten, approximately 3 miles west of Winterberg.

That afternoon, Bayerlein returned to Milchenbach and conferred with Model, who requested a briefing on the attack plans. Bayerlein provided an overview, which was met with criticism by the field marshal. During their briefing, General Dennert, commander of the 3rd Panzergrenadier Division, arrived, and the division was officially placed under Bayerlein's command. Dennert was ordered to recapture the town of Küstelberg, which had been occupied by American forces during the morning when they brushed aside the Volkssturm defenders. After regaining Küstelberg, Dennert's division was then to prepare to attack Medebach. The schedule of movement was very critical, and Dennert advised the officers that his division would not be arriving until the morning of 31 March and would have to immediately launch the attack. However, there were no other forces with which the attack could be supported. Exhausted, Bayerlein then returned to Winterberg. At 7:00 p.m., he issued the order to launch the attack as soon as the twelve tank destroyers of the Panzer Lehr arrived that evening.

On 30 March, Model's request for a general breakout of Army Group B, as he and his officers had planned, was denied by Kesselring; the forces were to remain on the Rhine. The threat of an American crossing between Bonn and Wesel was considered too great, and if it occurred, it would sever the remaining German units from their valuable source of ammunition, some of which was being delivered directly to the troops from the factories in the Ruhr. The great Silesian industrial area had already been lost to the Russians, and the Ruhr was the last available manufacturing center for war supplies.

To hold the Ruhr, the high command approved only a limited operation, thrusting out of the Winterberg area toward Kassel to reestablish the front and block the American thrust. Thus, the German divisions on the Rhine between Duisburg and Bonn remained in place while the columns of American divisions continued to pour east out of the bridgeheads, leaving the Ruhr industrial area behind.

Model, unable to secure permission to free his forces from the encircling U.S. First and Ninth Armies, continued with the preparations to break through the American columns east of Winterberg, now with the only goal being to link up with the Eleventh Army elements near Kassel.

SS Brigade Westfalen, ordered to proceed south of Paderborn from the Sennelager training areas in support of the breakout attempt, began its march toward the south. The tank destroyers of the Panzer Lehr arrived that evening; however, the unit's Battalion 2 was still missing. It was later discovered that the battalion had advanced too far to the east during its movement and was now outside the American forces that were in the process of closing the pocket.

The attack was launched at midnight without the Panzer Lehr Battalion 2. By morning, the German units attacking out of Winterberg had secured the Hallenberg-Medebach road and captured the villages of Liesen, Hesborn, and Medelon. The important road junction north of Hallenberg was taken before sunrise. Near Medelon, the attack by the splintered units of the Panzer Lehr ground to a halt, stopped by concentrations of American armored units. After a vicious exchange of fire, the Americans slowly began giving ground, and the German units pushed as far as the town of Küstelburg, where the heavy Tigers and Panthers regrouped and pushed onward.

From initial reports, it appeared that the breakout had succeeded. General J. Lawton Collins, commander of the U.S. First Army, reacted immediately to the German drive that threatened to sever his advanced elements. He pushed units of the 1st Division toward Büren, south of Paderborn, to block any breakout attempt in that area. If Bayerlein's forces succeeded in breaking through, they could prevent the planned linkup of the First and Ninth Armies and possibly foil the trap being set for the German army group.

Despite the Germans' poor morale and lack of supplies and transportation assets, isolated battles raged among the towns and villages in the Sauerland as Bayerlein's forces attempted to break through the closing ring. But as the morning dawned, the resistance from the shaken American units began to stiffen, and by midmorning, the attack had ground to a halt.

A turn of fortunes occurred on 31 March. As they had during the Ardennes Offensive, the German armored units, bereft of air cover of their own, relied on unfavorable weather to protect their columns from the marauding Jabos; the breakout attempt depended on penetrating the American columns before the weather cleared. As the skies opened, the German units winding their way through the hilly, wooded terrain of the Sauerland found themselves targets of the fighter-bombers that blanketed the skies. As always, the aircraft attacked any discernable movement, and the columns of vehicles, representing the final re-serves of the Panzer Lehr, were left burning by the roadsides. Antiaircraft batteries were destroyed by teams of fighter-bombers sweeping over the treetops, below the field of fire of the high-velocity guns. To the west of the town of Alt-Astenberg, a swarm of fighter-bombers descended on the spearhead of the panzer columns and left most of the tanks disabled.

During the night of 2 April, Fritz Bayerlein ordered a withdrawal of his corps back to Winterberg. The corps commander realized that the breakout attempt had failed, yet there was still a possibility that the Eleventh Army, outside the pocket, could somehow break through to the army group if his corps remained strong enough to tie American units to the Sauerland. The breakout operation had driven 8 miles into the American left flank and had temporarily disrupted a headlong race by the U.S. divisions toward the northeast. However, Army Group B had now expended its most valuable resources in a fruitless attempt to prevent being encircled by American forces. There were no illusions in the foxholes scat-tered throughout the woods and farmyards: even the most determined German staff officers, exasperated by their efforts to sustain the morale and fighting ability of the exhausted troops, now realized that they faced inevitable defeat.

One Sauerland resident, Fritz Zöllner, whose his fifteen-year-old son had been conscripted into the Volkssturm, was determined to save the boy from cer-tain death or captivity as the Americans approached. Zöllner was a veteran of World War I and knew only too well what the overwhelming forces the Allies were bringing to the front would mean to anyone opposing them. He and a neigh-bor set out to find their sons, both of whom had disappeared into the labyrinth of a collapsing army only several weeks before the Allied crossing of the Rhine.

The two men headed for the Reichsarbeitsdienst base near the town of Velmede, where they suspected the boys were undergoing basic military training. At 5:00 p.m., they cleared the last roadblocks before Velmede and began inquir-ing as to the location of their sons. It was no easy task. The civilian inhabitants, expecting the customary artillery barrage that accompanied the Allied advance, had taken shelter within their cellars, so the streets were devoid of civilians. The military situation exhibited a picture of absolute chaos, with varying units attempting to execute often conflicting orders. But the confusion of the final hours offered an advantage to the men in the search for their sons—no one stopped them in their quest.

At length, they succeeded in locating the boys in the Reichsarbeitsdienst compound. The teenagers were lying on their bunks, fully dressed and outfitted with field equipment awaiting their marching orders. The two men hastily devised a plan for their sons to slip over the back fence of the base under the cover of darkness. With luck, their unit would not receive orders for at least several hours. The escape worked as planned, and at 10:00 p.m., the boys climbed the fence at a specified location; by 11:00, the men, with the teenagers in tow, had cleared the last checkpoint leading out of town. They were on the outskirts of Meschede by midnight, having successfully circumvented three checkpoints manned by SS guards. At the town of Freienohl, they were unexpectedly halted at another checkpoint by a sentry who ordered them to wait while he examined the documents of several Wehrmacht vehicles that simultaneously appeared at the intersection. The first truck had hardly cleared the checkpoint when the two men and their teenaged fugitives broke into a run toward the Ruhr River. Surprisingly, they heard no shots behind them. At length, they paused to catch their breath and were relieved to see that no one had attempted to follow them in the darkness. During the remainder of their journey to Sundern, they only encountered forlorn, elderly Volkssturm troops, who paid them no attention. At daylight, they reached their homes, where the boys remained concealed for a week.[6]

The combined Rhine crossing and airborne landings in the Wesel sector, north of the Ruhr, had functioned as flawlessly as could be expected in war. By 26 March, the American Ninth Army was utilizing more than seven bridges over the Rhine, across which an endless flood of men and material poured. The breakout from the bridgehead was launched on the morning of 26 March, the main objective being the town of Dorsten. By 27 March, Dorsten had fallen, and American units were rapidly advancing toward Hamborn, Ruhrort, and Meiderich, all of which fell one day later. Haltern and Dülmen on the Lippe River were taken. The drive sliced through the southern flank of Blaskowitz's Army Group H, and units of the army group were pushed to the south, where they became trapped in the developing pocket with Model's Army Group B.

On 28 March, Blaskowitz dispatched a situation report stating that his units could delay the Allied advance only for a matter of days at most. Once his command collapsed, the Allies stood prepared to drive across the wide north German plateau and strike toward central Germany, cutting off the important ports of Bremen and Hamburg from the German heartland. The Allied drive was flanked by the Ruhr area to the south and Holland to the north, both of which held numerous, albeit weakened, German divisions that could not be moved to halt the Allied breakout. In the words of Blaskowitz, both areas on the Allied flanks were threatened with encirclement and were "no longer of any decisive meaning" at that stage of the war. In his situation report, the general took the risk of recommending the evacuation of his forces from Holland and the Ruhr. Like Field Marshal Model, he reasoned that "with a withdrawal of forces from both areas it would be possible to halt the enemy break-out in the Army Group B sector, to establish a defense of the Weser, to conduct an orderly evacuation of troops and equipment from Holland and to establish a defensive line in favorable terrain in the area of Groningen." Blaskowitz then recommended immediate approval of this proposal and requested orders to conduct the withdrawal. The response from Berlin was an abrupt denial: there would be no permission granted to conduct any withdrawal. Additionally, he was warned that he was not to submit negative situation reports in the future and that the army group was to be utilized more efficiently. The warning closed with the promise that reinforcements were en route from Denmark.[7]

By 30 March, less than a week after the breakouts of the Remagen and Wesel bridgeheads began, it was clear to Blaskowitz that the Allies could not be hindered from racing toward the east and ultimately encircling the Ruhr as well as severing his forces in Holland. The towns of Dorsten, Gladbeck, and Sterkrade fell to the Allied advance as the columns pushed toward Münster. Bottrop, Marl, and Herten were occupied, and units of the American Ninth Army passed to the north of Hamm toward Ahlen and Beckum.

As the Allied armies streamed toward the east out of their bridgehead at Wesel, any possible German defenses in the path of the advance were being neutralized by armadas of bombers. The city of Cösfeld was quickly rendered a field of rubble during a series of air strikes. Dülmen was reduced to burning ruins so extensive that Allied aircraft, attempting to conduct after-action reconnaissance operations, had difficulty locating where the city had stood only hours earlier. When attempting to conduct a photoreconnaissance after the last bombing raid, one experienced American pilot had trouble finding the city of Dülmen and described it as having been reduced to "a couple of ruins in the middle of a desert." As the American advanced elements secured the destroyed city, support units brought forward bulldozers to clear a path through the rubble for supply convoys. The heavy machinery quickly pushed piles of debris aside and constructed a wide path the GIs christened USA Street, which cut a swath from the western end of the destroyed town to the eastern approaches. More than 300 women and children were killed in Dorsten when a fleet of fighter-bombers struck the train station in a low-level attack. A local diarist wrote, "Corpses are still being found in the rubble-filled city, they have been completely shrunken by the heat of the flames."[8]

Within the rubble, there were not only rescuers at work. German soldiers—stragglers who were separated from their units or deserters from the Wehrmacht—worked alongside foreign laborers and German inhabitants in plundering the devastated neighborhoods. Following the air attacks, the fighter-bombers constantly circled the sea of ruins, searching for new targets. The local residents risked death in their efforts to recover any valuables from their bombed homes, racing against both the plunderers and the advancing Allied army to save what could be salvaged. With belongings piled onto small farm carts or simply tied in bundles and carried on their backs, the civilians carried carpets, clothing, linens, chairs, and anything that might be saved to a safer storage area.

The advancing Allies often met unexpected resistance. The stragglers and deserters, wandering eastward to escape the American and British troops, found themselves rounded up at checkpoints by the *Kettehünde*—as the German soldiers contemptuously referred to the military police. The motley collections of stragglers were assigned to makeshift units, where they were joined by the even less effective Volkssturm soldiers. The Volkssturm was organized into four groups, or "levels." The primary level, designated "uk" (or *unabkömmlich*), consisted of men with a semblance of military training. The second level was made up of men with health problems, the third level was composed of elderly men, and the fourth level consisted of Hitler Youth companies.

Under the direction of "resistance commanders," the fourth group often fought to the end. The teenagers who made up this group had, throughout their lives, been indoctrinated to serve the Führer, and in many cases, they could easily be convinced that the final victory was approaching. Near the town of Grütlohn, British forces drove directly into a deadly concentration of small-arms fire. After two hours of heavy fighting, the Allied soldiers finally suppressed a fanatical group of Hitler Youth teenagers armed with Panzerfausts and a smattering of automatic weapons. Many of the boys manning ambush sites and roadblocks were led by Wehrmacht or SS noncommissioned officers who continued to believe that victory was possible, despite the obvious collapse taking place around them. In Bocholt, an officer in command of a flak unit, manned by demoralized Volkssturm conscripts, declared, "We only need to hold out for three more days, then our new weapons will be put into action and everything will change instantly."[9]

The senior officer in Bocholt, Colonel Primus, was an experienced soldier who had witnessed and participated in the war at its worst, and he was aware of the combined power in men and material they were now facing. As soon as Primus discerned artillery fire echoing from the direction of Borken, he knew that Bocholt had been bypassed and that exit routes to the east were severed. At 6:30 p.m. on 28 March, he ordered the few remaining soldiers from Fallschirmjäger

Regiment 21 to withdraw from the city and establish positions behind the Aa River.

That evening, inhabitants of Bocholt caught the faint sounds of armored vehicles approaching from the south. At 11:30 p.m., the forward elements of a British armored unit probed the southern outskirts of the city and drew to a halt. With their approach, straggling Wehrmacht defenders demolished all bridges and telephone facilities within the city. Several city administrators convinced the Wehrmacht soldiers to spare the massive grain elevator holding 1,000 tons of wheat. The following afternoon, the last German soldiers filed out of the city toward the north, away from the oncoming Allies.

A number of the retreating soldiers were overtaken by the British mechanized units between the village of Rhede and Bocholt. A woman who witnessed British elements rounding up German stragglers recorded, "What one sees is enough to bring tears to our eyes. Our poor, abused, betrayed soldiers—they stand there with upraised hands, malnourished, badly clothed and hardly armed."[10]

The isolated bands of defenders often caused immeasurable suffering among the populace. With a seemingly endless supply of military equipment, the Allies used their resources unsparingly. Under the maxim of expending material to save lives, any shot fired by erstwhile defenders received artillery barrages in retaliation. Weather permitting, artillery spotters and reconnaissance planes patrolled the skies before the advancing columns, seeking out any hidden defenders and providing the oncoming troops with a concise picture of what lay ahead. After the Allies captured the town of Anholt on 29 March, a diarist noted, "My God—they have tanks! Tanks and always more tanks! They have everything, even mail trucks are rolling over the bridges!" A cleric in the village of Mussum recorded, "The Germans are still defending. Bombs and shells fly over us and impact all around. But at 17:00 it is all over—we can finally raise white flags."[11]

A Wehrmacht captain organized a makeshift combat unit from various troops collected between the villages of Borken and Ramsdorf during the search for stragglers. Having been awarded the coveted Knight's Cross shortly before the arrival of the Allies, he may have been inspired to organize resistance that otherwise would have been deemed useless. Throughout the night, the energetic captain tirelessly ordered the streets and bridges in the town mined, and he attempted to establish a defense line complete with roadblocks and tank trenches.

The local inhabitants were of another opinion, and they resisted his efforts: for them, the arrival of the Allies would mean an end to the torment that had befallen them since the tide had turned against Germany. The captain fiercely responded with threats of court-martial and immediate execution. At length, several older citizens succeeded in convincing him that the optimal location for a defense would be along a line running between the village of Lünsberg and

Sternbusch. The determined officer eventually collected his hapless forces and marched into the darkness.[12]

As the British forces were threatening Bocholt with encirclement, it suddenly occurred to a number of inhabitants that their savings were still held in the local banks and financial institutions. Some attempted to cross the gauntlet of artillery fire to the town's *Sparkasse* ("savings bank"), but they were forced to abandon their plan by the hail of shells. Others picked their way through the beleaguered town to the *Reichsbank* ("national bank"). There, they discovered that the bank manager still had the key to the fortified building—and he had been killed during a previous air raid. Undeterred, they located someone who knew where the body of the official was buried. A small group of men hurried to the grave site with shovels, and within several minutes, the corpse was exhumed. A cursory search located the keys to the building and vault. The body was unceremoniously rolled back into the grave and hastily covered with earth before the men hurried back to the Reichsbank. There, they recovered approximately half a million reichsmarks. Some 174,000 reichsmarks were hastily issued to the populace in accordance with their bank balances as the Allied tanks approached. The remainder disappeared in the haze of anarchy that swept the area as the Allies began entering the city. Unbeknownst to those who risked their lives to legitimately recover their money, the currency would become all but worthless when the enemy soldiers occupied the area.[13]

As the Allied forces were racing toward the east from the Remagen and Wesel bridgeheads, twenty-three-year-old Heinz Spenner assembled with more than 1,000 newly trained paratroopers on the drill field of the *Fallschirmjäger* ("paratrooper") training base in the ancient Prussian town of Stendal. In long ranks, the camouflage-clad paratroopers stood at attention while a company NCO paced the length of each rank and numbered each trooper—one ... two ... one ... two. After several minutes, the sergeants reported to the company commanders, who in turn marched to the battalion commander, rendered salutes, and conferred beyond the hearing of the troops. The officers saluted and returned to their companies. After a short speech regarding the training received, the duties expected of the men, and the sacrifices to be made, the actual purpose of the muster was announced: "Those who are designated number one will go to the Eastern Front ... those with number two will go to the Lower Rhine front."

Spenner risked a glance at the two men flanking him. The soldiers stood with set faces, expressionless. He himself heard the announcement with mixed emotions. He had drawn number two: he was going to fight the Americans or British—again. Spenner was not new to the paratroop battalions, and he was not new to battle. He had joined the Luftwaffe because he wanted to learn to fly. He dreamed of piloting airplanes and in a moment of youthful exuberance had been easily convinced that if he volunteered for the Luftwaffe, he would receive an assignment to flight school. It was not until after he had enlisted that he discovered, in the early stage of the war, that he was too young to qualify for pilot training. Instead, he was trained as a radioman. After flying combat missions between Greece and North Africa, he had lost his nerve. He reported to his commander, who had nodded and expressed understanding that he no longer wished to fly: aviators often lost their nerve after a series of combat missions. The squadron commander promised that he would look into what options might be available.

Several days later, Spenner had been called into the commander's office and was told that good news awaited. There was an easy solution for ending his career as aircraft crewman. The commander advised him that he could volunteer for another branch of service—he could report as a volunteer to the Waffen SS. Or he could volunteer for paratrooper training. For Heinz Spenner, there was no question; it would have to be paratroops.

After basic airborne training, he had been assigned to Italy, sunny Italy. But for Heinz Spenner that meant Monte Cassino and the months of grueling combat under appalling conditions during which Allied and German soldiers fought to the death on muddy hillsides. There was no way to escape the torment other than through severe wounding, capture, or death.

After several weeks, his decimated regiment was withdrawn, deemed to be no longer combat effective. The soldiers were sent to northern France to be reinforced and reequipped—and then came Normandy. During the night of 5–6 June, Canadian paratroopers descended out of a black sky directly on their position. Throughout the night, the Canadians and Germans fought at close quarters with submachine guns, grenades, entrenching tools, and knives. The antagonists remained inextricably mixed in close, savage combat for several hours, during which no quarter was given. For those who survived, sunrise brought a scene of horrid devastation. Mangled bodies lay entwined, camouflaged German corpses lying together with Canadians in olive green. Again, Spenner had miraculously emerged unscathed. The German forces consolidated their position and then began what became weeks of fighting for the Normandy beachhead.

Several weeks later, as a Sherman tank burrowed through a hedgerow in a frontal assault, Spenner had leaped over the impenetrable brush with a Panzerfaust to engage the armored vehicle just as the gunner fired. The resulting explosion almost severed his left leg just below the knee. He regained consciousness propped in a motorcycle sidecar with his leg swathed in bandages. The driver was forced to constantly veer from the road and seek shelter under foliage as marauding Jabos pounced on the motorcycle whenever it broke from the concealment of trees lining the narrow farm track.

Spenner's next seven months were spent in military clinics and hospitals as doctors labored to save his leg, which resisted all efforts to heal. At long last, he was again pronounced fit for duty. But the leg remained painful and sore, the wound often seeping fluid and resistant to all medication. Now, in March 1945, it appeared as though he was to be sent back into battle.

One evening in the last week of March, hundreds of paratroopers boarded a line of open railcars, and as night fell, the heavily laden train departed from Stendal for the west. By sunrise, they had rolled to the dark hills of the Sauerland, and as the train passed the village of Willebadessen, Spenner recognized that they were not far from his aunt's home, where he had spent weekend outings during happier days.

After proceeding beyond Willebadessen, the train slowed to a crawl. The paratroops lying on the railcars found themselves inching across a badly damaged viaduct over a deep gorge. The decrepit viaduct seemed to shudder with every car that traversed the chasm, but at long last, all the railcars cleared the gorge. The train was on the verge of continuing when it braked to a stop. After several long minutes, word was passed among the groups of paratroopers that the train had been halted by an army officer on the tracks ahead, who advised the rail engineer that the area before them was already occupied by American forces. To continue would take the entire train into the American lines and the load of troops into captivity.

With no other recourse, the engineer reversed the gears, and the train began inching slowly backward, moving over the damaged viaduct at a snail's pace. Spenner knew that they were only several miles from Paderborn and that it was perhaps only a matter of hours before they would be committed to battling an overwhelming enemy. The train cleared the viaduct and began to gain speed, for the engineer was desperate to find a suitable place to conceal the train before it became a target for Allied fighter-bombers.

Spenner realized that this might be his last chance to survive, to make it through a war that had already claimed so many of his comrades. He glanced about and pensively observed the paratroopers. Many of them lay dozing after a restless night in the open on the railcars. A few seemed to stare listlessly into the distance. Spenner reflected on the past months and years of war that had swept over Europe. His thoughts wandered to Monte Cassino, and he remembered the constant, gnawing fear and the days and nights spent among the dead and dying under a ceaseless hail of mortar shells as the Allies pressed relentlessly forward. He recalled the night of the Normandy invasion, the vicious, deadly struggle with *Kappmesser* gravity knives as the silent shadows of Allied paratroopers descended on the defenders. He heard the bursts of submachine guns and the deafening explosions of hand grenades thrown into the foxholes and earthworks. He recalled the morning sun rising to reveal a chimera of horror and carnage, the remains of the fierce struggle for survival that had raged throughout the night.

Glancing about him, Heinz Spenner viewed the camouflage battle smocks, leather and canvas magazine pouches, long belts of 7.92-mm machine-gun ammunition, and wooden-handled stick grenades tucked into field belts. He smelled the heavy odor of steel and cosmoline mixed with tobacco and sweat. His world had changed inordinately since he, as an eighteen-year-old recruit, had dreamed of flying airplanes. Carefully inspecting the reinforced buckle of his paratrooper helmet to ensure that it was secure, Spenner gathered up his heavy cartridge belt and grasped his assault rifle. After a furtive glance at the soldiers dozing about him in the early morning sun, he jumped from the moving train.[14]

After passing the city of Hamm on the Lippe Canal, units of the U.S. Ninth Army broke from the main thrust toward the city of Münster and swung toward the south in the direction of Soest. To even the most casual observer, it was clear that it was only a matter of hours before units of the Ninth Army heading south would meet up with the columns of the First Army that had wheeled north at Marburg. For the Wehrmacht officers tracking the movements of the two armies, the paths appeared to be taking the American units directly to Paderborn.

On 31 March, as the Ninth Army continued its eastward course toward Paderborn, the point elements of the U.S. 2nd Armored Division closed on the western approaches of the town of Ahlen. The small town had seen many changes during the war. What had been a small municipality with a few medical facilities had become an expanded hospital area. The numerous clinics were filled with more than 4,000 wounded. Hundreds more were inhabiting private homes requisitioned for the purpose. The senior medical officer was fifty-year-old Paul Rosenbaum, a veteran of World War I who soon found himself at the center of the controversy regarding the official status of the city.

The Nazi directives clearly specified that no city, no town or village, not a single yard of territory was to be left undefended, and the party officials were intent on obeying Hitler's edicts to the end. Rosenbaum knew that if the German forces attempted a defense of the city, the medical facilities would suffer devastation and that countless wounded soldiers and civilians would die.

As the Americans approached, the political functionaries proceeded to establish defenses throughout the area. Massive Red Cross flags were predominately exhibited at the facilities. However, the political officials were determined to obey Hitler's no-surrender policy and resist the oncoming Allies, regardless of the number of lives that might cost. Kreisleiter Wemhöner ordered the evacuation of all noncombatants from the city. A prominent area known as the Galgenberg was designated as an assembly point, where all evacuees were to meet for transport from the town in farm carts. Leaflets were hastily printed and distributed throughout the area by officials, advising all residents of the evacuation order.

Rosenbaum had not been idle in his attempts to hinder the unnecessary destruction of Ahlen. On Easter Friday, the Volkssturm troops manning the roadblocks and checkpoints throughout the area began disassembling the obstacles. Placards appeared on buildings at the outskirts of the city proclaiming Ahlen an "open medical district" that was not to be defended. As the senior medical representative and ranking German army officer present, Rosenbaum was issuing instructions with potentially deadly consequences. His orders were in direct violation of Hitler's edicts, and as such, the doctor was subject to immediate arrest.

The inhabitants were relieved when it initially appeared that their city would be spared. As the Allied army approached, the populace observed columns of war-weary, retreating German soldiers filing toward the east, away from the front. In the wake of the retreating German troops, hordes of jubilant foreign laborers enjoyed their first breath of freedom in many years. Their guards and overseers had melted away, and thousands of laborers found themselves without supervision. They collected in groups according to specific nationalities. French, Polish, and Russian prisoners of war mixed with laborers from the same countries. The inhabitants, peering fearfully from behind curtains or gathering in small groups in their neighborhoods, could sense that the next hours would determine whether their city would survive the war intact or, like so many others, be destroyed in a senseless act of defiance.

On 31 March, the American advance elements reached the outskirts of the city. That afternoon, a column of Allied tanks bypassed Ahlen to the north and was streaming toward Münster. In the city's thirteen military hospitals, the staff officers, orderlies, nurses, and civilian volunteers prepared for the worst. Medical supplies were taken from the dwindling reserves and readied for use. Preparations were made to move some of the 4,000 wounded to cellars. There were no adequate transport facilities for the evacuation of more than 1,000 of the wounded from the area. The number of patients climbed as the straggling German units delivered their casualties before moving onward as they attempted to escape the Allied columns pursuing them.

Contradictory rumors raced through the city. Some said the city was officially declared an open medical center and would not be defended. Others affirmed that the defenses were being reinforced and that more German forces were en route to engage the Americans. Many of Ahlen's inhabitants were praying for the quick arrival of the Allied troops. The city was also filled with thousands of families who had fled the industrial centers west of Ahlen. Their homes and workplaces in Essen, Cologne, Düsseldorf, and Recklinghausen had disappeared under the deluge of bombs routinely dropped by armadas of Allied aircraft, and they knew what would occur should the remnants of the German army attempt a defense.

Rosenbaum continued to work feverishly to save the city and the thousands of wounded in the facilities. A medical orderly reported to him that a company of German tanks was at the rail yard and preparing to establish defense positions. Seizing his telephone, Rosenbaum managed to locate the commander of the German unit, a young lieutenant from Bielefeld, and explain the situation to him. The officer agreed that under the circumstances, it made no sense to fight in the city, and he promised to withdraw. A short time later, Rosenbaum received word that the tanks had rolled out of the city toward the east.

However, the political officials continued to believe that Ahlen should be defended. With the Volkssturm and police units under their command, they requisitioned farm carts and obsolete civilian vehicles to transport elderly soldiers, young boys, and lightly wounded soldiers to man the defenses. Quantities of Panzerfausts were loaded into carts in anticipation of defending the city at close quarters against Sherman tanks. Rosenbaum, intent on defying the party officials, arrived at the Buschhoff intersection at the western border of the town as a group of elderly Volkssturm troops were erecting a crude barricade. Accompanied by several of his staff members, Rosenbaum ordered them to dismantle the ridiculous structure and to return to their homes. The motley collection of Volkssturm soldiers, many of whom had survived the horrors of Verdun and the Somme some twenty years earlier, eagerly obeyed Rosenbaum's directions and disappeared into the surrounding neighborhoods. As retreating German units continued to flow through the intersection, Rosenbaum ordered the officers to take the combat units directly through the city and to refrain from establishing any defenses. A horse-drawn flak battery was ordered to proceed toward the village of Neubeckum. The makeshift defenses west of the city were rapidly dismantled, opening the way for the American tanks.

On the morning of 31 March, the U.S. 95th Infantry Division arrived at the approaches to the city. The U.S. 8th Armored Division was concentrated in the area of Selm, whereas the U.S. 2nd Armored Division bypassed Ahlen to the north and overran the villages of Sendenhorst, Enniger, and Wiedenbrück. In the face of the overpowering display of military strength, the Nazi officials began reconsidering their desire to fight for the Führer. Finally, at midday on 31 March, the party functionaries agreed to declare Ahlen an open city. For the first time since the invasion of Reich territory began the previous fall, a German city would not be defended.

Rosenbaum climbed into his vehicle and directed the driver through the deserted streets to the Quante-Portmann building on the Walstedder Strasse. With the doctor standing in the open vehicle holding a large Red Cross flag aloft, the car cautiously approached several ponderous Sherman tanks that had taken up positions along the street. Flanking the tanks in the shelter of doorways crouched dozens of heavily armed American infantrymen wearing rounded, olive-colored helmets and short, khaki jackets. After dismounting from the vehicle, the doctor was placed in a jeep and driven to the command post of Colonel Hinds in an ancient mill near Walstedde. The doctor was driven past a seemingly endless row of tanks and support vehicles. In the open field beyond the Quante-Portmann building, a company of Shermans was preparing to fire on the city with the first indication of resistance. Artillery batteries beyond the tanks were pulling into position, their long barrels pointed menacingly toward Ahlen. Dozens of black soldiers were in the process of unloading hundreds of high-explosive shells from the beds of massive trucks. The jeep bounced down the narrow road, and approximately 3 miles from the village of Walstedde, they arrived at a command post. As the doctor dismounted from the jeep, an American soldier approached and reached for the doctor's Iron Cross before being interrupted by a sharp command from an officer. Although Rosenbaum could not understand the exchange of words in English, it was clear that the souvenir-seeking soldier was being admonished for his unseemly behavior. The doctor was then taken to Colonel Hinds, the commander of the sector.

The German medical officer advised the grim colonel through an interpreter that the city was free of German combatants, and he managed to convince Hinds that he desired to surrender the city to the Americans. The colonel agreed to return to Ahlen with Rosenbaum, despite the shelling coming from German batteries located farther to the south near the industrial city of Hamm.

At 2:00 p.m., both officers drove toward Ahlen under the escort of Sherman tanks. As they approached the city, the vehicles were met by a sudden burst of machine-gun fire. The tanks moved into action and quickly decimated an SS reconnaissance unit that had fired on the advancing column. After recovering from the provocation, it was clear to Rosenbaum that the angry colonel suspected he had been led into an ambush. It took several minutes for the exasperated German officer to convince him that the SS patrol did not come from the city but had strayed into their path from the direction of Hamm-Heessen, farther south and beyond his jurisdiction. Thirty minutes later, American convoys, directed by German police positioned at the street intersections, were rolling through the quiet but undamaged city of Ahlen between blocks of buildings draped with white flags.

Six miles to the east, in the city of Beckum, a German officer was fulfilling another mission as the American forces were closing on Ahlen. On 4 March 1945, twenty-nine-year-old Major Rudolf Dunker had been assigned to the 116th Panzer Division staff for preliminary instruction as a General Staff officer; from there, he was to be assigned to the War Academy. Late in the afternoon of 30 March, he received word to contact the division commander, Major-General Siegfried von Waldenburg. Waldenburg advised Dunker over the telephone that the Americans had begun simultaneous movements from north and south to close a pocket around the army group. The northern wing of the American forces was pushing over Dülmen, Ahlen, and Beckum toward Lippstadt. The southern wing was advancing over Siegen, Winterberg, and Brilon toward Paderborn. The two armies were expected to attempt a linkup within the next several days in the area between Paderborn and Lippstadt. The 116th Panzer Division was to be withdrawn from the line for a drive toward the east to push clear of the rapidly developing pocket. The forces were then to be utilized to strike against the open flanks of the Allied forces that were continuing to move eastward. Dunker was assigned to take command of the field replacement battalion of the 116th Panzer Division and stop the American thrust toward Lippstadt and Paderborn long enough to permit the division to clear the pocket.

That evening, Dunker arrived at the command post of the field replacement battalion accompanied by a communications van and a courier on motorcycle. He received a briefing from Captain Inboden and learned that he would be commanding roughly 2,000 untrained, lightly armed troops who were improvised into eleven infantry companies, with whom he was expected to stop an entire American mechanized army.

Determined to obey his instructions, he set to work. Based on the latest reports, Dunker was aware of the approximate progress of the American advance. Scanning a map, he immediately knew where the optimal defense line would have to be drawn. The town of Beckum, just east of Ahlen, was built around an important road junction that would have to be taken by the Americans en route to their objective of closing the pocket near Paderborn. With the weak forces at his disposal, Dunker knew that the Americans could only be halted, albeit temporarily, at a tactically important terrain feature or in an urban area. He quickly folded his map, called the staff officers, and departed for the town of Beckum.[15]

Unlike Rosenbaum, who had chosen a humanitarian means of bringing the war to an end in his city, Rudolf Dunker was committed to carrying out his orders to defend Beckum. The major was fully capable of fulfilling such assignments. In addition to having earned the esteemed German Cross in Gold, he had been awarded the Iron Cross First Class and Second Class and the Close Combat Badge. He had also served as an officer with the renowned 116th "Windhund" Panzer Division, which had been opposing the Allies since the invasion of Normandy. Thus, he was experienced in fighting against heavy odds.

Dunker's orders were to defend Beckum to the last man if necessary to permit the escape of his division from the pocket. He had received these orders from three sources: from his division, from the district combat commander of Soest, and from the Reichs defense commissar. It appeared that he was left with no choice. The orders from the Soest district commander and the defense commissar to defend Beckum at all costs simply for the sake of not surrendering any ground were clearly irresponsible, and the major was prepared to ignore orders based solely on that premise. However, the order from the 116th had sound military purpose. The Americans had to be halted long enough to prevent the pocket from closing until as many German troops as possible could escape toward the east. With the defenses at hand, the major could only stop the Americans, if only temporarily, at Beckum. Therefore, he was left with a decision. To defend Beckum meant that the city would be reduced to rubble and that untold numbers of innocent people might lose their lives. To retreat from the city would bring the Americans much closer to sealing the pocket, thus trapping forces that could otherwise be used in establishing a defense farther east.

At 9:00 p.m., Major Dunker called a briefing for all of Beckum's civil authorities. Those present at the meeting were Deputy Bürgermeister Beumer, Senior City Inspector Kersting, City Planner Mey, Police Director Leggemann, Police Administrative Director Lienkamp, Senior Education Director Keuker as officer in charge of the "city" Volkssturm, SS Hauptsturmführer Klinger as officer in charge of the Beckum District Volkssturm, and attorney Dr. Illigens as representative of the district street and roadways commissioner in Münster.

After the short briefing, which began at 10:00, Dunker ordered the city planner, Mey, to prepare a map showing the locations of all facilities such as reinforced buildings, bunkers, and air raid shelters. When asked the whereabouts of the Bürgermeister, Beumer explained that the mayor was ill and could not be present. The major immediately appointed Beumer as interim Bürgermeister. Dunker then requested detailed information about the city—size, number of inhabitants, conditions of refugees, defense possibilities, and protection areas for civilians during artillery barrages and air raids. Beumer affirmed that he was responsible for the industrial facilities. When asked if any preparations had been made for destroying the facilities, he responded negatively. Dunker then requested that such preparations be completed no later than 6:00 a.m. When Beumer retorted that he could not carry out the duties of Bürgermeister and city planner simultaneously, the major turned to Illigens and appointed him interim Bürgermeister in Beumer's stead.

Dunker then briefed the officials on the military situation and explained that on the following day, a counterattack by German forces was planned and that heavy fighting involving armored units could be expected. The Germans were going to try to prevent the pocket from being closed in the area of Lippstadt-Beckum-Hamm. He added that the officials could also expect heavy shelling from artillery batteries as well as air bombardments, especially in the area of the main road intersections in Beckum. To spare needless civilian casualties, all civilians were to evacuate the city during the night; Illigens was to be responsible for carrying out the evacuation.

Dunker also advised the officials that white flags had been observed in the town and that a surrender was out of the question in view of the operational plans and the strategic importance of the location. He added that should more signs of capitulation be seen, he would be forced to take action against those responsible. Senior Inspector Kersting asked if sensitive documents could be destroyed at that time, and Dunker authorized the officials to immediately proceed with the destruction of all classified material. The officials then departed to conduct their assignments.

A stream of interruptions had disrupted the briefing. At one point, an officer arrived and announced that the Beckum distillery had opened its doors and was distributing liquor to the German soldiers. A number of the erstwhile defenders, sensing that the end was approaching, had taken advantage of the windfall and were now rendered unfit for combat. Dunker ordered that the distribution of alcohol cease immediately, and he directed that the owners of the distillery were to report to him. Predictably, the owners failed to appear prior to the major's departure to inspect the defense positions. During his inspection, Dunker ordered two reconnaissance patrols to reconnoiter the roads leading west and northwest toward Ahlen and Neubeckum.

One of Dunker's reconnaissance patrols probed slowly along the Beckum-Ahlen road until they reached the Rosendahl farmstead. From the farm, they observed the white flags flying in Ahlen and suspected that the Americans were now occupying the city. The officer in charge of the patrol advised the farm owner that the troops were planning to make a stand at the tiny cluster of farmhouses. The ancient homesteads offered a semblance of protection in an area that dominated the only improved route directly connecting Ahlen and Beckum. If the American armor could be delayed even for a few hours, it would mean more time had been won in keeping the pocket open. Rosendahl, knowing that any fighting would likely destroy his ancestral home and his livelihood, set about convincing the officer that resistance would not be fruitful. He emphasized that it would only cost the lives of the soldiers. The small German unit had no heavy weapons, and the Panzerfausts did not have enough range to inflict any damage on a convoy of tanks as they approached over the open fields. The American tanks, after receiving initial fire, would simply remain at a distance, he said, and destroy the farmstead with their heavy weapons, possibly killing everyone present. The officer reluctantly saw the logic in the argument and withdrew his men toward Beckum. A short time later, an American convoy, led by a platoon of tanks, approached the cluster of farm buildings. The lead tank quickly ground to a halt after being struck by a Panzerfaust. A small group of unseen German stragglers had unwisely fired on the advancing Americans.

The American armored vehicles responded instantly. With tracks sloughing through the soft earth of the surrounding fields, the heavy tanks maneuvered into a defensive position. The massive vehicles then methodically opened fire and ignited the buildings with 76-mm phosphorus shells. The farm buildings belonging to the Uthoff-Brune, Grieskamp, Grabenmeier, Nillies, and Dahlhoff families were consumed by flames. As the firing subsided, the American tankers dismounted and assisted in treating the wounded civilians; the dead were laid aside for burial. Bellowing cattle and panic-stricken horses were led from the burning barns before the GIs turned again to the task at hand. They remounted their Shermans, and with a clatter of tracks, the column continued east toward Beckum.[16]

To compound the dilemma he was facing, Major Dunker next learned through a phone call from Lippborg that the combat commander of Soest had ordered that the bridges over the Lippe River at Lippborg, Herzfeld, and Benninghausen be demolished at midnight. This action would leave Dunker's forces trapped against the Lippe River, with no route of retreat. He placed a call to the commander and became engaged in a verbal confrontation that lasted several minutes. During the heated exchange, he was finally succeeded in persuading the commander to agree to leave the bridge at Herzfeld intact.

The city of Ahlen was the scene of feverish activity as American columns continued to flow toward the east in the direction of Beckum. Colonel Hinds, the American with whom Rosenbaum had negotiated a peaceful surrender of the city, had been replaced by Colonel Bruno. The new American commander advised Rosenbaum that he had been directed to capture Beckum. Bruno requested that the doctor telephone the German officer in charge of the Beckum garrison and attempt to convince him to surrender the city.

Shortly after he had persuaded the Soest commander to leave at least one bridge over the Lippe intact to permit the reinforcement—or retreat—of his troops, Major Dunker received a phone call from Ahlen. The voice at the other end of the line introduced himself as Oberfeldarzt (Lieutenant-Colonel) Dr. Paul Rosenbaum. The doctor then began to explain in great detail that he was calling on a humanitarian mission. He said he was an old front soldier and an experienced battle surgeon who clearly understood the meaning of duty and sacrifice. However, he noted, it was also his duty to advise the major of what he had been observing throughout the day. He had passed countless armored vehicles and support vehicles during the drive into the American lines and had personally observed them in action at the outskirts of Ahlen. The doctor had seen even more columns arriving behind the advance elements when he drove forward to collect the soldiers who had been wounded during the short exchange of fire at approaches to the city. He advised the major that he had personally observed no fewer than 2,000 vehicles—consisting of tanks, self-propelled guns, reconnaissance vehicles, and personnel transports—streaming toward the east on four separate routes.

The Americans had almost completely encircled Ahlen from the west, and they were in the process of closing the circle at the city's eastern approaches. The doctor had been advised that the American artillery batteries would begin firing on Beckum at 11:30 p.m. Rosenbaum pleaded with the major to permit the 15,000 inhabitants of Beckum, who lacked bunkers or shelters, to survive the war with their homes and workplaces intact. In a telephone conversation that lasted several minutes, he described how he had already observed the ragged German units retreating from Ahlen toward Beckum and said that he knew that they had no chance of stopping the American advance. Should the American commander deem it necessary, he added, the Americans would flatten Beckum with bombers. The discussion ended with Major Dunker explaining that he was under clear and distinct orders. However, he agreed to place a call to the district commander in Soest, and he asked the doctor to call him again that evening at 11:15, at which time he would have an answer. Rosenbaum emphasized once more that time was of the essence, as the moment was fast approaching when the Americans would lose patience and Beckum would be reduced to rubble. Dunker responded that he understood but added that he had an obligation to confer with his superiors. He once more asked the doctor to call him at 11:15.

It was not possible for Major Dunker to communicate with the division over the radio to explain the situation. Furthermore, even if he was to request orders from the division regarding Beckum, the answer could not reach him in the limited time available. The answer would lie with the district commander in Soest, to whom he was also subordinate and with whom he had direct contact.

The major picked up the phone, paused, and dropped it back onto the cradle. After weighing the consequences of his actions for several seconds, he decided not to contact the commander in Soest. Dunker knew that his response would be an explicit order to defend the city to the last man: the colonel would never accept responsibility for surrendering the city to the Americans. Dunker therefore decided to take independent action. Beckum would not be defended. As he gazed pensively at the telephone on his desk, the major knew that he could face severe retribution for this decision.

Picking up the phone again, Dunker immediately ordered a conference with all of his subordinate unit commanders. He also requested that the city interim Bürgermeister, Illigens, contact him by telephone. A short time later, he received the expected telephone call from Rosenbaum. Dunker immediately demanded that the medical officer reconfirm what he had previously reported about American troop strength. The only solace that the major could have with his decision was that there were not dozens but hundreds of armored vehicles, followed by endless convoys of support units, approaching the city. He also demanded to know how Rosenbaum had knowledge of an artillery barrage that the Americans had threatened to initiate at 11:30.

Rosenbaum responded that he had attempted to call Dunker that afternoon, but the communications lines were interrupted. He wanted to relay to the major that his previous estimate of enemy strength fell far short of the actual number of tanks, half-tracks, and support columns headed their way. He also said that he was unable to tell the major how he knew of the artillery barrage but that the information was definitely reliable.

The major asked Rosenbaum to pass on to the American commander of the forces in Ahlen that he, the combat commander of German forces in Beckum, was requesting a cease-fire until 1:00 a.m. in order to establish communications with him and declare Beckum an open city. Rosenbaum agreed to pass the request on to the Americans, but he reminded the major that time was running short. He then asked if the decision originated with Dunker's superior or if the major was making this decision on his own accord. That information, he added, would be important to the American colonel. The major responded that he was making the decision himself and that he was assuming all responsibility for declaring Beckum an open city. He then asked if Rosenbaum could come to his headquarters as an emissary.

Rosenbaum agreed to a meeting if Dunker could assure him that, while en route, his party would not fall victim to "irresponsible elements." He well remembered the shock of being fired on as he approached Ahlen in the company of the American colonel. There were also many officials—and soldiers—who stubbornly continued to enforce Hitler's no-surrender policy. Dunker promised him safe passage and an escort.

A short time later, Illigens, the interim Bürgermeister of Beckum, and City Inspector Kersting appeared at Dunker's headquarters. The major explained what had transpired between himself and Rosenbaum in Ahlen. Soon, the military unit commanders appeared, and Dunker briefed them on the situation. He then reminded them of Hitler's *Führerbefehl* (a personal directive from the Führer) issued the past fall. In accordance with the directive, he asked the officers gathered about him if any one of them was willing to assume the duties as city commander and take responsibility for the defense of Beckum. The officers remained silent. Dunker then declared that since no officer was willing to take command, he was required to pose the same question to all enlisted personnel. He requested that the officers brief their troops on his decision to declare Beckum an open city. Furthermore, he said, all troops were to evacuate the city no later than 1:30 a.m. All units should report their status no later than 1:45.

Dunker reasoned that the Americans would probably occupy the city during the night and immediately push south to close the pocket within the course of the next twenty-four hours. He instructed all forces under his command to march over the Herzfeld bridge and establish defensive positions on the south bank of the Lippe between Lippstadt and Lippborg. His new command post would be established in Östinghausen after 5:00 a.m. He briefed them on the necessary route of march, the requirement for establishing new defense positions, the areas of defense, and the location of the new headquarters and communications center. After dismissing the officers, he called the communications center at Mackenberg, explained the situation to the senior communicator, and ordered him to destroy the communications facilities before withdrawing behind a line running from Wiedenbrück to Lippstadt. The forces occupying the areas of Wiedenbrück, Langenberg, Benteler, and Cappel would be verbally briefed. The adjutants of various units assigned to the Field Replacement Battalion en route to Beckum were given new orders to establish positions south of the Lippe.

At 11:40, Rosenbaum again called and advised Dunker that the Americans had accepted the cease-fire proposal. He then put the American colonel's translator on the telephone. The translator confirmed that the cease-fire had been agreed on but added that if fire was received from German positions, the Americans would launch an attack on the city at midnight. He reminded Dunker that the American artillery batteries were prepared to level the city if necessary. The German major explained that he had ordered his forces to evacuate the city but that the Americans could not enter the city prior to 6:00 a.m.; the risk of an engagement between the withdrawing troops and the oncoming Americans was too great. The translator agreed.

For Dunker, time was critical. He had no way to transport his troops, and the American forces were fully motorized. He needed a lengthy head start to ensure that his soldiers could cross the Lippe before the American advance elements arrived. At 11:00 p.m., he received another call from the translator, who advised him that the American colonel had refused Dunker's proposal; the American forces, the translator said, would enter the city at 2:00 a.m. Dunker replied that the proposal was unacceptable. He informed the translator that under these circumstances, he would be forced to defend the city following the temporary cease-fire. The only concession he could make to his initial proposal was to alter the schedule to allow the Americans to enter the city at 4:00 a.m. The translator passed the telephone to Rosenbaum and disappeared to advise the colonel of Dunker's statement.

Dunker and Rosenbaum discussed the situation further for several minutes. At the close of the conversation, the major presented an unusual request to the doctor. "I live in Husum, on the North Sea," he explained, "Osterhusmer Strasse 19. My mother is Frau Blanca Dunker, my oldest brother Carlos is probably still in Danzig. My second oldest brother lives in Santiago, Chile. I am the third son. My younger brother was killed in action, my second younger brother is also dead. Please tell my family what happened here, it may not be possible for me to do so later. Tell them that I also promised that I would not take my own life. That's all."[17]

Rosenbaum soberly agreed to contact Dunker's family and passed the telephone to the translator. The American told Dunker that the colonel had refused the proposal to remain clear of the city until 4:00 a.m.; it was necessary for the Americans to adhere to their own timetable. He again reminded Dunker that if the Americans were fired on, the city would come under artillery fire. He added that the American forces would abide by the Geneva Convention, but if they took fire, "there wouldn't be much left" of the city.[18]

Dunker stubbornly replied that the Americans' timetable was unacceptable. If not enough time was provided for the withdrawal, it was likely that German and American forces would make contact, with deadly consequences. He had to ensure that his troops had enough time to clear the city before the Americans entered, and this could not take place prior to 4:00 a.m. Dunker also requested the name of the colonel with whom he was dealing. The translator refused to provide the name, but he advised Dunker that that information was known to Rosenbaum. The translator then asked Dunker to wait a moment while he again contacted the colonel.

Within several minutes, the translator returned to the telephone to tell Dunker that his proposal was accepted: the American forces would enter the city at 4:00. Greatly relieved, the German officer again asked the name of the colonel with whom he was negotiating and reminded the translator that, for the conduct of the negotiations, he had already provided his own name. Once again, the translator departed and then, after several minutes, picked up the telephone one more time.

The translator stated that situation remained unchanged; for security reasons, he could not provide the colonel's name. But Dunker persisted and advised the translator that he would have to know the name of the officer with whom he negotiated. The translator refused yet again and explained that American policy prohibited the disclosure of personal information.

Dunker explained that he would instruct the Bürgermeister of Beckum to wait for the Americans at the Beckum city hall with a white flag to officially surrender the city. The translator stated he would advise the American colonel of those intentions. After several minutes, he returned to the line and stated that the colonel wanted emissaries to meet with him outside the city, prior to the entry by the American forces. Dunker agreed to send an emissary if he was given a guarantee of safe conduct. The translator thanked Dunker for his concern for sparing the civilian lives, and the negotiations came to an end. After placing the handset on the receiver, the harried major glanced at his watch. The time was 12:50 a.m. He did not have much time to withdraw his troops from the surrendered city.

Seconds later, the telephone rang again. The district commander was on the line from Soest, and he demanded to know why Dunker was more than two hours late in submitting his hourly situation report. The major explained what had transpired. The shocking news that Beckum would be given up without resistance left the commander speechless for several moments. After recovering, the colonel demanded that Dunker withdraw from the agreement and defend Beckum. Major Dunker met this order with steadfast refusal. He advised the commander that it was too late—he had to abide by the agreement with the American colonel. The district commander furiously demanded to know why Dunker had taken independent action in negotiations instead of contacting higher command. Dunker responded that had he sought permission, the request to negotiate would never have been granted. In view of the information available to him, he took responsibility for negotiating a withdrawal from the city.

Realizing that Dunker would not retract his agreement with the Americans, the colonel ordered him to establish a defense line south of Beckum. Major Dunker was aware that he had already violated standard procedures by disobeying the irrevocable order to defend all towns and villages. The major then continued to counter the district commander's orders. He stated that he could not establish a line south of Beckum, for the terrain was flat, open ground and he was without artillery or armor support. Additionally, he said, the troops were already conducting their withdrawal, and it would not be possible now to change directions.

The conversation took on a sharper tone. Dunker ended the dispute by saying that he had no more time to discuss the situation, but he advised the commander that he would report to the headquarters the following morning after establishing a defense line. Dunker suspected what the future held for him was not good.

Initial reports began arriving to inform him that his units had evacuated their positions and were on the march. At 1:45 a.m., it was reported that the rear guard had cleared the southern exit of Beckum. The major decided that, for the time being, any further communication with the district commander would only serve to exacerbate a grim situation. He radioed his parent command, the 116th Panzer Division, and advised the staff of the actions he had taken, the current situation, and his intended actions for the next twenty-four hours.

At 2:00 a.m. on 1 April, he climbed into his vehicle and ordered the driver to proceed to his new command post in Östinghausen. As they drove through the deserted streets of Beckum, he noticed that some of the residents, aware that the last German troops had withdrawn, were already hanging white flags from windows and doorways. He cleared the outskirts of the town and drove past long files of troops marching in the darkness, finally arriving at Herzfeld at 4:00 a.m. As they approached the bridge spanning the Lippe, the structure suddenly exploded several hundred yards in front of them. Dunker leaped from the vehicle and raced to the edge of the canal. He found only smoking ruins where, just seconds earlier, an intact bridge had stood. Exasperated, he ran back to his vehicle and pulled a map from his document case.

The only route now available for crossing the Lippe was by way of Lippstadt. Dunker's staff had been sent ahead, and he now had no means of contacting them. By driving back and forth among the columns of soldiers for two hours, he was able to organize and issue orders to the units to march over Lippstadt and to concentrate to the southwest of the city no later than 11:00 a.m. Even the small head start he had managed to wring from the Americans during the nerve-wracking negotiations was now probably insufficient to fulfill his intentions.

The horizon in the east was growing light as they proceeded onward. While traversing through villages, they observed small groups of churchgoers, reminding the weary troops that it was Easter Sunday. The exhausted officer arrived at his headquarters in Östinghausen at 7:00 a.m., where he rested for one hour before proceeding to Soest. At 9:00, he arrived at the Soest commander's headquarters, where he encountered Colonel Stripp, the officer with whom he had exchanged words throughout the previous day and night. Dunker was immediately showered with curses and abuse. The enraged colonel advised him that he could expect to be summarily court-martialed and shot. Colonel Stripp continued with the tirade until he was interrupted by a telephone call. From the expression on the colonel's face and the tone of his voice, Dunker perceived that it was an urgent report regarding the Allied troop movements, and he had the feeling that the situation was taking another turn.[19]

The staff officers at Field Marshal Model's headquarters knew that they were facing encirclement should the army group be denied permission to withdraw its forces from the Rhine. With the speed of the American advance out of the bridgeheads toward the east and the lack of transport for their own forces, it would only be a matter of hours before the army group, with twenty-five divisions, would be trapped in a massive pocket. The field marshal summoned Major Winrich Behr and instructed him to carry out an unusual mission. Behr was to drive to Berlin and, as a personal representative of the field marshal, request instructions regarding the withdrawal of the units on the Rhine.

The major was provided a communications van, a Volkswagen *Kübelwagen*, and a motorcycle with a sidecar with which to conduct his mission. The detachment departed in the early morning hours under darkness. By sunrise, the men had reached the outskirts of Paderborn, where they asked a local farmer for the latest reports on the American advance. The farmer stated that the Americans were already approaching Paderborn and that for Behr's group to proceed on their route would take them directly into the path of the armored columns. He volunteered to guide them along a route that would take them around Paderborn and through the American lines. The farmer took a seat in the Volkswagen, and the party proceeded along side roads and farm tracks on a meandering trail through wooded hills interspersed with open fields. The group passed Paderborn to the north and was soon east of the American lines, where the soldiers parted company with their guide.

By the next evening, they had proceeded as far as the university town of Göttingen in the Hartz Mountains. The radiomen lost contact with the army group in the mountainous terrain, and near an army post in Göttingen, the driver of the communications van reported that the vehicle was broken down. The exasperated NCO advised Behr that the van could go no farther without repairs and that there were no parts on the base. Though he was not convinced that the vehicle was truly disabled, Behr called the men together and advised them of the situation. He told them that the war was lost, and stated that some of them had family members. There were responsibilities that had to be fulfilled, he said, especially when facing a lost war and the unknown future that occupation would bring. There would be hardships, and their families would be in dire need. He ended his briefing by motioning to the battered vehicle. "Leave that thing here," he unceremoniously stated. "You can all go home." At the nearby personnel office, he prepared discharge papers, signed them under the direction of Army Group B, and stamped them with an official seal. Then, he and the other soldiers parted.

Accompanied only by his driver, Behr continued toward Berlin the next morning. Their immediate destination was the Oberkommando des Heeres (Supreme Command of Land Forces [German]) staff in Zossen, and they circumvented Berlin to the south to arrive at that location. In Zossen, Behr met with an old friend, Major Freitag von Lohringhoven, who escorted him to Colonel-General Heinz Guderian. Despite the dire situation, the personnel in Zossen projected an outwardly calm appearance and almost appeared resigned to the impending defeat. The somber mood reflected the reality of the situation. There was nothing to report to Guderian, nothing on which he needed to be briefed. Indeed, the chief of staff had more pressing problems than to worry about Army Group B in the Ruhr Pocket.

That afternoon, Behr and his driver departed in a column of vehicles for Berlin. Having been in the city numerous times throughout the war, Behr was not overly struck by the blackened ruins and expanses of total destruction in the heart of the city. Like so many other soldiers from the front, he had witnessed firsthand the devastation of the industrial cities such as Cologne, Essen, and Düsseldorf. The mountains of rubble, the sirens, the pounding of the flak batteries, and the casualties all blended into one nightmare. Berlin was no exception, and it did not make a more distinct impression on him.

The mood was somber in the Führerhauptquartier. Behr was escorted by Lohringhoven as their party descended into the labyrinth of a massive, dimly lit bunker. There, he observed Adolf Hitler from a distance of 15 feet and noted that the Führer exhibited a forlorn, dispirited appearance. His hair was uncombed, and one arm was encased in a bandage; his face was gray and haggard. Some twenty officers were present, but Behr noticed that Reichsmarschall Hermann Göring was absent from the briefing, as was SS leader Heinrich Himmler. The voices reciting production figures, enemy positions, and Wehrmacht situation reports droned through the darkened chamber like a distant, monotone recording. It struck the major as ridiculous that in the midst of the dismal briefings and the bleak atmosphere, he was to add to the immense problems by advising the dictator that Model was requesting instructions on how to avoid a total collapse in the Ruhr.

The army in the Ruhr was apparently written off; little mention was made of the Americans and British. Behr found it difficult to believe that the entire future of Germany—the fate of the nation and its millions of people—lay in the hands of the dejected group of individuals crowded below the earth in a dimly lit cavern. He was relieved that he was not called on to address the briefing. Guderian intervened and simply asked if there were further instructions for Model's army group and let the issue melt into the stifling surroundings.

After approximately one hour, the officers shuffled from the briefing room. In an antechamber, Behr was surprised to encounter a Luftwaffe colonel he had known in previous years. In the course of their conversation, Behr told him that he was present for a briefing, that his business here was concluded, and that he now wanted to return to the Lower Rhine. The journey would be a difficult, if not impossible, undertaking, he said, since the Americans now had the Ruhr Valley tightly sealed with mechanized armored divisions. The officer immediately said that he could get Behr back into the Ruhr. The following morning, two Heinkel 111s were scheduled to depart from the airfield at Werde to deliver a load of nitroglycerin to the Ruhr industrial area. If he so desired, Behr could fly into the Ruhr on one of the aircraft. But, the officer added, it was not without extreme risk—if the highly sensitive load of nitroglycerin should receive a direct hit, there would be a massive explosion, so Behr should give the opportunity careful consideration.

Behr immediately left the Reich Chancellery and drove through the destroyed city to visit his mother and father, who lived in the Fronau area north of Berlin. The journey took him through a dead city. There was no traffic on the streets, and no people were observed amid the ruins. All that was left was the empty, burned shell of a dead metropolis. Against the somber setting of devastation, the weather was greeting the spring with sunshine. The trees were turning green, the flowers in Fronau were in bloom, and the fruit trees were already covered with blossoms in an early spring.

The following morning, the major drove to the airfield in Werde. As Behr approached the expansive runways, he was stunned to observe Luftwaffe personnel engaged in a soccer match. Two teams wearing colorful jerseys sprinted across a groomed soccer field, kicking the black-and-white ball to one another. Their shouts contrasted sharply with the distant, soft thunder of Soviet artillery fire. Behr thought of the soldiers facing the Russians only a short distance away by vehicle, only a few hours' march for an infantryman. And his thoughts returned to Model's divisions trapped in the Ruhr, facing the world's mightiest industrial power.[20]

Chapter 8

Closing the Ruhr Pocket

The last week of March 1945, General Patton's Third Army crossed the Rhine at Oppenheim and was piercing the heart of Germany. Farther north, the U.S. First Army broke out of the Remagen bridgehead and, encountering little resistance, pushed through the hilly terrain of the Sauerland. Field Marshal Montgomery's Twenty-first Army Group crossed the Rhine at Wesel, and after establishing a bridgehead against sporadic but sometimes fanatic resistance, it moved eastward toward the Münsterland and the Teutoburg Forest.

As the two American armies were breaking out of their bridgeheads on the Rhine, farther to the east waves of bombers continued their relentless campaign to disrupt German transportation and communications centers. Twenty-year-old Werner Trienens was in Rheine recovering from severe wounds received in August 1944 when he was assigned to escort ten recruits to Iserlohn for induction into the Wehrmacht. On Monday, 26 March, they proceeded as far as a suburb of Münster by train and then marched by foot through the badly damaged city, which had received another bombing raid only hours prior to their arrival. No public transportation was available, and emergency crews were at work restoring water service and utilities. Locating a Wehrmacht vehicle that was en route to Iserlohn, the men finally arrived at their destination at dawn.

Trienens's orders were to report to the Seydlitz Kaserne (a military base) with the teenagers, but there, the group found only a forlorn remnant of the Wehrmacht facility; the base had already been destroyed by bombs. At length, Trienens located the administration offices in a nearby field, where he was directed to an adjacent row of bunkers. On delivering his recruits, his orders received the obligatory official seal and were duly signed, and he was released to find transportation back to Rheine. Inquiring at the train station, he learned that no trains were running and no scheduling was possible in the face of incessant air attacks. After failing to locate any transportation, the exasperated soldier decided to put an end to his participation in the war. Armed with his signed orders for delivering the recruits, he hitch-hiked and walked for some twenty-four hours before reaching the home of his parents, located on Widukindstrasse 31 in the city of Paderborn.

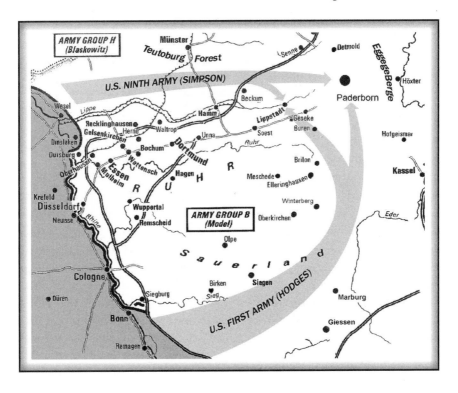

Trienens's father was disturbed by his son's unexpected appearance. The severe punishment for harboring deserters was well known. However, the young soldier was determined not to die for Hitler in the closing days of a lost war. Trienens found his home almost empty, many of the furnishings having been moved to the homes of friends and relatives outside the city where the danger of air raids remained remote. The kitchen was still sparsely equipped, and one bed remained in the house. His mother normally stayed with the Lummer farm family to escape the incessant bombing raids, while his father was working in Salzkotten. His sixteen-year-old brother, Heinz, had been called to the Paderborn Volkssturm, and to his relief, his youngest brother, Seppel, was working with a farmer in Neuhaus.

Trienens's mother was overjoyed to see her eldest son again and planned to celebrate the homecoming with what few provisions could be obtained. She advised him that they had been rasing rabbits in a hutch, one of which could be slaughtered for dinner. Late that afternoon, she sent him to the store with ration stamps to obtain something special "for the Easter holidays."

He was en route to the store when the initial air raid warning sounded. He turned and hurried back to the house and had just entered the kitchen when the full alarm sounded. No sooner had the sirens begun than the heavy throbbing of approaching Flying Fortresses could be heard, quickly followed by the dull, distant thudding of detonations. He and his mother hurried to the cellar as the bombs grew nearer.

Within seconds, they found themselves at the center of a maelstrom. Sitting on a bench, the soldier wrapped his mother's head in a blanket to block out the horror. Windows crashed, dust filled the air, and their eardrums throbbed from the earsplitting explosions that rent the atmosphere. The smell of flames engulfed them, and it became difficult to breathe. Trienens could discern human voices screaming somewhere in the distance. A final, massive explosion was followed by sheets of flames erupting from a forward storeroom, where incendiaries had penetrated a shattered window. Stumbling through the dust and smoke, they made their way up the stairs and onto the side street, where they ran past burning buildings to a nearby field. The shrieking of the rabbits burning in their cages could be heard above the crackling flames, and they rushed toward the middle of the open field where they could escape the fire and breathe cool air. As Trienens turned to look on the burning city, he observed the massive tower of the Paderborn Cathedral slowly tilt until, overtaken by flames and the force of gravity, it crashed to the earth, the sound of the falling structure rising above the waves of phosphorus explosions.[1]

General Fritz Bayerlein's attempt to break through the American units pouring east out of the Remagen bridgehead for a drive toward Kassel with his LIII Corps quickly ground to a halt. Using highly mobile forces in coordination with air reconnaissance and fighter-bomber patrols, the Americans succeeded in stopping the German drive within hours. The First Army's 3rd Armored Division again concentrated on proceeding north and northeast to meet advance elements of the U.S. 9th Army at Paderborn.

The American armored divisions were organized into three combat commands: A, B, and R. Each had the approximate strength of a regiment and consisted of two task forces (TFs). The TFs were further organized into combat teams and battle groups, which were identified by the name of the specific commander of the unit. For the advance toward Paderborn, the task forces were assigned four separate routes, numbered one through four. The four columns would advance north simultaneously and converge on Paderborn for the linkup with the U.S. Ninth Army. Combat Command R (CCR), under Colonel Howze, was assigned to push Task Force Hogan over the Wewer River toward Paderborn on the westernmost flank, designated as March Route 1. Task Force Richardson was to proceed along the Wünnenberg-Haaren-Nordborchen road over March Route 2. Combat

Command B (CCB), under Colonel Boudinot, was assigned the two easternmost routes, with Task Force Welborn advancing over the Niedermarsbert-Etteln-Paderborn road along March Route 3 and Task Force Lovelady advancing along the eastern flank over Arolsen–Rhoden Lichtenau–Paderborn on March Route 4. Task Forces Doan and Kane, designated as Combat Command A (CCA), were assigned to follow up in reserve, with Kane on the left in the wake of Hogan and Doan following behind Welborn. The TFs were to converge on Paderborn no later than 31 March, where they would join with units of the Ninth Army that were advancing toward the south. What the soldiers of the 3rd Armored Division did not know was that they were about to encounter a new enemy—one that posed a serious obstacle to the planned linkup.

Roughly 20 miles west of Kassel, in the small settlement of Arolsen, was a small military training center assigned to the Waffen SS Finance Administration School. Under the leadership of SS Sturmbannführer Thöle, the school nominally consisted of 70 staff personnel and had a student capacity of 1,100 troops.

Thöle had received orders in mid-March to provide a battle group of 900 men, under the leadership of Sturmbannführer Becker, to be dispatched to the 32nd SS Division facing the Soviet army south of Frankfurt an der Oder. The school facilities had been stripped of weapons and equipment to arm the soldiers transferred to the front. After the departure of the battle group, the school had just one automobile, two small motorcycles, and two wood-fueled trucks available. The only staff personnel remaining were those who had suffered severe wounds during the previous six years of war or members of the administration cadre whose presence was deemed essential. Among the students who stayed behind were convalescents who had had both legs amputated and had to be carried into the classrooms. Of the training officers still in Arolsen, three had lost an eye and most had suffered disabling wounds in combat; many of them walked with crutches. The rest of the staff consisted of approximately 200 support personnel who fulfilled supply and administrative functions.[2]

As the school prepared to meet the oncoming Americans, the training officers halted a troop train that was carrying soldiers from furlough to their various units. Taking command of the soldiers on the train, the school cadre formed two battle groups to be placed under command of the military district commander in Kassel. Before this could be accomplished, however, one of the groups received orders to proceed on foot as a battle group along the Frankenberg-Eder road toward Marburg in the south.

On 29 March, the battle group made its first contact with the Americans south of Korbach. An American unit, part of the U.S. 3rd Armored Division, was advancing north toward Paderborn to conduct the linkup with the Ninth Army when they collided with the group of students, instructors, and support personnel from Arolsen. In the short skirmish that followed, two American tanks were disabled.

Hearing the fighting in the distance, Sturmbannführer Thöle ordered Obersturmführer (First Lieutenant) Schmeykahl to lead the second battle group toward Korbach. As Schmeykahl entered that village, his vehicle was struck by fire from an oncoming Sherman. Soon after engaging the American force, the two SS battle groups found it impossible to hold a line, and Schmeykahl ordered the troops to fall back and regroup in Mengeringhausen.

By the evening of 29 March, the remnants of the SS battle groups from Arolsen had regrouped between Mengeringhausen and Twiste. The troops under Schmeykahl's command had scattered after the action at Korbach, and stragglers continued trickling in to be reorganized into combat units. The Americans' intent to close the trap around the Ruhr was obvious, and the Germans decided to retreat toward Landau, farther to the east, to avoid being caught in the encirclement.

Sturmbannführer Thöle, the SS force commander, now received intermittent orders by telephone from the military district commander in Kassel. Having escaped the encirclement by moving eastward, the battle group was directed to reinforce a line along the Eder River valley and wait to receive orders from SS Brigade Westfalen. Unbeknownst to them, the orders from Westfalen would never reach Thöle's embattled units.

The ancient city of Paderborn carried a long tradition as the site of military training facilities, and the Nazi government had continued to utilize and build on the training areas for Wehrmacht and Waffen SS units. As the Americans began their drive from the north and the south to close the pincers, military training commands in the Paderborn area were being organized under the auspices of SS Brigade Westfalen. Plans called for the brigade to leave the quarters in Sennelager, north of Paderborn, and proceed south into the Sauerland. The troops were then to combine strength with other German forces in the area to cut off the leading elements of Americans advancing out of the Remagen bridgehead.

Field Marshal Model, intent on preventing the linkup that would trap his army group in the Ruhr area, had ordered SS Brigade Westfalen to be placed under command of Lieutenant-General Hermann Flörke, whose LXVI Corps had been decimated during the retreat from the Rhine. Model ordered Flörke to regroup his forces, including SS Brigade Westfalen, in the area of Marsberg; then, no later than 31 March, they were to push toward the Eder reservoir. Unbeknownst to any of the Allied forces moving through the Sauerland, the main routes the SS troops planned to use were the same roads the three American columns pushing north toward Paderborn were taking. The powerful and confident U.S. forces were on a collision course with a dreaded, although vastly weakened, enemy.

In addition to the training personnel from Sennelager who formed the core of SS Brigade Westfalen, there was one unit that would severely handicap the American drive toward Paderborn. Heavy Panzer Battalion 507 had seen its first action in March 1944 near Tarnopol on the Russian front. Since that time, the renowned unit had been held in reserve until needed at critical points on the front, and it had thus been thrown into action time and again until its battle-scarred tanks were decimated. In January 1945, the battalion had lost its last Tiger tanks during the fighting on the Narev. Thereafter, the battalion's 2nd and 3rd Companies were ordered to Sennelager along with the battalion staff to be reequipped and trained in the use of new Tiger II tanks. The 1st Company was destined to remain on the Oder Front to support the Wehrmacht forces that were desperately attempting to block the Russian advance on Berlin.

The two companies of Heavy Panzer Battalion 507 that were withdrawn from the east began training with their new Tiger IIs in mid-March. The massive Tigers, delivered to the training area directly from the Henschel factory in Kassel, weighed almost 70 tons and were the heaviest operational tanks produced by any nation during the war. The Tiger II was similar to the Tiger I, but it carried heavier armor on the turret and bow; like its predecessor, it was equipped with a high-velocity 88-mm cannon. The rolling fortress was manned by a crew of five, who were protected by 150-mm glacis plates on the frontal armor. The enormous vehicle could carry almost eighty rounds of 88-mm high-explosive, armor-piercing, and hollow-charge ammunition. Despite its powerful 700-horsepower engine, however, the Tiger proved to be underpowered and less mobile than the earlier, lighter tanks, and it was encumbered by a maximum speed of less than 25 miles per hour. The tank could be easily identified by its long, low profile and massive, interlocking road wheels, similar to those on the favored Panther.

The Tiger was also plagued with mechanical problems. In a tank-on-tank duel, the machine could not be matched by any other tank in any theater. But in the confines of the Sauerland and the Teutoburg Forest, with thickly wooded hillsides and narrow, winding roads, the faster, highly maneuverable American Sherman tank had a distinct advantage. Many of the experienced German tank crews preferred the lighter, more maneuverable Panther. At this stage of the war, however, it was unusual for the German units to receive new equipment of any kind.

In mid-March 1945, the 507th received a large number of new recruits and twenty Tiger IIs with which they manned and equipped two panzer companies. During the following two weeks, they familiarized the personnel with their new tanks and trained the crews, adjusting the guns and drilling as intact armored companies. The battalion received additional reinforcement when it was joined by three Tiger tanks from Heavy Panzer Battalions 510 and 511. The commander of the battalion, Major Fritz Schöck, had assigned twelve of the new tanks to the

3rd Company under the command of then-Lieutenant Wolf Koltermann. The remaining Tigers and three Panther tanks were assigned to the 2nd Company, commanded by Lieutenant Bernhard Pfeuffer.

On the night of 24 March, Koltermann had reason to celebrate. In addition to being given command of a new Tiger tank company, the veteran from the Russian Front was marking his promotion from lieutenant to captain. His commander, Major Schöck, also awarded him with the coveted Knight's Cross. As the Allies were preparing their breakout from the bridgeheads on the Rhine, the new captain—with Germany's highest award for valor suspended from his neck by a wide red, white, and black ribbon—spent the night toasting and singing marching songs with his fellow officers and crewmen in Sennelager.[3]

The SS personnel of the Sennelager training units had been organized into two battalions, one under the command of one-legged Hauptsturmführer (Captain) Denker as an SS panzer reconnaissance battalion, the second under command of Hauptsturmführer Uhden. Both battalions consisted primarily of men recovering from wounds.

The staff of the hastily assembled Brigade Westfalen established a command post 3 miles east of Paderborn in the village of Dahl. Regiment Meyer moved into Hamborn, 4 miles south of Paderborn, and established a regimental command post. The two battalions under Fruehauf and Schaarschmidt began moving south. Regiment Holzer established a command post in Dörenhagen, 4 miles southwest of Paderborn, where they were joined by Major Schöck's Heavy Panzer Battalion 507.

Few of the SS or Wehrmacht personnel at the facilities near Paderborn were aware that they were now assigned to the newly organized SS Brigade Westfalen. The administrative offices were combed for personnel; weapons and equipment were lacking, and there was no means of providing rations and logistics in the field. Assigned to lead the brigade was Obersturmbannführer (Lieutenant-Colonel) Hans Stern, who had transferred to the Waffen SS from the Wehrmacht, where he had earned the Knight's Cross in 1941 while serving as company commander with Panzer Regiment 11. The brigade consisted of two regiments that retained the designation of their regimental commanders. The commander of the first regiment was Sturmbannführer Meyer, who had been severely wounded while serving with the 3rd SS Panzer Division "Totenkopf" in Russia. Meyer's regiment consisted of two battalions, SS Panzer Reconnaissance Training and Replacement Battalion 1 under command of Sturmbannführer Fruehauf and SS Panzer Reconnaissance Training and Replacement Battalion 2 under command of Hauptsturmführer Schaarschmidt. On 31 March, Meyer's regiment was joined by an SS Panzer Reconnaissance NCO Training Battalion, led by Hauptsturmführer Sonne.

The second regiment of Brigade Westfalen was commanded by Sturm-bannführer Friedrich Holzer, who had won the Knight's Cross in 1943 while serving on the Eastern Front with the 2nd SS Panzer Division "Das Reich." Holzer had been assigned to command the SS Panzer Training and Replacement Regiment in Augustdorf after suffering numerous wounds as a tank commander on the Eastern Front, and like many officers at this stage of the war, he was well accustomed to fighting in adverse conditions and against formidable numbers. Holzer's regiment consisted of five battalions, each made up of two or three roughly assembled infantry companies with 120 soldiers each.

On 29 March, Panzer Battalion 507 received mobilization orders and was officially integrated as a component of SS Brigade Westfalen. The 2nd Company was assigned to move toward Dörenhagen and Eggeringhausen. Koltermann's 3rd Company was ordered to advance to the village of Kirchborchen and strike the oncoming Americans on their eastern flank.

As the 507th prepared its tanks for battle, word was unexpectedly received at the nearby SS Panzer Reconnaissance Training and Replacement Battalion 2 in Staumühle that all personnel were to assemble and organize for combat. The companies, hastily collected by the training cadre, were made up of seventeen-year-old recruits with only three or four weeks of rudimentary training and elderly miners from the area of Aachen. The groups of recruits were organized into impromptu infantry platoons; the elderly men were assigned to provide supply functions.

The groups from the Staumühle facility were issued weapons from the various training armories available to them. Small arms consisted of MG-34 machine guns, K98 rifles, Italian submachine guns, Belgian pistols, and shoulder-fired Panzerfausts. In addition to their field uniforms, the troops were provided with black leather trousers and jackets to be worn over the uniforms. The unusual leather garments had been salvaged from a German navy depot in France during the rout in late summer 1944. The thick leather uniforms, well suite for armored vehicles and U-boats, proved to be too cumbersome and heavy for infantry use and were soon discarded. All other belongings that could not be easily carried were assembled and stored in laundry bags. The companies possessed no vehicles, although the battalion supply unit was assigned two wood-fueled trucks. The staff retained several automobiles and motorcycles.[4]

The SS unit located in nearby Augustdorf also lacked basic equipment and supplies. Incoming recruits had no bedding, lockers, chairs, or tables, and their empty barracks were devoid of furnishings at the time of their arrival. Unfazed by the lack of facilities and equipment, Obersturmführer Walter Ott, the battalion communications officer, had purchased supplies for the recruits. He obtained straw from a nearby farmer with his own funds and had it delivered by horse-cart for bedding. The remainder of his bank account was used for rations. While serving in Normandy with the 17th SS Panzer Division "Götz von Berlichingen," Ott had witnessed the immense material support the Americans were able to bring onto the battlefield. Now, facing the Allied onslaught as it rolled deeper into Germany, he held no illusions regarding the outcome of the war. Even if he survived, Ott concluded, in defeat he would no longer need the money anyway.[5]

The training companies in Augustdorf were also equipped with a wide array of foreign and German weapons. Each platoon was issued a light machine gun and a limited number of submachine guns. The majority of the recruits retained their bolt-action carbines. Despite the fact that they were being produced cheaply and in great quantities, few Panzerfausts had filtered through the erratic supply chain to reach the Augustdorf facility. The runners who carried communications between companies and higher commands were issued bicycles, many of which were plagued with flat tires, but there were no replacements for worn-out equipment. The communications unit possessed one mobile radio that was pulled in a wooden hand-cart. No infrastructure for logistics or support was available. Even the most rudimentary infantry clothing and equipment was sparse; the men were mostly clad in traditional black panzer uniforms. The short, double-breasted tunics, cut narrow at the waist, were of excellent design for maneuvering in and out of the narrow confines of tank turrets, but they were poorly suited to infantry operations.

On the night of 29 March, the mixed array of young, aging, and convalescing soldiers departed their barracks. They arrived in Augustdorf early the next morning. A quick but thorough search of the SS depot in Augustdorf, where they had hoped to find needed uniforms and equipment, produced only a few mottled-camouflage SS battle smocks and field-gray overcoats. The supply of weapons and ammunition had long since been depleted.

In Augustdorf-Nordlager, the SS Panzer NCO Training and Instruction Battalion, under command of Hauptsturmführer Burmeister, was busy preparing for battle. The students and instructors buckled on heavy leather cartridge belts and field gear, filled their magazine pouches, and shared the burden of carrying the heavy belts of machine-gun ammunition.

At 6:15 p.m., they began to march south under darkening skies. A light rain started to fall as they passed the village of Haustenbeck, and they marched through Paderborn's deserted streets. The city was still burning from the massive air raid of 27 March, and the darkness was punctuated with sporadic explosions and collapsing buildings that hurled glowing embers and large fragments of masonry skyward from the rubble. Although Paderborn had previously experienced bombing raids during the course of the war, the most recent air raid had been the largest and had fallen on a defenseless city that was stripped of any means of repelling the bombers. Within twenty-seven minutes of the appearance of the Allied bombers, Paderborn had suffered almost complete destruction.

Bomb craters and collapsed buildings marked the path of the marching grenadiers and students. The stench of dead cattle and burned vehicles choked the air, and no sign of life could be discerned as they made their way through the blackened city. After several hours, it was noticed that two erstwhile soldiers were already missing. Both had been recovering from wounds and could have been unable to keep pace or perhaps had decided to simply end their war by disappearing into the darkness.

The column cleared the city of Paderborn, and the order was soon given to load and secure the weapons. At about 2:00 a.m. on 30 March, the column arrived at the village of Nordborchen, south of Paderborn, and bivouacked. More troops arrived from the Sennelager training facilities throughout the night. By dawn, the entire combat group from the training battalion had settled into Nordborchen; platoons and squads of soldiers were sleeping in barns, garages, and private residences.

Shortly after arriving in the darkened village of Nordborchen, Untersturmführer Ahrens was ordered to march his platoon to the Alfen-Wewer road to ensure that it was secure and to relieve the outposts. At 4:00 a.m., he gathered the weary students assigned to his platoon and started off through the darkness. The platoon began digging defenses adjacent to the road south of Wewer, and a reconnaissance patrol was dispatched toward Alfen. As the eastern horizon grew light, the patrol returned and reported that the other SS units had established security positions in Alfen. Knowing that any enemy from that direction would first encounter the security detachment in there, the soldiers removed their heavy battle gear and earnestly engaged in preparing defenses.

At approximately 9:30, they were startled to hear the sound of tank fire from the south, at a distance of 4 or 5 miles. The men sprang to their feet and prepared their weapons for battle as the erratic sound of small-arms fire began drifting through the still morning air. At 10:00, Ahrens and another soldier, named Öhler, set out toward Alfen on an antiquated motorcycle that they had discovered nearby. Minutes later, they came on sentries nervously anticipating the arrival of the enemy. They cautiously proceeded south toward the farthest outposts, where the secondary road joined Reichsstrasse 480 in a sharp curve. As the motorcycle slowly turned the corner, they found themselves face to face with a massive, olive-colored Sherman tank, in front of which a GI was standing with a machine pistol trained at them. With little other choice, Öhler stopped the motorcycle and raised his hands. Ahrens raised his hands, dismounted the motorcycle, and obediently walked toward the American, who was motioning with the submachine gun and calling good-naturedly, "Come on boys, come on."[6]

When the American soldier momentarily averted the muzzle of the submachine gun, Ahrens sprang into the thick undergrowth lining the road. He was immediately followed by a burst from the American's weapon. The deafening fire from the GI's weapon was joined by a burst from the tank's machine gun. Unscathed, Ahrens cleared the field of fire, dodging, ducking, and running until he disappeared into the surrounding woods.

He paused to catch his breath and to get his bearings as the shots and curses of the GIs faded behind him. Peering from the copse of woods, he observed an immense column of olive drab tanks and half-tracks streaming northward toward Kirchborchen. The sounds of erratic but heavy fighting echoed over the hills as the American column began encountering the SS units. After attempting to estimate the strength of the column, Ahrens struck out in a northerly direction toward Nordborchen, taking advantage of the cover offered by the woods.

That same morning, at 4:00, the 2nd Company of Fruehauf's battalion, led by Obersturmführer Hoffmann, departed Staumühle and headed south. Shortly after sunrise, the ragged troops were south of Nordborchen when they encountered a panic-striken Wehrmacht paymaster, who reported that the Americans were moving toward them with heavy armored columns. Hoffmann immediately ordered his troops to dig in along both sides of Reichsstrasse 480. He then turned command of the company over to Oberscharführer (Sergeant) Gedaschko while he rode forward in a sidecar to reconnoiter the road ahead.

After 3 miles, Hoffmann encountered four Sherman tanks, swung the motorcycle about, and fled before the tank crews could react. Within ten minutes, he had reached the battalion headquarters in Etteln, where he reported the American presence to Sturmbannführer Fruehauf. Fruehauf ordered him to take a Volkswagen Kübelwagen and two Panzerfausts, return to the American column, and attempt to delay its advance while he organized the units. Hoffmann leaped into the Volkswagen and rattled away toward Kirchborchen.

A short time later, he engaged a Sherman and a half-tracked personnel carrier from a location south of Kirchborchen along Route 2. The entire area erupted in fighting as Hoffmann's company attempted to halt the American armored column without the support of antitank guns. The soldiers of one platoon west of Reichsstrasse 480, led by Unterscharführer Zabel, were killed to the last man. Many of the Americans gave SS troops no quarter; indeed, some of the GIs, having fought their way through SS units from Normandy to the Rhine, practiced a policy of killing the SS troops wherever they found them. Under heavy losses, the remaining soldiers of Hoffmann's company began withdrawing toward Etteln, where they quickly established defenses and continued to hold their position until dusk. As the sun set and darkness descended on the ragged band of survivors, the men in the company, now numbering only fifty, collected their equipment and filed toward Grundsteinheim.

The 2nd Company, Battalion 2, of Regiment Meyer, also began hastily preparing to move in the early morning hours of 30 March. The troops were delayed for several minutes; the modified ignition systems of the wood-burning trucks required some time before the engines were warm enough to function. Eventually, the troops proceeded south through Paderborn to Henglarn, where they dismounted from the trucks; the vehicles returned to transport the other companies to their destinations. The 2nd Company was the only intact unit yet to arrive at Henglarn. As the company established defenses, one platoon was ordered to take positions approximately 200 yards south of Atteln along the Henglarn-Atteln road. Soon after the company established a position, the rattle of tracked vehicles was heard in the distance. Suddenly, six Shermans roared down the road toward the positions before coming to an abrupt halt several hundred yards from the concealed Germans. With throbbing engines, the tanks remained stationary along the road for several minutes while the tank commanders carefully examined the terrain with binoculars from their turrets.

Untersturmführer Weber, one of the platoon leaders, had just crawled closer to the stationary Shermans with an antitank weapon when the vehicles rocked forward and resumed their advance at a rapid pace. The column rumbled past the hidden soldiers, unaware that they were being observed from a short distance by an improvised combat group of SS grenadiers. Behind the six Shermans rolled an immense convoy of trucks, jeeps, and half-tracks. Unbeknownst to Weber and the others, they had met the forward elements of Task Force Welborn of the U.S. 3rd Armored Division.

Unable to engage the convoy with their light, shoulder-fired antitank weapons from a distance of 200 yards, the men of the company remained motionless under concealment until nightfall. Throughout the day, the American units continued to roll past in a terrifying exhibit of military power. As night descended, the platoon made its way over the ridge toward the east. There, the soldiers met the rest of their company, which had already suffered heavy losses while engaging Welborn's unit in Henglarn.[7]

On 30 March, Regiment Holzer marched along the Paderborn-Lichtenau-Scherfede road toward the south. Obersturmführer Walter Ott accompanied the battalion toward Scherfede, where the men were directed to establish defenses to halt the oncoming Americans. The battalion consisted of Ott's communications unit, made up of a few radiomen and a modified Panzer II chassis as a mobile communications vehicle, and three hastily assembled infantry companies and a panzer company. The armored unit consisted of a dozen obsolete tanks of various models that had been used for training. Ott established his communications center near Scherfede in a forestry building, where they could establish telephone communications with the command post in the town.

That morning, the men of Task Force Lovelady were proceeding from Rhoden toward Scherfede when they suddenly encountered Holzer's Battalion 1. The task force had been assigned to proceed north on the right flank on March Route 4, secure the road junction in Scherfede, and head for Paderborn through Kleinenberg and Lichtenau. As the task force neared the village of Wrexen, it encountered German soldiers who were determined to halt the advance.

The Americans soon lost a Sherman to an antiquated MKIII, and the GIs dug in under heavy fire to await reinforcements. Throughout 30 March, the sound of fighting rang from the woods surrounding Wrexen. As darkness fell, the grenadiers continued to block the advance with small arms and Panzerfausts. The fighting continued into the night, and before sunrise, Lovelady's columns had lost five tanks to the scattered German units. It was not until the morning of 31 March that the GIs could reach their objective of Scherfede.

Task Force Richardson continued to meet stiff resistance in Kirchborchen and Nordborchen. Nestled in the rolling hills 6 miles south of Paderborn, the twin villages of Nordborchen and Kirchborchen were strategically important to the task force's advance, as either could provide a staging area for any German units preparing to attack the flanks of the American columns. Task Force Richardson had first met resistance to the west of Etteln as it collided with the mixture of troops constituting Hoffmann's company. After rolling through the weak defenders, Richardson's tanks then proceeded toward the village of Kirchborchen. Preparing to meet the American column was a force of more than 200 Hitler Youth, augmented by Waffen SS veterans, who were hastily establishing defenses.

The tanks of Richardson's columns were supported by infantrymen of the U.S. 36th Infantry Regiment, who fought their way into the outskirts of Kirchborchen. As they attempted to penetrate the first line of houses, they were met by a hail of small-arms fire and Panzerfausts, used as direct-fire weapons and as improvised artillery between the buildings. The Americans were forced to a halt and were soon compelled to evacuate their positions and abandon the town.

On the left flank of the U.S. 3rd Armored Division, Task Force Hogan pushed to Wewer with little resistance. The American occupation of Wewer threatened to cut off any route of retreat for the German troops in Kirchborchen. To avoid being encircled, the SS and Hitler Youth defenders withdrew from Kirchborchen, which by then was referred to as "bazooka-town" by the GIs of Task Force Richardson, who had experienced the engagement there. The Americans followed in the wake of the withdrawing Germans and occupied the heavily damaged buildings recently used by the defenders. After a brief delay to reorganize the units, they moved forward in pursuit, again meeting resistance from the withdrawing Germans. The night rapidly erupted with the sounds of small-arms fire over the crackle of burning buildings and intermittent bursts from Panzerfausts as the grenadiers withdrew through deserted streets. The surrounding structures were illuminated by two American armored vehicles burning with white-hot intensity, ignited by Panzerfausts fired at close range in the narrow, cobblestone streets. By midnight, most of Kirchborchen had been secured by the Americans. The GIs attempted to consolidate their gains at dawn, while German snipers set to work from the surrounding woods, making any movement difficult.

As Richardson's units fought fiercely in the streets of Kirchborchen, other units assigned to his combat command circumvented the town on the main road to the west. The U.S. 3rd Armored Division had been ordered to reach Paderborn by 30 March, and the mechanized units were bypassing pockets of resistance to meet their goal.

Between 10:00 and 11:00 a.m., the units bypassing Kirchborchen collided with SS troops at nearby Nordborchen, where troops of Holzer's Battalion 3, under command of Hauptsturmführer Burmeister, had prepared to meet the oncoming Americans. One of the grenadiers preparing to engage the American columns was Waffen SS Grenadier Wolfgang Huber. To his right was Unterscharführer Diner, to his left Unterscharführer Schröder. The soldiers nervously inspected their weapons and secured their combat gear as artillery and tank shells began impacting the area, showering them with dirt and fragments of masonry from nearby buildings. Soon, the high, rounded profiles of Sherman turrets appeared, accompanied by half-tracks loaded with infantrymen.

As the Americans neared, the grenadiers opened fire from their hidden positions. A hail of small-arms fire was returned. One member of the platoon, Hiermeier, fell with a shot to the head. He was quickly carried by the withdrawing grenadiers to a nearby church, where he died within minutes. Grenadier Quast received a shell fragment in the skull. Untersturmführer Pozorsky, the platoon commander, was severely wounded as a bullet tore through his thigh and severed an artery. Schröder, Grewel, Peitler, and Raffelberg soon fell with head wounds. Thiejung, Lack, Breitenstein, and Hauptscharführer Wulfes were all wounded. Nachtrab and Nitsch continued to pour fire toward the moving Americans with their MG-42 as Schnellmoser and another soldier fell to American snipers. Huber and Rottenführer Ungemach continued to engage moving tanks and fleeting silhouettes of infantrymen.

A German medical officer, assisted by the Scandinavian nurses Else-Katrin and Inger, busied himself readying a barn in the center of the village to serve as an aid station. The pastor of the local church agreed that the wounded could be carried into the relative safety of the church; the Americans should respect its sanctity. With a touch of irony, the medical personnel improvised a Red Cross flag by tearing apart a large Nazi banner for use of the scarlet fabric. The flag was draped from the church bell tower to identify the impromptu medical facility. They then set about their grim task of caring for the wounded who arrived limping or carried on makeshift litters. That evening, there remained thirty-five survivors in the company.[8]

As the fighting raged in Nordborchen, Untersturmführer Ahrens, after having escaped the American with the machine pistol by springing into the woods south of Kirchborchen, arrived at the scene. As he entered the village under heavy fire, one of the grenadiers rushing toward the fighting told him that a fellow officer, Untersturmführer Christian Schwab, was lying either dead or wounded in the village church. Ahrens hurried to locate his friend and found the church full of dead and dying soldiers. He assisted the Danish nurse, Else-Katrin, in carrying a badly mangled corpse from the building before finding Schwab. Seeing that the severely wounded officer would probably not survive, he departed the improvised hospital in search of his company.[9]

On the morning of 30 March, reconnaissance units of the U.S. 3rd Armored Division's Task Force Welborn departed from Niedermarsberg and pushed north, running parallel to Task Force Richardson farther to the west. The forward reconnaissance units met German resistance at the village of Meerhof, which they reported and bypassed, leaving it to the main task force to mop up the enemy units.

Near Husen, the American reconnaissance units then clashed with the forward elements of Meyer's regiment, who were in the process of establishing defenses along a line running from Haaren-Helmern-Husen. Welborn's tanks, followed closely by infantry in half-tracks, quickly eliminated weak opposition in Husen, Atteln, Henglarn, and Etteln and proceeded on a route through a wooded area northeast of Etteln toward the main Eggeringhausen-Kirchborchen road.

General Maurice Rose, commander of the U.S. 3rd Armored Division, worried about the resistance his forward units were unexpectedly encountering, decided to commit more forces to the area east of Nordborchen. The German armored units that had been reported on his flank continued to present a danger that could not be ignored. He ordered Task Force Welborn to engage the German units from the rear and thus eliminate the threat. At approximately 5:00 p.m., the tanks and half-tracks of Task Force Welborn pressed on toward the northeast through a wooded area between Etteln and Eggeringhausen; there, they again encountered SS grenadiers, who were supported by elements of Heavy Panzer Battalion 507. After penetrating the weak resistance in Etteln, Welborn's force swung toward Eggeringhausen, where they encountered tanks of the 507th's 2nd Company. A sharp engagement between the American and German tanks ensued before the Americans disengaged and swung toward the west. They were unaware that Wolf Koltermann's 3rd Company was lying in wait for such a movement to occur. Lieutenant Jähn, commanding one of the 2nd Company tank platoons, immediately radioed Major Schöck and advised him that the American column had turned and was heading directly toward Koltermann's location.

Captain Koltermann had positioned his company of tanks on a wooded hill known as the Kühlenberg, situated between Kirchborchen and Schloss Hamborn, where his unit could observe any advance toward Hamborn or Kirchborchen from the southeast. Koltermann ordered his 1st and 3rd Platoons to take positions to the north and the south of the road, where they could engage the oncoming column's flanks after the point elements had passed. He situated his own 2nd Platoon where the men could observe the tanks on the enemy's point, after they were well within range of the other platoons lying in concealment. The approaching sounds of heavy tracked vehicles could be heard as dusk was falling on the hills and valleys of the lower Teutoburg Forest.

At length, Koltermann observed an American armored reconnaissance vehicle as it cautiously emerged from the forest, proceeded about 100 yards into the open field, and halted. After several minutes, the reconnaissance vehicle was followed by fifteen or twenty Sherman tanks. The column rumbled past the reconnaissance vehicle and took up a wedge-shaped formation along the roadway. The formation then remained stationary, with engines idling for several minutes, before continuing toward his position.

Koltermann permitted the point elements to come well within range before ordering his company to open fire. The platoons on the left and right flanks of the American column fired simultaneously. Within minutes, practically all of the tanks in the formation as well as the support vehicles moving forward from the woods were rendered immobile wrecks. Flames shot skyward from hundreds of gallons of burning fuel and exploding ammunition. With the firing of weapons floating over the hills, the 2nd Company of the 507th advanced from Eggeringhausen to join the engagement.

By 7:30 p.m., Welborn's advance column was destroyed. Vehicles had careened in all directions across fields and into the nearby woods to escape the deadly fire. The vehicles rendered immobile were rapidly abandoned as the GIs sought shelter. Armored vehicles remained burning on the fields and along the road. Koltermann reported the action to the battalion staff and ordered his company to advance. The company had previously been assigned to secure the flank of the battalion and prevent the SS troops in Kirchborchen-Nordborchen from being outflanked from the south; for the Tigers to abandon their positions would have risked leaving the troops still battling in Kirchborchen and Nordborchen open to encirclement by other American columns.

However, Koltermann's request to make a limited thrust approximately 1 mile to the end of the woods was approved. At 7:45, the company received orders for the 2nd Platoon to comply with the original assignment of securing the flank while the 1st and 3rd Platoons were to reengage the enemy and ensure the complete destruction of the devastated column.

Koltermann's tanks began clearing the area strewn with American vehicles. The crewmen of the Shermans and the infantrymen in the half-tracks had sought cover in the woods. The tanks began coming under small-arms fire, which only served to reveal the positions of the infantry. One Sherman tank belatedly attempted to conceal itself behind a farm building at the edge of a field, where it was discovered by a Tiger commanded by Senior Sergeant Fritz Breitfeld. Breitfeld's Tiger advanced beyond the barn, turned on its tracks, and fired into the hidden tank. The Sherman was immediately engulfed in flames and exploding ammunition.

By 7:45 p.m., the American point element was destroyed. The route taken by Welborn's column was now choked with destroyed, damaged, and abandoned vehicles for several hundred yards. Small-arms fire and isolated explosions continued to echo throughout the area as the scattered Americans engaged the German infantry in isolated firefights on the thickly wooded hillsides. Other German soldiers took the opportunity to quickly inspect the wreckage lining the roads in their search for K rations and cartons of American cigarettes. Koltermann ordered the two flanking platoons to withdraw in the direction of Dahl. His 2nd Platoon delayed in withdrawing to cover their retreat.[10]

With the 3rd Armored Division staff following in the wake of the task force, the Americans pushed through Atteln and Henglarn to Etteln, where a command post was established on a high terrain feature with excellent communications reception. The fighting was still in progress when General Rose received word that problems had developed for Task Force Richardson in Kirchborchen.

Like most soldiers, Richardson did not desire to have his commanding general present during an engagement, particularly when he had to focus his full concentration on the situation at hand. The colonel attempted to persuade Rose not to come forward. He first radioed that he had no jeep to spare for escorting the general to his location. When advised that the general was proceeding forward, he notified the staff with the dire warning, "Don't send 'Big Six' this way!" With the unexpected situation with the enemy far from resolved, the woods, hills, and ravines seemed to be swarming with Germans, and the concerned task force commander did not want the general to risk traveling unknown, unsecured roads after nightfall.[11]

As dusk was approaching, General Rose left his command post on the heights near Schloss Hamborn and advanced with two jeeps, a motorcycle, and an armored reconnaissance vehicle. He first intercepted Colonel Welborn's column, which was advancing 5 miles from Richardson's task force on a parallel route, as the sounds of small-arms fire and explosions echoed through the heavily wooded area.

Welborn's combat command had encountered Koltermann's Tigers of the 507th, four of which had been previously sighted by fighter-bombers and supposedly destroyed. The massive German tanks had emerged onto the road and were firing into the column, leaving burning trucks, tanks, and half-tracks illuminating the sky in their wake. Welborn had succeeded in bringing his lead vehicle and several follow-up tanks into a depression that offered cover, but seven Shermans remained burning on the roadway and the nearby fields. As General Rose approached the location of Welborn's column, he was able to discern the glow of burning vehicles on the distant ridge line. Flares sizzled skyward intermittently, illuminating the horizon for several seconds before drifting behind the terrain features. Rose ordered Task Force Doan, held in reserve, to quickly move forward for support as more of the 507th's Tigers moved toward the sounds of battle reverberating across the darkened landscape.

The Tiger tanks of Panzer Battalion 507 sliced between Welborn's burning column and Task Force Doan. Within several minutes, the remainder of Welborn's unit—and General Rose—found themselves cut off by the Tigers that materialized out of the twilight. The sound of small arms crackled over the roar of tank engines and the rattle of heavy tracks on asphalt. Exploding ammunition and cannon fire resounded through the hills and ravines as scattered German infantry platoons engaged the American columns. German tanks, emerging from the tree line, raked the columns with machine-gun fire. With the advance route clearly blocked and the road behind them now severed by the German tanks, Rose's staff artillery commander, Colonel Braun, recommended that they leave their exposed position on the road and take cover in the nearby woods. Rose, noticing that there were no sounds coming from the direction in which Welborn had disappeared, ordered the two jeeps, the motorcycle, and the armored reconnaissance vehicle to follow Welborn's route. The small convoy wheeled onto a side road and proceeded almost 1,000 yards before approaching a crossroads in the darkness, where they were met by a hail of small-arms fire pouring from both sides of the narrow road. Wheeling their vehicles, they retreated toward the main road, where they observed a massive tank emerge from the darkness onto the roadway ahead of them, followed by the silhouette of another. Then a third tank wheeled onto the road.

With a mixture of relief and trepidation, the staff officers assumed that the tanks were the new Pershing models that had recently been delivered to the division. As the column gave way and permitted the lead tank to rumble past, one of the soldiers in the jeep noticed something ominously unfamiliar. The vehicle was equipped with twin exhaust pipes rising from a 700-horsepower engine. The new Pershings had only one exhaust. With shouts of alarm, those in the staff vehicles immediately took action to clear the enemy column. The first jeep sped from the road and bounced across an open field into the darkness. The second jeep, the vehicle in which the general was riding, was stopped by the third Tiger when the tank swerved into the path of the vehicle. The armored car following close behind General Rose's jeep, with eight members of his staff, halted abruptly. A hatch cover instantly flew open, and a tank commander wearing a black panzer uniform appeared in the turret with a schmeisser submachine gun trained directly on the jeep. The occupants of the vehicle—General Rose, his driver, Corporal Stevens, and his aide, Major Robert Bellinger—raised their hands in surrender.

As the three men exited the jeep and stood by the roadside with their hands over their heads, they heard the German tank commander shouting commands over the heavy throbbing of the Tiger's engine. None of the three Americans by the roadside could speak German, and Rose, unable to discern what the German was shouting, called out to the threatening silhouette with the machine pistol that he did not understand. After several seconds, he advised his driver and aide that they should drop their sidearms. Bellinger and Stevens gingerly reached for their shoulder holsters, pulled the harnesses bearing the pistol holsters over their heads, and dropped the weapons to the ground. Rose, unlike his aide and driver, was wearing a standard-issue belt holster on a web belt, an item that is difficult to loosen with one hand. The general dropped his arms to unbuckle his belt. As the general's hands went to his waist, the nervous German tanker opened fire with the submachine gun, instantly striking and killing him.[12]

As Rose pitched forward, mortally wounded with a shot through the head, Stevens plunged out of the line of fire behind the tank and Bellinger leaped into the ditch lining the road and disappeared into the darkness. The eight staff personnel in the armored vehicle, still under the muzzles of the Tiger tank's guns, exited the vehicle with their hands above their heads. Within seconds, they were surrounded by German infantrymen who had arrived to support the tanks.

The Tiger immediately rumbled forward and continued down the road toward the sound of battle, leaving the general's body lying by the roadside. The jeep and the armored staff vehicle remained untouched until they were later recovered by American forces; the classified documents in both vehicles, hidden in the dark, went undiscovered by the Germans. With General Rose's death, Brigadier General Doyle O. Hickey took command of the 3rd Armored Division, and Colonel Doan assumed command of Hickey's Combat Command A.

At 10:00 p.m., Koltermann's company received orders to withdraw. The tank commander reported no casualties but noted that twenty-four enemy armored vehicles and numerous light vehicles had been destroyed. The tanks had driven into combat with their last reserves of gasoline, most of which was now almost depleted. At 11:00, the Tiger platoons were en route to Eggeringhausen in a search for fuel and supplies.[13]

The early morning hours of 31 March found Kirchborchen and Nordborchen, so fiercely defended during the previous hours, deathly quiet as GIs moved through rubble-strewn streets lined with burning houses. The previous afternoon, the Americans had been able to bring their armor to bear on the German defenders again, and in the nearby hamlet of Jammertal, intense fighting had occurred that left armored vehicles in flames and the streets of the village littered with corpses. The burned-out hulks of five American tanks and two German panzers remained as evidence of the fierce engagement in the twin villages of Nordborchen and Kirchborchen. Running low on fuel and having expended much of their ammunition, the Tiger companies were now threatened with encirclement by American units advancing toward Wewer, and so they withdrew under cover of darkness. In a scene reminiscent of the Napoleonic Wars, some sixty wounded Germans were loaded onto horse-drawn farm carts piled with straw, and the creaking wagons slowly plodded through the night toward the medical facilities in Bad Lippspringe, Bad Meinberg, and Detmold.

At dawn, as the Americans cautiously felt their way through the abandoned villages of Nordborchen and Kirchborchen, they found streets and buildings littered with more than 100 dead still lying where they fell. Homes, outbuildings, and barns contained wounded soldiers who had died; a thorough search of the villages revealed only a handful of wounded Germans who could be taken prisoner.

The American forces entering the destroyed villages were not in a magnanimous mood. Many of the war-weary GIs found it unfathomable that, at this stage of the war, so many German soldiers continued to fight bitterly, and they reacted accordingly. They regarded the persistence of some German military units, particularly the Waffen SS units, as a cause of unnecessary casualties among combatants and noncombatants alike. Many of the GIs who had been killed or wounded in the fierce fighting south of Paderborn had survived the long march through France, endured the bitter fighting during the Battle of the Bulge, and slogged to the Rhine only to be killed or suffer permanent mutilation in nondescript towns of the Sauerland and isolated villages south of Paderborn.

The GIs involved in the fighting were largely unaware that the forces collected under the dubious title of SS Brigade Westfalen were represented by a motley collection of Luftwaffe ground personnel from the airfields around

Paderborn, poorly trained Volkssturm draftees, teenaged members of the Hitler Youth, and convalescents bolstered by a handful of combat-hardened veterans from Waffen SS and Wehrmacht units. The Tigers that had inflicted so much damage on the U.S. task forces were the tanks of Heavy Panzer Battalion 507 — a regular Wehrmacht unit. The German army tank crews wore a special black uniform with a menacing silver skull insignia on each lapel in the tradition of their pre–World War I predecessors, the elite Leibhussar cavalry regiment of Kaiser Wilhelm and his forebears. The distinctive uniforms often caused their opponents to mistake them for SS troops. And the Americans were painfully aware that many of the units with which they had collided during their drive toward the north were Waffen SS, who had a reputation for ruthlessness.

The news of General Rose's death by the roadside on the evening of 30 March spread rapidly. Many of his soldiers had been unaware that the general was Jewish and the son of a prominent rabbi in Colorado. Not all generals are liked and admired by the frontline soldiers, most of whom lead a relatively miserable, unenviable existence, being exposed to the elements while eating bad food, suffering from exhaustion, and catching minimal moments of sleep in the mud. General Maurice Rose was an exception. He believed in leading from the front and by example, and he did not request of his soldiers what he himself was unwilling or unable to do.

Soon, rumors flew among the units that the popular general had been taken prisoner and shot because he was Jewish. Other soldiers, remembering the massacre of American prisoners by Waffen SS forces in a field near the Belgian town of Malmédy during the Battle of the Bulge, suspected that another massacre was intended the night Rose was killed. Newspapers promptly reported that the general had been murdered after surrendering. Predictably, reprisals began.

A war crimes investigation regarding the incident, conducted in the months following the shooting, concluded that the general was shot in the heat of battle and that the German tanker had mistaken Rose's actions in unbuckling his web belt as an attempt to resist capture by drawing his weapon.[14]

It was clear that the Germans on the scene did not know a general had been killed. In the fading light, his rank insignia would have been difficult to distinguish under even optimal conditions. The nervous German tank commander never realized that he had killed the commander of the U.S. 3rd Armored Division. General Rose was tall, athletically lean, and wearing a standard-issue field uniform with simple stars of rank on his helmet and collars. The Tiger crewman was only familiar with Rose's German counterparts, who were easily distinguished by their distinctive crimson-and-gold collar tabs, gold-trimmed peaked caps, and riding breeches marked by twin crimson stripes. Combat troops usually have a very limited knowledge of the enemy rank insignia, and it was unusual for an

American general to be so close to the front in hours of darkness at the height of a confusing battle. Maurice Rose's body lay by the roadside for the next several hours, and his personal papers, as well as the classified documents accompanying him, remained undisturbed at the scene.

Many GIs immediately assumed the worst. Numerous German prisoners were shot where they surrendered, and some wounded were shot where they lay or were left to die. Soldiers seldom die instantly in battle: unless they receive a massive wound in a vital organ, they often survive for hours of intense agony, growing weaker while their bodies slowly hemorrhage and soak their uniforms and the ground on which they lie. Depending on the severity of the wound, they often writhe and convulse in pain, with involuntary muscle spasms racking their bodies as their hearts fight to continue their work. Often, they cry for relief for hours before their pleas gradually subside with the onset of unconsciousness and death.

The corpses of twenty-seven Germans who apparently had been shot after surrendering were discovered behind the village cemetery of Etteln by civilians emerging from their shelters. The bodies of eighteen executed German soldiers were found in the wake of the American advance by civilians in Dörenhagen. In retribution for the fanatic resistance they encountered and for the death of their general, the Americans forebade German civilians to immediately bury the dead. Sometimes gathered by the local inhabitants and taken to a collection point, the decomposing corpses lay exposed in full view of the townspeople for days as a ghastly reminder of what Hitler's war had brought them. The roadsides and orchards south of Paderborn remained dotted with foxholes and makeshift defenses containing empty shell casings, discarded field equipment, and dead Germans whose bodies were eventually covered by a few spadefuls of dirt and forgotten.[15]

The evening that the 3rd Armored Division encountered fierce resistance south of Paderborn, the commander of SS Brigade Westfalen reported to the commander of the LXVI Corps, Lieutenant-General Flörke. The commander directed Obersturmbannführer Hans Stern to push the SS brigade toward the southwest to meet with units from Army Group B that were in the Winterberg area. They would join forces to attack toward the west in order to break through the Allied forward elements and disrupt the American's linkup attempt. Stern doubted the attack and subsequent joining of forces would be possible. To accomplish that, his brigade would have to detach from their current engagements with the enemy, traverse some 60 miles, receive supplies, and then reorganize and coordinate plans with the Wehrmacht units from Army Group B.

Within hours of the fierce engagement with Welborn's column, Heavy Panzer Battalion 507 received orders to again meet the American forces. On 31 March, American armored units were collecting in the area near Schloss Hamborn for a final drive toward Paderborn. At 3:00 p.m., the 507th's 2nd Company rolled across the Haxterberg Heights, from which they observed columns of American infantry advancing in loose formation. The Tigers immediately formed an assault wedge and advanced, firing from all barrels. One American tank was discovered by Sergeant Wilhelm Voss at the edge of a wood-line, and a high-velocity round from Voss's 88-mm gun ripped the Sherman's turret from the chassis. As the Tigers approached the trees, they filed onto the only roadway leading through the thickly wooded region. The lead Tiger was commanded by the company commander, Lieutenant Bernhard Pfeuffer; the second by Sergeant Voss; the third by Sergeant Fritz Ebner; and the forth by Sergeant Willi Wolf.

The column slowly wound through the woods until the men suddenly found themselves in the midst of an American assembly area near Schloss Hamborn. To the right of the roadway was a long column of vehicles of every description: tanks, armored reconnaissance vehicles, half-tracks, communications vans, and supply trucks lined the road for hundreds of yards.

Reacting immediately, Lieutenant Pfeuffer opened fire toward the front of their column. The following tanks fired to the right. GIs swarmed in all directions as they attempted to escape the inferno, and within seconds, fuel tanks and ammunition were exploding among the burning vehicles. Voss's Tiger, the second in the column, followed Pfeuffer's lead tank and passed an apparently disabled Sherman near the narrow bridge leading over the Ellerbach streambed. As Voss's tank rumbled past, the turret of the Sherman suddenly rotated toward the third Tiger, commanded by Fritz Ebner. Voss shouted a warning to his gunner, Sebastian Hüpfl, who frantically attempted to bring the long 88-mm barrel on target. Before Hüpfl could bring the gun to bear on the Sherman, the American tank opened fire, with the third Tiger directly in its sights. Ebner's tank was struck at point-blank range on the turret, killing the commander instantly.

At that moment, the lead Tiger reached the narrow road leading to Schloss Hamborn, where the vehicle was fired on by numerous American tanks. Several 76-mm projectiles impacted against the heavily armored turret without result. At length, a round struck the road wheels, rendering the Tiger immobile. Sergeant Voss's Tiger quickly moved into position to support the damaged lead tank. Voss's gunner, Hüpfl, was unable to discern individual targets in the gathering dusk and began firing on muzzle flashes that pierced the darkness. Suddenly, a loud explosion filled the interior of the Tiger, and the turret was enveloped in flames. The Tiger's driver, Ertl, was screaming into the microphone as Voss tore the hatch cover open and pushed himself free of the burning tank. Hüpfl could see a dark sky through the hatch above the flames and attempted to follow Voss in springing free of the tank. But he quickly fell back into his seat as his strength left his knees—he had placed his hands directly on the glowing steel of the turret and now watched helplessly as his hands, the skin burned from the flesh, began to cramp and curl into themselves. Realizing that he was going to burn alive in the fiery coffin, he mustered his strength and forced his way through the hatch. He was followed by gun loader Wolfgang Bloss.

The two soldiers fled from their tank and quickly joined the Tiger's commander. The men made their way up the streambed until they recognized the familiar throbbing of a Henschel engine. They cautiously moved in the direction of the engine and came on the only surviving tank of their column. Taken aboard Willi Wolf's Tiger, the wounded were evacuated to their command post, from where they were transported to a field hospital in Neuenbeken, some 3 miles northeast of Paderborn.[16]

As the task forces of the U.S. First Army were meeting fierce resistance from SS Brigade Westfalen south of Paderborn, several miles to the west in the village of Wewelsburg, Nazi officials were feverishly preparing an evacuation. In 1934, Himmler had leased the 350-year-old Wewelsburg Castle for the purpose of establishing an imposing SS center for research and education. The entire castle and the surrounding area were acquired with a ninety-nine-year lease for the token sum of one reichsmark per year. The Reichsführer had immediately initiated extensive renovations. For several years, the labor at the castle was provided by Reich Labor Service volunteers. SS Obergruppenführer Siegfried Taubert directed the administrative management of the castle, its neighboring facilities, and the SS Research and Education Center. Taubert labored tirelessly on the project for years. With the onset of the war, labor was provided by concentration camp inmates, most of whom were members of the forbidden Jehovah's Witnesses. The laborers were quartered behind barbed wire in the neighboring village of Niederhagen.

By 1943, renovation to the castle had largely ceased. Construction materials were difficult to obtain, the escalating construction costs had exceeded the budget, and the armaments industry had a higher priority for the allocation of scarce resources. An SS staff had remained assigned to the castle, and although the expansion was far from complete, the castle already housed an extensive library, a large collection of antiquities, and Himmler's personal arms collection. During the war, the massive structure had received a coat of camouflage paint and had thus escaped damage. It appeared that the Allies remained oblivious to the significance the Reichsführer placed on his favored project.

In the latter phases of the war, the number of inhabitants in the castle increased significantly. The Gestapo office from the Ruhr city of Gelsenkirchen moved into the facility following the destruction of the unit's former building during a bombing raid. Various officials and party organizations, forced to evacuate the heavily bombed cities to the west, filled every available space in the castle.

Now, despite efforts to protect the imposing structure throughout the war, it appeared that the area would soon be overrun by the American forces.

As American troops closed on Paderborn, Obergruppenführer Taubert made preparations to evacuate the castle. The family members of the SS staff residing in the nearby villages were ordered to prepare for evacuation to Bad Frankenhausen in Thuringia. The immense collection of antiquities and artworks were carefully packed and transferred from the castle to the nearby Boddeker estate. Many of the valuables were hidden within the walls of the estate's buildings; others were distributed to various facilities and nearby homes for concealment. It was assumed that the Allies were aware of the castle's significance and would attempt to capture it and its contents as soon as possible.

On 30 March, Taubert ordered a member of the SS staff to reconnoiter the Büren-Paderborn and Salzkotten-Wewelsburg road intersection to ensure that the American units had not blocked the route to the east. Within minutes, word was received that the crossroads remained open, and a convoy of vehicles departed the castle grounds and proceeded toward Paderborn.

Far to the east, in the town of Prenzlau, south of Stettin, Reichsführer SS Heinrich Himmler was preparing to dispatch one of his most trusted adjutants on a special mission. Twenty-five-year-old SS Hauptsturmführer Heinz Macher was no novice to war and was well suited for the task. The tall SS officer was a recipient of the Iron Cross, the German Cross in Gold, and the Oak Leaves to the Knight's Cross. While serving in Russia and France, he had more than proven his ability to accomplish difficult assignments under the most adverse of circumstances. Himmler now assigned the battle-hardened officer to take a detachment of SS engineers through the American cordon surrounding the Ruhr area and destroy the castle before it could be seized by the Allies.

On Saturday, 31 April, Macher arrived at Paderborn at the head of the engineering task group. He was forced to dodge a gauntlet of fire from American tanks before making his way through the ruins of the recently bombed city. At length, he located the Paderborn city commander at his command bunker on the Wilhelmshöhe. Macher then advised the commander that he was under personal orders from Reichsführer Himmler and requested a briefing on the enemy locations. He also asked to be assigned a driver who was familiar with the area and could take him on the most direct route to the village of Wewelsburg. The short briefing was interrupted by the unexpected arrival of SS Obergruppenführer Taubert, who had left Wewelsburg the day prior to Macher's arrival. Taubert expressed astonishment and outrage on hearing that Macher had arrived under special assignment from Himmler to destroy the castle. "What?" he exclaimed in disbelief. "You want to destroy my castle?" He then shook his head emphatically. "You can't do that!" "I have my orders," Macher replied with characteristic detachment. He then turned and departed to fulfill his mission.

As Macher's convoy proceeded southwest along narrow, secondary roads, the hillsides and woods were marked with stillness. An uneasy calm had settled onto the surrounding villages and hamlets in the wake of the vicious fighting that had occurred only hours before between the American forward elements and SS Brigade Westfalen. In the village of Wewelsburg, now devoid of SS staff, Bürgermeister Karl Dierkes raised a white flag to greet the American forces. It was already known that the Americans had captured the nearby villages of Brenken, Tudorf, and Haaren, and they were expected to roll into Wewelsburg and thus bring an end to an era.

At 3:00 that afternoon, the sounds of approaching motors could be heard. Residents peered from behind curtained windows or dared to glimpse from the cellars where they had sought refuge from the foreign soldiers, whom they expected at any moment. As the vehicles rumbled through the narrow, cobblestone streets of the seemingly deserted town, many inhabitants were shocked to observe the arrival of dozens of soldiers clad in familiar field gray.

Hauptsturmführer Macher ignored the numerous white flags that greeted his arrival and drove directly to the castle. On eyeing the massive structure, he knew that far more explosives would be needed than he had at his disposal. After departing from the city commander's bunker in Paderborn, Macher had driven to the SS training facilities in Senne, where he had located a cache of Panzerfausts to augment his small supply of explosives. He now set to work. The SS troops placed charges in the main turrets of the castle and in the administration offices. Filling the facility with piles of straw, the soldiers then ignited the curtains and detonated the charges. As the structure burst into flames, the men then fired Panzerfausts into the buildings. Within an hour of the squad's arrival, the complex was blazing fiercely.

As flames enveloped the complex, inhabitants of Wewelsburg gathered in disbelief to witness the destruction of their landmark. The local cleric rushed from his church and called the village fire department, which raced to the scene. The SS troops permitted the fire department to safeguard the nearby homes from the flames but ordered the firemen to remain clear of the castle. The stone structure of the church, standing adjacent to the castle, was relatively undamaged, but a number of its large, leaded-glass windows were pushed inward by the enormous blasts. The explosions rocked the village, and numerous large, gray slates were shaken from the roof of the church and crashed to the earth.

At 5:00 p.m., two hours after its unexpected arrival, Heinz Macher's SS detachment drove out of Wewelsburg, accompanied by a number of family members of the castle staff. The return route took them back to Paderborn, where they deposited the civilians with Taubert. The detachment then proceeded to Bad Meinberg, where Macher located a Wehrmacht command center and dispatched a message to Himmler's headquarters reporting that he had fulfilled his mission.

As the SS detachment withdrew from the castle, the facility was stormed by onlookers intent on plundering any remaining valuables from its interior. Although the castle had suffered extensive damage, many rooms and offices within its cavernous interior survived intact. Village inhabitants, refugees from the Ruhr, and foreign laborers swarmed the castle and began carting away rugs, furniture, works of art, liquor, tableware, and linens. The plunderers elbowed their way through the narrow stairwells in the massive wine cellar and waded ankle deep in wine, liquor, and champagne as they dragged cases of bottles toward the castle doorways. Looters ran back and forth with their plunder, depositing items in a secure location and returning for more. The frenetic plundering continued into the night. Early Sunday morning, the flames mysteriously reignited and destroyed more of the interior, filling the corridors and chambers with smoke and driving many of the looters from the scene.[17]

The first Americans appeared at Heinrich Himmler's partially destroyed castle on Monday, 2 April. A Polish laborer had reported to the U.S. 3rd Armored Division headquarters that a concentration of about fifty German soldiers, accompanied by numerous vehicles, had been observed at the intersection of the Salzkotten-Wewelsburg and the Büren-Paderborn roads. The Americans immediately dispatched a reconnaissance patrol to obtain information and to occupy the village of Wewelsburg. A short time later, another report arrived indicating that the German unit was also supported by as many as ten armored vehicles. Within minutes, the reconnaissance patrol troops reported that they had secured the village and had encountered no enemy forces other than three dejected German soldiers, whom they had captured. The Americans then began a systematic search of the village.

Soon after occupying Wewelsburg, the 83rd Reconnaissance Battalion established headquarters at the nearby Böddeken Manor, where, prior to the abandonment of the castle, the SS staff had hidden part of Himmler's art collection behind a false wall. As knowledge of the significance of the ancient castle spread among the American troops, the hunt for valuables, documents, and souvenirs increased. The false wall at the Böddeken Manor was demolished, and the contents vanished. Officers from the U.S. Monuments, Fine Arts and Archives Group arrived to inspect the facility. An American intelligence officer discovered and expropriated a cigar-box-sized container filled with silver SS rings bearing the death's-head emblem. The rings had previously been awarded to SS officers and were returned to the Wewelsburg after their deaths at the front, where they were intended to be exhibited as part of an honor monument after Germany's eventual victory. Of more importance to the Allies, the intelligence officers discovered numerous intact files and documents within the castle. Other files and SS materials were located during the search of the village.

Hidden deep within the west tower of the castle was Himmler's personal vault. The vault had been constructed under secrecy during the prewar years, and its existence was known only to a select cadre of SS officers. The Americans, unable to open the vault's complicated locking mechanism, used explosives to gain entrance. They then carried bundles of files to the main hall of the facility, where a number of intelligence personnel sorted the documents.

On 9 April, the location of the huge vault was discovered by Müller-Wettin, one of the concentration camp inmates who had labored at the castle. The door had already been blasted open, and the floor of the vault was scattered with documents and administrative files that had apparently been considered unimportant by the military officials. All other traces of the contents had disappeared.

Despite the chaos that enveloped the castle and its environs, the newly liberated Jehovah's Witnesses attempted to salvage as much of the contents of the castle as possible. A collection center was established in the concentration camp's kitchen, where the inmates collected and cataloged all items they could recover. The collection was eventually turned over to the occupation authorities, where the trail came to an ignominious end. The Americans quickly located the crates and cases of antiquities and valuables at the Böddeken Manor. The extensive collections were cataloged, crated, and later transported to an Allied collection facility in Wiesbaden, where all traces of the entire inventory, including Heinrich Himmler's personal arms collection, simply vanished.[18]

As the American First Army units were closing on Paderborn from the south, the U.S. Ninth Army continued its relentless drive from the north. Farther to the west of Paderborn, in the city of Soest, Major Rudolf Dunker found himself under a torrent of abuse from the district commander, Colonel Stripp, for having failed to defend Beckum. Stripp advised Dunker that he was to be placed immediately under arrest and would undoubtedly be shot for his traitorous actions.

The tirade was suddenly interrupted by the ringing of the telephone on the commander's desk, and by the tone of the conversation, Dunker suspected that his situation was about to change. After a brief, grim conversation, the commander slammed the telephone back on the receiver. The caller had advised him that the Americans were now pushing out of Paderborn toward the west after having conducted a linkup. The encirclement was complete, and American units were advancing toward Soest. There were no organized defenses between Paderborn and Soest with which they could be stopped, so they had an open area through which their mechanized units could move at will. The commander turned to Dunker and asked him the location of his troops. The major replied that he had little idea. The troops that had not already been overrun during their withdrawal by the fast-moving American armored columns were somewhere in the area southwest of Lippstadt. This response brought another torrent of abuse from the colonel.

At length, Dunker was able to interject. He advised the commander that the troops had been directed to assemble southwest of Lippstadt no later than 11:00 a.m. and that the bulk of the forces, those who had not been captured or had not deserted, were likely already concentrated in that area. The commander pulled Dunker over to his map table and ordered him to establish a defense line along the Rüthen-Erwitte-Lippstadt railroad line and to defend it to the last man. As Dunker gathered his map case to leave Soest, the commander added that his conduct in defending this line would influence how the previous problem would eventually be addressed.[19]

On the south perimeter of the Ruhr Pocket, the Freikorps Sauerland militia prepared to engage the enemy. The Freikorps companies marched from Dielfer Furt toward Breitenbach before halting in a wooded area. Six men were ordered to conduct a reconnaissance patrol for the purpose of locating any American patrols that might lie ahead. That evening, they identified American units along the Kaan-Marienborn rail line and returned to their unit, the headquarters of which was located in the Bürbacher schoolhouse.

On returning, the reconnaissance unit troops received another mission. They were ordered to proceed to the area of Feuersbach, where it was believed an armored unit under the command of a highly decorated Wehrmacht captain was located. After departing from the makeshift headquarters, they proceeded through the darkness toward their objective. At dawn, they observed American outposts and the brown canvas tents that characteristically marked the Allied positions. No sooner had they stumbled onto the Americans than they were taken under fire. The small band successfully escaped without losses by fleeing through the underbrush.

After realizing that they were not pursued, the patrol headed for the Hasen train station through a field overgrown with 12-foot spruce trees. As they crept toward the train station, they observed American sentries, beyond which were numerous American soldiers preparing coffee. The GIs had dug numerous foxholes and positioned several machine guns adjacent to the woods. Freshly disturbed earth indicated that mines had been laid for additional security. Making their way through the evergreen thicket, they came on several soldiers from the town of Siegen. The soldiers had withdrawn from a previous position and told the Freikorps men that they were awaiting nightfall before proceeding further.

They then advised the Freikorps members to move cautiously and to refrain from excess movement; the Americans were known to open fire at any movement within the undergrowth. The Freikorps reconnaissance unit then returned to the headquarters to discover the schoolhouse was vacant; there was no trace of the battalion. They now stood abandoned and leaderless. During their absence, the battalion had marched toward the west in the direction of Lüdenscheid.[20]

As the Americans closed on the central city of Paderborn, the inhabitants of the towns, villages, and settlements to the east of the city prepared to meet the invaders. The town of Bad Driburg was a concentration of military clinics and hospitals, and thus, the war had largely left it untouched. The former military commander of the German garrison, Lieutenant-General von Hase, had been incriminated in the 20 July 1944 assassination attempt against Hitler and had thus accompanied many of his comrades to the gallows. Most of the inhabitants of Bad Driburg were first directly affected by the war on 21 February 1944. Following an aerial battle between German fighters and Allied bombers, the pilot of a German aircraft noticed that his landing gear was no longer operational. Ahead, he observed a badly damaged American bomber attempting to maintain altitude as it made its way toward the English Channel and the British Isles. The German pilot ordered his navigator to bail out of the damaged aircraft. He then rammed the Allied plane. The bomber crashed in a field near Driburg, where the action was observed by farmer Albert Koch. The explosion of fuel and ordnance on board the bomber shattered windows as far away as the Langen Strasse, 2,000 yards away. The German fighter impacted between Donhausen and Rothehaus, some 2.5 miles from the bomber's crash site. The American bomber crew and the German pilot were subsequently buried in the Stellburg Cemetery in Bad Driburg.[21]

The inhabitants of Bad Driburg were reminded that the war was approaching when Paderborn was destroyed by a fleet of bombers on 27 March. Two days later, American tanks were reported to be in Brilon, and the town received numerous wounded soldiers who had been engaged in the fighting near Wrexen and Scherfede. The wounded had been evacuated directly to Bad Driburg from the scene of fighting, and the inhabitants knew that the situation was more than serious. The Bad Driburg medical facilities had undergone a transformation from rehabilitation clinics to battlefield hospitals.

Wild rumors circulated among the settlements of the Eggegeberge. Stories of ill-disciplined, rampaging American soldiers sent inhabitants scrambling to conceal food and valuables in expectation of widespread looting. The defenses west of the town consisted of remnants of a division transferred from Denmark, reinforced by a small number of hastily organized reservists. The reservists were mostly seventeen-year-old Hitler Youth from Northeim and Hildesheim who had been thrust into Wehrmacht uniforms and told that they would receive instructions on the use of their weapons while on the march toward the American units.

The Nazi officials were determined to follow Hitler's edict and defend the town to the last man. They ordered the erection of a barricade, defended by twelve Volkssturm members, near the approaches to the town. The defenders were armed with a total of four antiquated Italian rifles and twelve rounds of ammunition. Their weapons inventory was completed with one Panzerfaust, the proper operation of which remained a mystery. The intensity of their defense would determine whether the Americans would roll over a pile of ruins or simply drive through an intact community while en route to Berlin.[22]

Beyond the village of Bad Driburg lay the settlement of Brakel. Like other small settlements in the Eggegeberge, the war had largely passed the inhabitants by, apart from isolated tragedies that befell individual families who lost their sons in distant combat. On 22 February 1945, the small town's rail yard was the target of a limited air raid in which fifty-five-year-old railway worker Franz Fröling was killed. The brief attack proved to be the onset of a series of raids that occurred almost daily thereafter. The constant air alarms interrupted the once-mundane lives of the inhabitants and disrupted school classes and shopping hours and served to make life generally unpredictable. Even the tilling of farmers' fields became difficult as the front drew nearer. Fighter-bombers routinely patrolled at low altitude in search of targets, and farmers in their fields offered a temptation that was apparently difficult to resist. In one air raid, the Americans succeeded in striking a troop train carrying a combat group of Waffen SS troops who were en route to the front. Seven of the SS grenadiers died in the attack. Their bodies were placed in makeshift coffins, and two days later, the local Nazi Party officials held a memorial for the fallen before they were transported to the local cemetery for burial.

During the last days of March, long files of desolate refugees were observed fleeing from the enemy approaching from the west. One early afternoon, residents were shocked to see a column of concentration camp inmates painfully winding their way east along the Hanekamp and Ostheimer roads toward an unknown destination. The sixty or seventy skeletal figures, clad in ragged blue-and-white-striped uniforms, were escorted by approximately eight armed SS guards. Horrified onlookers watched as, at the end of the column, one particularly weak inmate was desperately clinging to the figure ahead of him in an attempt to keep pace with the group. The prisoner managed to hang on to a fellow inmate until they reached the nearby Lobbenberge heights, where he collapsed in the road. An SS guard approached the motionless figure, a shot rang out, and the column continued crawling toward the east without pause.

The body was collected by local inhabitants and taken to the St. Vinzenz Hospital morgue. No documents or personal effects were found on the victim, and the following morning, the unidentified man was buried in the village cemetery. However, a Polish Catholic prayer book was found on the body, and thus, the local Catholic church community maintained the grave.[23]

While the fierce fighting south of Paderborn between SS Brigade Westfalen and the task forces of the U.S. 3rd Armored Division echoed through the valleys and hills of the Sauerland, defenses were being constructed in Paderborn. A General Staff captain had been assigned as combat commander of the city, and he established a command post in a bunker on the Wilhelmshöhe. The captain, accompanied by a one-armed lieutenant as his second-in-command, had vainly attempted to receive additional reinforcements to stem the inevitable tide of American forces.

On the evening of 30 March, the news arrived that American forces were advancing on Warburg, some 15 miles to the south. All defenses in the Paderborn area were placed on alert. Sporadic reports continued to arrive, providing a patchwork glimpse of the battles raging in the villages to the south. The one-armed officer, a former Hitler Youth commander, was determined to defend the city against all odds. The defenses received reinforcements by the arrival of remnants of a flak regiment, consisting of 10 officers, 47 NCOs, and 260 enlisted personnel. The battalion headquarters was established near a tank barricade on Reichsstrasse 1 between the train station and a nearby bridge.

In the early morning hours of 31 March, the battle commander of Paderborn received a message that some 1,000 American troops had arrived between the airfield and the panzer base. As fighting erupted on the southern outskirts of the city between the American advanced elements and the defenders, the German forces began to give way. Exhausted soldiers filtered into the city from the front, carrying their wounded. By nightfall, the Americans were firmly entrenched on the outskirts of the city, and their artillery batteries began firing into the ruins, taking strategic crossroads and possible defense positions under fire. The civilians who remained in the tormented city cowered in their cellars as explosions continued throughout the night. On Sunday, 1 April, the Americans advanced into Paderborn. An eyewitness recorded:

The tanks that were reported are now entering the city and shooting at everything they see. It is raging from all corners of the city, the exhausted [soldiers] have taken cover in bomb craters. They also quickly give up the hopeless fight and flee. Tank battles are taking place on the airfield and in the surrounding area. Tanks from both sides are being left in the path. Fighter-bombers chase the retreating units and smoke out the isolated resistance. It is no longer a fight, but is a running conflict between firing steel giants. Soon it is quiet, and the unequal fight was very short. The Americans now cautiously enter the dead, destroyed and partly burning city.[24]

The city was soon bedecked with white flags; the combat commander followed the earlier example exhibited by the Nazi officials and fled his headquarters on the Wilhelmshöhe to disappear in the direction of Neuhaus. By 5:00 p.m. on Easter Sunday, the guns had fallen silent in Paderborn. The remaining Wehrmacht troops in nearby Sennelager soon evacuated the area, leaving the path open for American units to close the area around Paderborn. The young, one-armed battle commander, who had left Paderborn to establish defenses in Neuhaus, resisted the efforts of a cleric to convince him to surrender the city. When the pastor persisted, the officer threatened to shoot him if he continued to exhibit defeatism.

The fanatic lieutenant remained true to his word. The German forces under his command continued to hold Neuhaus until the evening of 3 April. The final defenses began collapsing under a heavy artillery barrage and ended with the deaths of ten inhabitants and some sixty German soldiers. The young lieutenant chose death through suicide over captivity.[25]

Chapter 9

Sealing the Trap

As the American forces poured toward the east along both flanks of Army Group B, the other German army groups in the west were collapsing under the weight of the Allies. In the sectors of Army Group G, to the south of Model's reeling forces, the Americans crossed the Kinzig and Fulda Rivers and pressed toward Eisenach and Würzburg. To the north, in the Army Group H sector, the combined British and American forces were flowing past Münster. Desperate attempts to prevent the Americans from closing the pocket had stripped Army Group B of any possible reserves, and the German high command continued to insist that its forces remaining in position on the Rhine could not be moved.

Even if Model's pleas for permission to withdraw his forces from the Rhine to prevent their encirclement had been approved, it is doubtful that efforts to move the divisions would have succeeded. Transportation resources were lacking, there were no fuel reserves available, and American aircraft had immobilized the railways. Moreover, the intense fighting had decimated the few German units remaining on the front. Between the Teutoburg Forest and the Sauerland, just as between Paderborn and Dortmund, there were no mobile German units in sufficient strength to prevent the Americans from closing the ring.[1]

At the VII Corps headquarters, Major General J. Lawton Collins was concerned about the situation on 31 March. He was still unaware of Model's counterattack near Winterberg that had driven almost 8 miles into the flank of the 3rd Armored Division, although he was aware through intelligence reports that the Germans were planning to strike against his left flank. He was also unaware that the forward elements of the 3rd Armored Division had been severed from the main drive by the German attack. He was more concerned that the Germans would be able to escape the developing pocket. Any attempt by them to move east, out of the enveloping pincers that were forming around the army group, could only be foiled by rapid movement of the U.S. Ninth Army, north of the Lippe River. Collins was concerned that Montgomery's slow, methodical advance along the north flank of the Ruhr might afford the Germans the opportunity to escape.[2]

On the afternoon of 31 March, Collins called General Simpson, commander of the U.S. Ninth Army, and requested his support. For a corps commander to call the commander of another army and ask for support was an unusual breach of protocol and doctrine, for professional soldiers avoid breaking the official chain of command. However, in view of the rapidly developing situation facing the 3rd Armored Division, Collins felt the urgent need to circumvent formality.

He candidly advised Simpson that he was concerned Montgomery was proceeding too slowly. He was worried that the Germans would be able to slip through the corridor at Paderborn if the Allied forces did not act quickly. He was also concerned that his own forces had become too widespread during their headlong advance, and he asked that a task force from Simpson's 2nd Armored Division be pushed toward Paderborn immediately. Collins advised the Ninth Army commander that he, too, would begin a rapid advance from his southern area. Without conferring with Field Marshal Montgomery, Simpson agreed to act in coordination with Collins's request. The orders were delivered to the 2nd Armored Division immediately.

From the south flank of the pocket, Collins issued orders to his staff for the operation. Task Force Kane from the 3rd Armored Division was selected to lead the drive toward Paderborn. Simultaneously, Collins reinforced his left flank and ordered parts of the U.S. 1st Infantry Division to advance toward Brilon-Büren. These units immediately began a movement toward the north, and on 31 March, they reached the southeast borders of the Lippstadt district in the area of Rüthen-Hemmern. The units were to secure all important streets and crossings and to protect the area against any German thrust that might endanger further operations toward Paderborn.[3]

There was little German opposition between the Lippe and Möhne Rivers to disrupt the American advance. The Wehrmacht's 476th Infantry Division had arrived in the area several weeks earlier to be reequipped, and it occupied a number of weakly defended positions. However, most of the division had already been withdrawn to defend the approaches to the Teutoburg Forest, and other units were detached from the command and transferred to the area between Arnsberg and Menden.

The local inhabitants between Lippe and Möhne followed the latest developments with trepidation. For several days, heavy artillery could be heard in the direction of Wesel as the Allies breached the Rhine, and in the south, the news of the American arrival at Brilon had raced through the towns and villages scattered between Paderborn, Soest, Lippstadt, and Warstein. Roadblocks had been constructed from concrete slabs and were reinforced with felled trees. The obstacles were manned by elderly inhabitants who found themselves conscripted into local Volkssturm units.

In the closing days of March, the towns of Erwitte, Geseke, and Lippstadt had seen streams of bedraggled Wehrmacht soldiers coming from the direction of Soest and Meschede intermittently in an attempt to escape the closing pocket. The columns were especially active during the hours of darkness when the Jabos were unable to patrol the skies along the Hellweg and the connecting rail lines. On 30 March, the Reichsbahn ceased rail traffic between the lines connecting Lippstadt-Warstein and Lippstadt-Neubeckum. The last trains moved out of the station in Lippstadt at 1:00 that afternoon to avoid becoming caught in the pocket. The trains moving along this route were in acute danger from aircraft, especially along the Soest-Lippstadt-Paderborn line. One attack occurred on 28 March along the Soest-Hamm route, during which a train loaded with Hitler Youth members was struck by a band of fighter-bombers; more than forty of the teenagers were killed or wounded.[4]

Thousands of refugees fled before the oncoming American army. They moved with every available asset on foot and with horse-carts, and a few were still in possession of dilapidated motor vehicles. Simultaneously, large columns of prisoners were on the move. Allied POWs consisting of Russians, Poles, French, British, and Americans were being marched to less threatened areas. Laborers from every occupied country in Europe could be observed in the long, ragged ranks shuffling toward the east as their captors attempted to evade the relentlessly advancing armored columns.

The Americans encountered no resistance in the area of Salzkotten, although a few isolated German troops occupied the area. A German lieutenant-general had remarked to Bürgermeister Seidler that he had observed an American infantry column advancing toward Wünnenberg and Fürstenberg from the heights near Haaren at 7:00 p.m. He stated that he intended to request that the commander of the Sennelager training facility defend the heights south of Niederntudorf.

On Friday morning, German officers appeared, assigned to secure the road crossing south of Neiderntudorf, the Alten Hellweg before Wewelsburg, and the Alten Hellweg in front of Schloss Brenken. With this development, the danger to Salzkotten increased. In addition to the regular inhabitants of the town, the war had brought some 500 nuns, 1,200 refugees, and 900 wounded being cared for in a reserve medical facility. Most of the wounded were amputees from the various fronts throughout Europe.

The Salzkotten Bürgermeister immediately drove to Oberntudorf and explained to an American officer the situation in the town and requested that the town be spared from an attack. He asked that Saltzkotten be declared an open city, as there were no German combat forces in the vicinity.

On Saturday morning, two German companies appeared and occupied positions on the road toward Oberntudorf on the Herrenhaus Hosenholz Heights and along Upsprunger Road. The population began to flee the town, certain that there would be fighting. The Kreisleiter of the Büren district mobilized the local Volkssturm. The Bürgermeister contacted the Kreisleiter and explained that he had spoken with the Americans and requested that the Kreisleiter not endanger the civilians or the hundreds of wounded in the hospital. The Kreisleiter agreed to drive to Sennelager to coordinate efforts with the military authorities in an effort to spare the town. The German military units occupying the road positions were informed of the intentions of the Bürgermeister and Kreisleiter, and the soldiers of one unit immediately shouldered their weapons and departed from the area.

During the afternoon, four Sherman tanks appeared from the direction of Oberntudorf and advanced toward Salzkotten over the Bosenholzer Heights. On the heights, there was a brief but intense exchange of fire in which a German soldier was killed. During a lull in the engagement, the officer in charge of the unit, Lieutenant Günther, was informed of the Bürgermeister's intent to surrender the city, and he was asked to withdraw his forces. He responded that his unit did not fall under the chain of command of the Sennelager commander. The officer then placed a call to his regimental commander in Lippstadt and requested instructions. The call resulted in the arrival of an 88-mm battery and orders to defend Salzkotten to the last man.

The tension increased with the arrival of German reinforcements. At 10:00 that evening, the sound of a detonating Panzerfaust was heard. Some twenty minutes later, it was reported that several American tanks had pushed past the German defenses and that one tank advancing along Oberntudorfer road near the edge of town had been disabled. The Bürgermeister again pleaded with Lieutenant Günther to withdraw his forces and offered to take full responsibility if the officer would withdraw toward Verne.

The 88-mm flak battery, dispatched to reinforce Günther's troops, was reportedly moving in the vicinity of Thüle. The Bürgermeister succeeded in stopping the battery from advancing beyond that point; from there, it later continued toward Sennelager. The German units occupying the Bosenholzer Weg as well as the Wewelsburger road were now cut off; facing insurmountable odds, the troops soon emerged from their positions with their hands held high over their heads. The unit occupying positions on the Upsprunger road began withdrawing toward Verne. To Bürgermeister Seidler's immense relief, Salzkotten was finally free of German combat troops by midnight.

Seidler met with the city officials in front of the Rathaus as Sherman tanks were heard approaching in the distance. At 12:10 a.m., the first tank was observed advancing along Vielser Strasse in front of the French POW compound behind the district finance building. The elated French prisoners demolished the locked doors from within the structure and greeted the American columns.

The first Americans dismounted from tanks after drawing to a halt before the Rathaus. The Bürgermeister and Dr. Reineke advised the soldiers that there were no combat troops in the town and that the city would be surrendered. An American officer explained that he had been told by his superiors that the local facilities contained some 900 wounded and that his forces were not to fire on the city. When the officer asked why they had received fire during their approach, Seidler explained that he had no authority over the German troops and that the civil authorities only represented the local populace.

Immediately after the meeting between Seidler and the American point element, some thirty-five tanks took up strategic positions throughout the city. After nightfall, the Bürgermeister received instructions to display white flags from the buildings and that all weapons, regardless of type or function, were to be surrendered to the American authorities. The city's inhabitants first experienced the occupation the following morning as they made their way to Easter Sunday services.

As the units of Task Force Hogan secured strategic positions in Salzkotten, American reconnaissance patrols established contact with Task Force Boles east of the city. The next morning, Task Force Kane, lying in wait for daylight within the tree line of Böddeken Forest, prepared to advance toward the northwest. Promptly at 6:00 a.m., the long, olive-colored columns emerged from the forest and rolled through Niederntudorf toward the settlement of Geseke.

The political Ortsgruppenleiter in Geseke was prepared to defend the town against the American army. He previously had received some seventy-five Panzerfausts from Lippstadt, with which he intended to arm his Volkssturm units. However, unbeknownst to the Nazi officials, members of the fire department had already concealed the weapons—and no one was willing to reveal the location.

On 31 March, the town's Reichsbahn office halted local rail traffic. Roadblocks were constructed at the Sosternschledde and on the Osttor and the Delbrücker roads by filling concrete culverts with soil and gravel. Isolated German soldiers, in small groups or alone, were seen retreating in the direction of the outlying villages. The citizens of Geseke watched from the Brenker Mark, a local geographic location, as an armored reconnaissance vehicle rolled along the Alten Hellweg between Erpernburg and the Bürener road. The Steintor was blocked with tree trunks, and a small force of SS troops prepared positions for defense. On Friday, 30 March, a citizen had hoisted a white flag on the church tower, and tension continued to build as the enemy neared. Weapons, uniforms, and Nazi documents were buried or burned, and food was hidden. German soldiers who were in the town on leave or had been discharged from service took flight or were hidden by friends and relatives after removing and concealing their incriminating uniforms.

On Saturday, 31 March, it was rumored that the Americans were closing on Salzkotten. Armed German soldiers were observed passing through Geseke toward the west. At 7:00 p.m., a group of about 100 citizens approached the SS troops located at the Steintor in an attempt to persuade them to withdraw. Predictably, an altercation ensued, during which the heavily armed SS clearly held an advantage. Finally, the Ortsgruppenleiter persuaded the stubborn troops to withdraw. At 11:00 p.m., the Ortsgruppenleiter received disappointing but expected instructions from his superior, Kreisleiter Lücke in Lippstadt, to defend Geseke.

Between 7:00 and 8:00 the following morning, Easter Sunday, the first Sherman tanks rolled over Tudorfer road toward Geseke. Several women stood at the Osttor with white flags to greet the tanks, which could be clearly identified by the imposing white stars painted on the olive-colored turrets. At the last moment, the women flagged down a vehicle packed with German soldiers who were obviously fleeing toward Salzkotten and warned them that they were heading into the path of the tanks. The vehicle immediately wheeled about and sped away. As the American tanks advanced along the Kapellenweg toward the town's outskirts, the women walked toward the column. Several of them hoisted their white flags to indicate their intent and to signal that Geseke was not defended. As the lead American vehicle reached the city's eastern approaches, an artillery shell impacted nearby, bringing the advance to an abrupt halt as the soldiers sought cover. After several minutes of cautious waiting without further incident, the soldiers returned to their idling vehicles and proceeded into the town.

No one could determine from where the artillery shell had come. The projectile had struck a residence on the Völmeder Strasse, behind the railway embankment, but otherwise inflicted little damage. The American troops advanced through the quiet town to the Westtor where they positioned tanks on the south and west walls. From these locations, they had an open field of fire on the Eringerfeld airfield.

After securing the roadways leading from the town, the Americans collected their first prisoners in Geseke. They assembled all police officers on the Rosenstrasse, from where the prisoners were marched to the Lappe barnyard at the intersection of Lüdischen Strasse and Ecke Kuhstrasse. Intermingled with the police officers were soldiers from the Eringerfeld airfield and from the airport on the Hölterklee, an adjacent meadow. They were soon joined by a small collection of Wehrmacht deserters who had been discovered during the searches or were betrayed to the Americans by local inhabitants who hoped to ingratiate themselves with the victors.

The Americans met light resistance in the southern and southwest areas of Geseke. As they were entering the town from the direction of Büren, an American tank was greeted by a high-velocity, armor-piercing shell fired from a hidden gun. The Sherman was enveloped in flames, and a member of the crew was killed. The entire crew of the German flak gun, consisting of four teenagers who had recently been conscripted into the mobile flak battalion, were shot by enraged American soldiers in reprisal. A German officer who attempted to escape toward Bönninghausen was shot, as was an Austrian Luftwaffe soldier who tried to warn the crew of another 88-mm flak gun on Tudorfer Weg of the approaching American column.

Geseke was cleared by U.S. forces by 11:00 a.m., following the deadly encounter with the antitank position at the town's southwest approaches. The GIs captured two 88-mm flak and four light field guns during the clearing action. As they proceeded into the town, a flak battalion manned by almost 300 Hungarian soldiers emerged from concealment to surrender without resistance.

The Americans then moved on toward the village of Störmede, which was not occupied by German troops. However, the column met resistance southwest of the village on Reichsstrasse 1 and the Störmede-Eringerfeld road, where they captured two flak guns manned by labor service workers. The two guns were taken under fire by American tanks from the Linde road between Störmede and Geseke and quickly knocked out of action. The tanks then proceeded to the road crossing southwest of Störmede, where American infantry troops quickly captured forty members of the crew and support soldiers from the Störmede-Eringerfeld airfield. Two Germans were killed and several were wounded during the short exchange; the remainder were taken prisoner. Among the prisoners was Freiherr Wilderich von Ketteler auf Schwarzenraben, who, despite his noble heritage, had been serving at the airfield as a staff corporal. The aristocrat experienced the dubious honor of being taken prisoner on his own property.

No damage was inflicted on the village, but on Reichsstrasse 1, a house was burned and two others were lightly damaged as result of small-arms fire. From Störmede, the American tanks advanced to the airfield located on the southern side of the road to Östereiden. No resistance was encountered at the airfield, in part because there was little left to defend. The airfield facilities had already suffered heavy damage during the series of air raids on Saturday, 24 March, when waves of American bombers had pounded the field and leveled Paderborn. The field had been occupied by Gruppe I, Jagdgeschwader 27, and Gruppe III, Nachtjagd-Geschwader 1, under command of Major Drewes until late March. Some 1,800 bombs had fallen on the facilities, destroying the runway, the barracks, and the administrative buildings. During the night of 30–31 March, the garrison personnel had evacuated the ruins to seek shelter in the nearby village of Ehringhausen.

The forward elements of Task Force Kane left Störmede and advanced west, where they soon reached the village of Langeneicke. There, they encountered no resistance until they reached the area north of the village. From the neighboring village of Ehringhausen, a number of German soldiers attempted to escape the advancing column by fleeing in trucks. As they entered the open road heading south toward the hills and forests of the Sauerland, they were quickly discovered by an American reconnaissance patrol. Several Sherman tanks rolled across the fields between Störmede and Ehringhausen and opened fire on the German vehicles. Unable to proceed along the road, several of the Germans fled into a farm building owned by Anton Meilfes. The farmhouse received several impacts from tank fire, forcing the soldiers to seek refuge in the cellar, where the farmer's family was hiding. Within minutes, all of the fugitive German soldiers were taken prisoner and their vehicles were destroyed by the Americans.

After leaving a small security force in Langeneicke, Task Force Kane continued to push west and soon reached the village of Bökenförde. Meeting no resistance, the main force continued toward Lippstadt, leaving several tanks and infantry units at strategic points in the village. Bökenförde was the westernmost point reached by the task force, and from there, the Amis turned north and continued on toward Lippstadt.

Sixteen-year-old flak assistant Erich-Wilhelm Riekenbrauck, from the neighboring village of Westernkotten, found himself in the path of the advancing Americans. He had been assigned to the airfield at Eringerfeld near Störmede, where he experienced a heavy bombing raid on 24 March. As the column of Sherman tanks and half-tracks approached, he and several friends fled eastward. The group evaded the American units by turning north and traversing familiar ground toward the west. During the late evening of Easter Sunday, Riekenbrauck was stopped by an American sentry on the Giseler Bridge at the western approach to Bökenförde, scarcely fifteen minutes from his parents' house in Westernkotten. The group had approached the bridge at 10:00 p.m., where the boys failed to notice a tank concealed in the darkness on the Westernkotten bank of the river. While crossing the bridge, they found themselves blinded by a searchlight. Rough commands in English halted them in their tracks, and they knew their only recourse was to raise their hands above their heads.

After a cursory search of their pockets, the boys were taken by truck to Lippstadt, where they were confined in a cellar. Unable to determine where in the city they were being held, they remained locked in the cellar for the next three days. On 3 April, they were removed from their makeshift cell and, after climbing aboard a truck driven by black soldiers, were taken through the ruins of Paderborn. At length, they arrived at Bredelar-Niedermarsberg, where they joined an immense number of German soldiers, Volkssturm members, Hitler Youth, police officers, and rail employees caged in an open field. They remained in the barbed-wire enclosure for eight days, during which it rained heavily. The inmates dug caves in the soft soil in an attempt to escape the icy rainfall. As the saturated ground received more water, the caves filled with mud and collapsed, leaving the prisoners in freezing, rain-sodden uniforms.

Eventually, they were ordered aboard a convoy of trucks for transport through Marburg to Koblenz, Andernach, and then Remagen. At Remagen, they found themselves in an even more massive open-air camp, where they remained for fourteen days before being transported by rail to Namur, Belgium. Riekenbrauck returned home to Westernkotten on 1 October 1945.[5]

While Task Force Kane of the U.S. 3rd Armored Division pressed on toward Lippstadt from the south, another task force farther north was driving from the Münsterland toward Lippstadt to close the pocket. A telephone call from Lieutenant General Simpson to Major General Collins's VII Corps had resulted in an agreement for the two forces to meet. Combat Command B of the U.S. 2nd Armored Division now received orders to detach from the main body of the unit and to drive to Lippstadt. Most of the division would continue toward the east from the area north and west of Hamm.

When Major Rudolph Dunker evacuated Beckum on 31 March and 1 April, the forward American armored columns were able to occupy the important transportation crossing without resistance. The combat elements of Combat Command B rolled through the city of Beckum in the early morning hours and closed on the village of Diestedde.

Small German units had withdrawn before the rapidly moving American columns. During the previous day, a group of approximately 600 SS troops appeared at the Düllo farm from the direction of Beckum. They situated a number of armored vehicles among the village houses and prepared defenses. That evening, the inhabitants of Diestedde discerned the ominous rattle of small-arms fire across the open fields from the north, and they gathered white flags and prepared to hoist them from buildings at dawn. At 6:00 the next morning, a brief engagement erupted on the outskirts of the village, after which a white flag appeared from a nearby church tower. By 6:40, the shooting had ceased, and an uneasy silence descended on the cluster of buildings. Unbeknownst to the Americans, the SS troops had been forced to abandon their armor due to a lack of fuel; the soldiers in the approaching column, who had engaged the SS on the previous day, were unaware that the German tanks had been abandoned.

As the Americans drew near, they resumed firing on the settlement, and three buildings soon erupted in flames from tracer bullets and incendiary rounds. Heinrich Beermann, whose house was also burning, hoisted a bedsheet and approached the American positions. After being eyed suspiciously by a number of GIs, he convinced the officer in charge of the detachment that the tanks the Americans were targeting were unmanned and immobile and that the soldiers had evacuated the village more than two hours earlier. To Beermann's relief and astonishment, the American captain apologized for the damage to the homes, explaining that he and his troops were unaware that the SS troops had departed.

After capturing the village of Diestedde, the first units of the 67th Armored Regiment proceeded toward Wadersloh, meeting little resistance. On the Lippstadt-Wiedenbrück road, the forward elements intercepted a large German convoy and took several hundred prisoners. Units from the regiment then swung toward the south and proceeded toward Lippstadt. As they approached the town, D Company of the 67th Armored Regiment, under the command of Lieutenant Glass, surprised more than 100 exhausted German soldiers while they were sleeping. The company took the entire group prisoner and captured thirty trucks, three half-tracks, eight passenger vehicles, and a large quantity of small arms. The intersections and exits to the town were quickly secured to prevent any remaining German soldiers from escaping.

Other units from the 67th Armored Regiment closed on Lippstadt from various routes. The 2nd Battalion advanced from Diestedde toward Liesborn, closely followed by the 1st Battalion of the 41st Armored Infantry Regiment. The advance was delayed by poor road conditions, and a number of ragged German columns moved along the roads toward the east ahead of the American units. The advance continued in order to construct a solid line along the Lippe River from Lippstadt to Herzfeld. As the infantry units reached the outskirts of Lippstadt, they soon occupied the town and secured intersections, effectively blocking the five exit roads leading south.

The inhabitants of Lippstadt met the incursion with great concern. The town had thus far escaped major damage throughout the war. The nearby airfield had been heavily bombed, and on 10 March 1945, a number of bombs had struck the city to the south of the rail station. The inhabitants were aware of the events that had taken place over the past several days. Paderborn had suffered a large bombardment from the air, after which the Americans had pushed over Brilon to the outskirts of the city. During the week leading up to Easter, the intermittent sounds of distant artillery could be heard floating from the direction of the Rhine. For several days, the sounds of battle grew louder as the combatants approached Münster and Paderborn.

In January 1945, Lippstadt had more than 26,000 inhabitants, including approximately 1,000 foreign laborers. The town possessed three large industrial complexes: the Westfälische Metall-Industrie, the Westfälische Union, and the Lippstädter Eisen- und Metallwerke. The area had been rapidly filling with refugees over the past weeks. Many came from the east to escape the Soviet army. Others were fleeing the bombing in the heart of the Ruhr, some 60 miles to the west. The thousands of recently arrived prisoners and foreign laborers from every country in Europe, who were transported from the approaching front, added to the swelling population.

The Lippstadt airfield had been established in 1936, and the area again became a garrison center with fighter squadrons stationed at the airfield north of town. A flak regiment was stationed in one of the two bases situated along the southern road, dating from time of the Kaiser's army. The fighter squadrons had been decimated during the course of the war; any able-bodied soldiers of the flak unit had long since disappeared into the ranks of the Wehrmacht. The Volkssturm had been mobilized in October 1944, and the district's teenaged boys and older men had been called to fill the ranks. Their uniforms consisted of a simple armband printed with the word *Volkssturm*. Weapons and military equipment were almost nonexistent for the reluctant conscripts. On the first day of April—Easter Sunday 1945—there were no regular units present in the city.

The leader of the Volkssturm battalion in Lippstadt, Reserve Infantry Captain Wilhelm Oberwinter, was already determined to avoid fighting in his town. Also in Lippstadt were two Freikorps Sauerland companies. The demolition of the Lippstadt bridges spanning the Lippe River had also been dutifully prepared. On about 20 March, Engineering Captain Friedrich Gerke, who was a patient in a Lippstadt medical clinic, received orders from the local Nazi Kreisleiter to prepare to defend Lippstadt. After discussing the order with members of the city council, Gerke decided not to carry out the directive. He then passed the information on to his immediate superior, Senior Medical Officer Dr. Schlaaf. Shortly thereafter, Gerke was ordered to report for duty to the flak base, where he was to be assigned to the command of a paratroop lieutenant-colonel.

The colonel directed Gerke to prepare for demolition of the bridges at Jahnplatz, on the Cappeltor, and on the Lippertor (three city crossings or gates), as well as the Rhedaer rail bridge and the bridge in Lipperode. Aviation bombs that remained in storage in airfield magazines and detonating materials from the flak base were to be used for the demolitions. The medical facility was combed for engineering personnel, and a small unit was eventually assembled to carry out the destruction of the bridges. Captain Gerke and Engineer Captain August Knoop established a command post in the Tivoli inn, where they organized a defense of the bridges and prepared them for demolition.

The Nazi Kreisleiter had also established a command post in a wooden barracks building near a water tower. The officials organized a team of women for duty in the command post, under the supervision of the Nazi Party. The purpose of the command post was to notify the local party officials of impending air raids so that teams could be alerted for clearance and rescue operations. A direct telephone line to the senior commander of the Nazi district, in place since 1944, enabled instant communications in the event of a regular switchboard failure.

A conference was held in the Lippstadt flak kaserne following the heavy air raid of 27 March 1945. Present were the lieutenant-colonel of paratroopers, a small number of flak and Luftwaffe officers, Bürgermeister Friedrich Fuhrmann, and Dr. Schlaaf. The discussion focused on the defense of the town. Bürgermeister Fuhrmann vehemently argued that the defense plans would only result in senseless destruction. The conference abruptly ended after the heated debate. Attempting to calm the distraught mayor, the lieutenant-colonel took his hand and commented, "Herr Bürgermeister, we will hold the town for our Führer." Within several days, most of the officers who attended the meeting had simply disappeared.[6]

The thrust of U.S. forces on Brilon on 29 March severed the telephone lines in the southeast Sauerland from the rest of Germany. The political district office in Lippstadt received instructions from the Nazi Party chief in Harkortberg to dispatch a reconnaissance unit toward Olsberg-Brilon in an attempt to gain information regarding enemy movements. The reconnaissance force returned the following morning at 7:00. Based on its report, Kreisleiter Lücke relayed a message to the command post on the Harkortberg (a local terrain feature) that Lippstadt was in danger of encirclement.

The Lippstadt Volkssturm was mobilized to build barriers on the main approaches, primarily along the northern perimeter of town. Demolitions were placed on the bridges, and on Friday, the explosives were prepared by the engineers for detonation. Fleeing German columns had been passing through the town for several days in an attempt to escape the developing pocket. The streets were crowded with horse-carts and vehicles of every description and isolated groups of German soldiers and staff personnel who were being transferred outside the threatened areas. Within Lippstadt, no single battle commander was made responsible for the defense of the city, and so, for the inhabitants and officials, the military situation remained unclear.

After leaving Colonel Stripp's office in Soest, Major Rudolph Dunker set about locating his forces near Lippstadt. Dunker's troops had safely conducted the move from Beckum to the southwest of Lippstadt, with the exception of one company. When the major arrived at the assembly area at 11:00 a.m., he learned that the very event he was attempting to avoid had occurred. During the withdrawal, the company had come in contact with an American armored unit and had been decimated in a brief but intense engagement. While Dunker was organizing his force to carry out the instructions received from Colonel Stripp, the communications personnel were receiving repeated messages in broken German asking, "How situation Beckum?" and "Where own forces? ... Where enemy?" The source of the questions remained a mystery, and the queries remained unanswered. Dunker radioed the division and provided an updated situation report;

the division responded that they concurred with the directions he had received from the colonel. However, to Dunker's relief, the headquarters advised him that he was now back under the jurisdiction of the division.[7]

On Easter Sunday, 1 April, a general alarm was sounded in Lippstadt. Enemy tanks were reported to be approaching from Cappel, and the sound of engines could be detected in the distance. The Volkssturm units and Freikorps Sauerland personnel manned their positions at the approaches to the city. Kreisleiter Lücke jumped into his vehicle and sped toward Cappel to investigate the rumors of approaching tanks. As he observed the first olive-colored reconnaissance vehicle near the Ense distillery in Cappel, he turned and sped back to his command post. As Lücke braked to a halt before his headquarters, he was advised that an American column had been reported approaching Geseke. Lücke immediately relayed the report to Gauleiter Hoffmann on the Harkortberg and requested instructions. He received the ambiguous answer that the situation could not be judged from the Harkortberg and that he would have to act on his own.

Lücke, his determination to defend every foot of ground eroded by the sight of American armored vehicles, dispatched a courier to the Volkssturm units manning primitive barricades and trenches at the city's approaches with the order to fall back toward the town. Sometime between 6:00 and 7:00 a.m., Captain Friedrich Gerke was replaced at the local military command post by Captain August Knoop. Gerke, relieved that his duties at the command center were at an end, returned to his residence.

Bürgermeister Fuhrmann set out on his bicycle early in the morning on Easter Sunday, determined to fulfill a mission. He was intent on preventing the senseless destruction of the town and the bridges within its environs, for which he, as Bürgermeister, was responsible. Fuhrmann encountered a colorful array of worshipers en route to Easter services at the various local churches. Columns of retreating German troops wound intermittently through various streets, intermingled with less disciplined groups of POWs and foreign laborers, all moving ahead of the oncoming Americans. The religious services were soon interrupted as word raced through the populace that the Americans were approaching.

In Lippstadt, the sound of battle drifted through the still morning air from the direction of Cappel. The occasional faint rumble of engines and heavy tracks grating against pavement could be discerned amid the distant and sporadic rattle of gunfire. An American observation plane flew low over the northern quarter of the town, the pilot almost visible to curious onlookers. A horse-drawn battery of German field guns was observed retreating from Cappel. The teams and caissons soon halted and established a firing position on the lower Bastion Strasse in front of the Friedrichschule, a local school. A group of Volkssturm soldiers withdrew from the northwest sector of town toward the Lippe bridge near the intersection

of Friedrich and Bückeburger Strasse. As they began preparing defenses at the
bridge, the head physician at the nearby Dreifaltigkeit medical center attempted
to persuade them to relocate farther from the hospital. The doctor requested that
a 300-yard perimeter be established free of troops around the medical facilities.
He was eventually successful in persuading the troops to relocate to the southern
branch of the river at the Soesttor-Hellinghaeuser Weg.

By midmorning, the westward streets and the fields to the northwest of the
town had come under a slow but methodical barrage of artillery fire. Shells impacting the fields along the Barbarossa Strasse and Rüdenkuhle could be seen
from the roof of the Evangelischen clinic. The shelling abated at 11:30 a.m.
As the shelling subsided, the first Sherman tanks approached from Cappel. An
immobile German tank fell victim to a Sherman on the Cappeler Landstrasse,
and the point elements of the armored column soon arrived at the first Lippstadt
roadblock. The obstacle was immediately opened by several elderly men, and
the American tanks clattered through the ineffective barrier into the town. As the
first tanks penetrated the outskirts of the town, an explosion reverberated across
the open fields and through the now-deserted streets. The bridges over the Lippe
on the Bückeburger Strasse, on the Cappeltor, and at the north train station were
demolished by the retreating Wehrmacht.

Volkssturm leader Wilhelm Oberwinter was near the town post office as the
first Americans approached from the direction of the Rathaus. Springing on his
bicycle, Oberwinter pedaled to the flak kaserne in the southern part of town.
There, he burst into the battalion briefing room, grabbed a teenaged courier, and
ordered him to relay an important message to various Volkssturm units. Providing
the youth with exact locations, he instructed the courier to spread the word that
the Volkssturm troops in Lippstadt were officially ordered to evacuate their positions, disband, and return to their homes.

At 11:50 a.m., the chief medical doctor at the Evangelischen clinic was informed by telephone that white flags were hanging from windows throughout the
city. At 12:40, three American tanks appeared in the street adjacent to the medical
complex. The doctor noticed the tanks assume tactical positions that gave them a
clear field of fire, and their turrets rotated to train their guns directly on the clinics
and medical facilities. Unable to predict what the next minutes might bring, the
doctor emerged from the building with his hands held high above his head. A GI
emerged from one of the armored vehicles, and the doctor explained to him that
there were no troops in the hospital complex. The soldier appeared satisfied with
the doctor's report and advised him that all firearms on the premises were to be
surrendered immediately.

The garrison manning the airfield north of Lippstadt prepared various facilities for demolition, using a number of 500-kilogram bombs stored in magazines

nearby. The plan resulted in a halfhearted effort by Luftwaffe personnel that left most of the structures intact. A number of them were preparing to defend the west end of the airfield, but, experiencing a change of heart as the American columns drew ever nearer, they eventually withdrew ignominiously toward Detmold. Soon afterward, the first Sherman tanks rolled onto the airfield and took as prisoners two German soldiers who either had been left behind or had decided to end their participation in the war and go into captivity. The entire north half of Lippstadt was under American control; the southern neighborhoods remained unoccupied.

A pair of unidentified German tanks were seen in front of the flak kaserne that morning, but they had since departed toward the east. The withdrawal of the tanks was soon accompanied by the exodus of the last groups of officers and soldiers, some on hastily requisitioned bicycles, all heading east and away from the oncoming Americans. The departure of the garrison troops left the facilities without security personnel, and storage and supply buildings were soon being plundered by civilians. Locals converged on the abandoned facilities and left carrying armloads of uniforms, various articles of clothing, blankets, boots, and shoes. Even entire rolls of gray-green Wehrmacht uniform fabric were dragged from storage bins in an effort to seize anything of value prior to the arrival of the Americans.[8]

At 1:30 p.m., a resident on the outskirts of Lippstadt met a neighbor who had hurried home from the city center. The acquaintance fearfully spoke of American tanks approaching the Erwitter-Overhagener Strasse. Adding to their growing concern were the long files of German soldiers moving along the Overhagener Strasse. Unlike so many soldiers they had seen that morning, these men were advancing *toward* the oncoming Americans. Some eighty heavily armed landsers moved in a single column. In marked contrast to the Luftwaffe garrison soldiers who had fled, these troops appeared determined to fight, and they were laden with machine guns, rifles, and antitank weapons.

The soldiers dug defense positions at the Erwitter-Overhagener Strasse intersection, chambered belts of ammunition into the feed trays of automatic weapons, primed hand grenades, and patiently waited. As the first American tanks approached, the shooting began. Within seconds, several white flags appeared on nearby buildings. But the effort to spare the buildings from destruction brought only retribution, as the German soldiers turned and fired on the flags. The flags disappeared into the structures as quickly as they had appeared. The German soldiers fired from corners of buildings and from positions entrenched along the railbed of the Westfälischen Landeseisenbahn toward Erwitte Strasse. Several frightened citizens watched from a cellar window as one of the defenders, lying prone behind the railbed, was struck by a bullet. An American reconnaissance vehicle approached the corner of the Overhagener Strasse without firing, appeared to observe the skirmishing for several seconds, and then withdrew. Several minutes later, a large number of American tanks appeared. Slowly, as if reluctant to cede the field to the enemy, the German soldiers began to withdraw in the face of the oncoming tanks and half-tracks. A voice shouted in German through a loudspeaker, telling the citizens to surrender: further resistance was futile. The shrill voice added that should resistance continue, the town would face destruction from squadrons of aircraft.

Simultaneously, another American column left the city center and rolled toward the southern part of town. Task Force Kane from the 3rd Armored Division approached the town from the direction of Bökenförde after having broken out of its positions in Böddeken Forest that morning. These units, one within the city and the other coming from the south, were directed toward one another by the reconnaissance aircraft.

Also in the southern part of the town was Major Dunker, the German officer who had defied orders and evacuated the town of Beckum to spare the medical center's needless destruction. Dunker observed the American tanks approach from two directions and meet at the southern end of the town shortly after noon. He was now resigned to the fact that the Ruhr Pocket was closed. Army Group B was trapped, and the major could not help but wonder how many Wehrmacht soldiers may have escaped to the east had he delayed the American advance by choosing to defend Beckum.[9]

Friz Moos, a member of Flaksturmabteilung 98, had been assigned to drive from the area of Siegen to Lippstadt and Güterloh and attempt to locate fuel for his antiaircraft battalion. Moos crossed the deserted town of Meschede and reached Lippstadt at approximately 6:00 that morning. He immediately began seeking his family, aware that they had not left Lippstadt during his absence. After locating his relatives, he and several members of his battalion reported to the nearby flak kaserne at 7:30, only to find the base in stages of evacuation. There was no duty officer, no one in charge to whom he could report. As he attempted to drive through the gate of the compound, he was suddenly confronted by a sentry, who advised him that it was now forbidden to leave the kaserne. Argument and confrontation with the guard produced no results, and there was no one available with whom he could speak regarding his assignment.

Abandoning their vehicle, Moos and the men accompanying him slipped through the base perimeter fence at the first opportunity. Spurred on by the fear of what their actions might bring should they be discovered, they raced across the open field and made their way toward his residence in Lippstadt. En route, they encountered a number of local inhabitants who were returning to their residences from Easter Sunday worship. The pastor had interrupted services and dismissed the congregation on receiving word that the Americans had captured Cappel and were now approaching Lippstadt.

As rumors spread that the Americans were approaching, Moos and his fellow fugitives, along with members of his family, took shelter in the Weissenburg distillery. The expansive cellar offered an excellent refuge in case fighting broke out. En route to the distillery, they met a young boy who told them that the Americans had retreated and would not enter the town. Skeptical of the unlikely news, Moos climbed a nearby tower while the others sought refuge in the distillery. From the tower, he observed a long column of olive green vehicles winding through the southern sector of town on Westernkötter Strasse and Bökenförder Strasse. He knew that the column was headed directly toward the town water reservoir. Climbing from the tower, he advised the others of the approaching American column. The small group huddled expectantly in the cellar for several hours before deciding to return to their home on the corner of Bökenförder and Josefstrasse.

From an upper-floor window, they watched immense columns of Allied material rolling through the streets from Bökenförde. Soon, the first houses were searched by soldiers clad in khaki and olive uniforms. The door to the house in which the fugitives were hidden burst open, and several soldiers noisily entered. On seeing Moos and his comrades, an American asked in a friendly tone if they were soldiers. The nervous group admitted that they had been members of a flak unit. They were then instructed to leave the residence. As they stepped through the front door, each soldier received kicks from a number of GIs waiting outside. They were shoved against a nearby wall, where they stood with upraised hands for an undetermined period of time before being led to a factory storage facility on the corner of Erwitter Strasse that evening. They were eventually joined by a growing number of ill-fated prisoners from various areas of Lippstadt, including railway and postal employees. Two days later, they were transported by truck through Paderborn to Niedermarsberg, where they were held in an open field for several days before being sent to France.[10]

Kurt Becker was serving as an impromptu soldier with the Freikorps Sauerland unit detailed to assist in the defense of Lippstadt. The band of German civilians hastily pressed into service were sparsely uniformed with a mixture of Wehrmacht and civilian clothing. Many of the erstwhile soldiers sported only an armband bearing the words *Freikorps Sauerland* to identify them as combatants. They had recently been equipped with antiquated French rifles, most of which lacked ammunition. On Easter Morning, Becker found himself occupying a shallow defensive position hacked into the ground near the Beckumer Strasse, directly behind the railbed in Lippstadt. He and his fellow conscripts had spent an uneasy night in a soccer field near their position, and now, the unkempt group prepared to defend Lippstadt against the U.S. Army.

An observation plane appeared overhead and circled lazily above the town, and soon, they could hear the muffled sounds of tank engines and the clatter of distant tracks from the direction of Cappel. As the sounds grew louder, the first American soldiers appeared unexpectedly between a nearby row of houses. Becker, like the other reluctant soldiers with whom he been ordered to stop the armored advance, immediately tossed his weapon aside and raised his hands. He was motioned forward and was soon being marched to a collection point at Beckumer Strasse with other prisoners.

Several hours later, the captives were loaded onto an ammunitions carrier and driven toward the town center to the Marktplatz. After dismounting from the vehicle, they were again searched before being locked in the Rathaus. Throughout the afternoon and night, they could hear foreign voices as the city was being plundered by foreign laborers enjoying their first, euphoric hours of freedom. The next morning, the prisoners were ordered to form columns and were then paraded past newsreel teams before being loaded onto trucks and driven to Ahlen. After a series of searches, during which they were stripped of anything of value, they were transported over Lüdinghausen to the massive POW cage at Rheinberg.[11]

Prior to the arrival of the Americans, Erna Wiegelmann and her neighbors were aware that the end of the war was rapidly approaching for the inhabitants of Lippstadt. The streets had swarmed with columns of refugees and foreign laborers, most of whom appeared to be coming from Lipperode, east of Lippstadt. However, Erna and the others awoke on Easter Sunday to an empty, seemingly abandoned town. The faint sounds of distant detonations and scattered gunfire resonated softly. Erna collected her family members and, together with several neighbors, descended into the cellar. Their main concern was whether Lippstadt, as prophesied by Propaganda Minister Joseph Goebbels, would be defended to the last bullet. In the cellar, they were surprised to find two young, bedraggled German soldiers, who pleaded for civilian clothing. One of the women hastily departed and soon returned with work coveralls, for which the soldiers exchanged their threadbare uniforms before slipping away into the surrounding neighborhood.

At length, they dared to crack open the door from the cellar leading to the Poststrasse, only to observe a street still empty of traffic or pedestrians. They soon observed a heavily armed soldier making his way slowly along the edge of the street, followed at a distance by several others. The men moved silently, on quiet, soft-soled combat boots, as opposed to the hobnailed jackboots commonly worn by the soldiers of the Wehrmacht. The soldier saw the faces peering from the doorway, prompting the inhabitants to close the door and scurry back into the cellar. Erna and her family cowered on the wooden bench there among the other women and children as rifle butts pounded against the door and an angry voice demanded that it be opened.

Two Americans entered the cellar with flashlights, shined the lights in the faces of women and children, and conducted a cursory search before leaving. The women waited for several hours before daring to again peer outside. The streets were now crowded with what appeared to be hundreds of American soldiers and myriad vehicles. One of the women hurried upstairs and hung a bedsheet from a window—the first white flag to be seen on Poststrasse. It was 11:00 a.m., Easter Sunday.[12]

On Saturday evening, 31 March, paratrooper Bernd Kampert had slipped out of the military infirmary with several friends to visit acquaintances in the town. The group returned early the next morning by climbing over the wall that surrounded the medical complex grounds. At about 10:00 a.m., they were awakened by other patients, who advised them that churchgoers had reported American tanks moving from the south toward Lippstadt. The group of soldiers discussed their options. They could either remain in the hospital and await capture or attempt to slip away. Deciding to avoid captivity, the group hurriedly donned their uniforms and slipped from the compound. They immediately struck out to the north, unaware that the American columns were also closing from that direction. Following deserted streets through the town, they had gone several blocks when they came on a group of Wehrmacht soldiers who were clearly in retreat. They conferred with the soldiers momentarily and compared information gleaned from various rumors sweeping through the town. The apprehensive soldiers heard gunfire in the distance, and any plans for slipping out of the town dissipated. Kampert and his fellow escapees wandered dejectedly back to the medical compound, all thoughts of evasion temporarily forgotten.

A short time later, Kampert watched a file of American soldiers patrolling along the Fleischhauerstrasse with weapons at the ready. White flags had mysteriously appeared throughout the neighborhood and hung limply from buildings. The senior medical officer entered the ward and announced that the lazarette was now in the hands of the American army and that everyone should remain calm and not resist being taken into captivity.

The following day, the patients and medical staff heard that foreign laborers were plundering the Kisker distillery. Several patients managed to steal out of the medical compound with an ambulance, which they drove to the distillery. Loading the vehicle with bottles of schnapps concealed beneath rolls of bandages, they drove back to the clinic. On returning, they explained to the American guard that the vehicle contained hospital supplies. For the next several weeks, the patients conducted a surreptitious but lucrative trade, exchanging schnapps for American cigarettes with the GIs, whom they routinely met behind a storage building in the rear of the hospital grounds.

After an inspection of the medical facility, all nurses were ordered to accompany the American medical personnel to an unknown destination. A number of them returned after several days and reported that their services had been needed to care for Russian and Polish laborers who had consumed pure alcohol. Many of the foreigners had subsequently died in agony. Word also circulated among the military patients that a young German medical officer at the facility was performing surgery on Waffen SS soldiers to remove the blood group tattoo on their inner left arm. The doctor allegedly was able to conduct the procedure in a manner that left a scar resembling a bullet wound.

The inhabitants of the hospital attempted to linger in the wards as long as possible, for there was an abundance of food and the soldiers could receive visitors. After several weeks, however, it became obvious that many of the soldiers were no longer in need of medical care, and the doctors were ordered to release any recuperated patients.[13]

In one of the leading Sherman tanks that entered Lippstadt was an American soldier named Werner Ostheimer. For Ostheimer, entering the town brought his life full circle. His family, forced out of Germany under Hitler's draconian anti-Jewish policies, had emigrated to the United States in 1937. Like so many other young Americans, Werner heeded the call of his adoptive country and entered the U.S. Army in 1943. In February 1945, he found himself serving as a tank sergeant assigned to C Company, 2nd Battalion, 67th Armored Regiment. Attached to Combat Command B of the 2nd Armored Division, Ostheimer was traversing an area that was very familiar to him. His home in Germany, until he was forced to emigrate, had been in the Westphalian town of Lippstadt.

During the night of 31 March–1 April, Sergeant Ostheimer's tank had rumbled through the area between Ahlen and Beckum. The early morning hours brought the column through Diestedde, from where they had pressed on through Liesborn and Cappel to Lippstadt. Being familiar with the town, Ostheimer was assigned to lead the column, which consisted of six tanks, a number of trucks, and numerous half-tracks. Between Cappel and Lippstadt, the column had fired on a German tank crouching ominously in the distance. The Americans were unaware that the immobilized vehicle had been abandoned by its crew hours prior to their arrival. At approximately 10:00 a.m., Ostheimer's tank rolled into Lippstadt without meeting resistance. The few roadblocks were open, and the column rolled over the Beckumer Strasse, crossed the heavily damaged but still passable bridge on the Cappeltor, drove along the Cappelstrasse to the intersection with Marktstrasse, and stopped near the Marktplatz. The streets remained empty, without a trace of German soldiers.

An additional column from the 67th Regiment took a different route into the town. Wehrmacht Captain Friedrich Gerke observed an American tank on the Wiedenbrücker Strasse from a window of his residence. The tank came in from the direction of the Lippestrasse, turned toward the town, and drew to a halt before the damaged bridge at the north train station. The captain watched as a soldier clad in khaki emerged from an open turret hatch and climbed from the tank. The soldier cautiously walked on the damaged bridge, stopped momentarily, and gazed at the surrounding buildings. He then jumped up and down several times, as if to test the stability of the bridge, before shouting and motioning for the tank to cross. The massive steel vehicle slowly rumbled across the structure, rolled farther into the town, and halted at the Marktplatz. As the hatches opened, the tank was immediately swarmed by a mob of jubilant French prisoners of war, many of whom began to dismantle additional roadblocks.[14]

Farther to the west, another American armored unit crossed the northern tributary to the Lippe River and entered Lippstadt over Friedrichstrasse and Cappelstrasse. The first GIs soon arrived at the Catholic hospital and at the Landeszentralbank in the city center. Another column rolled from the north train station toward the city center and cautiously approached the Marktplatz. From his office in the Rathaus, Bürgermeister Fuhrmann observed the first heavily armed American soldiers as they moved carefully behind Haus Mock. Warning the police officers who were present in the Rathaus of the arrival of the Americans, Fuhrmann then left the building with a white handkerchief held high overhead. As he neared the oncoming Americans, a burst of automatic-weapons fire suddenly cracked over his head. Throwing himself to the ground, he lay prone for several seconds, not daring to move. At length, the shaken Bürgermeister pulled himself to his feet and dashed back into the Rathaus, where he again warned the police not to offer resistance.[15]

After a brief halt in the cobblestoned square of the Marktplatz, the column of tanks and support vehicles, led by former resident Werner Ostheimer, continued over the Lange Strasse and moved from the town in a westward direction along the Erwitter Strasse. They had expected to meet units of the U.S. First Army, and Ostheimer suspected that they would locate the First Army units somewhere along that street. The sergeant then heard over his radio that the two American armies had linked up in Lippstadt. He immediately turned his column around and returned to Lippstadt.

As the column wound its way through the town, Ostheimer observed several vehicles laden with GIs. A tank commander, when leading a formation through months of combat, can usually recognize vehicles from his own unit. However, among these vehicles was a Sherman tank that appeared unfamiliar to him. Pulling close to one tank, which was accompanied by a number of infantrymen, he immediately identified the tactical insignia of the U.S. 3rd Armored Division. The division was assigned to the U.S. First Army. With relief, Ostheimer realized that the linkup between the First and Ninth Armies had succeeded. It was Easter Sunday, 1 April 1945; the time was 4:09 p.m. The Ruhr Pocket was now closed.[16]

Climbing from the turrets of the tanks, the soldiers calmly conversed for several minutes. They probably were unaware of the significance or scope of their meeting in the nondescript Westphalian town of Lippstadt or of the fact that they had successfully closed an armored ring around Field Marshal Walter Model's Army Group B. Trapped between the American armies and the Rhine were the Wehrmacht's Fifteenth Army, the Fifth Panzer Army, two corps of the First Parachute Army, and large numbers of flak units, as well as innumerable artillery, engineer, supply, and replacement units. Enclosed in the pocket were some 325,000 German troops, among them 26 generals and an admiral. The number of surrounded Wehrmacht soldiers exceeded the number of troops killed and captured at Stalingrad or in North Africa.

A German family anxiously observes Allied airborne forces from their home near Wesel. A fallen German soldier lies in the foreground. (Photo courtesy Imperial War Museum)

Forces of the U.S. Ninth Army cross the Rhine as Allied B-24 Liberators conduct resupply missions to units on the east bank of the river. The units of Field Marshal Bernard Montgomery's Twenty-first Army Group conducted a crossing of the Rhine near Wesel on 23 and 24 March 1945. (Photo courtesy Imperial War Museum)

British commandos secure their position in Wesel. The town was almost completely destroyed by artillery and bombing raids prior to the crossing of the Rhine by Montgomery's Twenty-first Army Group. (Photo courtesy Imperial War Museum)

Major-General Deutsch, commander of the German forces in Wesel, was killed during the fighting for the heavily destroyed town. One account of his death states that he was shot by British commandos when he refused to surrender; another account claims that he died during an exchange of fire. The absence of gold-braid shoulder boards and cap insignia indicate either that the general removed them to be less conspicuous to the enemy or, more likely, that they were collected from the body by souvenir hunters. (Photo courtesy Imperial War Museum)

British infantrymen file past a row of fallen German soldiers as they secure objectives on the east bank of the Rhine. (Photo courtesy Imperial War Museum)

British soldiers inspect German dead near Wesel. In addition to being looted for souvenirs and valuables, enemy dead were often searched for identification documents and intelligence materials. Personal letters, photographs, and other possessions strewn about the bodies were usually an indication of those activities by opposing troops. (Photo courtesy Imperial War Museum)

(Above) Two fallen German soldiers lie along a roadside as a third, less severely wounded, awaits evacuation and medical treatment. (Below) American airborne troops and British armor meet in Münster as they proceed toward the east after crossing the Rhine. (Photos courtesy Imperial War Museum)

(Above) German children near the town of Friedrichsfeld watch from the roadside as a group of Wehrmacht prisoners are led along the autobahn to a prisoner-of-war enclosure. (Below) Troops of the U.S. 17th Airborne Division depart from the German town of Appelhülsen on a Churchill tank of the Guards Armored Division as they advance toward Münster, some 9 miles to the northeast. (Photo courtesy Imperial War Museum)

(Above) Vehicles of the U.S. 83rd Infantry Division enter the town of Ahlen, Saturday, 31 April 1945. Paul Rosenbaum, the Wehrmacht commander of the numerous medical facilities in the town, successfully negotiated a peaceful surrender of Ahlen with U.S. forces after a lengthy and heated dispute with local Nazi Party officials. (Right) Major Rudolf Dunker of the 116th Panzer Division, who was threatened with execution after he disobeyed Hitler's directive and agreed to evacuate his troops from the town of Beckum to avert the destruction of the extensive medical facilities there. Dunker was spared a court-martial only by the rapid American advance toward Lippstadt, and the major was later taken prisoner after escaping encirclement in Hamm by U.S. forces. (Photo courtesy Willi Mues)

An American patrol is ambushed by a German unit concealed near the Lenne River on the outskirts of Oberbrügge, 12 April 1945.

Wounded personnel of the U.S. 8th Armored Division are evacuated as infantrymen move into the heavily damaged town of Dorsten on 29 March 1945.

(Above) A German nurse assists a U.S. Ninth Army medic in bandaging a wounded Wehrmacht soldier in the town of Unna on 11 April 1945. The original Signal Corps caption stated that Unna was heavily defended by SS units, and it mistakenly identified the wounded soldier as an SS trooper. Such errors were common during the engagements that enveloped the towns and villages when defended by various components of Waffen SS, Wehrmacht, and Volkssturm troops. (Below) German troops captured by the 194th Airborne Regiment are assembled in the town of Appelhülsen for evacuation to prisoner-of-war enclosures west of the Rhine.

(Above) A 20-mm flak crew of Panzer Brigade 106 awaits the appearance of Allied forces in the Ruhr Pocket. (Below) A rare photograph from late in the war shows a heavy Panzer IV accompanied by an armored reconnaissance vehicle of Panzer Brigade 106 rolling through the deserted streets of Bonn. The location of the armored vehicles is ironically named Friedensplatz, or "Square of Peace." (Photos courtesy Willi Mues)

(Above) A Sherman tank of the U.S. 7th Armored Division cautiously enters the heavily contested village of Oberkirchen in early April 1945. The body of a slain Wehrmacht soldier is indicative of the vicious engagement that occurred in the Sauerland village as American units raced to secure the pocket. (Below) Sergeant Raymond Daum and Private First Class Ralph Dudrow accompanied by Dr. Karl Wilkes examine a medieval Gobelin tapestry discovered in the castle of Count Wildernich von Spee near Brilon, Germany. The Signal Corps photo caption stated that the Gobelin was valued at 150 million marks.

Soldiers of the U.S. First and Ninth Armies meet in Lippstadt on Easter Sunday, 1 April 1945. The linkup sealed the Ruhr Pocket and encircled Field Marshal Model's Army Group B and elements of General von Blaskowitz's Army Group H, trapping some 325,000 German troops.

(Above) Soldiers of the U.S. 83rd Infantry Division leave the village of Horn near the Teutoburg Forest as American forces secured their hold on the Ruhr Pocket. (Below) A massive German Jagdtiger sits abandoned in the village of Netphen, probably immobilized by lack of fuel. (Photo courtesy Willi Mues)

Sherman tanks of the U.S. 8th Armored Division neutralize German positions as they prepare to advance into the town of Kirchhellen on 28 March 1945.

(Above) After sealing the pocket at Lippstadt, American armored units penetrated the Teutoburg Forest and advanced toward the east. On 2 April, the forward elements of the U.S. 2nd Armored Division entered the town of Lemgo. The infantrymen taking shelter along the buildings and the lack of civilian onlookers indicate that German troops remained active in the area. (Below) An American soldier is held aloft by jubilant Russians when a Soviet prisoner-of-war camp is liberated by the Ninth Army south of Bielefeld on 2 April 1945. Some 900 emaciated prisoners were liberated from Stalag 326, and it was reported that mass graves nearby held the bodies of 30,000 prisoners who had died of starvation and disease or had been executed. (Photo courtesy Imperial War Museum)

(Above) Ecstatic Russian and Polish laborers flock through the Rathausstrasse in Lippstadt on 1 April 1945 as word spreads of the arrival of American forces. (Below) Liberated Russian laborers in the town of Soest celebrate the surrender of Germany on 8 May 1945. Soest was captured by the U.S. Ninth Army on 6 April 1945.

A shepherd approaches soldiers of the First Army near the village of Wewelsburg. The Wewelsburg Castle, seen in the distance, was chosen by SS leader Heinrich Himmler to become a primary National Socialist research and education center. As American forces closed on the area, Himmler ordered his SS aide, Heinz Macher, to destroy the facility. Macher and an SS detachment set the castle ablaze, causing damage but leaving much of the facility intact. The contents of the castle, including Himmler's personal antique arms collection, were confiscated by U.S. forces but subsequently disappeared without a trace.

As American forces reduced the Ruhr Pocket, mass graves containing the bodies of hundreds of Gestapo victims were discovered. Former Nazi Party members were forced to unearth the bodies of seventy-one political prisoners who had been removed from the prison at Remscheid-Lüttringhausen on 13 April and executed near the town of Ohligs. Citizens of Ohligs were compelled by occupation authorities to observe the reburial of the bodies in a memorial service conducted near the Ohligs town hall on 1 May 1945.

(Above) Wehrmacht troops surrender to American forces in Bonn. With the dissolution of Army Group B by Field Marshal Model, large numbers of German soldiers drove to U.S. checkpoints to surrender or simply waited for the Americans to arrive. Others attempted to evade capture by donning civilian clothes, but few escaped. (Below) A small number of the German troops who surrendered following the dissolution of the army group by Field Marshal Model on 17 April 1945. The prisoners are assembled in an open field near Iserlohn, and an American MP is seen on the left among the prisoners.

A German military cemetery in the Sauerland. As the combat troops departed, residents were left to clear their towns, villages, and farmsteads of Wehrmacht dead. This small cemetery was typical of those found throughout Germany in the closing weeks of the war. Most bodies were exhumed and transferred to larger regional military cemeteries in the decades following the war. (Photo courtesy Willi Mues)

Chapter 10

Death in the Eggegeberge

The thickly wooded area of rolling hills and winding roads east of Paderborn is known as the Eggegeberge. The Höxter District encompasses much of this region from the eastern edge of Paderborn to the Weser River, some 30 miles to the east. The Eggegeberge is located at the southernmost tip of a larger series of densely wooded hills historically referred to as the Teutoburg Forest, which extends southeast from Osnabrück and is joined to the Sauerland by the Eggegeberge east of Paderborn.

An invasion of the Teutoburg Forest was not without precedent. On a late summer evening in the year A.D. 9, a Roman general named Quinctilius Varus was lured from his encampment by a Germanic chieftain named Arminius. Once a friend and ally of the Romans, Arminius had succeeded in unifying large numbers of feuding tribes for the purpose of halting Rome's encroachment east of the Rhine. During a deadly struggle that extended over a period of several days, no less than three Roman legions, some 20,000 troops and auxiliaries, were annihilated in the foreboding forests by the forces of Arminius. Varus did not survive his defeat, preferring to fall on his own sword than endure the ignominy of defeat at the hands of barbarians. On hearing of the crushing defeat, Caesar Augustus was said to have pounded his head against a door in anguish, crying, "Quinctilius Varus, give me back my legions!" Never again did Roman forces bear the designations of the XVII, XVIII, or XIX Legions that were lost in Germania. Emperor Tiberius, the successor of Augustus, abandoned any further plans to make *Germania magna* a Roman province. Some 2,000 years later, the defeat of invaders at the door to Germany would not be repeated.

The day before the American forces had closed the pocket at Lippstadt on 1 April, Easter Sunday, the Höxter District Nazi Party officially announced that any persons exhibiting a white flag as the enemy approached would be shot. Furthermore, anyone who hindered or refused service with the Volkssturm would be punished, this punishment would extend to family members, and any cooperation with the enemy would be punished by death.

The directive was not an empty threat. On 4 April, Bürgermeister Gräfe of Lemgo was arrested in the village of Lügde by Wehrmacht officers. He was held in the local police jail for several hours before being taken before a military tribunal. Found guilty of subverting the scorched-earth directive, he was sentenced to death. The rapid withdrawal of German troops from the village preempted the execution, so the sentence was not carried out in Lügde. Instead, the Bürgermeister was transported east toward the Weser River amid streams of refugees and retreating Wehrmacht troops. The following morning, Gräfe was shot in the Bodenwerder churchyard, and his body was hung from a nearby tree as a macabre warning to the populace. The corpse could not be removed for twenty-four hours. The Bürgermeister's crime had been to protect his town from destruction by surrendering it to approaching American forces.[1]

The day after the tank duel at Schloss Hamborn, the three wounded Tiger tank crewmen from Heavy Panzer Battalion 507 were admitted to the field hospital in the village of Neuenbeken, some 3 miles northeast of Paderborn. The tank's commander, Sergeant Voss, had escaped the blazing vehicle with burns to his hands, and gunner Hüpfl had suffered severe burns to his hands and face. But Wolfgang Bloss had received the most serious injuries of the three. The gun-loader's face had been burned beyond recognition. The burns of the crewmen were hastily treated with cod-liver oil, which did little to alleviate the pain. On Easter Sunday, the day following the tank battle, the sounds of distant engagements could be discerned from the direction of Paderborn as the U.S. 3rd Armored Division assaulted the city. By 5:00 p.m., Paderborn was in the hands of the American forces.

On Monday, a large number of heavily armed GIs appeared in the Neuenbeken field hospital. They moved through the ward examining the patients closely before pulling two wounded SS infantrymen from their beds and dragging them from the building. Shoving the soldiers to the side of the street, the GIs pushed them forward so that they lay face down. Two of the GIs raised their weapons and fired into the men's backs before continuing on their way. A German doctor rushed to the scene and discovered one of the men was still alive. With assistance from staff personnel, he returned the badly bleeding soldier to the clinic, where the doctor was able to save him. The soldier was seventeen years old. It was rumored that the Americans were taking revenge for their medic having been fired on during a previous engagement near Paderborn.[2]

As the American forces from the First and Ninth Armies were meeting in Lippstadt on Easter Sunday, a German battery took up position in a field to the south of Bad Driburg, east of Paderborn in the Eggegeberge region. The gunners took the Paderborn-Lichtenau road under fire to block the path of American units approaching from Paderborn. Within minutes, the Americans began to return fire. Incensed at the callousness of the German gunners for endangering the medical facilities, a German medical officer in charge of a surgery team convinced the artillery unit to withdraw. In another attempt to break the ring around the Ruhr, two attacks were launched from Driburg during the night of 3–4 April by a weak panzer battalion consisting of eight tanks supported by a mixture of Wehrmacht and Waffen SS infantry. Three battle-damaged tanks limped back to their stations near the town at dawn. The supporting infantry units had taken heavy casualties, and there were no reserves to reinforce the decimated units.

On 4 April, the military authorities in Driburg received orders to initiate the evacuation of the medical facilities. The town was to be defended. The American advance elements were expected to approach from the direction of Buke. The Volkssturm unit guarding the roadblock at the entrance to the village was relieved by a number of young soldiers. The order to evacuate the medical facilities was an impossible task, as there were no means to do so, yet despite the lack of transportation assets, the medical officers were ordered to evacuate all ambulatory patients and staff on foot. Within hours, a column of medical personnel and convalescents was trailing along the road eastward to Höxter.

Meanwhile, two of the village inhabitants were advancing in the opposite direction toward the American lines. Two fourteen-year-old boys had heard rumors that black American troops were occupying the panzer base near Paderborn, and they mounted their bicycles and pedaled toward the west to catch a glimpse of the Americans. They met the first American unit near Brocksberg and were permitted to pass without question. In the area of the panzer base, they encountered American armored units. The excited boys were greeted by the GIs, who provided them with scarce items from their rations. The boys were permitted to ride on one of the Sherman tanks as far as Buke, where they dismounted and proceeded to pedal toward home. A communications station assigned to the staff at Bad Driburg was located in the Bendfeld Hotel in Buke. At 1:30 p.m., the communications personnel in Buke radioed to their headquarters that American tanks were on the street and that five crewmen had exited one tank to familiarize themselves with the surrounding terrain. The radio then went silent as the observer hastily concealed the telephone and disappeared through a rear entrance of the hotel.

A number of German soldiers had withdrawn from the area of Buke across open fields and were bypassed by the tank column. The Allied armor halted long enough to fire on a roadblock that had been erected on the road leading to Bad Driburg. Before long, other American vehicles overtook the two teenagers who had excitedly ridden a tank near Paderborn. However, on this occasion, the boys were not greeted with gifts. Taking the teens into custody, the Americans herded them, together with a group of civilians who had inadvertently encountered the armored column, into a nearby barn. Within minutes, the boys found an opening in the back of the building, through which they pushed their bicycles and fled across the fields toward the concealment of the Eggewald, a local wooded area. As they took shelter in the thick underbrush of the woods, the noise of heavy fighting rose along the road where the American column was engaging German units between the barn and the village. The Americans blanketed the area in smoke as they advanced along the road and through the woods lining the flanks of their advance.

The political officials who had established a command post in a medical administration building in Bad Driburg began to show signs of nervousness. They moved the staff to a forestry building some distance from the gunfire. The Ortsgruppenleiter, who, in a drunken rage, had threatened to shoot several members of the local Volkssturm for refusing to carry out his orders, fled from the Americans on a bicycle. After traveling several hundred yards, he encountered a local farmer who had left his fields when he heard gunfire and was en route to his home. The Ortsgruppenleiter forced the farmer at gunpoint to undress. He then put on the man's work clothes, exchanging his decorative but very obsolete Nazi Party uniform for the civilian garb.[3]

One of the units encountered by the American armored column as it neared Bad Driburg was Observation Battalion 6. A member of this unit recalled:

> We lay under the trees, without cover … An armored vehicle approached above us on the road and took us under machine gun and cannon fire. I was lying no further than thirty yards from the vehicle; Lieutenant Pehling and Meineke lay next to me. They were killed immediately; Pehling with a head shot, Meineke with an abdominal wound. He lived for a period of time, many were screaming for help, but no one was able to help anyone. Then I got it, too. I suddenly received a heavy blow against my right leg, and everyone who could move began withdrawing. Someone waved for me to follow, but I was then struck in the left upper arm. The Americans came forward slowly as the others withdrew. One of them motioned for me to come with them; only I and Corporal Beck were wounded. The Americans searched us from top to bottom, ignoring the fact that we were wounded. They also robbed the dead. A German medic was captured later, and he bandaged my wounds and carried me to the road … I was eventually taken to the hospital in Neuenbeken.[4]

On encountering resistance at the approaches to the settlement, the American armored unit began blanketing the surrounding homes and buildings with gunfire. Shattering windows, slamming through brick and timber walls, and setting farm buildings alight with tracer fire, the Americans slowly but relentlessly crawled forward. The occupants of buildings remained crouched in their cellars, terrified at the maelstrom that had erupted among their homes. The civilian driver of an

ambulance was called to evacuate some wounded. As he left the volunteer fire
department with his vehicle, he observed an olive-colored tank in front of the
Heinemann-Pilster home. Several soldiers in unfamiliar khaki uniforms waved
to the vehicle sporting large red crosses, and the driver halted. He was directed
to proceed to the Stellbergheim clinic, where he was astonished to find a large
number of American soldiers. The strangers were well behaved, and several of
the GIs were sharing chocolate and cigarettes with the medical and administrative staff. More wounded were delivered to the clinic as the engagement faded to
sporadic eruptions of small-arms fire.

Slowly, the streets of Bad Driburg fell silent. The surviving Wehrmacht and
Volkssturm members withdrew through the woods and farm lanes toward the
east as the sound of intermittent shots faded behind them. Scattered German
stragglers remained in the woods around the cluster of villages and isolated farmhouses in the area. Numerous small groups of Waffen SS remained along the
route of the American advance, and they busied themselves laying mines and felling trees behind the most forward elements of the Allied column. That evening,
the Volkssturm commander issued orders for his troops to withdraw to Höxter. All
communications between the outlying units and the command center in the city
had been severed, so homes and public buildings were without electrical power.
The residents began to breathe easier as the presence of the American armored
forces increased and the U.S. troops consolidated their positions in the village of
Bad Driburg. For the local people, it appeared that the war had finally come to an
end. The threat of a German counterattack, an event that would only inflict further damage on the village, was becoming more remote with each passing hour.

An American artillery battery was established near the Stellberg Cemetery,
and from there, the heavy guns fired over the village toward the east. The
American soldiers quickly occupied the offices of the Nationalsozialistiche
Deutsche Arbeiterpartei (NSDAP), the German Labor Front, and the post office.
The soldiers searched the abandoned home of the Ortsgruppenleiter, in which
they found a list of some sixty-two persons who had fallen out of favor with the
Nazi authorities and were to be arrested.

A cleric of the Driburg Mission House left the village en route to Brakel,
where he had been told his services were needed. En route, he encountered a
Wehrmacht combat unit commanded by a twenty-year-old lieutenant, marching
confidently toward Driburg. The cleric advised the officer that the town was occupied by American armored units, and the group of soldiers made an immediate
about-face and returned in the direction from which they had come. For Driburg,
the war was over, and the occupation was soon to begin.[5]

Beyond Bad Driburg, the citizens of Brakel had experienced bombing raids
through February, but March was remarkably quiet. On 1 April, the inhabitants

observed Easter Sunday with no disturbance from the Allies. Rumors abounded that the Americans were approaching from somewhere in the west, and telephone contact with towns and villages confirmed the reports that Allied spearheads had passed by the demolished city of Paderborn and had linked up in the town of Lippstadt to encircle the Ruhr.

The Wehrmacht forces in Brakel consisted of Convalescent Battalion 398 from the medieval Harz Mountain town of Goslar. The soldiers of the battalion, many of whom had not fully recovered from serious wounds, were responsible for manning the roadblocks on the western approaches to the village. The barrier consisted of 20-foot logs rammed upright into the earth on either side of the road, leaving a narrow pass that could be closed as enemy columns drew near. The barrier was equipped with a massive, barrel-shaped wooden drum that could be rolled into place and filled with gravel to block the passage through the primitive palisade. A number of such barricades had been erected along the approaches to the village; indeed, many of the trees lining the roadway had been sacrificed for that purpose.

In the first days following Easter, there was an influx of German troops traveling west to meet the oncoming American forces. Simultaneously, refugees from threatened or destroyed towns in the path of the Americans were arriving in the Eggegeberge. On Wednesday, 4 April, the first artillery rounds landed in Brakel. The Allies had established a firebase near Peckelsheim and were directing 155-mm artillery fire at selected targets from that location. One of the first rounds impacted directly onto the shop owned by businessman Heinrich Meyer-Eckemeyer. The windows shattered as the heavy shell penetrated the building, pierced the floor, and detonated in the cellar stairs, near the spot where the entire family had taken shelter. Others were in the cellar with the Meyer-Eckemeyer family. Anna Ruthe, Antonie Louise Kersting, and student Elisbeth Klahold had fled there from the adjacent playground. And several customers were in the shop when the first rounds fell on Brakel. As all of the store personnel and customers converged on the cellar, Heinrich Meyer, a veteran of the trenches of World War I, saw the danger in concentrating so many people in one room, so he ordered half of the refugees into an adjacent chamber. Hardly had the group separated when the large-caliber shell struck the building. Ten civilians in the cellar died from the impact, but all of the people led by Meyer into the neighboring room survived.

Another artillery round struck the dining room of the Tilly restaurant. Two young girls had been working in a back room when the first rounds fell, and they dashed toward one of their homes nearby. Just as they entered the back garden area, a projectile impacted nearby, killing both girls instantly.

The barrage lasted from 3:00 to 6:00 p.m., after which the shelling lifted and silence descended on the village. Throughout the night, the distant rumbling of shelling could be heard as the American gunners took other targets under fire, but Brakel remained free of further damage.

Most of the following day was quiet as well. However, at 3:00 p.m., a sudden, ripping burst from a machine gun echoed through the hills near the village. On the outskirts of the settlement, several soldiers of the convalescent battalion had unwisely opened fire on an approaching American armored column. Within seconds, the Americans replied with overwhelming force. A heavy-caliber tank projectile hit an ancient fortress tower in the town. This impact was immediately followed by an intense artillery barrage and withering machine-gun fire that swept the area between the armored column and the village. Machine guns raked the tree line, and tanks maneuvered into combat formation. Within minutes, a barn was set alight by tracer bullets, and the air filled with thick, black smoke produced by barrels of crude oil stored in the barn as the contents were consumed by flames. After several minutes of intensive fire, the tanks resumed their relentless movement toward Brakel. The rapid response by the Americans had caused numerous casualties, and corpses of dead and dying soldiers were scattered along the tree line.

Twilight was settling on the eastern slopes of the Eggegebirge as the forces moved relentlessly toward Brakel. The telephone operator in the village post office received a call from a nearby residence reporting the movement of countless American vehicles. The operator reacted immediately, informing the local officials that U.S. forces were moving through the nearby village of Istrup in force. By Friday morning, all German forces in Brakel had withdrawn eastward, and the small settlement was soon filled with jeeps, tanks, trucks, communications vans, ambulances, and half-tracks towing massive artillery pieces. Fourteen members of the convalescent battalion that was ordered to defend the village had been killed by the shelling and machine-gun fire. Their corpses lay scattered throughout the woods for several days before being collected by residents and buried in a common grave in the Brakel cemetery.

The retreating Germans attempted to stay clear of the main roads, and isolated bands moved eastward across fields and through wooded areas to avoid detection. In the area between the villages of Alten Hain and Grevenhagen, a farmer fertilizing his fields suddenly came upon a number of heavily armed, exhausted SS troops. They asked him for directions, and he provided them with information that would take them farther east while avoiding the main intersections and possible checkpoints. The group then departed, crossed the nearby rail line, and descended into a nearby village. They halted along the first row of houses there long enough for shoemaker Johannes Göke to repair the ragged boots of one of the soldiers before the men disappeared into the countryside.

On Wednesday, 4 April, the inhabitants of the tiny village of Pömbsen were extremely anxious about the fate of their homes and families. An enormous German tank had entered the village and come to a halt near several homes, where the crew had a view of the approaches from the west. Unable to persuade the crewmen to move to another position, the inhabitants of the nearby homes busied themselves in moving all valuables out of their dwellings to a safe location.

The village cleric was alerted to the new situation, and he approached the vehicle with cautious interest. Atop the turret was a young blond SS trooper engaged in preparing the tank for action. His curiosity satisfied, Pastor Sommer returned to his office and began packing his files and reference materials. If the tank crew refused to move, he reasoned, it would probably mean the destruction of the village. After packing the office material, Sommer began moving the religious artifacts to the sanctuary cellar.

That evening, gunfire echoed along the hills of the Eggegebirge as the Americans encountered splintered German units. As fighting swept toward the village, the inhabitants began seeking shelter in cellars or fled to the nearby woods, certain that their homes would be destroyed. A number of the families took refuge in the nearby Kirchgrund forestry house, located far enough from the village to be secure yet still within easy walking distance. Bursts of firing continued for several hours before silence descended. The night then passed without further incident.

Before dawn, several women in a home near the village outskirts heard cries and moans coming from their garden: they found a badly wounded German soldier, who had apparently been fleeing the Allied troops before collapsing near the residence. After sunrise, the bloody corpse of the blond SS tank crewman was found between the Rüschemeyer and Budde-Wellner homes. The body of a middle-aged German medic was also found in the vicinity. Pastor Sommer approached a building in which Americans had established a temporary command post and requested permission to gather the bodies for burial. Permission was granted, but the American officer advised the pastor to carry a white flag when recovering the bodies, as the area remained volatile and dangerous. Later that morning, inhabitants observed a small group of GIs kneeling on the street rolling dice. At their feet, the soldiers had piled large amounts of German currency.

The town of Nieheim barely escaped serious damage as the American columns drew near. The announcement by the Höxter party leaders that every town would be defended had had a sobering effect on the populace. Within Nieheim, one particular officer was determined to defend the town against the Allies. An SS colonel from Duisburg was confronted by a Wehrmacht colonel from Moers, who saw the senselessness in mounting a defense of the town. The SS colonel, backed by official Nazi Party directives, remained unmoved. Many of the young soldiers, most of whom had been bearing arms for only a few days, were confident in their ability to stop the Allies. The local women, providing the young soldiers with provisions, heard optimistic comments regarding the arrival of secret weapons and new divisions that would soon turn the tide of the war.

On Easter Sunday, the inhabitants of Nieheim were accorded a respite. The SS colonel who had insisted on defending the town ignominiously departed, together with district military headquarters staff, toward the illusion of safety behind the Weser River in the east. The Hitler Youth district office in Höxter issued a directive announcing the mobilization of all fourteen- and fifteen-year-old boys and required that they be ready to march within four hours. Under pressure from their families, the Hitler Youth members in Nieheim, as in many other of the small towns and villages in the district, ignored the instructions and remained at home.

On Tuesday, 3 April, a large warehouse filled with textiles, food, clothing, and various rationed articles was opened to the public. Previously administered by the "Dr. Goebbels Assistance" program for providing essentials to refugees from the bombed cities, the cache was made available to the citizens, who could take whatever they needed. The official orders to the military authorities required that the large depot and its contents be destroyed, but the instructions were not carried out. By the following day, American armored units had reached Merlsheim, only several miles distant. That evening, as the locals attempted to sleep fully clothed and prepared to flee at the first sign of danger, a Wehrmacht major ordered soldiers to man the barricades. At 2:00 in the morning, the troops inexplicably withdrew from their forward positions, leaving the barricades untended. A number of middle-aged men from Nieheim frantically dismantled the primitive obstacles.

Before dawn, a platoon of Wehrmacht soldiers entered Nieheim and established positions in barns and public buildings. It was rumored that the American armored columns were advancing along numerous main routes, and at 8:00 a.m., the first tanks appeared outside Nieheim. As heavy small-arms fire resounded through the area, the parishioners of the Catholic church interrupted their Mass to take refuge in their homes or behind the heavy walls of the church tower. The streets of Nieheim rapidly emptied as inhabitants sought shelter.

Within minutes, reports swept through the town that various buildings had been set ablaze by the tanks and the small-arms fire that was sweeping the town from its western outskirts. Fire department personnel trying to extinguish some of the larger fires scrambled for cover as they found themselves under a torrent of bullets fired from the American positions: from a distance, their dark blue uniforms closely resembled those of German military personnel. A medical aid station was hastily established in the cellar of the town hall and was manned by volunteer nurses. Bürgermeister Lücking and Department Inspector Hanses also sought shelter in the cellar. The first of the wounded to be brought for treatment was a soldier with a bullet wound through his arm. The sound of small-arms fire increased as the windows of the town hall and surrounding buildings began to shatter under machine-gun bursts and hand-grenade blasts.

Suddenly, an American soldier appeared in the stairwell of the makeshift aid station, his weapon pointed at the villagers. Seeing that all of the occupants were waving white handkerchiefs and bandages, he turned and pounded up the stairs as the sporadic bursts of gunfire grew to a deafening roar. One of the nurses tied a triangular bandage to a broomstick, cautiously ascended the stairs, and placed it through the shattered front window. The gunfire that had been directed at the building ceased immediately. Within several minutes, the American tanks had established positions at various strategic points in the town. Homes where the Americans had seen German soldiers fleeing continued to receive fire. The pastor's office was hit by a heavy-caliber machine-gun burst when two curious girls unwisely peered from a window, resulting in extensive damage to the structure.

By 10:00 a.m, the town hall was occupied by Americans. As the intensive firing waned, the entire building was searched for hidden German soldiers and weapons. The official town files were seized, and a German soldier with a serious bullet wound to his abdomen was evacuated by American medics. The residents began to take stock of their losses. Eight wounded and five dead German soldiers were found lying in the streets and within various buildings. Fifteen civilians, including seven foreign laborers, were also killed in the fighting. It was rumored that more than a dozen Americans had fallen in the engagement; the dead and wounded U.S. soldiers were rapidly transported from the scene.

As calm settled on the town of Nieheim, a number of the inhabitants made their way to the textile warehouse. A trickle of looters rapidly increased to a swarm as news of the wealth of material there, free for the taking, spread through the town. The storage facility soon filled with civilians of every age scrambling to seize articles, many of which they had not seen in abundance throughout the war. Containers were broken open, and clothing, rolls of textiles, bedclothes, stockings, suits, and foodstuffs were tossed about. Citizens began arriving with horses and hand-carts, and the streets filled with people carrying goods toward their homes. By that afternoon, the entire warehouse stood empty.

The five dead Wehrmacht soldiers were collected, and their corpses were searched for identification. The Americans permitted the villagers to bury the bodies but announced that only close friends and relatives could attend any memorial service for the fallen. Unbeknownst to the Americans, the soldiers were strangers to the local inhabitants, but nevertheless, a large segment of the population attended the burial. Under instructions from the senior American officer, no subsequent gathering of civilians was permitted without permission of the occupation forces.

The Americans began collecting isolated groups of German soldiers who had taken refuge in cellars and barns during the engagement. The prisoners were assembled in the square in front of the town hall, where they stood in ranks for several hours with their hands clasped on top of their heads. Their field equipment and the contents of their pockets and rucksacks were piled nearby. Sandwiches that had been provided to the soldiers only hours earlier by Nieheim residents lay scattered on the ground and were intermingled with spare clothing, personal effects, letters, and photographs. Also strewn through the area were mess tins, helmets, canteens, and the typical heavy leather Wehrmacht belts and field equipment.

The Americans continued their search for German soldiers. Informed that a farmer at the Emmerbrock home had been sheltering deserters, an American patrol dragged him from his home and forced him to dig his own grave while other soldiers searched the buildings on his property. Not finding any hidden soldiers, the Americans fired some shots in the air to emphasize their intent to punish anyone breaking the rules established by their commander and then released the terrified farmer.

The war continued its course through numerous villages of the Eggegeberge. Any resistance by German forces was met with overwhelming firepower, and the Americans often exhibited little sympathy for German soldiers who attempted to surrender following an engagement. On 6 April, the village of Tietelsen inexplicably came under heavy artillery fire as Americans approached the outskirts. The five-hour artillery barrage set barns, homes, and businesses alight, killing inhabitants and cattle. As the barrage finally lifted, the villagers were shocked to observe a heavily armed SS unit advancing between the timber-framed buildings. The soldiers also brought grim rumors that Tietelsen was to be defended to the last man: the village was already identified as one of the bridgeheads west of the Weser that had to be held. The SS unit abandoned a tank in front of the Saggel home, where it remained immobilized with a broken axle and served as an impromptu roadblock. The citizens breathed easier as the SS unit departed from the settlement and moved to the hills surrounding the western approaches to the village.

That evening, inhabitants detected the faint but unmistakable sounds of approaching American armored columns. Before dawn, small-arms fire resounded through the village as the American columns came in contact with the defenders in the nearby woods. Without warning, the abandoned tank at the Saggel home erupted with a massive explosion as the crew destroyed the disabled vehicle. The explosion totally demolished the residence and destroyed its contents, including the entire administrative records of the village. The vicious fighting continued for several hours, during which some areas of the village changed hands four times. At last, the gunfire faded as the German troops withdrew farther to the east.

The residents fearfully emerged from their cellars to observe the destruction that had occurred during the fighting. The village streets and alleys were littered with dead and wounded; American armored vehicles continued to burn and explode where they had been disabled at close range by SS troops armed with Panzerfausts. A surviving German tank took the village under fire from the nearby Elisenhöhe ridge line. Tragedy struck a small group of American soldiers who were clustered near a barn when a German shell impacted in their midst.

The resistance encountered by the Americans had resulted in numerous casualties among their ranks, and the GIs reacted bitterly. The angry infantrymen began systematically combing all buildings of the village in search of straggling German soldiers. A young SS trooper, expecting to bring his participation in the war to an end by deserting his unit, had taken refuge behind a damaged wall to wait for the Americans to pass beyond the village. When discovered by an American soldier, he emerged from his concealment pleading for mercy with upraised arms. He collapsed under the burst from a submachine gun. The bodies of thirteen German soldiers were later found by residents in the nearby woods; all had been killed by shots to the head. The villagers surmised that they had been taken prisoner during the fighting and had subsequently been marched en masse to the wooded area, where they were executed by enraged GIs.

Pastor Plümpe was traveling from Steinheim to Rolfzen when he came on a decimated company of some forty young soldiers resting by the roadside. Cold, dispirited, and exhausted and frightened by their previous encounter with the U.S. Army, they stared listlessly as the pastor approached. The tattered soldiers informed Plümpe that they had come from Detmold, where they had engaged American forces throughout the previous night. They remarked that they would rather die there by the roadside than be forced to defend another town. The pastor, able only to provide words of reassurance, left them by the road.

The small village of Amelunxen lies some 15 miles to the east of Brakel. Situated on the narrow Nethe River, the village rests in the Weser Valley, where the hills of the Eggegeberge become less foreboding and open along the narrow river valley to expanses of rolling, green pastureland. Amelunxen had been identified by German military officers as the site where a new bridgehead would be established; consequently, the village could not fall to the Allies.

The first indication to the inhabitants of Amelunxen of the decision to defend the village occurred on 2 April. A small Wehrmacht unit, reinforced with combat engineers, unexpectedly arrived and began constructing defenses. They dug trenches, erected roadblocks, and readied the rail lines and the river bridges for demolition. The situation grew more ominous on 5 April when some 130 Waffen SS troops arrived from the south. Rumors began circulating that Amelunxen was to be held as a bridgehead on the west bank and that every structure was to become a fortress.

That evening, the first shots were heard in the village as an American reconnaissance patrol, approaching from the village of Ottbergen, met resistance at the village's approaches. The enemy patrol withdrew, and many inhabitants spent a nervous night shivering in their unheated cellars, not knowing when the Americans would reappear. Others chose to flee the settlement and sought shelter in the surrounding woods and nearby farms. Friday, 6 April, would determine the fate of the village.

The SS unit established a command post in the home of shepherd Josef Struck. At 4:00 the next morning, his family was forced to leave the home to seek refuge elsewhere while the determined troops prepared their defenses. Josef Struck decided to return to the large barn where he had herded his flock of sheep. He had been told that the Americans, when advancing along their route toward Paderborn, had not fired on the numerous flocks they came across, so he assumed it would be best if his own sheep were left outside. Opening the large doors, he herded 200 sheep from the barn, leaving two dozen ewes that had recently dropped lambs in the shelter of the building.

A heavy artillery barrage descended on the village after Struck's departure. A number of projectiles impacted the field where his animals grazed, causing them to panic. Suddenly, the barrage ceased as quickly as it had begun. As the shelling fell silent, the only sound to be heard was the soft droning of a reconnaissance plane circling above the Weser Valley. The aircraft was trailing several colored flares, which had been released to halt the shelling after the aircraft crewmen recognized the presence of Struck's herd. Within minutes, artillery fire could again be heard along the Weser. The new barrage was directed on the west end of the village, and the damage to homes, barns, and shops increased with each impact. Fires began to spread, ignited by white-hot shell fragments that struck the highly flammable, centuries-old structures. It was impossible for the inhabitants to even attempt to extinguish the flames under the deadly barrage that continued unabated. Unheard and unseen by the villagers, American infantry units slowly worked their way, under the protection of numerous tanks, along the Nethe River toward the village.

Not all Amelunxen residents had sought refuge in surrounding forests or in their cellars. A small number of citizens had attended early Mass in the Catholic church. As they were leaving the church, the first machine-gun bursts broke out in the west end of the village. A gigantic explosion rocked the clusters of buildings as German forces detonated the explosives on one of the river bridges. American tanks, flanked by infantry, slowly began penetrating the perimeter of the village as the German forces withdrew under heavy fire.

One of the first buildings reached by the American soldiers was a farmstead inhabited by a number of refugees. At the height of the small-arms engagement, forty-three-year-old Minna Klaproth left the cellar of the home and raced to the upper floor. On the second floor, she tried to close an open window from which curtains were billowing. A short distance away, the family's barn was engulfed in flames, and the nearby Lingemann farm was burning. As Minna leaned from the window to close the shutters, a rifle bullet struck her, fatally penetrating her lung.

The barn housing Josef Struck's ewes fell victim to the vicious small-arms fire. An American rifle grenade penetrated the building, and the structure immediately began to burn fiercely. Within the barn were a number of German soldiers who were engaging the Americans in a vicious exchange of fire. More German soldiers were firing from the cover of a nearby stone wall and from the Klaproth and Lingemann farm buildings. The bodies of four German soldiers lay sprawled in the entrance of one structure, all having fallen to American marksmen.

After Minna Klaproth failed to return to the cellar, her husband left the safety of that shelter to search for her. Finding her bleeding profusely from the wound to her lung, he raced down the stairs and burst out through the door of the dwelling with his arms high in the air, frantically calling for help. He located an American medic after almost falling victim to the gunfire pouring from nearby buildings. At length, he was able to convince the soldier that his house did not contain any German troops and that his wife was in desperate need of medical assistance. Both men raced through ricochets and bouncing tracer rounds as they sprinted to the Klaproth home. Despite the efforts of the medic to save her, Minna Klaproth died on the floor. Her only son had fallen in Russia only months earlier.

At midmorning, another massive detonation ripped through the air as the rail line leading to Drenke was demolished in the face of oncoming infantry. Fortunately for the houses clustered nearby, only half of the prepared explosives detonated, sparing the buildings extensive damage but shattering windows throughout the area. The debris from the explosion blocked a nearby spillway, causing the current of a stream to overflow its banks. Seventy-three-year-old Karl Behler fled from his cellar as water from the stream began flowing into low areas around the homes. As he left his cellar, he was immediately struck by small-arms fire. The severe wounds proved to be fatal, though he would not die until 2 May 1945.

By 11:00 a.m., the Americans had succeeded in traversing the wreckage of a bridge and were searching homes covered by a tank that continued to fire into areas suspected of sheltering German soldiers. Burning homes collapsed on their foundations, and the crash of walls and timbers could be heard among the incessant pounding of gunfire as the fighting continued to rage within the small village. Eventually, a light drizzle began falling, slowing the spread of the flames and dampening the sounds of battle. By noon, two-thirds of the village was occupied by American forces, albeit after fanatical resistance from SS troops who were determined to hold their positions until nightfall. The German soldiers continued to defend the area containing the churches and the exits leading to Godelheim and Wehrden. The Catholic church was used as a makeshift hospital and was quickly filling with wounded soldiers and civilians.

At midday, the Mühlen-Nethe Bridge was demolished by the defenders. The explosion damaged nearby structures and destroyed the power transformer that provided electricity to the village. The fighting continued through the afternoon and raged from building to building and house to house as the Germans slowly gave ground to the American forces. At 5:00 p.m., the Germans began to withdraw to the southeast, toward the village of Wehrden, several hundred yards away. American tanks were positioned on a terrain feature at the eastern edge of the village, and they began firing indiscriminately in the direction where the defenders had last been observed.

The home of the Menke family was the last structure on the eastern exit of Amelunxen, and it had served as the final command post for the German troops before they withdrew from the village. A large number of residents sought shelter in the cellar of the Menke home, where they remained throughout the twelve hours of fighting for control of the village. At 5:00 p.m., American forces moved into the Menke residence in the wake of the withdrawing SS troops. The German soldiers had continued to fire from the structure at the oncoming Americans until they abandoned the position. As the Americans took control of the embattled home, a GI ran down the stairs, kicked open the cellar door, and fired a burst from a submachine gun into the room. Miraculously, none of the civilians cowering in the shadows was injured.

The American soldiers were not in a magnanimous mood after the vicious fighting that had occurred throughout the day. They discovered a young SS trooper who had tried to conceal himself among the civilians in the cellar and drove him up the stairwell with kicks and shouts. They pulled three local teenagers—Josef Kornfeld, Hubert Menke, and Vinzenz Schmidt—from the group of frightened civilians and ordered them to follow the SS prisoner. The three teens, with arms held high over their heads, stumbled at gunpoint behind the prisoner toward the center of the village. Just behind the SS soldier was Vinzenz Schmidt, followed by Hubert Menke; Josef Kornfeld trailed the column. As they marched in single file, flanked by a heavily armed infantryman, fifteen-year-old Kornfeld began to sob with fear, and he pleaded with Menke to let him walk ahead. The terrified prisoners had marched some 100 yards from the Menke home when, without warning, an American soldier fired his weapon point-blank into the SS trooper. The captive collapsed to the ground, mortally wounded. The three boys froze with terror until the Americans ordered them to continue walking. Ignoring the dying German soldier writhing on the ground, the group silently filed past the convulsing figure. Suddenly, Schmidt, fearing that they were all facing the same fate, sprang into a roadside ditch and, scrambling frantically over the rough ground, disappeared into the darkness. Cursing loudly, the American soldier fired again, and Kornfeld collapsed dead on the road. Schmidt eventually reached a narrow tunnel leading under the rail line, where he remained hidden for several hours.

Hubert Menke, remaining under the eyes of the American guards, was marched to a nearby home, where a temporary command post had been established. As he stood near the house under guard, more Americans approached. One of the soldiers pulled a knife from his belt and pressed it against Hubert's neck as he stripped the teenager of his watch and a fountain pen. The GI then punched him in the face and proceeded to pummel him with kicks as he lay on the ground. After an indeterminable length of time, he was pulled to his feet and pushed into the command post, where he was questioned amid kicks and punches from his captors. Eventually, he was shoved into a nearby room to join a flak soldier who had suffered a severe gunshot wound to the head. Hubert was ordered to carry the wounded soldier on his back and was marched to the home of a local construction contractor. In the cellar of the Schlüter home, he joined seven captive SS troops. The prisoners remained in the home for the remainder of the night.

Later that evening, Vinzenz Schmit dared to venture from his concealment in the railway tunnel. Shivering from cold and terrified of being seen by the American troops, he carefully picked his way through the village cemetery and safely reached the Menke home. After determining that soldiers were no longer occupying the house, he entered the residence to find several families cowering in the building. Among the civilians were the mother and father of Josef Kornfeld. He told the distraught parents what had occurred. The next morning, Josef's body was found where he had fallen after being shot.

Hubert Menke spent the rest of Friday night lying on the floor of the building with the seven SS prisoners. At midmorning the next day, the captives were ordered out of the home and assembled in front of the building to await their fate. The local building contractor, Schlüter, recognized Hubert Menke among the prisoners. Hurriedly seeking a translator among the milling Americans, he advised the guards that Hubert was a local teenager who had never served in the military; the boy was not a soldier. At length, Hubert was released to return to his home as the other prisoners were marched away.

On Saturday, the populace began picking up the debris from the fighting of the previous day and evening. The corpses of fifteen German soldiers were collected from various locations where they had fallen. The inhabitants counted the bodies of thirteen American soldiers that were being transported by their countrymen to a distant location. The occupiers refused to permit the bodies of the German soldiers to be buried in the Amelunxen cemetery, but they were loaded onto heavy U.S. Army trucks and taken to an undisclosed location. Several days later, the corpses of four more German soldiers were discovered in a nearby field. After collecting identity documents and personal effects, several men loaded them onto hand-carts, with which they were transported to the Amelunxen Evangelical cemetery for burial.[6]

Farther to the southwest, where the Eggegeberge and the southern end of the Teutoburg Forest merge and create deep ravines and ragged ridge lines, Heinz Spenner found himself again looking for shelter. The twenty-one-year-old paratrooper grimaced with pain as he lay along the railway embankment after jumping from the troop train transporting his regiment toward an inevitable battle with the Allies. The train had been retreating slowly along the tracks after the news had reached the engineer that American forces were in Altenbeken, some 5 miles ahead. The jump onto the steep embankment had caused the wound in Spenner's lower leg, a souvenir of the fierce fighting in Normandy, to reopen. The paratrooper lay quietly without moving, hesitant to raise his head in case he had been observed springing from the flatbed railcar. His jump did not provoke any response, and the train continued rolling slowly southward. After several minutes, the train cleared his location, and the surroundings grew silent. He listened as the sound of the heavy rail wheels grew faint and at long last disappeared in the morning fog.

Pulling himself to his feet, he attempted to ignore the pain emanating from the bleeding wound in his leg as he adjusted his ammunition and equipment belt, slung his assault rifle, and cautiously observed his surroundings. He knew that it could not be far to his aunt's residence in the village of Willebadessen; the train had been traveling at a slow pace after passing the isolated settlement, and he was convinced that he would find food and refuge with the relative with whom he had spent vacations as a child. He would have to avoid the rail line: a rail network converged at Altenbeken, only a few miles away, and would likely be subject to regular security patrols. Traveling along main roads was liable to bring an unwelcome encounter with military units. Above all else, he feared falling into the hands of the Americans or the SS, either of which would mean imprisonment or execution. After several minutes of listening intently for any sounds of military activity, he was comforted by the silence around him and then plunged into the forest.

After several hours, Spenner came to the familiar residence of his relative in Willebadessen. In response to his knock on the door, the weary paratrooper was greeted by the familiar visage of his aunt. The woman stared at him cautiously from behind the slightly opened door before expressing horror and surprise at Spenner's appearance. Then she hastily and unmistakably informed him that he was not welcome at her home. Glancing fearfully about as she opened the door to admit him into the foyer, she explained that the road alongside the home led to Hardehausen, a nearby village in which an ammunition depot was located. The road was regularly traveled by the Waffen SS, and she was terrified that his presence in her home would become known to them. Feverishly stuffing some food into a rucksack, she led him to the door as she explained that the risk was simply too great; a military patrol or an SS resupply convoy could happen along at any moment. After coaxing her nephew out, she closed the door behind him and watched cautiously from behind white-laced curtains as he limped into the nearby hills.[7]

With his leg continuing to bleed from the wound received in Normandy, Spenner hobbled along the rough terrain toward the south. The experienced paratrooper knew that either the SS or the Americans would be guarding road crossings, so he made his way through thickets and copses of dense forest until he found a suitable place to rest. Rolling himself in his shelter-quarter, the soldier ignored his throbbing wound and eventually fell asleep.

The following morning, he arose stiffly and continued south toward the settlement of Sherfede; he had other relatives in the area who might exhibit more courage than the fearful aunt in Willebadessen. Having spent summer vacations in the area, he soon recognized the paths and roads where, under far happier circumstances, he had once ridden his bicycle through fields and forests. As he neared the heights close to Sherfede, Spenner froze momentarily and listened intently. The sound of engines wafted softly through the ravines and trees, growing more distinct with each passing minute. With a pounding heart, he realized that he could not continue on his present course. The sounds emanating from the valley below were not the familiar throbbing of Henschel panzer engines but the ominous growling of Detroit motors. Some ten months earlier, he had heard those engines on almost a daily basis as the Allies battled their way yard by yard through the Normandy hedgerows. It had been an American-manufactured tank that had almost cost him his leg, inflicting the wound that continued to plague him. Easing his way slowly along a tree line, he advanced cautiously until he could observe the northern approaches to Sherfede. There, on the road where he had ridden his bicycle as a child, he saw a column of Sherman tanks interspersed with jeeps, trucks, and long files of infantrymen. Soldiers in khaki and brown were entering and exiting several buildings, and it was obvious that the Americans were in Sherfede to stay; to attempt to seek shelter with any remaining relatives in or near the town was out of the question. After watching the enemy column for several minutes, Spenner turned and made his way north. The Americans would probably be moving east, toward the Weser River, and to head north was the best way to avoid capture.

Spenner limped through the forests of the Eggegeberge until nightfall, leaving Sherfede and the American tanks far behind. Throughout the day and evening, the sounds of distant artillery, punctuated by momentary flashes illuminating the far-off hills, indicated the direction of the American advance. Again wrapping himself in his shelter-quarter and consuming what was left of his food, he slept for several hours. On awakening, he realized that the artillery had fallen silent. Knowing that it would soon be dawn, he proceeded along the tree line toward the north. As the horizon grew lighter in the east, the paratrooper knew that he would have to find concealment—and hopefully a source of food—before full daylight arrived. As he edged along a pasture clearing, he was brought sharply to a halt by a loud command. With a mixture of relief and trepidation, Spenner obeyed the instructions, shouted in German, to raise his hands and advance into the open. As he cleared the shadows, several camouflaged figures stood and ordered him forward. Spenner immediately recognized the mottled-camouflage smocks and helmet covers of the Waffen SS.

The paratrooper responded obediently but cautiously to their commands and called out to them not to shoot. His actions provoked a torrent of curses. "What in the hell are you doing here?" one of the troopers exclaimed. "I almost killed you … I thought you were an Ami." The mistake was understandable. Wearing his Luftwaffe paratrooper battle smock and the short-rimmed, rounded jump helmet while carrying a Fallschirmjäger assault rifle, all of which were only vaguely familiar to the SS in the dim light, he could easily have been mistaken for an American soldier.

Spenner feigned gratitude in coming on the sentries, and while trying to conceal his nervousness, he explained that he had been attempting to avoid capture by the Americans. Ignoring more soldiers concealed beneath the undergrowth, one of the sentries ordered the paratrooper to accompany him to a command post. Spenner was relieved that they had not disarmed him—an indication that they believed he was, in fact, attempting to locate a German military unit.

The soldier escorted Spenner along a wooded trail to a command post several hundred yards distant. They entered a wooden building, where the paratrooper was presented to a highly decorated SS officer sitting behind a desk. The officer appeared weary and was visibly annoyed. After explaining that the sentries had observed Spenner emerging alone from a tree line, the guard was dismissed by the officer, who then demanded an explanation from the paratrooper. Spenner explained that he had been trying to locate a German unit and that he had been hospitalized in Erwitte; on hearing that Americans were approaching the town, he said, he had gathered up his equipment and fled to avoid becoming a prisoner of war. The officer demanded to know why he was in the hospital; Spenner replied that the wound received in Normandy was proving to be resistant to heal. The officer leaned forward and observed the blood-stained trouser leg. He then demanded that Spenner detail the route he had taken since leaving Erwitte. Having been raised in the Paderborn-Erwitte area, it was not difficult for the paratrooper to describe a route by which he might have escaped the closing pocket and thus found himself in the Eggegeberge and Teutoburg Forest outside the pocket. The officer asked about the sighting of American forces, and Spenner explained that the Americans were in Sherfede and added that he had turned farther north to avoid capture.

Exhibiting surprise that the Americans were already in Sherfede, the officer indicated he would send Spenner with a reconnaissance patrol toward Sherfede to confirm the presence of enemy troops to the south. Spenner then explained that he could no longer travel on foot; his wound was continuing to bleed, and further activity would only exacerbate the condition.

The officer motioned for the paratrooper to sit in a chair, and he called for one of the soldiers in an external office. He ordered the trooper to organize and conduct the reconnaissance patrol. Relieved that the officer was inclined to believe him, Spenner leaned against the wall and promptly fell asleep.

The paratrooper awoke several hours later as word arrived that the patrol had confirmed Spenner's information: American armored units were indeed south of their position. The officer ordered one of the soldiers to escort Spenner to a medical clinic to receive care for the wound.

As he and the soldier walked toward an impromptu aid station, Spenner observed some half dozen corpses, clad in brown Reich Labor Service uniforms, strewn haphazardly near a building. From their appearance, the bodies were fresh, and the victims appeared to be very young. The workers had obviously been shot during the hours prior to Spenner's arrival, and the shocked paratrooper could only assume that they had deserted from their unit to avoid being mobilized for combat.

He was taken to an SS staff surgeon, who began cleansing and binding the wound. After dressing the leg, the doctor advised him to wait nearby for transportation to a field hospital. As the doctor was assisting his patient toward the door, he asked the paratrooper in a hushed voice if he was aware of how the Americans received SS prisoners. Spenner furtively glanced about to confirm that the two of them were alone. "I would not want to be in your situation," he replied, "if the Americans show up here and find those bodies out there."[8]

Close on the heels of Heinz Spenner were the forward elements of the U.S. First Army. Pushing southeast out of Paderborn, the armored columns drove through the Teutoburg Forest toward of the medieval town of Warburg. The inhabitants of the town had watched the ominous signs of war grow more obvious over the previous weeks as the American forces drew nearer. Waves of bombers passed overhead en route to larger, more lucrative targets in the area of Kassel, and a number of isolated raids were launched on the town. The railway junction was attacked numerous times, and the station bore ever-increasing scars from the fighter-bombers that screamed over rooftops to machine-gun the freight trains below. On calm, quiet days, the Warburg residents could hear distant attacks on the Scherfede rail junction, and any movement along the Nörde-Eissen-Borgholz rail line was open to unexpected assault. During one attack, a fully loaded train near the Warburg station was set ablaze by fighter-bombers; the sheets of flames rose from camouflaged railcars and illuminated the surrounding buildings for hours as tons of war material exploded and burned.

Warburg was intended to be a central point for a defensive line forward of the Diemel River. Numerous tank barriers were erected on the Ossendorfer Strasse, on the Germete road, on the Mennerstrasse, and along the Kasselerstrasse near the Kamm laundry facility. Woodcutters were dispatched into the Asseler woods to obtain massive tree trunks for the construction of the barriers. As the men and boys from the Volkssturm assisted prisoners of war and foreign laborers in erecting defenses, rumors flourished that the Americans had already bypassed Marburg and were advancing on the nearby villages of Korbach and Arolsen. Observers positioned in the belfry of the Neustädter church reported artillery fire hitting the Rhoden-Wrexen road.

A Wehrmacht cavalry captain was assigned to serve as combat commander for the town, and the officer established his headquarters in the cellar of the Rosenmeyer building along the south wall encompassing the medieval structures. On Friday, 30 March, the commander held a situation briefing in his headquarters, where he issued orders to Volkssturm units defending the town. The outlying areas were occupied by Wehrmacht and Waffen SS troops; the Volkssturm was assigned to establish defenses between the outlying villages and the township. The soldiers were expected to defend their positions to the last man; whoever failed to do so would be shot. The company commanders would be held responsible for ensuring that their forces carried out this order.

Intermittent reports of rapidly closing American units continued to arrive throughout Friday, 30 March. It was also reported that white flags were displayed in some areas. The Volkssturm was detailed to construct defenses on the northwest edge of the city, as American units were now presumed to be coming from the village of Ossendorf. The next day, the locals took shelter in their cellars or fled to outlying areas to the south, away from where the oncoming Americans were expected; the Volkssturm worked hurriedly on barricades that were yet to be completed. As reports arrived that the Americans were entering nearby villages, the local Nazi Party officials piled into a waiting car and disappeared.

The Americans did not enter Warburg from the west or the southwest, as had been expected. The first American tank appeared in the front yard of the Sauser family, the home of a horse trader on the southeastern outskirts of the town. Frau Sauser immediately draped a white flag from the upper floor of the house. More tanks approached and rolled onward, capturing the Diemel bridge on the Kasselerstrasse without incident.

The arrival of the enemy column took the inhabitants completely by surprise. The forward element, consisting of a reconnaissance vehicle followed by several tanks, drove unopposed through a still-open barrier. Onlookers stared in shock and amazement as the olive-colored vehicles lumbered through the narrow, cobblestone roads toward their objectives. Some inhabitants took cover in roadside ditches, fearing that shooting would erupt at any moment. Elderly Volkssturm soldiers unbuckled their field gear and raised their arms in surrender. The advanced elements continued over the Diemel bridge along the Kasselerstrasse, closely followed by convoys of support vehicles. Stunned villagers watched as columns of communications vans, bridge-building units, massive trucks, and bulldozers snaked through the tight confines of the streets. The primitive barriers, constructed so laboriously by squads of Volkssturm members, laborers, and POWs, were simply pushed aside by the bulldozers that rolled from flatbed trucks. Infantrymen worked their way forward on either side of the road as the columns penetrated deeper into the town.

Taken completely by surprise, the battle commander, who had positioned his forces on the western edge of the town, attempted to bring his troops to bear on the east. A rapid-response unit was dispatched from the command post to patrol through the Sternstrasse and make their way to the Neustädter market. At the market, they were to establish contact with defenders in the western sector of town, and from there, they were to conduct a counterattack.

Frightened residents observed a small group of German soldiers carrying Panzerfausts slinking along the Sternstrasse toward an American tank that had halted near the Café Eulenspiegel. Before they could get within range of the tank, they were spotted by the GIs, who immediately opened fire. The group scattered, leaving only shattering windows and flying debris in their wake. Other defenders were observed by an American tank as they made their way up the

Hauptstrasse. The soldiers attempted to engage the tank with Panzerfausts but were fired on through the corner window of the Fischer grocery store.

The fighting continued on and off for several hours as Germans and American GIs sought one another through the maze of buildings. A large number of civilians had taken shelter in the crypt beneath the Burg chapel, where they cowered as the sounds of machine guns and rifle fire resounded from the Brüder churchyard. The Fischer and Hartmann homes went up in flames, as did the Schmidt hair salon. The city fire department equipment was nearby, but it was out of reach of the inhabitants, who remained confined to their cellars as the fighting continued. Eventually, one resident sought out some American soldiers, who assisted the civilians in retrieving the fire pump. Throughout the fighting, the GIs were searching the buildings in the medieval sector of the town.

As the engagement intensified, a Wehrmacht colonel who had been wounded earlier and was being treated in one of the local clinics ordered a German medic to exhibit a large Red Cross flag and to proceed to the city hall, where the deputy Bürgermeister, Phillipp Schlüter, was located. Holding the large red-and-white banner high overhead, the medic was permitted to pass through the combatants without incident. He soon found the mayor and informed him that Colonel Dropmann requested that he contact the Americans to surrender the town.

However, Schlüter did not relish the idea of approaching enemies who had just suffered numerous casualties and would obviously not be in a benevolent mood. To exacerbate the problem, neither he nor the medic could speak English. The medic reminded Schlüter that he was not a party member and was thus well suited for the mission. The soldier also advised Schlüter that the Americans would have an interpreter. Additionally, while combing the buildings, the Americans had already let it be known that should the fighting continue, they would launch an air raid no later than 3:00 p.m. This information was enough to force Schlüter, who had seen Paderborn following the massive raid of 27 March, to gather his courage and approach the foreign conquerors. After all, Warburg was a smaller town and might be completely obliterated by such an attack.

The two emissaries made their way through the battle-scarred streets holding the Red Cross banner aloft. They made first contact with the Americans near the Schönen Aussicht inn, where Schlüter's purpose was relayed through an interpreter to an American officer. As expected, the officer asked the civil administrator if he was a member of the Nazi Party, to which Schlüter replied that he had never joined the Nazi ranks. The officer then asked if he was prepared to guarantee that no further fighting would occur. Schlüter guaranteed that the Germans were prepared to cease firing. The two emissaries were ordered onto a half-track, which rumbled through the cobblestoned streets to the town hall;

there, the American guards searched the empty rooms of the building. They then left the building and drove through streets already bedecked with white flags to the Warburg district administration building, where Schlüter was soon released.

The American dead were gathered from the streets and buildings and taken to the district farm agency building, from where they were transported that evening. The German dead were collected for burial in the Breuna cemetery. Numerous homes and buildings had suffered damage from small-arms and grenades. The town hall had been all but razed, with doors kicked open, windows shattered, and walls riddled with bullet holes. Podiums, desks, and cabinets had been broken into, the contents scattered throughout the offices. The city treasury offices had been looted. Especially desired by the American troops were postage stamps bearing the image of Hitler, and the temporary mayor was compelled to escort numerous soldiers to the post office, where they obtained sheets of the colorful stamps. A growing pile of civilian and military weapons appeared in the center of the town hall as firearms were surrendered by inhabitants at the direction of the occupation authorities.

Soon, the sounds of heavy trucks resumed as convoys rolled through the ancient town. Large, olive-colored vehicles bearing the white star of the Allied forces careened along the streets, packed with prisoners of war en route to a large, open enclosure near Welda. The local citizens attempted to pass food to the hapless captives, and neighborhood children were assigned as look-outs to report the approach of trucks carrying prisoners. The local bakeries prepared hundreds of fist-sized loaves that could be thrown onto the back of the trucks to the disheveled Wehrmacht soldiers.

The American troops did not remain in Warburg in strength but pushed onward toward their next objectives. In the village of Welda, the inhabitants hung white flags from all buildings until a party official named Lamoller appeared. Halting on the outskirts of the village in front of the Müller home, which openly displayed a white flag, Lamoller and his driver ordered a girl to identify the owner of the house. As Müller appeared, the party official pulled his pistol and shot him at point-blank range, killing him instantly. The two Nazis then drove through the town firing wildly at any buildings that exhibited signs of surrender.

Near the village of Wormeln, a German machine gun opened fire on an American ambulance. The incident immediately resulted in the appearance of several American tanks that established positions near the Twiste bridge and fired into the village with machine guns and cannons. The armored vehicles then moved on, quickly neutralizing weak German defenses and occupying the village. In the settlement of Ossendorf, the German defenders retreated toward Menne-Hohenwepel with the first appearance of American armored units. Scherfede was occupied after a brief but intense defense by SS troops. The Americans advised the defenders through loudspeakers that the town would be leveled if resistance did not cease within two hours. The fighting continued between the SS troops and the Americans as the inhabitants fled their homes to the safety of the surrounding forest. At length, the SS troops withdrew in the direction of Paderborn. A local citizen then climbed the church belfry and hung a white flag. In Ikenhausen, a battle between American Shermans and German Panthers resulted in the deaths of some thirty-six German and twenty-six American soldiers. German stragglers continued to appear from concealment to surrender or were captured by carefully positioned mechanized units who were responsible for blocking any escape routes. By the evening of Easter Sunday, 1 April, the fighting in the Warburg district was all but over.[9]

Chapter 11

Reducing the Pocket

Despite Walter Model's repeated attempts to gain permission to withdraw troops from the positions on the Rhine, Hitler ordered them to remain in place to protect the Ruhr industries. A subsequent plan to attack the American forces from within the pocket with the entire army group was weighed by the field marshal and his staff. An optimal location of the breakthrough was considered to be at the point where enemy forces were weakest or where the German forces outside the pocket were close enough in sufficient force to enable a linkup. An analysis of the troop strengths and locations revealed that both criteria did not exist in one single location. The American advance toward the east and the positions of the German forces made it impossible to carry out both options simultaneously; one or the other would have to be chosen.

The American ability to repel a breakout attempt was deemed to be weakest in the south, through the U.S. First Army. However, this option offered little opportunity to link up with Wehrmacht forces outside the pocket once the American lines were penetrated. A breakout to the west would mean confronting the strongest enemy units, and the distance to German forces made this option even more questionable. The German officers considered whether a simultaneous breakout by various units in different directions would be feasible. It was decided that this option would incur heavy and irrecoverable losses and would be tantamount to disbanding the army group.

A capitulation of the army group was discussed between Model and Major-General Carl Wagener, the Army Group B chief of staff. Both officers agreed to continue resisting. The time was not right for a capitulation: the army group still had the ability to fight, and relief from outside the pocket was pledged by Hitler. However, the emphasis on protecting the vast industrial area was little more than an illusion. The Ruhr was surrounded and cut off from the rest of the Reich, just as the army group was, and it was no longer of any use to the beleaguered Wehrmacht. By continuing to resist, Model's isolated army group was forcing a large number of enemy forces to remain committed in northwest Germany. OB West, Field Marshal Albert Kesselring, relayed Hitler's order to Model that all

breakout attempts were to be delayed; further, the Ruhr area was now to be designated the *Ruhrfestung* ("Ruhr Fortress") and was thus to be defended.

The Ruhrfestung encompassed an area approximately 80 miles in diameter,
with the western boundary on the Rhine. It included the heavily populated Ruhr
industrial area; the hilly, heavily forested regions of the Sauerland on the southern border of the pocket; and the open, expansive Münsterland along the northern perimeter, bordered by the Teutoburg Forest in the east. Much of the region
was well suited for defense, with rolling hills and thick, wooded areas intermittently cut by rivers and streams. Because of the geographic conditions, the Army
Group B staff concluded that the main threat to the German units in the pocket
would probably come from the east, where heavy concentrations of Allied forces
were preparing to press further toward Berlin.

One of the most important issues at hand was the immediate assessment of
food and supplies available in the pocket, for no assistance could be expected
from without. With the exception of a few aircraft carrying vital industrial supplies, no air resupply was possible. It was determined that there was enough food
for troops and civilians for three to four weeks, assuming that what was immediately available in storage depots was secured and rationed.

The army group was limited to two sources for obtaining ammunition. A
minimal amount could be produced inside the pocket within a number of days;
other munitions would have to be flown into the pocket at night. It was estimated
that, with no large-scale engagement developing, enough ammunition could be
provided to last two to three weeks. In the industrial regions, there were large
quantities of aviation fuel and crude oil that, if correctly mixed, could be used
in some gasoline and diesel engines. The army group found the industrialists in
the area eager to ignore or circumvent Hitler's scorched-earth edict, and many
of the installations and bridges not already destroyed by Allied aircraft could be
spared.[1]

For most of the Army Group B staff, consisting of highly trained, experienced
officers who were well aware of the shortfalls facing their troops, the situation
seemed hopeless. The forward elements of the British Second Army were pushing north of Münster toward Rheine and Osnabrück. The XII Corps of the U.S.
Ninth Army was nearing Bielefeld. Münster was encircled by units of the U.S.
17th Airborne Division advancing from the south. The U.S. 84th Infantry Division
was preparing to move toward the east after crossing the Rhine. The U.S. 30th
Infantry Division was preparing to push forward from Hamm and Drensteinfurt.
North of Lippstadt, the U.S. 83rd Infantry Division was securing the pocket
while other units were continuing to move toward the east. The forward elements of the U.S. 2nd Armored Division were at the approaches to Örlinghausen
in the Teutoburg Forest. Forward units of the U.S. 8th Armored Division were

pushing toward Paderborn and Senne. Other divisions of the XVI Corps of the Ninth Army were crossing the Rhine.

After closing the pocket at Lippstadt, the First Army's VII and V Corps were holding a line from Geseke over Paderborn and Warburg to Kassel. Before Kassel and Fulda stood the foremost units of General George Patton's Third Army. Units of the U.S. XVIII Airborne Corps were concentrating on the southern perimeter of the pocket. Numerous divisions assigned to the U.S. III Corps were still pouring over the Rhine at Remagen.

The elation felt by the Americans on closing the pocket in Lippstadt was short-lived; they soon had to resume the deadly business of winning a war. Staff officers from the U.S. First and Ninth Armies met in Lippstadt on 2 April to plan the destruction of the Wehrmacht forces trapped in the Ruhr Pocket. The encircled area represented an enormous, horizontal, egg-shaped region. The large end of the oval was formed by the Rhine in the west; the tip of the small end was at Paderborn, near where the First and Ninth Armies had linked to trap the German army group.

The decision was made to split the pocket from the small town of Nuttlar, in the southeast near Brilon, by driving through the eastern Ruhr area to the industrial city of Duisburg, where the Ruhr River met the Rhine. The operational area north of the Ruhr River was assigned to the Ninth Army. It was geographically smaller than the area assigned to the First Army in the south, but the northern sector was more densely populated and was strewn with numerous industrial towns and factories, each of which would have to be cleared of any remaining enemy forces. It was expected that the Ninth Army's advance through the industrial heartland of Essen, Dortmund, and Duisburg would involve heavy house-to-house fighting. Additionally, the cities had been largely destroyed by months of intense bombing; thousands of the inhabitants had fled the industrial areas and were scattered throughout the Ruhr area. The ruined cities also exacerbated Allied concerns regarding the remnants of the German forces trapped in the pocket, as the ruins of the abandoned cities provided excellent terrain for a stubborn defense.

Simultaneous with the First Army's attack from Brilon at the southeastern sector of the pocket, an attack was to be conducted from the northeast corner of the Ruhr Pocket near Paderborn. This plan called for the U.S. 8th Armored Division, assigned to the Ninth Army, to push forward to Paderborn and to concentrate north of that city.

After the meeting of the First and Ninth Armies in Lippstadt, the Americans in the town consolidated and strengthened their positions. It was rumored that SS units in the small town of Erwitte, some 3 miles to the south, were preparing to counterattack. The Americans strengthened their positions at crossroads and strategic buildings. An American artillery unit in the southern part of the city established battery positions with the guns pointing menacingly southward.

Foreign workers, exuberant in their first hours of freedom, feverishly began to plunder Lippstadt without interference from the American troops. The German soldiers who did not go into captivity when the Americans moved into Lippstadt withdrew over Westernkotten toward Erwitte.

On Monday, 2 April, following the capture of Lippstadt, German soldiers arrived at the town of Weckinghausen and prepared defenses. Foxholes were dug, and a 37-mm antiaircraft battery was established nearby. At midday, the village received its first incoming artillery shell, fired from distant American positions. The shelling continued intermittently until evening. At sunset on 3 April, the first American soldiers appeared from the direction of Lippstadt, and they occupied the Büker and Könighaus estates on the northeast edge of Weckinghausen after herding all inhabitants into a cellar. The remaining sections of the settlement remained in German hands.

The inhabitants in Esbeck observed dejected Volkssturm units passing through the village on Easter Sunday. As the last of the forlorn conscripts disappeared, the villagers began exhibiting white flags in preparation for the arrival of the Americans. They were alarmed at the sudden appearance of an SS unit in the process of withdrawing to a new defense line. In reprisal for the display of surrender, a seventy-year-old villager was shot by an SS soldier before the unit continued its retreat.

In Rixbeck on Sunday, 1 April, the village was crowded with columns of civilians fleeing from the direction of Lippstadt. A group of German soldiers who had taken quarters in the local schoolhouse suddenly departed, and villagers began burying valuables in preparation for the arrival of the enemy. By midday, silence had descended on the settlement, and rumors soon flourished that the Americans had left Lippstadt and were advancing directly toward Rixbeck. That afternoon, the first olive-colored reconnaissance vehicle, conspicuously displaying a large, white star on its armored chassis, rolled into town.[2]

The village of Benninghausen did not experience the end of the war peacefully. On 1 April, American troops arrived at the northern bank of the Lippe and established artillery batteries near Göttingen. A Wehrmacht captain with twelve men was determined to hold the village, and his first measure was to demolish the nearby bridge spanning the Lippe. As a result of the massive explosion, the Becker Gasthaus and the Marx home were badly damaged. Within minutes, the far-off American battery launched phosphorus shells into the village, setting the local church ablaze. The Mueser farmhouse soon stood in flames, and the Osthof barn followed. Advancing American units came under fire from the determined defenders, causing the forward elements to halt before the besieged village.

As the Germans continued to resist, the Americans announced that the village was to be obliterated if resistance continued into Monday night. A number of inhabitants took advantage of a lull in the engagement to flee to neighboring Eickelborn, where they felt secure in the vicinity of a hospital. In Benninghausen, a group of foreign workers fled from building to building in attempts to find shelter from the shelling. Their guards had fled, and the confused laborers were abandoned and leaderless. The threatened bombing raid on Benninghausen never occurred, and at length, the German forces withdrew. With the departure of the Wehrmacht troops, several residents timidly approached the Americans and advised them that the defenders had retreated. Minutes later, the narrow streets were choked with massive vehicles and swarms of English-speaking soldiers.

The traditional Easter Mass in the village of Wadersloh was interrupted by the sound of approaching tanks in the distance. The inhabitants hastened to their homes to hang white flags as the last Wehrmacht stragglers withdrew toward Langenberg. The first American jeeps navigated the narrow streets of the village at approximately 7:00 a.m., quickly followed by numerous tanks and troop transports. The village was occupied without resistance, and after a short respite, the tanks rolled on toward Langenberg-Wiedenbrück, which also ended the war peacefully. The conquerors established an artillery battery in Wiedenbrück, and the Americans organized a command post in the village administration building. Their presence was followed by immense columns of men and material that rolled through the village for two days. The arrival of the Americans was marked by the characteristic search for alcohol and Nazi souvenirs, all of which were eagerly surrendered by the inhabitants without incident.[3]

The Americans continued to dispatch patrols and occupy villages along the Lippe River as they concentrated on severing any escape routes for the Germans. One of the first villages under Allied control after the closure of the pocket was Lipperode. The settlement had suffered limited damage during the earlier bombing of the nearby airfield. As the American units approached, a band of German soldiers established positions in the town, supported by the threatening presence of a tank. The villagers remained awake throughout Saturday night anticipating the arrival of the enemy and praying that their village would be spared destruction. Early on Easter Sunday, detonations were heard in the distance, and the villagers fled to their cellars. Other detonations occurred throughout the morning as bridges were demolished by the retreating Wehrmacht. A number of young Labor Service workers entered the village with small arms and threatened the villagers who implored them to move on. An elderly man was heard chastising them. "If you want to inflict more misery on everyone, go ahead, shoot," the aged veteran remarked. "But think about your own parents ... my sons are also soldiers."[4]

Undeterred by the reproach, the new arrivals assailed the local Volkssturm members with threats when they attempted to resist bearing arms. At length, one of the inhabitants arrived with the news that Americans were already in the town. The messenger added that he had even spoken to some of the foreign soldiers on the Delbrücker Weg. His report was confirmed by the sound of a small-arms engagement that drifted across the slate-tiled rooftops, and the villagers again sought the security of their cellars. A German tank hidden near one of the farmhouses on the fringes of the village suddenly opened fire. A German officer appeared in a vehicle before a group of curious inhabitants who had ventured out. He demanded that the white flags be removed from sight. The citizens implored him not to defend the village, and the officer simply glared at them for several seconds before careening away. An observation plane circled lazily over the village, and a voice from a concealed loudspeaker ordered civilians to seek the safety of their cellars.

An elderly inhabitant approached the American positions with the intent of surrendering the town. However, since he was not an official representative, his pleas for a cease-fire were ignored. Artillery shells began falling again, and the disheartened civilians who had emerged from their cellars scrambled to seek shelter from the explosions while cursing Hitler and praying to God.

The barrage damaged the steeple of the evangelical church, and the school received a number of impacts that destroyed all windows in the structure. Several houses on the Friedhofstrasse and the Tack Gasthof were damaged. Soon, the first tanks arrived, rolling cautiously through the streets, halting at crossroads, and listening and scanning the surroundings before proceeding. Files of heavily armed infantry crouched in the shadows and prowled along the sides of buildings, flanking the tanks as the turrets turned and halted momentarily on suspicious structures that might shelter German soldiers.

At length, the inhabitants breathed with relief. The soldiers following in the wake of the advance elements searched homes for uniformed personnel and weapons. Intermittent shots floated through the still air as Americans fired at isolated groups of German soldiers who were withdrawing from the village. Within several hours, an ominous silence descended on the rows of red-brick structures, pierced only by the rumble of Detroit engines. By 5:30 p.m., the village was firmly in American hands following the destruction of a lone German tank on the Landstrasse. A large number of ecstatic Russian, Polish, and French prisoners were freed from their bondage, but the Americans kept the foreigners under tight control. As a result, little plundering was suffered by the inhabitants.[5]

Easter Sunday also brought the war to the tiny village of Mettinghausen, situated on the Lippe River. The village had been occupied by a small group of German soldiers on 27 March, supported by four tanks. On the early afternoon of 1 April, the Americans pressed toward Mettinghausen from the direction of Lipperode and immediately encountered resistance from the German tanks east and northeast of the village. Three of the tanks had to be abandoned when they ran out of fuel during the brief but intense engagement, and the Germans who did not go into captivity withdrew toward the east. The Haselhorst barn fell victim to incendiary bullets and burned to the ground during the fighting.[6]

The last German stragglers entered the village of Mantinghausen on Easter Sunday at 10:00 a.m. To the consternation of the inhabitants, a Wehrmacht anti-tank unit positioned its guns at three separate locations in the village. The villagers fled to a nearby wooded area between Mantinghausen and Westenholz to wait out the engagement, but they soon found themselves caught in the line of fire as the Americans unexpectedly appeared from the direction of Westenholz. After approximately three hours, the German antitank unit withdrew toward Boke, abandoning their positions to the Americans, who entered the village without further resistance. The lead Sherman tanks sprayed the area with machine-gun fire as the vehicles approached the first buildings, but they were initially met only by a chilling silence and empty streets. As tanks and half-tracks rumbled into the settlement, they were greeted by numerous white flags and foreign laborers who emerged to welcome their liberators.[7]

The remaining settlements in the area fell without resistance, with the exception of the tiny village of Scharmede. The local inhabitants had taken refuge in the church as artillery rounds began striking the roads leading to the settlement. The sporadic firing continued for several hours, and by 6:30 that evening, seven farmhouses belonging to the Schulte-Alpmann, Nölleke, Fecke, Koch, Eikel, and Werning families were in flames. American tanks appeared shortly thereafter, supported by files of infantrymen and guided to their objectives by the brightly burning structures. The few German soldiers who had been compelled by a young lieutenant to defend the village soon surrendered, and the inhabitants set to work attempting to save the remaining dwellings from the flames.

After a cursory inspection of the area, the American column continued toward the west. A large mob of Polish laborers emerged from the surrounding countryside as the forces departed, and in the absence of any armed authorities, they proceeded to ransack the village.[8]

Many of the residents of Paderborn had fled to the nearby village of Elsen during the bombing of the city. On Easter Sunday, the last of the tattered German units had withdrawn from Elsen, and shortly thereafter, white flags appeared from doors and windows. The community leaders—Pastor Mentrup, Bürgermeister Timmerberg, and town engineer Schröder—all agreed to meet the Americans at the first opportunity in order to surrender the village. Equipped with white flags, the three men walked cautiously along the road toward Paderborn without encountering any American units and returned to the village empty-handed. However, the following day, villagers observed dozens of tanks and columns of vehicles suddenly appear in the streets. A number of the vehicles halted; others continued their advance along the main road. Unbeknownst to the villagers, the tiny village of Elsen had been identified as the assembly area to prepare for the attacks on Neuhaus and Sennelager.

Numerous homes were requisitioned for billeting the soldiers, many of whom took advantage of the quick evacuation of civilians and helped themselves to valuables left behind by the inhabitants as they were evicted from their homes.[9]

In the neighboring village of Gesseln, Pastor Hermann Bieker was holding Easter Sunday services when the Americans arrived. On Saturday, both he and Pastor Mentrop of Elsen had suspected that the Americans might arrive the following day, so it was agreed that Bieker would hold Easter Mass for the inhabitants of Gesseln, thus sparing them the dangerous trip to the Gesseln church. The clerics prepared to hold Mass in the Güllenstern farmhouse; an altar was erected, and word was spread from house to house that the service was to be held on Easter Tuesday.

The building filled with worshipers on Tuesday morning, and the village children assisted with the services. The main doors were closed to block an icy wind that swept across the area, but a side door was open. Several minutes into the Easter observance, the assembly fell ominously silent. The singing halted abruptly, and the multitude of worshipers instinctively pressed toward the protection of the altar. The heavy rumble of massive engines quickly filled the air, faded momentarily, then increased as numerous vehicles began filling the streets beyond the farmhouse.

The priest, undeterred, continued with the service without pause. At length, several women nervously tapped on the altar. "Herr Vicar, they are here!" they exclaimed nervously. "They are already here!"[10]

The priest glanced up and said quietly, "We will continue." He went on reciting the Mass, and the congregation responded in turn. The hushed atmosphere was suddenly filled with the muffled rumble of engines and the grinding of steel tracks on brick streets. Stealing a glance through a window, the priest observed a massive green tank approach the building and clatter across the street. The cleric continued his recitation with bowed head as the heavy steel turret rotated toward the building. The vehicle rocked into motion again and rolled toward the doorway as the voice of the priest droned on, barely discernable over the sound of the enormous machine.

The twin doors of the building shuddered as the tank moved against the doorway and halted. Voices shouted commands in English, and suddenly, the door opened. Through the doorway, the congregation observed more tanks grinding past. The ominous black muzzle of a 76-mm cannon was trained directly at the altar. As the priest completed his service, he looked over the bowed heads of the congregation through the doorway and saw the tank crewmen kneeling before their vehicle, bareheaded in the morning air. The tension instantly evaporated, and the villagers began to unpack the bags that they had readied for their flight before the enemy.

With the village of Neuhaus in American hands, the U.S. First and Ninth Armies began to concentrate their forces in preparation for the thrust toward the east—the push that would split the massive pocket into two sectors. The Ninth Army, still assigned to Field Marshal Montgomery's Twenty-first Army Group, received orders to turn its forces 180 degrees and push to the west. Intelligence reports indicated that some twenty German divisions trapped in the pocket were planning to attempt a breakout in the area of Soest. The 8th Armored Division was ordered to secure a line along the Ruhr River and to remain in contact with the First Army elements with whom they had linked in Lippstadt, in order to secure the left flank. The division's Combat Commands (CC) A and R moved first, with Task Force Poinier on the front of CC A. Group Poinier led the way through the villages of Salzkotten, Geseke, and Eikeloh and halted short of the village of Erwitte. Combat Command R, led by Major Artmann, struck out from Lippstadt on 3 April but soon met strong German resistance near Weckinghausen, which forced the foremost units to halt.

The American columns occupied a number of nearby villages as they rolled from Lippstadt on 3 April. Tanks, half-tracks, jeeps, and canvas-covered trucks rolled through Hörste, Mönninghausen, Ehringhausen, and Dedinghausen. Artillery batteries were positioned between Lippstadt and Esbeck, and windows rattled and splintered in the village of Rixbeck as rows of heavy guns fired toward German positions in Erwitte, Weckinghausen, and Overhagen. Isolated German units continued to offer sporadic resistance, and engagements were fought between the areas of Westernkotten, Weckinghausen, Stirpe, and Lippstadt.

The American drive toward the west encountered strong resistance from a German unit occupying the Warte estate southwest of Lippstadt. The residents of the isolated farmsteads in the area were awakened on 2 April by a group of heavily armed German soldiers who arrived from the direction of Stirpe-Weckinghausen. The unit consisted of landsers from Panzergrenadier Regiment 156 from the 116th Panzer Division. A young officer who appeared to be in command of the group stated that they planned to break through the American ring. In response to his questions, the inhabitants provided him information regarding the locations of American units. They advised him that the American tanks were on the southern perimeter of Lippstadt. Part of the battle group departed in the direction of Overhagen; the remainder stayed behind at the farm and prepared defenses.

Foxholes were dug adjacent to a small stream, and machine-gun positions were established while officers and NCOs studied the surrounding terrain.

During the evening of 3 April, an artillery barrage fired from the direction of Lippstadt blanketed the farm. As the shell-bursts faded, the sound of American armored vehicles could be heard as a column neared the farmstead. A barn was soon enveloped in flames, and windows and roof tiles in the houses shattered and crashed to the ground over the rattle of automatic-weapons fire as the Americans encountered the German defenders. Despite the continued firing by German soldiers from the windows and foxholes, the residents began hanging white flags from the buildings. An exhausted German soldier soon appeared in a cellar entrance, where he quickly concealed himself, exclaiming, "What's the point in this … I have a wife and children."

Soon, tanks ground to a halt before the farmyard, and the German fire abruptly ceased. GIs began searching the buildings, and prisoners with hands clasped behind their heads were assembled in the cobblestoned farmyard. The mangled bodies of four German soldiers were carried from their bullet-riddled positions and laid in a row nearby.[11]

After burning documents and destroying the communications equipment in Lippstadt, Kreisleiter Lücke and several members of the local Nazi Party staff had fled through Bökenförder Feld toward Erwitte. Some members of the Freikorps Sauerland made their way to the city's imposing, granite water tower after the Americans captured the northwestern sector of Lippstadt. At the tower, they were joined by leaderless Wehrmacht soldiers, Reich Labor Service members, and assorted officials seeking further instructions. They were told to simply make their way to the Reichsschulungsburg in Erwitte, where they would be organized by a Wehrmacht army officer. The Reichsschulungsburg, a Nazi education center, had been designated an assembly point for stragglers and retreating German units.

In Erwitte, the situation was not calm at the Reichsschulungsburg. Members of every Wehrmacht service branch, minor political functionaries, members of the Reich Labor Service, and splintered groups and individuals from every conceivable military or political organization had collected in Erwitte. At the Reichsschulungsburg, they received soup from a horse-drawn Wehrmacht kitchen. The commander of the education center had disappeared, and despite an intensive search of the area, no trace of him could be found.

While waiting for orders, the members of Freikorps Sauerland eventually lost patience with the obvious lack of organization. A group of conscripts gathered at the entrance to the complex. After several minutes of milling about the imposing structure, they were finally confronted by a Wehrmacht major, who rudely asked them if they had forgotten how to salute senior officers. The major demanded to know their unit and then ordered them to proceed to the Hellweg intersection to intercept any straggling Wehrmacht soldiers and direct them to the Reichsschulungsburg. He also instructed them to take into custody any Soviet prisoners of war, thousands of whom were now wandering aimlessly throughout the countryside. If any evidence of looting was found in their possession, the looters were to be summarily shot.

The men complied with the major's orders and subsequently directed a number of Wehrmacht stragglers to the facility. Two NCOs of a flak unit whose guns were situated near the Glasmer farm brought five Soviet prisoners of war to the crossroads and explained that they had been taken into custody near their battery. A search of the prisoners revealed that they had several hand-grenade detonators and fuses. Unable to explain where they had obtained the explosives, the hapless Russians were turned over to several Wehrmacht soldiers. One of the soldiers departed with the prisoners and later returned, reporting that they had been shot in accordance with the major's orders.

Early that afternoon, a soldier whom the Freikorps members had directed to report to the education center returned and advised them that he had found no one in charge at the facility. The Freikorps commander promptly left the checkpoint and went to the center to investigate. To his chagrin, he was unable to locate the major. A solitary SS officer was finally found in the midst of feverishly packing his personal belongings. The officer explained that he was in a great hurry; he was also taking leave of family members before fleeing toward the Sauerland. The officer merely commented that he had no time to speak with the men, and no further orders were issued.

The town of Erwitte became a massive traffic jam as columns of vehicles and people attempting to flee the pocket converged on the small settlement. Added to the military traffic were flocks of refugees, POWs, and foreign laborers from various cities in the Ruhr. With no one in charge, chaos reigned. The local inhabitants were gravely concerned over rumors that Erwitte would be defended, and word of the shooting of the Soviet prisoners only fueled their anxiety.

The Erwitte Volkssturm had been mobilized and organized into three companies. During the last week of March, the massive elm trees along the Anröchter road were felled for use in constructing roadblocks and tank barriers, and the Volkssturm was assigned to man the series of obstacles. Their equipment was sparse and their training cursory. They had been afforded the opportunity to fire a machine gun at a nearby gravel pit, and the members who had been issued firearms found themselves in possession of antiquated French rifles. They were later issued ammunition, but it was of Czech manufacture and of a different caliber and thus useless to the hapless conscripts. Some of the Volkssturm members eventually received German arms, but the weapons were ancient rifles dating from the Franco-Prussian War. Many of the Volkssturm soldiers were wearing civilian clothes and were issued armbands on which was printed *Deutsche Wehrmacht* to provide a semblance of uniform. It was rumored that the Volkssturm thus equipped would spearhead an attack through the American columns to break out of the pocket.

Most of the Volkssturm members were local inhabitants who unexpectedly found themselves combatants within sight of their homes, and many of them simply disappeared into the countryside or took refuge with family or friends at the first opportunity. The roadside ditches and hastily dug foxholes were littered with Panzerfausts and assorted weaponry, much of which had been discarded by the erstwhile defenders. Some areas were being defended by fanatic young officers, many of whom had never experienced combat and were acting under the influence of a lifetime of Nazi propaganda.

The regular Wehrmacht units assigned to defend Erwitte consisted of two companies from Panzergrenadier Regiment 60 and a unit from Field Replacement Battalion 146 of the 116th Panzer Division. Numerous stragglers were collected and loosely organized. The soldiers represented a variety of all arms of the services. The ranks of gray-green army uniforms were sprinkled with the blue-gray tunics of the Luftwaffe. The combination of various unaffiliated units, augmented by untrained Volkssturm conscripts, offered a poor military force of dubious reliability.

The roadblocks on the main approaches to Erwitte were reinforced with large tree trunks. An 88-mm flak had been positioned along the road to Berge but was withdrawn on 31 March. The inhabitants of Erwitte watched with growing anxiety as small groups of soldiers aimlessly wandered along the roads.

The Erwitte defenses were concentrated around the cemetery on the east side of the village, adjacent to the road leading north to Lippstadt. Situated among the hedgerows and lines of trees near the cemetery were two 37-mm antiaircraft guns and an 88-mm high-velocity flak. Foxholes and trenches were dug along the approaches to the cemetery, and an isolated position was located in a small copse on the road leading to the village of Berge.

The American columns approaching Erwitte, some 5 miles south of Lippstadt, initially met strong German resistance from the Erwitte cemetery. The GIs halted for the night and dug foxholes along Reichsstrasse 1 and established positions in the numerous fields and fruit orchards dotting the plain between Lippstadt and Erwitte. Shells fired from unseen American batteries to the north struck the town on Monday afternoon. A lull in the shelling brought several hours of ominous silence until nightfall, when the shelling renewed with greater intensity. The anxious residents remained awake throughout Monday night and Tuesday morning. At approximately 4:00 p.m., artillery fire began falling on the town again. One of the high-explosive projectiles struck the corner of the Catholic church's rectory. The intense bombardment that blanketed the vicinity of the church unnerved an aged priest, Eberhard Klausenberg, who suffered a fatal heart attack during the engagement. The German artillery battery, at the cemetery east of town, first returned fire that evening, but the gunners soon began rationing their quickly depleted supply of ammunition. The American artillery fire intensified and continued throughout the night. The inhabitants of Erwitte remained huddled in their cellars until the following afternoon.[12]

On Wednesday, 4 April, the American units prepared to capture Erwitte from several directions. As the tanks began to move toward the town from the north, they were engaged by hidden 88-mm flak positions. The antiaircraft guns opened fire on GIs attempting to approach the town by advancing behind hedgerows that were scattered across the open ground. An observation plane droned overhead, directing the fire and reporting every movement and location of German forces.

The inhabitants of the neighboring village of Eikeloh witnessed the assault on Erwitte and watched as the tanks, situated on the eastern perimeter of their village, fired into the neighboring town. They then observed the tanks moving forward, accompanied by infantrymen cautiously advancing under the protection of the hedgerows and fruit trees flanking both sides of Reichsstrasse 1.

A number of families had fled the village of Westernkotten to take shelter in the Domhof farmhouses, approximately 2.5 miles southeast of Erwitte, and as the tanks closed on Erwitte, they hung white flags from the farm buildings. The display of capitulation immediately brought fire from the German guns positioned at the approaches to Erwitte, for the gunners assumed that with the display of white flags, the American forces were occupying the farm buildings.

During the early morning hours of 4 April, the American columns approached from the north. However, the tanks quickly withdrew on encountering renewed fire from the Erwitte cemetery. In response, a hail of artillery fire again descended on the cemetery and the fruit orchards. As the shell-bursts slowly faded, the Americans again approached, now under less resistance, and soon advanced toward the town, followed by endless convoys. At 2:30 p.m., the firing suddenly ceased, and the tanks, half-tracks, and infantry entered the town.

The approach of the American forces was also observed by Wehrmacht Captain Wolfgang Königsbeck, commander of the 9th Battery, Artillery Regiment 146 of the 116th Panzer Division. Since ammunition for the battery was in very limited supply, the gunners were ordered to engage only targets that could be taken under direct fire. The battery's primary objective was to report any enemy activity to headquarters; thus, the unit was relegated to an intelligence role. The battery was situated in a cement quarry south of Erwitte, which offered a commanding view of the open plain between Erwitte and Lippstadt.

The artillery captain descended from his observation post on the cement factory tower and raced to the telephone to call the switchboard in Erwitte. He received a full report of the American strength from a switchboard operator, who told him that "large numbers" of American tanks were passing through the town and were stopped outside the building where the operator was and that the streets were swarming with American soldiers. The operator then added, "I have to hang up now, an American officer will be returning at any minute."

Realizing that to remain in his exposed location would prove fatal, Königsbeck ordered an evacuation of the battery position, and the unit was soon moving west under sporadic fire from liberated Russian prisoners who had armed themselves with discarded Volkssturm weapons.[13]

In Erwitte, white flags soon appeared from windows and doorways. A search of the homes and buildings in the town produced a small group of German prisoners, who were assembled in the market square, standing in ranks with hands clasped behind their heads. Small arms and assorted military field equipment lay strewn about the red-brick pavement as GIs searched the pockets and rucksacks of the dejected captives.

As the American forces approached Erwitte, sixteen-year-old Gretel Klara huddled in her family's cellar with five neighbors, awaiting the outcome of the gun battle. The explosions of antiaircraft artillery mixed with the vicious chatter of machine-gun fire as the engagement near the Erwitte cemetery, some 1,000 yards away, raged throughout the morning.

As the gunfire faded and eventually fell silent, the anxious refugees waited in the darkness of the cellar, fearing what the next minutes would bring. At length, the group heard voices shouting commands in English at close proximity to Gretel's parent's grocery store. Gretel cautiously climbed the staircase and peered fearfully toward the locked door. Suddenly, the butt of an American infantry rifle crashed through one of the adjacent windows. A hand reached through the shattered glass and unlocked the door, and a fearsome GI bedecked with combat equipment was silhouetted in the doorway. The olive-and-khaki-clad figure wore a round steel helmet, and grenades hung from his cartridge belt.

The soldier entered the store as Gretel hastily retreated back into the cellar. The GI followed close behind her into the darkened room, where he halted to scan the huddled figures in the light from a flashlight. He then turned and wordlessly departed.

The other women and children soon left the cellar and made their way through streets now filled with columns of American trucks and combat vehicles. Gretel Klara remained in the cellar, frightened of the strangers in foreign uniforms. Suddenly, the door to the cellar burst open again, and she was horrified to see a number of Russian laborers ransacking the store shelves. After several seconds of chaotic looting, several of the Russians spied the girl peering at them from the cellar and stormed down the steps toward her. Gretel turned and raced up an adjacent stairwell leading to the street to seek the safety of the conquerors.[14]

The GIs quickly requisitioned homes and office buildings for billeting. The local inhabitants hastily evacuated their homes and searched for lodging with friends and relatives. The German troops who had escaped capture or death withdrew toward the villages of Anröchte, Klieve, and Waltringhausen. The Americans continued their methodical advance toward Anröchte and beyond, in the direction of Haar. Task Force Poinier, the unit that led the attack on Erwitte, advanced toward Anröchte, its progress impeded by destroyed bridges.

On the Tuesday following Easter, as American task forces were preparing to assault Erwitte, a German infantry company farther south marched into the village of Berge. The unit, consisting of some 100 soldiers armed with light weapons and commanded by a tall, blond lieutenant, began digging trenches and preparing defensive positions. The young officer established a command post in the Mendelin home on the southeastern perimeter of the village. A communications center was established, and foxholes were dug in a wide arc around the house. A German armored vehicle was concealed behind a stone wall near a barn on the southern end of the village.

On Wednesday, 4 April, Wehrmacht Sergeant Max Reng was lying in wait for the American column as Task Force Goodrich of the U.S. 8th Armored Division moved on Bergen from the direction of Hoinkhausen and Nettelstaedt. The German NCO fired a Panzerfaust as the first tank passed his position at the crossing of Weickede-Hoinkhausen and Nettelstaedt roads. The conical, high-explosive projectile struck the vehicle at close range, and the tank sloughed to the side of the road and ground to a halt. The other armored vehicles immediately opened fire on the German position, fatally wounding Reng. Three soldiers accompanying him were taken prisoner as the tanks opened a barrage on buildings in the village. A German observation team in the church tower was forced to retreat as the structure came under heavy fire. After several seconds of intense firing, silence descended on the area, and the column cautiously rolled into the village. The heavy tracks of the Shermans tore paving stones from the roadway as the crews navigated the narrow streets leading to the center of the village. At length, the concealed German tank opened fire, disabling two American vehicles before being struck by an armor-piercing projectile. The panzer crew jumped from the burning vehicle and disappeared into the smoke-filled streets.

The engagement in Berge was of short duration, and the German defenders, including the blond lieutenant, quickly surrendered after the Americans sealed the exits to the village. The surrounding homes were left riddled with bullet holes, and soon, the Americans had assembled several dozen prisoners who were later transported to Weickede. The Americans suffered no casualties in the brief exchange. The armored and infantry units that captured Berge on Tuesday morning were quickly followed by a heavy artillery unit. The artillery battery established fire positions east of the village, where the heavy weapons began firing toward the northwest. The firing continued intermittently for the rest of the day and throughout the night. On 5 April, the villagers observed the battery troops breaking their position and moving onward, leaving only a few GIs occupying the village.

With the capture of Berge, large numbers of Russian prisoners of war and laborers were liberated. The malnourished prisoners were soon looting the outlying farms and small villages, some taking revenge on former overseers for the treatment received during four years of servitude. The Russians obtained an abandoned German army motorcycle and sidecar equipped with a machine gun, with which they careened about the surrounding countryside, shattering windows and riddling walls with bullet holes at random. On 14 April, a confrontation ensued between the Russian motorcyclists and inhabitants of Berge near the Albersmeier farmstead. Farmer Heinrich Albersmeier was killed and several villagers were wounded as a result of the encounter.[15]

American units consisting of A and B Companies of Armored Infantry Battalion 58 advanced toward the village of Horn on 4 April. As dusk approached, Colonel Wallace and his driver, Corporal Robert J. Buss, cut through a field to link up with their unit, which they assumed was occupying Horn with Task Force Walker. As their jeep neared the village, they came under heavy infantry fire from German soldiers concealed along a hedgerow. Quickly throwing classified documents into the dense undergrowth, both the colonel and the driver raised their hands in surrender.

When the colonel failed to appear at Major Artmann's command post, units were dispatched to search for the commander. One of the patrols returned several hours later with a frightened young German soldier, who cooperated in describing the prisoners. The U.S. officials learned that Wallace and his driver had been captured between Horn and Bochum by a reconnaissance patrol from the 116th Panzer Division. They were then taken to Schmerlecke and delivered to the command post of Major Tebbe, commander of a panzer battalion assigned to defend the sector. Despite the freezing temperatures that descended on the Sauerland after sunset, Wallace had steadfastly refused to don the German army jacket that his captors offered; he was concerned that he and the driver would be shot as spies.[16]

Villagers in Horn displayed white flags as the American columns approached, but the German soldiers were not prepared to surrender and instead opened fire on the file of vehicles. The enraged Americans ordered a heavy concentration of artillery and tank fire on the settlement. The village church tower was extensively damaged, and impacts threatened to obliterate entire blocks of residences and barns.

Three Horn citizens—Wilhelm Becker, Josef Kleegraf, and Eduard Kerker—departed from the beleaguered village under darkness and sought out the city commander in Lippstadt. After meeting with a series of other officers, they were finally taken to the commander. The weary officer was awakened from a deep sleep to hear the pleas of the men. The resolute villagers, who had already risked death in traversing the battle-torn area at night, offered to serve as hostages in order to assure the Americans that Horn presented no danger. The commander listened as they explained that the display of surrender was by no means intended as a subterfuge and that the German soldiers who had opened fire were not associated with the village inhabitants. The commander agreed to attempt to save the settlement from further destruction; in return, the three men would have to remain in Lippstadt, and if another shot was fired on American troops from Horn, they would indeed be shot in reprisal.

The anxious emissaries waited out the night perched on stools in the Severin house, awaiting the outcome of the American advance on Horn. The next day, the commander told Horn's residents, through an interpreter, "You have a good Bürgermeister. If he hadn't gotten me out of bed, Horn would not be standing now."[17]

On Wednesday evening, Anne Sommer observed a file of American infantrymen entering Horn from the neighboring villages of Ebbinghausen and Berenbrock. The heavily armed and determined GIs began thoroughly searching residences, barns, and public buildings. They pierced beds, chests, sacks, and haystacks with bayonets. Wardrobes were broken into and the contents strewn about the buildings. A number of homes were requisitioned for the billeting of soldiers; the inhabitants were compelled to find shelter elsewhere.

The following day, a general curfew was in effect; the inhabitants could neither return to their homes nor tend to their livestock. A substantial increase in military traffic was noted. All male inhabitants were ordered to assemble in the town square, after which a number were taken into custody and transported to an unknown destination. Within forty-eight hours, most of the troops had departed, and hordes of plundering Russians and Poles followed in their wake. The foreign laborers embarked on an orgy of destruction and vandalism, throwing food onto manure piles and destroying furnishings and equipment. In response, a local emergency unit was organized. When the church bells rang, men armed with clubs or other makeshift weapons assembled to protect property from the marauders. American patrols occasionally appeared and attempted to bring order to the lawlessness that prevailed following the departure of the combat troops.[18]

On 4 April, the U.S. 8th Armored Division joined the push toward the west, deep into the pocket. The German unit in their path, the 116th "Windhund" Panzer Division, was trying to hold a line more than 40 miles in length. On the same day that the 8th Armored Division struck, the XXXXVII Panzer Corps, under which the 116th was subordinate, received a message to hold all ground at any cost. Preparations were being made from outside the pocket to break through the American ring.

The 116th Panzer Division was too weak to consider obeying the order. The entire division now comprised less than 5,000 troops. One of the division's foremost units, Panzergrenadier Regiment 60, was attempting to hold a 9-mile front with less than 600 troops. The division had received no reinforcements since the Allies had crossed the Rhine at Wesel. Many of their isolated positions defending crossroads, villages, and strategic terrain features consisted solely of a single tank or artillery piece and a handful of grenadiers or Volkssturm.[19]

The 116th Panzer Division had largely evacuated Anröchte, which had once held the command post of Panzergrenadier Regiment 60. The regiment's units had been reduced to dispersed bands of stragglers and miscellaneous troops, including several naval officers. But a young German officer commanding a handful of forces equipped with Panzerfausts was determined to defend Anröchte. When several villagers sought to discuss the futility of defending the villlage, he responded, "My homeland in East Prussia has gone up in flames. Anröchte can also go up in flames."[20]

On the morning of 4 April, an American unit under the command of Captain McGafferey left the village of Berge, advanced to Anröchte, and occupied the eastern routes into the village. An obsolete German tank, concealed near the Berghoff stone quarry, opened fire on American units as they closed on the village, and the column immediately withdrew. Within minutes, Anröchte was blanketed with artillery projectiles. The artillery fire struck the church tower, and a woman in the vicinity was fatally wounded by shrapnel. As the barrage lifted, the Americans entered Anröchte from two directions and occupied the town. The German officer from East Prussia had disappeared, as had his ragged band of defenders. The Americans immediately ordered all male inhabitants to assemble in the town square, and after a short and cursory interrogation, the men were sent to their homes, except for three officials who were retained as liaison personnel. A curfew was immediately put into force, and the customary search of homes and buildings began.[21]

One of the last towns to fall to the American units assigned to seal the ring around Army Group B was the ancient village of Kallenhardt. The Sauerland settlement, 3 miles east of Warstein, occupied a commanding height that overlooked a road junction in the Arnsberger Forest. Some sixty soldiers—mostly Wehrmacht convalescents, Volkssturm conscripts, and stragglers who had hoped to escape the last days of the war—found themselves under the command of a fatefully energetic, nineteen-year-old lieutenant. The young officer was convinced that the road junction north of the Kallenhardt heights was of great strategic importance, and he was thus determined to defend the position. The motley force was armed with a variety of foreign rifles, several machine guns, two mortars, and a tank. Roadblocks were erected on the Nuttlar-Rüthen road, and local men were conscripted into an impromptu security force.

On the Tuesday following Easter Sunday, a patrol of four American tanks approached the road junction north of the village from the direction of Nuttlar. The solitary German tank, concealed below a nearby terrain feature, opened fire on the advancing Shermans. The German vehicle was disabled following a brief skirmish. During the engagement, a machine-gun crew just outside the Finger residence opened fire from the heights commanding the valley to the north. As machine-gun bursts echoed along the length of the streambed below, Mathilda Finger observed a local teenager with a Panzerfaust balanced over his shoulder slinking along the row of houses toward the American patrol. Before the boy could make his way to the tanks through the orchard below the heights, the American patrol withdrew into the woods in the direction from which they had appeared. Shortly thereafter, Mathilda's husband arrived home, breathless and exhausted. He had fled his work detail at the onset of the engagement to return home, where he excitedly reported that the Americans had disappeared behind the woods to the north of the village.

Several of the soldiers from the small Kallenhardt garrison arrived at the Finger residence and requested a bedsheet to use as a white flag. It was obvious to the inhabitants that they had been given only brief respite; the Americans would eventually return. The Finger house held a commanding view that overlooked the valley and streambed where the Americans had first appeared. If they were to return from the same direction, the white flag would immediately come into view and, it was hoped, the war would end for the conscripts and Kallenhardt residents without further tragedy. Finger unhesitatingly agreed to hang the sheet from his home. Other residents followed suit and displayed bedsheets from their upper windows in an attempt to spare the village the destruction they knew was certain in the event the Americans suffered any casualties.

Within minutes, the young German lieutenant appeared, furious at the display of capitulation. Drawing his pistol from its holster, he wildly threatened to shoot whoever was responsible for displaying the flags. A vehement protest arose from the crowd of women and elderly men. At length, the officer returned his firearm to its holster, but he ordered the removal of the flags and threatened to shoot anyone responsible for any further attempts to surrender.

Friday afternoon brought a barrage of artillery and mortar fire to Kallenhardt, followed by an assault by American armored units from three directions. Mathilda Finger and her children fled to her basement, which became crowded with neighbors and relatives as the shells impacted nearby. As the explosions of artillery projectiles and bursting mortar rounds lessened, Mathilda picked her way through the crowded basement and peered from a ground-level window. Advancing cautiously along both sides of the street were several soldiers in olive-drab uniforms, crouching in doorways and taking momentary refuge behind the corners of the dwellings as they penetrated deeper into the narrow roadway toward the church.[22]

Several Americans climbed into the church tower at the center of the village, where they continued to direct the attack through a loudspeaker. As the rattle of small-arms fire drifted over the medieval rooftops, German resistance quickly collapsed. Seven of the defenders were killed in the engagement, including a forty-seven-year-old flak crewman who was the father of four children. He had been trying to make his way home to his family in Freienohl when he was conscripted into the force at Kallenhardt. More than fifty Germans were taken prisoner, many of whom were wounded in the skirmish. A small number escaped toward Suttrop. The angry GIs herded the German prisoners to the center of the village, where they shot the headstrong lieutenant and set the local schoolhouse ablaze in retribution for the resistance they had encountered.

Shortly after the sounds of small-arms fire ceased echoing through the narrow river valley, a squad of American soldiers entered the Finger residence. They inspected the home for weapons, searched for any lingering German soldiers who may have taken refuge in the building, and then ordered all inhabitants to evacuate the residence. The Finger family hurried to collect some clothing before the Americans occupied the home in larger numbers.

After the initial retaliation for the resistance they had received from the Kallenhardt garrison, the Americans exhibited a nonchalant attitude. At the Fingers' home, the soldiers stacked their field equipment in the living room, and several reclined on the furniture while others prepared food at the stove in the kitchen. They occupied the home for several days before continuing along the valley to an unknown destination. When Mathilda Finger returned, she found the cellar stripped of all food, including a large ham that she had been carefully hoarding for a special occasion. Entering her kitchen, she saw the family dog, which had remained in the residence during the occupation by the Americans, sleeping contentedly in the middle of the room. Scattered about the floor were the sparse remnants of the ham, indicating the generous treatment given to the animal by the American soldiers during their stay.[23]

The tanks of the U.S. 8th Armored Division advanced 28 miles on 6 April. The task force, under the command of Major van Houten, bypassed Soest to the north and established positions behind the city. The XIX Corps of the U.S. Ninth Army, also to the north of Soest, prepared to use the troops of the 95th Infantry

Division, commanded by Major General Devine, to capture Soest. Under relentless pressure from the oncoming Americans, the troops of the 116th "Windhund" Panzer Division continued to fall back, eliminating any hope of breaking out of the pocket.

At 12:30 p.m. on 6 April, Bad Sassendorf was occupied by van Houten's forces as they advanced toward Soest. The Americans rolled to the center of the town as white flags appeared from buildings lining the main roadway. The GIs were met at the town hall by Bürgermeister Schröder, who assured them that no German troops remained in the town. The soldiers took the Bürgermeister into custody and continued search and clearing operations in the area. Schröder's body was later found near the town of Delbrück, but the reason for his death remained a mystery. Before they departed, Town Councilman Hermann was hastily appointed chief of police by the Americans, who then continued their advance until drawing to a halt at Ostönnen.[24]

As the Americans headed west, Task Force Goodrich occupied Neuengesecke, Enkesen, Brüllingsen, and Ellingsen. At 3:30 p.m., a combined unit from Task Forces Goodrich and van Houten fought their way into the village of Echtrop. During the engagement, a German tank was destroyed by the American troops, who captured thirty prisoners as the firing quickly diminished. Three German tanks rolled out of the woods and fired on a supply convoy as the Americans were passing the village of Berlingsen. A number of American half-tracks and trucks were hit before an armored column arrived to beat back the German troops.

Units of the U.S. 8th Armored Division resumed the reduction of the pocket on the morning of 8 April. During their advance toward Westendorf, Task Force Goodrich found all bridges over the Möhne River in Allagen demolished. Task Force Poinier entered Mülheim-Möhn and progressed toward Belecke. The column halted at a roadblock, where Lieutenant Colonel Arthur D. Poinier dispatched a prisoner of war into Belecke to request that the town surrender. The anxious Bürgermeister eagerly complied, greatly relieved that the Wehrmacht had failed to establish a defense in his town.

American columns west of Belecke rolled into Sichtigvor-Mülheim and searched all buildings for weapons. The GIs discovered eight ceremonial salute rifles in the Mühle-Krick-Schöne area, which they promptly smashed before crowding all local inhabitants into the room of an adjacent home for several hours. The soldiers raided numerous henhouses for fresh provisions during their sweep through the village and established quarters in several homes. In the nearby settlement of Brüllingsen, a farmer named Schülte-Böhmer was fatally shot by a GI.

En route to Sichtigvor, American troops watched several German soldiers fleeing into nearby woods. They immediately collected a number of local inhabitants, who were compelled to walk in front of the GIs as they combed the dense underbrush in search of the fugitive landsers. At length, the civilians were released after the Americans deemed their search fruitless.

The war did not end without incident in the village of Am Liermond. The withdrawing Wehrmacht troops positioned two machine guns in front of the village chapel to slow the American advance. The point element of the American column discerned the machine-gun nests from a distance. Seizing local residents Georg Strop and Heinrich Cramer, the soldiers forced the villagers to approach the chapel as shields in front of American patrol. The landsers manning the weapons withheld their fire as the civilians neared and at length rose from their positions with upraised hands. That evening, more American forces poured into Am Liermond. The newly arriving troops located a generous source of alcohol, after which they embarked on a frenzy of vandalism, looting cellars of food and stealing valuables from homes. Sentries were eventually placed in front of the houses that had suffered severe looting, and much of the lawlessness soon abated.

The city of Warstein had been prepared for defense by Nazi Party officials. Roadblocks were erected and defense units organized despite the wishes of the inhabitants to surrender. A Wehrmacht officer in the town, Major Hass, finally ordered the Volkssturm to dismantle the barriers. The afternoon of 6 April brought artillery rounds that struck at random throughout the town, resulting in a brief artillery duel when German batteries began returning fire.

Major Hass was soon relieved of his command and replaced by another officer. The newcomer was determined to defend Warstein. He ordered the tank barriers to be reconstructed and placed under guard by police and fire department personnel. That evening, the Bürgermeister of Kallenhardt was dispatched by the Americans into Warstein to attempt to persuade the new major to surrender. The officer was determined to defend the town, and all efforts to reason with him were in vain.[25]

Warstein was shelled throughout the night as anxious residents huddled in their cellars and bunkers. The impacts of heavy-caliber artillery projectiles were concentrated on the center of town. The church received several direct hits, as did the large Cramer brewery. The city soon lost electric power and water. The shelling continued for several days, erratically and with varying intensity. Eventually driven out of their cellars by squalid conditions, inhabitants began to risk the artillery barrages to flee the city. More than 100 citizens took refuge in nearby caves, while others simply fled into the woods. A small number stubbornly clung to the uncertain shelter of the cellars.

When the American forces finally began their slow and methodical advance into the urban area, the Wehrmacht defenders began withdrawing, with heavy losses. Within hours, GIs were searching houses as columns of tanks rolled through streets devoid of civilians. Following the armored units rolled hundreds of vehicles of every description that soon packed the streets and jammed the town center.

As the town filled with khaki-clad soldiers, numerous residents were ordered to evacuate their homes for use by U.S. forces. The inhabitants were initially required to assemble in the town square. After two hours, the women and children were released to return to their homes. All military-age males were marched to the Volksschule, where they were retained until sunset.

The area of Warstein and Suttrop marked the southernmost point of the operation area of the 8th Armored Division. Farther south, units of the First Army's III Corps continued to push west through Meschede and deeper into the pocket. On 7 April, a full week following the closure of the pocket at Lippstadt, it was still unclear to the Wehrmacht's Fifteenth Army staff whether Warstein remained in German hands.

The village of Borgeln stood in the path of American armored columns that were pressing toward Soest. The inhabitants of Borgeln received their first indication that the area was encircled from the local postman, Albert Walter. He had been dispatched to transport sacks of mail toward Brilon, and en route to his destination, the postman was met by columns of Sherman tanks.

Walter's report of oncoming Allied troops was accompanied by wild rumors. The local newspaper, the *Soester Nachricht*, was last delivered on 28 March, and the other newspaper, the *Westfälische Landeszeitung*, had not appeared for several weeks. Even the daily army reports, often a main source of local news, became sporadic. Two days after Easter Sunday, electric power was disrupted, leaving the inhabitants without lights or radio reports, thus reducing news sources to intermittent rumors.

Road obstacles were erected at the approaches to the village and were reluctantly manned by Volkssturm members armed with Panzerfausts. The weak gesture was generally considered by the local populace to be not only fruitless but also a danger to their homes and families. Although children were ordered to be evacuated beyond the reach of the oncoming Americans, parents resisted the directive. Subsequent orders to comply with the evacuation were again ignored. On the Friday before Easter Sunday, Reichsbahn officials were directed to leave Soest and relocate beyond the occupied area. The railway workers proceeded as far as Bad Driburg—and promptly returned home after finding the route blocked by the American advance.

The Easter services held in Soest on 1 April were interrupted by loud explosions. On Tuesday, sounds of battle could be discerned: distant engagements resounded softly over the horizon, and artillery rounds impacted nearby. Inhabitants sought refuge in cellars as the artillery impacts increased. Two large Wehrmacht trucks transported supplies to Borgeln for a command post that had been established in the vicinity. The German sergeant in charge turned the remaining provisions over to the Bürgermeister with instructions to issue items as needed to evacuees if he failed to return. Shortly thereafter, local inhabitants broke into the gymnasium where the supplies were stored and looted shoes, canned goods, and clothing. Casks of wine were broken into, the contents disappearing among the populace. A local pastor was successful in dissuading a mob of refugees from plundering the church clothing collection. The cleric managed to drive the throng, led by a drunken individual from Dortmund named Bech, from the churchyard before returning the clothing to the storage rooms. That evening, the rooms were again broken into, and numerous items, particularly blankets, were stolen. The pastor then advised the Bürgermeister that he could no longer accept responsibility for the supplies. That night, vehicles arrived from a panzer regiment and retrieved more items.[26]

On Thursday, German infantrymen appeared and took up positions near the north and west approaches to Borgeln. Tanks and armored vehicles trickled through the narrow streets of the village, the heavy vehicles loosening the brick paving stones and rattling windowpanes as they passed. That evening, artillery rounds increased, forcing inhabitants to remain in their cellars as pressure waves from the impacts rocked the houses. At 9:45 Friday morning, the village was assaulted by the Americans.

A large group of teenaged students from the Mommsen-Gymnasium in Berlin-Charlottenburg had been transferred to the Soest area to serve as flak assistants. In addition to their duties with the heavy flak batteries, they continued their lessons under the tutelage of their elderly instructor, Dr. Möller. On 6 April, the students were taken prisoner and assembled along with Wehrmacht soldiers who had been captured near the Markhoff farm. Möller rushed to the scene and pleaded with the GIs to free his pupils. The grim soldiers were unmoved and unconvinced that the teenagers should be released. Failing to gain their freedom, the distraught teacher was determined to accompany his charges into captivity. Möller was seen clinging desperately to the side of a truck bearing the prisoners as it departed from the farmyard and headed toward an ominous destination. The grief-stricken instructor finally dropped to the ground when the American guards beat him away with rifle butts.[27]

As American units cleared the village of Borgeln and pushed on toward Soest, they encountered Matthias Lücke, a veterinary officer serving with Veterinary Replacement Battalion 6 near Maas. Their orders for him to raise his hands in surrender were repeatedly and inexplicably refused. With little alternative, one of the GIs shot the officer. His body was later collected by Red Cross nurses, wrapped in a sheet, and transported by farm cart to Borgeln.[28]

The American forces sweeping toward Soest were followed by mobs of foreign laborers recently liberated by the GIs. Fritz and Anna Oberhoff observed
a number of Russians outside their window demanding "Zvibulla, Katoschki!"
The couple passed several items of food through the window until, frustrated
that the food was provided too slowly, the Russians lost patience and began forcing their way through the window. The farmer and his wife fearfully gathered up
their two children and fled to a nearby field, abandoning their farmstead to the
mob. Several hours later, they dared to venture back to their home only to find
it looted of all provisions. The furnishings were destroyed, beds were overturned,
wardrobes were splintered, and all their possessions had been strewn throughout
the house. The Russians had packed food into a baby carriage and filed up the
street in search of additional loot. The family spent the remainder of the afternoon salvaging torn photographs, documents, and muddy clothing from the ditch
lining the road where the gang had discarded what they decided not to take with
them.[29]

Some American units initiated efforts to control the hordes of laborers. A massive collection of property was confiscated from the Russians and placed under
guard for disposal. Some of the items were eventually returned to the original
owners. Many residents hid valuables from the plunderers. Dietrich Jaspert succeeded in concealing jewelry between the double roof of a dog house. He also
hid ham and sausages beneath a woodpile. Friedrich Oberhoff hid his hunting
rifles by bricking them behind the wall of a storage building.[30]

Thirty-eight-year-old Erna Neuhaus in Soest huddled in her home with a
number of neighborhood women and children as the first American troops entered the town. She was prepared to hang a white sheet out of an upper story
window but hesitated to display this sign of surrender because no one was sure
whether party officials would return. Several days earlier, she had quietly cleared
the home of Nazi regalia. National Socialist books and Nazi flags were burned,
and her brother's Wehrmacht uniform and medals were hastily buried.

At length, she heard a voice calling, "They're already here!" Seconds later,
Erna observed several American soldiers edging cautiously up the street, weapons
at the ready. After noticing the women peering from the upper-floor window of
the house, the GIs burst through the door and then inspected the home, exploring all rooms. They then appeared to relax and made themselves comfortable.

Chewing gum and gesturing to other new arrivals, the soldiers had an am-
bivalent manner and casual demeanor that lent an air of comfort to the anxious
inhabitants. The GIs smiled at the children and gestured to the women as they
rubbed the stubble of beard on their chins. The women correctly concluded that
the soldiers wanted water for shaving, and they quickly brought pails of heated water for the conquerors. The soldiers nonchalantly shaved and washed their faces

and spoke with one another in open, friendly tones in English; the wide-eyed children crowded around to watch the strange giants in khaki and olive green from a respectful distance.

The newcomers seemed astonishingly at ease. Compared to the tattered remnants of the Wehrmacht, the strangers exhibited an air of health, satisfaction, and confidence. The women dared to exhibit traces of smiles; they began to speak with one another in hushed tones. Long seconds passed, and the discourse grew bolder and louder as the women spoke with growing optimism. Suddenly, everyone began to speak with an outpouring of emotion as the realization fell on them that it was over.

As more Americans arrived, the soldiers in muddy boots and soft, cotton uniforms toured the centuries-old home with curiosity. They made themselves comfortable in the dwelling, resting on chairs and sofas or reclining on the floor. Suddenly, Erna remembered the photograph of her brother hanging on the wall and could not help but cast a fearful glance at the framed picture. Following her eyes, one young American saw the photograph of Erna's brother in uniform. He strode across the room and stopped before the picture. The portrait peered forlornly from the frame, a young man in Wehrmacht field gray, an Iron Cross pinned on his breast. "A Nazi," the American remarked confidently. "Do you know him?" Erna answered through a translator, "Yes … my brother." She continued hesitantly, "He was killed in Italy … he was twenty-six." An officer rose from his seat, carefully removed the photograph from the wall, and, with a slight bow, solemnly extended it to her.[31]

By the following afternoon, the Americans had moved on to a new objective. Freed laborers, primarily from Russia, Poland, and Serbia, flooded in their wake. Many of the ecstatic workers had previously toiled in the neighboring farms and knew the area intimately. Some laborers exacted revenge on their former lords. Others plundered every corner of every building in their search for valuables. Many simply sought food. The hordes of uncontrolled workers exacted a grievous toll on the neighboring farms and villages. For local inhabitants, there was safety only in large numbers, and many farms and villages were abandoned to the roving swarms of pillagers.

With no knowledge of how or when an end to the torment might arrive, if it arrived at all, many inhabitants in outlying areas were overwhelmed with hopelessness. Reports of murder and rape abounded, and no authorities appeared willing or able to bring the chaos under control. Two neighboring farmers near the Hiddingser estate shot or hanged their families in despair. Inhabitants were shocked at the conditions they found on returning to their outlying homes. Featherbeds were lacerated, the goose-down stuffing strewn throughout the buildings. Articles of clothing not stolen were smeared with the contents of the canned goods hauled from basement shelves. Windows were smashed, and furnishings were destroyed or, in many instances, used to fuel cooking fires. Clumps of threadbare, barely recognizable Russian military uniforms lay scattered where the prisoners had exchanged their lice-ridden rags for clothing found in the homes. In the warm spring weather, many of the foreigners were observed wearing pajamas as they roamed the streets; some sported stylish top hats and elegant evening clothes.[32]

Within Soest, rumors flowed through the city about whether the Wehrmacht garrison would capitulate, withdraw and leave Soest to the Americans, or attempt a defense. It was rumored that the city commander, Lieutenant-Colonel Schuster, had decided to withdraw and leave the city to the Americans. He lacked artillery with which to conduct a defense, and no armor was available. For his forces to attempt to defend a city that had already been reduced, in large part, to a field of ruins would serve no strategic or tactical purpose. However, the local Nazi Party officials were determined to resist. As the Americans drew nearer, Schuster removed himself from duty, citing illness. The command of the troops was assumed by a Knight's Cross holder, Colonel Siggel, who agreed with the party officials that the city should be defended.

At 4:00 p.m. on 4 April, the Soest train depot came under a hail of artillery rounds fired from batteries in the area of Lippborg. The barrage continued into the night before abating in the early morning hours. The following day, formations of aircraft appeared over the city and loosed a number of bombs on its western sectors, and the artillery resumed in an effort to clear the piles of rubble of any erstwhile defenders who might have remained lurking within the ruins.

The artillery blasts continued throughout the night, striking the western sector that had escaped major destruction from previous bombing raids. The Münster Tower, the roofs of the St. Petri Cathedral, the St. Pauli Cathedral, and the Brunstein Chapel received direct hits. Numerous fires sprang up within the neighborhoods but were confined to certain city blocks.

By the following day, 6 April, the defenders had had enough. At 9:00 a.m., a white flag appeared on the Münster Tower as the German soldiers filed out of the city toward the town of Meiningsen. Still, the shelling continued intermittently throughout the morning and afternoon. As sunset approached at 6:30, the guns fell silent. A French captain from the POW compound was dispatched to the Americans, whose units had already reached the nearby village of Meckingsen. At 7:00, the first American tanks appeared, followed by the endless convoys. The American commander established a command post in the district administration building on Nöttenstrasse. The Oberbürgermeister was immediately advised that he was relieved of his duties.

Along the southern perimeter of the pocket, American units began tightening their hold on the Ruhr, slowly moving north and northwest and driving the scattered German units into dense concentrations of unorganized bands as they attempted to escape captivity. The American units began overrunning Sauerland villages filled with wounded German soldiers, who lay in cellars, hallways, and private homes. The entire area had been under constant air attacks for days, and the harried medical personnel were exhausted from lack of sleep and constant physical exertion. With the onset of the air raids, it was necessary to carry hundreds of badly wounded on stretchers into the cellars, where patients were packed together in close quarters.

The medical staff of the Augusta-Victoria facility was first aware that the torment was at an end on 9 April, when the front door to the hospital was hurled open. An American officer in battle dress wordlessly strode into the entrance hall, where he was quickly joined by a sergeant. Armed with a submachine gun and accompanied by the sergeant, the officer gazed about for several seconds before strolling the length of the halls in apparent good humor. His slightly staggering gait suggested that his mild disposition was the result of alcohol consumption. The two soldiers cursorily inspected the facility before entering the administration office. In expectation of the Americans' arrival, the medical officers had piled their sidearms on a large desk in the center of the office. The two soldiers each selected a pistol from the pile and stuck them in their web belts. The officer then handed his submachine gun to the sergeant and jokingly saluted the large, obligatory portrait of Adolf Hitler hanging on the wall. With that, the two GIs departed through the door.[33]

As the American soldiers made their way through the towns and villages of the Sauerland, they began encountering immense stores of goods previously evacuated from the heavily bombed Ruhr cities. The extensive contents of the Dortmund city museum were stored in the Grafschaft monastery and in the villas of the Fürstenberg estate. The entire inventory from the Essen Heimat Museum was packed in dozens of crates for safekeeping. Other rare items came from numerous private collections. Among the priceless artworks and antiquities were vast quantities of consumer goods and clothing. The entire inventories of businesses were transferred to various public facilities, and retail firms from Bochum, Essen, Iserlohn, and Cologne had transported shipments of textiles, shoes, jewelry, and clothing out of the heavily bombed regions. A major wholesale firm from Cologne secreted thousands of pounds of coffee, 43,000 bottles of cognac, and 40,000 bottles of wine throughout the area.

As the German authorities fled before the Americans, foreign workers and German inhabitants took advantage of lawless conditions to help themselves to whatever was available. No one knew what the future would bring: one had to be prepared for any eventuality. Warehouses were looted of valuable contents during the uncertain phase following the withdrawal of defenders and prior to the arrival of the conquerors. A German supply sergeant near Graftschaft opened his vast stores of coffee to the withdrawing Wehrmacht soldiers. Word quickly spread among locals, dozens of whom converged on the facility and helped themselves to the contents. To the horror of the civilians, the following day saw the unexpected appearance of the dreaded Wehrmacht Feldgendarmerie, the military police. The authorities immediately announced their presence by declaring that anyone found hoarding coffee would be prosecuted under a law that permitted the death penalty for plunderers. Some returned their spoils in exchange for amnesty. Others, sure that the threatening officials' presence was temporary, simply concealed the contraband. Two days later, the military police were taken into captivity by the advancing Americans.

Many of the Americans were remarkably disciplined and correct in their behavior. In the town of Nordenau, the inhabitants refrained from displaying white flags of surrender out of fear that the Americans would not arrive before German forces returned to occupy the area. The oncoming Americans first clashed with German defenders in the nearby village of Nesselbach before entering Nordenau. The following morning, a tall American went into the Gnacke Hotel and strode from room to room in search of hidden German soldiers. Cautiously pushing open each door to the hotel rooms with the muzzle of his submachine gun, the soldier remarked to the frightened inhabitants in broken German, "Guten Morgen ... Alles kaput, Deutschland kaput, Hitler kaput, guten Morgen." Other Americans spread quickly through the village, searching homes and businesses. The occupation of the village proceeded without incident, apart from the customary pocketing of watches, jewelry, and swastika-bedecked souvenirs. Within hours, the men of the American unit who had so correctly handled the occupation were followed by hordes of Russian and Polish laborers who celebrated their freedom by thoroughly sacking the wine cellars and liquor stores.[34]

As the Americans pressed beyond Nesselbach, German defenders began to concentrate in the area of Schmallenberg. Major Bauch, the German commander assigned to defend Schmallenberg, situated his command post in an imposing house at the Nordstrasse and Weststrasse intersection. Throughout 6 April, the town endured barrages of artillery fire that destroyed a number of houses as more defenders flowed into the town. Trenches were dug between homes and in gardens, machine guns were placed in upper-floor windows, and platoons of landsers shouldering Panzerfausts and MG-42s wound through the streets en route to their assigned locations. A number of tanks and self-propelled guns entered the town and established positions on the nearby terrain features and in front of the local school, in the Wiethofschen estate, and between numerous houses. Several tank crews carefully selected locations where they were afforded an open field of fire along the approaches of the Graftschaft road.

The increasing number of defenders was of particular concern to the senior medical officer, Dr. Maurer, who was a prewar inhabitant of Schmallenberg and commander of the medical facilities. The recent days had seen a larger influx of patients, notably wounded soldiers who had been evacuated from the ever-closing front. The doctor approached Major Bauch and implored him to withdraw his defenders and declare the town an open area. The major stubbornly replied that he had no authority to do so; only the supreme commander was authorized to take such an action.

Despite all arguments, the major could not be moved to withdraw the entrenched defenders. Maurer was left with no alternative but to attempt an evacuation of the wounded, most of whom were nonambulatory. With no transportation available, the medical staff succeeded in moving severely wounded patients from the exposed schoolhouse into less threatened buildings. During the mortar barrage that soon followed, the school burned to the ground and the surrounding buildings were extensively damaged.

On 9 April, the inhabitants of the village of Sallinghausen were surprised by the appearance of Panzer Lehr Division troops, who began establishing defenses. The very same unit had departed from the area a week earlier to participate in the failed breakout attempt. They were now accompanied by a horse-drawn artillery battery that had recently withdrawn from a base near Soest. The artillery unit erected two large-caliber mortars and an enormous howitzer, with which they opened fire toward the American lines. They moved onward after firing a total of eight rounds from the mortars. Predictably, American artillery projectiles began falling throughout the area shortly after their departure. The civilian populace took refuge in cellars or in the bunkers they had laboriously shoveled out of the earth and roofed with logs. Shivering in the unheated shelters, they anxiously waited for the shelling to cease.

The shelling resumed at dawn the next morning, accompanied by the ominous drone of an observation plane overhead. After lengthy discussions with the German troops, a number of residents began displaying white flags from their homes. Eventually, a German soldier agreed to act as an emissary, and he approached the American lines with a white flag of his own. He soon reappeared with instructions to return to the American positions with all German military personnel in the village. Bread bags were filled with provisions in preparation for the long, uncertain journey to the POW cages. As the soldiers prepared to march toward the American lines, one of the landsers remarked, "They won't take me prisoner. In Russia I was able to make it through situations like this, and I'll make it through this one." After buckling on his field equipment, he shouldered his weapon and disappeared into the nearby forest.[35]

Chapter 12

Total Collapse

As the heavy artillery pieces continued shelling towns and villages on the perimeters of the ever-shrinking pocket, the Nazi propaganda machinery was desperately attempting to harangue the inhabitants in hopes of inducing them to resist. A continuous radio broadcast announced:

> German men and women: In this most dangerous hour cowards and deserters are attempting to save their pathetic lives. Any person who assists such individuals without immediately notifying the proper authorities of their presence is guilty of assisting them in their criminal behavior. Keep your eyes open for the contemptible traitors, you will recognize them by their demeanor. Refuse these cowards and criminals any quarter. Do not offer them assistance, throw them from the trains, turn them over to the police or military authorities! They are betraying you, they are betraying millions of brave soldiers on the front, they are betraying your own fathers and sons, men and brothers and they betray your children. They are worthless, refuse them your assistance![1]

The town of Hamm was the site of an important industrial rail junction and thus had suffered extensive damage from bombing raids throughout the war. The approaches to Hamm were first reached by American forces on 31 March, after strategic points in the vicinity were shelled. At 9:00 p.m., a barrage began falling on the city center, and during the night, American tanks rumbled through the town's northern approaches. At 2:00 a.m. on 1 April, retreating Wehrmacht troops demolished the Hamm bridges over the Lippe River.

The Nazi officials in Hamm had attempted to organize a defense prior to the arrival of the American forces. Roadblocks were hastily erected, and remnants of a Wehrmacht unit retreating from the western areas of the Münsterland were instructed to prepare defenses. The locals were ordered to store food and to take up residence in their bunkers and reinforced cellars.

As the American armored columns closed on the town, all women and children were ordered to evacuate the city. However, few inhabitants obeyed, preferring to remain in their homes to await the fate of the town. The residents who chose not to abandon their homes for outlying areas soon found themselves in the midst of vicious fighting that lasted more than a week and further devastated the besieged city.

Bürgermeister Deter of Hamm argued desperately against the plan to defend his city. His attempts to persuade the forces to abandon their defenses and declare Hamm an open city resulted in an order from the Gauleiter that he be arrested and taken to Harkortberg, where he was to stand trial and face execution for his defeatism. However, the district Reich defense commissar argued that Deter should be assigned to a combat unit, where he could demonstrate his loyalty to Germany and the party.[2]

On 1 April, the XXXVII Panzer Corps received the order to attack out of the Werne-Hamm area in a northern direction toward Münster. The corps was also directed to initiate a cautious withdrawal behind the Dortmund-Ems Canal. The elements of the 116th "Windhund" Panzer Division that were still mobile were ordered to concentrate to the south of Hamm during the night of 1–2 April. However, with the unexpected approach of American armored columns, the 116th was forced to move toward the north and northwest in the direction of Soest. The 1st Company of Panzer Pionier Battalion 675 was ordered to Nateln, between Soest and Hamm, with instructions to destroy all autobahn bridges between Hamm and Wiedenbrück. The company failed to complete the destruction of the bridges before being quickly ordered to Hamm's eastern approaches, where it was combined with other units of the 116th Panzer Division to create a defense of the city.

Throughout the night of 1 April, the Americans pushed cautiously forward from the northern approaches to the rail station, while the southern sectors of the town continued to receive heavy artillery fire. The inhabitants remained huddled in their bunkers as tons of high-explosive shells rained on the city. As the Americans penetrated the heavily populated quarters, they encountered resistance, and both sides, including troops from various Waffen SS units, suffered dead and wounded.

At the height of the engagement, a prominent local citizen was successful in dissuading an SS major from erecting a command post in the Feidik Bunker, as the structure was rapidly filling with the dead, wounded, and dying. The thorough destruction of the town's bridges had almost eliminated the possibility of moving freely throughout the rubble-filled area, with the exception of the large rail bridge. With the rail bridge damaged but still intact, the Americans were able to penetrate deep into the marshaling yards and the industrial sector of the city. From this strategic location, the attackers were able to drive deeper into the city center.

The Americans occupied the rail bridge in Hamm, which greatly hindered German attempts to push the determined GIs from the town. In time, a plan was formulated to detonate several trucks laden with explosives under the massive, eleven-track bridge, after which an assault force of two battalions would push forward and seize the strategic area from the Americans.

While the German defenders were planning to recapture the immense railway marshaling yard, the battle-weary troops from the U.S. 83rd Infantry Division holding the rail junction were relieved by fresh units from the 95th Infantry Division. The Americans were expecting a counterattack and were determined to hold their ground. The GIs established defensive positions among the ruins of the rail facilities, and reconnaissance patrols noted an ominous concentration of German forces that coincided with an unusual increase in German artillery fire on the American bridgehead.

The landsers, under an umbrella of artillery fire, pushed from the eastern sector of the town with several heavy trucks loaded with explosives. Accompanying the vehicles were several half-tracked, armored transports packed with infantry. A German tank supporting the mission fired from the east into American positions. One of the operation's main objectives was to sever a long, concrete underpass beneath the rail lines that served as an access and egress route to the railhead for the American forces. The tunnel was defended by a platoon of GIs from E Company of the 378th Infantry Regiment.

The three Wehrmacht trucks were loaded with almost 9 tons of high-explosive Donarit. They were supported by a platoon of combat engineers led by Lieutenant Fütterer. The plan called for the three trucks to approach the bridge just before sunrise and halt beneath the rail facility. The time fuses would then be ignited, and the vehicle drivers and support personnel would make their way through the rubble of the destroyed town until they reached the safety of their own positions.

The operation began at 5:30 a.m., following a heavy barrage from artillery batteries and mortar positions. The trucks traversed the battle-torn area and approached within 20 feet of the bridge before being stopped by a massive bomb crater. The lead truck, led by Lieutenant Fütterer, struck a mine, completely blocking the roadway. The second vehicle attempted to bypass the disabled truck but quickly became immobilized by the tons of rubble that created impenetrable obstacles. The crew abandoned the truck under heavy small-arms fire while the tank assigned to escort the team opened fire on the deserted vehicles. The city center shuddered as an earsplitting explosion reverberated for miles when the tons of Donarit were detonated.

As the smoke and dust slowly settled, the silhouette of the bridge was still visible against the sunrise. The German assault team retreated through the ruins, with several of the landsers bleeding profusely from their ears, their eardrums ruptured by the enormous blast. One of the armored half-tracks accompanying the party was disabled by a projectile fired from a carefully camouflaged American tank. The crew immediately scrambled from the burning vehicle with superficial wounds. The lieutenant was the only member of the team unaccounted for. A German NCO, together with a Wehrmacht medic, set out through the field of ruins to locate the missing lieutenant, but no trace of the officer was ever found.

The approach of the Germans had been detected by American outposts when they were approximately 100 yards away from the bridge. When the GIs opened fire from the tunnel and from foxholes adjacent to the structure, the German tank opened fire on the tunnel position, wounding most of the soldiers. However, the Germans were held back by fierce small-arms fire when the lead truck struck the mine that had been laid to secure the American defenses in the tunnel. The Americans had targeted the vehicle just as it struck the mine, and the troops scrambled for cover as the vehicle exploded with a massive roar. After the Germans were forced to retreat under heavy small-arms fire, the Americans began evacuating their twenty-two casualties.

After the Germans' failed attempt to destroy the bridgehead, American reinforcements began streaming over the Lippe River, forcing the Germans to abandon plans for capturing the rail facility. By daylight of the following morning, the XXXXVII Panzer Corps issued the order to abandon the attack.

Despite the loss of the Hamm railhead, the vicious fighting for the remainder of the city continued. For six days, the inhabitants crouched in their bunkers and cellars as mortar and artillery shells showered the ruins. In the western sector of the city, some 6,000 haggard civilians cowered in a massive bunker, awaiting an end to the torment. As the fierce engagement continued, food and water supplies were soon expended. Despite the adverse conditions in the bunker, the refugees could not leave the concrete shelter without risking death or injury.

At length, several teams of men eased their way from the bunker during hours of darkness and searched the rubble for food, which they transported back to the masses waiting underground. They explored collapsed homes, cellars, and shops for dwindling rations, which were ravenously consumed as soon as they were delivered to the bunker. On the Wednesday following Easter Sunday, a battered truck carefully navigated through the rubble with a team of men who had decided that food would have to be found elsewhere; all immediate resources had been exhausted.

They dodged shell-bursts and the sharp, deadly impacts of mortar rounds as they made their way through rubble-strewn streets toward the nearby village of Herringen, an area still free of fighting. Their main concern was not only to make it through the barrage to safety but also to reach Herringen, collect supplies, and then navigate the gauntlet of fire and return to the bunker.

The truck's fuel gauge remained on empty, and using the last drops of gasoline, they made their way to the supply area of a mining administration facility. The officials there initially refused to assist the anxious men. As dialogue degenerated to threats, they were finally provided a 5-gallon canister of fuel. After refueling the truck, they continued on their mission to Herringen. There, they drove from bakery to bakery, loading cartons of bread onto the truck before returning to the bunker, where they delivered 2,000 loaves to the famished refugees.

The American forces holding strategic positions in the Hamm marshaling yard soon counterattacked. B Company of the 378th Infantry Regiment became engaged in heavy fighting while breaking out of the bridgehead and soon lost five men killed and numerous wounded in the rubble. The German resistance collapsed after the GIs progressed some 300 yards beyond the railhead. Simultaneously, C Company launched an attack to the left. After silencing a heavy German machine-gun position, the company fought their way through the buildings until they reached a favorable artillery observation point, where they directed deadly fire onto the German defenses. All resistance soon ceased as the companies continued to advance. Within hours, the GIs had captured more than 200 prisoners, with C Company having two men killed and four wounded in the engagement.

By midday, the attack ground to a halt. Patrols were dispatched to collect German stragglers. The rail junction was firmly in American hands, and the 378th Infantry Regiment had captured nearly 1,000 railcars filled with rations, supplies, and ammunition. However, the western sector of the town continued to offer resistance throughout the morning. In the early afternoon, a German police officer volunteered to go through the lines to attempt to convince the remaining Wehrmacht forces to surrender. He slowly but resolutely picked his way through the rubble, occasionally coming under isolated sniper fire, until he reached the headquarters of an SS lieutenant-colonel. The SS officer stubbornly refused to discuss a surrender, declaring that the American forces were not sufficiently strong for him to justify an honorable capitulation. The officer eventually disappeared into the ruined city.[3]

While the battle for Hamm was raging, other American units were heading southwest to sever any escape routes out of the city for German forces. During the night of 3 April, the 331st Infantry Regiment pushed over the Lippe River near the town of Dolberg without meeting resistance. As they crossed the Lippe, the forces dispersed into the wooded area northeast of Hamm and prepared to capture the rail bridge over the Lippe Canal, near the village of Haaren.

The village was taken without incident, but the American forces met strong resistance as they approached the bridge. After being forced to withdraw from the Haaren rail trestle, reconnaissance patrols quickly discovered that all bridges spanning the canal were heavily defended by Wehrmacht infantry armed with automatic weapons and Panzerfausts. After several attempts to capture the Haaren Bridge, which was defended by approximately seventy-five landsers, artillery fire was ordered onto the positions. Under the protection of heavy-caliber shell-bursts, a platoon rushed the bridge, and the German defenders quickly began surrendering. Two Americans were killed during the engagement. To the east of the rail trestle was a road bridge, which was taken after a brief defense with small arms. As the firing died, one German officer and sixty-eight other defenders were taken prisoner.[4]

The Americans strengthened their hold on Hamm throughout 5 April. The patrols combing the battle-scarred streets encountered little opposition; occasionally, they were compelled to suppress erratic and isolated small-arms fire as forlorn stragglers continued to emerge from the ruins with their hands held high in surrender. The bulk of the remaining troops assigned to the 116th Panzer Division had withdrawn after the failed attempt to destroy the rail bridge. American artillery units began laying fire on the area south of Hamm, and in the nearby town of Rhynern, inhabitants huddled in their cellars and makeshift bunkers to await the inevitable.

During the night of 6–7 April, artillery fire was directed on Rhynern, several miles south of Hamm. At 4:00 in the morning of 7 April, the Americans moved toward the village of Osttünnen, situated 2 miles northeast of Rhynern. Near Osttünnen, they surprised a force of twenty exhausted Germans sleeping in huts on the edge of a large field and seized an 88-mm flak battery and a number of 20-mm antiaircraft guns. The Americans then pressed on toward Rhynern without resistance until they met a group of approximately twenty-five Hitler Youth who were determined to stop the American advance. During the ensuing engagement, ten of the teenagers were killed and eight were taken prisoner. The others fled in the direction of Rhynern.

Nineteen-year-old Ilse Schulze-Velmede huddled in the cellar of her family's farmhouse on the southern outskirts of Rhynern as the sounds of battle grew nearer. She listened apprehensively to the rattle of distant gunfire throughout 4 and 5 April, and the heavy-caliber artillery shells began creeping toward the farmstead and were soon exploding in the nearby fields and gardens.

Ilse's father, a battle-tested veteran who had survived the monumental barrages at Verdun during World War I, commented on the distance of each impact as the explosions echoed across the farmland and inched ever nearer. The family had buried a large canister of provisions in the nearby garden. Hunting rifles and shotguns had been concealed under the rafters of a storage building, and silver, porcelain, and other valuables had been buried or carefully hidden in anticipation of the enemy's arrival. Suddenly, an immense shell impacted some 50 yards behind the home, shattering windows and sending clouds of dust raining from the rafters of the cellar. The shell impacted directly on the buried canister of preserved food, sending it flying several hundred yards into a nearby orchard, where remnants of smoked ham and sausages were scattered among the pink-and-white apple blossoms.

The family remained in the cellar throughout 6 April, occasionally stealing a glance out the ground-level window as isolated gunfire, accentuated by extended bursts of automatic-weapons fire, swept over the farm and nearby town. The next morning, the rattle and explosions of close-quarters battle grew more intense. At length, the huddled family discerned the growl of engines and grinding tracks of armored vehicles. Faint voices, speaking barely discernable words in English, drifted through the adjacent fields and orchards. In the late afternoon, as silence descended on the tiny group of civilians huddled beneath the home, the family was alerted by a sudden, heavy pounding on the front door. Ilse's father limped up the stairs and cautiously opened the door, and for several seconds, rough voices could be heard by those anxiously waiting in the cellar. The door to the cellar suddenly burst open, and strangers in olive-colored uniforms shouted unintelligible commands. It was clear that they were being ordered to leave the safety of their cellar. The group of seven women and children were directed into the farmyard, where they joined Ilse's father, their hands held high.

The heavily armed strangers in round helmets proceeded to search the home. An American soldier raced into the farmyard and began shouting in Polish. The soldier then leaped on Ilse's father with punches, kicks, and verbal outbursts. A Polish laborer who had joined the group in the farmyard rushed forward, desperately shouting and gesturing until the punches ceased. The two exchanged comments in Polish as the laborer explained to the soldier that the workers at this farm had been treated well.

More soldiers began arriving, and numerous vehicles roared into the brick-paved farmyard. Imposing vehicles of every description, with white stars and numbers stenciled on green bodies of the trucks and tracked vehicles, were parked haphazardly throughout the area. With more shouts, the family was ordered inside the farmhouse, where they were met by a shocking scene of random destruction. Armoires were overturned, and feather comforters had been pierced with bayonets in the search for hidden weapons and valuables. The contents of shelves, chests, and armoires were strewn throughout the house. Ilse, the only member of the family with a rudimentary knowledge of English, was directed to interpret for the Americans, and she relayed to her family instructions to remain inside the house until further notice.

A burly American sergeant asked if there were any Wehrmacht soldiers hidden on or near the premises and if there were any weapons on the property. Shortly thereafter, the Americans discovered the hidden shotguns and hunting rifles, which they angrily smashed against nearby fruit trees. In response to their questions, Ilse explained that the weapons had been taken from the house many weeks ago and that she had assumed they were disposed of or destroyed. Apparently satisfied with this explanation, the sergeant disappeared into the milling mass of GIs.

One of Ilse's primary concerns was the brood of newly hatched chicks she had been nurturing in a small brooder near the barn. The nights and mornings were still bringing frost, and she knew that unless she was permitted to tend to the small, wood-burning incubator, the chicks would perish.

On the morning of 8 April, the family was permitted to leave the residence for one hour to care for the livestock and to conduct necessary business. Ilse immediately rushed to the brooder to find the chicks huddled in a small, yellow mass but still alive. Hastily gathering a handful of twigs, she fueled the heater and provided them with a small amount of feed and water. Ilse then left the farmyard and headed to the nearby store in hopes of obtaining milk.

The disappointed teenager soon returned empty-handed, for the store had already been looted of all provisions. Her route took her past the nearby cemetery, where the girl observed several elderly men unloading a number of dead soldiers from a horse-cart. Now fully in control of the village and the surrounding area, the Americans had instructed the inhabitants to gather the German dead for disposal. The men had collected the bodies where they had fallen during the previous engagement: the dismal remains lay scattered among the buildings, in the streets, on the roadsides, and in farm orchards. Ilse observed the corpses, wrapped in gray Wehrmacht blankets, lying in a long row beneath the trees lining the cemetery. She was able to discern the gleaming hobnailed boots of several corpses that extended from the sodden gray shrouds. Other wrapped bodies displayed glimpses of tousled hair; an occasional limb extended cold and lifeless from beneath the blankets. The old men strained under the weight of the fallen soldiers as they pulled them from the wooden cart and placed them on the wet earth. The gray blankets, soaked from a light rain and bearing large red-brown patches of blood, clung to the corpses like sodden shrouds, presenting macabre ranks of blood-and-rain-soaked cocoons as they awaited burial. Averting her eyes from the gruesome scene, Ilse hurried onward, preferring the now-dismal sanctuary of her home to the foreboding atmosphere of defeat.[5]

While the American units were moving into Morsbach, the 4th Battery of the 388th Volks-Artillery Corps was in the process of dissolution. The unit had been created in October 1944 in the ancient military district of Güstrow-Mecklenburg. The 4th Battery was equipped with nine 88-mm antitank guns and first saw action in the area of Aachen under the command of Lieutenant Siegberg Fiola. Following the Ardennes Offensive debacle, during which the battery was engaged in the area of St. Vith, the unit joined other decimated Wehrmacht units in retreat to the Rhineland. Eventually, it withdrew over the Rhine and was positioned near Altenkirchen, northeast of Remagen.

During the breakout of the Remagen bridgehead by American forces on 25 March, the unit was ordered to engage the Americans near the towns of Bruchertseifen and Breitscheid. There, it became decimated, losing the officer in charge as well as seven NCOs, numerous gunners, and the entire inventory of 88-mm guns to the American tanks and aircraft. The remnants of the force—four NCOs, twenty-seven crewmen, three trucks, a field kitchen, a radio van, and a maintenance vehicle—withdrew to Au on the Sieg River. Sergeant Wimmer, one of the surviving NCOs, was instructed by radio to transport the battery to the area of Morsbach to await further orders. The gun crews took quarters in the village of Bitze, near Morsbach, where they established communications with the headquarters, which was located in Böcklingen-Lichtenberg.

On 3 April, a Wehrmacht engineering unit prepared to destroy the large railway bridge near Heide as well as remnants of a V-2 rocket train that had been transported to the area from Volperhausen. Wimmer attempted to persuade the sergeant in charge of the engineering squad not to destroy the bridge, However, his endeavors met only stubborn refusal. The engineer explained that his orders were clear; there was also the danger that refusing to carry out the orders would result in his arrest by the police unit in Morsbach.

The following day, Wednesday, 4 April, a courier arrived from Böcklingen-Lichtenberg with instructions for the 4th Battery to remain at its location and to integrate with any infantry unit and engage in defending the village. Three days later, the air was rent by a massive explosion as the Morsbach-Heide railway bridge was demolished, after which the engineering unit withdrew. Wimmer discussed the general situation with the other NCOs of the battery, and they reached a consensus as to what action should be taken next.

At 2:00 p.m., the battery personnel were assembled, and the senior NCO briefed the ranks of landsers on the decision they had reached. In view of the overwhelming Allied forces they were now facing, any further resistance was deemed senseless. The battery would be disbanded. Those who desired to do so could attempt to make their way through the American lines to reach their homes; discharge papers could be obtained from the administration NCO. Wimmer advised the others that he planned to stay in place and simply await the arrival of the Americans. The battery provisions were distributed to the soldiers and local civilians. The soldiers who chose not to retreat were advised to remain within homes.

That afternoon, the residents and battery crews watched from behind shuttered windows as a solitary platoon of German infantrymen, heavily laden with combat equipment, filed through the village and disappeared toward the north. The fugitives knew that they had just observed the retreating rear guard. The settlement of Bitze was now a no-man's-land.

The night passed without incident. At dawn, Wimmer donned his field uniform, concealed his pistol, and settled in to await the Americans. At 9:00 a.m., he observed a file of infantrymen, wearing khaki and olive green in place of the familiar Wehrmacht field gray, winding slowly along both sides of the Rhein-Bitze road toward the village. The column of soldiers carried rifles at the ready and were spaced at a combat interval. They passed the residence where he waited without halting and were soon followed by a number of vehicles bearing more soldiers. Within several minutes, the village was occupied by American troops in company strength, and squads of soldiers set about searching the homes.

Wimmer moved from his observation place at the window and seated himself on the sofa, resigned to his fate. At length, a heavy crash resounded from the front door of the residence. a large, black soldier entered the living room and, surveying the contents of the home, was startled by the silent image in field gray sitting before him. After recovering from his initial surprise at the uniformed figure on the sofa, the GI commanded him to raise his hands. Wimmer obediently placed his hands above his head and rose to his feet. The soldier, now joined by more GIs, nervously searched his uniform pockets, discarding any items they found. The American then demanded that Wimmer surrender his watch. The Wehrmacht sergeant resisted, for which he received a sharp blow in the ribs from the soldier's rifle. The watch was stripped from his wrist, and Wimmer was then driven outside, where he joined the other men of the battery. The group of prisoners were marched to the nearby village of Rhein, where they spent the night enclosed in a chicken coop and awaited transportation to the massive prison compounds on the Rhine.[6]

The village of Wiehl came under heavy artillery fire on the evening of 10 April, in which the neighborhood of the church and the rail station suffered much damage. The town hall and the village school were damaged, as were numerous homes and shops. Inhabitants tried to extinguish the flames, but the artillery shells that continued to fall hindered all firefighting efforts.

The local Volkssturm members abandoned their weapons in the cellar of the town hall and disappeared. Hugo Weber and several others discovered the rifles strewn about the building prior to the arrival of the first American reconnaissance patrols. The men hauled the weapons, along with incriminating Nazi paraphernalia (including an imposing Hitler bust), to the nearby cemetery, where the items were quickly buried.

At midday on 11 April, the first Sherman tanks drove over the Wiehl Bridge near the Hans and Company factory; within two hours, the town was firmly in the hands of the Americans. The point elements were quickly followed by columns of trucks, jeeps, and half-tracks carrying dozens of soldiers. During their search of the village, the GIs discovered large quantities of provisions and liquor that had been stored beyond the reach of the Allied bombers by wholesale firms, and within a short time, the streets were teeming with drunken soldiers.

Weber and his compatriots remained concerned about the buried weapons, and their anxiety increased when it was revealed that they had been observed by a Polish laborer while they concealed the contraband. Other inhabitants were also aware that the weapons were buried nearby and could at any moment reveal the location of the cache to gain favor with the occupiers. The apprehensive men eventually returned to the cemetery and disinterred the weapons, which they loaded onto a wagon and delivered to the American command post.[7]

At Model's Army Group B headquarters in the village of Schalksmühle near Lüdenscheid, the field marshal's operations officer, Colonel Günther Reichhelm, was surprised to receive an immediate priority message from the high command. The unexpected message, from the Führerhauptquartier in Berlin, read: "General Staff Colonel Reichhelm is required for an assignment that will determine the destiny of Army Group B. His transfer is to take effect immediately." The terse message was signed "Adolf Hitler."

Reichhelm advised Model of his new orders and showed him the unusual message. He also advised the field marshal that he had no intentions of flying to Berlin or anywhere else. He was determined to remain with the army group to the end.

Model did not react at once. In the course of their discussion, during which Reichhelm refused to accept the orders to Berlin, Model sarcastically but half-jokingly asked the colonel if he was afraid to risk flying out of the pocket. Reichhelm understood that Model was giving him no alternative. He departed to make arrangements for his transfer.

An hour later, he returned to advise Model that he had arranged for a flight out of the pocket in a twin-seated Klemm, a small, single-engine observation plane. The field marshal immediately interjected that to use that type of aircraft was far too dangerous. The slow, low-flying plane would present an excellent and irresistible target for the marauding fighter-bombers. Additionally, the Americans were known for establishing antiaircraft batteries at all tactically important terrain features, and thus, the plane could easily fall victim to ground fire. Model advised the colonel that he would arrange other transportation.

The field marshal remained alone in his quarters for the next two hours, composing a lengthy letter to his wife for Reichhelm to take out of the pocket with him. As Reichhelm appeared to receive his final instructions, Model, in his typical fashion, advised the colonel that he was to be in proper uniform for his departure. Reichhelm was wearing the official duty uniform, albeit without the prescribed pistol, and he returned to his quarters to retrieve his sidearm. When he returned, Model then requested that Reichhelm join him for dinner before his departure. In the staff guest book at the officers' mess, the field marshal carefully wrote *"Der beste K.I.K. wird K.A.K.* (The best *Kamerad* inside the pocket will be the *Kamerad* outside the pocket)." He then told Reichhelm that he had arranged for his transport in a Junkers JU-52. Several days earlier, fifty of the transport planes had been assigned to deliver essential tools to a facility within the pocket for the ongoing munitions production. Seventeen of them had survived the gauntlet of Allied fighter-bomber and antiaircraft fire, and these aircraft would be departing to return to their base as soon as darkness fell.

Following the meal, Model accompanied Reichhelm to the vehicle that was waiting to carry him to the airfield. He then passed the colonel an envelope. "This is for my wife," he said. "Try to see that it is delivered to her." Reichhelm accepted the letter with a nod, saluted, and wordlessly turned on his heel and climbed into the vehicle.

The aircraft left the Ruhr pocket during the middle of a cloudy night, protected from the relentless fighter-bombers by a shroud of darkness. The primary destination was the airfield at Staaken. However, as the crew made their approach, they found the airfield was being pounded by a bombing raid. The pilots of the transport aircraft banked and flew back to the field at Jüterbog, where they landed at the height of another bombing raid. As the aircraft rolled to a halt amid massive impacts from a torrent of heavy bombs, Reichhelm sprang from the plane and leaped into a bomb crater, where he stayed until the air grew silent. The colonel then made his way to the administration buildings of a nearby artillery school, where officers provided him with a vehicle and driver for the 35-mile journey to Zossen, south of Berlin.

In Zossen, he was met by Colonel-General Alfred Jodl, to whom he gave a short but descriptive briefing on the situation at Army Group B. Jodl then told him to get some sleep, for he would be going to Berlin that afternoon and he needed to be rested for the briefing in the Führerbunker. Reichhelm sought out a cot in a nearby duty room and quickly fell into a deep sleep.

That afternoon, he was awakened by General Walther Wenck, the old acquaintance who had requested that Reichhelm be assigned as chief of staff for the newly established Twelfth Army. Wenck had personally requested Reichhelm for several reasons. They had known one another many years, and Wenck was aware of the colonel's competence and trusted him fully. In searching for the most capable staff officers for the Twelfth Army, Wenck had used his influence with the chief of the Army General Staff, General Hans Krebs, to order Reichhelm's transfer from the Ruhr Pocket. Also of importance to the Twelfth Army's mission, Reichhelm, as Army Group B's operations officer, knew the situation in the pocket better than any other soldier, and the Twelfth Army was assigned to break through the cordon to Model's army group.

After a short discussion, Wenck advised his new chief staff officer that he had to depart, but he instructed Reichhelm to meet him later in Bad Kösen, where the Twelfth Army staff was assembling. Wenck had already made the necessary arrangements for administrative support through the district commander in Magdeburg. During the conversation, Reichhelm was struck by his old friend's appearance. The once-jovial officer, who had been nicknamed *Sonnenvögel* ("Sunbird") by his friends, appeared haggard and solemn. In addition to the burdens of his new assignment, Wenck had not wholly recovered from a vehicle accident that had occurred several weeks earlier while he was en route to Army Group North on the Eastern Front.

At 5:00 that afternoon, Reichhelm was met by Colonel Kleiser of the OKW staff, and together with a driver, they proceeded along the dismal route to Berlin. Their journey was uneventful. The spring air was unusually quiet and was uninterrupted by the fighter-bombers that routinely harassed any moving vehicles. In Berlin, Reichhelm found a city paralyzed and racked with destruction. They were compelled to navigate through entire city blocks of buildings reduced to rubble by the heavy bombing raids; the streets remained choked with rubble, and the omnipresent stench of decay filled the air.

The small party eventually arrived at the Reich Chancellery on the Bendlerstrasse, where they were immediately escorted into the cavernous Führerbunker. They descended into the cavern, where Reichhelm was struck by the stale air and the glare of artificial lighting that bathed the somber surroundings in a pallid hue. In the corridors, he recognized a number of old acquaintances whom he had not seen in many years as they hurried about their duties.

The officers were provided with a simple meal of sandwiches before Grand Admiral Karl Dönitz made his appearance. Reichhelm was not personally acquainted with the admiral and was greeted with characteristic formality. He was then warmly embraced by General Krebs, with whom he had served on the Ninth Army staff in Russia and, more recently, in Army Group B under Model. General Krebs was wearing an eye patch due to an injury received during an air raid on the Wehrmacht headquarters in Zossen.

Colonel Reichhelm was struck by the stark contrast of environments that he was witnessing. Outside the bunker, the city was in ruins, and all life appeared to be at an end. Within the cold confines of concrete walls, however, the General Staff officers were meticulously appointed in rich crimson and gold-trimmed uniforms. Numerous Wehrmacht generals, bedecked with gleaming decorations, crowded the narrow chambers, their appearance contrasting with the occasional civilian officials in business suits. Orderlies and adjutants and SS officers with polished boots and spotless uniforms hurriedly paced the corridors with documents and briefcases, greeting the staff officers with formality.

The group of officers gathered before a large map table in a cavernous briefing room. Slumped listlessly in a massive chair on the opposite side of the table was Reichsmarschall Hermann Göring. The table, which was approximately 8 feet wide by 12 feet in length, was covered with an impressive layer of maps. The colonel was immediately taken by the fact that the size of the German Reich had been reduced to an area that could be examined on a series of 1:25,000-scale maps, a scale normally used by company-level officers on the front.

Adolf Hitler shuffled into the briefing room shortly after Reichhelm's arrival. The colonel was shocked by his appearance. His entire body trembled, and he shuffled as he walked, with his body bent and stooped. Reichhelm had seen Hitler on other occasions, most recently at Berchtesgaden during the briefings for the 1944 summer offensive and while planning the Ardennes Offensive. He had earlier observed him numerous times at the Wolfschanze ("Wolf's Lair") in Rastenburg—Hitler's headquarters in East Prussia where briefings had been conducted throughout the course of the Russian campaign. Now the Führer appeared to be the broken shell of a once-captivating leader and energetic orator. In many ways, his changed appearance was representative of Germany's transition.

Hitler shuffled his way through the throng of officers and selected his seat at the table. To the left of Hitler stood Field Marshal Wilhelm Keitel, to his right was Jodl. Behind Jodl stood Dönitz, Albert Speer, Wilhelm Burgdorf, and others. Jodl opened the briefing with a general situation report. The Eleventh Army was mired in the Harz Mountain region, he said, east of the Ruhr Pocket. The Twelfth Army was being assembled under the command of General Wenck in the sector north of the Eleventh Army. Reichhelm was then requested by Jodl to brief the Führer on the situation with Army Group B.

Reichhelm explained that although Model bore the responsibility for defending the Ruhr, he possessed no more strength with which to carry out his duties. There no longer existed a means of preventing the Allies from capturing the entire Ruhr should they launch a determined attack with the intent of doing so. After a short description of the army group's condition, concentrating primarily on the lack of essential military supplies and the fact that all food resources were becoming exhausted, the room filled with silence. After a pause, Reichhelm continued. He explained that the soldiers were "sitting on the piles of coal" in the

Ruhr and that the civilians were pleading with them to throw away their arms and uniforms, don civilian clothing, and anonymously disappear from sight. He added that the army group's ammunition was depleted, that there existed no ammunition reserves for either rifles or machine guns, that vehicles and tanks were immobilized for lack of fuel, and that even if they had fuel they would be of little use because the tanks lacked ammunition. He continued to emphasize that the means of supply had disintegrated and that many units simply disappeared when overrun by the American armored columns. He brought his description to a close by noting that, in his opinion, the army group was finished.

Hitler remained stiffly seated at the table, staring ahead and seeming not to acknowledge Reichhelm's words. His body trembled, and he grasped the edge of the table tightly with both hands. Silence filled the room with foreboding, and no one dared to glance at one another, in apprehension of how the news would be met. After a long pause, during which Hitler appeared to remain transfixed on the table before him, the Führer finally broke the silence as he uttered a single sentence, "Model was my best field marshal."

Again, a long silence descended on the chamber. Then suddenly, Hitler looked up from the table and stated emphatically, "Army Group B can be relieved!" He abruptly seemed to have found new strength, adding with excitement, "I have assembled the Twelfth Army for this purpose, and it will be led by one of my best generals. General Wenck is experienced in guiding his troops through the most adverse conditions. I have total faith in his ability to lead the young soldiers, who are still fresh and who are being led by experienced officers and non-commissioned officers." Hitler almost rose from his seat as he declared, "The Eleventh Army will be joined by the Twelfth, together they will be able to strike the Allies between the American and British sectors, where they are the weakest."[8]

Reichhelm was shocked by Hitler's failure to grasp the meaning of what he had just explained. He realized that he was listening to illogical statements born solely from desperation, but nonetheless found it difficult to believe what he was hearing as Hitler continued with a rising voice: "The Eleventh Army will have to be transferred over the Elbe and the Mülde into the Harz to meet up with the Twelfth."[9]

Hitler's diatribe was soon interrupted by Jodl, who cleared his throat and calmly said, "That won't be possible, mein Führer." Hitler shifted his gaze and looked at Jodl expectantly. The general elaborated, "The Eleventh Army is already too weak, and they cannot fight against tanks in the Harz." Hitler's gaze hardened, and he glared frostily at Jodl for several seconds. Then he blurted out that he was familiar with the Hartz from the early days of the Reich party rallies, that he knew it was thickly wooded, and that the troops could easily stop the tanks simply by felling trees across the narrow, winding trails. Hitler's voice rose, and his words came faster as he asserted that the soldiers could just mine the roads, thus rendering the Harz impenetrable to mechanized units.[10]

Jodl spoke again, more emphatic in his attempt to explain the hopelessness of such an attempt. Hitler responded with ever-sharpening vigor, and the confrontation continued for several minutes. At length, Jodl rebutted Hitler's diatribe with the comment, "Mein Führer, perhaps you know the Harz, but I know the situation." As Jodl and Hitler continued, Reichhelm happened to glance across the table, where Reichsmarschall Göring, the highest-ranking military officer in Germany, was seated. At some point during the heated exchange, Göring had placed his head on the table and pulled a large map over it. His massive bulk, clothed in an elegant, soft gray uniform with imposing marshal batons mounted on heavy, gold-brocade shoulder boards, remained slumped in his seat; he sat motionless and apparently oblivious to the confrontation. Reichhelm was unsure of whether the Reichsmarschall, possibly under the influence of sedatives, had fallen asleep or was simply unable to accept the bizarre situation; perhaps he was illogically attempting to block out the ongoing, catastrophic predicament by concealing his head beneath a map.[11]

Jodl continued to defend Reichhelm's position, and it was not necessary for the colonel to attempt to explain why the army group was finished. Jodl explained to the disbelieving Hitler that even the Eleventh Army, currently situated southeast of the pocket in the area of Kassel, was not in a position to move. Even if it was possible to set the troops in motion and even if the Allied aircraft did not pounce on every moving vehicle, constantly disrupt rail lines, and render the acquisition of every gallon of fuel almost impossible, the Eleventh Army would still lack the strength to break through the Americans' armored blockade to free the army group. To do so would require a thrust through the Sauerland as far west as Soest, some 50 miles from the Elbe. There were simply no means for the army to advance on such a wide front, especially with inexperienced troops who lacked the resources to carry out such an undertaking.

Hitler continued to counter Jodl's arguments. He added that the German forces would have to use the tactics of the Russians and become more flexible in their improvisation, just as the Russians had defended Moscow. The German forces would have to infiltrate through the ring the Allies had forged around the Ruhr. In small groups, he asserted, they could make their way through the rough terrain of the Sauerland until they had assembled enough forces to break the line and free the trapped army group. He triumphantly announced that, for the purpose of transporting the forces, he was providing Wenck's army with 200 Volkswagens that were available from the training command in Döberitz.

Reichhelm continued to listen to the exchange with disbelief and astonishment. He was shocked that Hitler now expected the battered armies, equipped with Volkswagens, to defeat endless columns of Sherman tanks and thousands of healthy, fresh troops. Even if fuel was available, each of the tiny vehicles Hitler spoke of were only adequate for transporting three or four lightly equipped soldiers each across favorable terrain.

At length, Reichhelm was able to exchange words with several members of the staff. He advised them that he was expected to report to Wenck as soon as possible but that he first had to retrieve his 200 Volkswagens. Relieved that the surreal experience was at an end, the colonel left the bunker, met the driver assigned to him, and departed from Berlin. As he made his way out of the bunker, he glanced at his watch and realized that the ordeal that had seemed to last for an eternity had actually taken only one and a half hours.

In the southwest area of the shrinking Ruhr Pocket, American units reached the village of Spurkenbach at midday on 6 April. The file of GIs was observed through binoculars by Herr Dehler, a local resident who initially spotted the foreign soldiers as they approached along a wood-line adjacent to the Euelscheide field. Dehler watched as three squads of infantrymen, with some twenty men each, filtered cautiously into the southern edge of Spurkenbach before disappearing behind distant residences.

As the American patrol was entering the village, a Wehrmacht communications vehicle pulled up at the Wilma residence next to Dehler's home. A lieutenant, accompanied by several soldiers, entered the house and announced that he was establishing a command post in the building. The officer advised Dehler that the Americans were approximately 2,000 yards away. Dehler replied that, in fact, the Americans were already in Spurkenbach, adding that he had seen them only a few minutes before the Wehrmacht unit's arrival. Stunned for several seconds, the officer recovered from his surprise and stated that it did not matter. He had "chased them from Blankenberg," he said, boasting that he would chase them from Spurkenbach, too.

At 2:00 p.m., Dehler alerted the lieutenant that the Americans were again on the move. Through field glasses, they observed the patrol approaching along a row of massive oak trees. The officer seized the handset to a radio and requested reinforcements. Within thirty minutes, a truck carrying a mixed squad of Wehrmacht soldiers and Volkssturm troops arrived. As the truck halted and the occupants sprang from the vehicle, they suddenly came under a burst of fire from a machine gun concealed in the Merten residence. Eight Germans soldiers fell in the hail of bullets. A second truck arrived with reinforcements, but this vehicle halted behind a curve in the road, and the occupants swarmed into nearby cover. The second truck was followed by a self-propelled assault gun, and the heavy, tracked vehicle took a position where it could cover the approaches to the village.

Soon, artillery shells began impacting throughout the area. German artillery batteries were firing toward the south from Oberzielenbach; the high-explosive projectiles whistled over Spurkenbach to block the advance route that would be taken by American reinforcements. American artillery pieces returned fire from Oettershagen, and the area soon resounded with explosions and heavy-caliber impacts. A Sherman tank advanced toward the village and halted behind the Käsberg barn. Several minutes later, the German assault gun and the Sherman were engaged in a duel that lasted through the afternoon and destroyed both the Käsberg barn and the Dehler home. The engagement continued until dusk as the antagonists probed their opponents' positions and fired from concealment, with neither side finding a decisive turning point. At length, the German lieutenant fell mortally wounded, and the landsers and Volkssturm withdrew into the woods near Grunewald, leaving a rear guard along the curve north of Spurkenbach.

Eleven Germans died in the engagement. A German machine gunner who had established a position near the Wilma residence was struck in the back by a burst from an automatic weapon. The soldier dragged himself into the house, where his body was found the following morning.[12]

During the evening of 7 April, a column of Sherman tanks drew up to the village of Erblingen. Concealed beneath a towering chestnut tree was a German self-propelled gun. The American column encountered a roadblock and paused for several minutes before circumventing the obstacle and entering the village. As the lead Sherman turned onto the narrow streets of the village, a German soldier hidden near the Krämer residence fired a Panzerfaust but missed the tank. Simultaneously, the self-propelled gun opened fire, and the village instantly erupted in gunfire and explosions.

The residents remained in their cellars, terrified that their homes—and their lives—might be lost at any moment. However, the firing ceased as quickly as it had begun, and an ominous stillness enveloped the area. Within minutes, the abrasive rattle of steel tracks on pavement echoed through the bullet-riddled homes and barns. The Krämer home went up in flames, and the inhabitants were prevented from trying to extinguish the fire.

The next morning, the GIs returned and searched the village for weapons and German stragglers. The bodies of five German soldiers were found among the bullet-scarred buildings, and two residents died of wounds received in the short but intense engagement. The crew of the German assault gun had attempted to retreat along the Lambach streambed, where the weapon had become inextricably mired in the soft soil and was abandoned.

The Americans appeared to be in good humor, and as a resident attempted to speak to them in English, one of the soldiers announced that his father was from Germany. The strangers in khaki and olive uniforms behaved correctly and helped themselves only to fresh eggs and liquor.[13]

The last German unit near the village of Baumen was a light flak battery, the crew of which was quartered in nearby Hufen. The battery had received instructions to expend a limited amount of ammunition daily, to be fired toward the American positions to the south or at Allied aircraft. However, the flak crew made a conscious effort to fire the weapons only when no aircraft were observed, as to do so would just bring unnecessary danger to themselves and the neighboring villages.

As the American units approached, the battery withdrew northward. The Allied fighter-bomber activity increased, and farmers began working their fields by moonlight to avoid the attacks from enthusiastic fighter pilots. The first American troops arrived during the evening of Saturday, 7 April. Their presence was announced by a burst of machine-gun fire as they entered the village from the direction of Herfen and Wiesental-Pochstrasse. The automatic-weapons fire was followed by 76-mm tank projectiles that drove the populace into the shelter of their cellars.

Within minutes, the Americans were searching for weapons and German soldiers. They requisitioned residences for quarters, herding the inhabitants into their cellars while they prepared food and rested in the homes. In one of the houses was a local teacher named Waffenschmidt, who served as translator. The atmosphere grew relaxed as he and other inhabitants began conversing with the soldiers. A young woman with a four-month-old child was permitted to leave the crowded confines of the cold cellar, and several GIs relinquished her bedroom so that she could care for the infant in relative comfort.[14]

On the outskirts of Waldbröhl, Sergeant Hans-Joachim Schulz drew his self-propelled gun into cover along the Diezenkausener road and waited for supporting infantry to arrive. His unit had just broken off an engagement with American forces near Waldbröhl. The Americans were determined to capture the town and thus free some seventy wounded and sick U.S. prisoners of war who were hospitalized in the lazarette. Retreating from Waldbröhl, the gun crew concealed the heavy tracked vehicle near the village of Happach and awaited further orders.

At approximately 4:30 p.m., the interior of the vehicle chassis suddenly erupted with an earsplitting explosion. The gun commander, Sergeant Schulz, screamed for everyone to evacuate. The vehicle had been struck by an antitank shell fired from an unseen opponent. As three members of the crew scrambled from the vehicle, Schulz attempted to restart the engine and thus bring the vehicle into cover. Rapidly scanning the horizon and nearby terrain, he could see no sign of enemy activity between Boxberg and Waldbröhl and surmised that the attack came from behind them, in the direction of Hermesdorf.

After several seconds of desperately trying to start the damaged engine, Schulz climbed through the hatch and leaped from the chassis. At that moment, a second high-velocity projectile struck the assault gun and exploded on impact with a thunderous report. A fragment of the heavy shell ricocheted from the armor and sliced cleanly through Schulz's right leg.

Four Sherman tanks had emerged from the village of Biebelshof, where they had spotted the waiting assault gun. The first projectile had struck the vehicle squarely on the stern, damaging the motor but failing to ignite the fuel. As Hans-Joachim Schulz lay badly wounded next to the heavy vehicle, tank rounds began impacting into the soil nearby.

The family of Hans Pönitz, together with several neighbors, observed the engagement from their nearby home in Diezenkausener. Sixteen-year-old-Bruno Brix raced across the field to the vehicle, where he found Schulz hemorrhaging from a wound that had all but severed his leg. Running back through the exploding projectiles, he reported what he had found to the family. In the meantime, a pause in the firing enabled the three uninjured crewmen to pull Schulz to cover.

Seeing what had occurred, the residents Pönitz, Barth, and Pampus exhibited a large, white flag and approached the fallen soldier. They carried Schulz back to the shelter of the Pönitz greenhouse and nursery. A physician who had previously been evacuated from Bonn, Professor Baltes, immediately set to work binding the wound and advised the others that the limb had to be treated in a hospital immediately.

The hospital in Waldbröhl was inaccessible, for the American troops had severed the approaches to the town. The men decided to evacuate Schultz to the Luftwaffe clinic in Denklingen. A woman mounted a bicycle and set out by a circuitous route to that village. On arriving, her initial requests for assistance were met with refusal. The senior medical officer did not want to dispatch the sole remaining ambulance to the area, which was still experiencing sporadic but heated skirmishes between Wehrmacht and Allied troops. At length, however, her pleas were rewarded, and the vehicle set forth through the growing darkness.

The driver was compelled to return to Denklingen via the villages of Bröhl, Dickhausen, and Eiershagen as the medical assistants worked to stabilize the badly wounded soldier. Arriving at the clinic after sunset, Schulz underwent surgery, during which the remnants of the leg were removed.[15]

On 8 April, the remaining German troops evacuated Waldbröhl. Following in their wake were units of the U.S. 78th Infantry Division, moving cautiously to avoid casualties in suspected mined areas. The headquarters of C Company of the 309th Infantry Regiment was established near the Waldbröhl clinic, where they liberated seventy-eight American POWs.

The approach of the U.S. troops was observed by Justice Official Jeske, as was the northward withdrawal of the German troops during the same evening, 8 April.

A German sentry had been posted at the doorstep of the Justice Department building, and at 10:00 p.m., Jeske noticed that the sentry had disappeared. The official then saw that the windows in the building under military occupation were shuttered, indicating that the evacuation had taken place.

The next morning, the inhabitants were awakened at 4:00 by artillery shells randomly impacting throughout the town. The explosions faded at 5:30 a.m., and within thirty minutes, the shrill sound of a loudspeaker could be heard through the neighborhoods as an American patrol, accompanied by a truck, drove through the streets making an indiscernible message to the inhabitants. Jeske observed six American soldiers approaching along the Kaiserstrasse toward the town hall with rifles at the ready. The patrol then turned and filed along the Gerichtstrasse, where they discovered a number of abandoned Wehrmacht rifles that they smashed against the heavy stone steps of the building.[16]

The Americans entered the village of Morsbach on 8 April with platoons of infantry riding atop the turrets of Sherman tanks. As Dean Strack heard the rumors that the Americans had arrived, he hurried to the village church and saw a massive tank parked on the Dorfstrasse. American soldiers were searching the office buildings and residences for German soldiers and weapons, and as several of the khaki-clad GIs approached the church, Strack explained to them that no German soldiers were inside. Satisfied with his report, they moved onward. Shortly thereafter, another squad of infantrymen entered the church, and one of the soldiers removed his helmet respectfully before entering the portal. Several of the GIs climbed the bell tower, where they established an observation post complete with communications equipment and a tangled web of land lines.

Soon, the first prisoners arrived on the scene. The Americans drove a small band of local police officers to the village square, where they stood for several hours with their hands clasped on their heads. The policemen had been engaged in security duties at the nearby Reich Labor Service camp and had surrendered to the advance patrols without resistance. While the prisoners stood in ranks under guard, a number of the GIs entered the church and lounged nonchalantly on the furnishings. The soldiers dropped their heavy web combat belts and leaned their weapons against the walls; several removed their muddy boots and reclined on the church pews. The group pulled rations from various packs and calmly but wearily consumed provisions, smoked cigarettes, and rested in the shadows of the ancient structure, taking no notice of the centuries-old architecture that sheltered them. Eventually, some hours after the prisoners were removed from the village to a unknown fate, the Americans donned their equipment, shouldered their weapons, and filed toward their next destination.[17]

Prior to 12 April, elements of the 7th Flak Division had established defenses in the village of Drabenderhöhe, including eight heavy, 88-mm antiaircraft guns and numerous 20-mm and 37-mm guns, for a total force of thirty-six weapons. Most of the positions were located along the Pappelallee, near the cemetery, behind the Schloehann residence, and on a nearby height known as the Höher Berg. Accompanying the flak units were remnants of the 353rd Volksgrenadier Division, which moved into the area from the south after engaging American advance elements. The division commander, Lieutenant-General Höcker, established his command post in nearby Hillerscheid prior to transferring it to a less conspicuous location in a forestry cabin southeast of Engelskirchen. The flak and Volksgrenadier forces were reinforced with the surviving paratroopers from the 3rd Paratroop Division, many of whom had fallen casualty to the U.S. 97th Infantry Division while retreating from the area of Siegburg. The combined number of troops assigned to defend Drabenderhöhe was roughly 700, which quickly declined to approximately 300 as units began withdrawing before the approach of the Americans.

The first engagement near Drabenderhöhe occurred on 11 April, when elements of the U.S. 309th Infantry Regiment clashed with Wehrmacht defenders in the settlements of Jennecken and Niederhof, resulting in casualties on both sides. Throughout the remaining daylight hours, soldiers of the 353rd Volksgrenadier Division withdrew from the Drabenderhöhe area toward Engelskirchen, leaving some 300 men of the flak units under the command of Captain Kanski as a rear guard.

Late that afternoon, a large number of the flak soldiers had assembled in the parking lot of the Klein restaurant to receive further instructions when small-arms fire erupted from the direction of the cemetery and on the Marienberghausen road. American reconnaissance units had approached through the woods and across the open fields of the Horberig area and were probing the eastern perimeter of the village. The engagement became more intense as additional troops from both sides joined the skirmish. The Americans halted outside the village until the afternoon of the following day, and the Lang home and an adjacent barn went up in flames. The area of the cemetery suffered extensive destruction, during which the large trees lining the road were destroyed.

The fighting slackened during the hours of darkness, but dawn brought renewed machine-gun bursts and explosions from hand grenades and mortars. The area echoed with bursts from the flak positions as the gun crews attempted to force the American units to withdraw. The GIs brought heavy mortars into position in the area of Hillerscheid, from where they dropped high-explosive projectiles throughout the village and surrounding defenses. An attempt by the Americans to circumvent the resistance by rolling over the village of Forst to the northeast with a platoon of Sherman tanks was halted by three German assault guns concealed in the heavily wooded roadsides. By midafternoon, the Americans had withdrawn toward Kaltenbach-Ründeroth, leaving three fallen German soldiers in their wake.

As the fighting around Drabenderhöhe intensified, an American machine-gun crew established a position in the foyer of the Muth home, from where they attempted to engage German defenders in Drabenderhöhe. During a lull in the firing, an inhabitant of the home, elderly "Oma" Muth, descended the stairs to find the GIs repositioning their weapon and preparing for the next round of fighting. The grandmother was shocked to notice that one of the Americans, while engaged in the vicious fighting, had been compelled to relieve himself in the corner of her living room. Enraged, she stormed to the machine-gun position, shook her fist at the crew, and soundly reproached them for their uncivilized behavior. The soldiers only grinned in response, and with the renewal of the fighting, the woman disappeared again into the interior of her dwelling. Shortly thereafter, Oma Muth's handsome grandfather clock was riddled with bullet holes when a German machine gun returned fire.

As the fierce engagement swept back and forth through the village, neither side could force the other to withdraw. Lieutenant Colonel Schellman, commanding the U.S. unit, sent word to his opponent, Captain Kanski, that continued resistance was useless. However, the captain stubbornly held his positions.

At length, a temporary cease-fire was agreed on to recover the wounded, and some farmers took the opportunity to emerge from their cellars to feed and milk their cattle. A number of villagers assisted with efforts to recover the wounded. E. Dreibholz hitched a team to a farm cart, in which wounded were transported to the Höler residence in nearby Scheidt for medical care. The improvised aid station was occupied by a German medical officer, Dr. Althoff, and two Wehrmacht medics, who worked feverishly to save the lives of the many wounded that were taken to the location. They were assisted by a number of local men and women who rendered first aid until the wounded could receive professional care.

At approximately 5:00 p.m., the fighting inexplicably renewed, and resident Wilhelm Ruhland, who was helping to recover the wounded, was killed by a bullet. Several inhabitants approached Captain Kanski and implored him to cease his resistance and withdraw. Again, the officer adamantly refused to accede to their pleas. The vicious engagement took a turn when an American bullet pierced Kanski's arm, severing a main artery. After the mangled arm was crudely bandaged, the officer was evacuated to Scheidt, where Dr. Althoff tried to staunch the flow of blood and save the limb.

As the staff doctor was bandaging the badly wounded arm, he admonished the captain for refusing to withdraw his troops and thus inflicting unnecessary suffering on the inhabitants. The officer remained unmoved, and the doctor ordered him evacuated from the area, claiming that without further, immediate medical treatment, the wound would be fatal. Kanski was transported over an isolated logging track through Engelskirchen to Lindlar.

Immediately on Kanski's departure, Althoff ordered the remaining defenders to withdraw. Some of the soldiers retreated through the Loopetal streambed, but others chose to remain and wait for the opportunity to surrender. Several Wehrmacht soldiers disappeared into nearby homes, where they removed their uniforms and quickly donned whatever civilian attire was available. In the Muth residence, field-gray uniforms lay strewn throughout several rooms, and the garden and street outside were littered with abandoned rifles, pistols, and field equipment.

Local resident Kurt Nohl raced to Kanski's command post, which the captain had established in the cellar of the Müllenbach Gasthof. Scattered throughout the building were weapons, typewriters, uniforms, and miscellaneous Wehrmacht equipment. The cellar floor was strewn with documents and files. Nohl suddenly remembered that at the Lang inn, where some Nazi officials fleeing from the encroaching U.S. Army had established their latest headquarters, a large swastika banner and a framed Hitler portrait were hanging from a dais. The teenager raced to the restaurant, tore the two incriminating items from the wall, and threw them behind the podium. He then turned and dashed to the relative safety of his home.

Within minutes, the first files of American infantry troops were cautiously probing the bullet-riddled streets, now bedecked with white sheets, and they began searching the homes and buildings. The Muth family remained huddled in their cellar until the Americans entered the home. A GI immediately discovered the frightened residents and drove them into the street, where they were questioned by an American soldier speaking broken but intelligible German. The interrogator seemed to be well informed about the village and its inhabitants, including the Nazi Party members and the administrative officials. A French prisoner of war who had worked for the Muth family approached Herr Muth and passed him a letter. The former prisoner explained that, should Muth have difficulty with the Allies, he should show them the document. He then thanked the family for the treatment he had received throughout the war, indicating that his gratitude was also exhibited in the letter.

Residents of the village soon heard a strange cracking sound that echoed the length of the deserted streets as they waited anxiously in their cellars, uncertain of their fate. After being ordered from their cellar, Kurt Nohl, his father, and his mother were astonished to see an American soldier strolling along the rows of buildings while cracking a long, leather whip over his head. Discovered by the GI in a nearby barn, the whip had been used to drive the neighborhood cattle. Now it was entertaining the numerous American soldiers who gathered to watch the performance.

A large group of prisoners were soon collected between the steps of the church and the Heu bakery. Some of the soldiers were still wearing civilian clothing; most exhibited a forlorn appearance in threadbare German army gray or Luftwaffe blue uniforms. Before the men were marched away, a number of local families hastily provided the dejected prisoners with sparse provisions to help sustain them on their long journey. Several of the American soldiers made clear their intent to take Kurt Nohl into custody. They were unconvinced that he was not a Wehrmacht soldier, and many of the prisoners they had collected were no older than he. Several harrowing minutes elapsed while it was explained that he had not been conscripted into the Wehrmacht because his two older brothers had already been killed in action. Finally convinced, the occupiers left him in peace.

All male inhabitants were ordered to assemble in the village square, and the citizens feared that the men would be transported elsewhere, perhaps never to be seen again. Their fears were soon allayed, however, when the Americans released the men to return to their homes after informing them of the rules of occupation. They were advised that the regulations were to be strictly obeyed under penalty of severe punishment. They were also informed that the fierce resistance in Drabenderhöhe had ended in a very timely fashion. A bombing raid had already been scheduled for 6:00 p.m., and had the resistance continued, the entire village would have been left a pile of smoldering ruins.[18]

Chapter 13

Disintegration

On 8 April, Lieutenant-General Fritz Bayerlein, commander of the LIII Corps, was ordered to report to the headquarters of General von Lüttwitz's XXXXVII Panzer Corps for a briefing. Bayerlein was to receive instructions on a new plan to break out of the Ruhr Pocket by striking toward the northeast, penetrating the Allied ring around the army group, and linking up with Wenck's Twelfth Army outside the pocket.

At the briefing that afternoon, Bayerlein received his directive to make preparations for the breakout. The general was shown a message detailing the establishment of the Twelfth Army. As they discussed the situation, Lüttwitz expressed skepticism that the breakout attempt would succeed. The two commanders also spoke of the hopelessness of being trapped by the massive Allied force. Lüttwitz advised Bayerlein that he planned to surrender his forces at the first reasonable opportunity. Normally, such a statement from a Wehrmacht general would have been considered worse than disloyal or treasonous. However, as Lüttwitz saw it, the war was irretrievably lost, and there was no longer any reason for the killing to continue. Bayerlein agreed. The Panzer Lehr Division, the cream of Bayerlein's remaining force, was reduced to twenty battle-scarred tanks and ten half-tracks; it would be best to put an end to the struggle. After the two generals agreed to keep their decision strictly confidential, the meeting ended, and Bayerlein hastily departed for his headquarters.[1]

By 12 April, some German commanders, having expended their ammunition and gasoline, began disbanding their units. Lieutenant Schopper of the 9th Panzer Division portrayed the disintegration of many of the splintered German units when he recorded in his diary that "the armored radio vehicle has been demolished, we are disbanding and taking to the woods."[2]

The commander of the 12th Volksgrenadier Division, Lieutenant-General Engel, noted:

> West of Meinerzhagen there are still isolated engagements, none of which have any meaning. The splitting of the Ruhr Pocket is in full gear, there

has been no trace of any unified command structure since 10 April. Some final remnants of the division continued to fight near Gimborn; they fought until all ammunition was exhausted. Isolated groups are moving along a splintered front toward the east, in an attempt to reach the Weser where another front is supposedly being established.[3]

On the evening of 12 April, a meeting took place in Wipperfürth between the area commanders, Colonel Schaede and Major Leppel, and the civilian authorities of the town. The colonel demanded to know from Bürgermeister Jakob Krudewig how many Volkssturm troops were available to establish a defense. The Bürgermeister advised him that there were approximately 500 men available; however, weapons were almost nonexistent. They possessed a single machine gun and sixteen Danish and Italian rifles, for which there was only a small amount of ammunition. A quantity of Panzerfausts were stored in the Niedergaul bathing facility, but American reconnaissance troops had already occupied that area. Krudewig also elaborated on the abysmal lack of training of Volkssturm members; only one man had ever received instructions with a Panzerfaust.

The meeting lasted several hours. Colonel Schaede directed that minutes of the meeting be prepared. He then ordered it to be officially entered in the document that a defense of Wipperfürth would be irresponsible. The document was then signed by all officers and officials present.

During the night of 12–13 April, the last German soldiers withdrew from the town. Soon thereafter, German artillery shells began impacting strategic crossroads in the southwest area of the settlement. The road junctions in nearby Niedergaul and Gaulstrasse were blanketed with high-explosive artillery shells, as were the electrical power station, the Riesener bakery, and the machinery building of the Vorwerk company. A number of inhabitants were killed or wounded in the barrage, including Kalsbach, Kopp, and Gudelius, as well as a Polish girl; all of the victims were buried in the woods adjacent to the Stillinghauser road. The artillery fire compelled most residents to spend a restless night in their cellars.

As dawn broke on 13 April, an uneasy stillness had come to Wipperfürth. The streets were empty in anticipation of the arrival of the Americans. Jakob Krudewig cautiously left his home at 5:00 a.m. and walked toward Niedergaul, where, it was rumored, the Americans had already established positions. He found the roadblocks neither closed nor occupied; the Americans had failed to advance along the expected route from Dohrgaul but, fearing a possible ambush, had circumvented the area and approached from Lindlar. Niedergaul remained deserted and free of any troops. Krudewig eventually encountered a local inhabitant, who informed him that during the night, American soldiers had entered Niedergaul to awaken Egon Moser, a physician. A German woman was in need of medical care, and the doctor had departed with the soldiers. With no other information regarding the whereabouts of the Americans, Krudewig returned home.

At 9:00, he received a telephone call from Leo Zorn, the senior doctor at St. Joseph Hospital in Wipperfürth. The doctor recommended that Krudewig approach the Americans and advise them of his intent to surrender the town. The Bürgermeister refused, for he was unable to guarantee that there would be no resistance from straggling German troops when the Americans approached the settlement. Shortly thereafter, Krudewig noticed that white flags were hanging from numerous homes and shops.

Some two hours later, a team of American military vehicles drove along the Gaulstrasse, and the occupants of a jeep halted and asked a civilian to direct them to the Bürgermeister. Word soon reached Krudewig, who hurried to meet the soldiers. The first question asked of him was how long he had held his office. Krudewig replied that he had been Bürgermeister for two days. He was also asked about his predecessor, and the Americans were advised that the former Bürgermeister had disappeared two days previously. He was then questioned regarding the number and location of any remaining German troops, and he informed the Americans that a substantial number of sick and wounded Wehrmacht soldiers were in the Convent School and in the Gymnasium, both of which were being used as medical clinics. He also informed the soldiers that some 120 police officers remained in the town under the command of Lieutenant-Colonel von Wolf. The jeep immediately wheeled about and sped to the location he provided.

The Wipperfürth police force was taken into U.S. custody, and large trucks arrived within minutes and transported the men from the town. Several hours later, the police officers were returned to the village and turned over to Krudewig, albeit minus their wristwatches and rings.[4]

The Americans forces, in the process of destroying the remaining German units within the pocket, hardly paused after the collapse of resistance in the area of Hamm-Rhynern. From Hamm, they struck out in three directions: the southeast toward Soest, the south en route to Unna, and the southwest toward Dortmund. The armored columns crossed the autobahn south of Rhynern in the early morning hours of 7 April. Several tanks, accompanied by a small number of jeeps carrying a dozen soldiers, drove toward an airfield on the outskirts of Werl, where they encountered a large, imposing structure. Unbeknownst to the GIs in the lead elements, they had come upon the Werl prison, locally known as the Sicherungsanstalt.

The prison complex had come under heavy artillery fire early that morning, and the prisoners had been transferred from the upper floors to the cellars and lower facilities for safety. The cell doors remained open to facilitate a rapid evacuation of the inmates if it became necessary. Almost 2,000 prisoners were confined behind the massive gray walls; only a few had been evacuated prior to the arrival of the Americans. Transportation was lacking, and the few vehicles available were required for more pressing commitments.

Large numbers of women and children had taken refuge from the bursting artillery rounds in the air raid bunkers beneath the thick walls of the prison. There, a single telephone line maintained contact with the administration office near the prison entrance. At 4:00 on the afternoon of 7 April, the prison director was contacted over this line by a watchman at the entrance, who reported that the Americans had arrived. The director ordered the prison gate to be opened, and U.S. troops stormed into the complex.

An American officer ordered all members of the prison staff, including the guards on duty, to assemble in the courtyard at once. The soldiers searched neighboring houses, where they seized off-duty administrators and guards and then marched them at gunpoint to the prison. As a column of officials, some still in pajamas and slippers, walked through the streets toward the prison, they were joined by other members of the staff who had observed the ensuing event and unknowingly joined the procession, unaware of what was going on. The officials were accompanied by a number of German soldiers who had been discovered hiding nearby. Some 200 officials and soldiers were soon assembled in ranks in the prison courtyard.

In the confines of the courtyard, they were met by more incoming American soldiers, as well as journalists and cameramen who captured the surrender of the prison keys on film. The officials were ordered to file past a designated area of the courtyard before the cameras, where they were filmed ceremoniously depositing their keys in a growing pile on the ground. The act was repeated several times at the behest of the cameramen to ensure that the surrender would be portrayed in its proper context.

As the filming of the surrender of keys was closing, the courtyard was suddenly stormed by freed inmates, who leaped on the American soldiers in unbridled elation. Some fell on the pile of keys lying on the brick-paved courtyard, and others took out their fury on the prison officials, some of whom collapsed under the pummels and kicks as their American captors looked on with amusement.

The tumult lasted about thirty minutes. After the cameramen packed away their equipment, some of the soldiers busied themselves with organizing the inmates. Others, accompanied by a pair of Sherman tanks, led the column of officials through the gates of the prison. The guards, officials, and German soldiers felt increasing anxiety as, through the rapid English being spoken, they discerned the words *Gestapo* and SS. The prisoners were led to a large farmyard in the nearby village of Scheidingen, where it became obvious they were to be held for an indeterminate length of time. With the growing threat of mistreatment at the hands of their captors, who were growing more vocal, the prison director finally convinced the senior officer present that the prison had nothing to do with the concentration camp system but was a facility for German and foreign citizens who had been convicted of various crimes.

The following afternoon, the prison staff returned to the facility, where the inmates were instructed to select which of the assembled officials should remain in service. A large number of the inmates were placed in charge of the prison, and they immediately imprisoned all officials against whom any animosity was held. The now-liberated inmates remained in charge of the facility until July 1945, when the transfer from American to British jurisdiction took effect.[5]

On 6 April, the town of Siegen fell. Oberbürgermeister Alfred Fissmer remained in office as the Americans quickly established jurisdiction over the city, known for its extensive mines and tunnels. Although Siegen itself had been reduced to rubble during numerous bombing raids, the populace suffered relatively few casualties. Fissmer had tirelessly worked to modify the tunnel system into a massive shelter complex large enough to house the entire population of the city. Now, he was beset with other concerns. The danger of the air raids ended with the occupation by American forces. But few people were aware of an immense treasure concealed deep beneath the old city that had been evacuated from the cities of the Ruhr during the height of the Allied strategic bombing campaign. The Americans soon heard rumors of an extensive treasure hidden in the vicinity, and they were determined to locate it.

Several days after the guns in Siegen had fallen silent, a jeep bearing the American city commander and a young liaison officer halted at Fissmer's office in the imposing building on the Kaisergarten. The senior officer called to Fissmer, who dutifully approached the jeep with cautious expectation. Before the American commander could speak, the liaison officer brusquely demanded, in fluent, accent-free German, to be taken to the "stolen treasures." Fissmer countered that he knew of no stolen treasures but advised them that he had taken a large quantity of artwork into official custody for safekeeping.

The American commander, hoping to avoid a confrontation, diplomatically fended off the liaison officer's demands and, slapping the Bürgermeister on the shoulder, requested that Fissmer lead them to the items. Fissmer agreed to reveal the location but asked that armed guards be stationed at the tunnel where the treasures lay to protect the contents. A work camp with a large number of laborers was situated near the tunnel entrance, and Fissmer was concerned that if the inmates learned of the treasure, they would attempt to overrun the facility and plunder the contents.[6]

As the American forces consolidated their hold on Siegen, Field Marshal Model's staff, located to the northeast in the town of Olpe, was hastily preparing to evacuate the Army Group B headquarters. Olpe was only twenty minutes away from Siegen by car, and it was perhaps a matter of hours before the American columns would approach the town as they thrust toward Dortmund, Düsseldorf, Cologne, and the other major cities deep within the Ruhr industrial area. After just two weeks in Olpe, during which the town's communications facilities were utilized to retain contact with Berlin and Zossen, the army group staff, now reduced to some fifty personnel, loaded files, telephones, typewriters, and field equipment onto a few remaining trucks for transport to Schalksmühle near Lüdenscheid.

On 8 April, one week after the Ruhr Pocket was closed at Lippstadt, the Americans reached Olpe. Church services that Sunday were held by parishioners within the numerous bunkers and mines where the local inhabitants sought shelter from the marauding aircraft and the ominous, ever-closing impacts of heavy artillery shells. German military convoys, a strange mixture of dilapidated trucks, motorcycles, and horse-drawn caissons augmented by groups of soldiers on foot or bicycle, filed through the ruins of the town as they fled from the approaching Americans. Teams of military police—the Feldgendarmerie—conducted searches of homes and public buildings, collecting stragglers who had abandoned their units in an attempt to conceal themselves and wait for the inevitable arrival of the Americans. Some of the men caught in the searches fell victim to "flying courts-martial" and were quickly sentenced to be executed. As an example to other soldiers who entertained ideas of seeking refuge with locals to escape the oncoming clash with the enemy, four suspected deserters were shot several hundred yards south of Olpe near the village of Lütringhausen and were buried by the roadside. One of the victims was the father of five children.[7]

On 9 April, the rattle of small-arms fire was near enough to Olpe that residents could clearly discern the rhythmic pounding of the American Browning machine guns and the ripping response of the German MG-42s. The gunfire was accompanied by occasional grenade blasts and the methodical detonation of mortar rounds. Bürgermeister Wurm met briefly with several members of the city administration, and the decision was quickly reached not to defend Olpe. The main obstacle in preventing further destruction to the city was the military. The German force commander, Major Kramer, was prepared to evacuate his command post and turn it over to the city for use as a medical center. However, this did not relieve him and the city commander, Captain Rody, of their responsibility to prepare the city for defense against the oncoming Americans.

The citizens of Olpe spent most of the remainder of 9 April huddled in their shelters, nervously awaiting the arrival of the U.S. Army. In the early morning hours, during which random artillery shells impacted intermittently on the area, a local police officer telephoned Rody to inform him that the Americans had reached the outskirts of the town. On hearing this news, Rody simply stated, "My assignment here has now lost any further meaning. I'm going home to lie down and finally get some sleep." Before hanging up, he added, "I won't be able to avoid becoming a prisoner of war, anyway."[8]

As dawn broke on the horizon, the Bürgermeister and several members of the administration tied a white cloth to a staff and approached the foremost American positions. Bürgermeister Wurm was placed in a jeep and driven to an American command post, where he signed the official documents to surrender the town. Several days later, General Matthew B. Ridgway established his headquarters in the building that formerly housed the Nazi district command center.

The American units that overran Olpe continued on their thrust toward the northwest, deeper into the Ruhr. In the nearby mining town of Lüdenscheid, Kreisleiter Joost called the switchboard in Olpe for information regarding the situation and the locations of the American forces. Little did he realize that the end for the Nazi officials was rapidly looming. The Americans were pushing with record-breaking speed toward his district.

The stores in Lüdenscheid opened their doors on 9 April and began selling previously rationed food to all inhabitants. Some food items were obtained for the first time since the prewar years without presenting ration coupons. No one knew what the next hours would bring, and people were hoarding any available provisions. The military police continued their deadly work in searching out deserters and stragglers. Soldiers found without proper authorization were given short shrift, and eleven suspected deserters were executed following cursory trials. Their bodies were exhibited in the market square as a reminder to the civilians that Nazi directives were still in effect.[9]

In early April, a formerly high-ranking Nazi official fell into the hands of the U.S. First Army. Franz von Papen was the last German chancellor before the Nazi Party gained a majority in the Reichstag, paving the way for Hitler to become chancellor. However, Papen had remained in service as vice chancellor and later as special emissary to Vienna and ambassador to Turkey. After being sent into retirement due to his outspoken criticism of the Nazi policies, he returned to his home in the small settlement of Wallerfangen near Saarbrücken.

In mid-March, Papen was ordered to evacuate his retirement home, and he sought refuge at his daughter's residence in Stockhausen, concealed in the hills of the Sauerland. To escape the threat posed by fighter-bombers and the myriad dangers that the approaching front would bring, the former diplomat, his daughter, and her children then relocated to a small cabin the family owned in the forest. Papen's son and son-in-law remained in Stockhausen to protect their residence from the gangs of marauding foreign laborers that were plaguing the area.

On 9 April, the home was occupied by Americans, and Papen's son and son-in-law were marched into captivity. One day later, the stillness of the forest was interrupted by an American patrol led by Lieutenant Thomas McKinley, who appeared at the cabin door. The American officer confronted Papen, showed him a photograph, and asked if he was indeed the person identified as the former ambassador. Papen affirmed that he was the man they were seeking but argued that he did not know what the Allies might want from a sixty-five-year-old retiree.

During the curt discussion that followed, Papen bitterly stated that he wished only that the war was over, to which an American sergeant replied that about 11 million soldiers wished that as well. The sergeant then placed Papen under arrest. When Papen asked if he might join his daughter and her children for a last meal together, the Americans granted his request. After consuming a bowl of soup with the family, Papen packed some items into a rucksack, and, still wearing knicker-bockers and a feathered hiking cap, he climbed into a U.S. Army jeep and rode into captivity.[10]

The day following Franz von Papen's arrest in the forest near Stockhausen, the resistance within the pocket moved closer to collapse. General von Lüttwitz, commander of the XXXXVII Panzer Corps, arrived at the headquarters of Bayerlein's LIII Corps, some 8 miles northeast of Iserlohn. Bayerlein's front had been reduced to a thinly defended area running from Stokum, east of Unna-Kamen-Ostrich, and north of Dortmund. Bayerlein's remaining defenders consisted of remnants of the 180th and 190th Infantry Divisions and his former command, the renowned 116th Panzer Division. Lüttwitz again discussed the possibility of a surrender with Bayerlein, and he brought news that his chief of staff, Lieutenant-Colonel von Siebert, was being transferred to the Army Group B staff to serve as Model's operations officer in the wake of Reichhelm's departure.

Model arrived unexpectedly during the intense discussion at the headquarters and announced that the Panzer Lehr Division was to be resupplied immediately; he was ordering the division to spearhead a breakout toward the northeast. The field marshal outlined detailed plans for the resupply operation as well as operational plans for the breakout, which was to occur in the area of Unna. Bayerlein listened attentively, hardly believing that Model—the commander who had so emphatically protested Hitler's plan for the Ardennes Offensive because of a lack of strength with which to carry out the operation—was now expecting to conduct a thrust through the Allied armored divisions.

The following day, 11 April, Siebert reluctantly left Bayerlein's staff to assume duties as the Army Group B operations officer. His replacement with Bayerlein's LIII Corps was Colonel Neckelmann. The new chief of staff quickly made it known that not only did he view the general situation quite differently than his predecessor had but also that he was adamantly opposed to any surrender to the Allies. Neckelmann's bearing and attitude immediately distanced him from his commander, Fritz Bayerlein.

Also on 11 April, an order from Field Marshal Model arrived for General Siegfried von Waldenburg, commander of the 116th Panzer Division, directing him to lead the attack out of the pocket toward the northeast. All mobile assets under control of the army group were to be placed under Waldenburg's command for the purpose of the breakout. Every attempt to persuade the field marshal to abandon the effort was icily rebuffed: Model was intent on making one last thrust toward freedom, however temporary, for his army group. Bayerlein, distraught at the field marshal's stubborn refusal to cancel the breakout attempt, was now prepared to take the most drastic measure necessary to avoid further death and destruction. After the order to launch the attack was received by his headquarters, Bayerlein formulated a plan to place the field marshal under arrest should Model reappear at his headquarters.[11]

Several days later, the first American tanks appeared in the nearby village of Homert. Two olive-drab half-tracks approached the Neuenhof estate but quickly turned and disappeared toward the south when they received a burst of machine-gun fire from the red-brick farmyard. During the afternoon of 12 April, artillery rounds began falling in the town of Lüdenscheid. The pace of the American advance seemed to increase hourly, and at 3:00 p.m. on 13 April, the Americans dispatched emissaries into the tortured city to request its surrender. By 7:00 that evening, the town of Lüdenscheid was under American occupation. Ernst-Wilhelm Boland, a German medic working in the Baukloh medical facility within Lüdenscheid, noted in his diary, "This evening we heard in the Wehrmacht Supreme Command report that Lüdenscheid had fallen after a heroic defense. Our only comment: Not a single shot was fired from German defenses."[12]

On 12 April, the city of Unna fell to the Americans. Next, the inhabitants of Dortmund fled their homes in expectation of an oncoming attack. The army group command reported that Dortmund fell only after putting up heavy resistance, but the American units in fact rolled into the city without engaging the Wehrmacht forces, which continued to melt away before the Allied armored columns. An order from Field Marshal Model to retake the city was ignored. Model also issued orders to prepare the bridges over the Ruhr River for destruction, but Lüttwitz, aware that destroying the bridges would mean the end of water, gas, and electricity service for the inhabitants, refused to forward the order to his troops.

That afternoon, Bayerlein reappeared at Lüttwitz's headquarters in Hohenlimburg. The two generals continued to discuss the possible consequences of a capitulation. No one believed that the German troops in the pocket could continue resisting much longer. Indeed, it was only a matter of days before the remaining defenses were eliminated, regardless of how determined the forces might be to resist. The generals agreed that Model's demands to attempt a breakout were out of the question.

General von Lüttwitz also mentioned other repercussions. It was well known that General Otto Lasch, commander of the German forces that surrendered to the Soviets at Königsberg, had been sentenced to death by hanging, albeit in absentia, for the capitulation of that city. Lüttwitz did not fear Hitler's henchmen; in American captivity, he would be beyond their reach and retribution. But the notorious Sippenhaft order—the Nazi policy that relatives would be punished for crimes committed by their family members—was of great concern. The officers did not discuss details of how the surrender should occur; they could not know the next Allied move or intent, but they did agree on what they would not do—they would not put up a defense. This meeting was the last that the two corps commanders would have during the war.[13]

On the afternoon of 12 April, General Bayerlein visited a large POW camp near Hemer, in which some 25,000 Allied troops were confined. The rations in the camp had been exhausted for several days, and there was no means of resupply. The camp commander was instructed to feed the prisoners by requisitioning food from the local populace. Additional rations were obtained from a small supply depot that had been found in the area of Letmathe.

One day later, all direct communications between Bayerlein's command post and the army group staff was lost, although sporadic radio communications continued. The lack of communication exacerbated an increasingly confusing situation among the trapped German forces throughout the length of the chain of command. In the afternoon of 13 April, Bayerlein again appeared at the Hemer POW camp.

Shortly before his arrival, the camp had received artillery fire from the south, which killed or injured some seventy prisoners. Bayerlein spoke with the camp's senior officers, and an American major agreed to report to the American lines. The major was instructed to explain the situation to the officials there and to request that the artillery fire be lifted. The major was soon escorted through the lines to the U.S. 99th Infantry Division.

General Bayerlein also agreed to permit General von Waldenburg to establish contact with the American units opposite his position northwest of Iserlohn. He wanted to declare Hemer an open city, free of German armed forces, in order to avoid unnecessary loss of life and further destruction to the city's infrastructure.[14]

That evening, Bayerlein drove to his former command, the Panzer Lehr Division, the headquarters of which was now located near Werdohl. The purpose of this visit was to bid farewell to the soldiers of the division, whom he had commanded for many of the most perilous months of the war. Bayerlein had established the Panzer Lehr in January 1944 and had led the division for a year before relinquishing command. The division had only recently been halted during the breakout attempt near Winterberg. Just as it appeared that the breakout would succeed, the skies had cleared, and swarms of aircraft descended on the German columns. American armored units and swarms of fighter-bombers had materialized in great strength between the Sauerland towns of Langenwiese and Schmallenberg, bringing the advance to a halt. Major-General Horst Niemack, the division commander, was wounded in action and was flown out of the pocket for medical attention on orders from Field Marshal Model. The highly decorated Colonel Paul von Hauser, commander of Panzergrenadier Lehrregiment 901, had then taken command of the division.

During Bayerlein's final visit with the Panzer Lehr, he advised Colonel von Hauser to capitulate at the first reasonable opportunity: the time had come to spare lives and bring an end to the senseless destruction. Hauser agreed that on the following day, 14 April, he would contact the American forces to advise them of his intentions to surrender.

The POW compound near Hemer was officially turned over to the 99th Infantry Division that same day, 14 April, and thousands of emaciated Allied prisoners were liberated. The American forces then entered the town of Hagen, thus splitting the Ruhr Pocket in two. Bayerlein received a radio message from Model's army group staff ordering the corps to break through the American forces between the east and west pockets to reestablish contact between the German forces. Bayerlein disregarded the command; the message went unanswered. However, he was particularly concerned about the attitude of his chief of staff and operations officer, both of whom were vehemently opposed to any capitulation.

On 15 April, Hauser officially surrendered the Panzer Lehr Division, with 2,460 men, 8 tanks and self-propelled guns, 50 vehicles, and an 88-mm flak battery.[15] That evening, Bayerlein ordered his corps to evacuate the entire north bank of the Ruhr River. He advised his officers that the bridges over the river were to remain intact.

The former commander of the Army Replacement Command in Dortmund, General Büchs, was assigned by the army group as combat commander of Iserlohn. As the American ring tightened around the city, he was directed to defend Iserlohn to the last man. Then, on 15 April, Büchs received instructions from Bayerlein not to defend the city. Furthermore, he was advised that Bayerlein intended to surrender his corps to the Americans that very evening: Iserlohn had survived the war largely intact, and there was no reason to destroy it now. The landsers occupying defensive positions on the outskirts of the city began evacuating their defenses.

Bayerlein also shared his intent to surrender with General von Waldenburg, commander of the 116th Panzer Division. The surrender was to take place at the 116th's headquarters in a wooded area west of Refflingsen; the exact time for dispatching emissaries to the Americans was yet to be determined. The topic of their conversation was cautiously withheld from Bayerlein's chief of staff. Bayerlein also contacted General Ernst Hammer at his headquarters in Reingsen and advised him of the plan. Hammer agreed to cooperate.

At 9:00 p.m. on 15 April, emissaries were dispatched to the U.S. 7th Armored Division with a written message: "The LIII Corps is prepared to lay down its arms to avoid any further, useless bloodshed. It is requested that a cease-fire be initiated. Requesting further instructions. Bayerlein, Lieutenant-General."

General Bernhard Klosterkemper was also ordered to report to Bayerlein's headquarters, where he was advised of the plan to surrender. The outraged general adamantly argued against any capitulation; he was already preparing a counterattack over the Ruhr against American forces that had broken through near Engste, and he was determined to carry out the attack. The general was placed under arrest by Bayerlein, and Klosterkemper's operations officer agreed to cease combat operations.

Shortly after midnight, on 16 April, the emissaries returned from the American lines with a response from the U.S. 7th Armored Division: "Capitulation accepted. The division chief of staff will arrive at the corps headquarters at 07:00 to make further arrangements." At 3:00 a.m., the front fell eerily silent. The landsers huddling in their positions could no longer detect the thunder of artillery; the usual, distant chatter of small-arms fire no longer floated through the villages and forests. The U.S. 7th Armored Division's chief of staff appeared promptly at 7:00 and issued instructions for the surrender. The staff officers discussed the assembly point for the corps's troops and the surrender of weapons and ammunition. The American officers guaranteed that the prisoners would receive rations.

During the discussion, it was noted that the city of Iserlohn was not included in the capitulation proceedings. An officer was dispatched to advise General Büchs of the instructions to surrender his command along with Bayerlein's corps, and Büchs agreed to the measure. As the discussion continued, Colonel Zollenkopf, commander of the 9th Panzer Division, appeared at the scene. He had heard that Bayerlein was in contact with the American forces and that U.S. Army officers were at the LIII Corps headquarters. Zollenkopf was advised of the action in progress and was asked to include his division in the surrender. The colonel immediately agreed to do so.

By 11:00 a.m., the instructions and terms of the surrender had been disseminated to the various commands of the LIII Corps. At 12:30, the commanding generals and their staffs were taken to the U.S. 7th Armored Division headquarters, east of Menden. General Bayerlein was the senior officer among the German officers going into captivity. His chief of staff and operations officer were not present. The staff officers, both of whom were opposed to the surrender, had disappeared from the corps headquarters. General von Waldenburg and his operations officer, Lieutenant-Colonel Heinz-Günther Guderian, were in attendance, as were General Hammer, General Klosterkemper, and Colonel Zollenkopf. The generals were accompanied by their operations officers.

The capitulation encompassed an immense number of German soldiers and large quantities of equipment. Some 30,000 soldiers laid down their arms. The surrendered equipment included 40 artillery pieces, 30 battle-worthy tanks, and some 100 disabled tanks as well as several thousand miscellaneous motor vehicles. The generals and their staff officers were taken to a POW enclosure near Brilon. Generals Bayerlein and von Waldenburg were driven to the U.S. First Army headquarters, where Bayerlein was interrogated by the army intelligence officer, Colonel Dixon.

Bayerlein had experienced a long, stormy relationship with Courtney Hodge's First Army. The two men had faced one another in Tunisia, in Normandy, during the pursuit across northern France, during the Ardennes Offensive, throughout the Rhineland campaign, and finally in the Ruhr Pocket. During the interrogation, Colonel Dixon assured Bayerlein that the capitulation of his corps would not be publicized. The German officers were concerned that, under the Nazi Sippenhaft order, their families might suffer retribution for the generals' decision to lay down their arms.[16]

While the once-renowned Panzer Lehr Division was surrendering to the Americans in the Ruhr Pocket on 15 April, Major Winrich Behr was attempting to return from Berlin to Army Group B headquarters. On the airfield at Werde, near Berlin, Behr climbed into a waiting Heinkel 111. The sound of roaring engines drowned out the distant artillery fire rumbling ominously on the horizon as the Soviet army closed ever nearer, and the shouts of the Luftwaffe ground crews were still discernable as they kicked a soccer ball over the expanse of open field. The sun was unusually bright, and as the heavy aircraft rose into the air, Behr could observe the ruins of the German capital in the distance. With clear skies, it would be a flight of immense risk, as the Allied fighter-bombers would seal the Ruhr against all German traffic on the ground and in the air. Behr thought of the pilot's warning against making the trip. With the highly explosive nitroglycerin cargo, even one well-placed bullet could bring down the plane in dozens of pieces.

Within minutes, the aircraft had crossed the Elbe and the Harz Mountains and was flying at low altitude over the Sauerland. It landed unopposed near Wuppertal, where the major was transported to the Army Group B headquarters in Waldesruhe, only 1.5 miles away. Field Marshal Model awaited his arrival, and he was immediately greeted by the commander.[17]

The situation during Behr's absence, as expected, had steadily worsened. The army group staff had lost all contact with the remnants of Gruppe von Lüttwitz that had been holding out in the northern sector of the pocket. General von Zangen's Fifteenth Army had also evaporated, leaving urgent attempts to establish contact unanswered. The staff later learned that Zangen and the Fifteenth Army staff had surrendered on 13 April. The 272nd Volksgrenadier Division had been dissolved by order of the division commander on 12 April. The remaining staff officers of the division joined Model's staff, and the group of elderly miners who were intended to reinforce the division were sent home. The 183rd Volksgrenadier Division had disappeared after dispatching a final message from Wipperfürth on 13 April. The 353rd Volksgrenadier Division was no longer reporting from Dhünn after 14 April. On 15 April, the 3rd Parachute Division disappeared from the army group near Burscheid.[18]

The Americans had succeeded in splitting the pocket when the U.S. 8th Division drove from the south to meet the U.S. 79th Division driving from the north on the Ruhr River at Hohenlimburg-Hagen. Again, the staff of Army Group B had been compelled to retreat from the relentless American spearheads, and thus, it had taken new quarters in the tiny vacation town of Waldesruh near Wuppertal.[19]

Immediately on Behr's return from his odyssey to Berlin, Model suggested the two of them take a short walk, for the field marshal was anxious to learn the outcome of Behr's trip. They left the headquarters building and began pacing along a wooded trail. They moved slowly, navigating through the numerous bomb craters along the path.

Behr had served with the field marshal since the commander's arrival in Normandy, and Model had come to trust the twenty-five-year-old officer implicitly. The commander appreciated the forthright information he always obtained from one of his most trusted officers. Behr had experienced the way in which Model at times revealed his impatience and treated his officers brashly. He had observed firsthand how, during an important briefing, if a general failed to exhibit the attitude and alertness that Model demanded, the field marshal would exclaim, "Aide, bring this man a cognac! He is apparently asleep on his feet!" Such remarks served to embarrass both the target of Model's comments and his staff officers. Yet Behr had learned long ago that the field marshal respected immediate, direct answers, even when the information was negative.

The major now found himself in a position to break only disappointing news to Model. Without hesitation, he explained how he had been unable to even approach Hitler to discuss the fate of Army Group B. He described the sordid conditions at the Reich Chancellery and the way in which those at the supreme headquarters appeared oblivious to the disaster looming in the Ruhr.

During their discussion, the sound of distant fighter-bombers droned faintly, increasing in volume only to softly fade again as the aircraft relentlessly sought targets of opportunity. Suddenly, the faint drone of the powerful engines increased to a roar, and the aircraft were immediately above them. The field marshal and Behr leaped into a bomb crater as a pair of Allied fighter-bombers swept overhead. The air was rent with immense explosions as the staff buildings were hit with heavy-caliber machine-gun bullets and bombs. Model and Behr found themselves cling-ing to the sides of the crater, half filled with stagnant water, as the marauders banked and made another attack. Plumes of black smoke billowed upward in the aftermath of the explosions, and flames shot into the sky as the wooden structures ignited from tracer bullets and the detonations of high explosives.

The experienced pilots had obviously detected the arrival and departure of vehicles from the isolated structures and thus succeeded in almost eliminating the Army Group B headquarters. As the result of a direct hit on the main structure housing the personnel, dozens were killed and wounded. Official files and docu-ments disappeared in flames, and the staff worked frantically to recover any items that might still be of use. Despite their efforts, the official function of Army Group B appeared to have come to an end. That evening, in an attempt to avoid the ma-rauding aircraft, the staff moved to the Haan forest, southwest of Wuppertal.[20]

By mid-April, the Allies had succeeded in reducing the pocket, densely con-gested with the remnants of Wehrmacht divisions, to an area roughly 30 miles in diameter. The conditions enhanced the opportunity for fighter-bombers to seek targets of opportunity in the towns and villages on the perimeter of the Ruhr.

By the end of the second week in April, Model's forces were facing total de-feat. Yet on 17 April, he again decided to evade the inevitable surrender of his army group. The army group was to be dissolved, in three distinct categories. The very young and very old were to be discharged from the Wehrmacht and sent home. The officers, senior officials, professional soldiers, soldiers of normal military age, and supply units were to simply allow themselves to be overrun by the enemy. Those officers and soldiers who so desired could attempt to escape captivity by disarming themselves and penetrating the enemy lines to return to their homes. Others, on their own volition, could remain with units and under the leadership of the most senior officer present and try to fight their way out of the pocket. On the day this decision was made, the army group received an or-der from OKW granting permission to break out of the pocket. However, by that point, OKW messages were no longer heeded by anyone in the army group.[21]

On 17 April, Model and his chief of staff, General Wagener, met in the Haan forest to discuss their next actions. U.S. General Ridgway had sent an emissary,

Captain Brandstetter, to deliver a plea to surrender to the field marshal. The letter carried by Brandstetter mentioned how, in April 1865, two American solders had met in a small village called Appomattox. Ulysses S. Grant, commander of the Union army, had implored his counterpart, General Robert E. Lee, to spare further bloodshed and destruction by surrendering his army. Lee surrendered and thereby ended the bitter conflict. Ridgway now appealed for Model to follow the example of the leader of the Army of Northern Virginia and bring an end to the suffering faced by his own soldiers and the inhabitants of the Ruhr.

Model refused to accept the appeal to surrender. During his meeting with Wagener, he asked the general, "Have we done everything possible for us to perform our duty?" Wagener replied that they had. Model continued, "Then what is left for a defeated general to do?" Following an embarrassing silence, Model grimly stated, "In ancient times they took poison."[22]

General Wagener accompanied Captain Brandstetter to the American lines to deliver Model's terse message declining the request to surrender his army group. Wagener did not return to the staff and reportedly chose to go into captivity. Model dismissed most of the remaining staff personnel.

From the thickly wooded area near Haan, the remaining staff officers transferred to a renowned horse farm, the Mydlinghoven estate. Only a very small skeletal staff remained. Colonel Theodor Pilling (Model's personal adjutant), Colonel Michael, the Ic, three aides, several drivers, and Major Winrich Behr stayed with the field marshal. At Mydlinghoven, the aides were released to try to make their way home or to join a combat unit. The staff personnel quickly dispersed, leaving only several drivers, an Opel communications vehicle, a DKW Meisterklasse automobile, and an armored reconnaissance vehicle. A number of the staff officers proceeded to drive toward the area between Düsseldorf and Duisburg, where they evaded American patrols and took refuge in the thick forests between Lintorf and Wedau. American tanks had already sealed the roads through Lintorf, just over 1 mile from the field marshal's location.[23]

While en route to Mydlinghoven, Model's small group came on a Wehrmacht general speeding along a road in a staff vehicle, still in full uniform. He was coming from the direction of Ratingen, approximately 4 miles away. Pulling to a halt, the general advised Model that the Americans already occupied the strategic crossroads in Ratingen; the front line ran roughly from the Rhine toward the southeast. He explained how he had navigated through the American lines, and Model listened intently. After the general proceeded down the road, the small group of fugitives climbed into their remaining vehicles and continued toward Mydlinghoven. After establishing makeshift quarters, they returned to the vehicles and drove toward Düsseldorf. After several kilometers, they passed a farmhouse on the left, flanked by an open field. Adjacent to the field was a heavy antiaircraft battery. The field marshal motioned the convoy to a stop and then climbed from his vehicle, closely followed by Behr. They approached the four guns of the isolated battery and were met by a young Luftwaffe lieutenant.

Model glanced at the large, 88-mm guns concealed under camouflage netting and demanded that the battery commander identify the target. The officer replied that they were simply firing toward the east—in the direction of the American lines. The battery had been instructed to expend the remaining stocks of ammunition, after which the unit was to be disbanded. The field marshal told the officer to fire into the air if there was no specific target, and the officer responded with a sharp salute.

Model and his entourage returned to their vehicles and proceeded toward Düsseldorf. As the small column continued along the road toward the northern perimeter of the pocket, Model mused, "It would be a respectable death for a field marshal … to be able to die here fighting alongside a battery." Behr remained silent, suppressing the uneasiness he felt at this remark. Having experienced the war on three different fronts within a short, intense span of three years, the reconnaissance officer had no intentions of now, at the twelfth hour, needlessly sacrificing his life in a lost war. And as a professional officer, he was hardly able to simply agree with the field marshal—to say, "Yes, go right ahead." He was also fully aware that a lost war brings a different fate to field marshals than to twenty-five-year-old majors. Major Behr preferred to survive the end of the war if possible.

The officers in the vehicle remained largely silent as they approached the ruins of Düsseldorf. The once-bustling city now presented a forlorn air of abandonment. The officers had experienced such an atmosphere in previous months and years in France, in Belgium, and even in Russia. They had often encountered an eerie period of emptiness in the urban areas, when the opposing forces were no longer locked in engagements but were separated by a no-man's-land of rubble, roofless concrete structures, and shattered glass. The German army had fled, and the American army was approaching to fill the void left in the wake. The streets were empty of life; the few inhabitants remaining in the city dared not venture from the safety of their shelters in anticipation of the enemy's arrival and the unknown fate that would bring. Only the broken shells and scarred facades of the buildings indicated that a thriving city had once existed where now only skeletal remains were visible.

The small convoy of vehicles eventually located the well-known Düsseldorf Parkhotel, where Model suspected he could find Gauleiter Florian, the district Nazi Party chief. At the moment the vehicles pulled to halt before the imposing hotel, the Gauleiter was rapidly descending the stairs. Florian was still wearing his official brown uniform breeches and polished riding boots, over which he had quickly donned a civilian overcoat. A stylish fedora had replaced the crimson and brown Nazi Party headgear. In the face of the advancing American army that was relentlessly tightening the noose around the Ruhr Pocket, the Nazi official was obviously intent on abandoning his offices in hopes of disappearing into the surrounding rubble.

Florian was clearly embarrassed at the sudden encounter with Model and the staff officers, and it was obvious that he had been caught in the act of flight. It was particularly disturbing to have been seen by the field marshal, who demanded the unquestionable fulfillment of responsibility from others, just as for himself. Model left the company of his officers and spoke with the Gauleiter for several minutes. He then returned to the waiting vehicles. As they retraced the route on which they had come, the officers noted that the streets remained empty. However, many of the previously forsaken buildings now sported white flags in anticipation of the Americans' arrival.

Winrich Behr was relieved that the antiaircraft battery they had observed earlier was no longer firing. The heavy guns remained in their positions, with the mute barrels pointing skyward through the camouflage netting. The crews were nowhere to be seen; obviously, they had expended their remaining ammunition and disappeared into the countryside. Only the abandoned guns, accompanied by scattered, expended shell casings and woven-wicker projectile containers strewn about the battery, marked their previous activity.

The vehicles made their way back to the farm at Mydlinghoven. Behr proposed to the field marshal that he take the reconnaissance vehicle and drive to Ratingen. The general with whom they had spoken earlier had indicated that the Americans were withdrawing from their positions near the town. If the American troops were no longer controlling the crossroads in Ratingen, Behr felt it would be possible for the group to slip through the line at that point. Model agreed, and Behr departed, driving along the isolated road in search of a possible breach between the American positions.

Shortly before reaching Ratingen, he veered from the paved road and steered the vehicle cautiously through the woods. He came on a clearing that he immediately recognized as a former artillery position. Empty ammunition crates, K ration containers, and shell casings littered the area. The ground was clearly marked from heavy, tracked vehicles, and the experienced reconnaissance officer could see where the gun limbers had been set into the soft earth. Listening carefully, he could discern no presence of military units — no voices, no engine noises, no isolated gunfire. The Americans had apparently withdrawn. The major then proceeded carefully toward Ratingen. He approached a low ridge line, and from the slope of a terrain feature, he observed the town sprawled below in a low-lying area. The streets were abandoned, and large white flags hung limply from the buildings in the still afternoon air. The flags indicated that the town was already occupied or at least under the control of the Americans. Yet the Allied troops had obviously departed, leaving the captured town empty.

Major Behr slowly navigated his vehicle back through the woods until he reached the road leading to the farmhouse where the staff was located. Reporting his findings to Field Marshal Model, he explained that the route through Ratingen was apparently open and that from there, they could make their way out of the encircled area. To escape from the interior of the pocket was, in any case, a better alternative than to simply wait for the Americans to complete their campaign of eliminating any remaining German military presence.

The convoy again began moving. Driving the reconnaissance vehicle, Behr preceded the other vehicles transporting the field marshal, Colonel Pilling, and Colonel Michael. They soon arrived at the observation point from where Behr had surveyed Ratingen, and the group made a stop. For several minutes, they listened in silence. No sounds could be heard from the town. At length, they remounted their vehicles and proceeded into Ratingen.

Apparently, there were no troops in the town, and the apprehensive inhabitants remained behind shuttered windows and closed doors. The vehicles wound unimpeded through the streets until they cleared the perimeter of houses on the town's north side. Anxious to clear the main road, they proceeded north several miles toward Duisburg. On approaching a forested area between Ratingen and Duisburg, they left the improved roadway and entered the forest, continuing to make their way north. After following a lumber track for several miles, they suddenly came on a large construction site where the autobahn leading to Duisburg had been under expansion.

While attempting to circumvent the maze of trenches and concrete footings, the reconnaissance vehicle became immobilized in the deep, rain-soaked morass. Forced to abandon the heavy vehicle, the party of fugitives proceeded farther in the two remaining vehicles. After traversing the wooded terrain for some 3 miles, they came to the village of Lintorf on the southern outskirts of Duisburg.

To the south of Duisburg, between Lintorf and Wedau, two large lakes formed a secluded area that was approachable only from one direction. The bridges from Duisburg that spanned the lakes had been demolished, thus creating an isolated, favorable area in which the group could stop. The lakes were an impassible barrier between the woods and Duisburg, and the woods were a formidable barrier from the south. Few inhabitants dared to venture into thickly wooded areas during the initial stages of collapse, and even the heavily armed Americans would not penetrate the area without a specific goal.

Driving deeper into the forest, they located a site from which the vehicles could not be observed by marauding aircraft. As the sun set, the four officers prepared to rest for the night. Field Marshal Walter Model, his adjutant, his

intelligence officer, and a war-weary reconnaissance officer were all that remained of the Wehrmacht's once-mighty Army Group B. It was 20 April, Hitler's
fifty-sixth birthday.

That evening, the tiny group tuned in the Wehrmacht receiver in an attempt
to learn any news regarding recent events. They listened in silence as Joseph
Goebbels, the Reich propaganda minister, began his traditional speech marking the Führer's birthday. In an extensive harangue, he explained to his listeners
how the new wonder weapons were ready to be set against the enemy to wring
a last-hour victory from the impending collapse. He disparaged the people who
had greeted the arrival of the Allies with white flags and little resistance. The propaganda minister made specific mention of the "traitorous Ruhr Army" that had
been demobilized by Field Marshal Walter Model.

At last, the diatribe came to an end, leaving the four weary listeners silently
swatting mosquitoes and staring into the darkness. The field marshal finally broke
the silence. For the first time, the officers heard Model speak of the political situation in which Germany had become engulfed. "I sincerely believe that I have
served a criminal," he stated. "I led my soldiers in good conscience ... but for a
criminal government." No further words were uttered as the staff officers considered what the field marshal had said. They had all served with Model for many
months, and he was known for refraining from making any political statements or
exhibiting overt preferences for any subject other than military duties.[24]

That night, they slept on the ground, wrapping themselves in canvas shelter-
quarters. The next morning, Model asked Behr to accompany him on a walk for
a few minutes. As they paced along the forest path, Model began to speak: "Behr,
you are the one who I believe has the best chance to make it out of here; you are
young and I have always trusted your experience." He paused for several seconds
before continuing. "I am sure you will make it through this, and I have some
things I would like for you to give my wife."[25]

Model extended an envelope containing a letter, his wedding ring, and several other objects. Behr, unwilling to resign himself to such an ignominious end
for the field marshal, replied, "Herr Feldmarschall, I think we will be able to
make it through this." Model remained silent for a moment before responding.
"Behr," he said, "I cannot imagine that I, as a field marshal, the one who out of
conviction in victory for my country am responsible for the deaths of hundreds
of thousands of my soldiers, should now emerge from these woods to approach
Montgomery, or the Americans, with my hands in the air and say 'Here I am,
Field Marshal Model, I surrender.'"[26]

Again, Behr responded that there was still hope of evading the encircling
forces. Model simply responded that this was something he would have to carefully consider; it was obvious that he was resolute in his refusal to go into captiv-

ity. Just over two years earlier when the news was reported that Field Marshal Friedrich Paulus had surrendered the Sixth Army at Stalingrad, Model had remarked to his son, Hans-Georg, "A German field marshal doesn't surrender. Such a thing is just not possible."[27]

As the two officers returned to their makeshift bivouac, Behr mentioned that they were exhausting their food supply and suggested that he drive toward Duisburg to obtain provisions. Nearby were several farm buildings, and it was likely that they could obtain food there. In any case, a reconnaissance of the area was needed to determine what their next move should be. The field marshal agreed. Behr climbed into the one of the vehicles and set out through the forest.

The major returned to the isolated site between Lintorf and Wedau that afternoon. As he pulled to a halt, he was met by Lieutenant-Colonel Michael. "The field marshal shot himself with his pistol," the colonel simply stated. "We buried him over here." He led Behr a short distance to the grave site. Concealed in the forest was a low mound of earth topped by a small, improvised cross. For Major Winrich Behr, his service with the Third Reich, with Field Marshal Walter Model, and with Army Group B was a closed chapter.[28]

Chapter 14

Defeat and Occupation

With the laying down of arms, the burial of the dead, and the incarceration of prisoners, a new but equally difficult phase began for both conqueror and defeated. The official U.S. policy for the occupation of Germany had traversed a maze of bureaucratic developments before its eventual implementation in 1945, yet the Allies were still poorly prepared for the immense task of governing the conquered areas.

The instructions regarding arts and archives were limited to directions to make all reasonable efforts to preserve historical archives, museums, libraries, and works of art. This directive excepted those items deemed to promote Nazi ideology under the "denazification" instructions. Thus, the Allies immediately launched a campaign to purge all public institutions of Nazi emblems or any designs that were interpreted as glorifying militarism.

This effort was only partially successful as Allied armies swept through Germany. Allied propaganda had led many U.S. soldiers to believe that Germans were a people with no culture of their own, that any works of art worth preserving had been looted by the Nazis from their victims, and that the taking of any valuables by Allied soldiers was therefore justified "liberation." For many GIs—hardened by months of combat against the Wehrmacht and coming from a continent and a society far distanced from the confines of Europe—the Germans represented something less than civilized beings.

A U.S. First Army report revealed that as new units passed through previously undisturbed areas, the troops took "radios, food, bicycles, crucifixes, doors, cooking utensils, and cattle."[1] As the forces moved farther into Germany, crimes ranging from simple theft to widespread looting became commonplace. Groups of soldiers waited expectantly outside headquarters facilities to intercept civilians bringing in the radios, cameras, and weapons that, by order of the occupation authorities, they were required to surrender. An American soldier summarized the chaotic situation by reporting, "It was a unique feeling ... You can't imagine how much power we had. Whatever we wanted, we just took."[2]

Looting in the western theater of operations was not limited to American soldiers. In retribution for the misery inflicted on them by the Nazis, British and Canadian troops also participated in instances of senseless destruction and theft. British reports reveal the wanton slaughtering of livestock, pillaging of museums, and looting of banks. Churches, monuments, and works of art were damaged and desecrated; valuable archives were intentionally destroyed. Major General G. W. R. Templer, the British director of military government, reported personally viewing the site where troops had maliciously destroyed an immense collection of porcelain in a medieval castle.[3]

The early actions of the occupiers varied greatly from place to place. In some towns and villages, the inhabitants escaped looting, theft, and damage to personal belongings. Inexplicably, some nearby settlement would experience a high degree of criminal activity at the hands of either the occupiers or the bands of foreign laborers, by then officially designated as DPs—displaced persons. The town of Holzweiler saw a great deal of destruction by American GIs as the occupation began. They first systematically searched all residences, commercial buildings, and other structures for weapons, cameras, and radios. The entire population of the town was assembled and placed under guard in two large warehouses. The men were separated from their families and taken to nearby barns. Any males suspected of being German soldiers were rounded up and transported to the massive POW enclosures on the banks of the Rhine. After a local cleric intervened, the women and children were finally released to return to their homes. The relief they felt when permitted to return to their homes soon turned to disappointment; the soldiers had systematically searched the blocks of houses while the inhabitants were absent. All items of value were missing. Radios that were not taken were destroyed. Linens, down comforters, blankets, and anything else that the soldiers needed were removed.

The homes that had not suffered serious destruction were requisitioned for quarters by the occupiers, and the owners were compelled to seek shelter elsewhere. Some 700 civilians were transported to Holzweiler from the village of Wanlo and were housed in the Holzweiler church. They huddled together for warmth in the badly damaged church as a heavy rain streamed through the roof and saturated all belongings. Some 50 small children and infants clung to their mothers for warmth and cried of hunger and thirst. Milk was provided for the children on the second day, and the adults shared the sparse rations they received from the soldiers. The church remained occupied by the civilians from Wanlo and Holzweiler for five days, after which they were permitted to seek shelter elsewhere.

In Rheindahlen, the American authorities ordered all eighteen- to thirty-year-old residents, who were under guard in a hospital at the time, to assemble in the town square. Without explanation, they were then ordered to return to their homes. There was no milk for the infants and young children, and mothers were feeding their babies with water. There were no diapers or towels. During the two days of incarceration, each adult was provided one or, in some instances, two slices of dark bread. The elderly in one room took turns sleeping on the only mattress remaining in their quarters. After several days, the authorities authorized 200 inhabitants to return to their homes, but the release was mysteriously halted after 130 detainees left the premises. Shortly afterward, most of the inhabitants who had departed returned of their own volition. To their great disappointment, their homes had been requisitioned and were now occupied by American soldiers.[4]

Within several days, Herr Esser was named Bürgermeister of Rheindahlen by the occupation authorities. His position permitted him to move about the town during the hours of curfew, armed with an identity card and a white armband. On his first visit to his home, he found that the American guards had vanished. After entering the residence, he was shocked to discover furniture, utensils, bedding, linens, stockings, shoes, dresses, photographs, books — everything in the home — lying in chaos. In the nearby school, he found decaying cabbages, potatoes, onions, preserves, and canned goods; broken jars, bottles, porcelain, and destroyed sewing machines were strewn throughout the classrooms.

Mönchengladbach suffered severe destruction during the course of the war. Of 130,000 prewar inhabitants, only 49,000 battered citizens remained at the end of the conflict. Most of the people had been evacuated, had fled before the Allies, had been drafted into the Wehrmacht, or had lost their lives under the hail of bombs and artillery projectiles. More than 40 percent of the housing had been destroyed, and an additional 20 percent had been badly damaged. The shortage of habitable dwellings was exacerbated when the American forces requisitioned most of the remaining houses for the billeting of troops. Entire blocks of homes that had escaped major destruction during the war were off-limits to German citizens. The borders were marked by tangles of concertina wire and secured by guards, through which no German was permitted to pass. When their homes were confiscated, the inhabitants were notified that they had to leave the premises within a specified period of time, depending on the needs — and, apparently, the disposition — of the occupation authorities. They were permitted to take with them what possessions they could carry on their persons.

The occupation authorities routinely posted placards outlining regulations, which, under threat of punishment (including execution), were not to be circumvented. The signs announced that a military government was now in effect; every person was required to follow the regulations without question. Other than between 9:00 a.m. and noon, everyone was to remain in his or her home. During the three morning hours, one person per household was permitted to move freely for the purpose of obtaining food or water. A blackout was to be strictly enforced between sunset and sunrise. The use of cameras or binoculars was forbidden. Communications equipment, firearms, munitions, explosives, and any other war materials were to be delivered to the military authorities.

Certain infractions of the rules established by the occupation forces could result in capital punishment. Those that brought severe punishment included contact with German military personnel; armed assault or armed resistance against Allied personnel; assisting German military personnel or nationals allied with Germany to avoid capture; the sabotage of military equipment belonging to Allied powers; the destruction, removal, altering, or concealing of files or archives of any kind; plundering, arson, or theft; the intentional hindrance or deceiving of Allied personnel; any assistance rendered to the enemy; and endangering the security of Allied personnel. Individuals accused of violating the regulations were to be tried in a court of the Allied military powers.

The disarming of the German population exacerbated the lawlessness that pervaded the conquered areas in the wake of the Allied forces. In accordance with occupation policy, all firearms, regardless of function, were to be surrendered to the authorities. The possession of firearms could, under certain circumstances, be punished by death. In the Münsterland, as in other areas, an amnesty period was offered in hopes of disarming the public and clearing the area of the war material that lay everywhere. Other forbidden articles that were to be surrendered included carrier pigeons, gasoline, lubricants, and fuel oil.

The search for weapons gave Allied soldiers an official purpose for entering homes and buildings at will. Depending on the disposition of the searchers, little might remain intact after the inspections. One inhabitant in the town of Viersen watched while GIs wantonly destroyed valuable porcelain as they made their way through his home. At length, he disappeared into his cellar and returned with a bottle of cognac and offered it to the soldiers, explaining that this was the only weapon in the home. The contented GIs immediately ended their search and disappeared with the bottle to engage in less destructive behavior.

Predictably, many American soldiers were disinclined to participate in wanton theft and the destruction of personal property. Six Americans entered a home in Lobberich and herded the inhabitants into one room, where they remained under guard until the house was searched. After a few minutes, one of the soldiers returned with a wristwatch that had been hidden under a pillow. Returning it to its owner, the soldier warned her that she should conceal it more effectively—and added that other soldiers would have taken it.

The male citizens in Kempen were ordered to assemble in the town square, and from there, approximately 300 were marched to the cellar of the local finance office and held until the following day. While the men were being held, all other inhabitants were ordered to remain in their homes with the doors open. American soldiers began systematically searching the buildings for German soldiers and weapons. No deserters or firearms were found, but the GIs eagerly confiscated Nazi paraphernalia; Hitler photographs; flags; and large quantities of wine, beer, and other liquor.

After the departure of the first Americans to enter the town of Hüls, Bürgermeister Peter Knippen was advised by a citizen that a Hitler bust and a party banner was still in the district's National Socialist Assistance Office. Knippen hurried to the office and removed the items, placing the flag in the coal stove, where it would be burned. Soon, Americans reappeared and, during a search of the building, discovered the Nazi banner in the stove. Angry soldiers demolished the interior of the building. Not until an American officer known only to the inhabitants as Captain Cohn appeared and took control of the town did the destruction abate.[5]

In the Sauerland village of Siedlinghausen, teenager Margarete Lütken anticipated the arrival of the Americans with a mixture of excitement and trepidation. The war was clearly lost, and despite the rumors and propaganda to which the inhabitants had been subjected over the previous months, the end of the war would mean a change from the misery and uncertainty the fighting had brought. In her imagination, the young girl had even romanticized how the first American stranger she encountered might appear. Her fanciful expectations were met with disappointment. A massive, unshaven GI cautiously pushed open the front door of her home with the muzzle of a rifle. As the helmeted stranger entered the foyer, Margarete noticed that his sweat-stained combat blouse was bedecked with brooches and pins. The soldier immediately pulled a brightly colored scarf from the coat rack in the foyer and crammed it into his jacket pocket. After exploring all of the ground-floor rooms, he commanded her to proceed up the stairs before him. They ascended the narrow staircase, and the soldier began pocketing various items that pleased him. He picked up a "dynamo" flashlight that she had placed on a table just moments before his arrival and affixed it to his web belt. Slinking into her parents' bedroom, the GI emptied her mother's jewelry box, rifled through the contents, and selected several pieces, which promptly disappeared into a pocket. The ominous figure then discovered her father's small coin collection, and it, too, disappeared. Margarete painfully watched as he found her mother's most prized possession, an heirloom oboe. The instrument was crammed into his belt. It was then that she noticed the soldier's left arm was decorated with watches extending from wrist to elbow. Shocked at the conduct of the first American she met, she looked into his face disapprovingly and exclaimed in schoolyard English, "You are a robber!" The GI, unfazed by her reproach, grinned and continued his search of the home, pocketing more valuables.[6]

The American soldiers often assumed that every city hall had been utilized as a Gestapo headquarters, and they exhibited their hatred for the Nazi regime accordingly. Often, the entire contents of official files were confiscated and trucked to an unknown destination by military personnel. Currency was removed from tax offices and strewn about the streets or handed to passers-by at the whim of the soldiers. A curfew was immediately instituted, but it changed unpredictably according to the rumors of resistance or sabotage activity. When the German civilians were permitted to leave their homes during specified hours to obtain necessities, their excursions typically involved hurrying through the streets and forming lines at all facilities where food might be obtained; the inhabitants were anxious to be off the streets prior to the onset of curfew, after which infractions were punishable by arrest. The effort to obtain food, water, and other necessities was also hindered by a regulation forbidding the assembly of more than five persons; in the circumstances, the rule had to be ignored, although infractions could result in arrest. Assembly for worship was permitted as an exception to the regulation, and American army chaplains often performed religious services for the public.

Appointments to the position of Bürgermeister occurred at random and were made by the officers in command of the first units to occupy towns and villages. In accordance with Allied occupation policy, officials who had held public office under the Nazi regime were usually removed from their positions and arrested. The appointment of a Bürgermeister was often marked by a hastily drawn, semiofficial document identifying the individual as the new town official. The Bürgermeister of one Rhineland town received his identity document in the middle of the street; the document was a page torn from a notebook. The initial appointments hardly reflected administrative skills or experience, and the positions changed hands at random intervals: either the initial officeholder appointed by the Americans would resign, the occupation authorities would replace the individual for uncooperative behavior, or replacement became necessary when the military government attempted to enforce often vague and conflicting occupation regulations.

The city of Cologne remained divided for a period of six weeks, with the Rhine River representing the dividing line between the occupied western half and the half under Nazi rule in the east. In the west bank area of Cologne, the occupation came early, for the Americans had captured that portion of the city on 6 March. The occupation authorities immediately imposed a curfew, the violation of which could be punishable by death. Patrols quickly set about combing the intact residences and commercial buildings in search of German soldiers, hidden weapons, radios, and cameras. During the searches, jewelry, watches, and other valuables often disappeared into the hands of the searchers as they consolidated their rule over the conquered areas.

Cologne resident Wolfgang Schmidt and his parents were in their residence on the Merheimerstrasse when an American patrol arrived. They suddenly heard the deafening sound of rifle butts against their door, accompanied by shouts of "Open up! Open up!" Wolfgang's mother was paralyzed with fear, but his father quickly moved toward the door to admit the soldiers. Wolfgang grabbed his father's arm to restrain him, frantically reminding him in a hushed voice, "The Hitler portrait! Let them wait!" The boy ran into the living room, removed the incriminating portrait from the wall, and hastily slid it behind the piano.

After the portrait was safely out of sight, his father opened the door. Standing before the frightened occupants were two American soldiers in full combat gear, submachine guns at their hips. One of the soldiers was nonchalantly smoking a cigarette; the other was chewing gum. Unable to understand the demands of the soldiers, the family discerned from their attitude that the soldiers were intent on searching the dwelling. Wolfgang's father led the soldiers from room to room as they inspected the contents of wardrobes and cabinets. They emptied drawers onto the floor, upended bedding, and tossed the contents of wardrobes into the middle of the room.

Suddenly, one of the soldiers emerged from a bedroom holding his father's blue Reichsbahn railway cap. "Nazi! Nazi!" the soldier shouted, gesturing at the swastika emblem on the peak of the cap. The cap was thrown to the floor, and the soldier trampled it while he continued to shout unintelligibly. In his classroom English, Wolfgang desperately attempted to explain that it was only a railway worker's cap and that his father was an employee of the Reichsbahn. The soldier finally grasped the meaning of his explanation and immediately calmed down. Ignoring the family's antiquated radio, the soldiers left the apartment without further incident and moved to the nearby residence of a minor Nazi Party functionary. The official had fled with his family shortly before the arrival of the Americans, but he had neglected to sanitize his home of incriminating paraphernalia. The Americans came across his Nazi Party uniform and a bust of Adolf Hitler. In a rage, they proceeded to vandalize the home. The uniform and Hitler bust were thrown through a window onto the street. The entire contents of the home quickly followed. Leaving the apartment uninhabitable, the soldiers moved on.[7]

The village of Siedlinghausen was struck particularly hard by American soldiers. On the first day that U.S. troops occupied the village, the soldiers began their customary search for Wehrmacht deserters and hidden weapons. During the search, feather beds were slashed and wardrobes, suitcases, and trunks were broken open; the contents were scattered throughout the dwellings. Linens were torn and riddled with holes; porcelain was raked from china cabinets onto the floor or thrown through windows. Many of the troops were less interested in obtaining material goods than in locating stores of alcohol, and the cellars and barns were combed for whatever schnapps or wine might be stored. The wanton behavior took a remarkable turn for the better once the combat troops had departed and the rear-echelon troops took up residence in the village.[8]

The inhabitants of the large cities often suffered more personal loss than those living in the smaller towns and villages in the outlying areas. In the immediate aftermath of defeat, the Americans often pressed on toward their next objective, taking police officers and public authorities into custody and leaving anarchy in their wake. The German citizens sometimes contributed to the lawlessness. Unable to predict what the future would bring, the inhabitants sought to stockpile anything of use against shortages in the future. Railyards and storage facilities were plundered for food and valuables. Freight cars were forced open, and the contents were strewn along the rail lines. The storage facilities of department stores and small grocery stores were plundered. Laden with clothing, sacks of foodstuffs, textiles, and abandoned military equipment, throngs of civilians loaded hand-carts and carried on their backs anything they could find. Official government buildings were not spared. Nazi Party offices, once plundered by Allied soldiers for souvenirs and valuables, lay open to civilians in search of anything of use. Postal facilities, which often contained piles of military mail destined for German soldiers serving in an army that no longer existed, were plundered of their contents. With the collapse of the transportation systems in the closing weeks of the war, letters and packages piled up at postal facilities and were abandoned by authorities as the Allies approached.

The Americans were often as generous as they were undisciplined. In Siedlinghausen, the village children, enjoying the freedom that came with the lack of school since the occupation began, often returned home laden with chocolate, white bread, and tins of corned beef obtained during their forays among the Americans. However, the inhabitants, accustomed to the strict regulations that had governed all activities in Germany, were shocked at the fishing methods used by the Americans. The soldiers were observed placing electric wires into the streams, after which they would engage a generator and scoop out stunned fish by the basketful.[9]

As they devised policies that affected the German economy and the standard of living, the American authorities became concerned with fraternization between Americans and German citizens. In preparation for dealing with the populace of an enemy country, Eisenhower's troops had been provided with a booklet entitled *Pocket Guide to Germany*. The booklet outlined the War Department's official policy on Germany and attempted to prepare GIs for the challenges of occupation. It advised the reader that Hitler's policies had widespread support among the citizens, and it explained the so-called miscreant cultural and national traits of the German people. According to the guide, World War II had occurred, in part, because of the breakdown of nonfraternization policies set after World War I. The friendly relations U.S. service members had developed with German civilians were deemed partly responsible for the outbreak of the war, and the mistake was not to be repeated.[10]

American troops had first set foot on German soil when they crossed the German-Belgian frontier southwest of Aachen on 11 September, 1944. On 22 September, 1944 General Eisenhower received a telegram from Washington expressing a matter of great concern to the president:

> There have appeared in the press photographs of American soldiers fraternizing with Germans in Germany. These photographs are considered objectionable by a number of our people.
> It is desired that steps be taken to discourage fraternization by our troops with the inhabitants of Germany and that publication of such photos be effectively prohibited.[11]

Despite efforts to prohibit fraternization between U.S. soldiers and Germans, social interaction, particularly with young women, could not be halted. One of the difficulties regarding the prohibition was that it only served to promote contact between those Americans and Germans who were willing to risk engaging in prohibited behavior. The policy essentially limited lonely American soldiers to contact with illicit elements and unlicensed prostitutes. According to one civil affairs report on the reasons for evoking the ban:

> The troop were no longer billeted on inhabitants where they could enjoy the feminine society of the household, but were lodged in barracks … The result was that the venereal rate, which had been surprisingly small … now are amazingly large … the Commanding General determined to revoke the anti-fraternization order, in order that soldiers might again associate with decent women.[12]

One of the arguments put forward by Secretary of the Treasury Henry Morgenthau, a highly influential and vocal proponent of the ban, was that despite the effectiveness in increasing morale and reducing the rate of venereal disease, fraternization had also resulted in "an epidemic of requests for permission to marry German women."[13]

Eisenhower had previously received Combined Chiefs of Staff Directive 551, "strongly discouraging" any forms of fraternization between U.S. soldiers and the civilian population in Germany. The terse message from President

Franklin Roosevelt, however, provided an impetus for more stringent measures. Eisenhower immediately replied through Chief of Staff George C. Marshall, requesting that Marshall assure the president that Eisenhower had repeatedly emphasized the orders against fraternization. Additionally, all commanders had been issued explicit orders "insisting that fraternization be suppressed completely."[14] In his directives to his troops, Eisenhower stressed that the directive and spirit of the *Pocket Guide to Germany* were to be followed, advising them that "Germans had learned since early childhood to use force, deception, and ruthlessness to gain a position of dominance over all other peoples of the world." He also stated that "however sick of the Nazi party, the Germans have sinned against the laws of humanity and cannot come back into the civilized world by merely sticking out their hands and saying—'I'm sorry.'"[15]

In addition to the policy outlined in the handbook, Eisenhower issued a nine-page directive reinforcing the tone of the guide and leaving no room for circumventing the official policy of nonfraternization. The directive was explicit in prohibiting any social interaction with Germans involving "friendliness, familiarity or intimacy," whether in groups or as individuals, in either official or unofficial exchanges. Social interaction such as attending German-American church services, visits in homes, shaking hands with Germans, participating in sports with them, exchanging gifts, attending social events, accompanying Germans in public in any capacity other than official business, and holding any forms of discussions were all explicitly forbidden. Violations of the directive were punishable by a fine of $65 and the possibility of a court-martial.[16]

Other problems related to the prisoners of war. In the immediate aftermath of their capture, the situation of POWs remained perilous until they could be removed from the combat area. On 7 April, for example, a number of straggling German soldiers from the 116th "Windhund" Panzer Division filtered into the settlement of Budberg near Werl. The ragged and hungry soldiers found shelter with local farmers, and ten members of the group were provided haven by Bürgermeister Becker. The following morning, the village came under fire from an American artillery battery, which killed a number of the inhabitants in their cellars. As the barrage lifted, American infantrymen entered the village, securing the buildings and capturing the soldiers without resistance. Two of the soldiers were shot as they attempted to flee. Among the prisoners were seventeen-year-old Friedrich Schmidthausen and a badly wounded officer, Captain Gerling. Over several hours, the prisoners were joined by other captives as the Americans cleared the village of Wehrmacht stragglers.

The captives were taken to the Borg house at the perimeter of the village, where they were lined up with their faces to a wall. Almost instantly, the soldiers and their prisoners found themselves in the midst of ricocheting bullets and shattering windows as concealed German soldiers opened fire on the group of captors and captives. In the wake of a short-lived engagement, in which several Americans became casualties, the prisoners were marched into the Borg house, where they remained under heavy guard for the rest of the day. Several hours later, a number of American soldiers who had been killed in the exchange were placed in a row beneath the window, and the prisoners were periodically compelled by their captors to view the bodies. A lieutenant was later separated from the group for interrogation. On his return, he advised the other prisoners that the Americans were preparing to execute the prisoners that evening.

During the afternoon, the seven youngest of the prisoners were separated from the group, ostensibly to be executed. The soldiers were returned to the group following an energetic protest by the Wehrmacht lieutenant. At 6:00 p.m., the prisoners were ordered from the building; carrying the wounded captain on a dismantled door, they marched to a nearby command post. There, they were again questioned by an American officer. The soldiers, unable to comprehend the interrogation in English, could not respond satisfactorily to the questions. The officer angrily ordered the prisoners to be taken away. As the fourteen captives were marching through Budberg, one of the guards suddenly gave the order for them to be placed against a wall. After the men lined up along a structure with their hands behind their heads, the soldiers opened fire. Bodies tumbled to the ground, and the shooting stopped as abruptly as it had begun. Of the fourteen prisoners, three remained alive as the Americans quickly faded into the darkness. At daylight, the dead were piled onto a truck by U.S. Army personnel and driven to an unknown location. Two of the wounded soldiers—an elderly Volkssturm member and an officer candidate—were found the next day in a nearby barn by U.S. soldiers and taken into captivity. Friedrich Schmidthausen, who had fallen with seven wounds, had feigned death until the GIs disappeared. He then escaped with assistance from a Russian laborer and a teenaged girl who transported him to a medical clinic.[17]

On 13 April, as American forces surrounded the small settlement of Spitze, they met unexpected resistance from a flak battery that had been established near the village. The flak crewmen, who had refused the appeals of the inhabitants to surrender or withdraw, were determined to offer resistance. The German soldiers had reportedly been drinking heavily throughout the time they were at the village. As the American columns approached the nearby village of Biesfeld, where white flags were displayed, the battery opened fire with 105-mm antiaircraft guns. The barrage destroyed a house and killed a woman, a young girl, and two German soldiers who had taken refuge in the building to await the arrival of the U.S. troops.

A column of American tanks, seeing white flags waving from buildings in Biesfeld and Spitze, expected no resistance and were unaware of the presence of the flak battery. When the column approached the village from the direction of Herrenstrunden, it was also taken under fire. The tanks and support vehicles immediately turned and took up positions from which they could fire on the village. The exchange lasted throughout the night, during which reconnaissance patrols from both sides attempted to discern the positions of their opponents. At dawn, the village was assaulted and captured by American soldiers, and the flak position was quickly neutralized. As the firing subsided, the Americans herded all inhabitants, foreign laborers, and German prisoners of war together. The angry Americans separated the detainees and prisoners into three groups and began questioning them as to why the U.S. troops had been led into an ambush. One of the French laborers, Roger Vidal, explained that the civilians in the village were not responsible for the incident; none of the inhabitants had offered or wanted any resistance. He also explained that the foreign workers in the village had always experienced good relationships with the inhabitants. Shortly thereafter, the Americans released the civilians and marched the captured soldiers and a number of uniformed police to a nearby field along the Gladbacher road, where the twenty-one prisoners were machine-gunned.[18]

The death of German prisoners at the hands of war-weary, battle-hardened GIs was only one of the problems facing both the victors and the conquered in 1945. Under the terms of the Geneva Convention, the signatories were required to feed POWs rations equal to those provided to their own troops. Both Germany and the United States had signed the convention, which held the same legal ramifications as a treaty. As the war in Europe approached its end in spring 1945, the Allied forces were facing an unexpected problem of unforeseeable proportions.

In May 1943, Eisenhower had had to deal with immense numbers of German prisoners of war in Tunisia when the Afrikakorps surrendered. In a letter to Chief of Staff Marshall, he lamented the difficulties associated with handling prisoners, stating that West Point had never prepared him for the task and remarking that "we should have killed more of them."[19] Little did he realize that the future would bring a problem much more acute than that facing the Allied supply system in 1943. At the beginning of May 1945, Supreme Headquarters, Allied Expeditionary Force (SHAEF), reported holding a total of 4,209,000 German prisoners of war. By June 1945, the figure had risen to 7,614,794 POWs and "disarmed enemy forces."[20]

The term *disarmed enemy forces* held a special meaning for Eisenhower and the U.S. government. Facing a staggering food shortage throughout their areas of responsibility, the governments of the United States and Britain had found a means of circumventing the Geneva Convention. The British changed the status of the prisoners flooding into the POW enclosures from prisoners of war to surrendered enemy personnel (SEPs). Eisenhower, at the request of the Joint Chiefs of Staff in Washington, initiated a policy of redesignating prisoners as disarmed enemy forces (DEFs). This policy permitted the Allies to provide rations to German prisoners at a level lower than that prescribed by the Geneva Convention. Because no regulations existed for personnel under the DEF designation, this move essentially meant that the prisoners could be treated in any manner deemed necessary by their captors.[21]

Following the surrender of Germany in early May 1945, there was no longer a German government that could intercede or negotiate on the prisoners' behalf. Other countries, including those that had remained neutral during the war, had little inclination to assist prisoners who had served a regime that inflicted immeasurable misery and death throughout Europe. Consequently, the prisoners were abandoned to the mercy of their captors. Exacerbating the situation was the personal animosity felt by Eisenhower toward the Germans, an attitude that was widely shared by the ranks of American soldiers serving as guards and administrators of the massive camps. The guards "tended to be young, recently arrived recruits, men who had not been in combat," and as veterans noted, the new arrivals were "most likely to find a means to show how tough they were."[22] The attitude of indifference or malice was exacerbated by senior officials who selected Jewish officers to administer the camps—an opportunity that, as one Jewish officer remarked, enabled them to "get a little revenge."[23]

For thousands of the German troops who surrendered in the spring of 1945, the preliminary treatment they received in captivity did not bode well for their future. Usually exhausted, dispirited, and very hungry, many felt an initial relief to finally see their war come to an end, especially in the western theater where, in contrast to the Eastern Front, captivity meant an extremely high likelihood of survival. If they survived their final encounter with Allied troops in combat, they were usually immediately relieved of their wristwatches, wedding rings, and any other items of commercial value. As they emerged from foxholes, bunkers, and bullet-riddled buildings with their hands held high, field badges and decorations were torn from their uniforms by souvenir-hungry GIs. One GI wrote home to inform his parents that he had obtained "pistols, knives, watches, fur-lined coats, camouflaged jump jackets." He further reported that "a pistol flashed ... can persuade anybody" to surrender his watch.[24]

The prisoners were usually marched singly or in columns, hands clasped behind their heads, to a nearby collecting point. The makeshift POW pens gradually filled as they were joined by other recently captured soldiers to await transport to a large POW enclosure. Each step in the journey involved more searches. By the time they arrived at the massive enclosures, which were simply fields sur-rounded by barbed wire, watch towers, and numerous armed guards, they usu-ally possessed only the uniforms they wore—having been divested of all other personal and official items, often including identity documents.

After being delivered to the POW cages, the prisoners frequently received nothing to eat or drink for days. In 1945, the entire German population was facing starvation, and the prisoners in the hands of Allied captors were not a priority in terms of the scarce food resources. By the end of the war, crop levels had fallen by some 30 percent.[25] The extensive destruction of the German rail-roads and other transport systems exacerbated the already bleak situation. Many densely populated areas had become dependent on horse-carts for the delivery of whatever food that was available. Roving bands of DPs, following in the wake of the invading enemy forces, decimated the food stocks and stripped the farms of anything edible that remained after the troops departed. The severing of the area east of the Oder-Neisse line from Germany by the Soviet Union also denied the population of food that might have been obtained from traditional sources in Silesia. The resulting shortages left the prisoners at the bottom of an extensive supply chain, and the denazification procedures only delayed the release of thou-sands of POWs who could have contributed to the reestablishment of transporta-tion and food-production facilities.

The military governor of Bavaria, General Patton, vehemently disagreed with the Allied occupation policy regarding German POWs. In September 1945, he wrote to his wife, Beatrice:

> I am frankly opposed to this war criminal stuff. It is not cricket and is Semitic. I am also opposed to sending PW's to work as slaves in foreign lands [in particular, to France] where many will be starved to death.[26]

Not all senior officers shared Patton's sentiments. Brigadier General Philip S. Gage, Patton's former roommate at West Point, wrote:

> I read in the paper of how you required the civil population of Weimar to visit the Buchenwald prison camp and see for themselves the horrors of the Nazi regime … I do hope that wherever and whenever you can, you will do what you can to make the German populace suffer. For God's sake, please don't ever go soft in regard to them. Nothing could ever be too bad for them.[27]

The denazification controversy spelled the end of a tumultuous career for the most popular U.S. general. Exasperated by Patton's noncompliance with U.S.

policy, Eisenhower relieved him of command, replacing him with General Lucian Truscott, Patton's former subordinate. Eisenhower's instructions to Truscott were to be stern in his treatment of the Germans and to provide "preferential treatment" to Jews.[28]

For the hundreds of thousands of prisoners filing into the POW enclosures along the Rhine, the future was very uncertain. Prisoners were usually stripped of all belongings on capture and were searched again prior to entering the cages. Mountains of articles confiscated from the hapless POWs grew at the entrance to the cages: razors, cigarettes, canned goods, spare clothing, rucksacks, blankets, canteens, ponchos, loaves of bread, mess tins, sandwiches, laundry bags, crackers, pocket knives, scissors, eyeglasses, letters, pocketbooks, and anything else that a landser may have carried to help him endure the war and, if he survived, the subsequent, inevitable imprisonment. All items were thrown together in heaps with little semblance of order. The columns of prisoners filed through the transit camps day and night, and the piles grew larger with each passing hour. The prisoners watched with astonishment and dismay as the mounds of belongings, personal documents, and assorted equipment were periodically doused with a flammable liquid and set alight.

The riches of the Americans—the immense material superiority—became more apparent to the prisoners each day. Seventeen-year-old Wehrmacht private Kurt Stasyk had attempted to avoid imprisonment by eluding the enemy soldiers along the northern fringes of the Sauerland as he made his way toward his home in Drolshagen. Hiding during the hours of daylight and traveling at night, he was aroused from an exhaustion-induced sleep early one afternoon by the nudging of an American soldier's boot. After being searched, he was marched with upraised hands toward a farmstead, where he joined a growing group of prisoners being held for further transport. The following morning, a large truck pulled to a stop in the farmyard, and the prisoners, after being stripped of baggage and equipment, were directed onto the vehicle. Packed closely in the open bed, they swayed at every curve as the driver sped along the twisting roads of the Sauerland.

Suddenly, the truck jolted to a stop on the side of the road. Cursing GIs descended from the cab and ordered several prisoners from the truck. Kurt, standing at the rear of the truck bed, jumped to the roadside and was joined by several other soldiers. Directed by their captors to change a flat tire, they set about wrestling the spare and tools from the chassis as other trucks in the column rumbled past. After completing their task, Kurt and another soldier were struggling to slide the spare onto the rack beneath the chassis when they were stopped by an impatient guard. To their astonishment, the GI picked up the flat tire by the rim and heaved it into a nearby hedgerow. The unbelieving landsers climbed onto the truck and were soon barreling toward their destination. Kurt Stasyk could only imagine what would have happened to a Wehrmacht landser had he been observed discarding a perfectly good tire.[29]

The search for German military stragglers, the rumors of resistance activity, and the pursuit of Nazi authorities in hiding brought tens of thousands of civilians into captivity. In the village of Steinheim, the occupation troops ordered all former German soldiers to report to the home of the local cleric for registration. Some twenty local men reported as required. The registration consisted of one simple question: each man was asked if he had served as a soldier. Those who answered in the affirmative, many of whom were World War I veterans, were immediately placed in custody to join a growing number of internees at the Steinheim furniture factory, where they remained under close guard by GIs carrying rifles with fixed bayonets. The group was eventually transferred to a barn belonging to Konrad Lödige. After several hours, the men were ordered onto a truck that transported them to Brackwede by way of Bad Pyrmont and Detmold. Brackwede was apparently a transit camp, from which the mass of prisoners were destined for the immense enclosures at Rheinberg for further processing and distribution. Many of them did not return home for several years.[30]

The POW camps along the Lower Rhine continued to fill as more convoys of prisoners arrived each day. The Rhine camps and those of nearby tributaries extending from Rheinberg near Wesel in the north to Bad Kreuznach in the south soon held more than half a million German prisoners. The cages near Rheinberg, Wickrath, and Remagen became especially notorious for hunger and deprivation. Initially, they contained the 325,000 prisoners from Army Group B who surrendered during the latter days of April, but these men were soon joined by prisoners from other areas. As the Americans continued east, they captured thousands of German soldiers in Bavaria, Saxony, and Thuringia. Hordes of German soldiers surrendered en masse to the American forces after crossing the Elbe in an effort to escape Soviet captivity. These prisoners, too, were soon on their way to the camps along the Rhine.

By June 1945, the Americans reported that there were more German prisoners than U.S. troops in the American zone. The teeming masses of POWs quickly exhausted the resources of the Allies, who, as victors and occupiers, were also responsible for feeding the civilian population. The weeks-long deprivations in the prison cages sometimes revealed unexpected traits within the ranks of the once highly disciplined Wehrmacht. One prisoner of war wrote in his diary:

> Last night I awoke, went walking around the enclosure and discovered
> a swarm of my comrades trading with the American guards. They now
> disgrace themselves in front of the very same men that they describe as
> common criminals, scraping their bits of English together and motioning

through the wire ... two cigarettes for one Iron Cross, First Class; four cigarettes for a gold wedding band; two packs of twenty cigarettes for a good wristwatch. One of us knows of a German soldier in our transport group, who is apparently in possession of cigarettes and conducts business for himself. He now has seventy rings. Later at home they will say that the Americans took their rings from them.[31]

While imprisoned in one of the *Rheinwiesenlager* ("Rhine meadow camps"), another German soldier recorded:

We curse the weather along the Rhine and four of us cower under a single shelter-quarter. Then come the others, who pace about the entire, long night, restless, hour after hour. This is the camp: a field encircled with pilings rammed into the earth by massive machines, bound together with barbed wire, secured with double and triple rolls of wire, flanked by watch towers, patrols of armored vehicles, and guards with dogs. We dig into the earth like on maneuvers, but not with shovels, but with ration cans, broken spoons, bare hands; like moles at work throughout the day. In Remagen there stand two fruit trees in the middle of the camp. Within a few hours all that remains of them are white stumps without bark; the landsers found a use for everything. A beet-root is consumed within a short time. An elderly man cuts slice after slice from a half-rotten beet. His shoulder boards exhibit silver braid. Within the camp that holds thousands are the remains of a farm shed. In the cellar lie those sick with diarrhea. They pass only blood and water. Hundreds make their way to the medical station to the young German medic. There is a shortage of medicine. Bulldozers periodically roll through the immense camp and push earth over the holes, quickly eliminating the results of endless hours of digging. The camp is like a massive, teeming, human horde.[32]

As the guns in the Ruhr Pocket fell silent, other dramas continued to play out across the scattered villages and towns. Almost 9 million DPs, mostly foreign workers from eastern Europe, swarmed over Germany and Austria following their liberation from farms and factories where they had been employed as forced laborers. The Allies were ill prepared to care for and control the millions of displaced slave laborers in the areas they conquered. Usually, the workers were set free on the arrival of Allied forces. Not being subject to the curfews and numerous restrictions required of the German civilians, they were at liberty to roam. The workers had often undergone years of deprivation at the hands of brutal overseers, and they reacted accordingly. They fled their camps and places of work and struck out along roads and trails aimlessly. Banding together, they armed themselves with weapons found in abundance in German military establishments or where they had been tossed by the thousands along the roads by fleeing Wehrmacht soldiers. Thus armed and working together, they raided outlying farms and villages. By day and night, hordes of mostly Poles and Russians swarmed throughout the countryside, stripping the inhabitants of all items of use or intrinsic value.

Following the surrender of Germany in May 1945, the Allied authorities concentrated their efforts to gain control of the areas under their jurisdiction. When the Allied forces encountered roving bands of DPs, they were taken into custody and transported to nearby collection points for further disposition. Many of the roaming laborers were citizens of countries allied with the United States against Germany and thus retained rights according to their official status. However, not all Allied personnel regarded the swarms of Poles, Russians, and Jews, recently freed from concentration camps, with favor. In his description of the Russian DPs located within a temporary camp near Aachen, an exasperated U.S. major wrote:

> In Aachen there were thousands of Russian DPs … They ruined the light wires every time they were installed; telephones were ripped out; windows were broken as soon as they were installed; fires broke out "accidentally"; a liaison officer was murdered; and the camp was in a constant state of chaos. The tactical troops assumed "responsibility" for the camp. They issued passes every afternoon for a group of DPs to visit the town. The visits were looting expeditions. The DPs would leave the camp with empty baskets and briefcases and return at nightfall loaded down like camels with all manner of goods … Murders, rapes, and robberies abounded. Several Russians were put in prison, but they caused so much trouble they had to be turned over to the penitentiary in Eberach. Everything was run on a hands-off kid-glove policy, which was not conducive to discipline.[33]

Some of the DPs found their new status advantageous. As DPs, they were impervious to German law and beyond the jurisdiction of German police officers, and their special status often fostered "indolence, irresponsibility, and organized criminality."[34] With the clothing issued to many of them by American forces from U.S. Army supplies, they had an excellent cover for moving at will and intimidating the local populace. Some of the former concentration camp inmates, once the object of pity among the U.S. soldiers, persisted in wearing their striped concentration camp uniforms to draw the attention of touring journalists, to whom they would repeat accounts of abuse. The necessary enforcement of law and order, accompanied by the reincarceration of numerous DPs, created resentment among the foreign laborers and concentration camp inmates. The abuse of displaced persons detained by U.S. forces became a popular, albeit short-lived, theme for journalists. A torrent of reports in American newspapers described the abuse suffered by the detainees—first at the hands of the Nazis and now at the hands of the American government.[35]

The reports spurred a visit to Germany by the U.S. representative on the Intergovernmental Committee on Refugees, Earl G. Harrison, who toured the camps under the auspices of a special emissary of the president. His negative report, coupled with a similar report by Saul S. Elgart of the American Joint Distribution Committee, resulted in additional food resources being funneled to the Jewish camps, where the rations exceeded 3,000 calories a day during a period when the general populace was starving under conditions that had reduced the average daily intake to less than 1,000 calories.[36]

The provision of additional food did not alleviate the situation, and the American press continued to publish scandalous reports on the abuse of DPs by the occupation authorities. Eisenhower ordered his generals to personally inspect all camps; the subsequent reports revealed that living conditions in the camps surpassed those of the general civilian populace. In September, hoping to stem the flood of reports of abuse, Eisenhower ordered that housing be requisitioned from Germans to accommodate the DPs; he also ordered an immediate lifting of any restrictions on their movement. The immediate result was a wave of looting throughout the vicinity of DP establishments. In Bavaria, the U.S. Army reported 1,300 DP raids against the civilian populace during just one week in October.[37]

General Patton, the postwar military governor of Bavaria, was more outspoken in his disdain for the displaced persons. In response to Harrison's report and Eisenhower's insistence that liberated Jews be placed in German homes, he wrote in his diary on 15 September 1945:

> One of the chief complaints is that the DPs are kept in camps under guard. Of course, Harrison is ignorant of the fact that if they were not kept under guard they would not stay in the camps, would spread over the county like locusts, and would eventually have to be rounded up after quite a few of them had been shot and quite a few Germans murdered and pillaged …
> The brilliant Mr. Harrison further objected to the sanitary conditions, again being ignorant of the fact that we frequently have to use force in order to prevent the inmates … from defecating on the floor when ample facilities are provided.[38]

The DPs continued to be a political and logistical problem for the Germans and occupation authorities for months. Following the surrender in May 1945, the DPs constituted 4 percent of the civilian population in Munich but were reportedly responsible for 75 percent of the crime. Between 1 June and 30 October 1945, the military government convened 2,700 trials for DPs accused of murder, robbery, rape, and looting. In the North Sea port city of Bremen, some 6,000 DPs committed 23 murders, 577 robberies, 319 burglaries, and 753 thefts within several months. After the murder of 13 Germans by a gang of DPs armed with automatic weapons in November, U.S. soldiers raided their camp and discovered massive quantities of slaughtered beef and stolen U.S. property, in addition to valuables looted from the civilians in the surrounding area. As a result of the raid, the inmates raised black flags and posted large signs at the entrance to the camp that read "American Concentration Camp for Poles."[39]

Many of the workers—poorly educated, surviving on starvation rations, and having toiled for years in the German war industry—were seeking only to return to their homes. Yet they knew only that their homes were somewhere in the east: they had little or no knowledge of what had occurred either in their homelands or in eastern areas of Germany since their departure. They set out aimlessly to separate themselves from the factories and mines where they had endured years of misery and found themselves in villages and towns that were unprepared and unable to provide either food, shelter, or clothing. The roaming bands were so commonplace that they became universally termed the *Russenplage*—the Russian plague. Initially, the freed laborers plundered outlying areas in search of food. Near the village of Ampen, for example, wandering waves of laborers swept along the roads during the second week of April and raided farmhouses and estates in a desperate search for provisions. A large inventory of wallpaper, glue, and accessories was discovered by laborers in a barn near the village, where a businessman had stored the items to prevent their destruction by air raids. The starving mob tore open wrappings and boxes and consumed the contents in quantity—with horrible consequences for many. The glue and adhesive paste, which they had believed to be edible, caused a painful and slow death. Other deaths occurred when the laborers consumed fertilizer that farmers had been hoarding in the face of shortages: potassium nitrate, needed for fertilizing fields, was also essential for the war industry. While the barn was emptied of its contents, other laborers assaulted the farmhouse. The owner was forced to hand over all contents of his home.[40]

The homes and farms along the Ampener Chausee were especially hard hit, as most of the laborers approached the village from the direction of Ostönnen. The gangs usually pounded on doors and demanded food. If the situation allowed, they would storm into the home, ransacking the entire residence. At one home, the inhabitants succeeded in barring the door against the swarm of invaders for several minutes before they were overcome by the mass of plunderers. Meanwhile, marauders converged on the nearby barn and slaughtered the family goat, a hog, and numerous rabbits. Fowl were slung against a barn wall. A teenager rushed from the chaos in the farmhouse and attempted to stop the Russians' slaughtering only to be threatened with a pitchfork. Some of the intruders grasped chickens and, after wringing their necks, began roasting them over open fires without plucking or dressing the animals. One astonished farm family peered fearfully from their windows as a group of laborers fell on the entrails of a hog that the family had set aside a day earlier to be processed as animal food. The ravenous workers consumed the entire pile of waste. The sugarbeets, stores of potatoes, and grain for livestock were consumed raw by starving laborers desperate to fill their stomachs.[41]

The Allies did not find only surrendering German soldiers, roving foreign workers, and cowed inhabitants as they tightened their grip on the Ruhr and Rhineland. In the waning days of the war, Nazi officials had sought to eliminate any surviving "undesirable" elements. In the Dortmund city park and the nearby Bittermark woods, the American forces uncovered evidence of mass murders committed by the Gestapo. Some 200 political detainees, foreign workers, and petty criminals had been confined in the Hörde prison, among them German and French resistance members. During the week of 7 March, 29 political prisoners were transported by truck from the Gestapo facility in Hörde and marched to an open field in the Bittermark woods, where, in small groups, they were led to a large bomb crater for execution. After all of the prisoners had been shot, the crater was covered with a thin layer of earth. The second mass shooting of prisoners in the Bittermark woods occurred in the days prior to 24 March, when 21 prisoners were killed, again in a bomb crater. The third such execution took place on the morning of 24 March; on that day, 25 prisoners were shot. These prisoners had been bound together in twos and threes and marched to the execution site. Other executions occurred in other locations. On 30 March, 42 prisoners were executed in Romberg park; in early April, 15 prisoners were shot near Hacheney. The bloodletting continued. On 8 or 9 April, more shootings occurred in Romberg, with some 60 more killed in a nearby field, and 3 murders were committed at the Dortmund-Hörde rail facility.[42]

The Americans learned of the executions after their arrival on 19 April. The initial reaction was to arrest all local Nazi Party officials, who were then compelled to exhume dozens of bodies from mass graves. Under the watch of German resistance members, the bodies were removed, the identities were confirmed as accurately as possible, and the remains were then reinterred in collective graves in nearby cemeteries.

Many foreign laborers were shot simply for being in the way. In the area of Warstein, a group of SS executioners commanded by Dr. Kammler, an SS Obergruppenführer in charge of the V-weapons operations in the Sauerland, committed terrible atrocities on the foreign workers that fell into their hands during the final weeks of the war. Recognizing that the roving bands of foreign workers who had fled the Ruhr industrial area threatened the security of the inhabitants in outlying areas, Kammler took action. He issued his first execution orders on 20 March. As a result, 57 laborers, including 21 women and a child, were removed from their temporary holding camp in the Suttrop school and transported to isolated woods between Warstein and Kallenhardt, where they were shot and hastily buried. The process was repeated the following day when 71 individuals were transported from the massive labor camp in the Sauerlandhalle in Warstein to an execution site in Langenbachtal. The 14 men and 56 women, one of whom carried a year-old child, were lured onto trucks with promises of better living and working conditions. A day later, on 22 March, some 70 workers were drawn to their deaths in the same manner. The workers were transported to the Eversberger Heide, an area of open fields, where they were stripped of all identifying documents and valuables before being shot.[43]

The massive barracks in which the foreign laborers were being held, the Sauerlandhalle, also fell to the wrath of the Nazis. The barracks had been divided into two separate facilities, with French workers on one side and Russians on the other. After barring the doors and windows to prevent escape, the section housing the Russians was set on fire. As the panic-stricken laborers attempted to flee, they realized that the exits had been sealed. The situation would have ended with a disaster of immense proportions if the French workers had not managed to tear an opening in the wooden wall separating the two groups, through which the Russians were able to escape the inferno. No lives were lost in the incident, but the Sauerlandhalle was completely destroyed by the fire.

After capturing the town of Ohligs near Solingen on 13 April, American authorities discovered a mass grave containing the bodies of 71 Gestapo victims. The grave was located in a sand quarry, and the bodies had been covered with a thin layer of sand. Exhumation of the remains began on 30 April under the command of Lieutenant Edwin Rosenzweig of the U.S. Army. The corpses were exhumed by local Nazi Party members, who were warned to exercise caution in uncovering the corpses so as not to deface the remains; many of the party officials were compelled to unearth the bodies with their bare hands. Examinations of the remains revealed that each prisoner had been shot in the back of the neck, and it was noted that the dead were dressed in their best clothing. Eventually, 64 of the bodies were identified as political prisoners from prisons in Wuppertal and Lüttringhausen. Among the dead was a well-known bank executive who was one of the wealthiest citizens in the Ruhr. Some 1,000 inhabitants from the area were ordered to witness the exhumation of the corpses. The following day, the victims were buried in a grassy area near the Ohligs town hall, with about 3,000 citizens in attendance. The local inhabitants were compelled to view the remains before burial, and the funeral continued for more than two hours. Men, women, and children filed past the long rows of bodies, pressing handkerchiefs against their faces in a vain attempt to stifle the overwhelming smell of decay. After the viewing, services were held by Catholic, Protestant, and Jewish clerics.[44]

EPILOGUE

The death of Field Marshal Model brought an end to the existence of Army Group B. Within the Ruhr Pocket, the Allies had succeeded in encircling and destroying twenty German divisions and capturing 325,000 troops, among them twenty-six generals and one admiral. In the wake of the fighting, the villages along the river valleys of the Sauerland, on the expansive northern plain of the Münsterland, and in the foreboding Teutoburg Forest were left in ruins. The sporadic resistance left hundreds of homes and administrative areas little more than piles of rubble. Cadavers of livestock and corpses of soldiers lined the roadsides, intermixed with burned-out hulks of motor vehicles. The mangled bodies of defenders clad in field-gray uniforms were carried to village cemeteries and buried as soon as the occupation authorities permitted; the remains of GIs who had fallen in the countless villages, orchards, and fields were entered in official records before being transported to other, faraway cemeteries. Eisenhower had decreed that no American soldier was to remain buried in Germany, and many soldiers found their final resting places in the soil of those countries they had died to liberate.

Sergeant Hüpfl, the tank commander whose detachment of Tigers had surprised the American armored column in an assembly area near Schloss Hamborn, continued to be plagued by the events that had occurred at that time. After their escape from the burning tank, the three surviving members of his crew, like hundreds of thousands of other German soldiers, eventually went into Allied captivity. Corporal Bloss was delivered to a burn clinic to receive surgery for his severe burns, and Sergeants Voss and Hüpfl were incarcerated in the prisoner-of-war camp in Eselheide, some 6 miles northwest of Paderborn. The three soldiers had escaped the burning hulk of their tank at the height of confusion during the intensive engagement. However, the fate of crewmen Walter Ertl and Werner Schurig remained unknown to Hüpfl; perhaps, he thought, they had been captured by the Americans and were now prisoners of war.

The main question that plagued him concerned his own actions during the terrifying moment when the tank became enveloped in flames. The turret of a Tiger tank must be stationary at the 11:00 position to facilitate opening the driver's and radio operator's hatch cover from within. Escaping the tank under such conditions had been practiced repeatedly — it was critical to react instantly and instinctively, for during an engagement, tank crewmen have no time to think of what actions to take to ensure their survival. Yet Hüpfl continued to question whether, in the final moments when flames began racing through his tank, he had instinctively moved the turret into the correct position to give his two crewmen a chance to escape the inferno.

As the weeks passed, thousands of prisoners languished in the camps, awaiting an undetermined future. The incarceration became more relaxed under British supervision, and the prisoners were afforded a greater degree of freedom from their barbed-wire enclosures. After imploring his captors to let him seek out the nearby site of his last engagement, Hüpfl received permission to leave the camp under the condition that he return no later than 10:00 that evening. The former Tiger commander set out toward Schloss Hamborn in search of answers to the lingering questions that haunted him. After several hours, he arrived at the Haxterberg Heights, near the area where his final clash with the Americans had occurred. He slowly made his way along the vaguely familiar road toward the site of the engagement. At the edge of the woods, he observed the abandoned hulk of a Sherman tank, with the turret ripped from its cupola and the 76-mm gun staring silently skyward. He then came on a dispersed column of trucks; several tanks and reconnaissance vehicles lined the narrow road in various stages of destruction and decay, still lying where they had fallen victim to the Tigers' guns. Within several minutes, he reached the sharp curve in the road in front of the bridge the Tigers had traversed at the height of the engagement. Sergeant Fritz Ebner's Tiger was still poised where it had received a direct hit on the turret. As memories of the encounter flooded back, Hüpfl increased his pace and crossed the bridge. At last, he found his burned-out tank sitting askew by the roadside, the massive steel glacis plates streaked with rust. With relief, he saw that he had, indeed, abandoned the burning tank only after moving the turret to the 11:00 position to give his crewmen a means of escape. He cautiously climbed onto the scorched wreckage and observed the forward hatch cover in the closed position, burned and scarred from projectile impacts. Despite strenuous efforts, Hüpfl could not move the steel cover; the impacts of heavy-caliber projectiles had apparently caused the plate to become tightly jammed, and he realized that the two crewmen had been unable to escape the burning vehicle after all. He climbed onto the turret and slowly lowered himself into the commander's seat.

The entire interior of the tank had been reduced to little more than a blackened carcass. He moved deeper into the chassis of the tank as memories of the screams, the smell of burning paint and rubber, and the earsplitting blasts of exploding ammunition came flooding back to him. He crawled past the commander's seat and, in the dim light, saw the scorched, virtually unrecognizable remains of Sergeant Ertl still sitting in the driver's position. A shriveled right hand grasped a service pistol; trapped within the confines of the steel behemoth, Ertl had apparently shot himself as the interior became enveloped in flames. Unable to discern the fate of the radioman in the dim light cast by the setting sun, Hüpfl departed from the grisly scene, determined to return and recover the remains of his comrades.

The following day, he returned to the tank, carrying a metal box in which to place the bones of the crewmen. In the stronger light of midday, he located the remains of radioman Werner Schurig curled near the half-open floor hatch, through which he had apparently attempted to free himself. After pulling the skeletal remains of the two men from the tank, he carefully sealed them in the box and then delivered them to the pastor of nearby Nordborchen for burial.[1]

Major Rudolf Dunker, the erstwhile battle commander of Beckum, continued to resist captivity or death in the Ruhr Pocket. After declaring Beckum an open city and withdrawing his forces from the area, he had been threatened with a court-martial and execution before events overtook any official action to initiate disciplinary procedures. He was ordered to report to his division commander on 3 April, and he reported to Lieutenant-Colonel Guderian for further instructions. Nothing of the incident in Beckum was mentioned, although Dunker expected to be detained for questioning—and probably punishment—regarding the surrender of the city. Within several days, a written report of the incident did appear, and the major was cautiously advised by the commanding general and the operations officer to make his way to the American lines: this was a situation that, given Hitler's no-surrender orders, they could not assist him in resolving. The major refused to desert, despite repeated, cautious urging from the staff officers. That afternoon, a court-martial was assembled for Dunker's case and an investigation into the incident was initiated. Witnesses were questioned, and all evidence was dispatched to the corps headquarters for disposition. Dunker remained at the division headquarters to await his fate. On 7 April, after the towns of Hamm and Soest fell to the Americans, he was ordered by the division commander to assume duties as battle commander of Werl. One day later, Werl was surrounded and overrun by American forces, and it appeared to the division staff officers that Dunker had either fallen or had found refuge in American captivity. Consequently, the case was shelved. Then, to their astonishment, the major, along with fifty of his soldiers, resurfaced at the division in the middle of the night. Assigned to lead another unit, Rudolf Dunker finally surrendered to the Americans on 14 April following a short but intense engagement near the village of Appricke, south of Menden. Field Marshal Model dissolved the army group two days later.[2]

Lieutenant Heinz Bauer had received severe burns when his tank was struck by an 88-mm projectile fired by a Wehrmacht gun crew during the American breakout of the Remagen bridgehead at the end of March. After receiving treatment for the burns on his face and hands, he remained with his battalion, which was assigned to the 3rd Panzer Division. The ring around the divisions in the Ruhr was closed: there was no escape route. On 17 April, his unit received Model's order to disband the army group. Intent on making his way out of the encirclement, Bauer, still suffering from intense pain due to the burns, joined up with several officers of his unit. Climbing aboard an American jeep captured in an earlier engagement, they spent several hours bouncing along back roads in search of a route that would enable them to clear the American checkpoints. As dusk was approaching, one of the officers opened a pocket knife and carefully cut a deep furrow in his left hand. Covering the bandages around Bauer's head and face profusely with fresh blood, the officer then wrapped up his own hand, and they proceeded up the road to an American checkpoint.

On approaching the intersection, occupied by an armored vehicle and some half dozen soldiers, the jeep was waved to a halt by a sentry. An American soldier examined the blood-soaked bandages covering Bauer's head and face. Other GIs eyed the German officers, clad in black panzer uniforms bearing the traditional hussar skull and crossed bones, with curiosity. After an exchange between the driver and several sentries in a mixture of broken English and German, the Americans spoke among themselves for several seconds until, with a shrug, a sentry ordered the vehicle and passengers to proceed to a medical facility about a mile away. The driver nodded and drove through the line as directed.

After proceeding several hundred yards, the jeep rounded a curve and was lost to sight of the checkpoint. The sun was setting, and the officers knew they had to find refuge quickly. Veering from the road onto a forest track, the jeep bounced across thickly wooded hillsides and ravines, occasionally stopping so the men could listen intently for any sounds of activity. The searing pain suffered by Bauer had increased, and his bandages were now stained by fluid oozing from the burns. They would have to find a means of cleaning the raw wounds and a source for sterile bandages. Full darkness had settled on the Sauerland when they dared to turn onto an isolated road that led them to a farmyard enclosed by red-brick structures. As they pounded on the farmhouse door, an upstairs shutter flew open and a gruff-voiced farmer leaned out, demanding that they go away. The officers explained that they had a badly injured soldier with them who needed medical care, and within seconds, the door opened to admit them.

The farmer's wife set about preparing food. The bandages covering Bauer's wounds were changed, but that did little to alleviate the pain. The soldiers expressed concern when they learned that a Polish laborer was on the farm; the farmer attempted to ease their suspicions by explaining that the man had worked there for several years and was reliable: he would not betray them to the

Americans. Concealing the jeep in the barn, the group to decided to rest for the night before proceeding onward.

The fugitives were awakened several hours later by the roar of approaching vehicles and hammering on the door, accompanied by shouts in English. The officers quickly realized that the farmyard was surrounded and that more vehicles were arriving. Knowing that further resistance would be futile, they proceeded into the farmyard with upraised hands, suppressing the frustration they felt at having ignored their instincts. The Polish laborer had, indeed, betrayed their location, and thus, their war came to an end.[3]

After leaving the grave of Field Marshal Model in the isolated forest, the three staff officers—Major Winrich Behr, Lieutenant-Colonel Roger Michael, and Colonel Theodor Pilling—parted company. Behr and Michael drove to a farmstead some distance away; Behr knew the farmer from previous contact. After concealing their vehicle, they exchanged their Wehrmacht uniforms for common work overalls. Behr left Model's personal effects and the final letter the field marshal had written to his wife with the farmer, who promised to keep the items safe until Behr's eventual return. Filling the pockets of their coveralls with various hand tools, the two men set out on a journey through the American lines. They did not carry any excess provisions or clothing: local workmen would not have such things in their possession, and to be found with those items would have revealed their identities as fleeing German soldiers to any suspicious authorities.

Their ruse succeeded. The two officers, disguised as simple farm laborers, simply walked through the American lines. Michael returned to his home in Heidelberg. Behr, whose home in Berlin was now firmly in the hands of Soviet forces, remained with friends who were willing to risk harboring the fugitive officer. After several months, he realized that he would have to report to the authorities in order to obtain identity documents, ration cards, and other verification necessary to survive in occupied Germany. He checked in at an American headquarters, where he was surprised to find a former classmate serving as an American intelligence officer. The Jewish classmate had fled Nazi Germany with his family prior to the war and took refuge in the United States. The two officers discussed various topics regarding their shared past. The American officer then asked Behr about his activities during the war, which Behr described in detail—rising through the ranks as a cavalry officer, serving with Rommel in Africa, the debacle at Stalingrad, Normandy, the Ardennes, and the final days in the Ruhr. They discussed the various commanders with whom Behr had served, such as Paulus, Rommel, von Kluge, and Model. At length, the intelligence officer assisted his former classmate in obtaining identity and discharge documents. That fall, Winrich Behr began studying at the University of Bonn. The postwar developments in Europe would serve him well. He soon exhibited extraordinary management and diplomatic skills, similar to the exceptional military talents he had displayed as a soldier, and eventually, he served as the assistant general secretary of the Europäische Wirtschaftsgemeinschaft (EWG, or European Economic Union) Commission in Brussels.

Major Michael took refuge with his parents in Heidelberg. His mother was English, so he passed the weeks immediately following Germany's surrender in relative safety. One midsummer afternoon, he was slowly guiding his bicycle over the remains of the destroyed Neckar River bridge when he was obliged to give way to an American officer. For several seconds, their eyes met, and he was surprised to see a familiar face. Like Behr, he, too, had run into a former classmate. The two men spoke at length, balanced on the ruins of the bridge. The American officer was now working with an intelligence unit—and he and his colleagues were interested in recruiting officers with Michael's abilities. The American scribbled an address on a scrap of paper and requested that Michael pay him a visit; he was certain they could use him in their organization. Michael did as the officer asked and soon found himself working with the Gehlen Organization. The roots of the Cold War—Western capitalism versus Eastern communism—were rapidly polarizing. Michael continued to work deep within the shadows of the intelligence community for a number of years until, departing on another assignment into the netherworld behind the Iron Curtain that had fallen across Central Europe, he simply disappeared without a trace.[4]

Hans-Georg Model, the field marshal's seventeen-year-old son, soon learned of his father's fate while serving with the Panzer Brigade Grossdeutschland on the Eastern Front. His commander, Hasso von Manteuffel, ordered that the young officer candidate be removed from combat duty at once: Germany was clearly defeated, and the Model family did not have to lose their sole surviving son. Hans-Georg objected to the transfer and expressed his desire to stay with his unit on the line. Manteuffel emphatically advised him that, as Hans-Georg was the last living son of the Model family, his commander had the official authority and the moral obligation to order the transfer. Hans-Georg survived the war and followed in his father's footsteps, becoming a professional army officer and rising to general's rank with the Bundeswehr, the Federal Republic of Germany's armed forces.[5]

Heinz Spenner, the paratrooper who had fled from the troop train in the Eggegeberge only to be taken into custody by an SS unit, awaited the end of the war in a military hospital near the town of Minden. Lying in a ward with other sick and wounded soldiers, Spenner awoke early one morning to hear several physicians conducting their daily inspection. It was several seconds before the soldier realized that the voices were not speaking German—the staff surgeon was escorting a team of American medical officers through the facility and briefing them on the patients and the general situation in the wards. With the capture of the medical facility, the Americans also brought with them penicillin, with which his injured leg could be saved. Heinz Spenner's odyssey came to an end in the summer of 1945 when he was released from captivity to return to his home in Erwitte.[6]

Colonel Günther Reichhelm who, on personal orders from Adolf Hitler, had flown out of the Ruhr Pocket to assume duties as chief of staff with General Wenck's Twelfth Army, eventually succeeded in linking up with the general near the Elbe River. After leaving the morose atmosphere of the Reich Chancellery in Berlin, Reichhelm had driven to Döberitz, where, according to Hitler's instructions, he was to receive the 200 Volkswagens with which the Twelfth Army would break through to Army Group B in the Ruhr. The logistics officer at the Döberitz training command had a total of 20 vehicles, and in typical bureaucratic fashion, he refused to surrender the Volkswagens without proper authorization. After a short but intense confrontation, a reluctant Reichhelm was uncharacteristically compelled to resort to open threats in order to obtain the vehicles. The colonel then proceeded toward the Elbe with the tiny column of Volkswagens in tow. As he neared the town of Bad Kösen, the column came under direct fire from an artillery battery situated farther ahead along the road. Wheeling the vehicles about, the drivers in the column retreated to the cover of a wooded area. Reichhelm studied a map to discern where Wenck might be located. The name Dessau-Rosslau immediately drew his attention. The colonel remembered from his prewar training days that an army engineering school was located in Dessau-Rosslau, directly on the Elbe. Reichhelm knew the training command would have a communications facility. Dessau-Rosslau was at the center of the Twelfth Army's operational area, and he was aware that no communications battalion had been assigned to the staff. Thus, it was possible that General Wenck would have established his makeshift headquarters at that location.

That afternoon, he found General Wenck and the hastily organized staff of the Twelfth Army. Reichhelm energetically set about constructing an army from remnants of the various units that could be found in the area. The two officers, having known one another for many years, did not engage in any unrealistic plans to break through to the army trapped in the Ruhr.

The entire area east of the Elbe was a chaotic sea of retreating Wehrmacht soldiers, miserable hordes of refugees, swarms of liberated prisoners, and hundreds of thousands of Red Army soldiers intent on avenging the destruction and death inflicted on their homeland by Germany. Following a massive battle on the Seelöwe Heights west of the Oder River, the Soviet army had succeeded in pushing to Berlin and was engaged in encircling the city. Hitler ordered Wenck's Twelfth Army to establish contact with the Ninth Army south of Berlin. The order was ignored. Field Marshal Wilhelm Keitel appeared at Wenck's headquarters and personally directed that Hitler's orders be obeyed.

Wenck and Reichhelm remained steadfast in their refusal. To launch an attack toward Berlin would be fruitless; it would only cause more death in a war that was long since lost. Wenck was intent on holding the Red Army at bay long enough to attain several objectives, none of which involved saving Hitler in Berlin. He and his officers intended to contact the remnants of the Ninth Army and help them cross the Elbe to the American lines. They were determined to retrieve the thousands of wounded personnel lying in the Beelitzer medical facilities and evacuate them over the river to the west. Their most important objective was to assist the countless refugees in escaping the wrath of the Soviet army. The entire operational area was filled with women and children who had fled from East Prussia, Pomerania, Silesia, and the Sudetenland—all areas overrun by the Soviet forces. The thousands of civilians had to be provided with food and shelter and, if possible, moved over the Elbe to the west. Thus, while Hitler's demands remained ineffective, some 100,000 soldiers and countless refugees succeeded in crossing the river.

As the advancing Soviets converged around the final remnants of Wenck's army, the general and Reichhelm, together with a handful of soldiers, climbed into a rubber boat and began crossing the Elbe. Reichhelm's aide, Melcher, refused to get on the boat. The soldier was from Pomerania, and he explained that he would have to give himself up to the Soviets, stating that he could never live anywhere other than in his homeland. The officers paddled the tiny boat across the expanse of the Elbe with machine-gun bullets and sniper fire cracking about them. One of the fugitives was fatally struck by a bullet during the crossing and died soon after reaching the opposite shoreline.

On reaching the west bank, the small group wandered a short distance before coming on an American unit. Approaching the soldiers, Wenck introduced himself as the commander of the Twelfth Army. The soldiers, unsure how to handle their high-ranking captives, relieved them of their pistols and military decorations before calling for an officer. For Colonel Günther Reichhelm, the war ended with American captivity.[7]

The fate of Field Marshal Model remained concealed from the Americans for a number of weeks, and they continued their search for the elusive commander. An imposing Mercedes limousine was discovered in the Ruhr Pocket and exhibited to the news media; it was announced that the vehicle had been the field marshal's staff car. It is likely, however, that the extravagant automobile was the property of a wealthy Ruhr industrialist, for such indulgences, particularly in the waning months of the war, were habitually disdained by Walter Model. Model's chief of staff, General Wagener, was questioned relentlessly about the whereabouts of the field marshal. Wagener had gone into captivity on 17 April and had no knowledge of the field marshal's intentions or location beyond that date. Omar

Bradley, commander of the U.S. Twelfth Army Group, offered a decoration to any soldier who captured the field marshal. The reward remained unfulfilled.

Several months after Germany's surrender, Winrich Behr, the General Staff major whom Model had entrusted with his personal belongings, cautiously journeyed back to the farmstead to retrieve the items for Herta Model, the field marshal's widow. The farmer had kept his word: the small parcel of items was safely returned to Behr. However, the farmer advised Behr that the British authorities had searched his farmyard and buildings thoroughly and discovered his uniform and decorations. The British soldiers continued to resurface on unpredictable visits in hopes of finding the owner of the belongings, which they had left on the premises. Behr thanked the farmer for the information and quickly left with Model's effects, abandoning the incriminating and obsolete uniform.

Many years later, the former cavalry officer reappeared at the farmstead, curious as to the final fate of his possessions. To his surprise, the farmer still retained the field-gray cavalry uniform. He advised Behr that every Christmas since the end of the war, he had received a telephone call from a British sergeant asking whether the mysterious major had ever returned to recover the items. The farmer was pleased to know that when the sergeant again made his customary telephone call that year, the issue could finally be put to rest.[8]

The skies over the Ruhr finally fell silent during the last hours before Germany's unconditional surrender on 8 May 1945. Over the course of the war, the Allies flew more than 2.5 million fighter-bomber missions and 1.5 million bomber missions against Germany. The Allies dropped almost 1.5 million tons of bombs on Germany or on areas under control of the Reich, of which more than 500,000 tons fell on the heavily populated cities. More than 3.5 million homes were destroyed, and 300,000 civilians died as a result of the raids. Another 780,000 were injured, and 7.5 million were left homeless. During the final sixteen-week period of the war in Europe, from 1 January to 26 April 1945, more than 400 air missions were flown against German cities.[9] The Americans had dropped 971,762 tons of bombs on Germany's cities; the British had followed closely with 657,647 tons. In a vain attempt to destroy enemy morale and bring an early end to the war by conducting a stepped-up bombing campaign, some 160,000 Allied airmen became casualties, and approximately 430,000 civilians died beneath the rubble of their cities and villages.[10]

With the passage of time, the relics of the war that had once cluttered the villages and hamlets of the Sauerland, littered the roadsides of the Ruhr, and rusted away in the Teutoburg Forest slowly disappeared. The burned carcasses of massive armored vehicles—remnants of the violent clashes between the German and American armored units in the hills and valleys surrounding Paderborn and along the narrow road near Schloss Hamborn—were eventually dragged away to an ignominious fate in the scrap yards; it was an irreverent end for the battle-scarred chariots of warriors. Roads and trails once scarred and torn by the heavy tracks of German Panthers and Tigers and American Shermans and half-tracks were resurfaced and refinished, thus erasing the traces of the paths taken by desperate soldiers. Battle-torn country hamlets were reconstructed; cities of the Ruhr were rebuilt. The Wehrmacht dead were removed from temporary graves in village cemeteries for reinterment in various *Ehrenfriedhöfe*, the traditional German military cemeteries. There, rows of black granite crosses marked the burials of the named and nameless who had fallen for an iniquitous cause. The thousands of foreign laborers were eventually repatriated to their homes throughout Europe. The surviving Jews had, for the most part, little desire to remain in the haunted land that had consumed their friends and families. Many of them emigrated to Palestine, where they assisted in creating the new nation of Israel; others joined the postwar wave of newcomers to a realm of promise and affluence in the United States.

A decade after the war, Hans-Georg Model, together with Winrich Behr, sought out the burial site of the field marshal in the isolated woods south of Duisburg. The grave was difficult to locate: contrary to postwar myth, Field Marshal Walter Model had not chosen a location between two imposing oak trees for his suicide and burial place. The area was quite nondescript. It was choked with copses of thick undergrowth and bore no tell-tale markings to reveal what had occurred there during the somber afternoon of 21 April 1945. After several hours of searching, they located a shallow depression and discovered unmistakable evidence of the field marshal. The grave had been hastily dug without proper tools; it was shallow, and that area of the woods was inhabited by numerous wild boar. Behr was certain that they had found the grave of the field marshal, and the location was soon positively identified by the remains and effects located there. The district forester had previously told Hans-Georg that his father's grave could remain in place, but he did not recommend that it be left so. Bands of unruly teenagers frequented the isolated area, where they sometimes engaged in activities unbefitting a grave site; one could not guarantee the sanctity of the location. Model's remains were reinterred in the German military cemetery at Vossenack, where he was reunited with hundreds of his soldiers who had fallen in the Ardennes, in Holland, in the Hürtgen Forest, in Aachen, and in the Ruhr Pocket.

In the village of Erwitte, some 15 miles from Lippstadt, where elements of the U.S. First and Ninth Armies met to seal the fate of Army Group B, a hungry ten-year-old named Willi Mues eyed a dark-skinned American soldier with curiosity. The black GI was sitting on the hood of a parked jeep and had several unfamiliar round orange globes. Willi looked on with interest as the American removed the soft peel and consumed slices of the fruit. At length, the GI took notice of the boy, who persisted in examining the activity from a distance. Grasping one of the oranges, the GI tossed it to him. The throw was not carefully aimed, and Willi watched with disappointment as the orange rolled onto the road and was immediately crushed to a shapeless, flattened pulp beneath the wheels of a passing convoy. Disheartened, the boy turned to his benefactor, who grinned and tossed him another orange. Willi grasped the strange fruit carefully and imitated the soldier's method of removing the peel. Only days earlier, the boy had seen frightened local teenagers hastily conscripted into the Volkssturm and ragged, dispirited Wehrmacht soldiers assembled in the market square as abject prisoners, at the mercy of the conquering army. He had observed foreign laborers as they roamed and looted his neighborhood at will. The collapse of Adolf Hitler's Third Reich had left the inhabitants trapped between the netherworld of an undeniable, shameful past and a fearsome, uncertain future. But now, biting into the first orange he had ever tasted, Willi realized that it was truly possible, after all, that the strange soldiers in their round helmets, cotton-cloth uniforms, and massive trucks were bringing with them a new destiny.[11]

NOTES

Chapter 1. Retreat to the Reich

1. Omar N. Bradley, *A Soldier's Story* (New York: Henry Holt, 1951), 344.

2. Ibid., 341.

3. Ibid., 375.

4. Ibid., 378.

5. Winrich Behr, interview by Derek S. Zumbro, 23 January 2002, Düsseldorf, Germany. Tape recording in the author's archive, Hattiesburg, MS.

6. Walter Görlitz, *Model: Der Feldmarschall und sein Endkampf an der Ruhr* (Munich, Germany: Universitas Verlag, 1993), 194.

7. Ibid., 194.

8. Ibid., 197.

9. Ibid.

10. Ibid., 198.

11. Wilhelm von Schramm, *Aufstand der Generale: Der 20. Juli 1944 in Paris* (Munich, Germany: Wilhelm Heyne Verlag, 1977), 270.

12. Ibid., 271.

13. Heinrich Springer, interview by Derek S. Zumbro, 24 May 2000, Ölixdorf, Germany. Tape recording in the author's archive, Hattiesburg, MS.

14. Görlitz, *Model*, 199.

15. Bradley, *Soldier's Story*, 316.

16. Springer interview.

17. Görlitz, *Model*, 203.

18. Bradley, *Soldier's Story*, 415.

19. Görlitz, *Model*, 205.

20. Springer interview, followed by letter to Derek S. Zumbro from Heinrich Springer, undated (June 2000). During the postwar years, Hans Speidel became commander of all North Atlantic Treaty Organization (NATO) land forces in Europe.

21. Bradley, *Soldier's Story*, 416.

22. Ibid., 418.

23. Görlitz, *Model*, 209.

24. Ibid., 210.

25. Ibid., 212. According to General Schack's postwar report, Schwerin intended to allow himself to be overrun by the American forces and taken prisoner rather than to submit to the People's Court.

26. Springer interview. The case was investigated, and Schwerin was exonerated. However, he was relieved of his command of the 116th Panzer Division and took command of an armored corps in Italy.

27. Görlitz, *Model*, 212.

28. Ibid., 214.

29. Ibid., 216. Leyherr was killed in action in 1945 on the front in southwest Germany.

30. Ibid. Reichhelm, Model's former operations officer, was not assigned to Army Group B at the time of the battle for Aachen. His opinion, however, is that German defenses would have held better had Aachen been declared an "open city" and had a defensive line been established to the east. This move would have freed those forces used in the city for defense in

other sectors where they were badly needed.

31. Ibid., 219.

32. Günther Reichhelm, interview by Derek S. Zumbro, 18 January 2002, Murnau, Germany. Tape recording in the author's archive, Hattiesburg, MS.

33. Behr interview.

34. Hans-Georg Model, *Generalfeld-marschall Walter Model, 1891–1945: Dokumentation eines Soldatenlebens* (Osnabrück, Germany: Biblio Verlag, 1991), 324.

35. Görlitz, *Model*, 224.

36. Reichhelm interview.

37. Görlitz, *Model*, 225.

38. Model, *Generalfeldmarschall Walter Model*, 337.

39. Jean Paul Pallud, *Battle of the Bulge Then and Now* (London: Battle of Britain Prints International, 1984), 331.

40. Charles B. MacDonald, *The Mighty Endeavor: American Armed Forces in the European Theater in World War II* (New York: Oxford University Press, 1969), 404.

41. On hearing reports of the discovery, Field Marshal von Rundstedt ordered Army Group B to conduct an investigation into the massacre. In the wake of the failed offensive, the investigation produced no results. A postwar investigation and trial conducted by Americans failed to conclusively determine who was responsible for the shooting of prisoners at Malmédy.

42. Springer interview.

43. Reichhelm interview.

44. Ibid.

45. Springer interview.

Chapter 2. Destroying the Ruhr

1. Max Hastings, *Bomber Command: The Myths and Reality of the Strategic Bombing*

Offensive, 1939–1945 (New York: Dial Press, 1979), 338.

2. Sir Charles Webster and Noble Frankland, *The Strategic Air Offensive against Germany, 1939–1945*, vol. 2, *Endeavor, Part 4* (London: Butler and Tanner, 1961), 57.

3. Ibid., 11.

4. Ibid., 14.

5. Ulrich Borsdorf and Mathilde Jamin, eds., *Überleben im Krieg: Kriegserfahrungen in einer Industrieregion, 1939–1945* (Reinbek, Germany: Rowohlt Taschenbuch Verlag GmbH, 1989), 92.

6. Major General Sir George Aston, "Future Wars," *New York Times*, 18 April 1920, E2.

7. Richard Overy, *Why the Allies Won* (New York: W. W. Norton, 1996), 113.

8. Borsdorf and Jamin, *Überleben im Krieg*, 181.

9. Air Force Historical Foundation, *Impact: The Army Air Forces' "Confidential" Picture History of World War II*, 6, vol. 3, no. 2 (Washington, DC: February 1945), 14.

10. Richard H. Kohn and Joseph P. Harahan, general eds., *Condensed Analysis of the Ninth Air Force in the European Theater of Operations*, USAF Warrior Studies (Washington, DC: Office of Air Force History, USAF, 1984).

11. Borsdorf and Jamin, *Überleben im Krieg*, 181.

12. Helmut Müller, *Fünf vor Null: Die Besetzung des Münsterlandes 1945* (Münster, Germany: Aschendorffsche Buchdruckerei, 1980), 49.

13. Borsdorf and Jamin, *Überleben im Krieg*, 182.

14. Roger A. Freeman, *The Mighty Eighth: Units, Men and Machines (A History of the US 8th Army Air Force)* (New York: Doubleday, 1970), 235.

15. Borsdorf and Jamin, *Überleben im Krieg*, 94.

16. Ibid., 95.

17. Ibid., 96.

18. Ibid.

19. Willy Niessen, *Frontstadt Köln: Endkampf 1945 an Rhein und Ruhr* (Düsseldorf, Germany: Droste Verlag, 1980), 18.

20. Hans G. Kösters, *Essen Stunde Null: Die letzten Tage März/April 1945* (Düsseldorf, Germany: Droste Verlag, 1982), 46–53.

21. Borsdorf and Jamin, *Überleben im Krieg*, 97.

22. Ibid.

23. Max Wind, interview by Derek S. Zumbro, spring 2000, Munich, Germany. Tape recording in the author's archive, Hattiesburg, MS.

24. Ibid.

25. Kösters, *Essen Stunde Null*, 51.

26. Kurt Stasyk, interview by Derek S. Zumbro, 17 May 2002, Drolshagen, Germany. Tape recording in the author's archive, Hattiesburg, MS.

27. Ibid.

28. Ibid.

29. Ibid.

30. United States Strategic Bombing Survey—Summary Report (European War), 23.

31. Kösters, *Essen Stunde Null*, 51.

32. Elenore Kötter, interview by Derek S. Zumbro, 17 July 2002, Dornstetten, Germany. Tape recording in the author's archive, Hattiesburg, MS.

33. Klaus Marcus, *Die Botschaft aus dem Dunkel: Alliierte Flugblattpropaganda über dem Niederrhein, 1940–1945* (Viersen, Germany: Schriftenreihe des Kreises Viersen, pamphlet no. 37, n.d.), 25.

34. Ibid., 26.

35. Ibid., 29.

36. Karl Peukert, *Die Amis kommen: Das Kriegsende im Ruhrkessel 1945 nach Dokumenten zusammengestellt* (Soest, Germany: Westdruck, 1965), 33.

37. Ibid.

38. Kösters, *Essen Stunde Null*, 40.

39. Ibid.

40. Niessen, *Frontstadt Köln*, 21.

41. Borsdorf and Jamin, *Überleben im Krieg*, 111.

42. Ibid., 115.

43. Ibid., 118.

44. Ibid., 190.

45. Niessen, *Frontstadt Köln*, 28.

46. Ibid.

47. Borsdorf and Jamin, *Überleben im Krieg*, 190.

48. Müller, *Fünf vor Null*, 68.

49. Borsdorf and Jamin, *Überleben im Krieg*, 126.

50. Kösters, *Essen Stunde Null*, 98.

51. Borsdorf and Jamin, *Überleben im Krieg*, 137.

Chapter 3. Into the Rhineland

1. Walter Warlimont, *Inside Hitler's Headquarters, 1939–45*, trans. R. H. Barry (New York: Frederick A. Praeger, 1964), 500.

2. Walter Görlitz, *Model: Der Feldmarschall und sein Endkampf an der Ruhr* (Munich, Germany: Universitas Verlag, 1993), 231.

3. Hans-Georg Model, interview by Derek S. Zumbro, 12 May 2001, Rheinbach, Germany. Tape recording in the author's archive, Hattiesburg, MS.

4. Ludwig Hügen, *Der Krieg geht zu Ende: Niederrheinische Berichte zur Operation Grenade 1945* (Viersen, Germany: Schriftenreihe des Kreises Viersen, pamphlet no. 37, 1987), 30.

5. Görlitz, *Model*, 236.

6. Hügen, *Krieg geht zu Ende*, 31.

7. Görlitz, *Model*, 238.

8. Hügen, *Krieg geht zu Ende*, 32.

9. Eric Taylor and Willy Niessen, *Frontstadt Köln: Endkampf 1945 an Rhein und Ruhr* (Düsseldorf, Germany: Droste Verlag, 1980), 67.

10. Ibid., 72.

11. Ibid., 86.

12. Ibid., 85.

13. Ibid., 89.

14. Werner Haupt, *Das Ende im Westen: Die Chronik vom Kampf in Westdeutschland* (Dorheim, Germany: Podzun-Verlag, 1972), 66.

15. Taylor and Niessen, *Frontstadt Köln*, 98.

16. Ibid., 107.

17. Ibid., 38.

18. Hügen, *Krieg geht zu Ende*, 83.

19. Ibid.

20. Ibid., 84.

21. Ibid., 90.

22. Ibid.

23. Ibid., 111.

24. Ibid., 115.

25. Franz Kurowski, *Die Panzer-Lehr-Division: Die größte deutsche Panzer-Division und ihre Aufgabe: Die Invasion zerschlagen — Die Ardennenschlacht entscheiden* (Bad Neuheim, Germany: Podzun-Verlag, 1965), 196.

26. Winrich Behr, interview by Derek S. Zumbro, 23 January 2002, Düsseldorf, Germany. Tape recording in the author's archive, Hattiesburg, MS.

27. Ibid.

Chapter 4. Crossing at Remagen

1. Charles B. MacDonald, *The Mighty Endeavor: American Armed Forces in the European Theater in World War II* (New York: Oxford University Press, 1969), 406.

2. Lothar Brüne and Jacob Weiler, *Remagen in March 1945: Key Factors of Events Leading Up to the End of World War II* (Meckenheim, Germany: Warlich Druck, n.d.), 15.

3. Ibid., 20.

4. Ibid., 21.

5. Ibid.

6. Manfred Michler, *Die verhexte Brücke: Die Wahrheit über den Brückenkopf von Remagen* (Koblenz, Germany: Manfred Michler, 1981), 10.

7. Ibid., 11.

8. Ibid., 13.

9. Ibid.

10. Brüne and Weiler, *Remagen in March*, 26–27.

11. Ibid., 29.

12. Ibid., 30.

13. Michler, *Verhexte Brücke*, 14.

14. Brüne and Weiler, *Remagen in March*, 31.

15. Michler, *Verhexte Brücke*, 15.

16. Ibid., 16.

17. Brüne and Weiler, *Remagen in March*, 33.

18. Ibid., 34.

19. Ibid., 35.

20. Walter Görlitz, *Model: Der Feldmarschall und sein Endkampf an der Ruhr* (Munich, Germany: Universitas Verlag, 1993), 244.

21. Brüne and Weiler, *Remagen in March*, 35.

22. Ibid., 37.

23. Ibid., 38.

24. Ibid., 43. Although this description of events does not correspond with later reports, it is possible that he was cut off from Bratge immediately on leaving the tunnel when the Americans appeared at the exit. If so, he would have barely escaped capture and would not have been able to initiate further communications with Bratge. According to all accounts, the time between Scheller's disappearance and the capture of the tunnel exit by the Americans was no longer than fifteen minutes. Scheller's account of personally assisting the engineers in their attempts to demolish the bridge with the emergency demolitions charge conflicted with other witness accounts.

25. Ibid., 44.

26. Görlitz, *Model*, 246. Görlitz suggested that this remark may have been meant as sarcasm.

27. Albert Kesselring, *Soldat bis zum letzten Tag* (Bonn, Germany: Athenäum-Verlag, 1953), 337–338.

28. Ibid., 338.

29. Ibid., 340.

30. Marcel Stein, *Generalfeldmarschall Walter Model: Legende und Wirklichkeit* (Bissendorf, Germany: Biblio Verlag, 2001), 304.

31. Ibid.

32. Brüne and Weiler, *Remagen in March*, 47–48.

33. Stein, *Generalfeldmarschall Walter Model*, 304.

34. Günther Reichhelm, interview by Derek S. Zumbro, 18 January 2002, Murnau, Germany. Tape recording in the author's archive, Hattiesburg, MS.

35. Michler, *Verhexte Brücke*, 31–32.

36. Ibid., 32–33.

37. Ibid., 33.

38. Ibid., 34–35.

39. Reichhelm interview.

40. Brüne and Weiler, *Remagen in March*, 53–54.

41. Ibid., 52.

42. Winrich Behr, interview by Derek S. Zumbro, 23 January 2002, Düsseldorf, Germany. Tape recording in the author's archive, Hattiesburg, MS. "*Es war uns völlig Wurst* ... Of course it was a great story for the Allied journalists and press, and it did cause a great deal of excitement because of the way it was reported, but to us, at that phase of the war, it really was meaningless."

43. Görlitz, *Model*, 247.

44. Hans-Martin Flender, *Der Raum Siegen im Zweiten Weltkrieg: Eine Dokumentation* (Siegen, Germany: Hans-Martin Flender, 1979), 74.

45. Hans G. Kösters, *Essen Stunde Null: Die letzten Tage März/April 1945* (Düsseldorf, Germany: Droste Verlag, 1982), 58.

46. Ibid.

Chapter 5. Crossing at Wesel

1. Charles B. MacDonald, *The Mighty Endeavor: American Armed Forces in the European Theater in World War II* (New York: Oxford University Press, 1969), 444.

2. Heinz Leiwig, *Deutschland Stunde Null: Historische Luftaufnahmen 1945* (Stuttgart, Germany: Motorbuch Verlag, 1987), 18.

3. Alexander Berkel, *Krieg vor der eigenen Haustür: Rheinübergang und Luftlandung am Niederrhein 1945* (Wesel, Germany: Selbstverlag des Stadtarchivs Wesel, 1994), 27.

4. Helmut Müller, *Fünf vor Null: Die Besetzung des Münsterlandes 1945* (Münster, Germany: Aschendorffsche Buchdruckerei, 1980), 16.

5. Generalleutnant Steinmüller, "Infanterie-Division 'Hamburg': Maerz–April 1945," Bundesarchiv Freiburg, MA-BA B-314. Steinlager Allendorf, Summer 1946, 2.

6. Annegret Dahmen and Doris Rulofs-Terfurth, eds., *Schutt und Asche: Dokumentation zum fünfzigjährigen Gedenken* (Wesel, Germany: Selbstverlag des Stadtarchivs Wesel, 1996), 14.

7. Ibid., 15.

8. Alexander Berkel and Doris Rulofs-Terfurth, eds., *Heimatfront Wesel, 1939–1945: Frauen und Männer erinnern sich an den Krieg in ihrer Stadt* (Wesel, Germany: Selbstverlag des Stadtarchivs Wesel, 1994), 141.

9. Ibid., 42.

10. Ibid., 166.

11. Ibid., 171.

12. Ibid., 199.

13. Leiwig, *Deutschland Stunde Null*, 18.

14. Ibid.

15. Berkel, *Krieg vor der eigenen Haustür*, 32.

16. Winston S. Churchill, *The Second World War*, vol. 6, *Triumph and Tragedy* (Boston: Houghton Mifflin, 1948–1953), 416.

17. Berkel, *Krieg vor der Eigenen Haustür*, 45.

18. Ibid., 46.

19. Ibid., 58.

20. Ibid., 58–59.

21. Ibid., 60.

22. Ibid., 52.

23. Müller, *Fünf vor Null*, 30.

24. Ibid., 40.

25. Ibid., 33.

Chapter 6. Operation Varsity

1. Alexander Berkel, *Krieg vor der eigenen Haustür: Rheinübergang und Luftlandung am Niederrhein 1945* (Wesel, Germany: Selbstverlag des Stadtarchivs Wesel, 1994), 69.
2. Ibid., 91.
3. Ibid., 93.
4. Ibid., 99.
5. Alexander Berkel and Doris Rulofs-Terfurth, eds., *Heimatfront Wesel, 1939–1945: Frauen und Männer erinnern sich an den Krieg in ihrer Stadt* (Wesel, Germany: Selbstverlag des Stadtarchivs Wesel, 1994), 188.
6. Berkel, *Krieg vor der Eigenen Haustür,* 106.
7. Ibid., 107.
8. Ibid., 125–133.
9. Berkel and Rulofs-Terfurth, *Heimatfront Wesel,* 202.
10. Ibid., 203.
11. Berkel, *Krieg vor der eigenen Haustür,* 155.
12. Berkel and Rulofs-Terfurth, *Heimatfront Wesel,* 204.

Chapter 7. Breakout toward the East

1. Helmut Müller, *Fünf vor Null: Die Besetzung des Münsterlandes 1945* (Münster, Germany: Aschendorffsche Buchdruckerei, 1980), 44.
2. Karl Peukert, *Die Amis kommen: Das Kriegsende im Ruhrkessel 1945 nach Dokumenten zusammengestellt* (Soest, Germany: Westdruck, 1965), 17.
3. Ludwig Bauer, interview by Derek S. Zumbro, 17 January 2002, Künzelau, Germany. Tape recording in the author's archive, Hattiesburg, MS.
4. Peukert, *Die Amis kommen,* 21–22.
5. Gustav von Zangen, "15. Armee: Amerikanischen Grossangriff aus dem Brückenkopf Remagen (23.–30.3.45)." Bundesarchiv Freiburg, BA-MA B-848, 26 May 1948.
6. Peukert, *Die Amis kommen,* 15.

7. Helmuth Euler, *Entscheidung an Rhein und Ruhr 1945* (Stuttgart, Germany: Motorbuch Verlag, 1995), 116.
8. Müller, *Fünf vor Null,* 29.
9. Ibid., 51.
10. Ibid.
11. Ibid., 42.
12. Ibid., 61.
13. Ibid., 45.
14. Heinz Spenner, interview by Derek S. Zumbro, 27 April 2002, Erwitte, Germany. Tape recording in the author's archive, Hattiesburg, MS.
15. Günter Wegmann, *Das Kriegsende zwischen Niederrhein, Emsland und Teutoburger Wald im März/April 1945,* Part 1, *Mitteilungen des Vereins für Geschichte und Landeskunde von Osnabrück* 83 (Osnabrück, Germany: Meinders & Elstermann, Osnabrücker Mitteilungen, 1978), 132.
16. Willi Mues, *Der grosse Kessel: Eine Dokumentation über das Ende des Zweiten Weltkrieges zwischen Lippe und Ruhr/Sieg und Lenne* (Erwitte/Lippstadt, Germany: Selbstverlag, 1996), 101.
17. Ibid., 113.
18. Ibid.
19. Wegmann, *Das Kriegsende zwischen Niederrhein,* 132–152.
20. Winrich Behr, interview by Derek S. Zumbro, 23 January 2002, Düsseldorf, Germany. Tape recording in the author's archive, Hattiesburg, MS.

Chapter 8. Closing the Ruhr Pocket

1. Werner Trienens, "Vor der Flammenhölle auf das freie Feld geflüchtet," Aus Stadt und Land (From City and Countryside) insert, *Westfalenpost,* 17 March 1995.
2. Wilhelm Tieke, *Aufstellung, Einsatz und Untergang der SS-Panzerbrigade "Westfalen" März–April 1945* (Gummersbach, Germany: Selbstverlag, 1990), 8.
3. Ulrich Saft, *Krieg in der Heimat … bis zum bitteren Ende im Harz* (Walsrode,

Germany: Militärbuchverlag Saft, 1994),
22–23.

4. Tieke, *Aufstellung*, 14–15.

5. Walter Ott, interview by Derek S.
Zumbro, undated, Gettdorf, Germany. Written
notes in author's archive, Hattiesburg, MS.

6. Tieke, *Aufstellung*, 17.

7. Ibid., 19.

8. Ibid., 20–21.

9. Ibid.

10. Saft, *Krieg in der Heimat*, 27–28.

11. Charles Whiting, *Battle of the Ruhr
Pocket* (New York: Ballantine Books, 1970).

12. War Department Classified Message
Center: Incoming Classified Message,
Headquarters Communications Zone,
European Theater of Operations, U.S. Army
Paris, France, to War Department, 8 April
1945. U.S.A. War Crimes Office File
12-407-5, 14 April 1945.

13. Waldemar Becker, *Das Kriegsende
1945 im ehemaligen Hochstift Paderborn*
(Paderborn, Germany: Volksbank Paderborn
Heimatkundliche Schriftenreihe 25, 1994), 18.

14. War Department Classified Message
Center, 14 April 1945.

15. Georg Vockel, "Als General Rose starb,
begannen Hinrichtungen!" *Westfalen-Blatt*
no. 81, 31 March 1992, KS16.

16. Saft, *Krieg in der Heimat*, 30–32.

17. Jost W. Schneider, *Heinrich Himmler's
Burg: Das weltanschauliche Zentrum der SS*
(Essen, Germany: Heitz and Höffkes, 1989),
183–187.

18. Ibid.

19. Günter Wegmann, *Das Kriegsende
zwischen Niederrhein, Emsland und
Teutoburger Wald im März/April 1945*, Part
1, *Mitteilungen des Vereins für Geschichte
und Landeskunde von Osnabrück* 83
(Osnabrück, Germany: Meinders &
Elstermann, Osnabrücker Mitteilungen,
1978), 153.

20. Hans-Martin Flender, *Der Raum Siegen
im Zweiten Weltkrieg: Eine Dokumentation*
(Siegen, Germany: Hans-Martin Flender,
1979), 75.

21. Hans Bölte, *Der Kreis Höxter "In jenen
Tagen": Das Kriegsende 1945 zwischen Weser
und Egge* (Herford, Germany: Bussesche
Verlagshandlung, 1979), 59.

22. Ibid., 60.

23. Ibid., 68–69.

24. Werner Niehaus, *Endkampf zwischen
Rhein und Weser: Nordwestdeutschland 1945*
(Stuttgart, Germany: Motorbuch Verlag,
1983), 111.

25. Ibid.

Chapter 9. Sealing the Trap

1. Günther Reichhelm, interview
by Derek S. Zumbro, 18 January 2002,
Murnau, Germany. Tape recording in the
author's archive, Hattiesburg, MS.

2. Charles Whiting, *Battle of the Ruhr
Pocket* (New York: Ballantine Books, 1970),
74–75.

3. Ibid., 74–76.

4. Wolf-Herbert Deus, ed., *Soester
Chronik, zugleich Bericht der Stadtverwaltung Soest über die Zeit vom 1. April 1942
bis 31. März 1948* (Soest, Germany:
Kommissionsverlag Mocker und Jahn, 1951),
25.

5. Letter to Willi Mues from Erich-
Wilhelm Riekenbrauck, October 1982, Mues
archive, Erwitte, Germany. See also Mues,
*Der grosse Kessel: Eine Dokumentation über
das Ende des Zweiten Weltkrieges zwischen
Lippe und Ruhr/Sieg und Lenne* (Erwitte/
Lippstadt, Germany: Selbsverlag, 1996), 165.

6. Mues, *Der grosse Kessel*, 160–169.

7. Günter Wegmann, *Das Kriegsende
zwischen Niederrhein, Emsland und Teuto-
burger Wald im März/April 1945*, Part 1,
*Mitteilungen des Vereins für Geschichte und
Landeskunde von Osnabrück* 83 (Osnabrück,
Germany: Meinders and Elstermann,
Osnabrücker Mitteilungen, 1978), 152–153.

8. Mues, *Der grosse Kessel*, 171–176.

9. Wegmann, *Das Kriegsende*, 153.

10. Mues, *Der grosse Kessel*, 178.

11. Ibid.

12. Ibid., 180–182.

13. Ibid., 178–180.

14. Ibid., 173.

15. Ibid., 173–178.

16. Sources disagree as to the exact time the two armies met. Toland wrote that the meeting was recorded by reporters and photographers at 1:00 p.m., but Task Force Kane reported the time as being 4:00 p.m. An after-action report prepared by members of the task force stated that they entered Lippstadt after encountering little resistance and made contact with units from the 2nd Armored Division at 4:00 and that the town was fully in American hands by 7:00 p.m.

Chapter 10. Death in the Eggegeberge

1. Hans Bölte, *Der Kreis Höxter "In Jenen Tagen": Das Kriegsende 1945 zwischen Weser und Egge* (Herford, Germany: Bussesche Verlagshandlung, 1979), 101–102.

2. Ulrich Saft, *Krieg in der Heimat … bis zum bitteren Ende im Harz* (Walsrode, Germany: Militärbuchverlag Saft, 1994), 32.

3. Bölte, *Der Kreis Höxter*, 63.

4. Waldemar Becker, *Das Kriegsende 1945 im ehemaligen Hochstift Paderborn* (Paderborn, Germany: Volksbank Paderborn, Heimatkundliche Schriftenreihe 25, 1994), 35–36.

5. Bölte, *Der Kreis Höxter*, 65.

6. Ibid., 60–140.

7. Heinz Spenner, interview by Derek S. Zumbro, 27 April 2002, Erwitte, Germany. Tape recording in the author's archive, Hattiesburg, MS.

8. Ibid.

9. Werner Niehaus, *Endkampf zwischen Rhein und Weser: Nordwestdeutschland 1945* (Stuttgart, Germany: Motorbuch Verlag, 1983), 110–124.

Chapter 11. Reducing the Pocket

1. Günther Reichhelm, interview by Derek S. Zumbro, 18 January 2002,

Murnau, Germany. Tape recording in the author's archive, Hattiesburg, MS.

2. Willi Mues, *Der grosse Kessel: Eine Dokumentation über das Ende des Zweiten Weltkrieges zwischen Lippe und Ruhr/Sieg und Lenne* (Erwitte/Lippstadt, Germany: Selbstverlag, 1996), 200.

3. Siegfried Schmieder, *Geschichte einer Gemeinde im Münsterland* (Wadersloh, Germany: Archiv d. Kreises Beckum, 1982), 228–229.

4. Mues, *Der grosse Kessel*, 202.

5. Ibid.

6. Franz Hoppe, interview by Willi Mues, September 1981, Mettinghausen, Germany. Manuscript in the Mues archive, Erwitte, Germany.

7. Mues, *Der grosse Kessel*, 204.

8. Ibid., 205.

9. Ibid., 235.

10. Ibid.

11. Ibid., 242.

12. Willi Mues, interview by Derek S. Zumbro, 9 April 2002, Erwitte, Germany. Tape recording in the author's archive, Hattiesburg, MS.

13. Mues, *Der grosse Kessel*, 246.

14. Gretel (née Klara) Spenner, interview by Derek S. Zumbro, 27 April 2002, Erwitte, Germany. Tape recording in the author's archive, Hattiesburg, MS.

15. Mues, *Der grosse Kessel*, 248.

16. Charles R. Leach, *In Tornado's Wake: A History of the 8th Armored Division* (Chicago: Eighth Armored Division Association, 1956), 157.

17. Mues, *Der grosse Kessel*, 256.

18. Ibid., 257.

19. Heinz Guderian, "Die Kämpfe der 116. Panzer-Division in der Zeit von 24.3.–16.4.1945 (Ruhrkessel)," Bundesarchiv Freiburg, BA-MA B-713, 21 November 1947, 11.

20. Mues, *Der grosse Kessel*, 258–259.

21. Ibid., 259.

22. Mathilda Finger, interview by Derek S. Zumbro, 27 April 2002, Kallenhardt,

Germany. Tape recording in the author's archive, Hattiesburg, MS.

23. Ibid. Other accounts, including the official U.S. Army after-action reports, stated that the officer died in the engagement. Kallenhardt residents who were present during the incident and subsequently interviewed by the author insisted that the officer was shot by American soldiers after surrendering. Frau Matilda Finger emphatically stated, "He was shot by the Americans, but no one cared ... He had even threatened to shoot my husband."

24. Mues, *Der grosse Kessel*, 271.

25. Ibid., 274.

26. Gerhard Köhn, *Bomben auf Soest: Tagebücher, Berichte, Dokumente und Fotos zur Erinnerung an die Bombardierungen und das Kriegsende vor 50 Jahren* (Soest, Germany: Westfälische Verlagsbuchhandlung Mocker and Jahn, 1994), 61.

27. Ibid., 260.

28. Ibid., 262.

29. Ibid.

30. Ibid.

31. Ibid., 292–293.

32. Ibid., 293.

33. Albert Huyskens, ed., *Der Kreis Meschede unter der Feuerwalze des Zweiten Weltkrieges* (Bielefeld, Germany: Druck W. Bertelsmann Verlag, 1949), 8.

34. Ibid., 51.

35. Ibid., 109.

Chapter 12. Total Collapse

1. Helmut Müller, *Fünf vor Null: Die Besetzung des Münsterlandes 1945* (Münster, Germany: Aschendorffsche Buchdruckerei, 1980), 54.

2. Willi Mues, *Der grosse Kessel: Eine Dokumentation über das Ende des Zweiten Weltkrieges zwischen Lippe und Ruhr/Sieg und Lenne* (Erwitte/Lippstadt, Germany: Selbstverlag, 1996), 277.

3. Ibid., 285.

4. Ibid., 287.

5. Ilse Schultze-Velmede, interview by Derek S. Zumbro, 29 April 2002, Rhynern, Germany. Tape recording in the author's archive, Hattiesburg, MS.

6. Wilhelm Tieke, *Bis zur Stunde Null: Das oberbergische Land im Krieg, 1939–1945* (Gummersbach, Germany: Verlag Gronenberg, 1985), 201–204.

7. Ibid., 218.

8. Günther Reichhelm, interview by Derek S. Zumbro, 18 January 2002, Murnau, Germany. Tape recording in author's archive, Hattiesburg, MS.

9. Ibid.

10. Ibid.

11. Ibid.

12. Tieke, *Bis zur Stunde Null*, 163.

13. Ibid., 169.

14. Ibid., 174.

15. Ibid., 178–180.

16. Ibid., 181.

17. Ibid., 195–196.

18. Ibid., 222–228.

Chapter 13. Disintegration

1. Fritz Bayerlein, "Die Kämpfe des 53. Korps im Ruhr Kessel Nordostfront Raum Unna-Dortmund-Hagen-Iserlohn," Bundesarchiv Freiburg, BA-MA B-836 (Ober Ursel), 15 January 1947, 2.

2. Wilhelm Tieke, *Bis zur Stunde Null: Das oberbergische Land im Krieg, 1939–1945* (Gummersbach, Germany: Verlag Gronenberg, 1985), 275.

3. Ibid., 276.

4. Ibid., 280–282.

5. Karl Peukert, *Die Amis kommen: Das Kriegsende im Ruhrkessel 1945 nach Dokumenten zusammengestellt* (Soest, Germany: Westdruck, 1965), 23.

6. Ibid., 34.

7. Ibid., 36.

8. Ibid., 37.

9. Ibid., 45.

10. Helmuth Euler, *Entscheidung an*

Rhein und Ruhr 1945 (Stuttgart, Germany: Motorbuch Verlag, 1995), 187–189.

11. Bayerlein, *Die Kämpfe des 53. Korps,* 4–5.

12. Peukert, *Die Amis kommen,* 45.

13. Bayerlein, *Die Kämpfe des 53. Korps,* 6.

14. Ibid., 8.

15. Franz Kurowski, *Von den Ardennen zum Ruhrkessel: Das Ende an der Westfront* (Herford, Germany: Maximillian-Verlag, 1965), 134–135.

16. Bayerlein, *Die Kämpfe des 53. Korps,* 8–14.

17. Winrich Behr, interview by Derek S. Zumbro, 23 January 2002, Düsseldorf, Germany. Tape recording in the author's archive, Hattiesburg, MS.

18. Tieke, *Bis zur Stunde Null,* 292.

19. Walter Görlitz, *Model: Der Feldmarschall und sein Endkampf an der Ruhr* (Munich, Germany: Universitas Verlag, 1993), 263.

20. Behr interview.

21. Görlitz, *Model,* 263.

22. Ibid., 265.

23. Ibid., 266.

24. Behr interview.

25. Ibid.

26. Ibid.

27. Ibid.

28. Ibid. See also Hans-Georg Model, interview by Derek S. Zumbro, 12 May 2001, Rheinbach, Germany. Tape recording in author's archive, Hattiesburg, MS.

Chapter 14. Defeat and Occupation

1. Earl F. Ziemke, *The U.S. Army in the Occupation of Germany, 1944–1946,* Army Historical Series (Washington, DC: Center of Military History, United States Army, 1975), 147.

2. Günter Bischoff and Stephen E. Ambrose, eds., *Eisenhower and the German POWs: Facts against Falsehood* (Baton Rouge: Louisiana State University Press, 1992), 277.

3. F. S. V. Donnison, *Civil Affairs and Military Government North-West Europe, 1944–1946: History of the Second World War* (London: Her Majesty's Stationery Office, 1961), 212.

4. Ludwig Hügen, *Der Krieg geht zu Ende: Niederrheinische Berichte zur Operation Grenade 1945* (Viersen, Germany: Schriftenreihe des Kreises Viersen, pamphlet no. 37, 1987), 137–138.

5. Ibid., 127–140.

6. Hartmut Platte, ed., *Kriegsende 1945: Wie Werler Bürgerinnen und Bürger das Frühjahr 1945 erlebten* (Werl, Germany: Verlag der A. Stein'schen Buchhandlung, 1995), 65.

7. Willy Niessen, *Frontstadt Köln: Endkampf 1945 an Rhein und Ruhr* (Düsseldorf, Germany: Droste Verlag, 1980), 111.

8. Platte, *Kriegsende 1945,* 65.

9. Ibid., 66.

10. Petra Goedde, *GIs and Germans: Culture, Gender, and Foreign Relations, 1945–1949* (New Haven, CT.: Yale University Press, 2003), 46.

11. Ziemke, *The U.S. Army in the Occupation of Germany,* 98.

12. Henry Morgenthau Jr., *Germany Is Our Problem* (New York: Harper and Brothers, 1945), 195.

13. Ibid.

14. Ziemke, *The U.S. Army in the Occupation of Germany,* 98.

15. Goedde, *GIs and Germans,* 47.

16. Ibid., 51.

17. Helmuth Euler, *Entscheidung an Rhein und Ruhr 1945* (Stuttgart, Germany: Motorbuch Verlag, 1995), 198–199.

18. Ibid., 199–200.

19. Bischoff and Ambrose, *Eisenhower and the German POWs,* 8.

20. Paul Carell, *Die Gefangenen: Leben und Überleben deutscher Soldaten hinter Stacheldraht* (Frankfurt, Germany: Verlag Ullstein, 1980), 149.

21. Bischoff and Ambrose, *Eisenhower and the German POWs,* 9.

22. Ibid., 13.

23. Ibid., 16.

24. Stephen E. Ambrose, *Band of Brothers: E Company, 506th Regiment, 101st Airborne, from Normandy to Hitler's Eagles Nest* (New York: Simon and Schuster, 1992), 275.

25. Bischoff and Ambrose, *Eisenhower and the German POWs*, 11.

26. Martin Blumenson, ed., *The Patton Papers, 1940–1945* (New York: DaCapo Press, 1996), 750.

27. Ibid., 709.

28. Bischoff and Ambrose, *Eisenhower and the German POWs*, 36.

29. Kurt Stasyk, interview by Derek S. Zumbro, Drolshagen, Germany, 19 May 2002. Tape recording in the author's archive, Hattiesburg, MS.

30. Hans Bölte, *Der Kreis Höxter "In jenen Tagen": Das Kriegsende 1945 zwischen Weser und Egge* (Herford, Germany: Bussesche Verlagshandlung, 1979), 97–98.

31. Erich Kuby, *Das Ende des Schreckens: Januar bis Mai 1945* (Hamburg, Germany: Ernst Kabel Verlag, 1984), 86.

32. Ibid., 144.

33. Ziemke, *The U.S. Army in the Occupation of Germany*, 202.

34. Ibid., 356.

35. Ibid., 357.

36. Ibid.

37. Ibid.

38. Blumenson, *The Patton Papers*, 751.

39. Ziemke, *The U.S. Army in the Occupation of Germany*, 357.

40. Gerhard Köhn, *Bomben auf Soest: Tagebücher, Berichte, Dokumente und Fotos zur Erinnerung an die Bombardierungen und das Kriegsende vor 50 Jahren* (Soest, Germany: Westfälische Verlagsbuchhandlung Mocker and Jahn, 1994), 254.

41. Ibid., 255.

42. Euler, *Entscheidung an Rhein und Ruhr*, 191–192.

43. Ibid., 194.

44. Ibid., 195–196.

Epilogue

1. Ulrich Saft, *Krieg in der Heimat … bis zum bitteren Ende im Harz* (Walsrode, Germany: Militärbuchverlag Saft, 1994), 33.

2. Willi Mues, *Der grosse Kessel: Eine Dokumentation über das Ende des Zweiten Weltkrieges zwischen Lippe und Ruhr/Sieg und Lenne* (Erwitte/Lippstadt: Selbstverlag, 1996), 581–582.

3. Ludwig Bauer, interview by Derek S. Zumbro, 17 January 2002, Künzelzau, Germany. Tape recording in author's archive, Hattiesburg, MS.

4. Winrich Behr, interview by Derek S. Zumbro, 23 January 2002, Düsseldorf, Germany. Tape recording in the author's archive, Hattiesburg, MS.

5. Hans-Georg Model, interview by Derek S. Zumbro, 12 May 2001, Rheinbach, Germany. Tape recording in the author's archive, Hattiesburg, MS.

6. Heinz Spenner, interview by Derek S. Zumbro, 12 May 2001, Erwitte, Germany. Tape recording in the author's archive, Hattiesburg, MS.

7. Günther Reichhelm, interview by Derek S. Zumbro, 18 January 2002, Murnau, Germany. Tape recording in the author's archive, Hattiesburg, MS.

8. Behr interview.

9. Helmut Müller, *Fünf vor Null: Die Besetzung des Münsterlandes 1945* (Münster, Germany: Aschendorffsche Buchdruckerei, 1980), 27.

10. Heinz Leiwig, *Deutschland Stunde Null: Historische Luftaufnahmen 1945* (Stuttgart, Germany: Motorbuch Verlag, 1987).

11. Willi Mues, interview by Derek S. Zumbro, 9 April 2002, Erwitte, Germany. Tape recording in the author's archive, Hattiesburg, MS.

BIBLIOGRAPHY

Interviews

Bauer, Ludwig. Interview by Derek S. Zumbro, 17 January 2002, Künzelzau, Germany. Tape recording. Author's archive, Hattiesburg, MS.

Behr, Winrich. Interview by Derek S. Zumbro, 23 January 2002, Düsseldorf, Germany. Tape recording. Author's archive, Hattiesburg, MS.

Finger, Mathilda. Interview by Derek S. Zumbro, 27 April 2002, Kallenhardt, Germany. Tape recording. Author's archive, Hattiesburg, MS.

Hoppe, Franz. Interview by Willi Mues, September 1981, Mettinghausen, Germany. Manuscript. Mues archive, Erwitte, Germany.

Jacobs, Franz. Interview by Derek S. Zumbro, 29 March 2002, Erwitte, Germany. Tape recording. Author's archive, Hattiesburg, MS.

Kötter, Elenore. Interview by Derek S. Zumbro, 17 July 2002, Dornstetten, Germany. Tape recording. Author's archive, Hattiesburg, MS.

Model, Hans-Georg. Interview by Derek S. Zumbro, 12 May 2001, Rheinbach, Germany. Tape recording. Author's archive, Hattiesburg, MS.

Mues, Willi. Interview by Derek S. Zumbro, 9 April 2002, Erwitte, Germany. Tape recording. Author's archive, Hattiesburg, MS.

Ott, Walter. Interview by Derek S. Zumbro, undated, Gettdorf, Germany. Written notes. Author's archive, Hattiesburg, MS.

Reichhelm, Günther. Interview by Derek S. Zumbro, 18 January 2002, Murnau, Germany. Tape recording. Author's archive, Hattiesburg, MS.

Schultze-Velmede, Ilse. Interview by Derek S. Zumbro, 29 April 2002, Rhynern, Germany. Tape recording. Author's archive, Hattiesburg, MS.

Spenner, Gretel (née Klara). Interview by Derek S. Zumbro, 27 April 2002, Erwitte, Germany. Tape recording. Author's archive, Hattiesburg, MS.

Spenner, Heinz. Interview by Derek S. Zumbro, 27 April 2002, Erwitte, Germany. Tape recording. Author's archive, Hattiesburg, MS.

Springer, Heinrich. Interview by Derek S. Zumbro, 24 May 2000, Ölixdorf, Germany. Tape recording. Author's archive, Hattiesburg, MS.

Stasyk, Kurt. Interview by Derek S. Zumbro, 17 May 2002, Drolshagen, Germany. Tape recording. Author's archive, Hattiesburg, MS.

Wind, Max. Interview by Derek S. Zumbro, Spring 2000, Munich, Germany. Tape recording. Author's archive, Hattiesburg, MS.

Official Reports in Bundesarchiv Freiburg

Bayerlein, Fritz. "Die Kämpfe des 53. Korps im Ruhr Kessel Nordostfront Raum Unna-Dortmund-Hagen-Iserlohn." BA-MA B-836 (Ober Ursel), 15 January 1947.

Guderian, Heinz. "Die Kämpfe der 116. Panzer-Division in der Zeit von 24.3.–16.4.1945 (Ruhrkessel)." BA-MA B-713, 21 November 1947.

Steinmüller, Generalleutnant. "Infantrie-Division 'Hamburg': Maerz–April 1945." BA-MA B-314. Steinlager Allendorf, Summer 1946.

Zangen, Gustav von. "15. Armee: Amerikanischen Grossangriff aus dem Brückenkopf Remagen (23.–30.3.45)." BA-MA B-848, 26 May 1948.

Official U.S. Sources

Air Force Historical Foundation, Assistant Chief of Air Staff, Intelligence. *Impact: The Army Air Forces' "Confidential" Picture History of World War II: Book 6.* Washington, DC. New York: James Parton and Company, 1980.

Headquarters Communications Zone, European Theater of Operations, US Army Paris, France to War Department, 8 April 1945. USA War Crimes Office File 12-407-5, 14 April 1945. Subj: Rose, Maurice 08439 Major General. Supplementing ourad E 30047 following report from 1st Army.

United States Air Force. *United States Strategic Bombing Survey—Summary Report (European War).* Reprint, Maxwell Air Force Base, Montgomery, AL, 1987.

Published Primary Sources

Berkel, Alexander, and Doris Rulofs-Terfurth, eds. *Heimatfront Wesel, 1939–1945: Frauen und Männer erinnern sich an den Krieg in ihrer Stadt.* Wesel, Germany: Selbstverlag des Stadtarchivs Wesel, 1994.

Blumenson, Martin, ed. *The Patton Papers, 1940–1945.* New York: DaCapo Press, 1996.

Bradley, Omar N. *A Soldier's Story.* New York: Henry Holt, 1951.

Churchill, Sir Winston. *The Second World War,* vol. 6, *Triumph and Tragedy.* Boston: Houghton Mifflin, 1948–1953.

Dahmn, Anneet, and Doris Rulofs-Terfurth, eds. *Schutt und Asche: Dokumentation zum fünfzigjährigen Gedenken.* Wesel, Germany: Selbstverlag des Stadtarchivs Wesel, 1996.

Dearnaley, E. J., and P. B. Warr, eds. *Aircrew Stress in Wartime Operations: Papers from the Flying Personnel Research Committee of the Ministry of Defence.* London: Academic Press, 1979.

Donnison, F. S. V. *Civil Affairs and Military Government North-West Europe, 1944–1946, History of the Second World War.* London: Her Majesty's Stationery Office, 1961.

Kesselring, Albert. *Soldat bis zum letzten Tag.* Bonn, Germany: Athenäum-Verlag, 1953.

Kohn, Richard H., and Joseph P. Harahan, general eds. *Condensed Analysis of the Ninth Air Force in the European Theater of Operations: United States Air Force Warrior Studies.* Washington, DC: Office of Air Force History, 1984.

Model, Hans-Georg. *Generalfeldmarschall Walter Model (1891–1945): Dokumentation eines Soldatenlebens.* Osnabrück, Germany: Biblio Verlag, 1991.

Warlimont, Walter. *Inside Hitler's Headquarters 1939–45.* Translated by R. H. Barry. New York: Frederick A. Praeger, 1964.

Ziemke, Earl F. *The U.S. Army in the Occupation of Germany, 1944–1946.* Army Historical Series. Washington, DC: Center of Military History, United States Army, 1975.

Newspapers and Periodicals

Aston, Major General Sir George. "Future Wars." *New York Times,* 18 April 1920, E2.

Deus, Wolf-Herbert, ed. *Soester Chronik, zugleich Bericht der Stadtverwaltung Soest über die Zeit vom 1. April 1942 bis 31. März 1948.* Soest, Germany: Kommissionsverlag Mocker und Jahn, 1951.

Dunker, Alfons. "Momente, Berichte und Episoden." *Geseke: Geseker Album* 1, 1976.

———. "Momente, Berichte und Episoden." *Geseke: Geseker Album* 2, 1977.

Trienens, Werner. "Vor der Flammenhölle auf das freie Feld geflüchtet." Aus Stadt und Land (From City and Countryside) insert, *Westfalenpost,* 17 March 1995.

Vockel, Georg. "Als General Rose starb, begannen Hinrichtungen!" *Westfalen-Blatt,* no. 81, 31 March 1992, KS16.

Wegmann, Günter. *Das Kriegsende zwischen Niederrhein, Emsland und Teutoburger Wald im März/ April 1945,* Part 1. *Mitteilungen des Vereins für Geschichte und Landeskunde von Osnabrück* 83. Osnabrück, Germany: Meinders & Elstermann, Osnabrücker Mitteilungen, 1977.

———. *Das Kriegsende zwischen Niederrhein, Emsland und Teutoburger Wald im März/April 1945,* Part 2. *Mitteilungen des Vereins für Geschichte und Landeskunde von Osnabrück* 84. Osnabrück, Germany: Meinders and Elstermann, Osnabrücker Mitteilungen, 1978.

Secondary Sources

Ambrose, Stephen E. *Band of Brothers: E Company, 506th Regiment, 101st Airborne from Normandy to Hitler's Eagles Nest.* New York: Simon and Schuster, 1992.

Bartov, Omer. *Hitler's Army: Soldiers, Nazis, and War in the Third Reich.* New York: Oxford University Press, 1991.

Becker, Waldemar. *Das Kriegsende 1945 im ehemaligen Hochstift Paderborn.* Paderborn, Germany: Volksbank Paderborn, Heimatkundliche Schriftenreihe 25, 1994.

Berkel, Alexander. *Krieg vor der eigenen Haustür: Rheinübergang und Luftlandung am Niederrhein 1945.* Wesel, Germany: Selbstverlag des Stadtarchivs Wesel, 1994.

Bischoff, Günter, and Stephen E. Ambrose, eds. *Eisenhower and the German POWs: Facts against Falsehood.* Baton Rouge: Louisiana State University Press, 1992.

Bölte, Hans. *Der Kreis Höxter "In Jenen Tagen": Das Kriegsende 1945 zwischen Weser und Egge.* Herford, Germany: Bussesche Verlagshandlung, 1979.

Borsdorf, Ulrich, and Mathilde Jamin, eds. *Überleben im Krieg: Kriegserfahrungen in einer Industrieregion 1939–1945.* Reinbek, Germany: Rowohlt Taschenbuch Verlag, 1989.

Brüne, Lothar, and Jacob Weiler. *Remagen in March 1945: Key Factors of Events Leading up to the End of World War II.* Meckenheim, Germany: Warlich Druck und Verlagsgesellschaft, n.d.

Carell, Paul. *Die Gefangenen: Leben und Überleben deutscher Soldaten hinter Stacheldraht.* Frankfurt, Germany: Verlag Ullstein, 1980.

Craven, Wesley Frank, and James Lea Cate, eds. *The Army Air Forces in World War II.* Chicago: University of Chicago Press, 1955.

Euler, Helmuth. *Entscheidung an Rhein und Ruhr 1945.* Stuttgart, Germany: Motorbuch Verlag, 1995.

Flender, Hans-Martin. *Der Raum Siegen im Zweiten Weltkrieg: Eine Dokumentation*. Siegen, Germany: Hans-Martin Flender, 1979.

Freeman, Roger A. *The Mighty Eighth: Units, Men and Machines (A History of the US 8th Army Air Force)*. New York: Doubleday, 1970.

Fritz, Stephen G. *Endkampf: Soldiers, Civilians, and the Death of the Third Reich*. Lexington: University Press of Kentucky, 2004.

Goedde, Petra. *GIs and Germans: Culture, Gender, and Foreign Relations, 1945–1949*. New Haven, CT: Yale University Press, 2003.

Görlitz, Walter. *Model: Der Feldmarschall und sein Endkampf an der Ruhr*. Munich, Germany: Universitas Verlag, 1993.

Hastings, Max. *Bomber Command: The Myths and Reality of the Strategic Bombing Offensive, 1939–45*. New York: Dial Press, 1979.

Haupt, Werner. *Das Ende im Westen: Die Chronik vom Kampf in Westdeutschland*. Dorheim, Germany: Podzun Verlag, 1972.

Hügen, Ludwig. *Der Krieg geht zu Ende: Niederrheinische Berichte zur Operation Grenade 1945*. Vierson, Germany: Schriftenreihe des Kreises Viersen, pamphlet no. 37, 1987.

Huyskens, Albert, ed. *Der Kreis Meschede unter der Feuerwalze des Zweiten Weltkrieges*. Bielefeld, Germany: Druck W. Bertelsmann Verlag, 1949.

Köhn, Gerhard. *Bomben auf Soest: Tagebücher, Berichte, Dokumente und Fotos zur Erinnerung an die Bombardierungen und das Kriegsende vor 50 Jahren*. Soest, Germany: Westfälische Verlagsbuchhandlung Mocker and Jahn, 1994.

Kösters, Hans G. *Essen Stunde Null: Die letzten Tage März/April 1945*. Düsseldorf, Germany: Droste Verlag, 1982.

Kuby, Erich. *Das Ende des Schreckens: Januar bis Mai 1945*. Hamburg, Germany: Ernst Kabel Verlag, 1984.

Kurowski, Franz. *Die Panzer-Lehr-Division: Die größte deutsche Panzer-Division und ihre Aufgabe: Die Invasion zerschlagen—die Ardennenschlacht entscheiden*. Bad Neuheim, Germany: Podzun-Verlag, n.d.

——. *Von den Ardennen zum Ruhrkessel: Das Ende an der Westfront*. Herford, Germany: Maximillian-Verlag, 1965.

Leach, Charles R. *In Tornado's Wake: A History of the 8th Armored Division*. Chicago: Eighth Armored Division Association, 1956.

Leiwig, Heinz. *Deutschland Stunde Null: Historische Luftaufnahmen 1945*. Stuttgart, Germany: Motorbuch Verlag, 1987.

MacDonald, Charles B. *The Mighty Endeavor: American Armed Forces in the European Theater in World War II*. New York: Oxford University Press, 1969.

Marcus, Klaus. *Die Botschaft aus dem Dunkel: Alliierte Flugblattpropaganda über dem Niederrhein, 1940–1945*. Viersen, Germany: Schriftenreihe des Kreises Viersen, pamphlet no. 37, Herausgegeben vom Oberkreisdirektor, n.d.

Michler, Manfred. *Die verhexte Brücke: Die Wahrheit über den Brückenkopf von Remagen*. Koblenz, Germany: Manfred Michler, 1981.

Morgenthau, Henry, Jr. *Germany Is Our Problem*. New York: Harper and Brothers, 1945.

Mues, Willi. *Der grosse Kessel: Eine Dokumentation über das Ende des Zweiten Weltkrieges zwischen Lippe und Ruhr/Sieg und Lenne*. Erwitte/Lippstadt, Germany: Selbstverlag, 1996.

Müller, Helmut. *Fünf vor Null: Die Besetzung des Münsterlandes 1945*. Münster, Germany: Aschendorffsche Buchdruckerei, 1980.

Niehaus, Werner. *Endkampf zwischen Rhein und Weser: Nordwestdeutschland 1945.* Stuttgart, Germany: Motorbuch Verlag, 1983.

Niessen, Willy. *Frontstadt Köln: Endkampf 1945 an Rhein und Ruhr.* Düsseldorf, Germany: Droste Verlag, 1980.

Overy, Richard. *Why the Allies Won.* New York: W. W. Norton, 1996.

Pallud, Jean Paul. *Battle of the Bulge Then and Now.* London: Battle of Britain Prints International, 1984.

Peukert, Karl. *Die Amis kommen: Das Kriegsende im Ruhrkessel 1945 nach Dokumenten zusammengestellt.* Soest, Germany: Westdruck, 1965.

Platte, Hartmut, ed. *Kriegsende 1945: Wie Werler Bürgerinnen und Bürger das Frühjar 1945 erlebten.* Werl, Germany: Verlag der A. Stein'schen Buchhandlung, 1995.

Saft, Ulrich. *Krieg in der Heimat … bis zum bitteren Ende im Harz.* Walsrode, Germany: Militärbuchverlag Saft, 1994.

Schmieder, Siegfried. *Geschichte einer Gemeinde im Münsterland.* Wadersloh, Germany: Archiv d. Kreises Beckum, 1982.

Schneider, Jost W. *Heinrich Himmler's Burg: Das weltanschauliche Zentrum der SS.* Essen, Germany: Heitz and Höffkes, 1989.

Schramm, Wilhelm von. *Aufstand der Generale: Der 20. Juli 1944 in Paris.* Munich, Germany: Wilhelm Heyne Verlag, 1977.

Stein, Marcel. *Generalfeldmarschall Walter Model: Legende und Wirklichkeit.* Bissendorf, Germany: Biblio Verlag, 2001.

Taylor, Eric, and Willy Niessen. *Frontstadt Köln: Endkampf 1945 an Rhien und Ruhr.* Düsseldorf, Germany: Droste Verlag. 1980.

Tieke, Wilhelm. *Bis zur Stunde Null: Das obergische Land im Krieg, 1939–1945.* Gummersbach, Germany: Verlag Gronenberg, 1985.

———. *Aufstellung, Einsatz und Untergang der SS-Panzerbrigade "Westfalen," März–April 1945.* Gummersbach, Germany: Selbstverlag, 1990.

Webster, Sir Charles, and Noble Frankland. *The Strategic Air Offensive against Germany, 1939–1945.* Vol. 2, *Endeavor: Part 4.* London: Butler and Tanner, 1961.

Whiting, Charles. *Battle of the Ruhr Pocket.* New York: Ballantine Books, 1970.

INDEX